orgetown University Round Table
Selected Papers on Linguistics
1961-1965

compiled by
Richard J. O'Brien, S.J.

Georgetown University Press, Washington, D.C. 20007

INTRODUCTORY NOTE

Since 1950 the annual Georgetown University Round Table Meetings have provided a forum for the discussion of linguistics and other disciplines related to language study. Each year the proceedings of these meetings, edited by the Chairman of that year's meeting, has been published as a separate monograph in the *Georgetown University Monograph Series on Languages and Linguistics.*

The present volume represents an effort to make some of the papers presented at the Round Table Meetings from 1961 to 1965 more easily available in an inexpensive format. The papers contained in the present volume originally appeared in Monographs 14 (1961) to 18 (1965), edited respectively by Michael Zarenchnak and Allene Guss (14), Elizabeth D. Woodworth, Robert J. DiPietro, and Allene Gus (15), Robert J. DiPietro (16), C. I. J. M. Stuart (17), and Charles W. Kreidler (18). Although the original editors are not responsible for the selection of the papers included in the present volume, each paper is presented exactly as it was originally prepared by its editor except that the published account of the discussion which followed the original presentation of each paper has been omitted.

Richard J. O'Brien, S.J.

iii

CONTENTS

CONTENTS

ON SOME RECURRENT TYPES OF TRANSFORMATIONS

Emmon Bach

University of Texas

In recent years there has been a great increase of interest in language universals. Some idea of the variety of approaches and linguists involved in this interest can be gained by reading through the contributions to the symposium on *Universals of Language* held at Dobbs Ferry in 1961. From the point of view of tagmemics Kenneth Pike has called for and put into practice a search for syntactic universals ("etic" concepts). And programmatic statements about universals have come from the proponents of transformational theory.[1] It is from the latter point of view that I would like to discuss some parallel situations in several different languages in order both to show how universals enter into and are justified by the description of particular languages and to make some suggestions about certain universal syntactic concepts.

I assume as a background this framework: a general theory of language which states what the linguistic theories for individual languages are like, in particular that each such description consists of at least three parts— a syntactic component, a semantic component, a phonological component—; further a statement of the structure of these components and the way in which they operate to give representations of the structure, meaning, and phonological shape of possible utterances on the three levels; an evaluation procedure for selecting the "better" of two equal comprehensive descriptions; a stock of universal concepts for filling in the substance of each such descriptive theory.

There are two kinds of universals in linguistic theory. When we state that linguistic theories for particular languages will have such and such a form, that the rules must obey such and such formal constraints, and so on, we are positing universal features of the structures of individual languages.

---

[1] Joseph H. Greenberg, ed., *Universals of Language* (Cambridge, Massachusetts, 1963); Kenneth L. Pike, "Dimensions of grammatical constructions" *Lg* 38.221-244 (1962) and elsewhere; Jerrold J. Katz and Paul M. Postal, *An Integrated Theory of Linguistic Descriptions* (Cambridge, Massachusetts, 1964), especially section 5.3.

Such universals have been called "formal universals." [2] They are parallel to statements like "all languages have phonemes and morphemes," but recent linguistic theory goes considerably beyond such statements in the detailed description of the nature of possible linguistic systems.

On the other hand, when we consider the items that enter into the rules for particular languages, we must ask whether there are any universal categories or statements here too. These have been called "substantive universals." [3] What they might be has been clear for some time in phonology. The description of the phonology of every language makes a selection from a stock of universal phonetic concepts and parameters. We do not have to state over and over again for each new language what a velar stop is (if the language has one), but only what is peculiar about velar stops in that language. The currently most widely used set of concepts (in transformational phonologies) is based on the distinctive feature theory of Roman Jakobson. [4] Besides offering a stock of categories from which particular languages choose, it provides a way of stating universal laws about relations among these categories. Thus, if a language has an opposition between vowels and consonants, then the vowels will have the feature of voicing. Exceptions to this law can be stated for the particular languages involved, leaving the typical pattern for general phonological theory. Japanese has voiceless vowels but the feature is completely redundant and predictable at a low level of the phonology (and note that even the particular rule about Japanese makes use of general phonetic concepts). Comanche is reputed to have a true opposition of voiceless and voiced vowels but this is a peculiarity of the language which will not stop us from stating our general law, just as the existence of the platypus and echidna or viviparous snakes does not destroy the usefulness of the categories of mammal and reptile in zoology (or the general statements we make about them).

Until recently it has not been clear just what the substantive universals in syntax might be or on what basis they could be justified. To posit such universals would be to turn the abstract symbols and categories of the syntax into interpreted symbols. When we set out to describe some new language we are usually pretty sure about what things we will call nouns (or substantives, etc.), or verbs, adjectives, and so on, but we have not known

---

[2] Katz and Postal, p. 160.

[3] Ibid.

[4] Morris Halle and his students have done the most in working out phonological theories within this framework. It is interesting that none of the linguists who object to the use of Jakobsonian features has offered an alternative set.

why and have either been very apologetic or have invented all sorts of obscure terms—e.g. "pure relational suffixes" for cases—in order to avoid the charge of glottocentricism. It seems likely that part of this justification will come from semantic theory.[5] I would like to concentrate here, however, on *syntactic* characteristics that might enable us to define such categories in general linguistic theory.

My discussion will be devoted primarily to the problem of nominal modifiers. In many languages (I should be bold and say "all") there are transformations which operate on two sentences to embed a version of one sentence into the other as a modifier of a "word" which occurs in both of the underlying sentences.[6] In English such transformations yield sentences with relative clauses, attributive adjectives, possessive constructions, and a few other types as illustrated here:

(1) I live in the house.
(2) Michael lived in the house. }>I live in the house that Michael lived in.

With the same embedding (matrix) sentence and various second sentences we have:

(1) + (3) The house is big.   >I live in the big house.
"   (4) My brother has the house. >I live in my brother's house.
"   (5) The house is by the bridge.>I live in the house by the bridge.
"   (6) The house has a red roof. >I live in the house with a red roof.

Since we can also have sentences with relative clauses matching each of the sentences with shorter modifying words or phrases—*I live in the house that*

---

[5] Compare Katz and Postal, *loc. cit.* and *passim,* as well as various statements in the writings of Noam Chomsky, e.g., "Current issues in linguistic theory," in Jerry A. Fodor and Jerrold J. Katz, edd., *The Structure of Language*, p. 82, fn. 28.

[6] A number of extensive revisions in transformational descriptions have been suggested recently, in Katz and Postal (see footnote 1), in Chomsky's lectures at the Linguistic Institute at Indiana University in 1964 (to appear in T. Sebeok, ed., *Current Trends in Linguistics,* III, in an announced book by Chomsky on *Aspects of the Theory of Syntax,* and in Edward S. Klima, "Current developments in generative grammar," to appear in *Kybernetika* I (Prague). The discussion in this paper follows the more familiar form of earlier transformational grammars, since most of the relevant work has been done in that framework. In some details the statements would have to be modified, although I think that the main conclusions will remain unchanged by more recent work. On the other hand, it seems to me that the possibility to state such similarities and differences as those discussed below places an important condition on any suggested revisions of transformational descriptions. If the conclusions about the syntactic definitions of such categories as Noun, Noun-Phrase, Verb, REL, RM are unstatable in the newer revisions of transformational grammars, then this seems to me to constitute a possible argument against such revisions.

is big, etc.—the question arises whether to relate these two types of modifiers in a direct way, that is, whether to derive the structures underlying the reduced modifiers from already embedded modifying clauses or to treat them separately. From the beginning the former course has been chosen.[7] The reasons can be seen by comparing the two transformations that would be necessary in each analysis for phrases like *the house on the corner.* With an independent rule we would have roughly:

$$\left.\begin{array}{l} X + Noun + Y \\ T + Noun' + Aux + be + Loc \end{array}\right\} \Rightarrow X + Noun + Loc + Y$$
$$\text{where } Noun = Noun'$$

Following the usual course we need only the singular transformation:

$$X + WH + Noun + Aux + be + Loc + Y \Rightarrow X + Loc + Y$$

This may not seem like a dramatic savings in simplicity, but the situation is a good deal clearer when the whole battery of such rules is considered, since we can deal with a more general symbol "Pred" and take care of adjectives, appositive noun phrases, and so on by the same rule. Additionally, the problem of getting the correct derived phrase structure is much simpler in the second alternative, since the operation is a simple deletion. (If the recent suggestions to eliminate generalized transformations are adopted, the details of the argument just given will have to be modified but the conclusions remain untouched.)

Let us look next at the general rule for relative clauses in English. It may be given more or less as follows:

$$\left.\begin{array}{l} X + Noun + Y \\ W + NP + Z \end{array}\right\} \Rightarrow X + Noun + WH + NP + W + Z + Y$$
$$\text{where (1) } NP = T + Noun' \text{ and } Noun' = Noun$$
$$\text{(2) } NP \text{ is not "part of" another } NP$$

The last part of the condition is to prevent, for instance,

*He was standing on the bridge that I live in the house by.

Notice first of all that we leave the second occurrence of the noun-phrase in the output of the rule in order to formulate general rules for such different forms as *who* and *which.* Further, the item WH has no particular phonological meaning, it might as well be THAT or 236 or RM or any other arbitrary symbol at this point. Finally, notice that there has been a shift of the NP to initial position and that ultimately the second occurrence of the NP will be deleted or replaced with WH by *which,* etc.[8]

---

[7] Cf. Robert B. Lees, *The Grammar of English Nominalizations* (Bloomington, Indiana, 1960), pp. 85-94.

One further detail may be mentioned. In English we distinguish between restrictive and non-restrictive relative clauses. One difference between them is that the class of sentence adverbs like *of course, unfortunately, probably, possibly* cannot occur in restrictive clauses. Compare the two sequences [9]:

Dogs, which of course bark, don't bite.
*Dogs that of course bark don't bite.

(or more clearly with *of course* after *bark*). Further evidence for this restriction (which has not been studied very much) comes from ambiguous forms like *hopefully* (which seems to have gone through a recent loan-shift from, presumably, German). The following sentence is ambiguous when standing alone:

The people are hopefully waiting.
Also in a non-restrictive embedded clause:
Send in the people, who are hopefully waiting.
But the sequence is unambiguous in a restrictive clause:
Send in the people who are hopefully waiting.
(I realize of course that with differences in order and intonation the first example can be made unambiguous.)

Summarizing then, the following characteristics of relative clause embedding in English can be listed:

(a) condition of identity of nouns in the embedded and embedding sentences;

(b) condition that the occurrence of the noun phrase in the embedded sentence not be part of another noun phrase;

(c) introduction of a grammatical morpheme which marks the relative clause;

(d) shift of the shared noun to the head of the embedded sentence;

(e) further changes in the embedded sentence, some obligatory, some optional, including formation of various relative pronouns or markers (*who, which, that,* etc.), deletion of *that,* reductions of clause, preposing of some adjectives, formation of possessives, etc.;

---

[8] This seems to be an instance of a more general restriction that might be imposed on all transformations, namely, that whenever an item "Q" is named in the structural description of a transformation, the proper analysis of a string undergoing the transformation must analyze the string at the "highest" Q possible at that point in the string, cf. N. Chomsky, "The logical basis of linguistic theory" in *Preprints of Papers for the Ninth International Congress of Linguists,* pp. 520-522.

[9] This example is adapted (in English translation) from Wolfgang Motsch, *Syntax des deutschen Adjektivs,* Studia Grammatica III (Berlin, 1964), p. 68.

(f) restrictions on the occurrence of sentence adverbs and the like (including apparently some restrictions on modal auxiliaries—*dogs that may bark don't bite*) in some kinds of relative clauses.

If we look at a closely related language like German, we find not surprisingly that many of the details in the rules for embedding relative clauses and the various constructions derived from them are the same. The differences result in part from details of the obligatory machinery of each language (e.g. cases and gender in German), partly from different options available (e.g. preposing of a wider variety of modifiers in German). I shall not dwell on the German rules except to point out that in both languages it is useful to posit a dummy element ("REL") which occurs in the expansion of the noun phrase in the PS and that there is some question as to whether this item (which is connected with the occurrence of the articles) should be positioned before or after the noun. (Once again, if we follow the recent suggestions of Chomsky or Klima, the item "REL" would be replaced by a direct introduction of "S" possibly with a relative marker in noun phrases in a cyclically ordered set of PS rules.)

Let us look instead at some sentences in Japanese.[10] The following sentences parallel (as closely as possible) the first set of English sentences quoted before (I use plain forms to simplify the discussion):

(1) boku ga uti ni sumu		⎫ >boku wa Taroo ga (*or* no) sunda
(2) Taroo ga uti ni sunda		⎭ uti ni sumu
(1)+(3) uti ga ookii		>boku wa ookii uti ni sumu
" (4) ani ni wa uti ga aru		>boku wa ani no uti ni sumu
" (5) uti wa hasi no soba ni aru		>boku wa hasi no soba no uti ni sumu
" (6) uti ni wa akai yane ga aru		>boku wa akai yane no uti ni sumu
or (6′) uti wa yane ga akai		>boku wa yane no akai uti ni sumu

Just as in English or German the description of Japanese syntax can be simplified if we posit a rule introducing such de-sentential modifiers ("relative clauses") quite generally and then give additional rules to yield the more specialized constructions illustrated above (and others). As a first approximation we might have something like this:

---

[10] I am grateful to Mrs. Akiko Ueda for checking and discussing with me my Japanese examples. I make no attempt here to discuss the suggested analyses in the light of the already rather extensive literature on the transformational analysis of Japanese.

$$\left.\begin{array}{l}X+\text{Noun}+Y \\ W+\text{NP}+Z\end{array}\right\} \Rightarrow X+\text{RM}+W+Z+\text{Noun}+Y$$

where (1) $\text{NP}=P+\text{Noun}'+Q$ and $\text{Noun}'=\text{Noun}$

(2) NP is not "part of" another NP.

There are several things to notice about this rule. First, it is very close to the rule for English given above, much closer than would be the individual rules for the special constructions derivable from its transforms. Second, the conditions stated are almost identical (as a matter of fact the first restriction as stated here will still be correct for English). Just as the second condition on the English rule was necessary, so also here to prevent, for instance, a derivation like the following:

kare ga hasi no ue ni tatta   'he was standing on the bridge'
boku ga hasi no soba no uti ni sumu   'I live in the house by the bridge'
*kare wa boku no soba no uti ni sumu hasi no ue ni tatta
*'he was standing on the bridge that I live in the house by'

And again we find certain restrictions (not dealt with further here) on the carrying-over of "sentence adverbs". The result of carrying over *sikasi* 'however' in the embedded sentence yields ungrammatical strings:

*boku wa ano sikasi Taroo no sunda uti ni sumu.

What I want to suggest next is that we deliberately exploit the similarities in the two general rules and state a rule which will have exactly the same form in the two grammars for Japanese and English. Assuming the amendment to the phrase structure mentioned above (i.e. the introduction of an optional item "REL" occurring in noun phrases) and the use of a dummy symbol "md" (with "REL → md" in the phrase structure) which provides the actual substituend in the rule (so that the substituted second sentence takes on the analysis "REL")[11] we may state a general rule as follows:

T 1. Relative Clause Embedding

            1   2   3   4
SD: S_1: X + Noun + md + Y
            5   6   7
    S_2: W + NP + Z
SC: 3 > 5 + 6 + 7 in S_1
where (1) 6 contains 2
      (2) 6 is not part of another NP

---

[11] The use of an item like "REL" is suggested in Charles J. Fillmore, "The position of embedding transformations in a grammar," *Word*, 19.208-231 (1963). See also Katz and Postal.

The "matrix dummy" *md* will be dominated by the universal symbol "REL" so that the general rule for substitution transformations will have the desired effect of giving an analysis of the substituted sentence as a "REL" (or if this is not possible an additional condition may be stated to the effect that *md* is dominated by REL).[12] Now we can extract this rule from the grammars of the two languages and state it as a universal transformation which is implied by the use of the symbol "REL" in any particular grammar and does not need to be stated for each language separately.

Before continuing let me point out several consequences of this attempt at stating a universal transformation for relative clauses. First, such a rule can obviously not be stated unless the categories mentioned in the structure index occur in the phrase structure rules of the particular languages for which it is claimed to hold. That is to say, the postulation of such universal rules has a direct bearing on the search for syntactic definitions of such items as "noun" or "noun-phrase". Second, I mentioned before that there was some question in describing English and German as to whether to position the item "REL" before or after the noun to which it is attached. It is clear that the rule just given must be supplemented by a special rule for Japanese which will reposition the reflex of the "relative clause" before the noun. If on the other hand we position "REL" before the noun, we will have to have a special rule for English and German. It would follow from the intent of my remarks that decisions about the particular details of our analysis for one or another language will be made in part on the basis of what we find out about many other languages. In other words, far from trying to describe each language "in terms of its own structure alone", we must try to describe each language in terms of the structure of all other languages. Third, we can see how universal implications in the spirit of Greenberg will find a place in general linguistic theory. Suppose, for example, that it turns out that most languages with the basic order Subject-Object-Verb (like Japanese) also have preposed desentential nominal

---

[12] This rule provides an example of the sort of empirical evidence that may be brought to bear on questions about the general rules for derived constituent structure. From this example and similar rules one could derive arguments about whether or not a substitution for an item "Q" in the SD should replace Q in the derived P-marker and take on its "higher" analysis, or whether it should replace what is dominated by "Q" and thus receive the analysis "Q" in the derived P-marker. If the latter course is followed then the SD could use "Rel" in place of the item "md" and, whether or not "md" might occur after a "Noun" when "md" is derived from other sources (e.g. "COMP"), the rule would apply properly only to those "md" derived from "REL" and still remain open to the application of rules like T5 below.

modifiers.[13] Then we do not have to state the rule shifting "REL" to a position before the noun for Japanese separately but can state in our general theory that this rule is predictable from the basic order of Japanese sentences.

By applying the rule to both English and Japanese sentences we have produced strings like the following:

I + Pres + live + in + the + house +
$$RM + Michael + Past + live + in + the + house$$

or

boku + ga + uti + RM + Taroo + ga + uti + ni + sum + ta + ni + sum + u

Let us next look at the steps that might be followed in reaching well-formed sentences in the two languages and at the same time parenthetically consider what happens in a few other languages if we assume the operation of the same general rule in them. Before beginning, however, I would like to point out both the syntactic and semantic relation between the strings just mentioned and the results of conjunction transformations. It would seem fruitful to pursue the question whether such structures as embedded relative clauses in English might not be derived from conjoined sentences to explain sets of paraphrases like the following:

I live in the house and the house is by the bridge.
I live in the house and it is by the bridge.
I live in the house that is by the bridge.
I live in the house by the bridge.

Consider first the relation between the structures discussed and pronouns. Suppose we give as a first rule for deriving relative clause and related constructions a rule which marks the repeated noun for pronominalization:

X + Noun + RM + Y + NP + Z → X + Noun + RM + Y + PRO + NP + Z
where NP = P + Noun' + Q and Noun = Noun'
    Y ≠ W + PRO (and further restrictive conditions on Y)

Now the interesting thing about this is that except for the presence of "RM" it is exactly like a more general rule that might be formulated for pronominalizations (I mean here real substitution forms). In other words, we

---

[13] See Joseph H. Greenberg, "Some universals of grammar" in *Universals of Language,* pp. 48-90.

do not have to state a special rule for this step but merely add a condition to the general rule:

T2 Pronominalization

$$1 \quad 2 \quad 3 \quad 4 \quad 5$$

SD: X+Noun+Y+NP+Z

SC: 4>PRO+4

where 4 contains 2; 4 is not part of another NP; and Y≠W+PRO; optional except where Y contains RM.

As a matter of fact if we want to characterize sentences like "I went down to the sea and the sea was black" as special, we can state a more general condition based on whether or not Y contains a sentence boundary. Now I would submit that this rule is valid both for English and Japanese. In English, the rule marks the shared noun for a shift to initial position in relative clauses. If this shift is considered optional for English we will generate sentences like "I was living in the house that Michael was living in it." Such sentences occur fairly often especially if the embedded clause is long and complicated. (I have heard one of the participants at this Round Table say something like this: "I was working on 61 languages that I was describing the sound structures of them.") Moreover, we have in some special varieties of English—e.g. mathematical writing—a relative marker *such that* which goes with clauses of precisely this form. Compare also the semi-grammatical *"He was standing on the bridge that I was living in the house by it."* As for Japanese, I would argue that the ordinary kind of pronominalization is simply a deletion of the pronominalized noun-phrase. But we have seen that one of the steps in deriving "relatives" in Japanese is precisely such a deletion. I do not know enough about different languages to adduce many parallels here, but (if I have the facts straight) Malay seems to have at least one such modifying structure which would result directly from the rules given so far with appropriate extensions: RM is *yang* and the pronominalized form yields (obligatorily in some sentences) a substitute *nya* which occupies the position held before by the shared noun.

The next rule is more restricted. In other words, it has to be referred to at least in the description of individual languages (unless it can be predicted from some other features of the languages which use it).

T3. Relative Pronoun Attraction

$$1 \quad 2 \quad 3 \quad 4 \quad 5 \quad 6 \quad 7 \quad 8$$

SD: X+Noun+RM+Y (Prep) PRO+NP+Z

SC: (a) 4+5+6+7>5+6+7+4

(English) (b)   4+5+6+7>6+7+4+5

where 7 contains 2.

The rule will hold for German and English with structural change (a). For English we may add (b) to provide for the possibility of both *the house that I live in* and *the house in which I live*.

In order to account for English sentences with the relative particle *that* we may next state a rule which has the effect of deleting the marked noun-phrase occurring immediately after the relative marker *RM:*

> T4. Deletion of Relative Noun Phrase
> $$1 \quad 2 \quad\;\; 3 \quad\;\;\; 4 \quad\;\;\; 5 \quad 6$$
> SD: X+Noun+RM+PRO+NP+Y
> SC: delete 4+5
> where 5 contains 2.

This is an optional rule for English. It will be correctly blocked when a preposition intervenes between *RM* and *PRO* (since we have no phrases like *the house in that I live* or *the house that in I live*). With no application of this rule we still have the noun for correct choice of *who* and *which,* etc. The rule will be obligatory for those languages like Norwegian that utilize an invariable relative particle (*som*). If the analysis of deletion as a general method of pronominalization in Japanese turns out to be untenable, then this rule would also hold obligatorily for Japanese.

Next we may state a special rule for Japanese which preposes the relative clause construction. It can be very simply given as follows:

> T5. Position of Relative Clause:
> $$1 \quad\;\; 2 \quad\;\;\; 3 \quad 4$$
> SD: X+Noun+Rel+Y
> SC: 2+3→3+2

Rules of this sort hold for many languages (e.g. Turkish). As mentioned above, it may not be necessary to state such a rule for individual languages. Instead, it may turn out that general linguistic theory would provide a "law" of the form:

> If NP NP (NP) Verb, then T5.

Notice, however, that such a universal implication will have a direct bearing on the details of order in setting up PS rules for individual languages. It is certainly premature to draw any conclusions at this point, but such a rule might show that the basic order of verb-end clauses which has been suggested for Modern German should be rejected.[14] Once again, particular

---

[14] Emmon Bach, "The order of elements in a transformational grammar of German," *Lg.* 38. 263-269 (1962); Manfred Bierwisch, *Grammatik des deutschen Verbs,* Studia Grammatica II (Berlin, 1963).

consequences of this preposing must be stated for Japanese (conclusive forms on verbs and adjectives, etc.). Even though this rule was made to take care of Japanese, by stating proper conditions and ordering the rule in our English grammar the same rule will account for the placing of attributive adjectives before the noun.

Our next rule deletes the relative marker *RM*. This rule is optional for English (and must be suitably restricted): *the man I saw* . . .

> T6. Deletion of Relative Marker
>   1   2   3
> SD: X+RM+Y
> SC: delete 2

The rule must follow all the rules for which we still need *RM* (for *who, whose, which, whom*). I think that it is better to state the rule in terms of the general symbol *RM* than in terms of *that* for several reasons. Not only is the rule still completely language-independent in its structural description, but if we state the rule in terms of the particular morpheme *that*, we must ensure by a more complicated SD that it is only that *that* that occurs in *that*-clauses that gets deleted.

Finally, in each grammar we must add rules like:

> $RM \rightarrow that$ (English)
> $RM \rightarrow som$ (Norwegian)

and (unless we assume the previous *RM* deletion has applied obligatorily) the rule giving *RM* a null phonetic representation in languages like Japanese.

Let me summarize what we have done so far in the form of a chart:

		English	Japanese
T1	embedding of relative clause (or comparable blocking T in new style grammars)	obligatory	obligatory
T2	pronominalization	obligatory (if RM)	obligatory (if RM)
T3	relative pronoun attraction	obligatory (in some styles optional)	(possibly obligatory)
T4	deletion of relative NP	optional	(possibly obligatory)

T5 preposing of REL	(obligatory if REL=Adj. otherwise not possible)	obligatory
T6 deletion of RM	optional	obligatory

Finally, for the individual languages we need phonological rules and further transformations, some interspersed among the above.

Now I think it is interesting to look at a totally unrelated language and one that is moreover rather different in general structure from English and Japanese, namely Swahili.[15] Let us assume that we use items like "Noun," "NP," "Verb" and so on in our Swahili grammar. If we take two sentences that fit the structural description of T1, say,

nilimwona m̀tu REL   'I saw the man' (plus REL)
m̀tu anaendesha shule   'the man runs the school'

and run them through rules T1 and T2 (both obligatory) we will obtain the following strings (I leave irrelevant parts unsegmented):

(T1) nilimwona m̀tu+RM+m+tu+a+na+endesh+a+shule
(T2) nilimwona m̀tu+RM+PRO+m+tu+a+na+endesh+a+shule

T3 will apply vacuously since the NP is already positioned next to its RM. If however we take another second sentence with *m̀tu* as object, say:

watoto walimwona m̀tu   'the children saw the man'

we will obtain by rules T1, T2, and T3 the following:

nilimwona m̀tu+RM+PRO+m+tu+wa+toto+walimwona

(Actually, these strings are a compromise between the final forms and the more abstract representations best suited to a description of Swahili syntax. For instance, there is good reason to consider the class prefix *m̀* on *m̀tu* as represented by "Sg+wa" at this point of the grammar.)

These strings have been obtained by using rules set up to account for Japanese and English. There is good justification for them both in English and Japanese separately and in the attempt to show their similarities. Now I think that it is rather remarkable that these strings seem to be in such good

---

[15] I am indebted to my colleague Edgard G. C. Polomé, for checking my statements about Swahili, and discussing them with me. My information about the language has been drawn primarily from his forthcoming *Swahili Handbook* and from E. W. Stevick, J. G. Mlela, and F. N. Njenga, *Swahili: Basic Course* (Washington, D.C., 1963).

shape for going on to describe Swahili relative constructions. We can accomplish the further description of such constructions by one special rule and a number of obligatory adjustments (that would have to be stated anyway, or incorporated into much more complicated individual rules). The one special rule is this:

T7. Obligatory Verb Shift

$$\begin{array}{cccc} 1 & 2 & 3 & 4 \end{array}$$

SD: $\overline{X + RM} + Y + \overline{Aux + Verb} + Z$

SC: $2 + 3 \rightarrow 3 + 2$

with suitable restrictions on Y (does not contain RM?)

This rule will give for our two examples:

nilimwona m̀tu + RM + a + na + endesh + a + PRO + m + tu + shule
nilimwona m̀tu + RM + wa + li + mu + on + a + PRO + m + tu + wa + toto

The further rules necessary are suggested by these:

PRO + Pre + Noun → Pre + o

(this yields the bound forms of the substitutive pronoun, as well as the "relative affix" forms)

Tns (Object-Marker) Verb + Pre + o →

Tns + Pre + o (Object-Marker) Verb

where Tns = li, na, ...

Rules for the reflexes of the prefixes (or class markers) with various forms, including in particular

$$Sg \begin{Bmatrix} wa \\ 1st\text{-}p \\ 2nd\text{-}p \end{Bmatrix} o \rightarrow ye \ in \ env. \ RM + SM + Tns((OM) \ Verb) \underline{\hspace{2cm}}$$

For the disposal of RM we can revert to our original list (T6) for a final deletion rule. This rule must be preceded by those rules which introduce the form *amba* optionally and obligatorily in various situations. If *amba* (with its proper affixes) is made a direct reflex of *RM,* then the final rule will be a deletion of all remaining *RM.* We thus obtain finally for our two examples:

nilimwona m̀tu anayeendesha shule

'I saw the man who runs the school'
nilimwona m̀tu waliyemwona watoto

'I saw the man that the children saw'

Notice that this sequence of rules provides just the order needed. In the included clauses object noun phrases remain in their usual place following the noun, but subject noun phrases are shifted to postverbal position (or rather the shift of verb—necessary anyhow—results in this order).

Now as a matter of fact, the last sentence (with postposed subject) is a rather bookish construction. Suppose we delete (or mark as optional for a certain style) T7, the only rule which has to be stated specially for Swahili just for this construction. Then with all other rules remaining and a rule changing RM into *amba* (needed in any case for some constructions in any style) we will have the more usual form:

nilimwona m̂tu ambaye watoto walimwona

I do not want to insist too much on the details of these analyses. I do want to underline, however, some general points.

(1) In working out rules for particular languages simplicity is often achieved by breaking down a number of complicated transformations into component steps. In this way a number of superficially disparate constructions turn out to be related as particular selections from the series of component transformations.

(2) Various unrelated and related languages seem to exhibit the same component transformations. The differences appear in the particular selections made, in the obligatory or optional character of the transformations, and in further special rules. The situation is exactly parallel to the situation in phonology, where languages differ mainly in the selection and low-level physical realization of phonological oppositions taken from a universal stock.

(3) By making reference to such universal transformations we can simplify the description of individual languages and at the same time build a general substantive theory of syntax. In order to do this we must use the same designations for various categories in different languages. Or— turning that statement around—because of the postulation of the universal transformations we can give some syntactic meaning to such terms as "noun," "noun phrase," "relative clause," "verb," and the like. It is important to disengage this search for universal syntactic concepts from the practical problem of choosing appropriate terminology. Linguists have reacted in the past to the use of a Latin or Indo-European terminology for describing languages of radically different structures. But I would submit that the particular words we choose are less important than the way we use and define them. A study of "the genitive in all languages" is silly only if we mean by "genitive" something specifically restricted to, say, Latin, or German. Once we have pinned down the concept in a suitably general way,

it is merely an interesting etymological fact that "genitive" comes from the Latin grammarians. As linguists we should be tolerant in etymological matters. "Paradigms" such as those listing the six "cases" of English and used as occasions for merriment in the linguistic in-group are to be rejected not because they attempt to list the reflexes of certain functions in a general syntactic framework taken from outside English, but because the general framework is wrong. Similarly, the term "relative clause" which I have used here to designate certain structures in three unrelated languages may be objected to as having the wrong connotations, and if desired may be replaced by a clumsier locution like "desentential nominal modifier." But this is, I think, a matter of convenience or rhetoric and after all not very important.

(4) Finally, just as the universal features of phonological systems are based on the common characteristics of sound systems as systems of oppositions realized by a vocal apparatus essentially the same in all humans, so also widespread or universal syntactic (and semantic) characteristics of different languages result from the universal needs of human speech communities. It is often said that all languages are equally complete.[16] Every language provides a means to capture in linguistic symbols any aspect of human experience whenever it becomes important enough to talk about it. The devices discussed above presumably have their counterparts in every language since their function is essentially to provide a new *ad hoc* expression for any person, place, or thing, experience, process, function or feeling that a human being may want to name.[17]

---

[16] Archibald A. Hill, *Introduction to Linguistic Structures* (New York, 1958), pp. 7-9.

[17] Robert B. Lees, op. cit., pp. xvii f.

THE BIOLOGICAL BACKGROUND OF MAN'S LANGUAGES

JARVIS BASTIAN

University of California, Davis

Most of us feel a certain ring of impertinence, irrelevance, and even irreverence to any discussion of the biology of man's languages. We can all see that languages are, first and foremost, cultural phenomena, especially in the light of the enormous linguistic diversity displayed by modern man. But as biology is the study of the achievement and maintenance of different modes of life, there is really nothing incoherent in thinking biologically about man's languages, for cultural phenomena are central to man's mode of biological adaptation. In fact, it is not possible to develop a clear understanding of man's biological status without considering cultural processes and products, for there are some very compelling reasons for believing that they have participated in the selective processes determining homonid evolution from its inception.[1] Thus, we may say that cultural forces have contributed to the shaping of the gene pool of the human population just as biological forces have contributed to the shaping of cultural communities, and our thoughts about man's nature can be terribly misled if we divorce human biology and culture, for they are interdependent parts of man's way of life in all its diversity.

In this light, human biology and man's languages are profoundly and mutually related, for human languages have become fundamental to most culture traits and particularly to those traits associated with technologies, which have the most direct biological consequences for man. There are at least two reasons why human languages are basic to technologies, and thus have such great biological importance. In the first place, cultural traits are transmitted from generation to generation by tradition, rather than genetical transmission, and as cultural trait-complexes become more complex, linguistic intercourse becomes the most important means of transmitting traditions, of assimilating new participants into them. An exceedingly im-

---

[1] See, for instance, "Culture and the Direction of Human Evolution: A Symposium", *Human Biology* (1963) v. *35* No. 3.

17

portant difference between genetical and traditional, especially linguistic, transmission is that the latter is not confined to transmission of traits across generations. Therefore, the diffusion and replacement of cultural traits may proceed at rates that are very much faster than genetically transmitted traits. The ever increasing pace of cultural history since Neolithic times bears ample witness to this possibility. Secondly, a good case can be made, as I will try to show in a moment, for thinking that man's languages are intimately connected with the processes from which novel cultural traits appear. In recent times, speaking paleontologically, man's cultural modes of adaptation have increasingly involved active control over his circumstances of life, rather than more passive accommodation to his environment, and this, of course, is the basis for the biological importance of technologies. Now, the development and expansion of biologically effective technologies rests upon increases in the scope and quality of information, or knowledge, about the circumstances of human life possessed by a cultural community. I hope to demonstrate later that the development of such new knowledge, or intelligence, is very much dependent on the nature of man's languages, just as is the assimilation and diffusion of the subsequent cultural innovations.

With these considerations in mind, it is easy to see that the feature of man's languages having the greatest adaptive significance to human ways of life is their openness. In any linguistic community, new utterances may be generated and effectively received without end. Not only that, but there does not appear to be any end to what such novel utterances may be about. That is to say, man's languages are not only open, but semantically open, and one of the especially interesting ways in which they are semantically open is that novel utterances may refer to previously novel utterances. The semantic openness of man's languages is in itself an innovation in biology, for all other animal signaling systems, including man's nonlinguistic signaling systems, that have been sufficiently studied have been found to be limited, either by restrictions on the occurrence and effective reception of novel signals or the semantic scope of novel signals.[2] It is not at all clear just how this semantic openness is effected in linguistic communities, but in view of its immense significance for human biology, it is important to try to reach some understanding of it, and the rest of my comments will be directed to an attempt of this sort.

In beginning, I would ask you to continually bear in mind that human

---

[2] J. Bastian, "Primate Signaling Systems and Human Languages" in I. DeVore (ed.), *Primate Social Behavior: Field Studies of Monkeys and Apes* (New York: Holt, Rinehart & Winston), (*to appear*).

linguistic systems, while integral parts of cultural complexes, are themselves adaptive complexes, most especially when we consider the constellation of traits that are shared by all of man's languages. Though these common traits may have very likely developed at different periods and rates, their nature and interrelations have been shaped by forces acting on the total complex, whatever it may have been at any point in time. This is a decisive reason for regarding the common features of linguistic systems as co-adaptive, because the adaptive outcomes of these systems are products of these features operating together as an integrated whole.

There is no doubt that the most potent forces shaping these shared features of linguistic systems have been connected with man's limited capacities for perceiving and remembering, or, in other words, analyzing, the stimuli that impinge upon him. In this regard humans do not appear to differ appreciably from other higher vertebrates, and this is why the openness of linguistic systems is so exceptional. How is it possible for man, with quite unexceptional analytic capacities, to effectively process the auditory signals he receives in his linguistic communities, where the number of different signals is essentially unlimited, the acoustic features fantastically complex and evanescent, and the rate of transmission exceedingly rapid?

I have already suggested that we should be prepared to find a number of characteristics of man's languages which operate together to effectively bypass his limitations in perception and retention. Chief among these is the grammaticalness of man's languages. Linguistic utterances do not have structural integrity. Instead of being complete and indivisible wholes, they are almost always concatenations of lexical items. However, the lexical items of any linguistic community are never concatenated with complete freedom, and an easy and valuable way of characterizing these restrictions is to say that the concatenations conform to rules governing the formation of well formed, or "permissible", chains of lexical items, and the transformation of one or more well-formed chains into other well-formed chains. Even though in any linguistic community the lexical items and rules of their formations and transformations are finite in number it is easy to see that there is no limit to the number of different well-formed chains conforming to these restrictions.

The most immediate biological consequence of this characteristic grammaticalness of man's languages is that instead of having to assimilate and retain a separate and distinct signal for every event that may be socially important to him, which is just not conceivable for even the most impoverished human circumstances we know today, the requirements of our languages are finite in scope and of a size befitting our limitations.

But language is a social phenomenon, and even though we can see that a speaker may generate an infinite number of well-formed utterances with a finite set of rules and a finite stock of lexical items, these utterances must be effectively received in order to be socially significant. And we have noted before that the acoustical events of linguistic intercourse are extravagantly complicated and transient. Furthermore, linguistic signals are essentially continuous, for though the acoustic wave-form is incessantly interrupted, the different lexical items into which the signal may be analyzed do not come floating to the listener as separate chunks of acoustic energy in the stream of time. Now we should all be aware of the often impressive performances non-humans may exhibit in coming to recognize many different linguistic signals. What evidence there is indicates that these performances in household pets, animal acts, and even prelinguistic children are often quite dependent upon the nonauditory contexts in which the signals occur and upon linguistically insignificant features of the acoustic signal, particularly prosodic features and voice qualities. But however many well developed discriminations may be attained, they are finite in number and each has its own history of conditioning. Furthermore, such performances are contingent on just the acoustic energies received, and therefore require rather narrowly defined conditions of listening. Another constraint on these performance capabilities is the fact that in any linguistic community different lexical items are very often as much alike acoustically as recurrences of the same lexical item. Indeed, homophony of lexical items tends to increase the more frequent their occurrence in the community. Such performance capabilities will clearly not do for the effective functioning of linguistic systems, yet we know that humans are not markedly different from many other animals in their ability to develop and maintain auditory discriminations.

The resolution of this paradox is, I think, to be found in the recognition that the effective perception of linguistic events is based on much more than well developed auditory discriminations. I am persuaded that the necessary extra ingredients for the perceptual processes arise from the fact that any really competent listener is also a competent speaker. I suggest that our appreciation of what is said to us derives in large part from the same processes involved when we are acting as speakers. If the lexical identities of some parts of the signal we receive can be established, we can synthesize a replication of the complete signal or a sufficiently good match to it, because in doing so we are operating with the same grammatical apparatus that generates the original signal. In other words, I am supposing that effective listening is very much a matter of the listener's own contribution. This supposition makes it quite easy to understand why linguistic signals may suffer really enormous degradations without affecting intelligibility, and why our understanding of what we hear depends upon a great deal more than just the passive quiverings of our ear drums, and why we may effectively process signals on their very first occurrence in our experience.

Thus, the competent listener, because he is interchangeably a competent speaker, does not, need not, nor is it likely he even can, instantaneously assess the lexical identities associated with all parts of the received wave train. He fixes lexical identities only to the extent required to synthesize a well-formed chain. When conditions demand it, he may need to narrow the matching error in his replications, but still his perception of what is said will be, in a sense, his own invention. Even so, his grasp of the productive apparatus of his language and the cumulative confirmation of his previous syntheses usually serve to make his inventions apposite. However, sometimes the circumstances of listening may be so unfavorable that the listener cannot assess lexical identities in the received signal sufficient for the syntheses of well-formed chains. Such conditions may stem from much more than adverse signal-to-noise ratios. The openness of linguistic communication is far more gravely threatened by the wide differences in the probabilities of occurrence of possible lexical items and concatenations thereof. For most people, most of the time, linguistic interchanges involve a relatively small part of the lexicon of the linguistic community. Such lexical items occur with sufficient frequency so that their acoustic-time complexes are well established identities easily recognized under most conditions. But the openness of man's languages requires the effective processing of signals that contain not only relatively rare but even completely novel lexical items.

The openness of linguistic systems, when jeopardized in this way, is preserved by the possibility of assigning non-lexical, but still determinate, identities to very rare or completely new lexical items. Such identifications are, of course, what we know as phonemic identification, and they enable the listener to accommodate unfamiliar lexical items on a provisional, non-meaningful, basis until their lexical status can be established. However, in view of the continuous nature of the acoustic products of linguistic acts, their enormous variability, and the human limitations in perception, retention and time, it is most difficult to develop an adequate understanding of the means by which phonemic identifications are achieved. To my mind,

the most appealing conceptualization of the processes of phonemic identification are the closely similar articulatory reference and analysis-by-synthesis
theories elaborated respectively by the groups at the Haskins Laboratories
and the Electronic Research Laboratory at M.I.T.[3] The intriguing thing
about these notions is that they suggest that the listener's competence as a
speaker may again serve to circumvent human limitations in the face of
the overwhelming perceptual demands of the task, for in any linguistic
community there is far more invariance in the articulation of linguistic
events than in their acoustic products.[4]

If these lines of speculation concerning the joint contributions of grammaticalness, interchangeability of listener and speaker, and the ever present
possibility of phonemic identification furnish a framework for understanding the openness of man's linguistic systems, they do not in themselves
accommodate the fact that man's linguistic systems are not only just pro-
ductively open, but semantically open as well. And as we noted before,
the immense biological significance of man's languages arises not so much
from his being able to produce novel grammatical utterances as from the
novel meanings that may be conveyed by them. To understand how this
potential may be realized we must examine the processes by which new
members, particularly the young, are assimilated into linguistic communities
because, as with all cultural traditions, it is through these processes that
their effective operation is maintained.

The initial stage of linguistic assimilation, in which the young come
to respond differentially to linguistic signals, does not appear to be governed
by processes different from those which affect the conditioning of dis-
criminative actions for many other animals and kinds of stimuli. However,
soon after this has begun, instrumental vocal acts start to appear. Again,
the processes by which these initial vocal acts are shaped and brought
under the control of both external and internal environmental states do
not seem to be biologically exceptional. The only really unusual feature
of these assimilative processes is that they are undoubtedly abetted by the
remarkable proclivity of human young for vocal play and mimicry, a
characteristic not occurring in any other mammals except perhaps for the
toothed whales. I think it is difficult to overestimate the importance of

---

[3] See, for example, A. M. Liberman, F. S. Cooper, K. S. Harris, and P. F.
MacNeilage, "A Motor Theory of Speech Perception" in G. Fant (ed.), *Proceedings
of the Speech Communication Seminar* (Royal Institute of Technology, Stockholm),
(*to appear*), and K. N. Stevens, "Toward a Model for Speech Recognition", *Journal
of the Acoustical Society of America,* 32 (1960), 46-55.

[4] J. Bastian, *op. cit.*

this characteristic. At any rate, the young soon begin to develop as speakers as well as listeners.

I cannot help but think that the interplay between the speaking and listening roles contributes to the development of control over the grammatical apparatus of the linguistic community because as competence in these two roles increases, and in my view this means they become more completely interchangeable, any skills acquired in one are directly transferable to the other. But I must say that I do not know of any really satisfactory accounts of the processes by which grammatical control is achieved. I think such accounts can be expected before long because this problem is now receiving the kind of attention and thought it deserves. Whatever the course by which command of grammatical operations is gained, as it begins to appear, a vastly different process of linguistic assimilation emerges which has extensive consequences for the semantic nature of linguistic systems.

Because the initial products of linguistic assimilation, for both speaking and listening, are conditioned by the different social outcomes attending the production and reception of different lexical items, these items have a direct reference to the sensory experience of the learner. But as more and more grammatical operations are assimilated, another mode of acquiring new lexical items becomes available that does not require separate histories of conditioning for each acquisition. Instead, novel lexical items may be introduced first as phonemic identities which may then be related to already assimilated lexical items through definitional, explicational, and inferential processes made possible through the grammatical operations of the linguistic system so that these new items acquire lexical status. This mode of linguistic assimilation may be described by following, with some liberties, Quine's distinction between meaning and reference.[5] Thus, new lexical items may be assimilated by developing an appreciation of their meaning, that is, their network of interrelationships with other lexical items and formations thereof in the linguistic practices of the community.

Once the meaning of such lexical items has been established, they may participate in turn in the elaboration of the meaning of still other lexical acquisitions, and this process may continue on and on with the result that lexical items may have reference only indirectly through their relations with other lexical items. Therefore, much of the lexicon of any linguistic community may have only the most remote connection, if any, with the domain of extralinguistic sensory experience. This semantic freedom of linguistic systems from any necessary sensory connection with

[5] W. V. Quine, *From a Logical Point of View* (Cambridge: Harvard University Press, 1953).

the environment has profound consequences for all aspects of human modes of life. Perhaps of most importance, it provides man with a repertory of actions that are not tightly bound to the immediate circumstances of his life, but which may nevertheless serve to mediate other actions of direct adaptive significance.

In closing, I would like to mention another consequence of the semantic openness of linguistic systems that is of particular interest to me, which is the bearing of this feature on the nature of human intelligence. Whenever we observe an animal acting differentially with respect to a particular condition of his environment, we may say without insult to the methodological canons of behaviorism that the animal has a concept of that condition, whatever the source of the animal's action may be. In this same way, we may ascribe concepts to humans if their actions, linguistic or otherwise, meet these requirements. Now there is a considerable body of evidence indicating that there are no qualitative differences among humans and some non-human primates, such as chimpanzees and rhesus monkeys, in their capacities for conceptual attainments when subjected to comparable training regimens. But when we consider the concepts that may be said to be associated with human linguistic actions, we find that because of the semantic openness of man's linguistic systems many actions have only an indirect connection, if any, to the immediate perceptual experience of the speaker or listener. The associated concepts in such cases are constructs rather than percepts. Yet when we look closely we find that most of the concepts connected to man's cultural adaptations are of just this kind, even though at first blush they appear to be percepts. So though there may be no decisive differences between man and other primates in their conceptual capacities, because of man's languages, there is a vast difference in the kinds of concepts they do form. There is no way by which you could bring a monkey to develop the concept associated with the English phrase "my uncle" because it is not in the nature of things that a monkey, or anyone else for that matter, may perceptually attend the criterial obstetrical events. Of course, it is conceivable that you might teach him to be competent in the English language, and thereby develop the concept; but if you can do that, I will be the monkey's uncle.

THREE MISCONCEPTIONS OF GRAMMATICALNESS

C. E. BAZELL

School of Oriental and African Studies, London University

Though I am concerned with three misconceptions of grammaticalness I shall have little to say of two of them. Both are rather common on either side of the Atlantic, but here at least they have been vigorously attacked by transformationalists, who unfortunately have done nothing to discourage the third misconception.

The first misconception is so absurd that I may be thought all too naive in considering it worthy of mention. It is the notion that the syntactic deviations of the 'colourless-green-ideas' type are not linguistic deviations at all, but (as it is variously expressed) are "ontological" deviations, or have something to do with the "real world", or are "aletheutic" rather than grammatical, and so on. The mere fact that such things have been said by otherwise quite reputable scholars is not a sufficient ground for my troubling to mention them. I mention them rather because this absurd view is apt to be attributed to anybody who attacks one of the other misconceptions.

The second misconception is that of grammar as tailor-made for the use of the semanticist. Each morpheme-class is a category of "values", and each morpheme has its fundamental meaning. The upholders of this view do not make the mistake of asserting that grammatical categories are arrived at by the use of meaning-criteria, and it is this that renders them dangerous. Our classes are set up on respectable distributional grounds, our morphemes are formal units. But once we have isolated the units, it is just these units for which we seek a meaning. Miraculously, the units which were singled out as appropriate for the simplest possible syntactic description, turn out also to be the units appropriate for semantic investigation. Any linguist who disbelieves in this miracle is considered to be a dullard who has no interest in semantics.

So once we have established a system of cases, we can then ask—what is the meaning of the accusative in Latin? of the instrumental in Russian? and so on, as though these questions must necessarily have an answer. Of course they **might** have an answer: a theory of the morpheme as a meaningless unit would be just as absurd as the theory of the morpheme as a meaningful unit. Morphemics does not commit us to semantic analysis, it also does not commit us not to make one. In respect of semantics, the morpheme is a neutral unit.

I would like to leave this question alone now. All the same there is one confusion which I may have often failed to castigate along with the other confusions. It is the confusion between meaning and what (for want of a better phrase) I shall call a **semantic tie-up.**

Semantic tie-ups are common enough in morpho-phonemics; for instance there are obviously such relations even in the English strong-verb formations—e.g. *wound, ground, bound,* have "circular action" as a common reference, but nobody wishes to say that it is part of the meaning of this formation. In morphemics this tie-up may be far more close: clearly the use of singular and plural verb-forms in English is strongly tied up with the potentially semantic distinction between singular and plural nouns. But neither is in itself a matter of semantics. The speaker can no more choose to say *the cats is* on the rare occasion that it might otherwise be appropriate, than he can choose to say *grinded* instead of *ground* when the action happens not to be circular. A semantic tie-up, so far from being a matter of meaning, is incompatible with meaning, for the speaker has no choice, apart from the choice of speaking his own language or not. Meaning implies choice; the meaning of a morpheme is what it contributes to the content of a sentence, and this meaning can be determined only by comparing otherwise similar sentences which lack this morpheme or have another instead. (The reverse does not hold: choice does not imply meaning—one can choose between 'he has' and 'he has got' but there is no meaningful distinction.)

As for the third misconception, I begin by reasserting a distinction which is intuitively obvious to all fluent and sensitive speakers of a language, but which has often been described in misleading ways. It is the distinction between what I have chosen to call **ungrammatical** and **non-grammatical** sentences. An ungrammatical sentence is one which is replaceable, *salvā significatione,* by a grammatical sentence. *He seems sleeping* is ungrammatical; on the most likely interpretation, the grammatical equivalent is *he seems to be sleeping. Colourless green ideas sleep furiously* is non-grammatical—there is no question of replacing it by a grammatical equivalent.

Ungrammatical sentences are **corrigible.** Their most obvious instantiations are sentences which violate an obligatory rule of transformation—e.g. the sentence *when he will come, I will see him.* This violates the rule which carries phrases of the type *when he will come* (or more strictly their generative antecedents) into phrases of the type *when he comes . . .* It would be useless to think up some context in which *when he will come* etc. would be appropriate, for the transformational rules provide precisely that any function performable by the ungrammatical sentence is taken over by its transform.

Non-grammatical sentences are not corrigible in the same way. Of course there are other ways in which they might be regarded as corrigible—*colourless green ideas* might be taken as a mistake for any other phrase one cares to choose. But so might any fully grammatical sentence.

There are many ways in which one may go wrong about the distinction I am making. One may make the distinction and describe it in a misleading way, as I think many sensitive linguists have done, to the glee of less sensitive linguists who cannot intuit the distinction. One can deny the distinction as such but attempt to tie it up with other, ostensively more real, distinctions. One can confuse the distinction with other quite different distinctions. Finally, one can make just the distinction I am making between the ungrammatical as opposed to either the grammatical or the non-grammatical, without recognising that the latter is also a genuine linguistic distinction.

First—misleading accounts of the genuine distinction. When Bolinger says that he could predict that the verb *seem* has no progressive form (except in unusual contexts), he is saying (I think) what I should express by calling a sentence such as *he is seeming good* non-grammatical rather than ungrammatical. There is some force in Chomsky's remark that this is circular; for (as he says) some characterisation of the meanings of *seem* stated without reference to its grammatical function would be needed, from which this function can be predicted. In the absence of this, Bolinger's statement reduces to the observation, misleadingly expressed, that *seem* does not occur in the progressive.

Yet this is very unsympathetic criticism. It is true that one cannot in any normal sense predict the distribution of a word from its meaning, since these are two aspects of the same thing, when (as in this case) it is a question of meaningful distribution. But this does not make the absence of *he is seeming good* from the set of normal English sentences in the least like the absence of *he seems sleeping* or *when he will come* etc. One would not even be tempted to say that the absence of sentences beginning *when he will come* can be predicted from the meaning of *will*. This is a mere **grammatical constraint.** I would like to say that the absence of *he is seeming good,* on the other hand, is due to a **grammatical restraint.** Accordingly, I make a distinction between **constraints** (constrictional rules) and **restraints** (restrictional rules).

Now what Bolinger is saying, in a way that Chomsky rightly calls misleading, is that the absence of *is seeming* is part of the semantic distribution of *seem* and the progressive, not a constraint which sets a limit to this distribution in the way that, e.g., the constraint whereby *if he will come* . . . is excluded from the set of gramamtical sentences, sets a limit to the semantic distribution of *will*.

It is no part of the semantics of *will* that sentences beginning *if he will come* . . . are ungrammatical. This is an easy case since sentences of the form *if he comes* . . . under one interpretation are transforms of pre-sentences of the form 'if he will come . . .' Hence the semantics of *will* can neglect this restriction anyway, dealing as it does merely with the pre-sentences: an obligatory transformation takes care of the rest.

The probable exclusion of *is seeming* is a far more difficult affair. Even if Bolinger is wrong in not taking this to be a matter of **constraint** we shall still not wish (for several reasons) to take *he seems* under any interpretation as a transform of 'he is seeming'. Even so, if the absence of *he is seeming* etc. is a constraint, *he seems* etc. may be said to fill a gap in the distribution of *seem* which would otherwise be filled by *is seeming,* much as *had to* fills a gap in the distribution of *must,* which otherwise would be filled by a normal past tense of *must*.

But suppose Bolinger is wrong, not only in his misleading expression of the situation, but also in his refusal to regard the absence (in normal contexts) of *he is seeming* as due to a constraint. Then Chomsky is also wrong in his assignment of the error. The error would then consist, not in making a vacuous prediction, or rather of specifying a form of prediction which would in all cases be vacuous, but in making an unjustified prediction, or rather of specifying a form of prediction, which would in all cases be unjustified (though it might often turn out right).

Take the case of the English morpheme 'must' (not of course the English word *must*). It is no part of the semantics of 'must' that this morpheme does not combine with the morpheme 'past'. The semantics of the two morphemes can be discussed without any implication as to the presence or absence of this combination.

Now is the absence of *is seeming* (the progressive of *seem*) from the set of phrases which the grammar will generate, similar to this, or is it rather similar to the absence of *colourless green ideas?* I do not know—I have heard arguments on either side. I suspect it to be a borderline case. It suffices that there is something to argue about.

The relations I am considering are all **linguistic** relations. Nothing could be more mistaken than the idea that the exclusion of phrases such as *colour-less green ideas* . . . from the set of grammatical sentences has something to do with the "real world". Yet this is just the idea which is attributed to scholars who continue to make the distinction between contraints and restraints. It is assumed that because they make the distinction between a grammatical constraint and a semantic restraint, they fail to make the distinction between a semantic restraint and what might be called a **referential obstruction.** Put crudely, it is supposed that a linguist distinguishing between the ungrammaticality of *the child seems sleeping* and the non-grammaticality of *colourless green ideas sleep furiously,* must also class *the cross-eyed elephant slept in the hotel bed* with the latter. As though there were only one distinction to be made!

One might compare the difference between constrictional rules and restrictional rules in language with a similar difference in a game: here the constrictional rules are the rules of play and the restrictional rules are the rules of good play. It is a constrictional rule of chess that one does not move the castle diagonally, and a restrictional rule that one does not put one's queen diagonally in front of the opponent's pawn. Both sorts of rules must be built into a machine designed for playing chess against a human opponent. It would be stupid to object that the machine does not recognise the difference between the two sorts of rules. Similarly, it is stupid to object that a transformational grammar does not distinguish between the two sorts of rules, if its object is just to generate precisely those sentences which are grammatical in the sense that they offend against neither sort of rule. But it is equally stupid to pretend that no distinction can be drawn.

Traditional grammar was in intention purely constrictional. Hence it is only to be expected that when traditional grammarians are confronted with the assertion that *golf plays John* is ungrammatical, they reply by adducing situations in which such a sentence might reasonably have a use. The objection is based on a misunderstanding, but it deserves a more sympathetic reply than the only too common: 'Well, if you say that *golf plays John* is perfectly grammatical, then I just can't speak with you any longer'.

This is rather like saying: 'Well, if you tell me that it is a perfectly correct chess-move to put one's queen diagonally in front of the opponent's pawn, then I just can't speak with you any longer'. Quite simply the move is correct by the rules of play, but utterly incorrect by the rules of good play.

Just as the restrictional rules of correct chess-play are far more complicated to formulate than the constrictional rules, so also are the restrictional rules of syntax. But it is a mistake to imagine that the difference lies just in this.

I am not arguing that semantics has to be introduced into one's grammatical considerations at the start; I am not even arguing that it has to be introduced at all. I leave it entirely to others to argue this. My point, while not irreconcilable with theirs, is quite different: that grammatical considerations should not intrude on semantics.

Of course there are relations between grammar and semantics, even when these relations are not built into the concepts in question. It is an empirical fact that certain allomorphs of the English plural (as represented by *oxen, children, feet, teeth*, etc.) all have to do with animals or their body-parts. Their interpretation as related allomorphs of the plural is independent of the fact that they have something in common semantically. There is also something in common semantically between *bound, wound* and *ground*, though not between any of these and *found*.

Yes (somebody may answer), but these are allomorphs, and by definition allomorphs have no semantic implications as such.

But my point is that morphemes may be in this respect quite similar to allomorphs. They have no semantic implications. The relation between the singular and plural form of English verbs is as such purely syntactic; it would be impossible to give the most elementary syntactic rules for the distribution of English verb-forms without this distinction being provided for. And in this particular case the morphemes are roughly in complementary distribution inter-verbally, much as allomorphs are in complementary distribution intra-verbally.

It cannot be said too often: morphemic analysis has no necessary implications whatsoever for semantics. People ask: 'If a morpheme is not a meaningful unit, what is it?' It is a unit which cannot be dispensed with in syntactic formulations: what more, at the moment, needs to be said?

It is very misleading, though not plainly wrong, to say that there is a close, though not a very close, relationship between syntax and semantics. It is misleading, since it gives the impression that there is one kind of syntax, rather close to semantics though yet not semantics. Whereas there are two kinds of syntax, one of which is not semantics at all, while the other is. The close but imperfect relationship is a loose compound of two different relationships, one of which is not merely close but perfect, and the other of which is not merely imperfect but rather non-existent. (E.g. the distribution of verbal *scatter* etc. and nominal *crowd* etc. is semantics, though it is also syntax; the distribution of the singular and plural forms of the verb in English is just syntax.)

Among the syntactic constraints some have a strong semantic tie-up, some little, and some none at all. It is this that leads to the confusion. Many linguists are tempted to look on a strong semantic tie-up as an approach towards semantic distribution. Certainly, the distribution of English verbal singular and plural appears more closely related to meaning than e.g. the distribution of the Latin genders. But this is merely a difference of degree; they are both constraints not restraints. It is pointless to ask why an English speaker has chosen to use the singular rather than the plural form of the verb in a given utterance: he has, if he wishes to speak English, no choice. Whereas when he says *the dog runs* etc. rather than *the dog scatters* etc., a reason can be given. There is no syntactic convention prohibiting *the dog scatters.*

Note—and I think this is behind the mutual incomprehension of people who would say that *the dog scatters* is entirely grammatical, and those who would say that it is entirely ungrammatical—that while there is no prohibition on the use of the phrase in any particular instance, it is not allowed that a speaker of English (as it now is) **generally** uses such a phrase. Meanings can be strained, but it is tautologically true that they cannot **generally** be strained. A strained meaning presupposes an ordinary meaning.

If you want to say that there is, in this sense, a constraint involved in the non-use of *the dog scatters* vis-à-vis *the dogs scatter* or *the crowd scatters,* of course I agree. But then one still needs to signal the difference between this sort of constraint and another form of constraint, and this is just the difference I make between a restraint and a constraint.

The distinction is a very old one. It has often been misleadingly described, and even more often drawn too absolutely or at the wrong places —and it is still uncritically accepted by many linguists and uncritically rejected by others. Yet so far as I know, it has been very little discussed, and a conventional vocabulary is not available for discussion. No doubt better terms are available for some of the concepts, and I should be grateful to hear of them.

AN APPLICATION OF PSYCHOLINGUISTICS IN LANGUAGE TEACHING: AN AUDIO-VISUAL INSTRUCTIONAL DEVICE

JOHN B. CARROLL

Harvard University

The teaching machine, or rather, the programmed instruction which it presents, is one of the more recent contributions of psychology to education. [1] The teaching machine may be looked upon as an attempt to provide a controlled environment for learning. By "environment" we refer to all the stimuli impinging upon the learner and all the means available to him either for the purpose of obtaining a feedback from his responses or for obtaining new stimuli. An "ideal" environment would presumably be one in which learning could occur most rapidly, efficiently, and conveniently. The simpler forms of teaching machines which have been exploited thus far, however, are not necessarily adapted to all kinds of learning; in particular, they do not seem well adapted to the teaching of spoken foreign languages.

Even before the advent of the teaching machine, many teachers have had the dream of providing an ideal environment for second language learning. Throughout the centuries, opinion has been divided as to what kind of environment for learning a second language might be ideal. Is it the foreign language milieu in which the individual simply immerses himself in the task of trying to communicate with a foreign people on their own terms? Is it the classroom, filled with able pupils directed by an able teacher? Is it the study, in which one works with a private tutor? We have no conclusive answer to this question—certainly no answer supported by empirical research. Many believe that the private tutor—other things being equal—can provide the best "environment" for learning a second language. Obviously, not everybody can have a private tutor, but electro-mechanical devices which could fulfill many of the functions of a private tutor might be the next best arrangement. The tape

---

[1] For a comprehensive survey of developments, see A. A. Lumsdaine and Robert Glaser (Editors), *Teaching Machines and Programmed Learning: A Source Book* (Washington, D. C.: Department of Audio-Visual Instruction, National Education Association, 1960).

recorder in language laboratory goes far towards meeting this need; sound films have been produced which go even further.

Neither the language laboratory nor the sound film, however, provides one critical element which should be present in any ideal environment for learning—namely, the possibility of an interaction between the pupil and his environment such that the environment responds to the pupil just as much as the pupil responds to the environment. That is to say, there must be a feedback between pupil and environment. In the process by which a child learns his mother tongue, such a feedback occurs almost constantly, for the child learns to make responses which be "reinforced" (rewarded) in specific ways by people in his environment. Such feedback occurs also for the adult set down in a foreign language milieu: eventually he learns language responses which get him food, drink, and shelter. In the classroom or the private tutoring situation, interaction between teacher and pupil depends upon pupil progress. The teacher corrects the pupil, gives him extra practice, and changes the approach when the pupil has difficulty.

The question we may now raise is the following: how much of the ideal learning environment, with all its linkages and interactions between pupil and teacher, can we simulate by electro-mechanical means? How much would we want to simulate in view of the cost and practical difficulties involved? It is clear that with present technology, we have no way of simulating one important element of an ideal environment for language learning—the ability of a skilled teacher to listen to the utterances of a pupil and evaluate them. The same problem, of course, has arisen in connection with the use of the sound film or the tape recorder in the language laboratory, and the only answer provided so far is that the pupil has to be taught to evaluate his own responses. We shall have to be content with this answer, and it may be a very good answer if we will exploit it to the hilt. Aside from this, however, we find that we can indeed simulate most of the critical elements of an ideal language learning environment. With electronic computers controlling various stimulus-presentation devices such as slide projectors, tape recorders with playback features, sound films or videotapes which respond to signals from the learner, an automated learning environment can be created which comes very close to the real thing, if we are willing to spend enough money.

My own explorations in the direction of an automated environment for language learning have taken me far short of the full electronic automation that might conceivably be attempted. My goal has been, simply stated, to develop an audio-visual device for individual self-instruction in language learning which could be built for no more than the cost of, say, a color-television receiver. I have achieved this goal, in the sense that a prototype model of the device now exists and is in working order.[2] It is pictured in Figure 1.

I have also devised a program in elementary spoken and written Mandarin Chinese to illustrate the possibilities of the machine, but the material has not as yet been tried out on volunteer subjects. At this time, therefore, I can only describe the device and present in outline the ideas on which it is based.

It is my assumption that it is convenient to divide the total content of instruction into manageably-sized units which we will call *loops*. A loop contains a short sequence of instruction which one may desire to present repetitively and with certain variations in procedure as will be described below. The loops will in turn be divided into *frames*, each frame presenting a small bit of instruction or practice—ranging from a single phonemic contrast, for example, to an utterance of three or four sentences. The learning of a complex skill like the speaking and understanding of a foreign language is usually acknowledged to require considerable repetitive practice. The design of the machine thus allows the student to work with a given loop in three progressively more challenging levels or modes of operation, called respectively (1) Familiarization, (2) Learning, and (3) Testing.

Let us describe how the student would typically proceed as he works with a given loop. He will start with the machine set to the Familiarization mode. Beginning in the frame zero, he proceeds through the successive frames of the loop. (This frame is numbered zero because it is both the beginning and the end of the loop.) The work with each frame consists of three phases: first, a *presentation* phase in which the student may be given instructions, new learning material, explanations, or any other content which may help in learning; second, a *question* phase in which he is given some definite task to perform, such as answering a question; and third, an *answer* phase

---

[2] This machine was designed by the writer and built by Mr. S. Kingsley Roby of Saddle River, New Jersey. The writer's work has been supported by a grant from the Society for the Investigation of Human Ecology.

FIGURE 1. Front view of the automated audio-viual instructional device described in the accompanying article. A Sample film loop is resting on top of the box containing the projection screen; a sample magnetic tape cartridge is resting against the wall of the same box (*center right*). To the left of the projection creen are (*above*) a small loudspeaker and (*below*) a box containing relays and auxiliary controls; in the foreground is the control panel operated by the student and (*bottom right*) the write-in paper tape.

in which he is given the opportunity of finding out whether the response he made in the question phase was correct or not. When he gets to the end of the loop (Frame zero), he checks the counters which show how many right and wrong answers he made during the loop. If he got too high a ratio of wrong answers, he proceeds through the loop again, and so on until he meets a suitably high standard of performance, say, two errors in the loop or less. As soon as the student meets this standard of performance, whether on the first or a later trip through the loop, he may set the machine to the Learning mode (called so for convenience—it is not implied that learning does not take place in the Familiarization mode also). This allows him to proceed through the loop again, but now the "presentation" phase of each frame is omitted; the machine now gives him only the question and answer phases, it being presumed that he no longer needs the instructions and practice materials supplied in the presentation phase. During the question phase of a frame, however, the student may call for "prompts"—that is, hints, or cues, or partial answers which will (it is hoped) help him recall the correct answer, not only during this trip through the loop but also when he meets the same question on the next trial. As before, the student may proceed through the loop in the Learning mode as many times as are necessary to achieve a specified standard of performance as exhibited in the response counters.

After the Learning mode, the student may proceed through the loop in the Testing mode. Here, he gets only questions. He must answer solely out of what he has learned, without support of prompts or of confirmations; the answers are "for keeps." (As yet is uncertain whether the Testing mode will be necessary for efficient learning; it may be useful only from the point of view of providing evidence of achievement.)

After mastery of Loop 1 in this fashion, the student proceeds to Loop 2 and works through it in the same manner, i.e., in the three modes, then to Loop 3, and so throughout the entire series. Tentatively, it is planned that each loop will contain about 40 frames, and one trip through such a loop may take anywhere from 20 minutes to an hour depending upon the complexity of the material put into the frames. If the student at any time wishes to go back in the sequence, he can refresh himself by operating an earlier loop in the learning or testing phase. One advantage of this system over the purely linear system now favored by many psychologists is that the student who wishes to "refresh" his knowledge does not have to retrace every step of the program. More important than this, however, is that it is not necessary to build into the program the repetitions which are apparently essential in the learning of a foreign language skill; the repetitions are a function of the way the machine is operated. This makes the programming and the storage of the program more economical than under a purely linear program. In a sense, the prototype of this machine is the memory drum, used for many years by psychologists in studying learning. [3] The program is contained in two elements.

First, the *visual* components are presented by means of a 35mm. film strip loop which is projected frame by frame. The film frame is divided into several areas, as indicated in Figure 2. The column of spaces at the right is not visible to the learner; instead, it is projected onto a bank of photoelectric cells which sense which spaces contain control marks. This information affects the operation of the machine; for example, markings may indicate whether the question presented in the frame is a constructed response question or a multiple-choice question, and if the latter, which answer is keyed correct. The remainder of the film frame is divided into a number of areas which can be exposed to the learner. One of these, the "reference area," is always visible and may contain any information or presentation which one desires to make available to the learner. Each of the others is exposed to the learner only if the corresponding shutter is opened. The order in which they are exposed will be further described below.

Second, the auditory components of the program are presented by means of a continuous magnetic tape loop cartridge. The tape contains two channels, one for the regular audio message to be heard by the learner and the other for control signals which mark the boundaries of tape segments, causing the tape mechanism to stop as soon as a signal is encountered.

Let us now move closer to the actual operation of the machine during a particular "frame." Suppose the learner is working with Loop One in the Familiarization mode. He has just finished with the introductory frame, "frame zero," and has pushed a certain button on the control panel, causing the film to advance to frame one. Immediately, the P-area of the frame one is exposed (see Figure 2), and at the same time the corresponding tape segment is played. For

---

[3] On this point, see David Zeaman, "Skinner's Theory of Teaching Machines," pp. 167-175 in Eugene Galanter (Editor), *Automatic Teaching: the State of the Art*, New York, John Wiley and Sons, Inc., 1959.

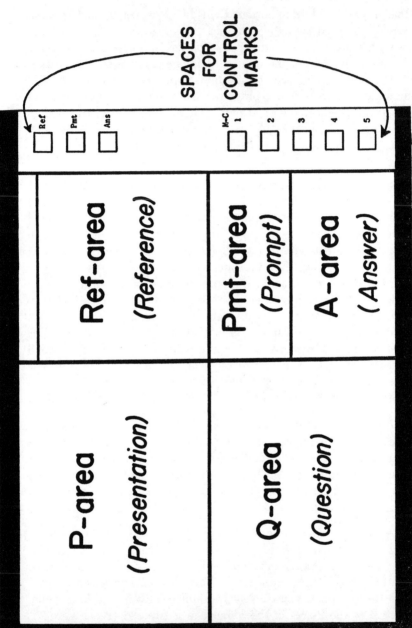

FIGURE 2. Design of film frame. The spaces for the control marks at the right are not seen by the student; each of the remaining areas may be separately exposed to him, except that the Ref-area is always visible.

example, the P-area might contain simply the printed instruction, "Listen and repeat," while the voice on the tape says, "Frame One. Repeat these words: . . . " The tape would play until a control signal on the tape is encountered. The reference area, also visible, might contain a picture to accompany the utterance. The learner would be expected to repeat aloud the foreign language utterance. Having done so, he would press a button to call for exposure of the Q-area, just below the P-area (see Figure 2) and the rendition of the corresponding tape segment. The Q-area shutter would open and the tape would again start to play, presenting some sort of question or task for the learner. It could be, for example, a multiple-choice question, in which case five buttons on the control panel would light up after the tape has finished playing, and the learner would have to press a button to signify his response. (In the Familiarization and Learning modes, the student is allowed to press one button after another until he finds the correct one, that is, the one which will advance the machine; only his first choice, however, is counted as right or wrong). If the Q-area presents a free-response task, i.e., requiring either a spoken or written response, the machine simply stops and waits for the learner to make this response to his satisfactions, after which the learner must push a buttton to advance to the next phase of the presentation. Whether the question is multiple-choice or free-response, the next phase of the presentation is the exposure of the A-area and the playing of a corresponding tape segment. These presentations furnish the learner with the correct answer, in either visual or auditory form (or both), together with any further information which one may wish to present at this time. For example, one may draw attention to some particular feature of the answer, or give special instructions concerning the evaluation of the student's response. For it is during the answer phase that the student must evaluate any free responses he was required to give during the question phase. If it was a spoken response, he will have to remember his response for a short time while comparing it with that rendered by the tape; if it was a written response, he has the opportunity of comparing it visually with what he sees in the A-area. He must then push one of two buttons which are lighted at that time, either the "R" (right) or the "W" (wrong) button, to indicate the correctness of his response. It is assumed that the student will not be tempted to cheat. He cannot cheat if the question was a multiple-choice question, for in this case the machine will already automatically have counted his first button-push (of the five lighted buttons) as either right or wrong, and the answer-phase serves only to reinforce or explain the correct choice which he will inevitably have come around to making even if his first choice was wrong (because the machine does not "advance" to the answer-phase until he finds the correct button).

When the learner has pushed either the R or W buttons (which would be lighted in case the question had been free-response) or another button, labeled "C" (which would be lighted in case the question had been multiple-choice), the machine will advance to the next frame, and the whole sequence is repeated in whatever variation is demanded by that frame. The learner proceeds in this way until he gets to the end of the loop, "Frame zero," at which time he can decide whether to repeat the loop in the Familiarization mode, or perform the loop in the Learning mode. If he decides the latter, he moves a lever to cause the machine to operate in that mode. As mentioned previously, the Learning mode omits the presentation phase; that is, the P-area is not exposed and the corresponding tape segment is omitted. Instead, only the Q-area and the A-areas of the frame are presented, in that order, together with the corresponding tape segments. During the learning mode the student may call for "prompts;" these are purely visual and are exposed in the "Pmt-area" (see Figure 2). In the testing mode the student sees only the Q-area, and the A-area if it is necessary for him to evaluate his own answer.

Although the above description probably seems complicated and formidable, the actual operation is very simple. The buttons to be pushed during a given frame are arranged in sequence from left to right, and the choices available to be pushed at any given time are always lighted. Young children can learn to operate the machine without difficulty. The operation is so simple that the learner can concentrate on the task of learning; there is no flipping of pages, manipulation of tapes, or other distraction.

Several minor points remain to be mentioned. One is that the machine will contain a device which will enable the student to hear again any auditory signal he has heard from the magnetic tape. He will not hear this replying from the master magnetic tape itself, but from an auxiliary tape device which continuously maintains a record of the last 30 or so seconds of audio signals which have been heard at any given time. The learner can rehear only as much as he wishes, however, and this will be immediate; i.e., he will not have to wait throughout the length of the auxiliary tape. At the same time, any signal on the auxiliary tape will gradually lose fidelity with repeated playing, thus discouraging the learner from over-use of this device.

Another point is that the machine as presently constructed contains no provision for the student to record and listen to his own spoken responses. This could easily be provided if it is found necessary, but it is believed that recording of the student's response would not be of any great assistance in learning; on the contrary, recording of students' incorrect responses may be a hindrance to learning. At any rate, there is up to now no convincing research evidence to the effect that the recording of student responses is a positive advantage in learning.

The machine contains a device whereby the student can write or draw responses on a continuous paper tape, each "frame" of written response moves up under a plastic window at the outset of the answer-phase, and then out of sight completely. The teacher or researcher can examine these tapes at a later time to get concrete evidence of student progress.

Programming for any teaching machine is tedious; programming for this audio-visual instructional device is at any rate not less tedious than for other machines, except for the fact that one is not required to program repetition as such. The materials for each loop must be carefully outlined and planned in advance. The program is prepared on large sheets of legal-size paper bearing the pattern shown in Figure 2 as well as space for drafting the script of the auditory program. These sheets are then photographed on Microfile film (negative) by an ordinary 35 mm. camera held in a special rig. The auditory program is recorded on a two-channel master tape; after this material is copied onto friction-free tape, it is packaged in continuous loop cartridges.

The basic principles underlying the design of the machine are simple:

(1) Provision is made for *maximal control* by the programmer (within feasible limits) of the stimuli impinging on the learner, particularly of their timing and sequencing; these stimuli may be either auditory or visual, or both.

(2) Provision is made for maximal versatility with respect to the kinds of responses evokable by the machine: spoken, written, or multiple-choice.

(3) The pacing of the machine is under the control of the learner, who can progress precisely as fast as he is able.

(4) The machine provides prompt confirmation of the learner's responses—normally not more than a few seconds after he has made his response.

Almost any type of foreign language instruction can be programmed for the machine. One can range from the purest of "direct-method" instruction in which all instruction is carried on in the target language with the aid of pictures and conventional symbols, to the most traditional form of grammar-translation teaching. One can program in "large steps" or in small steps. One can program so as to teach the student a knowledge of phonetics and phonemics to help him to learn a foreign language pronunciation; the audio-visual features of the machine make it amenable to programs in learning to read foreign scripts, such as Cyrillic or Arabic.

Ultimately, we may hope that experience and research will show how a machine such as this one can find its place in the equipment of the language teacher. One is given to doubt that a machine can fulfill all the functions of a teacher, even though it can go a long way. With suitable programming techniques, also, one may hope that language teaching can be made even smoother, easier, and more effective than it is under existing methods of instruction. But because this machine affords such good control over the manner in which language teaching material is presented, and indeed over the whole of the learning process, one of the most exciting possibilities of the machine is as a research tool. Since I am primarily an educational psychologist rather than a language teacher, it is with this use of the machine that I will be most concerned.

SOME INDETERMINACIES IN LANGUAGE

WALLACE L. CHAFE

University of California, Berkeley

One of the dogmas of American linguistics during the post-Bloomfield period and one that still exerts considerable influence on linguistic theory and practice has been that language patterning involves boundary lines which are wholly and in all cases impenetrable; that everything must be either this or that; and if this, then never also that as well. It is generally recognized that some aspects of language do in fact fall outside this restricted framework, but it has been assumed that such aspects do not form part of the self-contained system, usually called language structure, in which linguists are above all interested. This dogma looms behind the aphorism 'once a phoneme, always a phoneme', for example, and it explains the lack of enthusiasm shown in this country for the concept of phonemic neutralization. If a distinction exists between some elements, it has been assumed other elements cannot straddle the distinction or be ambiguous towards it. There is, of course, no justification for retaining such a doctrine if the facts of language refute it, and I will now suggest some ways in which they do.

There are four situations, I believe, all of them to be found in language, which are not in harmony with the doctrine of discrete boundaries as I have just stated it. I will refer to them as *neutralization, ambiguity, gradience* and *indeterminacy.* Let me define them briefly. Neutralization means that a distinction between A and B, significant in some environments, has no significance in others. Ambiguity means that X is sometimes A and sometimes B, depending on its environment. Gradience means that X stands somewhere between A and B. Indeterminacy means that X has some characteristics of A and some of B, but is not in all respects identifiable as either the one or the other.

Neither neutralization nor ambiguity is inconsonant with the doctrine of discreteness, if it is given a slightly broader interpretation than that with which I opened this paper. If such situations occur, and you may all be able to think of examples of them, it is still true that *in any particular environment* rigid lines are present. It is easily possible to relax the assumption that a boundary which exists anywhere exists everywhere in order to permit environmental variation in this regard. Gradience and indeterminacy, however, if we must take account of them in language as well as in paralanguage, mean that discreteness has indeed been a dogma, a deterrent to progress, and an example of the over-extension of mechanical principles which happens so often in the history of every science. A recent monograph by Bolinger has dealt with possible instances of gradience in language.[1] It is cases of the fourth type, of indeterminacy, that I wish to consider here.

But before I do, it is necessary to say some other things about language in order that we may have a common framework within which to proceed. There are so many conflicting theories now in the air that it is virtually impossible to talk about anything at all without a preliminary understanding on fundamentals. The most important assertion I want to make at this point is that there are two areas in which language has contact with the world outside itself, and that consequently there are two aspects of language which can be directly or indirectly observed: its sounds and its meanings. To attempt a description of language based on sounds alone is a course that I believe is foredoomed to failure, since it ignores at least half, and in a sense, much more than half of the behavior we want to describe. I would like to have you think of language, for just a minute, as if the observable part of it consisted of two streams flowing in the same direction, like the Potomac and the C & O Canal, except that they flow through time rather than through space. One of them is the stream of sound. Like the canal, this one is easy for us to control. We can record it magnetically and re-examine it whenever we wish. We can cut it up in pieces, stretch it, or compress it. We can produce it artificially and can make pictures of it on paper that include more detail than we know what to do with. The other stream is the stream of meanings, of which, as we are accustomed to say, the sounds are symbols. But, like the Potomac, meanings are considerably more difficult for us to handle. It is only in the minority of cases that we can observe them directly, as when Jack hands Jill the apple for which she has just asked. Most of the time we can only reconstruct their properties on the basis of indirect evidence, or, as is most often done, attempt imperfectly to relate them to our own internalized meanings through

---

[1] Dwight L. Bolinger, *Generality, Gradience, and the All-or-None* (The Hague, 1961). Kenneth L. Pike has also called for a broadening of linguistics beyond the restrictions of discrete categories; see for example his "Language as Particle, Wave, and Field," *Texas Quarterly* II, 2 (1954), 37-54.

translation. It is intriguing to think of the possibility of machines that would record the stream of meanings in speech as we now can record the stream of sound, of a semantic tape recorder or a semantic spectrograph, but how such machines might be constructed is beyond the range of imagination. Because, however, meanings are so hard for us to deal with, we are not justified in pretending, ostrich-like, that they are not there, or that we can describe language without them. It would be obvious folly for us to proceed on the assumption that the canal is the only route by which water flows past Georgetown.

If we have learned anything about language in all our systematic study of it, it is that while these two streams may seem laden with mud as they flow through the physical world where we can observe them, in their origin and destination they are limpid. Somehow, that is to say, within the mind of the speaker and the mind of the hearer, although certainly beyond the level of conscious awareness, they are patterned. I would like to say that patterning entails nothing more than the recurrence of relationships. Relationships, however, imply elements that are related, and we are used to dealing with elements such as phonemes and morphemes, syllables and words and various others. These elements are found to be arranged at different levels of inclusion, what Hockett calls 'size-levels',[2] yielding a kind of hierarchy of arrangements, although I believe it is an oversimplified distortion to visualize these hierarchies as a branching tree, as in traditional immediate constituent analysis and so-called 'phrase structure' grammar. In any case, we can look upon the origin and destination of the stream of sound as patterned within one hierarchy which can be called phonological and the origin and destination of the second stream, the stream of meaning, as patterned within another hierarchy which can be called grammatical. Joining these two hierarchies together, is the non-hierarchical realm of morphophonemics. And it is in morphophonemics that our first cases of indeterminacy occur.

These are familiar cases, and I don't want to spend much time on them. They are simply the numerous instances where it is impossible for us to decide whether a particular phoneme expresses one morpheme or another. Anyone who has attempted to describe a language in morphemic terms must have run into this situation. There is a fairly common kind of language change, the re-cutting of morph boundaries—whereby, for example, *a napron* became *an apron*—which is evidence that not only linguists, but

---

[2] Charles F. Hockett, "Ethnolinguistic Implications of Studies in Linguistics and Psychiatry," *Report of the Ninth Annual Round Table Meeting on Linguistics and Language Study,* Georgetown University (1958), 178-9.

also the speakers of a language may vacillate in this respect. The 'empty morph' and 'morph overlapping' have been suggested as devices for the handling of these situations, but whatever one does about them, the important thing is to recognize that morphophonemics does often present us with such cases, and to be able to accept them as part of the scheme of things. I would like to talk mainly about some ways in which indeterminacy may affect the very identity of grammatical elements, for somehow our preconceptions make it harder here to accept.

A question that frequently arises in grammatical analysis may be stated in this form: 'How do we know whether these two (or three, or more) different phoneme sequences express the same or different grammatical elements'? The question is an old one, but it has usually been treated as if it always had an answer. Let us begin by considering the English plural allomorphs /s/, /z/, and /ɨz/. There are two things about this set of phoneme sequences which lead us to equate them grammatically: first, the differences between them are phonologically predictable, a fact which suggests that they all three developed out of a single earlier shape; and second, they have, as we say, the same meaning. But the supposition that they have the same meaning is confirmed by the phenomenon of agreement: for example, by the fact that all three co-occur with the same plurally inflected verbs. The semantic criterion, thus supported by distributional dependencies, is sufficient in itself to convince us that the words *children, men* and *feet* contain this morpheme too, even though in these cases phonological predictability is wholly absent. There are other cases, however, where the supposed semantic identity is not independently confirmed: for example, in derivational affixes that show no agreement with external elements. Take the phoneme sequences /ayz/ in *legalize,* /ən/ in *widen* and the vowel difference in *fill* as opposed to *full.* The meanings of all three may be paraphrased 'to cause to be in the state denoted by the stem', but is identical paraphrase sufficient evidence of grammatical identity? Does it really matter whether we consider them one morpheme or three? It matters if we are concerned with counting morphemes, but if there is real indeterminacy here—if the question regarding grammatical identity or difference is actually a meaningless one—then counting morphemes cannot be a rigorous procedure. This consequence would be disturbing to language typologists, whose methods would then need some revision, but I think the rest of us might do well to accept it with equanimity.

Closely associated with this kind of indeterminacy, which might be called 'paradigmatic', is another kind for which the term 'syntagmatic' would be appropriate. I would like to illustrate it with the English numerals. When we begin counting—*one, two, three,* etc.,—we find a series of minimal grammatical elements which have the characteristics of morphemes. This situation holds at least through *ten,* and probably through *eleven.* Skipping *twelve* for a moment and passing on to the teens, we find now arrangements of two morphemes each, one of them identical with the already encountered *three, four,* etc., the other, the *teen* morpheme, having the meaning 'added to ten'. Before long we come to other two-morpheme arrangements, *twenty, thirty,* etc., in which we have the same initial elements again, but with a second element, *ty,* that means 'multiplied by ten'. I will leave out of consideration the possible identifications between *ten, teen,* and *ty*—all three partially similar both phonetically and semantically—and concentrate on *twelve,* where an analogous situation appears in especially clear-cut form. If *twelve* were not *twelve* but **twenteen,* we would most certainly know what to do with it, for it would be to *twenty* as *thirteen* is to *thirty, fourteen* to *forty,* etc. The first part of *twelve* might easily be associated with the first parts of *twenty* and *twice,* as well as with *two* itself. Is then its second part, /lv/, identifiable with the *teen* morpheme? There really is no good answer. The uniqueness of *twelve* makes us want on the one hand to fit it into the prevailing pattern and on the other hand to give some recognition to its place outside the pattern. Its relation to the teens is indeterminate; it belongs and it doesn't belong, both at the same time.

I would not like to rule out the possibility that there is even a gradient continuum of morphemicness, a nondiscrete scale of 'status as an independent grammatical element'. Toward the bottom end of the scale would be elements like the initial consonant cluster of *slip, slide, slick, slink, slither, slurp, slop* and *slush.* Towards the top of the scale would be the English plural morpheme, but its status might slip a little in *deer* and *sheep,* indicating that status also depends in part on environment.

The last kind of indeterminacy I want to mention is homonymy. Here, instead of several different phonological items expressing one grammatical element, we find several different grammatical elements being expressed by a single sequence of phonemes. Here, again, it is possible that there are degrees of indeterminacy. There seems little room for doubt that the phonological sequence /tuw/ in *too many* expresses a different grammatical element from the same sequence in *two men.* Indeterminacy is at a minimum because there is overwhelming external evidence of distinctness in the grammatical roles. But what about the /hed/ in *head of hair* and the one in *head of cabbage?* The semantic differences are evidently predictable; but if for that reason we identify the two *heads,* should we do the same with the *ears* in *earache* and *ear of corn?* The phonemic identity is a historical accident in this second case, but the semantic similarity and predictability are comparable to those found in the two *heads*. Has accidental phonological convergence coupled with accidental semantic similarity led to grammatical identity? How can we answer any of these questions with complete assurance?

I have a feeling that such questions are difficult to face because they are simply questions that should not be asked. They are like the question whether midnight belongs to the preceding or following day. We can arbitrarily decide what we want the answer to be, but we cannot thereby overcome the fact that the question is unanswerable because it is improper to the circumstances to begin with. Just as the science of physics in this century has moved away from a narrowly conceived materialism and blossomed out in all directions, it seems to me not unlikely, and more than a little intriguing, that linguistics may sooner or later also have to abandon its narrow framework of discrete pigeonholes, and that its ability to handle the elusive phenomena of language will likewise abundantly increase.

CODE-SWITCHING IN
GREEK-ENGLISH BILINGUAL SPEECH[1]

A. RICHARD DIEBOLD, JR.

The German linguist Albert Thumb, who worked extensively with the various modern languages spoken in the Greek homeland, early noted, as one must, that there is "ein heftiger Sprachkampf" between the collection of modern dialects which (together with an emergent colloquial standard based on some of them) has been called δημοτική /ðimotikí/ (hereafter *Demotic*), and a literary standard called καθαρεύονσα /kaθarévusa/ (hereafter *Katharevusa*).[2] The relationship between the two systems and their histories are not unlike other instances of diglossia, paralleling, for instance, the situation which Kučera has recently described for Literary and Colloquial Czech.[3] Later during these same meetings, I understand that Professor Householder will inform us in greater detail concerning this interesting case of Greek diglossia, which is euphemistically referred to in Greece as the γλωσσικόν ζήτημα /ɣlosikón zítima/, the 'language issue'. My only purpose in further mentioning it now is to indicate

---

[1] The research upon which this paper is based was supported by a research grant from the Laboratory of Social Relations, Harvard University. I acknowledge with thanks comments offered me by Eric P. Hamp, Charles E. Bidwell, and Fred W. Householder.

[2] Albert Thumb. 1895. *Handbuch der Neugriechischen Volkssprache.* Strassburg; Verlag Karl J. Trübner; and also his 1926 *Grammatik der Neugriechischen Volkssprache* (revised by J. E. Kalitsunakis). Berlin and Leipzig; Walter de Gruyter & Co. Thumb (1895:vii,viii) succinctly describes the Greek diglossia: ". . . man versteht bekanntlich unter 'Neugriechisch' *zwei* Sprachformen, einmal die lebendige vom Volke gesprochene, in Zahlreiche Mundarten gegliederte Sprache, welche eigentlich allein den Namen neugriechische verdient, dann die Schriftsprache, die καθαρεύουσα d.h., 'reine Sprache', welche eine literarische Wiederbelebung der mehr oder weniger modernisierten altgriechischen Gemeinsprache ist, also ein Kunstprodukt, allerdings nicht der neuesten Zeit, sondern das Ergebnis jahrhundertelangen, bis über Byzanz hinausreichenden Schriftgebrauchs: wie weit man in dieser erstarrten altgriechischen Sprachform neue, der Volkssprache entstammende Elemente zuliess und zulässt, was nicht nur in verschiedenen Zeiten verschieden, sondern wechselt auch jeweils nach Autor und Gegenstand."

[3] Henry Kučera. 1961. *The Phonology of Czech.* 's-Gravenhage; Mouton & Co., see especially pp. 11-20. The so-called spisovná čestina 'literary Czech' or spisovny jazyk 'literary language' is an analogue to Katharevusa; there is a colloquial "standard" (the hovorová čestina) which, like its analogue Demotic, is based on a multiple background of colloquial dialects such as the obecná čestina, and yet is influenced markedly by the literary language. Charles A. Ferguson has outlined four similar cases (including Modern Greek) in his 1959. "Diglossia", *Word* 15.325-340.

how it has obscured aspects of the subject which I want to discuss, namely, the nature of recent English-derived interference as this occurs in the bilingual speech of American Greeks, a variety of Demotic which Greek nationals are wont to label ἀμερικάνικα 'American'.

The language contacts which the Greek dialects have experienced during the past several centuries are many, and it is not unreasonable to assume that some of the observed linguistic changes in Greek, especially in the phonology and the lexicon, derive from those contacts; comparative procedures demonstrate, in fact, that many are. For the linguist restricted to written materials, however, there exists the problem of getting behind the facade of Katharevusa; the problem is similar to conjuring up an image of the ancient colloquial speech obscured behind a lattice of literary Attic, by examining, for example, Aristophanes's comic dialogues. Perusal of modern bilingual Greek dictionaries show considerable mixture at many points between Katharevusa and Demotic. The mixture, however, is not without a measure of order: when ever there is an actual rivalry between synonymous Katharevusa and Demotic members of a doublet, and the fact of rivalry is seldom reported, the problem of correct entry is cavalierly resolved by omitting the Demotic form. In these cases, *the Demotic form is frequently a recent borrowing.* We cannot welcome too eagerly, therefore, the appearance of dictionaries such as Swanson's *Vocabulary of Modern Spoken Greek*[4] since the Demotic entries contained therein provide an infinitely more reliable index of recent linguistic interference. It is difficult, to be sure, to assess the full effect of Katharevusa not only in fending off on-going linguistic interference but also in weeding out products of recent contact-induced changes. It is now known that there are a larger proportion of Katharevusa-derived loanshifts and induced creations than earlier realized. These are of the sort which enabled German-language sentimentalists to hold on to *Fernsprecher* before the onslaught of *Telefon;* and, like German, these forms especially abound in learned and technical vocabulary.

Loanword phonology has brought about a number of syntagmatic changes in the native phonology, both in the distribution and in the native phonology, both in the distribution and in the sequence con-

---

[4] Donald C. Swanson. 1959. *Vocabulary of Modern Greek*. Minneapolis; University of Minnesota Press. See also a study of loanwords by the same author, 1958. "English Loanwords in Modern Greek", *Word* 14.26-46. I have consulted, in addition, I. Kykkotis. 1947. (revised Edition, 1960) *English-Greek and Greek-English Dictionary*. London; Percy Lund, Humphries & Co. Ltd.

straint rules of the phonemes involved. For example, the distribution of the voiced stop series /b,d,g/ has changed as result of diaphonic identifications with various foreign models which had similar sounds in word-initial position; prior to this phonic interference, /b,d,g/ never occurred in word-initial. A brief examination of dictionary entries for /b,d,g/ will quickly betray their non-native provenance.[5] French and Italian loanwords certainly have been more influential in this syntagmatic change, but the Demotic forms μπούσι /búsi/ 'bus', ντόνατ /dónat/ 'doughnut', and γκρέϊπ-φρούτ /gréipfrut/ 'grape-fruit' are all replicas of English models. For another example, it is easy to reconstruct a morphophonemic code in many Greek dialects, for a period antecedent to the impact of French-Italian-English contracts, in which, between successive junctures, (1) nasal plus voiceless consonant becomes nasal plus voiced consonant, or in some cases, becomes voiced consonant alone (thus e.g. $n + t > nd$, $m + p > mb$); and (2) n before labial stops becomes m plus voiced labial stop, i.e. $n + p,b > mb$.[6] Syntagmatic changes in loanword phonology have altered these rules: e.g. nk (earlier $> ng$) occurs in English-derived loanwords such as τάνκς /tánks/ 'tank', np (earlier $> mb$) in πίνπον /pínpon/ 'ping-pong', nt (earlier $> nd$) in τζέντελμαν /dzéntelman/ 'gentleman'.

Loanword phonology has incurred little paradigmatic change from an analytic point of view; there have been no major changes in the status of distinctive features as opposed to determined or conditioned, i.e., redundant features in the phonological code. Minor exceptions include the change from conditioned to distinctive for the feature 'grave' (as opposed to 'acute') in the non-labial nasal /n/, such that phonemic split occurs between the acute allophones [n̪] [ñ] and the grave velar [ŋ]. Prior to the introduction of loanwords such as πίνπον /pínpon/ ['pi.ŋ₁pɔŋ], [ŋ] was in non-contrastive distribution with [n̪] [ñ], occurring only before velar consonants $(n + k,g> [ŋ]g; n + x,ɣ] > [ŋ]ɣ)$; they now contrast in syllable-final position. Phone-types novel to the earlier phonology have been

---

[5] The orthography recognizes the special status of these entries and reflects one of the morphophonemic rules discussed later in this paper: initial b is written μπ (mp, but $m + p > mb$, or sometimes $> b$); initial d is written ντ (nt, but $n + t > nd$, or sometimes $> d$); g is γκ but note that — γκ — (as well as — γγ —) is —ng— (and $n + g$ sometimes $> g$); in word-medial —μπ— $=$ —mb— and $=$ντ— $=$ —nd—. This is an interesting example, manifest orthographically, of the "psychological reality", not of phonemes (in the traditional sense), but rather of morphophonemes.
[6] Demotic morphophonemics is briefly discussed by Julian T. Pring: 1950. *A Grammar of Modern Greek on a Phonetic Basic*. London; University of London Press Ltd; see also Thumb 1895, op. cit., pp. 1-22.

imported: in some dialects, one regularly hears the fricatives [š] [ž] and the affricates [tš] [dž], which have come in with loanwords such as σιέρρι /šéri/ 'sherry', σάπ /šáp/ 'shop', τζέρκ /jérk/ 'jerk', not to mention in many non-English loanwords, e.g. γκαράζ /garáž/∼/garáz/ 'garage' (< French *garage* /garaž/). In other dialects, however, diaphonic identifications have substituted similar native sounds rather than importing these non-native ones; thus /séri/ /sáp/ /dzérk/ rather than /šéri/ /šáp/ /jérk/. Retroflexed vowels and English-like diphthongs have been imported also, but their frequency is low. Analytically, there is no compelling reason to set these importations up either as new phonemes or as constituting a separable coexistent system, a point to which I will return.

These changes, already integrated in the Demotic phonological code, are the common property of all American Demotic speakers, quite apart from their subsequent contacts with English. For those who do learn English, however, these integrated changes have paved the way for the assimilation of new loanwords with relatively little distortion of the phonological shape of the original English models. An extreme of distortion involving recent loans might be the replica ['pɛkɛdzdɔʀ],* but the shape of the English model *package-store* ['pækɨj ˌstɔˆ.] is nevertheless readily identifiable.

The generalizations which I want to make about the phonology of code-switching are based on the study of the diaphonic identifications which coordinate bilinguals make in their rendition of English words and phrases in the context of Greek discourses. [7] By 'code-switching' is usually meant the successive alternate use of two different language codes within the same discourse; it implies that the speaker is conscious of the switch. Although the research on which this report is based included the study of Greek forms in the context of English discourses, I will restrict my remarks here to the examination of English forms in the context of Greek discourses. The majority of idiolects which made up my sample was those of speakers who were coordinately bilingual in Greek and English, i.e., in whose Greek and English there were no features of foreign accent in one such as we might attribute to the dominance of the other. The sample did include, however, subordinate bilinguals who had obvious accents in English, their secondary language. Without excep-

---

[7] Analysis of these diaphonic identifications has followed the descriptive framework offered in Uriel Weinreich. 1957. "On the Description of Phonic Interference", *Word* 13.1-11.

* In the phonetic transcription, [ʀ]=apico- alveolar flap; [r]=any of the typical allophones of American English /r/.

tion the speakers had been born into families whose primary language was Greek. The coordinate bilinguals either acquired their Greek and English together as primary languages in childhood, or subsequent to having learned Greek as a primary language achieved perfect mastery of English as a secondary language. The description of the phonic interference which I observed, essentially listings of diaphonic identifications which account for the shape of Greek replicas of English models, is too lengthy to present here. The generalizations which the description yielded are more interesting.

One of the prevalent types of change in American Demotic is that which Haugen has called 'reborrowing',[8] a process which somewhat resembles dialect borrowing in the bilingual community and by which a replica-loanword becomes ever more alike in shape to its original model in the donor language. Reborrowing presumably operates on the basis of increasing proficiency in the secondary language and consequent greater familiarity with the models therein. The process is strikingly apparent in the case of those English-derived loanwords which are already integrated in Demotic (some so even before the 20th Century immigration to the United States), forms such as: (various written forms) /oloráit/ 'alright', μπάρ /bár/ 'bar', κέκ /kék/ 'cake', τσέκκι /tséki/ 'check', (various written forms) /gágzder/ 'gangster', τζάζ /dzáz/ 'jazz', σάντουΐτς /sándwits/ 'sandwich', σιέρρι /séri/ 'sherry', σόκ /sók/ 'shock'. Integrated loanwords such as these (I estimate that there are well over 100, some with high frequency of occurrence) are learned by the monolingual speaker as well as the bilingual during the normal childhood acquisition of his speech; they are a part of the Demotic *langue*. But many younger Greek speakers, coordinately bilingual in Greek and English, shortly acquire, as the Greek forms, not [ˈbaʀ] but [ˈbar], and [ˈɛɪk] for [ˈkɛːk], [ˈčɛk] for [ˈtsɛki], [ˈgæ.ŋstər] for [ˈgagzdəʀ], [ˈjæ.z] for [ˈdza.z], [ˈsænwič] for [ˈsandwits], [ˈšɛ.ri] for [ˈsɛːʀi], and [ˈšák] for [ˈsɔk].

It would be very interesting, working with a large sample of speakers, to ascertain whether there is a stratigraphy of replica-shapes from least to most resemblant of the model, co-varying with the proficiency of the speaker in the secondary language which con-

---

8 'Reborrowing' is discussed in Einar Haugen. 1950. "The analysis of linguistic borrowings", *Language* 26.210-231 (see especially section 12); see also Haugen's 1953. *The Norwegian Language in America*. 2 Vols. (Philadelphia; University of Pennsylvania Press) Vol. 2, Chap. 15 'The Process of Borrowing' and Chap. 16 'The Phonology of Loanwords', pp. 383-458, for many well-described parallel cases in American Norwegian.

tains the models.[9] I have noticed chains like (for ράδιο 'radio') [ˈřaðio] — [ˈʀɛːdio] — [ˈrɛɪ̯dio] which are thus correlated, [ˈřaðio] occurring in the speech of immigré subordinate bilunguals who learned English later in their lives, and [ˈrɛɪ̯dio] in the speech of young American coordinate bilinguals. There are a few loanwords which may continue to resist the effects of reborrowing; these are mainly place-names e.g., Νέα Ύόρκι/néa iórki/ 'New York', Βοστώνης /vostónis/ 'Boston', which were widely known and deeply integrated before immigration.

Examining the Greek of the coordinate bilinguals brought to light the following significant but not unexpected finding: that, with the exception of a very few forms, phonic interference always makes for perceptible differences between the replica and the model. This difference obtains independently of whether the speaker (1) produces the model without accent when speaking English or (2) is aware of the relationship of the English model and the Greek replica. I collected a short text in English from one coordinate bilingual, the subject of which concerned Boston weather reports. A detailed phonetic analysis failed to reveal any of the properties which might implicate a Greek accent, e.g., unaspirated phase-initial voiceless stops, substitution of [ɛ] for [æ], flapped for trilled r substituted for syllable-onset semi-consonant r, [ts] for č, s > z before voiced consonants, etc. A subsequent text in Greek was elicited, and the English-derived loanwords or code-switchings contained therein were subjected to detailed phonetic analysis. These included the following examples: [ˈuɛθəʀiˌpɔʀt], cf. his English [ˈu̯ɛðər+riˌpɔrt] weather-report, [ˈbɛkˌbɛɪ̯ˈstɛɪ̯sən], cf. his English [ˈbækˌbɛɪ̯ˈstɛɪ̯šən] Back Bay Station, [ˈmɔʀ dɛm znou̯], cf. his English [ˈmɔr dæ·m snou̯] more damn snow. The last example is a telling one: hearing the tape-recorded phrase in context of the Greek text, the informant was convinced that he had merely switched briefly into English, explaining that that had indeed been his intention. Hearing the two phases, one from the English text, the other from the Greek played in isolation, he was obviously astounded by his "accent." The informant's naive observation is partly true. The changes which affect the shape of the English models when they appear as replicas in Greek contexts, closely match the very changes in the English spoken by subordinate bilinguals which characterize a "Greek accent."

---

[9] This is a recurrent phenomenon in the American Norwegian described by Haugen 1953, *op. cit.*; e.g. cf. the older Norwegian speaker's [ˈtavan], an integrated replica for the English model *tavern* [ˈtævərn], and the younger speaker's replica [ˈtævəʀn].

Much of the distortion derives from disturbance in the lowest level rules of the phonology, i.e., to various changes in the occurrences of redundant features. Such phonetic distortions can make for alarming changes in the phonetic *substance* of a discourse, but without altering the basic *formal* properties of the phonology. It will be the purpose of a future paper to demonstrate that the phonology of Greek bilingual speech can be (must be) analyzed without establishing a coexistent phonological system.[10]

One conclusion which seems to emerge from this research has more relevance to the psychology of language: It has been my impression that code-switching, strictly defined, obtains only as a hypothetical endpoint in a typology of bilingual behavior. One of the linguistic correlates to the coordinate bilingual's purportedly being inputted with two separate codes, is his ability to keep the two language systems distinct with respect to linguistic interference.[11] Greek-English code-switching has convinced me that, even with a speaker's conscious efforts to offset interference, that Greek-English coordinate bilinguals cannot switch to one language in the context of the other without incurring phonic interference of the sort described in this paper. This suggests to me that we need to review our still imperfect notions of what is involved in the separability of two language codes in the same speaker.

---

[10] See the procedures suggested by Charles C. Fries and Kenneth L. Pike. 1949. "Coexistent phonemic systems," *Language* 25.29-50. It is curious that an earlier statement by Pike (1947. "Grammatical prerequisites to phonemic analysis", *Word* 3.155-172) to the effect that "one should hesitate to allow a small residue of words of foreign origin to prevent a general formulation" (p. 171) appears to be contradicted by the Fries and Pike 1949 paper.

[11] The psychological attributes of the coordinate bilingual have been discussed by Uriel Weinreich, 1953. *Languages in Contact: Findings and Problems.* (=Publications of the Linguistic Circle of New York, No. 1) [see pp. 8-10, 71-82], and by Charles E. Osgood and Susan Ervin in C. E. Osgood, ed. *Psycholinguistics: A Survey of Theory and Research Problems* (=Indiana University Publications in Anthropology and Linguistics, Memoir 10) [see pp. 139-145]. More recent literature is reviewed by Einar Haugen 1956. *Bilingualism in the Americas: A Bibliography and Research Guide* (=Publication of the American Dialect Society, No. 26) [see pp. 69-86].

LINGUISTICS AND CLASSIC PHILOSOPHY

Francis P. Dinneen, S. J.

Georgetown University

Modern linguistics and traditional grammar differ from each other markedly in the data they handle, in their methods and purposes. As a consequence of the linguistic description of languages, many scholars are convinced that most traditional views of language have been falsified. Most notable among these falsifications, it is generally held, is the rejection of the traditional parts of speech.

As a consequence of this falsification, a great deal of classic philosophy is also considered to fall by the wayside, since it is the opinion of many philosophers and linguists that just as traditional grammar is a reflex of the Latin and Greek languages, so too are the basic categories of classic philosophy.

It would be a waste of time to rehearse the excellent reasons we have discovered for denying the validity of an eight or ten part-of-speech basis for all languages. But there is a certain value in comparing notions of traditional grammar and classic philosophy with those of modern linguistics.

By classic philosophy, I have in mind the work of those thinkers who developed the insights of Plato and Aristotle, the Stoics and the medieval synthesizers of those views. Despite fundamental oppositions between different schools in the classic tradition at any given time, and certainly from one period to another, there is still a remarkable unity in all their speculation. This is a consequence of their logical framework, the set of descriptive categories or frames in which they set problems for solution.

There is one single book which is the chief source of this unity, the *Categories* of Aristotle. By considering the influence of this work, I think it can be shown at one stroke how different the approach of the classic tradition and that of modern linguistics is, and at the same time, that this difference need not have existed, since there is a surprising similarity in their descriptive methods.

The usefulness of such a comparison is twofold: first, we can only know clearly what we are doing, and what the traditional scholar is doing, when we are sure about what neither of us is doing; secondly, all linguists can probably be considered part-time propagandists, since we are eager to make linguistic methods and findings known, especially to as many educators as possible. The intellectual background of many educators in the field of language is traditional grammar; this traces back through a fairly straight line to the medieval logicians, the Roman grammarians and the ancient Greeks. Knowledge of this tradition would therefore seem to be useful for showing the advances we have made. This would be even more valuable if we could show, as I propose, that our methods are partially a development of a notion central to that tradition, but largely neglected by it.

The notion which traditional grammarians did not adequately exploit, which is an integral part of the inheritance of philosophy in the Aristotelian tradition, is the notion of Analogy. This notion played an important part in the speculations, logical and metaphysical, of the ancients and medievals. It was also a descriptive device of central and explicit importance in the work of the original Greek grammarians.

So what I would like to show in this paper is the similarity and differences of approach in classic philosophy and modern linguistics. This can be done by considering three main points: (1) the notions of Substance and Quality in the *Categories* of Aristotle; (2) the traditional definitions of 'noun' and (3) the pertinence of the notion of Analogy to both of them.

The method of this paper will therefore be to explain briefly what the *Categories* of Aristotle are about, then a comparison of logical and grammatical definitions of 'noun', and finally, the role of Analogy in both of these, with a comparison of structural descriptive methods and analogical.

The *Categories* of Aristotle is the first of three books which were part of the *Organon* or 'tools of science' as it was understood by the ancients and medievals. All three of these works were logical and therefore linguistic in orientation. The first of these three, the *Categories,* claims to deal with the meaning of any free form; the second, *On Interpretation,* treats of these forms in the syntactic construction known as 'predication'; the third, *Prior Analytics,* concerns the theory of the syllogism, three predications so arranged as to enable us to check the correctness of the third as a logical conclusion from the other two, because of its formal relationships to them.

In the first book Aristotle lists ten 'categories' or types of predicates. He says: "The meaning of any free form is either Substance, Quantity, Quality, Relation, Place, Time, Posture or position, State or condition, Action, or Affection." [1]

For our purposes the most important of these predicates are Substance

---

[1] *Categories* 1b.25.IV.

and Quality, since it is to these that the grammarians appealed in defining the noun. As far as the *things* meant by these predicates are concerned, there is this radical difference: Substance can be defined as what is not the other nine, but what is necessary for their existence. The other nine categories are called 'accidents' with respect to Substance, and the relationship was justified as follows: if there were no Substance to be the subject of the accidents, there could be no accidents; unless color, or size, or location, or a relation of equality were the accidents of some Substance, we would neither discover nor discuss qualities, quantities, locations and relationships.

Substance is distinguished into primary and secondary: "Substance in the principal and strictest meaning, in the primary sense of the term, is that which is neither predicated *of* a subject, nor can be found *in* a subject." [2] The subjects of which he speaks can either be physical or logical subjects. Examples of these are *man* and *horse*. By secondary substances he means the notions of genus and species. *Man* as a specific notion contains the individual man; *animal* as a generic notion contains both the species *horse* and the species *man* and therefore the individual *horse* or *man* as well. Both genus and species could therefore be predicated *of* an individual horse or man, even though they are not *in* them, since they were notions and not physical parts or properties. The nine accidents could also be predicated under the same conditions.

Quality is defined as "that because of which men are called such and such." [3] The notion was not restricted to men, of course, but applied equally to any substance. The examples he gives of this, however, principally concern human 'habits' such as wisdom, goodness, and other qualities such as dispositions, innate capacities or incapacities.

Both the notions of Substance and Quality were used to give a semantic definition of the 'noun' by later Greek grammarians. Their technical term for this was *onoma,* which has an instructive history. Its primary meaning is 'name' and it is in this sense that Plato gives the first important definition of it in Greek logic. It is the name of the actor. The other part of speech which he distinguished is *rhema,* which "names the action." [4]

Aristotle has a more general definition of *onoma:* it is "a sound having meaning by convention, which has no reference to time, no part of which has meaning separate from its whole." [5] This is distinguished from *rhema* in

---

[2] *Categories* 2a.11.V.

[3] *Categories* 8b.25.VIII.

[4] *Sophist* 261 ff.

[5] *On Interpretation* 16a.20.

two ways: what they have in common is that they name something; they differ because the *rhema* "has a particular reference to time" in addition, and it always means "something said or asserted of something:" [6] that is, it is always a predicate.

These definitions obviously do not fit any particular grammatical elements of Greek exclusively; they define a logical subject and predicate, even though the examples which Aristotle gives of the *onoma* are nouns, and those for the *rhema* are verbs.

Successors of Aristotle defined the *onoma* in a more restricted fashion. The Stoics, for instance, define it as what signifies Quality. And there were two types, proper and common.[7] It is worth noting in passing that although the Stoics were adversaries of Aristotle, they retained the same descriptive approach; instead of ten categories they said there were only four: Substance, Quality, State and Relation. The first two coincide with Aristotle's; the others include the rest of his list. The obvious difficulty with such an approach is in knowing when the list is sufficiently extended but closed, or sufficiently compact but inclusive.

We find significant grammatical work for the first time in Dionysius Thrax in the first century B.C. He defines eight parts of speech (for him they were really eight parts of a sentence, of course) and to the best of his ability he first gives a formal specification, and then adds a typical meaning. His definition of *onoma,* which could now be better translated 'noun' than the preceding definitions, is "a part of a sentence having case-inflections, signifying a person or thing, proper or common." In distinguishing proper and common nouns, he uses the notion of Substance: common nouns denote specific or generic substances, proper nouns individual substance. Examples were *stone* and *Socrates.*[8]

Thrax was succeeded by another Alexandrian grammarian, Appolonius Dyscolus, who improved on the grammar of Thrax by dealing with syntax, which had been completely neglected. In his definition of the 'noun', Dyscolus combines the Stoic and Alexandrian views: it signifies "Substance and Quality," the person or thing with their defining property.[9] This work of Dyscolus was the model for the most influential of Roman grammarians, Priscian. He uses the same definition of the noun but differently

---

[6] *On Interpretation* 16b.6.

[7] cf. Benson Mates, *Stoic Logic,* Univ. of Cal. Pub. in Phil., Vol. 26 (Berkeley, 1953).

[8] Text in I. Bekker, *Anecdota Graeca* II (Berlin, 1816).

[9] *Analecta Graeca* II.

worded: "The noun is a part of the sentence which assigns a common or specific quality of persons or things." [10]

The notion of Analogy is the term by means of which these concepts can be united. Basic to any analogy is similarity of relations, and a very general definition would be 'similar relations between terms'. This is especially significant when the terms are of different natures. The simplest and clearest analogies are mathematical proportions: $2 : 4 = 3 : 6$ illustrates the basic notions here. The terms are different ($2, 4, 3, 6$) but the relation is the same; here it is double.

This points up the most important and characteristic feature of analogies: to establish an analogy, certain aspects of the terms involved are declared irrelevant. Their existence, or their importance to some other point of view, need not come into question. By abstracting from undenied and inseparable features of a set of terms, we often discover a kind of unity which makes them all instances of the same relationship.

It is interesting to compare this notion of Analogy in general with its applicability in the logical and ontological speculations involved in the *Categories, On Interpretation,* and *Prior Analytics,* its role in grammar, and how this resembles modern structural methods of description.

First, it should be noted that Aristotle developed this notion of Analogy as a descriptive device of great generality; it was used to classify arguments, concepts, things, terms; later the medievals used it explicitly to answer the difficulties of Parmenides and Heraclitus. In discussing the meanings of free forms, for instance, he distinguishes between what we would call univocal, equivocal and analogical terms. Those which have a constant phonetic shape and constant meaning are univocal (e.g., proper names). Those which have a constant phonetic structure but different meanings each time are equivocal or homonyms. Those which have a constant phonetic shape, but whose meanings vary with the environment (terms which nevertheless preserve an important community of meaning despite the environmental differences) include the analogical terms. For the sake of this analogy, the higher unity of meaning, the differences are declared irrelevant.

A typical analogical term, one that is partially the same and partially different according to environment, is *substance*. The main defining note of Substance, as you will recall, is that properties are in or predicated of it; but Substance itself is not in or predicated of anything else. For Aristotle, this depends on the universe of discourse, with a sort of lower ontological limit for substances like man and animals.

---

[10] Priscian II, in H. Keil, *Grammatici Latini* II.

That is, in all non-mathematical analogies there is the prime analogate, the paradigm case of what is meant by a term. Other terms or uses are called analogical with relation to this clearest instance. In the case of Substance, the prime analogate or paradigm case is man himself, as the subject of various properties, without being the property of something else himself. Other things are called substances or are conceived substantially and are called 'subjects' if they have the required proportion or analogy to a man in relation to his possible modifications and relationships.

There is, therefore, a very clear distinction in principle, though often violated in practice, between the ontological and logical orders in Aristotle et al. between something that *is* a substance in the primary, ontological sense, and something that is conceived *as* a substance. For instance, there was a whole range of sciences whose *subjects* (i.e. things conceived substantially) were clearly recognized as ontological accidents. In mathematics, the *subject* of the science was taken to be Quantity, which as we have seen, was listed among the accidents: Aristotle and the others certainly did not think it was a substance like a man, but an obvious accidental property of bodies like men.

However, it had the required proportion or analogy to typical first substances: properties can be predicated *of* it, even though they are not *in* it, such as mathematical relations of equality and inequality. It is worth declaring the differences between subjects like numbers and men irrelevant, in view of the powerful unity of relationships that can be discovered: we can manipulate men in some circumstances exactly like numbers.

Analogy also played an important and explicit role in grammar. The Alexandrians were the scientific followers of Aristotle's Lyceum, which moved to Alexandria after his death. This thought-factory produced two of the most influential books of antiquity: the *Geometry* of Euclid and the *Grammar* of Dionysius Thrax, in both of which Analogy had a central role. He assigns as one of the six tasks of the grammarian the discovery of the analogies of the language. This was obviously his declaration of where he stood in the prolonged Anomaly-Analogy dispute.

Unfortunately, Thrax did not get below or beyond the level of words in his grammar, and the most important words in Greek are complex forms. He knew nothing of morphemes and had nothing to say about Greek syntax. He deals only with inflected and uninflected words, but does not inform us fully of how to group them. Dyscolus, his Alexandrian successor, did discuss syntax in a limited way, treating some aspects of government and concord; and Priscian, who modelled his work on Dyscolus, got no further.

He did make the lamentable mistake, however, of explicitly denying the morpheme grammatical status.[11]

In the work of Priscian, which builds on and borrows from Thrax and Dyscolus, we can see in detail the framework within which these men worked. It was almost exclusively the declarative sentence. This indicates an obvious and fateful inheritance from the prestigious logical study of language, but results in a narrow restriction of the patterns in which the functions of the so-called parts of speech can be studied. On such a basis it is not surprising that the 'noun' is defined as though its whole function is that of logical subject. This represents a failure to employ the full implications of analogical descriptive method. While we might admit that from some point of view—logically, for instance—the function of nouns as logical subjects could be considered as the prime analogate, the paradigm case of the use of nouns, there are many more functions that the same morphological set fulfills. In this sense, the definition might be admitted to be true, but uninformative.

The differences between the approach of classic philosophy and that of modern linguistics is therefore obvious. To the extent that much of traditional grammar relies implicitly on the work of classic philosophy and logic, we can discuss the same weaknesses. But the differences could be stated most clearly in terms of the data examined, rather than the methods used, although there are important divergencies here as well.

It could be said that classic philosophers and logicians looked *through* linguistic forms rather than *at* them, since they were studying the concepts, taken to be their meanings, as the most important defining qualities they had. Their purposes also differed from ours. We concern ourselves first and foremost with the description of languages; they claimed to be explaining language in some sense.

So despite these differences, the resemblance of structural methods of identifying units and the descriptive procedure in analogy is marked. Analogies are established by ignoring differences in the composition of the terms, because of the interest in the similarity of relations in which the terms are involved. Linguistic levels are established in the same way. The number and nature of aspects which are ignored defines the level of analysis. Phonemics ignores the non-distinctive, though patterned, differences of sounds in varied environments in order to discuss the restricted number of recurrent distinctive features. Unity is established among the variety of phonetic shapes of morphemes by setting out the analogies, the similarity of relationships among them, in terms of morphophonemic and distribu-

---

[11] Priscian II.3.14, in H. Keil, *Grammatici Latini* II.

tional regularities. A syntactic construction like English active or passive declares differences of person, number and gender irrelevant.

From these considerations, therefore, I would draw the three following conclusions: (1) Despite differences of data and purpose, there is a similarity in descriptive method to be found in classic philosophy and modern linguistics. (2) Descriptive categories are neither true nor false; they are either useful or useless, adequate or inadequate for some purpose. The methods and findings of modern linguistics therefore do not, because they cannot, falsify the descriptive categories of classic philosophy or traditional grammar. Given our extended data and purposes, however, the categories of classic philosophy and traditional grammar are shown to be inadequate. (3) It would appear that structural linguistics has exploited the analogical descriptive method of classic philosophy better than traditional grammar. Pointing this fact out may be one way of showing traditional grammarians the continuity between our methods and the methods of those logicians and philosophers to whom they could appeal for justification of their procedures.

THE EPISTEMOLOGICAL FUNCTION OF LANGUAGE

GEORGE L. FARRE

Georgetown University

*"The **Logos**, God whose altar is in the mind of man . . ."*
Euripides, Fragment 170

1. Introduction. One of the characteristic traits of the Greek genius has been the firm belief that all events, happenings, things and states of affairs in general make sense; that they have a meaning in terms of a few principles embodying a **Logos,** or central perspective within which all things are ordered.

Thus it is that the Milesians began the systematic search for the **Logos** of the cosmos. Euripides, Sophocles and the great playwrights of classical Greece displayed the tragedy inherent in the conflict which opposes the **logoi** of men to the **logos** of God.

In the long series of thinkers who preceded Plato, we may single out two who are of particular interest to us because their thought bears on Plato's notion of language—namely Parmenides and Pythagoras—I should say, the Pythagoreans. For the philosopher of Elea, the 'real', that is, what he calls 'being', is eminently knowable: "thought and being are the same thing;" and 'being' is simply, in his terminology, 'what is', or what we will call an 'existent'. For the Pythagoreans, another form of knowledge is attainable, namely the knowledge of relations—more specifically, what we would call 'mathematical' relations. Furthermore, this knowledge of relations is fully expressible by means of an appropriate language, while the knowledge of mathematical existents (i.e., the nature of numbers), though believed to be attainable, is not so expressible.

Thus, by the time Plato appeared on the scene, this much seems to have been acquired: there are two basic forms of knowledge: (a) knowledge of ideal existents, (b) knowledge of relations and of relational structures.

It is with Plato that the question of the expressibility of knowledge through language is first approached in earnest. It is neither the place nor the time to engage in a detailed study of Plato from the point of view of a philosophy of language, so we shall limit ourselves to a brief résumé of the conclusions that may be drawn from such an analysis. First, it is plain that Plato recognized both relations and existents as knowable. Furthermore, ideal existents—such as the 'Good', the 'Just', 'Man', 'Circle', etc.—are eminently intelligible in their own uniqueness by a sort of intellectual contemplation.[1] As for sensible existents, they are intelligible only in as much as they are innervated and informed by the ideas, i.e., by the intelligible existents themselves.

From a study of the dialogues, most especially the *Cratylus,* the *Phaedo,* the *Theaetetus,* the *Parmenides,* as well as the seventh Epistle, one may infer the following concerning Plato's views on the relationship between knowledge and language: The intelligible existents may be named and can be related to one another by means of language, but they cannot be described in themselves; they are, so far as language is concerned, ineffables. Indeed, the dialectical method—and before it the maieutical method of Socrates—is useful in demonstrating the inadequacy of nominal definitions and consequently, in pointing out the inherent incapacity of language to describe nonlinguistic entities.[2] On the other hand, the knowledge of relations and of relational structures is completely expressible linguistically since language itself is, by its very nature, relational. So that in Plato's view, it seems that language fulfills its epistemological function in the following way: to primitive atomic terms (such as 'man', 'good') are attached a signification and a denotation through the independently acquired knowledge of the corresponding intelligible existents (the **eidos,** or 'idea'). Such a term has a connotation, that is to say, a linguistic and therefore nominal definition linking its name to those of other existents in a way which is characteristic of the term defined. This linguistic relation will be called a 'concept'. It is worth emphasizing that the concept is not the same thing as the idea; it is simply its projection on the language.

The philosophical option directing our approach to the epistemological study of language is Platonic in the sense indicated above.

---

[1] ". . . as a result of continued application to the subject itself and communion therewith, it (i.e., knowledge) is brought to birth in the soul on a sudden, as light that is kindled by a leaping spark, and thereafter it nourishes itself. . . . " (seventh Epistle, 341 d-e), translated from the Loeb edition (London, 1929).

[2] cf. for instance the seventh Epistle (342 b-344 b), and in particular the following excerpt: "But in all cases where we compel a man to give the [intelligible existent] as his answer and to explain it, anyone who is able and willing to upset the argument gains the day . . . for they are ignorant sometimes of the fact that it is not the soul of the writer or the speaker that is being convicted but the nature of the [linguistic entities associated with the intelligible existent] which is essentially defective."

We will begin by giving a first definition of language as a sort of working hypothesis which we will later refine. By 'language' we shall understand 'a system of symbols developed and organized for the specific purpose of rendering intelligible certain aspects of human experience'. This definition states, among other things, that the characteristic feature of language is epistemological, and not communication. The important question of communication will not be touched upon at all here. We will assume throughout that language is perfectly 'public', a situation which is closely approximated by formal object-languages, as we shall define them later.

Language fulfills its role of introducing intelligibility into human experience through two specialized and correlative functions. These will be called, respectively, 'semantical' and 'logostical'. We shall turn our attention first to the semantical function, then to the logostical and finally to the relationship obtaining between the two.

2. The Semantical Function of Language. We begin by defining those terms which are used here in a sense which differs from the accepted practice of philosophers of language and logicians.

'What is the case' is an element of human experience, the existence of which is in no wise dependent on language. 'Facts', 'events', 'properties', considered in and by themselves, are simply the case. As such, they are meaningless, being neither 'this' nor 'that', but being, purely and simply. The totality of 'what is the case' will be referred to as 'the real', independently of any ontological or metaphysical status that one may wish to attach to that term.

A 'state of affairs' is an ordered set of elements of the real. It is directly apprehensible within a certain conceptual framework or perspective by means of appropriate experiential modes or techniques. Consequently, a state of affairs is linguistically describable in principle: in the sense that it is possible to define certain linguistic terms in a way that a proposition may be formed and asserted of the given state of affairs. A state of affairs has thus two characteristic features from our point of view: as an aspect of the real, it is a given of experience, and the existence of its elements is independent of the language. On the other hand, through the ordering principle which gives it intelligibility it is formally linguistic, i.e., its mode of existence is linguistically determined, though not its concrete existence. It follows that a given set of states of affairs, each determined by a common group of principles, constitutes a particular arrangement of the real as seen from the point of view embodied by the principles taken collectively. The totality of all states of affairs will be referred to as the 'natural referential R_n'.

If we consider the set of all states of affairs which are describable from a given group of linguistic principles, this set will be said to be 'homogeneous' (with respect to these principles), and one may refer to this restricted and specialized referential as a certain kind of 'reality'.[3] For example, by 'physical reality' we denote the set of all states of affairs which are formally definable within the linguistic framework of physics; similarly with 'biological reality', 'economic reality', 'ethical reality', etc., each qualificative indicating the nature of the ordering principles involved.

The set of semantical descriptions obtained from the referential will be referred to as the 'semantical universe of discourse U_s'. It constitutes the linguistic image of the nonlinguistic referential, there being a one-to-one correspondence between the two at least in principle.[4] The members of U_s must, by definition, fulfill whatever rules of semantical verification that are operative in the given language, and are consequently defined only within these limits.[5] They describe the formal structure of actual states of affairs by means of an appropriate terminology.[6] It is evident that such descriptions are purely linguistic entities both in form and in content, and that furthermore, they are always semantically true. For this reason, we will call them 'statements of fact'.

It must be observed at this point that U_s is devoid of any intrinsic ordering principle; it is simply a collection of unrelated descriptions. Whatever relations may obtain between the members of U_s come from elsewhere. In point of fact, the statements are correlated by means of a conceptual structure or theory. The development of such structures is the logostical function of language, just as the definition and description of states of affairs is its semantical function.

   3. *The Logostical Function of Language.* By **logos,** we mean an ordering

---

[3] It is quite evident that there is an important distinction between 'reality' and the 'real'. While the real is simply given as a multiplicity of irreducible existents, reality is its intelligible aspect. Therefore, there will be as many 'realities' as there are ordering principles for the elements of the real. This does not mean that every principle (or set of principles) must encompass the real in its totality. Most ordering principles—if not all—make a selection among the elements of the real. Those that are ignored in this process remain what they always were: meaningless. In this sense, it can be said (a bit paradoxically perhaps) that a language creates what it talks about.

[4] In principle only, since there is often little reason to describe every individual state of affairs; in most cases, such exhaustive description is not practically feasible, individual states of affairs being imbedded in time and distributed in space.

[5] For example, in a language like physics the descriptions of experimental states of affairs are governed by rules similar to those known as operational definitions and by the experimental techniques which define the states of affairs themselves.

[6] By 'terminology' we mean an algorithm and the semantical definitions of primitive terms.

and unifying principle which is susceptible of expression through a relational structure. In the case of an object language, the **logos** is the source of intelligibility from which meaningful states of affairs are definable and by means of which their descriptions may be correlated and ordered.

By 'theory' we understand the conceptual structure which incorporates a given **logos.** The conceptual structure is characterized by a set of inter-related propositions, some of which, called 'axioms', are primitive in the sense that they express the characteristic properties of the **logos** itself. We assume that a 'theory' is always formalizable, at least in principle.[7]

The logostical function of a language is thus the development and description of a given model or theory. This explicative process is done according to syntactical rules [8] appropriate to the nature of the theory and to its function.[9]

All propositions obtained by syntactical derivation form the logostical (or theoretical) universe of discourse U_L. Every member of U_L is thus L-determined in Carnap's sense and will be called an L-term. Furthermore, it describes a particular property of the model and nothing else.

At this point, it is desirable to classify the various types of languages that are distinguishable with the help of the notions so far introduced.

By 'object-language', we mean a language suitable for the description of nonlinguistic states of affairs. A language describing linguistic states of affairs is usually referred to as a 'metalanguage'.

Among object-languages, we can further distinguish two types according to the sort of referential they describe. An object-language describing a heterogeneous referential will be called a 'natural', or 'ordinary' language. English, French, etc. are such natural languages, since their referentials encompass the totality of human experience and therefore imply a whole bundle of different **logoi.** Because of its complexity, the philosophical study of ordinary language has not yet been carried significantly beyond the

---

[7] Actual axiomatization being mostly a metalinguistic requirement, it is seldom done in the linguistic system itself.

[8] The syntactical rules usually comprise the rules governing the algorithm used and the logical rules which govern the generation of the set of propositions as a system.

[9] In the case of an object-language, the semantical requirements may rule out certain algorithms. In other cases, it would appear that the nature of the theory itself requires a certain kind of algorithm, such as the tensorial calculus in the case of Einsteinian relativity. However, it is difficult to determine whether the theory conditions the algorithm, or whether the availability of a certain algorithm does not give the theory its particular form. What is beyond reasonable doubt is that both are intimately linked.

domain of pragmatics, wherein the principal method consists in the determination of the uses made of given terms. The British school of philosophic analysis has been most prominently associated with the study of ordinary language. An object-language describing a homogeneous referential R will be referred to as a 'formal object-language' because the theory of such linguistic systems is always susceptible to axiomatization. Physics, biology, the several behavioral sciences and the various philosophical disciplines are thus formal object-languages.[10]

A formal language which has no semantical dimension will be referred to as an 'abstract-language'. Its sole function is the linguistic expression and development of a particular **logos.** The different branches of mathematics are examples of 'abstract-languages'. Geometry, for instance, describes the properties of abstract space manifolds. It does not, in any way, either directly or indirectly, describe the properties of the real world.[11] The conspicuous absence of a semantical dimension does not, however, preclude the use of an abstract-language as an algorithm for a formal object-language. However, the abstract-language so used is no longer a 'formal' language, but simply a 'calculus', i.e., a set of convenient algorithmic rules dissociated from any original logostical meaning.

Finally, there are systems which have a linguistic structure though they possess neither a semantical nor a logostical dimension, being nothing more than simple syntactical systems. Such pseudolanguages will be referred to as 'linguistic matrices'. The different logical systems are of this type. They are called 'matrices', because any formal language, by the very fact that its logostical dimension is a relational structure, must, of necessity, be built around a syntactical skeleton.

What follows pertains specifically to formal object-languages. We think that it probably can be extended to encompass natural languages as well, despite the fact that the philosophical significance of such an extension is not immediately evident to us.

4. The Problem of Linguistic Verification. So far, we have encountered two types of linguistic molecular terms: the L-determined propositions

---

[10] This is actually an oversimplification. Physics, for example, is a family of languages usually related at the semantical level, although sometimes at the logostical level as well (so it is that relativity is part of classical physics on purely logostical grounds). To illustrate this, let us denote the different branches of classical physics as $L_1, L_2, \ldots L_k$ (e.g., mechanics, optics, thermodynamics, acoustics); then the language L_c, denoting classical physics, could be represented as the union of its sublanguages:

$$L_c = U_k L_k$$

[11] cf. for example: Poincaré's *Science and hypothesis.*

(or L-terms) and the statements of fact (or s-terms). It is quite evident that the logostical dimension of an object-language must be related to its semantical dimension by virtue of the definitions that we have given for these terms. Since each function of the language culminates in the formation of a corresponding universe of discourse, we can reasonably expect this relationship to be apparent at that level. The most obvious way for it to appear is undoubtedly as the overlap of the two universes of discourse so that the intersection $U_s \cap U_L$ is not empty. There must be elements in both sets that are formally identical despite the fact that they are different types of terms. $U_s \cap U_L$ will be referred to as the 'domain of adequation' of the language.

As we saw earlier, U_s contains only descriptions of actual states of affairs, i.e., of concrete individual elements of the referential. Their meaning is thus purely denotative and they are in the strict Kantian sense 'synthetic a priori'.

On the other hand, U_L contains only propositions which describe the properties of the theoretical structure characteristic of the language. As such, they are L-determined; whatever verification is required concerning them is a purely linguistic process (e.g., syntactical derivation) and in no way semantical. It is therefore quite proper to refer to these as 'analytic' in Carnap's sense.[12] The question which presents itself at this point is the following: how is it possible for such dissimilar linguistic entities as s-terms and L-terms to be formally identical? In attempting to answer this question, it must first be noted that 'statement' and 'proposition' as used in the present context refer to the way in which these terms are obtained and verified and not to their syntactical (or more precisely to their algorithmic) structure which may or may not be the same. Next it may be observed that in as much as a statement refers to a unique state of affairs and a proposition to the property of an abstract system, the possibility of their formal similarity requires some sort of proof. However, this possibility will become more evident when we note that, although L-terms do not describe actual states of affairs, they may describe classes of possible ones: provided of course that the atomic constituents of the propositions are susceptible of receiving a semantical interpretation. For if we say that 'all planetary orbits are conics' on the strength of the gravitational field theory, we describe a class of possible states of affairs—if, and only if, we can define semantically what we mean by a 'planetary orbit' and by a 'conic'. Still, the question of the adequation of the language has not been solved. Classes of possible

---

[12] cf. R. Carnap, *Meaning and necessity*, (Chicago: Univ. of Chicago Press, 1947). Enlarged ed. 1956.

states of affairs simply do not exist in the referential, although individual states of affairs do. The L-terms remain general and are consequently still incapable of semantical adequation. To achieve this goal one more step must be taken: the transformation of the still general term into a particular proposition describing no longer a class, but a single possible state of affairs. Not surprisingly, all formal object-languages possess the means of achieving this propositional particularization. To illustrate this process of particularization by means of an example taken from physics (which is a syntactically simple language), let us imagine that a student is observing the free fall of some object in a laboratory. He will describe this event in the following way:

$$y = y_0 + v_0 t + a_0 t^2 \qquad \qquad \text{(a)}$$

where 'y_0' denotes the altitude from which the said object was released, 'v_0' the release velocity and 'a_0' the acceleration during the fall. This description is quite evidently a statement of fact.

Let us assume further that our student wishes to find out whether or not the chap who taught him mechanics was right. Turning to his notes on gravitational field theory, he will find a general proposition describing the motion of any particle in the field of any other particle written as:

$$r^{-1} = C[1 + 1 \cos A] \qquad \qquad \text{(b)}$$

This general proposition describes a class of possible states of affairs, provided that 'r', 'C', 'E' and 'A' are semantically interpreted. At this point, comes the process of propositional particularization which will transform proposition (b) into another proposition which algorithmically is equivalent to (a). This will be done very easily by applying what are known as 'initial conditions' to (b), so that the transformation yields:

$$y = y_0 + v_0 t + a_0 t^2 \qquad \qquad \text{(c)}$$

Now (c) is a proposition, obtained by derivation on the theory; (a) was obtained by direct observation. It is quite evident that they are algorithmically identical, i.e., (a) = (c).

While the mode of propositional particularization varies with the different algorithms, all known formal object-languages have it. We are thus able to see how the semantical and the logostical functions of language are related through the domain of adequation. This enables us to redefine the notion of language from the epistemological point of view. Language, then, is 'a system of symbols and syntactical rules developed and organized for the definition and the description of states of affairs by means of an appropriate logostical structure'.

At this point, we might add a few remarks in the form of a conclusion. Whenever two sets overlap, three subsets are thereby defined: [13] (1) $U_L \cap U_s$ is the domain of adequation which was mentioned above. (2) $\tilde{U}_L \cap U_s$ is the set of all s-terms which are not subsumed under any L-term. It indicates the degree to which the language is 'semantically incomplete'. Ideally, all members of U_s should be in the domain of adequation. (3) $U_L \cap \tilde{U}_s$ is the set of all L-terms for the particularizations of which there are no semantical equivalents. As such, it may be called the 'set of logostical hypotheses'. Depending on the nature of the language, this set marks either its semantical limitations or its logostical inadequacy. However, it should be noted that $U_L \cap \tilde{U}_s$ can never be empty, even in the ideal case. This is due, in part, to the fact that not all logostical terms (atomic or molecular) are susceptible of receiving a semantical interpretation. But to pursue this matter further would take us too far from our announced purpose.

---

[13] We ignore in this paper the fourth subset $\tilde{U}_L \cap \tilde{U}_s$.

INTRODUCTION

CHARLES A. FERGUSON
Center for Applied Linguistics

In the article on Diglossia [1] I attempted to describe a certain
kind of language situation. This description or, let us say, the article
as a whole, was a result of my interest in describing the language situation, or more accurately, the socio-linguistic situation of the Arabic
speaking world. I felt that interesting though the situation was in
the Arabic speech community, it was not in all respects unique. That
is, in many ways this language situation was similar to the situation
in other speech communities. What I tried to do was to characterize
this situation in the hopes that here we would have discovered one
possible element in a general typology of socio-linguistic situations.
I mentioned about seven examples of diglossia and used four of them
as the defining languages or the defining speech communities. These
four were: Arabic, Modern Greek, Swiss German, and Haitian Creole. I tried to find the common features in the linguistic situations in
these four speech communities, and after a fairly careful examination
of this, I reached a definition which we will assume today as the
topic under discussion. It reads like this: "Diglossia is a relatively
stable language situation, in which in addition to the primary dialect of the language, which may include a standard or regional standards, there is a very divergent, highly codified, often grammatically
more complex, super-posed variety, the vehicle of a large and respected body of written literature, heir of an earlier period or in another
speech community, which is learned largely by formal education and
is used for most written and formal spoken purposes, but is not used
by any sector of the community for ordinary conversation." [2] That is
a fairly long and involved kind of definition. What it really did was
to list the characteristics which the four defining speech communities seemed to have in common. On our panel today we will listen
to specialists in each of the four languages that were used as defining languages in that original article.

---

[1] Charles A. Ferguson. "Diglossia," *Word* Vol. 15, 1959, pp. 325-340.
[2] Ferguson. op. cit., p. 336.

PROBLEMS OF TEACHING
LANGUAGES WITH DIGLOSSIA

CHARLES A. FERGUSON

Center for Applied Linguistics

In this discussion, I should like to outline the special problems involved in the teaching of languages with diglossia, as distinct from the general problems involved in all language teaching. The discussion will be limited to the kind of teaching which has as its aim enabling native Americans to understand, speak, read, and write a modern language in a manner approximating that of the educated native speaker of the language. The approach to language teaching which will be assumed for the discussion is roughly the so-called audio-lingual approach, which is currently accepted by many specialists as one of the best approaches to language teaching in terms of current educational aims and resources in this country. It may be worth while to summarize first some of the general assumptions of this approach. It is assumed that, other things being equal, the learning of a modern foreign language is more effectively accomplished if:

1. the learner concentrates first on understanding and speaking and later on reading and writing;

2. the learner has as a model a native or near-native speaker of the language he is studying;

3. the basic phonology and grammatical patterns of the language are learned to a great extent through extensive, carefully-planned drills intended to develop automatic responses similar to those of the native speaker;

4. the instruction is planned and supervised by someone with sound orientation in linguistics and is carried out with the use of materials prepared on the basis of sound linguistic analysis;

5. the learning is on an intensive basis, that is, involves at least ten contact hours a week with a model to be imitated;

6. audio-visual materials are employed to the extent feasible as an integral part of the course work, whether in the classroom or outside.

The acceptance of these assumptions eliminates or radically simplifies the discussion of many problems of procedure and content in a course of instruction in a modern language with diglossia. Some of the problems which remain, however, are serious and deserve careful examination.

1. *Learning two languages in one*

One point must be made at the outset. The problem of teaching a language with two major forms cannot be solved by teaching only one of the forms. I realize that there are teachers of these languages who feel that the only satisfactory solution is just this, and limit the aims of their courses to the mastery of just the H variety or just the L variety.[1] It is no doubt possibe that this solution is adequate for certain individuals who are studying the languages for certain limited purposes, but it is clear that this solution will not meet the needs of someone who wants to learn to understand, speak, read, and write these languages in a manner approximating that of the educated native speaker. The teacher and student alike must face the fact that there is more to be learned than one language; perhaps it is not as much as two full languages, but it is certainly more than is generally attempted in a single language course. All apart from considerations of the content and procedure of courses, it seems clear that more time will be required to achieve results comparable to those obtained in other language courses. An American college student or government official who undertakes a program of study of Arabic or modern Greek must be prepared to learn double sets of forms and vocabulary items for most of the language, as well as a whole set of skills involved in selection of the appropriate variety for a given context.

Three problems are immediately apparent for the one who is planning the language curriculum:

What is the relative emphasis to be accorded the two major varieties of the language?

In what order should the two varieties be studied?

How can skill in one variety be maintained when the learning is concentrated on the other variety?

Since about 1940, modern Arabic and modern Greek have been taught intensively along the lines of the audio-lingual approach at a considerable number of universities, government agencies, and pri-

---

[1] H=High variety. L=Low variety.

vate organizations in the United States. Haitian Creole has been taught very rarely in this way and to my knowledge there has been no intensive teaching of Swiss German in the United States. During these two decades of teaching, many shades of relative emphasis have been tried for the two varieties. It is probably correct to say that the trend in intensive Arabic teaching has been from courses where the emphasis was over 75% on the L variety, towards courses with exactly the opposite emphasis. In the teaching of Greek, the trend is less apparent, but it seems, if anything, to be mildly towards increased emphasis on the L variety.

In view of the heavy emphasis at early stages on understanding and speaking, it was only natural that most intensive courses in the 40's and 50's began with colloquial Arabic. Recently, some intensive or semi-intensive courses have attempted to begin with the H variety, making such oral use of H as the ability and inclination of the instructor would permit. One factor in the choice of order is the highly debated question of whether the transition and carry-over of knowledge is easier H to L or L to H.

Whether one begins with H or L, there is a serious problem in maintaining the skill acquired during the first part of the course while concentrating on a different set of skills in the second part. Students who have learned to converse fluently in some variety of spoken Arabic and have gone on to study the classical, often in a year's time lose their ability to converse. On the other hand, as people who have started with Classical Arabic acquire proficiency in the spoken language, they develop a tendency towards errors in the written language. No Arabic program with which I am familiar has solved this problem satisfactorily and only a very few of them have attempted any systematic solution.

It would be premature at this point to suggest promising ways of coping with these three problems, but at least one observation can be made. The nature of the problems is different in instances of diglossia such as Swiss German and Haitian Creole, where H is a standard language used as a medium of ordinary conversation in another speech community, and the instances of diglossia such as Arabic or Greek where this is not the case.

2. Dialect problems

Strictly speaking, the question of which dialect or dialects should be chosen for instruction in L is not a problem directly con-

nected with diglossia.   If there is a single standard variety of L
(as in Haitian Creole and Greek), this is obviously the one to be
chosen, but if there is no standard L the situation is parallel to a
language without diglossia which has no standard form.   In this
case the one who is planning the course must decide on the variety
of spoken language to be taught.

Often in the past the decision has been taken on the basis of
which dialect has the best instructional materials or has native
speakers most readily available for models or best prepares a student for work in a particular region or country.   While these are
all valid considerations, they probably should not be decisive in
any general curriculum planning for language instruction.   Additional criteria which may be suggested for dialect choice are: relative number of speakers; degree of intelligibility throughout the
entire speech community; ease of transition to H.   As an example
of a possible solution to this problem for Arabic, I would like to
repeat a suggestion originally made in 1951.

The solution suggested here for most American students of
Arabic is to concentrate on learning well the ordinary conversational Arabic of educated people of any of the important urban centers of the Arabic-speaking world.   The four such dialects which
are to be recommended because of the number of speakers, probable future importance, and availability of teaching materials and
native speakers, are:

Cairo ("Egyptian Arabic"), Baghdad ("Iraqi"), Damascus-Beirut-
Jerusalem ("Syrian"), Rabat-Salé-Fes-Meknes ("North Moroccan").
Specific recommendations would be:

a. For a particular company, project, or government agency:
   Where possible teach the most appropriate local dialect.

b. For universities, institutes, etc. offering a program of Middle East studies: choose Egyptian, Iraqi or Syrian Arabic
   and teach it regularly or, if facilities permit, alternate years
   among the three.

c. For universities, institutes, etc. offering a program of North
   African studies: teach North Moroccan.

One question not mentioned in the suggestion just quoted is
the need for facilitating the student's adaptation to a local dialect
when he goes to a part of the Arab world where the people do not

speak the kind of Arabic he has studied. This problem exists, of course, for native speakers of Arabic, but for them it is much less serious because of the far greater language resources at their command. It would seem that any responsible course of Arabic instruction at the college or university level should offer sufficient information on the nature and range of dialect variation, in particular lexical differences, to enable the student to make an adequate adjustment to a new dialect area within a matter of weeks, assuming that he has a solid basis in one particular variety of L.

3. *Intermediate forms of language*

Up to this point, we have not mentioned the existence of mixed forms of language intermediate between H and L which are used in certain kinds of situations. These actually constitute the most interesting problem from the point of view of those concerned with the theory of language learning and with general principles of methodology.

Most language teaching is based on the assumption of a single set of relatively stable forms and lexical items in the language being learned. Every language probably has alternative forms or constructions as well as synonyms when the choice depends on style, context, speed of utterance, and the like. But these alternates generally constitute a very small part of the whole language. The mixed varieties in a case of diglossia, on the other hand, involve exactly this kind of choice on a large scale. The native speakers mix elements from H and L in a highly variable way. In a semi-formal discussion a speaker may use the H word for "man" in one sentence and the L word in the next; he may use an H stem with an L grammatical ending (e.g. *raʔéto* "I saw him" = *raʔaytuhu* crossed with *šufto*). How does one teach a student to produce such mixed utterances? At a meeting on the teaching of modern standard Arabic (H) held at Harvard in the summer of 1958, it was agreed that the first step in answering this question would be the gathering of reliable data on intermediate varieties. One such study has appeared, but this is not yet enough on which to base the new materials and techniques required. The descriptive work is a job for the linguists, the subsequent work really would include the cooperation of linguists, language teachers, and psychologists.

4. *Suggested experimental programs?*

It is very difficult to use experimental methods to determine the most effective procedures for teaching one of the "neglected" languages in the U. S. Not only does the experimenter have the usual problem of numerous completely interrelated variables which make the construction of satisfactory experimental designs almost impossible in the language field, he also has such small populations of subjects to deal with that "pure" controlled experimentation is out of the question. What can be tried, however, is a careful clinical approach limited to several major plans. What I am suggesting is that specialists should try to work out programs of study which seem very likely to produce desirable results, although with major differences in content and procedure. Then as these programs are put into effect in a number of institutions, those concerned with the planning and with the actual teaching should meet from time to time to talk over points which emerge in the courses. By the end of a four or five year period of such limited experimentation, it ought to be possible to agree on a fair number of matters which are currently judged by guesswork and bias.

Plan No. 1

One such plan would be to begin with H, using the kinds of procedures and materials which are appropriate to the audio-lingual approach. In the case of Haitian Creole and Swiss German this is relatively easy since material produced for regular instruction in French and German could be used with only minor supplementation. For Arabic and Greek there are no materials available for such a course. It would take at least two years of collaborative work to produce a core of instruction in H which would emphasize learning the oral use of the language insofar as this can be done given the limitations on the spoken use of H. This first stage of the plan would constitute the first year's work at a college course of 8-10 hours per week.

The second stage of the plan would be directed primarily to L, but with a continued heavy dose of H. Something like one-fourth of the student's time and effort should continue to be focused on H, with the material concentrating now on the reading and writing and integrated as much as possible with the L material being presented for oral skills. This might constitute the second year of a college program.

The third and last stage of elementary instruction in this plan would consist of a course about two-thirds of which is devoted to reading in H with accompanying oral and written drills and about one-third to L, this time being taken up largely with planned conversation and discussion designed to review the oral material of the second year and to give conversational skill on certain topics met primarily in the reading.

At the end of such a course one would hope that the student would be able to make extensive use of the language for documentary research, travel to the country, listening to the radio, and so on. He would be ready to begin the serious study of literature in the language.

Plan No. 2

Another plan would be to begin with L and shift to H. Since this plan has been tried in a number of places, some instructional materials exist which could be used. Programs of this kind have in the past generally suffered from one or the other of two defects— either the study of L was dropped too soon, before the student had really acquired the basic structure, or no sysematic attempt was made to maintain competence in L after the shift. Some courses suffered from both these defects.

Here again it must be assumed that three years of college courses will constitute the minimum elementary program of instruction before the student is expected to make great use of the language or is encouraged to proceed to a study of literature or to advanced linguistic studies.

Plan No. 3

Of all the programs in Arabic instruction reported on in the U. S., only the Army Language School program has tried to present H and L simultaneously, or nearly so, with textbooks and recorded materials designed accordingly. This plan is well worth attention and its planners and teachers should participate in the discussion of the followers of the other plans. In this connection it must be pointed out that discussions and reports on courses are not sufficient —the instructors and planners must visit each other's programs often enough to get an adequate understanding of the problems and the results.

An Experiment

One final proposal: a group of specialists should design one or more experiments to throw light on the psychological and linguistic problems involved in teaching mixed varieties of languages when the variation is embarrassingly random and current methods of teaching are clearly inappropriate.

LINGUISTIC THEORY AND LANGUAGE LEARNING

Charles A. Ferguson

Center for Applied Linguistics

Scholars whose chief intellectual interest has been in the development of linguistic theory have generally looked on the problems of language learning either as of little concern to them or as an appropriate field for the application of linguistics. In this discussion today I should like to present the view that language learning is of great interest to the linguist and that the application can work the other way: the study of language learning has value for the construction of linguistic theory.

The first great advance in modern linguistics came in the nineteenth century with the historical and comparative study of Indo-European and other language families. The languages were studied chiefly from written documents and the principal procedures were the comparative method and internal reconstruction. Important notions such as genetic relationship and regularity of linguistic change entered the body of linguistic theory.

The second great spurt came in the 20's, 30's and 40's of this century in descriptive studies of dozens of languages all over the world. The languages were studied chiefly from spoken material elicited from informants, and the principal techniques were segmentation, matching, substitution and the other familiar "discovery procedures" of linguistic books and articles. Important concepts such as contrast, constituent and allo- became part of linguistic theory.

Continuing this oversimplified view of the history of linguistics, I want to hazard the guess that in the last few years a great new third period of development in our science has begun. I am not referring to the intensive work on grammatical analysis typified by the approaches of Pike, Chomsky, Trager-Smith and others, important and fruitful though this is. I am referring to the increasing concern with a new kind of diachrony, and new techniques to deal with it.

In what we may perhaps call now the "classical" kind of descriptive, synchronic linguistics, the analyst was concerned with the description of relatively homogeneous bodies of data, and the structuralist approach was most immediately concerned with single dialects and styles, often even idiolects or parts of idiolects. In spite of the application of structural principles to historical problems and the fitful development of techniques of dialectology and "over-all analysis," the successes of the past decades were most spectacular in the treatment of limited corpora of homogeneous data.

I have noted elsewhere[1] that this kind of language material represents only the exceptional situation, the special case, and that an adequate theory of linguistics—or even merely better sets of discovery procedures or "protocol sentences"—must be able to cope with the complex reality of interpenetrating styles, dialects and languages extending out both in social space and in time. Here, I want to refer to structural variation along the time axis.

Most work in diachronic linguistics has been concerned in one way or another with the change of one total structure to another, such as Old English to Modern English, or a proto-language to its daughter languages. The kind of diachrony I am now referring to is that which goes from zero structure towards full structure.

As the first example, let me take the child learning his first language, his "mother tongue." At the beginning, the child has no language and at age six, let us say, he controls close to the full structure of the language. The linguist's problem of diachronic description is to account for the development step-by-step, stage-by-stage, from the beginning to the chosen stopping point. Here the linguist cannot work with written records, as in 19th century diachronic work, and he cannot elicit spoken material with the same degree of assurance and verifiability he is accustomed to enjoying in his normal synchronic analysis. He must turn increasingly to new methods of observation, techniques of experimentation with complex control of variables, new uses of statistics.

But what has this to do with the linguist's understanding of the nature and function of language? What has this to do with linguistics, the theory of language? A great deal. If Roman Jakobson, for example, maintains that human beings speak and hear speech in terms of distinctive features, that these are in some sense universal and that they are arranged in a hierarchical order of some kind,[2] then he must maintain and, in fact, he has maintained that the child's learning to speak his own language must progress in terms of distinctive features and in accordance with the hierarchy he posits.

---

[1] *Word*, XIII,3 (1957), 479; *IJAL*, XXVI,3 (Publication 13 of the Indiana University Research Center in Anthropology, Folklore, and Linguistics, 1960).

[2] Roman Jakobson and Morris Halle, *Fundamentals of Language* ('s-Gravenhage, 1956), pp. 32-36.

Actual work with children has shown that Jakobson is in part right and in part wrong: for example, voicing and palatalization are often mastered as distinctive features and applied to a whole series of consonants almost simultaneously, then remaining available for use in new consonants learned subsequently, while on the other hand some other distinctive features are not learned this way. Of if he says that an [š]-type phoneme is learned before a [č]-type phoneme, he can be shown many counter instances of /č/ acquired before /š/ which will force modification of this hypothesis.

Without pushing this point any further, it seems clear at least that any comprehensive theory of phonology must include definitions and postulates accounting for the way children learn sounds and that such a general theory then becomes testable at least in part by actual observation and analysis of the changing structure of the child language.

Yesterday, Henry Lee Smith offered us as evidence of the universality of his "true word" that children begin their speech behavior with items closely similar to the "words" the linguist posits for the adult language.[3] This little piece of theory given us in passing was not of course phrased in such a rigorous fashion that it could be tested, but surely it is worth rephrasing with care so that it may become susceptible of controlled experimentation of the kind familiar to us from many other sciences. If it cannot be so phrased, then the material on child language can hardly be adduced as "evidence."

At several places in the work of Chomsky, there is the hint that he feels his kind of grammar writing reflects more closely the way a child learns his language. And it would be easy for us to go beyond this hint. For example, if transformation rules have any real validity in linguistic description it should in some sense be true that children learn in terms of them and in terms of the ordering of rules to which generative grammarians attach such great importance. Again, I would say: if there is to be a comprehensive theory of grammatical structure it must account for the way in which children learn the grammar of their language, and if this is so, one of the most pressing tasks of grammatical theorists is to phrase their theories in such a way that they are testable by accepted methods of controlled experiment. If it should turn out that such a phrasing or such experimentation is impossible—or for that matter trivial or uninteresting—then even the hints that one kind of grammar writing or another is more powerful in this respect should be eliminated.

So far we have been talking about the testing with child language learning of theory arrived at in other ways. There is another approach, the

---

[3] See above, p. 95. Reference to children not in Smith's revised paper.

direct study of child language learning for its own sake and for the development of linguistic theory from that. This is, in fact, already beginning to happen. This is not the occasion to report on these developments and, indeed, there are others much better qualified to do so than I, but I would like to refer to two instances of interest to me.

Three recent studies[4] carried out independently have agreed in giving this picture. When the child moves from the stage of one-word sentences to two-word sentences, it soon appears that the two-word combinations he uses have a grammatical structure consisting of a "pivot word," or "operator" and an "X-word," or "content word." The pivot word is one of a small number of high-frequency items, some of which do not occur as single word sentences, and the X-word is one of a larger class of less frequent words, all of which occur as single-word sentences. This is a remarkable indication of the importance at some level of the nucleus and satellite kind of phrase structure. It will be fascinating to see how future observations follow this and detail the expansion and change of structure. It will be most instructive to see the kinds of grammatical analysis which the investigators will be led to adopt to portray most effectively this changing structure.

The other instance is in the functions of language. In her recently published book *Language in the Crib* ('s-Gravenhage, 1963), Ruth Weir shows us the incredible extent to which at least one child played with his language in a purposeful and creative way. Her child in his tape-recorded evening monologs drilled paradigms systematically and created rhymed and rhythmic sequences which show that what Jakobson and others have called the metalingual and poetic functions of language can be surprisingly well developed at age two and a half. Even for the child, language is not just communication; it is grammatical analysis and artistry. Our theories of linguistics must cope with this.

In this paper we are discussing the linguistic analysis of change from zero towards full structure. Our first example was the child learning his language. Let us take a very different example: the creation of a pidgin language. Linguists have been acquainted for over a century with the kind of language called a pidgin, which, instead of continuing in the usual genetic way the language of a certain speech community, comes into being as a

---

[4] W. Miller and S. Ervin, "The development of grammar in child language," to appear in *Child Development Monographs;* R. W. Brown and C. Fraser, "The acquisition of syntax" to appear in *Child Development;* and M. D. S. Braine, "The ontogeny of English phrase structure: the first phase," *Language,* XXXIX, 1 (1963), 1-13.

means of communication among speakers of different languages by a process which seems to take over the grammatical structure of one language or set of languages involved and the lexicon of the other language or languages involved.

Linguists have become accustomed to brushing this phenomenon aside as something rare and isolated, the product of an unusual social situation, but it is becoming increasingly clear now that this process takes place fairly frequently in the world, in a variety of social situations, and that it deserves deeper study as an important type of human language behavior. From our point of view here today, there are two aspects of this I would like to note in particular.

One is the notion of simplification. Observers, including competent linguists, generally have the impression that a pidgin language is in some way "simpler" than its source languages. And it also seems true that there are remarkable structural similarities among pidgins no matter what their sources and uses. Even if it should turn out that the very close similarity of a number of French-, English- and Spanish-based creoles is really understandable by virtue of the apparently wild theory that they had a common origin in a Portuguese-based creole of the Cape Verde Islands subsequently relexicalized, I say even if this is true, the important point of simplification remains. If some features of language are to be regarded as simpler, hence presumably more basic and fundamental than others, this is an important matter for the linguist, and surely the intensive study of pidginization in various places, at various times, and from various source languages, should prove extremely instructive. Linguists could develop some very powerful pieces of theory if they had solid empirically-based notions of simplicity of structure.

The other point of relevance of pidgins to linguistic theory which I wanted to mention is in the realm of historical linguistics as traditionally practiced. Many months ago, Graham Stuart in a conversation put forward the hypothesis that many of the languages of Southeast Asia were originally pidgin languages. I do not know the evidence on which he bases this view, nor do I know how one could test its correctness with present techniques, but if there is any truth to the proposition that many apparently "normal" languages are in reality the descendants of creoles, then it should be very unsettling for linguists who are concerned with comparative linguistic work. It would seem that we could hardly rest until we had determined by careful sociolinguistic study the conditions under which a pidgin and then a creole is produced, or until we had determined by purely linguistic study the telltale marks of the pidgin origin of a language. If we cannot succeed in either of these efforts then we must reconcile ourselves to a degree of uncertainty in historical reconstruction much greater than we have hitherto been forced to do.

The obvious place to start is with the description of a pidgin language in the process of formation, beginning with no structure and progressing towards the full structure of a creole. This process is known to be taking place in such areas as parts of the Congo, and I hope linguists are beginning to work on it.

Let us turn now to a final example of diachrony of the zero-toward-full type, the learning of a foreign language in the classroom. A good deal of attention has been focussed on this situation in the last few years, but it has been almost completely in terms of the effectiveness of the language teaching, i.e., how to achieve optimum results in the learning process, or it has been in terms of discovering the basic principles of human language learning from the psychologist's point of view. These interests of the language teacher and the psychologist are both quite legitimate, but I find it a little surprising that the numerous linguists who have participated in studies along these lines have shown no interest from the purely linguistic point of view. With all the concern there has been for the teaching of French, for example, to speakers of English, I do not know of a single study which describes the linguistic structure of the French being learned by an English speaker. Starting from zero, how does this acquired structure grow step-by-step, stage-by-stage, towards full mastery?

No doubt the major variable in accounting for this diachronic progression will be the order in which the material of the target language is presented, and other variables will include the methods of instruction. Also, no doubt it will be difficult to elicit valid material by the normal informant elicitation techniques. But these particular aspects of the linguist's problem here do not detract from the general interest. People all over the world study languages in classrooms, and the careful *linguistic* study of this process should tell us something about the structure of the learner's language, and the structure of the target language, something about how language structures can change through time and perhaps some fundamental things about human language in general. And we need not be frightened of the variables mentioned and the difficulties of elicitation. These are in some ways an advantage: the presentation can be controlled for experimental purposes in this situation much more easily than in the natural child language-learning situation, and the problem of elicitation is, after all, only another way of looking at the important question of proficiency testing in a foreign language which teachers, psychologists and even linguists have been concerned with from other points of view.

More immediately productive, however, in this situation is the increasingly fashionable procedure of making contrastive studies between two languages to account for the learner's difficulties with his new language. Interestingly enough, we see these studies slowly changing their orientation. They are still concerned chiefly with analyzing and predicting the kind of interference which takes place in bilingual situations, including the classroom language-learning situation, but we are beginning to see concern with general typology of language structures, i.e., with linguistic theory.

As I have pointed out on several previous occasions, contrastive analysis presents the descriptivist with his basic dilemma in its sharpest form. He maintains, on the one hand, that every language must be described and its structure identified in the terms of the language itself, not by an imposition of categories from outside. He maintains, on the other hand, that comparison of two language structures will yield useful predictions on interference in bilingual situations. In order to contrast two language structures, however, the linguist must have some frame of reference into which both structures fit. One cannot compare, for example, the noun system of language A with the noun system of language B without making it clear *why* the term noun has been given to two classes differently defined and having different relationships within each language. The linguist is being called to create a new universal grammar, in other words, a comprehensive theory of linguistics. Some who are working on contrastive studies have taken the first halting steps towards this. Comparisons of demonstrative systems, of accentual systems, of relative clause types, for example, have suggested general typologies for further elaboration and verification.

To illustrate briefly what I mean, comparison of a few structurally divergent languages has yielded the following set of hypotheses about relative constructions, stated here quite unrigorously and without the necessary background of general theory and relevant definitions.

1. Every language has a construction in some grammatico-semantic sense equivalent to the English relative clause.

2. Either this construction involves a subordinate clause with connective morphemic matter, or it is an attributive phrase without such connective material. As examples of the latter type, one may cite the normal relative equivalents in Japanese and Turkish, such as Mr. Komai's example about the trout eater in Tokyo mentioned yesterday.[5]

3. If the construction involves a clause with connective, the connec-

---

[5] See above, p. 69ff.

tive material may lie outside the main and subordinate clauses, and in this case there is generally a resumptive pronoun when the connective corresponds to what would be the object of the subordinate clause in English. Arabic is a good example of this type.

4. If the connective lies within the clause, it may be either in the subordinate clause, as in English or most modern European languages, or in the main clause as in Bengali, most modern Indo-Aryan languages and possibly proto-Indo-European. In this latter case the relative connective normally precedes what is traditionally called the antecedent and is resumed by a demonstrative elsewhere in the main clause.

Along with such hypotheses, we may note interesting correlations such as the further hypothesis that if a language is of the type which has no relative clause but rather an attributive phrase, it generally has verb-final word order.

Typological hypotheses of this kind are stateable in forms which can be tested against further empirical data. Thus the process of contrastive analysis which has grown out of the problems of language learning leads towards the development of general theories of language.

This paper has suggested that the study of the acquisition of language from a purely linguistic point of view will help the linguist to a better understanding of the nature and function of human language and will contribute to the development of better procedures in the analysis and presentation of the structure and history of specific languages. Three examples were used as illustration: the child's learning of his first language, the formation of a pidgin language and the learning of a second language in the classroom. But it is the author's feeling that the purely linguistic study of almost any phenomenon of this general type can have the kind of value suggested, and further, that here is the growing edge of linguistic theory and methods of analysis where much of the effort of institutions and individuals should now be directed.

VARIETIES OF ETHNICITY AND VARIETIES OF LANGUAGE CONSCIOUSNESS [1]

JOSHUA A. FISHMAN

Yeshiva University

It is one of the puzzles of human behavior that much of what is close at hand, and even basic to one's own intellective concerns, is sometimes no better known than that which is more distant and peripheral. This puzzle—which philosophers of science and students of behavior have commented upon at length—was strongly underscored at the SSRC's 1964 Research Seminar on Sociolinguistics (held at Indiana University) when the linguists among us experienced considerable embarrassment in defining *languages* (as distinct from dialects, registers, patois, parlances, argots, etc.) while the sociologists among us experienced equally great difficulty in defining *ethnicity* (as distinct from nationality, race, religion, etc.). At the end of one heated discussion a distinguished linguist suggested that "ethnicity" be discarded as an unnecessary and confusing term. This met with the countersuggestion from a sociologist that the concept "a language" be discarded since it was not possible to define it in such a way as to help us answer such a simple question as "how many languages are spoken in area X?" Fortunately, this double suicide pact was never ratified and I for one came away from the summer's experience convinced that both terms were worthwhile but that both required considerable within-family scrubbing before they would be really fit for presentation before mixed company.

Ethnicity refers most basically to a primordial wholistic guide to human

---

[1] I consider this paper as being a minor supplement to John J. Gumperz' stimulating article "Types of linguistic communities," *Anthropological Linguistics,* 1962, 4, no. 1, 28-40, which I have reprinted in my *Readings in the Sociology of Language,* The Hague, Mouton, 1965. That paper, like the present one, is concerned with parallelism between social complexity and complexity of linguistic situations. However, while Gumperz spells out this parallelism in some detail, I merely treat the extremes of the continuum which Gumperz presents in order to utilize the obvious contrasts between socio-cultural settings for the purpose of examining the concept of ethnicity.

behavior. Its primary referent is to unmobilized man, to man living in a limited human and geographic environment uncomplicated by broader causes, loyalties, slogans or ideologies. For mankind under such limited social conditions we find it inappropriate to distinguish between those daily rounds that pertain to or derive from religion, nationality, or social class. As far as we can tell, peasant and tribal societies themselves make no such distinctions "from the inside" and their social structure, as viewed by us "from the outside," reveals no fully differentiated roles corresponding to those of pastor, politician, union leader, etc. Instead, we find a fully integrated set of beliefs, views and behaviors, a "way of life" that is "traditional" in that it invokes timeless custom as the directive guide to all the processes, problems and perspectives of life. This then is the initial and primary meaning of ethnicity: an all-embracing constellation, limited in its contacts with the outside world, limited in its consciousness of self, limited in the internal differentiation or specialization that it recognizes or permits; a "given" that is viewed as no more subject to change than one's kin and one's birthplace; a "given" that operates quite literally with these two differentiations (kinship and birthplace) uppermost in mind; a "given" in which kinship and birthplace completely regulate friendship, worship, and workmanship.

Language, as such, is usually not a conscious factor in the primordial world—except, on occasion, as a boundary-maintaining device—by which I mean to say that it is usually not something separately recognized, valued, loved, protected, cultivated and ideologized. Language norms exist, of course, as do minor variations in code, register or style consonant with the relatively minor distinctions in role relations and in social situations recognized in that world. But these norms of usage are symbolically unencumbered. They are transmitted as are other norms—those of planting and sowing, of dressing and eating—by example and by socialization within the fold, and they change slowly over time, usually without the help or hindrance of special caretakers such as language teachers, grammarians or professional bards. Ethnicity represents the primary guide to behavior in the "classical" folk society [2] and in even more limited tribal societies.

---

[2] The validity and utility of this category ("folk society") and the rural-urban continuum from which it is derived have been substantially discussed in the anthropological and sociological literature. For recent critical discussions see: F. Benet, "Sociology uncertain: The ideology of the rural-urban continuum." *Comparative Studies in Sociology and History,* 1963, 6. 1-23; also C. Geertz, "The integrative revolution: Primordial and civil politics in the new states," in his *Old Societies and New States,* (New York, Free Press, 1963), 106-159.

Many societies today exist at or close to this very level of primordial ethnicity and 50 to 100 years ago there were many more such. The bulk of the peasantry of Western Europe, including the peasantries of Britain and France, was not at all far from this level of social organization just a few centuries ago, at the very same time that their rulers and their city-cousins were living on a far different (though related) level of social organization, one that involved a transformation of unconscious primordial ethnicity in the direction of conscious nationality. The bulk of the peasantry of Eastern and Southern Europe was still close to the level of primordial ethnicity half a century ago when mass immigration to the United States from those regions was fully underway. Is it any wonder then that when Polish and Ukranian peasants were approached by census takers toward the end of the 19th century and asked to designate their "nationality" and "religion" they answered that they were "Kaiser's people" or that they were "local (indigenous) people"? Is it any wonder then that many late 19th and early 20th century immigrants to the United States gave very strange, un-reliable (and necessarily incorrect) replies to similar questions put to them by American immigration officers? [3] Is it any wonder that a Hungarian language census of the latter part of the 19th century (conducted and published in Hungarian) reported several thousand claimants of "Ungarisch" mother tongue? Is it any wonder that U.S. mother tongue census data for 1910 and 1920 reports thousands of claimants of "Slavish" and other non-existent or at least inappropriately labeled tongues? Is it any wonder that language statistics for India, Africa, New Guinea and other parts of the world today are confounded by the unawareness of the local populations (and by the ignorance of supposedly sophisticated census takers) as to just what to call the local vernaculars and populaces? It is a fact of primordial ethnicity that not only is there little language conscious-ness but that the languages employed may have no special designation or no better ones than "mother tongue," "our language," "simple language," "daily language," "high language," "book language," etc., i.e. terms with no group or societal name attached to them.

Let us briefly compare this state of affairs with another which evolved after many centuries in Western Europe but which was subsequently brought into being much more rapidly in other parts of the world as a result of much more rapid and externally pressured social change. Here we find a consciousness of national history, with its heroes and martyrs and national

---

[3] Further details and discussion of all of these examples may be found in "Ukranian language maintenance efforts" which constitutes chapter 12 of my *Language Loyalty in the United States,* The Hague, Mouton, 1965.

missions, national grievances, national ideals. Here we find a distinction between religion and nationality, even when everyone (or almost everyone) is of the same religion (or irreligion). Here we find pride in national literature with its poets and novelists and with its literary schools, periods and styles. Here we find a consciousness of national language, with its avowed beauty, subtlety and precision. Language (like the missions, the heroes, the ideals and the other national treasures to which it is explicitly related) becomes something to love, to fight for, to live for, to die for; something to safeguard, to develop, to enrich, to bring to others who are less fortunate. What has happened to (indeed, where is) primordial ethnicity under these circumstances?

Much has happened—much more than can be spelled out here—to the economy, to the political organization, to the social structure, to the communication possibilities, etc. As a result, there is both a broadening and a fractionization of concern. Instead of the local tribe or the local village, integrated on the basis of kinship and common, direct experience, there is the nation or the national group held together by symbols, instrumental organizations and ideological commitments. The formerly fully overlapping networks of kinship, friendship, worship and workmanship no longer fully overlap. In particular, there is a substantial distance between kinship-friendship networks on the one hand and broader economic and political networks (and allegiances) on the other hand. Not only are there farmers and shoemakers and carpenters and tailors (simple craftsmen—but, even so, far more specialized than the "do it yourself" inhabitants of primordial ethnic communities) but there are newspapers and movements and schools and unions and clubs. All of these provide the new, non-ethnic unity and the new non-ethnic diversity of modern "mobilized" society. As a result, both unity and diversity are organized and institutionalized at a symbolic level substantially beyond the reach of the family and the immediate community. It may still be there, but it is no more meaningful to ask the man in the street in Warsaw, Paris or Rome today to designate his ethnicity than it was to ask his peasant grandfather or great-grandfather to designate his nationality.

Primordial ethnicity is a construct that pertains to an all-encompassing web. This web comes apart and becomes segmentized, bit by bit, during successive periods of socio-cultural change. Its segments become separately transformed, symbolically elaborated and integrated via organizations, ideologies and political institutions. Nationalism—including language loyalty—is made up of the stuff of primordial ethnicity; indeed, it is transformed ethnicity with all of the accoutrements for functioning at a larger scale of political, social and intellectual activity. However, below the level of conscious symbolic behavior, bits and pieces of primordial ethnicity may still show through. Birthdays in France are not completely governed by the Great Culture of de Gaulle. Wedding ceremonies in Germany are not spelled out in detail by the values or mainsprings of German Kultur. Funerals of common folk in Quebec are French-Canadian in addition to being Catholic and they are somewhat different than Catholic funerals in Madrid, Warsaw, Rome and Mexico City. Even in the United States, after all of the de-ethnization that has marked our development as a nation, ethnicity is the substratum that continues to mark the food preferences, the family occasions, the pastimes, the residential patterns, the religious holidays, and a number of the most significant biological transitions in millions of 100% (and even of 150%) Americans.[4] These daily life patterns are ethnic at base, precisely because they are relatively untransformed, unideological, and unconscious. They provide us—and hundreds of millions of other so-called "enlightened" people throughout the world—with much of the color, the distinctiveness, the comfort, the folksiness, and the continuity in those aspects of daily life that are relatively untouched by national symbols and that are below the level of abstraction, organization and inclusiveness of the phenomena (and at the level of analysis) that most anthropologists refer to by the term "culture."

* * *

There is a particularly American (including American social science and American intellectual) discomfort and misperception with respect to ethnicity. The discomfort stems from our own¯ de-ethnicized national history relative to the national development of the more traditional nations of the world. The latter developed out of long centuries of *transforming* ethnicity, both as a result of internal unification and as a result of external demarcation and liberation. We have developed out of more recent, more heterogeneous, and more overtly and initially ideologized roots. Our common traditions are very largely symbolic and procedural rather than substantive in terms of detailed traditions and interactions of daily life. Our position as a "new nation" (in the sense that Lipset [5] uses this term) and our striving toward the "great society" (as this term and concept has recently become popularized) are both necessarily derived from non-ethnic

---

[4] For recent discussions of the surprising stability of residual ethnicity in American life see Nathan Glazer and Daniel P. Moynahan, *Beyond the Melting Pot*, Cambridge, M. I. T. and Harvard University Press, 1963; also Milton M. Gordon, *Assimilation in American Life*, New York, Oxford University Press, 1964.

[5] See Seymour M. Lipset, *The First New Nation*, New York, Basic Books, 1963.

roots and experiences. As a result, "ethnicity" is not a phenomenon with which most American intellectuals are really familiar (since they insist on confusing it with "American style" ethnic groups), it is not one in which they are really interested, (for isn't ethnicity "something old fashioned and unenlightened") and it is not one toward which they are sympathetic (since they themselves are "liberated from that kind of thing.")

In addition, ethnicity has suffered in American social science circles because, on the one hand, we feel uncomfortable about the terms "race" and "nationality," and, on the other hand, real "ethnicity" per se, is not something that can be simply asked for on a questionnaire. In sociolinguistic studies we frequently want to determine the background of our subjects in terms of the languages their parents speak or spoke and in terms of the traditions of their current as well as of their childhood homes and neighborhoods. Such information is needed to help us locate and describe particular speech communities, i.e. subjects with particular phonetic, lexical or syntactic features in their verbal repertoires and with particular language skills, attitudes and behaviors more generally. In the early years of this century it was not uncommon to attempt to secure such identifying background information by simply asking for "race." Replies such as "Norwegian," "Mexican," "Jewish (Polish)" etc., were not at all viewed as inappropriate to this query. Subsequently this term came under well-deserved scientific and popular opprobrium. The term "nationality" or "national origin" then came into vogue during the twenties and thirties, but it too ran into problems because by now the phenomenon referred to had become modified and attenuated. What was a third generation American of Norwegian or Germany ancestry to reply to a question concerning national origin? He was American born and so were his parents. Replies undoubtedly varied, some respondents claiming American "nationality" (including some respondents who had themselves arrived here from abroad as children), others claiming a "foreign" national origin (even when they were third generation). As a result neither of these claims, in and of themselves, were sufficiently predictive of language behavior, let alone being predictive of other less structured behaviors.

Finally, today, we find many investigators referring to "ethnic group membership." Unfortunately, on the one hand, this term is not a bit clearer to the man in the street than its predecessors. On the other hand, we are so surrounded by egalitarian convictions and pressures that we feel too embarrassed to talk of "race" (even when Negroes are involved) or to ask about "religion" (even when Catholics are involved) even though these terms are somewhat clearer. We often try to cover an entirely heterogeneous set of phenomena by referring to "ethnic groups," or to "ethnic backgrounds" other than entering upon the difficult path of measuring and describing "ethnicity." [6]

We must not misinterpret the fact that ethnicity cannot be discovered via a single item on a form or questionnaire, or the fact that it is not a term that the man in the street (our informant) understands (or uniformly misunderstands), or the fact that ethnicity has become a marginal aspect of modern American (and, more generally, of modern, urban, industrial, national) life, or the fact that ethnicity varies in the degree of its integration

---

[6] I have taken care to speak of "ethnicity" rather than of "ethnic groups" both because "ethnicity" is the more basic (and for Americans the more novel) concept and because "ethnic group" poses definitional and operational problems of its own. Ostensibly, ethnic groups are merely groups marked off from others by differences in ethnicity. However, the question immediately arises as to *when* a group is a group, i.e. how much "groupness" (and by whose standards) is required? Does an ethnic group become and remain an ethnic group when (and as long as) its own *members* consider it to be a separate group or when (and as long as) outsiders consider it to be such a group? Do individuals belong to an ethnic group when they themselves acknowledge such membership or when others attribute such membership to them? How is one to treat an aggregate of individuals who acknowledge no ties to each other, who practice few if any folkway that differ from those of their neighbors, but whose grandparents were clearly of the same ethnic background and who are viewed by their neighbors as constituting a group apart, even though they themselves have no such self-concept or self-aspiration?

The above issues represent genuine concerns in sociology and in social psychology for they obviously correspond to different social realities. Groups whose members acknowledge membership and groupness have different kinds and degrees of impact upon the behaviors of these members than do groups whose existence is externally rather than internally defined and determined. The consequences of different kinds and intensities of groupness are constantly being studied, particularly where acculturation, social disorganization and other processes of social change make it impossible to expect similar values and behaviors from most individuals to whom some common group-membership label is attached.

However, ethnic groups are of interest to linguists (and to many sociologists as well), *not* because of any concern with how groups are formed, dissolved and reformed, or with their varying impact upon their members, but because of an analytic need for categories by means of which subjects of predictably different values and behaviors can be easily located. My point is that such a "nominal" (categorical) approach to human groups is likely to be productive only in traditional settings where the groupness of groups is likely to be as real internally as it is recognizable externally. In other settings, particularly in modern and in modernizing societies, ethnic groups may not function in this fashion at all. They may have little impact on verbal behavior precisely because they do not correspond to real speech-and-behavior communities. As a result it becomes doubly appropriate to select and group subjects in accord with indices of ethnicity rather than in accord with attributed (and—from a functional point of view—often erroneously attributed) group membership.

and in its relationship with religion and language (to mention only two of its initial primordial constituents) in its various transformations beyond the stage of primordial ethnicity, or the fact that it may therefore, be more or less predictive of other behaviors—we must not misinterpret all of the the foregoing in such ways as to come to disregard the concept itself or the indisputable fact that certain stages of ethnicity have revealed very lawful relationships with certain kinds of language behaviors.

* * *

Perhaps it would be helpful to conclude what has thus far been a theoretical discussion with some empirical examples of how the concept of ethnicity has been utilized and has proved helpful in my own recent research.

Table I indicates how five "ethnic communities" in the United States (defined roughly in accord with Gumperz's "speech community") differed with respect to claimed routes and claimed success in transmitting their non-English mother tongues to their young in 1962.[7] A community of Mexican-Americans in San Antonio (Mex) and a community of Puerto Ricans in New York (PR) were the only ones of the five studied that claimed that home use and daily family life were still the major vehicles in this connection. A community of post-World War II Ukrainian immigrants in Newark (UK_1) were extremely sensitive to the falling off of language proficiency in their children. They had already begun to rely primarily upon non-religious language schools supported by their "ethnic community" for the transmission of their ethnic mother tongue (EMT), in view of the fact that "home use" had already become ineffective or unreliable after only 15 years of post-war American metropolitan life (this being a *much* more rapid rate of language shift than had obtained among pre-World War I immigrants to the USA). A community of second generation Ukrainian Americans living in a small Pennsylvania mining town

---

[7] For further details see chapter 8 of *Language Loyalty in the United States* ("Some community dynamics of language maintenance").

TABLE I

Mother Tongue Maintenance in Five "Ethnic Communities": Approaches and Accomplishments

(How) Do the Young Learn the EMT?	Community				
	Mex	PR	UK_2	UK_1	FR_2
Home Use	48%	62%	0%	0%	0%
Lang. Schools	6	3	17	26	0
Parochial Schools	0	0	45	3	76
Do Not Learn	46	35	38	71	24

(UK₂) and a community of second generation Franco-Americans in Fall River, Massachusetts (FR₂) had withdrawn one step further from direct control over language maintenance in that they had come to depend primarily on the services of an institution not even entirely within their ethnic community or under its control, namely, the Eastern Orthodox and the Roman Catholic churches respectively. My collaborators and I interpreted this Table (and several other related Tables not shown here) as indicating that our Mexican-American and Puerto Rican samples were still achieving an appreciable degree of language maintenance and, furthermore, that they were doing so primarily by operating within the traditional pale of ethnicity. On the other hand, we considered the second generation Franco-American and Ukrainian samples as being both least successful and most de-ethnicized in their approach. First generation Ukrainian Americans still occupied a middle ground between these two extremes. Their ethnicity (and their language maintenance) was no longer something merely and primarily to be *lived* but, rather, something to be organized, studied, valued, and appreciated. Other urbanized minorities who have embarked upon this route have found that it permits (indeed it often facilitates) mobility within the host society and, therefore, facilitates even more marginal ethnicity and language maintenance.

The degree to which ethnicity and language maintenance are related is also illustrated in Table II. Here we see that those parishes in the United States that still cling to ethnic mother tongues tend to do so for one set of reasons in connection with sermons and for another set of reasons in connection with their schools for children.[8] Non-English sermons are most often "justified" in very matter of fact terms. It is enough to say that sermons are in the language that the parishioners know best, in the language they speak most often at home and on the street, in the language that they and their parents and grandparents have always spoken, etc. These answers

---

[8] For further details see chapter 6 of *Language Loyalty in the United States* ("Mother tongue retentiveness in ethnic parishes").

TABLE II

Reasons Why Ethnic Mother Tongue is Used in Church Sermons and Taught in Parish Schools

Reasons	Sermons	Schools
Ethnic (native language, traditional language)	77%	29%
Other (beautiful language, practical language, cultural language)	23%	71%

imply that for many adults in these parishes (and it is for the adults that the sermons are intended) language and religion and daily ethnicity are still intimately linked, at least at the level of adult-adult interaction. However at the parent-child and at the child-child interaction levels this is most frequently no longer the case. Most parent-child and child-child interactions have drifted far away from the primordial ethnic context. As a result, children are taught the ethnic mother tongue not "simply" because it is theirs but rather because it is beautiful, cultural, practical, required by higher authorities, etc. Thus we see how language maintenance is differently rationalized (and differently actualized or realized) for generations that differ appreciably in their proximity to or infusion with primordial ethnicity. This difference between first and second generation rationales for language maintenance came up again and again in my study of language maintenance among American immigrants groups—whether rank and file members or intellectual-organizational leaders were at the focus of inquiry.[9]

I have chosen these two examples primarily because they illustrate my conviction that ethnicity is a matter of *degree* far more basically and far more provocatively than it is an all-or-none matter of *kind*. Linguists, in borrowing sociological concepts, have all too frequently asked *which* ethnic *groups* exist in a particular area (or what is the ethnic background of informant X) rather than inquire of the extent to which *ethnicity* is apparent in the behaviors of their subjects. The latter, admittedly, is a much harder question to go about answering. It involves a knowledge of the traditional rounds of daily life (as well as a knowledge of the conscious ideological elaborations and symbols that have been derived from as well as grafted upon simple ethnicity); a knowledge of actual observances, actual beliefs, actual friendship patterns, actual communication channels, etc. Ethnicity is a dynamic (I think you are accustomed to saying "a contrastive") phenomenon. It depends upon (interacts with) a larger setting to determine its exact nature at any particular time. It is not a pigeon-hole to which data can be assigned on the basis of superficial or "nominal" criteria.

You cannot be sure whether a certain phonetic range constitutes a phoneme in standard French (or whether "phoneme" is a useful construct) simply by asking an informant to answer "yes" or "no" on a questionnaire. You do not scrap the concept of "phoneme" merely because there are allophones. You do not become disgusted with phonemes simply because they are sometimes morphologically conditioned. You do not ridicule a particular phonemic contrast, let alone the analytic-descriptive construct of

---

[9] For further details see chapter 7 of *Language Loyalty in the United States* ("Organizational interest in language maintenance").

phonemes, merely because sound shifts occur. Nor do you expect all phonemic distinctions in language X to be present in the speech of all regional groups, all social classes, or on all social occasions entered into by the speakers of language X. Nor, finally, do you surrender your interest in phonemic description simply because sociologists do not understand it (as must be obvious to you from some of the above samples) or because it cannot be explained to them in one or even in a few brief lectures.

I do not know what lies ahead for the concept "ethnicity" as social scientists and linguists gain more experience in working together on socially imbedded language behavior in various parts of the world. On the other hand, I do not know what will happen to the concept "a language" either under those circumstances. However, I am more than willing to come back to Georgetown University 100 years from now (if you will have me) in order to find out.

LINGUISTICS AND READING

A Place for the Special Contribution of the Linguist

Charles C. Fries

University of Michigan

If "Johnny can't read," it is not because his teachers, or the principals of his schools, or the superintendents of his school systems, or the professors of education, or the directors of reading clinics have ignored or neglected the problems created by the innumerable and diverse Johnnies and Janes that must, for modern living, have an increasingly high standard of literacy. Whatever the causes of the "failures of modern education," no one can insist that they have arisen out of willful neglect of the problems or an unwillingness to labor hard in their study.

A linguist, who seeks to discover just where his special knowledge and experience might make a contribution to the understanding and solution of the many perplexing problems of learning to read and of teaching reading, finds not an empty field with a few inarticulate workers, but the floor of a Wall Street Stock Exchange on the eve of a financial crisis. The movement for what is called the "scientific study of education"—a type of investigation depending in large part upon statistical procedures applied to data gathered through the use of various types of "objective" tests and measurements— got under way during the first two decades of the twentieth century. In this accelerating trend toward the measurement-statistical approach to educational problems, the number of studies directed to the teaching of reading far exceeds that given to any other single subject of the school curriculum.

Through the patient work of men like the late William S. Gray, of the University of Chicago, Emmett A. Betts, formerly head of the Reading Clinic in Philadelphia—now of the University of Miami in Florida, and Arthur Traxler, of the Educational Records Bureau of New York City, in listing, classifying and summarizing these studies, the bibliographical resources in the field of "reading" are exceptionally good. These men deserve the gratitude of everyone who attempts to grasp coherently what this kind of research has contributed to an understanding of the nature of the reading process and of the materials and procedures for teaching. But even with the aid of Gray's *Summaries of Investigations Relating to Reading* (which cover more than 4,300 items from 1900 to 1962), Traxler's four volumes of *Research in Reading* (which though more highly selective cover 2,343 items from 1930 to 1958) and Emmett Betts' *Index to Professional Literature on Reading* (with its helpful information about more than 8,200 items)—even with such aids as these the very mass of the material creates great difficulty.

The difficulties, however, do not arise out of the volume of the materials alone. One comes away from a concentrated study of hundreds out of the thousands of these investigations much distressed and frustrated. He seeks in vain for the cumulative continuity that has characterized all recognized scientifically-sound research. He struggles hard, without success, to find strands of fundamental assumptions and accepted criteria of evaluation running through a series of studies attacking any of the major problems of the teaching of reading.

Quotations from men like Gray and Traxler, who have carried the main burden of recording and summarizing the published research on reading during the last thirty-five years, and who have sought diligently and sympathetically for the studies that have made sound contributions, give expression to some of the reasons for the feeling of distress and frustration with which one comes from an intensive study of these research materials.

W. S. Gray, Article, "Reading," in *Encyclopedia of Educational Research,* 1950, p. 966:

> "Unfortunately, much of the scientific work relating to reading has been fragmentary in character. . . . In the second place, there is far too little coordination of effort among research workers in the field of reading. . . . In the third place, many of the studies reported have been conducted without adequate controls."

C. Winfield Scott, "A Forest View of Present Research in Reading," in *Educational and Psychological Measurement* 14 (1943), 208-214:

> "In reviewing a recent summary of studies on mixed eye-hand dominance Gray concluded, 'Obviously final conclusions relating to this problem cannot be stated at present'. *This statement could be written large after every area of reading research.*"

Arthur E. Traxler, *Eight More Years of Research in Reading,* 1955, p. 6:

> "*Phonics*—The results of available research on phonics continues to be inconclusive as far as evidence of the value of phonetic training is concerned."

Arthur E. Traxler, *Eight More Years of Research in Reading,* 1955, p. 5:

"The findings in studies of reading speed and comprehension confirm earlier findings in that fast and slow readers appear to comprehend reading material about equally well. There is a small amount of evidence that fast reading is of advantage in the comprehension of pupils with high intelligence but is not advantageous for pupils of average and low mental ability."

In spite of the tremendous number of the published studies of reading, I have not been able to find the evidence to justify the frequent assertion that the findings of educational research since 1920 have provided the basis for most of the modern reforms in reading instruction. As a matter of fact, every one of the method-approaches and combination of method-approaches to the teaching of reading that are so vigorously and voluminously discussed today was in use, fully discussed and incorporated in textbooks and in teachers' manuals before 1890.

Perhaps the latest of the approaches to receive wide discussion is the one which uses the *Augmented Roman Alphabet* (ARA) for what the advocates of this approach call the *Initial Teaching Medium* (ITM).[1]

"This alphabet of 43 letters (so says the newspaper report) was designed by Sir James Pitman, grandson of Sir Isaac Pitman, who invented the Pitman shorthand system." Isaac Pitman, however, did more than invent a very successful shorthand system. He published his first *Phonography* in 1837. Five years later in 1842, with the assistance of A. J. Ellis (now well-known for his great work on English *Pronunciation*), he produced the system called *Phonotopy or printing by Sound.* This system of printing, using most of the letters of Romanic alphabet but augmented by seventeen new letters constituted a 'Phonetic print' which was then tried in the schools as a method of teaching beginning reading. The following statements are quoted from the journal *The Massachusetts Teacher* 6 (1853), 25-28, from the report of their committee appointed to examine this 'Phonetic system' as it was being used in 119 public and five private schools of Massachusetts.

"It has been found . . . that a wonderful gain may be made in teaching the reading, spelling, and enunciation of the common orthography, by the primary use of the Phonetic alphabet, and the Phonetic books. Not only should the child be taught to read by the means of the sounds of the language, which has been a favorite

---

[1] Introduced at the 27th Conference of the *Educational Records Bureau,* in New York, November 1963, by John Downing of the Institute of Education of the University of London. "A two-year experiment is nearing an end at 75 British schools where 2500 children aged 4 and 5 are being taught by the new method."

idea of many friends of education, but he should have a fixed character for every sound, or else, in the outset, he will be likely to have a natural tendency to dislike his book; a tendency sometimes, to be sure, overcome by a skilful teacher, but often irremediable.

"For the common orthography has such a variety of changes, not only in the sounds attached to each letter of the Romanic alphabet, but also in the number of combinations attached to each sound, that the child is liable to become so confused at the commencement of his educational career, as to render it extremely difficult, if not impossible, for him to progress with any degree of rapidity satisfactory to the teacher. . . . The Phonetic system of instruction, thus beneficial in its effects, has been introduced in 119 public and five private schools of Massachusetts."

The report then lists eight important Committees that have reported in favor of this system of Phonetic instruction.[2] This approach using the Romanic alphabet, augmented with seventeen so-called 'Phonetic' letters had considerable use in Britain and in the United States from 1842 to 1873. In addition to the report in the *Massachusetts Teacher* of 1853 just given, the *Journal of the Proceedings of the National Educational Association* had a similar report in 1873 (pp. 207-219).

But this use of an augmented Roman alphabet for the teaching of reading was by no means new in 1837. Two hundred and sixty-seven years earlier, John Hart had described his use of a quite similar alphabet. His book, which was published in 1570, had the title *A Methode or comfortable beginning for all vnlearned, whereby they may bee taught to read English, in a very short time with pleasure.*

Of the teaching he says, "The ease whereof is such, that so soone as one is able to name the .xxv. letters [of this alphabet] perfitly and readily, whersoeuer they present themselves to his eye, so soone shall he be able to reade."

Nineteen years earlier in 1551 he had discussed the *Unreasonable Writing of Our English Toung* and "had sought the meanes (herein writen) by which

---

[2] A Committee of the American Academy of Arts and Sciences, a Committee of the American Association of the Friends of Education, a Committee of the American Institute of Instruction, two Joint Committees of the Massachusetts Legislature on Education, a Sub-Committee of the Boston Primary School Committee, a Committee of the Ohio State Teachers' Association, a Sub-Committee of the School Committee of Cincinnati and various committees of divers associations in different parts of this country, as well as England, have reported in favor of this system of Phonetic instruction.

we may use a certaine, good and easi writing, only following our pronunciation and keping the letters in their auncient, Simple and Singular powers." [3]

Among the most important of those that followed Hart's approach to
the teaching of reading was Charls Butler (1633/34), who says of the use
of his 'phonetic alphabet', that "the learners attein unto a more perfect and
reddy reading in one year, than otherwise they have doon in three."

In 1768 Benjamin Franklin proposed his plan entitled *A Scheme for a
New Alphabet and Reformed Mode of Spelling* [4] as a means of solving the
difficulties created by English spelling. The Pitman-Ellis materials of 1842
carried on into the nineteenth century the approach to the teaching of
beginning reading devised by John Hart in 1570 and revised and tried by
his followers (I have named but three out of a considerable number in the
seventeenth and eighteenth centuries).

But the Augmented Roman alphabets, although tried enthusiastically,
did not solve all the problems of the teaching of reading.

In 1881 George L. Farnham, a school superintendent conscientiously
devoted to the search for the methods that would procure the most efficient
reading, wrote the following.

> "In 1858, the phonetic system was introduced into the schools
> of Syracuse, N.Y., and for a time it was thought that the true
> method of teaching children to read had been discovered. After
> a trial of five years, however, it was seen that while pupils learned
> to read by this method in much less time than usual, and attained
> a high state of excellence in articulation, their reading was nearly
> as mechanical as before, and few of them became good spellers.
> The two systems of analysis, phonic and graphic, had so little in
> common that permanent confusion was produced in the mind." [5]

Other so-called modern approaches to the teaching of reading reach back
into the nineteenth century. As early as 1842 the Word-method [6] was vigorously discussed and fully worked out in widely used textbooks published in

---

[3] See also his major book *An Orthographie, contayning the due order and reason,
howe to write or paint thimmage of mannes voice, most like to the life or nature.*

[4] "As to those who do not spell well, if the two difficulties are compared, viz., that
of teaching them true spelling in the present mode and that of teaching them the new
alphabet and the new spelling according to it, I am confidant that the latter would
be by far the least. They naturally fall into the new method already, as much as
the imperfection of their alphabet will admit of; their present bad spelling is only
bad because contrary to the present bad rules; under the new rules it would be good.
—The difficulty of learning to spell well in the old way is so great, that few attain it;
thousands and thousands writing on to old age, without ever being able to acquire it."

[5] Preface of his book on *The Sentence Method* (1881).

[6] See *The Common School Journal* 4 (1842), 90-96 and 27, 29.

1850, 1856, 1874 [7] and 1883.[8] As a general practice, these books also provided for the teaching of new words by using the methods of "word analysis by sound," usually preceded by a period of "preparation" activity to put the pupils "on their own" in approaching "new words" in their reading.[9]

The Sentence-Method received considerable discussion and practice from 1870 on. George L. Farnham's little book *The Sentence Method of Teaching Reading, Writing and Spelling* was first published in 1881, with later editions in 1886 and 1895. It was widely used in teacher-training institutes in the East, especially in Pennsylvania and New York State and in the Middle West, chiefly in Iowa and Nebraska. As explained and practiced by Farnham and his followers, this approach through the "whole sentence" was conceived and thoroughly worked out over a period of classroom trial lasting ten years—from 1870 to 1880.

This book of 1881 treated with considerable breadth the problems that face the teacher. It stressed the need for preparation exercises to make the pupils "ready" for reading, constantly insisted upon the getting of meaning and thought as the basic objective, made use of supplementary reading material and selection on the basis of pupil interest and in asserting that "True education is a growth," based the teaching of reading upon the experience of the pupils.

------

[7] *Webb's Normal Reader No. 1, A New Method of Teaching Children to Read.*
    Part I   Word Method
    Part II Teaching New Words, Reading, Spelling, the Alphabet, and the Sounds of the Letters
    Part III Union Method
[8] *Butler's Series,* 1883.
[9] See Webb's *Normal Reader No. 1,* p. 16ff. and Part II.
    See also Butler's Series—First Reader (1883) Preface p. 4.
      Suggestions to Teachers
"The first step in any work is the most important. Of no subject is this more true than of reading.
It is recommended that teachers using this book should employ the Word Method in connection with the Phonic Method. We are satisfied that the Alphabetic Method is a hindrance rather than a help. A child can more readily learn twenty-six words than twenty-six letters. Words have interest to a child because they mean something. Letters are merely arbitrary signs. . . . While advocating the Word Method, we would guard instructors against teaching words without first developing the ideas they represent.
To aid the teacher in this work, most of the lessons of this book are illustrated.
Begin the lesson by showing the children the picture. Let them tell all they see in it. Have a familiar talk about it. Call the word by which the object is known. Be careful to print the word as nearly like the one in the book as possible. Let the children find the word upon the page wherever it occurs, and pronounce it."

The leading teachers and administrators before 1890 did not conceive the task of teaching reading in any narrow fashion, and their practical classroom experimentation led to a continuing development in theory and method. The important changes in approach that characterize the history of the teaching of reading in the schools have grown out of the earnest struggle of the teachers and administrators themselves to find better ways— ways to achieve specific types of skills that the approach then in use neglected, ways to make their teaching measure up to their ideals of all that must be accomplished.

It is into this struggle, which has lasted approximately four centuries, that the linguist must come and find the place for his special contribution. The linguist, as a linguist, has a special competence in a special limited field. We assume that that competence includes *more than skill* in using the techniques and procedures necessary for the *practitioner of linguistic analysis*— that it does include the body of knowledge and understanding concerning the nature and functioning of human language built up by the devoted labors of a host of scholars, especially during the last century and a half. But we cannot assume that the well-trained linguist *merely by virtue of the fact that he is a linguist* is competent to deal with the applications of his science to the problems of teaching. As with the other sciences, I believe that the engineering applications of the linguist's special knowledge require an *additional* special competence which includes an understanding of the particular practical problems of the field of application and the status of the struggle to solve them.

From this point of view, there is a definite contribution that linguists can and should make in the struggle to make the program for the teaching of reading more adequate to meet the conditions that face the schools today.

Learning to read is learning to do something with language and we would assume that reading ability must be based on language ability. Children have learned to "talk" their language when they come to school (we assume an age of five).

The linguist competent to deal with the application of his special knowledge should be of use, first, in analyzing and describing with some precision the language achievement of the child as he enters the reading program.

Such a linguist should be of use, second, in defining, in relation to language, the nature of the reading process.

And third, such a linguist, with an added special competence in English, should be able to describe the special characteristics of English spelling as that spelling has been developed and is now used to represent the word-patterns of the language.

With respect to the language competence of the child, the linguist's approach would not be "word-centered" in the sense that he would consider primarily the number of vocabulary items the child "knows" (the Seashore calculation or the earlier estimates). He would be able to investigate the child's responses to the range of contrastive functioning units, the phonemes, that English uses to separate and identify the lexical items. His investigations would also include the range of contrastive markers that identify the basic structures to which grammatical meanings are attached.

With respect to the nature of reading he raises the question, "Just what must the child, who has learned to talk, learn in order *to add the skill of reading to his already attained skill of talking?*"

Learning to read is *not* a process of learning new language signals or other language signals than those the child has already learned. The basic difference between reading and talking lies in the medium through which the physical stimuli make contact with his nervous system. In "talk," the physical stimuli of the language signals make their contact by means of sound waves received by the ear. In reading, the physical stimuli of the same language signals consist of graphic shapes that make their contact with his nervous system through light waves received by the eye. The process of learning to read is the process of transfer from the auditory signs for language signals which the child has already learned, to the new visual signs for the same signals.

Learning to read, therefore, means developing a considerable range of high-speed recognition responses to specific sets of patterns of graphic shapes. In the transfer from a succession of sound patterns in a time dimension to a succession of graphic patterns in a space direction, there are many (often neglected) arbitrary features that must be specifically and thoroughly learned by much practice. Although the alphabet as used for English is phonemically based, it is not a 'phonemic alphabet', in the sense that there is a single letter for each phoneme and a single phoneme for each letter. Throughout the history of English spelling, the letters of the alphabet have never had a one-for-one correspondence with English phonemes. The phonemes, especially the vowel phonemes, have always been graphically represented by *spelling patterns*. English spelling today cannot be satisfactorily dealt with by trying to match individual letters with individual sounds. To say this, however, does not deny the basic relation that does exist between sounds and spellings. To grasp that relation, the beginning reader must learn to respond to the significant features of the major patterns of spelling rather than try to learn the many various sounds that each letter can be said to represent.

The spelling-pattern approach differs fundamentally from the phonics approach. Underlying the phonics approach is the assumption that much of learning to read is learning to match words as written, letter-by-letter, with words as pronounced, sound-by-sound (sounds produced in isolation with letters specified separately). It is perfectly true that for a certain range of spelling patterns, notably the first major set of spelling patterns, the phonics approach has been helpful, and this fact accounts for the persistence of phonics in the schools. But the 'phonics way' does not lay the basis for the kinds of responses to spelling patterns that can be used for all the materials. One can learn such words as MAN, MAT, MEN, MET the phonics way and project similar letter-sound correspondences through a substantial number of words, but even for the three-letter words like MAN, it is not the single letter A that indicates the vowel sound /æ/. It is the *whole-spelling-pattern* MAN in contrast with the *whole-spelling-patterns* MANE and MEAN that signals the different vowel phonemes that identify these three different word-patterns /mæn/ /men/ /min/, or the whole spelling pattern MAT in contrast with the spelling patterns MATE and MEAT.

Although the spelling-pattern approach always gives attention to whole words rather than to individual isolated sounds and letters, it differs fundamentally from any of the common "word-method" approaches in that there is no uncertainty in the identifying characteristics that mark off one written word from another. These are the identifying characteristics of the language itself as incorporated in the patterns of our alphabetic spelling.

The handling of these beginning materials need not be mechanical, but they must be subjected to rigorous criteria of selection and programmed into a progression of small, coherent contrastive steps. Even from the beginning, there must be complete meaning responses not only to words but to complete utterances. The *cumulative* comprehension of the meanings must become so complete that the pupil-reader can, "as he goes along," supply those portions of the language signals which the bundles of spelling patterns alone do not represent. The case for the use of a considerable amount of properly directed oral reading rests primarily on the need to develop this kind of *productive* reading.

In the preparation of materials for the teaching of reading there should be a place for more well-qualified linguists, well-qualified linguists who are willing to make the sacrifices necessary for them to become competent to assist in the application of their science.

LANGUAGE LEARNING IN THE FOREIGN AFFAIRS COMMUNITY

JAMES R. FRITH

Foreign Service Institute

I. The Era of Passive Diplomacy

The language problem in the foreign affairs community is as old as the republic itself. Benjamin Franklin, representing the U.S. in Paris during the Revolutionary War, complained that he could not speak or even understand the French language very well. A hundred years later in 1881 John A. Kasson, Minister to Austria, filed a dispatch in which he wrote:

". . . . We have few native-born Consuls who are really masters of any other language than English. Even after years of employment, when they have picked up shreds of a foreign language, they are often transferred to posts where the language and the usages are wholly unknown to them. . . . As a rule such agents content themselves with mere routine, and for ordinary intercourse depend upon some poorly paid interpreter of foreign origin, of whom the English language becomes in turn the victim. The same is true of some of our Legations. The real interpreter of our interests becomes at last an irresponsible and partially educated foreigner.

"It is to be greatly desired that the United States should escape from this condition of inferiority. . . ." [1]

The Cleveland Administration: First Official Action on the Language Problem. The language problem received top-level recognition for the first time in any official way in 1895 when President Cleveland issued an Executive Order requiring candidates for appointment to the middle grades in the consular service (salaries from $1,000 to $2,500) to pass an oral examination either in French or in the language of the post to which they were to be assigned. The order was hardly an effective solution to the problem. The Foreign Service was still in the throes of the "spoils system."

---

[1] William Barnes and John Heath Morgan, *The Foreign Service of the United States,* 1961, p. 139 ff.

When President McKinley took office in 1897, he continued the requirement of an examination, but it seems to have been a virtually meaningless
exercise: 112 candidates were examined and only one was rejected.[2]

The T. Roosevelt Administration: First Language Training. The first
solid provision for language proficiency among foreign affairs personnel
was made in March of 1902 when Congress authorized 10 "student interpreter" positions at the Legation in Peking. Interestingly, the officers
designated to these positions to learn Chinese were protected from the
"spoils system" and thus were among the first to have the opportunity of
planning a career in the foreign service extending beyond the next presi-
dential election. Similar legislation in 1906 established six student interpreter positions at the Embassy in Tokyo. Later, the program was extended
to Turkey with the result that, during the years from 1902 to 1926, 53
officers were trained in Chinese, 27 in Japanese and "a smaller number"
in Turkish.[3]

A significant fact about the early legislation was the recognition that
language training represents an investment of serious proportions which
must not be made casually and without assurance of an adequate return.
Any investment in training for members of a diplomatic and consular service
with the high rate of turn-over which ours had in the 19th and early 20th
centuries would have been hazardous indeed unless it was insured by
special legislation.

*The Coolidge Administration: Right Setting But Little Language Train-
ing.* The Rogers Act of 1924 provided this insurance throughout the
Foreign Service by establishing a non-partisan career Foreign Service
protected by law from the quadrennial threat of decimation. However, the
Rogers Act was followed by no great increase in the number of Foreign
Service officers who were assigned to language training. For the modest
numbers who were so assigned, Chinese and Japanese remained the most
popular languages. Turkish remained on the list, and Russian and Arabic
were added. Training in the Far Eastern languages was usually carried
out in the country where the language was spoken with the assistance of
special tutors over a period of two to three years. For the study of the
Near Eastern languages and Russian, officers were usually assigned for one
to two years at a university, notably the University of Berlin, l'Ecole des
Langues Orientales in Paris, and Harvard. During the ten-year period
from 1932 to 1941, a total of 58 officers received language instruction at

---

[2] *Ibid.*, p. 150 ff.
[3] *Ibid.*, p. 212.

government expense: 42 in Far Eastern languages, seven in languages of the Near East and nine in Russian.[4]

Small, Passive Diplomatic Corps: Twelve Languages Enough. There are three factors which explain, at least in part, the small numbers of officers assigned to language training during the years preceding World War II. *First,* the U.S. foreign affairs community was very small by present standards. In 1939, the Foreign Service of the State Department numbered slightly over 700 officers. The separate Foreign Services of the Departments of Agriculture and Commerce totalled a little more than 100 officers. Including the military attaches, the foreign affairs community in 1939 comprised fewer than 900 officers. *Second,* the U.S. maintained embassies or legations in only 58 countries in 1940 in contrast to 109 in January 1963. A dozen foreign languages would have sufficed to conduct virtually all official U.S. business in these countries. These would have included Arabic, Chinese, French, German, Italian, Japanese, Persian, Portuguese, Russian, Spanish, Turkish and possibly Thai. It was a normal, and usually rewarded, expectation that the officials with whom our Foreign Service dealt in most countries would speak English or, at worst, French, which many had learned through study abroad before entering the Foreign Service or contrived to learn through their own efforts because of its general utility. *Third,* this was still the era of passive diplomacy when the functions of the ambassador and his staff were largely limited to looking out for the few Americans who ventured abroad, reporting economic and political events and trends and conducting official U.S. business with the host government itself. The members of the foreign affairs community were not in any real sense participants in economic and political events in the host country, nor did they have much occasion to deal directly with its people in an official capacity.

II. The Era of Active Diplomacy

The New Diplomacy: Language Proficiency Gains New Importance. World War II changed all this completely and dramatically. The U.S. emerged from the war with responsibilities which demanded a new kind of diplomacy, an active diplomacy, a diplomacy which was to bring millions of Americans face to face with foreign peoples through new programs of economic, technical and military aid and through cultural and educational exchanges. Diplomacy before the war was a government-to-government relationship. Diplomacy after the war was to be somewhat more of a

---

[4] *Ibid.*

people-to-people relationship. Foreign languages were to take on more importance in several ways: the new diplomacy called for more proficiency in more languages on the part of more people.

The U.S. Foreign Service faced the new era only slightly better prepared language-wise than it had been at the turn of the century. Perry N. Jester wrote in the Foreign Service Journal in 1946: "One of the conspicuous deficiencies of our foreign service taken as a whole has been the lack of widespread and effective knowledge of foreign languages." His commentary was reminiscent of Minister Kasson's plaintive dispatch from Austria three generations earlier. This time, however, the observation was made as a prelude to action. The purpose of his article was to introduce the newly appointed Director of Language Studies, Dr. Henry Lee Smith, Jr., whose entry on duty June 1, 1946 was a landmark in the history of language learning in the foreign affairs community. It was, at long last, the beginning of a major effort to solve the language problem which had plagued the United States Foreign Service for a century and a half.

FSI School of Languages Established. In the same issue of the Foreign Service Journal, Dr. Smith, in a policy declaration, outlined the linguist's view of language and described a language teaching procedure which was novel—though not entirely new—in 1946: intensive instruction, stress on speaking, small classes, a linguist-native speaker team of teachers and use of audio aids. The organization which he proposed was a language school in Washington with a world-wide network of extension programs operating under its supervision at U.S. embassies and consulates. The Foreign Service Institute opened its doors officially November 13, 1946 with a School of Languages as one of its components. While the philosophy and plan proposed by Dr. Smith in 1946 have been refined with the advance of the science of linguistics and the art of language teaching, they have not been basically changed in the intervening 17 years.

Established by the Foreign Service Act of 1946 to provide instruction as necessary to meet the needs of the foreign affairs community, the Foreign Service Institute is the principal school for the civilian agencies responsible for the conduct of foreign affairs. Its two major branches are the School of Foreign Affairs and the School of Language and Area Studies (the School of Languages until a 1962 realignment of functions).

While the essential purpose of FSI is to prepare people for responsibility in the field of foreign affairs, FSI is only one of several sources of language training for personnel destined for positions requiring proficiency in a foreign language. Among others, the military services have maintained programs of language instruction at the Army Language School in Monterey, California, the Naval Intelligence School in Washington and in the Air

Force language program [5] conducted mainly at Indiana, Syracuse and Yale Universities and at FSI. Among the students in each of these programs are officers who are being prepared for duties of a diplomatic character, notably as attaches and military advisors to foreign governments. We shall be paying particular attention to FSI in the succeeding paragraphs since language learning in the foreign affairs community is a particular concern of FSI, but it should be noted that the language programs sponsored by the Department of Defense contribute significantly to the preparation of official Americans for duty abroad.

Foreign Affairs Community Grows. In the years following the establishment of the Foreign Service Institute, the foreign affairs community underwent an unprecedented growth. In 1948, the Economic Cooperation Administration came into being and has continued to operate in its subsequent reincarnations as the Foreign Operations Administration (1951), the International Cooperation Administration (1955), and the present Agency for International Development (1961). As the task of interpreting the U.S. to the world increased in size and importance, the U.S. Information Agency was established in 1953 as a separate agency. Military assistance programs became an important new arm of diplomacy. The Foreign Service Officer corps itself increased from 1,900 to 3,400 between 1954 and 1957 with the integration of 1,500 new officers including more than 600 who had previously held Civil Service positions in the Department of State in Washington.

The Lean Years: 1946-1954. It would be logical to suppose that the Foreign Service Institute would grow in stature and strength with the growth in size and responsibility of the community it was created to serve. Not so. The Institute fell on hard times before it had become firmly established. By 1954 it had reached such low estate that its continued existence was in some doubt. The Wriston Committee [6] reported in 1954: "The Institute at one time participated actively and valuably in research [in applied

---

[5] A recent development of major significance in the area of language learning within the military component of the foreign affairs community is the establishment of the Defense Language Institute as the central coordinating agency for all language training in the Department of Defense. DLI assumes full administrative authority July 1, 1963.

[6] The Secretary of State's Public Committee on Personnel, an *ad hoc* committee appointed in 1954 and chaired by Henry M. Wriston, then president of Brown University, to make recommendations concerning "the measures necessary to strengthen the effectiveness of the professional service to a standard consistent with the vastly increasing responsibilities in the field of foreign policy which have devolved upon the President and the Secretary."

linguistics] but that program has been virtually destroyed until now the work in language, though good within the limits permitted, is nowhere as distinguished as it should be."

The Committee strongly recommended that "the purposes of Congress as expressed in the Act of 1946 be fulfilled." This recommendation in 1954 marked the beginning of a vigorous new attack on the language problem in the foreign affairs community under the leadership of a revitalized School of Languages.

Language Learning Emerges. A survey of self-appraisals throughout the Foreign Service, completed in early 1956 at the instigation of Loy W. Henderson, then Deputy Undersecretary of State for Administration, revealed that less than half of the 4,000 regular, reserve and staff officers then on duty in the Foreign Service had a sufficient command of any foreign language to conduct official business in a satisfactory way in it. Plans were immediately laid for a "crash program" to provide substantial numbers of Foreign Service personnel with competence in French, German or Spanish. The facilities of the School of Languages were greatly expanded in Washington and temporary field schools were established in Nice, France, Frankfurt, Germany and in Mexico City.

On November 2, 1956, the Secretary of State approved a new language policy based on the premise that foreign language skills are vital to the conduct of foreign affairs. The policy read: "Each officer will be encouraged to acquire a 'useful' knowledge of two foreign languages, as well as sufficient command of the language of each post of assignment to be able to use greetings, ordinary social expressions and numbers; ask simple questions and give simple directions; and to recognize proper names, street signs and office and shop designations. The acquisition of a 'useful' knowledge, as defined, of one of the widely-used languages within the next five years or within five years of the date of appointment to the Foreign Service." As a measure of enforcement, promotions were denied to newly appointed Foreign Service officers until they had demonstrated proficiency in at least one language.[7]

The new language policy of the State Department was followed by new policy statements by ICA and USIA encouraging their personnel to achieve job-level proficiency in the local language of their posts of assignment. In 1960 Congress reinforced these policy statements with one of its own:

---

[7] It is worthy of note, as an aside, that the State Department had measured its language problem and had taken vigorous action to solve it well before Sputnik and "The Ugly American" made our national deficiencies in language education a table topic.

"It is the policy of the Congress that chiefs of mission and Foreign Service officers appointed or assigned to serve in foreign countries shall have, to the maximum practicable extent, among their qualifications, a useful knowledge of the principal language or dialect of the country in which they are to serve."

The Overseas Language Program. The composite effect of these policies was to increase language enrollments very considerably at FSI/Washington and to create a large demand for language instruction at overseas posts. In quantitative terms, the amount of language instruction provided by FSI in its world-wide program was to increase nine-fold from 1954 to 1962— from 120,000 student-hours of attendance in the fiscal year which ended in June 1955 to 1.1 million student-hours in the fiscal year which ended in June 1962.

FSI had sponsored a system whereby local instructors were hired to provide language classes for a few people at overseas posts almost from the beginning of its existence in 1946. This was still a very small program in 1954, numbering in all only a few hundred participants. Under the impetus of new language policies throughout the foreign affairs community, participation in the FSI overseas language program grew from about 750 in 1954 to about 9,000 in 1962, an increase of 1,200%. In order to provide professional guidance for this growing program, FSI started in 1958 to send Regional Language Supervisors into prescribed areas overseas to travel from post to post, organizing instruction along productive lines, training instructors, showing them how to use existing teaching materials (or devising new materials when necessary) and in other ways insuring that the Government had a worthwhile return on its now substantial investment in language training overseas.

These instruction programs at more than 200 sites around the world are generally one-hour-a-day classes. The students are representatives of the State Department, AID, USIA, the military attache systems, the Marine guard service and twenty other U.S. agencies. It is probably not surprising that over 1,600 foreign service personnel and their wives were enrolled in French instruction during a recent six month period, or that more than 1,100 were enrolled in Spanish. The demands that these growing programs are placing on the field of applied linguistics begin to be apparent, however, when it is noted that 335 were studying Arabic, that 117 were studying Turkish in Ankara, 114 Persian in Tehran, 124 Thai in Bangkok and 33 Cambodian in Phnom Penh. A look at the total picture brings the demands even more clearly into focus: 9,000 official U.S. representatives in a world in turmoil making an attempt, with such materials as could be found, to learn 60 languages in order to get their jobs done.

FSI Moves Into Textbook Production and Proficiency Testing. The increase in the volume of language training at FSI/Washington after the lull of the early 1950's was accompanied by a diversification of activities. The primary function of the FSI School of Languages was then, and is now, to teach. However, it was becoming increasingly apparent that the task took the School somewhat afield from the mere meeting of classes. Textbook problems and the need for measuring language skills were claiming increasing attention.

The Spoken Language series of textbooks from World War II days had become somewhat threadbare. These manuals were supplemented or replaced by more sophisticated texts as they appeared. However, new texts appropriate for the FSI student body were sparse, while new developments in language analysis and new techniques in language presentation were manifold. So, with its substantial staff of linguists, FSI moved seriously into the field of textbook production.

The publication of Volume I of the FSI Spanish Basic Course in 1957 was the beginning of a flow of new texts which have included French, German, Turkish and a dozen other languages, incorporating recent advances in the art of teaching foreign languages. In 1961, under NDEA sponsorship, FSI undertook an ambitious program of research and materials preparation with a commitment to produce textbooks in eleven African languages. The first three texts in this series—Igbo, Swahili and Twi—were published by the Government Printing Office in the early months of 1963 and are now available for public purchase. Yoruba is ready for printing as of this writing. The other seven [8] are scheduled to appear by mid-1965.

Meawhile, in 1958 the FSI Testing Unit was established to replace self-appraisals of language proficiency with more reliable estimates based on structured interviews by a linguist-native speaker team. The experience which the Testing Unit has gathered over the last five years is now being counted on for guidance in the calibration of new and hopefully less cumbersome tests under development by Professor Wilmarth H. Starr and others at New York University.

III. Stating the Language Problem

It is commonplace to talk glibly—and vaguely—about "the language problem." The foreign affairs community is exhorted in editorials, and

---

[8] Lingala, Kituba ("State Kikongo"), Bambara, More, Fula and Hausa. In addition to the eleven textbooks which are being developed through the support of the Office of Education under the National Defense Education Act, FSI will include an Amharic textbook in the African language series, bringing the total to twelve.

even in novels, to solve its language problem. But the difficulty with problems, to quote an aphorism, lies not so much in solving them as in stating them. Since 1955, FSI has had a hand in devising means for a usefully explicit statement of three aspects of the language problem which confronts U.S. representatives abroad.

Language Proficiency Scales. The first step was to devise scales for quantifying the language skills of people and the language requirements of jobs. Speaking and reading scales with levels from 0 to 5 were adopted by the State Department in 1955. Abbreviated definitions of the levels are as follows:

S-0 No practical speaking proficiency.

S-1 (Elementary proficiency)—Able to satisfy routine travel needs and minimum courtesy requirements.

S-2 (Limited working proficiency)—Able to satisfy routine social demands and limited office requirements.

S-3 (Minimum professional proficiency)—Able to speak the language with sufficient structural accuracy and vocabulary to satisfy representation requirements and handle professional discussions within a special field.

S-4 (Full professional proficiency)—Able to use the language fluently and accurately on all levels pertinent to foreign service needs.

S-5 (Native or bilingual proficiency)—Speaking proficiency equivalent to that of an educated native speaker.

R-0 No practical reading proficiency.

R-1 (Elementary proficiency)—Able to read elementary lesson material or common public signs.

R-2 (Limited working proficiency)—Able to read intermediate lesson material or simple colloquial texts.

R-3 (Minimum professional proficiency)—Able to read nontechnical news items or technical writing in a special field.

R-4 (Full professional proficiency)—Able to read all styles and forms of the language pertinent to foreign service needs.

R-5 (Native or bilingual proficiency)—Reading proficiency equivalent to that of an educated native speaker.

These scales have made it possible to talk about degrees of language proficiency within useful limits of accuracy without long and awkward descriptive phrases. It is thus possible to make a terse and meaningful summary statement, for example, that of the 3,162 Foreign Service Officers who had been tested as of last August 64.9% had S-3 or better and that 89% had S-2 or better in at least one language. Similarly, USIA can summarize the present inventory of language skills among its 700 Career Reserve Officers with the statement that 56% have either S-3 proficiency or better in French, German, Italian, Portuguese or Spanish, or else at least S-2 proficiency in one of the more difficult languages. The Director of our Foreign Aid Mission in Asuncion was able recently to state a reappraisal of the language needs of his organization by a brief message to Washington raising the prerequisite for 13 jobs from S-2 to S-3 R-3 in Spanish.

The Time Requirements Chart. The second major step was to relate the levels on the speaking and reading scales to time requirements for training. On the basis of its own experience and with advice from other schools and universities, FSI, working with others in the Government who were interested in the problem, prepared a chart showing the approximate period of training which well-motivated students would require to reach specified levels of proficiency starting from S-0 R-0. Taken into account are three variables: the aptitude of the student, the difficulty of the language and the intensity of training. The chart provides an easy if crude reference for administrators with no knowledge of language training, giving them useful, though approximate, information as to how much time must be allowed to prepare people for jobs which require language proficiency.

Classification of Local Languages. The third step was to devise a way of talking conveniently about the communication situation at overseas posts. FSI proposed three terms—*primary, primary alternate* and *secondary* languages—and assisted in preparing a questionnaire addressed to U.S. embassies and consulates in more than a hundred countries around the world to gather information on the communication situation at each post. The terms were defined thus:

Primary Language. Either an indigenous language used generally by the people, or an indigenous language used by a significant segment of the people and used officially by othe government, either as the sole official language or on a co-equal basis with another language. Examples: Spanish in Madrid, Japanese in Tokyo, French and Flemish in Brussels and Persian and Pushtu in Kabul.

Primary-Alternate Language. A non-indigenous language used widely by the government in conducting both internal and foreign affairs and by educated circles whether or not an indigenous language is also used officially or generally by the people. Examples: French in Saigon, Italian in Mogadiscio and French and Spanish in Tangier.

Secondary Language. Any language other than a primary or primary-alternate language useful in communicating with a substantial segment of the population or with a minority group that is politically, economically, or culturally significant. Examples: Chinese in Bangkok, Phnom Penh and Saigon and French in Athens, Ankara and Damascus.

An excerpt from the questionnaire will suggest the kind of information which was sought:

> "In the following questions if any language is definitely cor-
> related with any identifiable factor such as social class, minority
> cultural group, geographic subdivision or whatever, identify that
> factor.
> Language(s) decreed as official:
> Language(s) in which the Chief of State addresses the people:
> Language(s) in which the internal affairs of the government
> are conducted
> a) orally:
> b) in writing:
> Language(s) used in judicial proceedings:
> Language(s) used as the medium of instruction in schools
> (note differences in the various levels of instructions, if
> appropriate):"

The answers to the questionnaire provided the principal basis for classifying as primary, primary-alternate or secondary the languages which appeared, in 1962, to be significant from the point of view of present or potential need in the conduct of U.S. foreign affairs. As a practical necessity, the survey was, for the most part, restricted to investigation and description of the language situation at Foreign Service posts, i.e., *within the cities* in which the U.S. maintains embassies and consulates. An exception was the inclusion of 11 minority languages of the USSR as secondary languages although they are not widely useful in Moscow, the only city of the USSR in which the U.S. has diplomatic representation. The tentative list which this classification yielded added up to 154 languages exclusive of English (simplifying the complex dialect situation in Arabic to two general categories, Eastern and Western, and counting five variants of Chinese).[9]

---

[9] Tentative list of primary and secondary languages within cities in which the U.S. maintains either an embassy or a consulate (no primary-alternate language occurs which is not listed elsewhere as a primary language; asterisk marks languages which are primary at one or more posts; parenthetic enclosure distinguishes regional variants which may not be mutually intelligible; hyphen indicates mutually intelligible variants): *Afrikaans, Akan (*Twi), *Amharic, Arabic (*Eastern, *Western), Armenian, Assamese, Aymara, *Azerbaijani, *Bambara-Malinke, Basque, Bassa, *Baule, Beja, *Bemba, *Bengali, Berber, *Bulgarian, Bulu, *Burmese, *Cambodian, Catalan, Chinese (*Amoy, *Cantonese, *Fukienese, *Mandarin, Swatow), Chokwe,

Language	Number of Posts at Which Language is		
	Primary	Primary-Alternate	Secondary
Afrikaans	5	—	—
Arabic (Eastern)	17	—	7
Arabic (Western)	8	—	—
Chinese (Cantonese)	2	—	5
Chinese (Mandarin)	1	2	2
Dutch	4	1	1
English	46	36	41
French	15	30	31
Fula	1	—	6
German	15	—	8
Hausa	1	—	4
Hindi	2	—	4
Italian	9	2	4
Japanese	7	—	1
Persian	5	—	—
Portuguese	13	2	—
Russian	1	—	4
Spanish	48	1	4
Swahili	3	2	3
Tamil	1	—	5
Turkish	5	—	1
Urdu	3	—	3

By the same method of calculation, there were 97 primary languages. The tabulation lists the languages which are primary at one or more Foreign Service posts and useful in some degree for foreign affairs personnel at five or more posts.

Escaping "This Condition of Inferiority." The language list makes it

*Czech, *Danish, *Duala, *Dutch, Estonian, *Ewe, *Ewondo, Fanagalo, *Fijian, *Finnish, *Flemish, *Fon, *French, *Fula, *Ga, *Gaelic, Galla, Georgian, *German, *Greek, Guarani, *Gujarati, *Haitian Creole, *Hausa, *Hebrew, *Hindi, *Hungarian, *Icelandic, *Igbo, Ilocano, *Indonesian, *Italian, *Japanese, Javanese, Kannada, Kazakh, *Kikongo, Kikuyo, *Kimbundu, *Kinyarwanda, Kirghiz, *Kituba-Monokutuba, *Korean, *Krio, Kurdish, *Lamba, *Lao, Latvian, *Lingala, Lithuanian, Luba, *Luganda, Lunda, Luo, Macedonian, *Malagasy, *Malay, Malayalam, *Maltese, *Marathi *Martinique Creole, Masai, Maya, Mende, *More, *Nepali, *Norwegian, Nubian, Nyamwezi-Sukuma, *Nyanja, *Okinawan, Oriya, *Panjabi, *Papiamento, *Pashtu, *Persian, *Persian (Afghan), *Polish, *Portuguese, *Quechua, *Rumanian, *Rundi, *Russian, *Sango, *Sara, *Serbo-Croatian, Serer, *Shona, Sindebele, Sindhi, *Singhalese, Slovak, Slovenian, *Somali, Soninke, Sotho, *Spanish, *Susu, *Swahili, *Swedish, *Tagalog, *Tamil, Telugu, Temne, *Thai, Tigre, *Tigrinya, Tshwa, *Tsonga, Tswana, *Turkish, Ukranian, Umbundu, *Urdu, Uzbek, Vai, *Vietnamese, *Visayan, Welsh, White Russian, *Wolof, Yakut, *Yoruba, *Zarma-Songhai, Zulu, Zulu-Xhosa.

possible to measure approximately, but again within useful limits of accuracy, the diversity of the language problem of the U.S. foreign affairs community. It seems a reasonable estimate that the number of languages in which the Government would stand to gain by having at least a few people able to conduct official U.S. business abroad is something between 97 and 154. The foreign affairs community has vastly improved its foreign language competence in recent years, and scholars in the field of linguistics have provided the tools for further improvement in the form of descriptions and textbooks for growing numbers of the crucial languages. As it becomes possible to state the language problem of the foreign affairs community more explicitly, however, it becomes increasingly apparent that the U.S. can escape entirely from the "condition of inferiority" which Minister Kasson described in 1881 only after labor of heroic proportions has been accomplished in the field of applied linguistics.

SPECIAL VOCABULARIES IN THAI

WILLIAM J. GEDNEY
University of Michigan

One of the most interesting of the recent trends in linguistics is the search for features of semantic structure in the lexicons of languages. It is the purpose of this paper to point out in the Thai language an exceedingly simple structural feature manifested in various segments of the vocabulary. This feature is the conventional substitutability on a one-to-one basis of special terms in certain contexts for particular items of the ordinary vocabulary.

Perhaps the most obvious of these special vocabularies is the special set of forms used in speaking of and to royal persons. It is well known that Thai and many other languages of South and Southeast Asia have such special royal terms. They are often described by tourists and even scholars as a special royal language. This is an exaggeration, perhaps encouraged by the tendency of speakers of the language to grumble about the alleged difficulty in mastering and controlling these special royal forms. The royal terms do not constitute a special language, nor even a special dialect. They consist simply of a limited list of special lexical items, usually single words but sometimes phrases, which are substituted for corresponding items in the common vocabulary when speaking to or about a royal person.

This royal vocabulary is called in Thai *raachaasàp*, literally "royal words." The list has been published frequently in school textbooks. Perhaps the most authoritative version of the list is that formerly issued in pamphlet form for use by students in the Royal Pages' School. [1] This list contains 92 terms for parts of the body, a couple of dozen kinship terms, 66 terms for animals and miscellaneous objects, and 73 terms for actions of various kinds. These categories occupy roughly half of the small volume. The remainder consists of an alphabetical finder-list according to the ordinary synonyms.

Analysis of such published lists of royal terms are misleading in that they suggest that the special royal vocabulary is more exten-

---

[1] Royal Pages' School, *Raachaasàp*. Bangkok (2nd edition), 1932. 52 pages. (In Thai.)

sive than it actually is.   From our point of view the list is found
to be padded with various polite and euphemistic synonyms for
vulgar terms of ordinary speech, but these polite terms—comparable
to "limb" for "leg" in English—do not actually belong to the special
royal vocabulary.   Additional confusion for the lexicographer's purposes is that many of the entries in the published lists are not separate items at all, but merely illustrative phrases.

The failure in the past to perceive the special characteristics of
the royal terms and separate them out from such lists accounts for
the confused and wasteful treatment given the royal vocabulary in
existing dictionaries.

The key to the whole phenomenon is clearly the principle that
certain special terms are conventional substitutes in situations involving royalty for ordinary terms of the common vocabulary.   This becomes clear from the use of the special royal terms as substitutes for
the corresponding ordinary terms not only in straightforward literal
contexts but also in various idiomatic and metaphoric expressions;
that is to say, wherever the ordinary term would occur in ordinary
speech, the royal term is substituted for it if the situation involves
royalty.   It is as if the ordinary term were tabu in such a situation,
but the term tabu is hardly applicable.   For example one may use
the ordinary term for "hand" in speaking to royalty, but only the
special term in referring to the hand of a royal person, whether
speaking to royalty or about royalty.   Highly conventionalized eup-
hemism would perhaps be a more accurate characterization than
tabu.

These royal terms have been used in Thai at least from the time
of the oldest records of the language, beginning with the celebrated
Sukhothay inscription of 1292 A.D., and similar special sets of royal
terms are found in the languages of the other Southeast Asian countries that derived their higher culture from India.   In Thai some of
the royal terms are native Thai words; many are loanwords from
Cambodian; by far the greatest number is Indic.

No doubt in the days of the absolute monarchy they were one of
many devices which served the function of augmenting royal power
by marking with the utmost clarity the distinction between royalty
and subjects.   Other features of the traditional culture may be noted
which appear to have had a similar function.   Only royalty in the
old days could possess certain types of gold objects.   Only royalty
could, and indeed was expected to, marry within the family, while

for commoners incest was as adversely regarded as among other peoples elsewhere.

Although it seems clear that in the past the special royal vocabulary served this function of emphasizing the distinction between royalty and commoner, there is nowadays an opposite tendency to play down this distinction, to encourage the view that royalty is human. The result is that many now regard the special royal vocabulary as an unfortunate and awkward interference. It is not uncommon for princes who participate in public affairs, as many do, to ask their friends not to use the special royal terms. More than one Thai monarch of the twentieth century has turned to English in conversation and correspondence with Thai friends and relatives to avoid the complications of the royal terms. [2]

Use of the royal terms in the future will no doubt decrease. Journalists and others still try to use them properly, but slips are viewed leniently. Another factor which will also work for a decrease is the simple fact that the number of royal persons, formerly very large as a result of the polygamous royal marriages, is rapidly dwindling now that their numbers are not being replenished by the twentieth-century monogamous kings.

To return to the lexicographical aspect of the royal vocabulary, it seems clear that lexicographers, both Thai and foreign, have made unnecessary work for themselves by failing to recognize that the correct treatment of these terms is simply to mark them as part of the royal vocabulary and then give the synonym from the ordinary vocabulary for which they substitute.

Traditional Thai culture was characterized by the high value placed on decorum and convention. In social manners, in official conduct, in artistic composition, and in many other aspects of life in the traditional social system, one is struck by the striving not for originality or for unique individual achievement, but rather for grace and elegance in manipulating strictly conventional forms. With this in mind, one is tempted to seek further in the Thai lexicon for more such highly conventional phenomena as that exhibited in the royal vocabulary described above.

---

[2] One member of the royal family writes, "Members of the Chakri Family have often written to one another in English to avoid the elaborate language required for the different ranks even amongst relatives." Prince Chula Chakrabongse, *Lords of Life* (New York, 1960), p. 271.

A similar phenomenon is found in the forms used in speaking to or about Buddhist monks. These include a small number of special terms for "food," "to eat," "to sleep," etc., and here again it is clear that each special term substitutes automatically for a particular term of the ordinary vocabulary. Though the list of special terms for monks is much shorter than the list of special terms for royalty, the terms for monks have no doubt always had a much wider use, since most Thais seldom if ever have occasion to speak to royalty but virtually all Thais are in contact with Buddhist monks constantly throughout their lives.

Continuing our search, we find a similar lexical phenomenon in a particular segment of the literature, the large body of literary works dealing with the Panji romance, a story cycle of Javanese origin. Literary works on this theme include some of the major masterpieces of classical Thai literature, as well as many minor poems. [3] In all of these romantic tales dealing with Inaw, as the hero of the cycle is known in Thai, there occurs a special set of terms for "moon," "flower," and other similar items frequent in romantic stories. These terms occur only in works dealing with this story, and every youngster who studies classical Thai literature is required to memorize the list. Everyone is aware of the Javanese origin of the story, and the popular notion is that these special terms are loanwords from Javanese, but Thai scholars who have looked into the matter declare that these words are taken not from Javanese but from the local dialects of Malay spoken in the provinces adjacent to peninsular Thailand.

These terms are seldom so prominent as to impede comprehension. Their occasional occurrence must have served the function of reminding the readers or listeners that this is the Ĭnăw story, not the Rama story or any other of the various standard classics. Here again, as in the case of the royal terms and monks' terms, the obviously correct lexicographical treatment is simply to say "conventional synonym in the Ĭnăw story for—."

In seeking other sets of conventionally substitutable synonyms similar to those described above, one is tempted to identify in traditional Thai poetry another class of special vocabulary in the various sets of highly conventionalized synonyms upon which the classical

---

[3] A definitive study of Thai versions of this Javanese tale is found in Prince Dhani Nivat, "Siamese Versions of the Panji Romance," *India Antiqua, a volume of Oriental studies presented by his friends and pupils to Jean Philippe Vogel* . . .(Leyden, 1947), pp. 95-101.

poets drew. Many of the major poetic classics were composed to be sung as accompaniment to the ballet. Simplicity was desired in order not to distract attention from the dance and the music. Originality was valued only as it contributed to a more elegant treatment of what was conventionally expected. Poets had for such common meanings as "king," "lady," "army," "horse," "elephant," etc., whole sets of conventional synonyms to draw upon, and in most cases the choice clearly dependent upon nothing more than rhyme and meter. It seems clear that many of these conventional poetic terms are to be handled by the lexicographer in a way parallel to the treatment proposed above for the royal terms, monks' terms, and Malay terms in the Inăw story, that is, to gloss them by saying simply "conventional synonym in classical poetry for—." Even in cases where the earlier history of the word shows that it once had a somewhat different meaning, membership in one of these stereotyped sets of mutually substitutable synonyms seems to erase the semantic subtleties.

But although it seems clear that many terms in the poetic vocabulary are to be regarded in this way, they present a difficult problem in that it is frequently not easy to draw the line between sets of stereotyped synonyms on the one hand and on the other hand sets of near synonyms which cannot be said flatly to be mechanically interchangeable. Although many poets seem to have made their choices on arbitrary metrical grounds, undoubtedly the better poets were aware of and utilized connotational or associative values in choosing among available synonyms or near-synonyms. Further study of the poetic vocabulary may make it possible to decide whether some among these terms are to be regarded as conventional synonyms, parallel to the conventional sets of substitutes described above.

Turning finally to ordinary speech, we find another set of items somewhat similar to the above sets in this feature of conventional substitutability. Virtually all students of Thai speak of "pronouns." It is by no means clear, however, that Thai has a syntactic class of pronouns that can be identified on more objective grounds than the fact that they translate the pronouns of western languages; certainly the published studies that speak of pronouns have not demonstrated such a class.

But leaving syntax aside and approaching the so-called pronouns from a lexical point of view, one is at once struck by the similarity to the above sets in the feature of conventional substitutability. The pronouns often go in pairs; that is, choice of a particular form for "I" determines the choice of another form for "you," and sometimes the final sentence particle is involved as well. It has often been pointed out that the large range of choices indicating relative status of the speaker and the person spoken to reflects the stratification of social classes in the traditional social scheme.

The pronouns and associated final particles differ from the special vocabularies described above in that with the pronouns it is hardly possible to declare particular forms basic and then say that the others are conventional substitutes. The scope of this paper hardly permits us to deal properly with Thai pronouns, but it seems clear that they share somehow with the special vocabularies a feature of mechanical interchangeability.

It is perhaps no accident, in view of the many areas of the traditional vocabulary in which we find this feature of one-to-one interchangeability, that nowadays when new terms are coined to translate western technical terms each coinage is regarded as a conventional and arbitrary substitute for the western term on which it was modeled.

What does all this mean for the lexicographer? For practical dictionary-making purposes it means that in Thai, and perhaps in many other languages in parts of South and Southeast Asia where society and culture were formerly highly conventionalized, there are certain areas of the lexicon where the dictionary can and should take drastic short-cuts, merely indicating that the item belongs to a particular special set and in that set is a conventional substitute for a given item in the ordinary vocabulary. It is clearly an error to attempt, as all existing dictionaries do, to list again under the special terms all the meanings of the ordinary term for which it is substituted.

And on the theoretical level, it may be that in Thai and other languages of the area we have here a feature of lexical and semantic structure of a simple sort that should be dealt with first in our search for structure on these levels.

THE DEVELOPMENT OF THE BRAIN AND THE EVOLUTION OF LANGUAGE [1]

Norman Geschwind, M.D.

Aphasia Research Section, Neurology Service, Boston Veterans Administration Hospital, and the Department of Neurology, Boston University Medical School

Most students of the problem are agreed that there is something special about human language. The major alternative views may be summed up in two simple categories: (1) There is nothing *qualitatively* distinctive about human language; man only possesses *more* language than lower animals. The opposing group of views state: (2) Only man has language. Both approaches leave us with difficulties. If man has more of something than a monkey then just what particular function of the monkey's is it that is being multiplied in man? If only man has language then what is the essence of this new addition to the armamentarium of the activities of animals?

The first group of theorists are likely not to worry about the details of what it is in the animal that is multiplied in man. They tend to express their ideas as *Gedanken* experiments: Tell me what you want the animal to do and I can devise a training procedure to do it. The second group tend to phrase the differences in terms sometimes as ethereal as those of the first group are uncompromisingly untheoretical and practical.

Regardless of their particular position the adherents of each of these views have shared in common either an inability or a lack of interest in specifying what change in the design of the human brain permits of these quantitative or qualitative distinctions. This paper represents an attempt to bridge this gap in some small way. The linguist, even if he accepts the views presented here, may well find them disappointingly meager. The first day of this conference has been devoted to a series of papers representing much of the forefront of pure linguistic theory, and the overwhelming stress has been placed on aspects of syntax. The linguist would certainly wish to

[1] Some of the work discussed was done under a grant (MH 08472-01) from the National Institute of Mental Health to the Department of Neurology, Boston University Medical School.

133

know in what way the human brain has become adapted to the production of syntactic speech. Instead he will have to be satisfied—if indeed he is satisfied at all—by a theory of object-naming. Let me therefore hasten to state that I make no pretensions for what I say except insofar as it applies to object-naming. On the other hand an interest in object-naming is not ill-placed since much of the practical use of language rests on the basis of this rather unglamorous activity. Even object-naming in itself has its more interesting sides. Thus, workers in childhood development have tended to neglect the acquisition of names since this has been regarded as the simple enlargement of the lexicon, and have concentrated on the evolution of grammar. Yet the problem of the lexicon goes beyond the mere filling of the dictionary randomly. Thus, the naming of colors, which to the adult appears like a remarkably simple task, is often acquired late, long after the child can name remarkably complicated objects. The ramifications of this extend still further into language performance. Thus, there are reasons for regarding it as not unlikely that the time of acquisition of color-naming and of reading should be highly correlated.

There is perhaps one more reason to stress object-naming. While the mechanism suggested here for the naming of things throws no direct light on the acquisition of grammar, it does throw into relief some different ways of looking at the acquisition of grammar which may well be experimentally useful.

It is perhaps appropriate to put in one final comment on this type of theorizing. The linguist may wonder whether such a theory, even if correct, is any concern of his. Let me suggest some reasons which justify interest by linguists in this type of theory. In the first place it is reasonable that anything which throws some light on the nature of language should be of interest to the linguist. A second reason is that the linguist has the ability to provide help to the student of the nervous system. The theory of object-naming to be propounded here has certain implications which might conceivably be more effectively tested in a non-Indo-European language.[2]

There is a third reason which is perhaps the most cogent one for the linguist to take some interest in these matters. I gather from various sources, for example, from the proceedings of this conference a year ago,

---

[2] For example, the theory deals with the problem of color-naming as a corollary. The theory predicts that color-naming, if learned in a certain way, should be affected by certain lesions of the nervous system. In a hypothetical language in which there were no color-names, but in which the color of an object was stated as the color of some other well-known object, the theory would predict that this lesion should not have the same effect. A linguist is more likely to avoid the naive error that color-naming is done in the same way in all languages.

that the status of linguistic theories continues to be a difficult problem. In a sense the difficulty reduces to that of deciding whether the best theory is simply the most economical set of axioms from which the language be-havior can be deduced, i.e., in essence a condensed description. If this is true then theoretical linguistics might appear to be only a more efficient form of description. I would wish, cautiously, to make the suggestion, that perhaps a further touchstone may be added: to what extent does the theory tie in with other, non-linguistic information, for example, the anatomical aspects of language? In the end such bridges link a theory to the broader body of scientific knowledge. I would personally not see much virtue in the views of those theoreticians who feel that language and its disturbances must be viewed *separately* on the linguistic and biological levels. Let us now return to the main topic of this paper.

In order to specify what the differences are between man and subhuman primates let me first discuss some of the features of learning in these non-human forms. I hope I may be forgiven for some preliminary remarks about some elementary anatomical and physiological aspects which may not be familiar to all of you. If the discussion *appears* very remote from our topic please rest assured that it is all really germane.

Lying along the inner surface of the temporal lobes of the brain are a group of structures of extremely complex anatomy. For the sake of simplicity I will loosely use the term "limbic system" to refer to these and to their major connections in the **hypothalamus** and other structures lower in the brain. Included in the anatomical organization of this region are those parts of the brain which when stimulated give rise to sensations of taste or smell, and to certain emotions such as fear and their corresponding motor activities. For simplicity we may divide those aspects of the limbic system of interest to us into two groups: (1) **Limbic motor responses—** these are highly organized, essentially inborn motor sequences which mediate the motor responses involved in fear, rage, and sexual activities. (2) **Limbic sensory responses—**these are the subjective feelings of smell, taste, hunger and thirst and the corresponding feelings of satiation, sexual sensations, anger, and fear. It is not at all inaccurate to say that the limbic system mediates both the inborn motor sequences involved in those elementary activities intimately related to the survival of the organism or the species and the subjective experiences related to these activities.

Let us now consider by contrast the remaining "non-limbic" portions of the surface of the brain which, in fact, make up the bulk of the exposed surface of the hemispheres in the primates, including man. In particular we will concentrate on the sensory portions of this non-limbic brain.

There are three sensory regions which are to be specified here: the **visual cortex,** the **auditory cortex,** and the **somesthetic cortex** (which eventually receives the sensory information from the skin, muscles, bone, joints, and tendons—the term "touch" can loosely be used to designate this group of sensations). These three regions may be said to mediate the "non-limbic" modalities of sensation.

The zones we have so far considered, that is the "limbic" regions on the medial surface of the temporal lobe, and the primary centers for the "non-limbic" sensations of vision, audition and somesthesis, constitute only a small fraction of the surface of the hemisphere. These four regions, together with the classic **motor cortex,** are all, in the terminology of the great German neuroanatomist Flechsig, "primordial zones", that is, regions which mature early in the development of the individual. The most commonly used criterion for such maturation is the degree of myelination of the nerve fibers in these regions. These primordial zones also differ quite markedly from each other in cellular architecture.

If we contemplate the brain of a subprimate mammal, such as a rabbit or a cat, we find that these primordial zones make up the majority of the cerebral mantle. As we move up the phylogenetic scale we find the striking fact that these zones become increasingly separated by new areas of cortex. The cortex separating the primordial zones occupies a greater percentage of the surface in the primates and achieves its greatest extent in man where it clearly occupies most of the surface of the hemispheres. It is indeed the development of this **association cortex** which is responsible for the higher functions of the nervous system. The association cortex matures later in the life of the individual. Flechsig called these regions "intermediary zones" to indicate their later myelination. The different parts of the association cortex are more like each other in structure than are the different primordial zones.

Let us now turn to the problem of the connections between these different regions of the cerebral mantle. Flechsig (1901) stated an important principle for the brain of man which has in recent years been re-emphasized for the brain of the subhuman primate by Bailey and von Bonin (1951). The principle asserts that in man the primordial zones, i.e., the regions of early maturation, do not have any significant number of direct connections between them. Thus there are no significant direct interconnections between the limbic regions, the motor cortex, the auditory, somesthetic, and visual cortexes.[3]

---

[3] This principle holds to its full extent in man, the monkey, and chimpanzee, and probably in the other primates, at least the higher ones. It does not hold com-

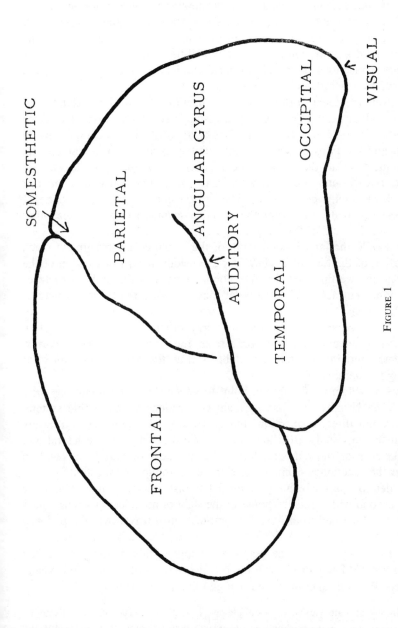

FIGURE 1

View of lateral (outer) surface of human left cerebral hemisphere. The frontal, parietal, temporal, and occipital lobes are indicated. In addition the arrows point to the primary somesthetic, auditory, and visual regions of the cortex. The region of the angular gyrus is also shown. Fuller explanation is given in the text.

Each primordial zone has a significant number of connections only to the immediately adjacent association cortex. The association cortex itself may have long connections to other regions. Let us now consider the connections of the non-limbic sensory modalities. In particular let us consider the connections of the visual cortex which are the best known and may serve as a paradigm for the others.

The primary visual cortex makes connections to the immediately adjacent visual association cortex. The visual association cortex has three important sets of connections, the first two of which I mention only in passing, and the third of which is immediately germane to our argument: (1) Connections to the visual association cortex of the opposite side via the **corpus callosum.** (2) Connections to the association cortex anterior to the classic motor cortex. (3) The largest connection and the one of most concern to us runs from the visual association cortex to the outer and inferior surfaces of the temporal lobe.

Why should the largest connection of the visual cortex eventually reach this portion of the temporal lobe? If we consider in turn this region of the temporal lobe we find that it makes connections with the limbic structures on the inner surface of the temporal lobe. In fact the limbic structures themselves constitute one of the primordial zones and therefore do not receive long connections directly from any other region of the cerebral cortex but receive connections only from the nearby association cortex. The lateral and inferior temporal lobe is thus the association cortex for the limbic structures.

Let us now sum up briefly the point to which these considerations have led us. The visual cortex has its main connections to the limbic system. These are not direct connections but go by way of the association cortex adjacent to the visual cortex and the association cortex on the lateral and basal surfaces of the temporal lobe. We are now prepared—at last—to consider the functional significance of these anatomical connections.

In order to approach this problem let us ask ourselves how a monkey would respond with a rage response to the sight of an object (such as a net) which he has learned to dislike. The impulse must travel over the pathway I have just specified from the visual cortex to the limbic structures and there arouse the inborn rage response. Suppose this pathway is broken at some point? The monkey will no longer respond with rage to this visual stimulus. We will have produced a visual-limbic disconnection.

---

pletely in sub-primate forms; for example, it is clearly not true of the cat's brain. It is therefore important to distinguish the species involved and not to generalize too readily to the human brain from that of lower forms, particularly when these lower forms are sub-primates.

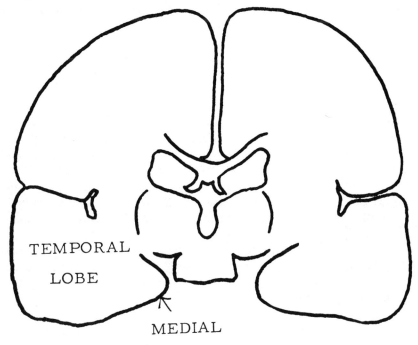

MEDIAL

TEMPORAL REGION

FIGURE 2

Cross-section in the vertical plane through the human brain. The temporal lobe is indicated. The medial temporal region (whose importance is discussed in the text) is also shown.

Consider now an example which is far more important for our purpose. How do we teach a monkey presented visually with, let us say, a circle and a cross to press the lever under the circle rather than that under the cross? We do this by what the psychologists call *reinforcing* one or another response. We may reinforce positively, i.e., reward the response we wish the animal to make, or we may reinforce negatively, i.e., punish the response to be rejected. I do not wish to go into the complexities of the question of reinforcement. For the sake of simplicity we may say that the primary reinforcers are limbic sensations, i.e., the rewards are such things as the taste of food, the satisfaction of hunger or thirst; the punishments are such things as the arousal of fear.

In effect then the visual learning paradigm in the monkey may be reduced to a simple formula: the animal learns to form associations of a visual stimulus to a "limbic" stimulus. In more general terms learning in the monkey consists in forming associations between a "non-limbic" stimulus and a "limbic" stimulus. This is true for vision, audition, and somesthesis. From the point of view of evolution this is reasonable: a stimulus in a non-limbic sensory modality is learned readily only to the extent that it arouses a sensation important to the survival of the individual animal or the species.

In order to look a bit more deeply at learning in the monkey let us now turn to a somewhat different test situation, the one reported by Ettlinger (1960). Here the monkey is taught to choose one of two patterns presented visually, let us say, a circle rather than a cross, by the technique already mentioned of rewarding the choice of one item. After the monkey has learned this to a high degree so that he chooses the rewarded circle on nearly all occasions, another experiment is performed. The monkey is now permitted to palpate two solid figures, a circle and a cross respectively, which are concealed from vision. The animal is again rewarded for choosing the circle rather than the cross. Curiously enough he shows no evidence of carry-over from the identical task done visually. The tactile task is treated by the monkey as a totally new one.

How are we to interpret this experiment and others which have essentially the same result? Ettlinger and others have argued that cross-modal transfers do not tend to occur in animals. But our previous discussion has already stressed that *all* learning in the monkey is cross-modal since the process of learning depends on the formation of associations between *non-limbic* and limbic sensations which is certainly a cross-modal task. The essence indeed of these experiments is that the animal has failed to form an association between two non-limbic modalities.[4]

The same task is, of course, remarkably easy in man who makes the transfer immediately in at least this particular experiment. What is the reason for the ease with which humans do this task which is so difficult for the monkey? Some authors say that man does it by means of verbal mediation. In other words, when one learns to choose a circle over a cross, one learns to choose the "circle". When the task is done we again choose the object which we have named "circle". The monkey's failure at these particular cross-modal tasks is thus attributed to his failure to use language.

---

[4] An objection might be raised that Ettlinger's experiment actually relates to cross-modal *transfer,* not cross-modal *association.* This problem is too complex to discuss fully at this point. Transfer is probably the simpler of the two, and therefore the failure of transfer probably also implies difficulty in association. In any case other evidence, e.g., from conditioning experiments, also points to the difficulty of non-limbic intermodal *associations* in subhuman forms.

A moment's reflection, however, shows that this argument which appears so plausible at first glance, has in fact been stated backwards. In order to call a seen object a circle we must have learned to associate the visual stimulus with the auditory stimulus "circle". In other words, to say that the ability to perform cross-modal associations depends on the ability to name misses the real point which is, as it were, the reverse: *The ability to name depends on the ability to form non-limbic cross-modal associations,* particularly *visual-auditory and tactile-auditory.*[5] One may go further: *The ability to develop language in man probably depends on his ability to form cross-modal associations* between two non-limbic modalities. One might raise the objection, however, that a deaf man might learn language without using cross-modal associations at all. Could he not learn to read by being shown the picture of the object which corresponded to each new written word? Indeed he probably could. In order, however, for him to be able to name (in writing) things with which he palpated he would at least have to be able to form tactile-visual associations. There is, however, a further consideration. Even a visual-visual association is a link between two non-limbic stimuli, and it is questionable that even this would readily be acquired by the monkey.

We have asserted then the thesis that man develops language because he can form associations between two non-limbic stimuli. Couldn't limbic stimuli be useful as language? The answer of course is no: a monkey would have a great deal of difficulty arousing in another animal a smell or taste, or a feeling of hunger or thirst. We communicate by producing non-limbic stimuli—auditory, visual, or tactile.

What is the basis for the difference in the ability of man and the monkey to form pure non-limbic associations? Let us return to our anatomical considerations. As we have pointed out there are three main connections from the visual association areas of a monkey—one to the symmetrical region of the opposite side, one to the motor association area, and the largest to the lateral and basal temporal lobe which is the association cortex for the limbic system. Thus none of the *main* connections are designed to mediate visual-auditory associations. There are, however, definite connections between some of the visual and auditory association areas, as shown for example in the experiments of Sugar, French, and Chusid (1948). These experimenters found clear evidence of fibers running from

---

[5] It is true that in adult man some visual-tactile associations may be done indirectly by the linking up of two separate cross-modal associations (visual-auditory and tactile-auditory). Each of these components is, however, itself an elementary non-limbic cross-modal association.

the auditory association cortex to the visual association cortex but none in the reverse direction; in other words they found no evidence for fibers which could mediate the arousal of auditory memories from a visual stimulus. Even the auditory to visual fibers they found constitute a group far smaller than the fiber systems mediating visual-limbic associations. The monkey brain thus probably contains visual, auditory, and somesthetic regions which, operating on the whole independently, feed into the limbic system stimuli which are used only to the extent that they more or less immediately affect survival.[6]

Even if a small number of fibers exist which have not been discovered between the visual and auditory regions, this would not affect the argument. The more information that must be carried between two cortical regions, the more fibers necessary to carry them. The more associations formed, the more cells are needed to store the memories. The monkey does not appear to have a sufficient basis anatomically to form extensive non-limbic intermodal associations. That a limited number of such associations could be performed perhaps with extensive training is probably correct, but there is probably an inherent limit to the speed of formation or the variety of such associations. One might say that the monkey lacks adequate "memory space" and "channel capacity" for this type of association.

It might be worth digressing for a moment to consider the great strain put on the facilities of a brain by a demand for non-limbic intermodal associations. Consider the situation that visual, auditory, and somesthetic association areas discharge independently into the limbic system via association cortex. In order to add visual-auditory and visual-tactile associations to the visual-limbic associations one would probably have to add at least twice as many fibers and cells as are now used for the visual-limbic connections alone. The probable minimum net effect of such an extensive addition of non-limbic intermodal fibers is therefore to triple the array of cells and fibers needed in the visual association system. It is no surprise that this uneconomical situation does not appear even in the subhuman primates.

What then of the human brain? What correlates with the newly acquired or at least greatly increased ability to form non-limbic intermodal associations and thus to develop language?

It is obvious that there has been marked development of the human

---

[6] There is a possible exception in the "curiosity" drive which has been studied by such workers as Butler (1953) and which does not appear to be quite so "primitive" as the other limbic reinforcers. Even this drive is very likely to depend on the limbic system.

brain in comparison to that of even the highest apes (Connolly, 1950). Thus the gorilla has the largest brain of any of the anthropoids, but it never even reaches half the weight of an average adult human brain. In addition the **cerebellum** makes up a higher percentage of the brain in the anthropoid apes so that the cerebral hemispheres of man (which constitute the part which is of concern to us) are relatively even larger than the discrepancy in whole-brain weights would suggest. Furthermore, a fully adult gorilla is a considerably larger animal than a human. An orangutan which when fully grown may weigh as much as a small human adult has a brain which is about one quarter as heavy as the human brain at maturity.

The human brain at birth is perhaps 40% of its adult size while that of the ape's is nearly 70% of full-grown size. This suggests that much of the human brain is evolutionarily late since it matures so late in the life of an individual. This supposition is amply borne out by closer inspection. The great increase in the size of man's brain is primarily in the association areas, rather than in the primary receptive areas. This growth is reflected in the **frontal pole,** the **temporal lobe,** and in the **inferior parietal region.** The greatest relative growth of the human brain compared to that of the subhuman primates is in the inferior parietal region, and it behooves us to look at this zone more carefully.

The impressive development of the inferior posterior parietal region (the region of the **angular gyrus**) is so great that some authors (e.g., Goldstein, 1927) even assert that this region is almost unique to man. Even those who deny this, such as Bonin and Bailey (1961), still stress that it is this region of the brain which has expanded most markedly in man compared to any of the apes. Its advanced state is testified to by the fact that it is one of the last regions to myelinate and was called by Flechsig one of the "terminal zones" in contrast to the earliest myelinating "primordial-zones" and the "intermediary zones" which myelinate at an intermediate period. According to Dr. Paul Yakovlev this region does not mature in its cellular structure until three or four years or even much later in childhood.

This region is ideally located for the purposes of our theory. It is placed between the association cortexes of the three non-limbic modalities: vision, audition, and somesthesis. It is thus admirably suited to play the role of acting as the way-station by which associations may be formed between these non-limbic modalities. This area may well be termed "the association cortex" of the association cortexes. By providing the basis for the formation of non-limbic associations, it provides the anatomical basis for language— or at least for object-naming. Other authors have stressed the importance of the posterior parietal region for language,[7] but I hope that I have been able to give a physiological basis to this localization.

There are many problems associated with the discussion I have just presented. Indeed, rather than use the word 'problems', I would perhaps have been more correct in saying that it raises many possibilities for further investigation. Much of the data now available does support the view advanced here. I will cite only a few examples of such data.

(Note to the reader: The following section contains rather technical material which can be omitted without violence to the main trend of the argument).

Very large lesions of the angular gyrus region produce an aphasic picture in which the patient speaks volubly but communicates little information. The speech is in particular remarkably poor in the names of objects. The reason for this clinical picture is readily deducible. The connections from the rest of the brain to the auditory association area are cut off. On the other hand since the auditory association area and the motor speech region and their connections are intact, the patient can still produce the automatisms of language freely—these are those aspects of language not demanding intermodal transfer for their use at a given instant. The comprehension of language is seriously impaired since the arousal of associations in other modalities by the auditory speech patterns is also cut off by the lesion. These patients, despite severe comprehension defect, may show perfect repetition because they have preserved the connections between the auditory association cortex and the motor speech region.

Even more revealing as to the importance of intermodal associations are certain more limited lesions. Thus in certain partial lesions of the angular gyrus (first described by Dejerine, 1891) there may be an isolated loss of the ability to comprehend written language and to write (the so-called "pure alexia with agraphia"), while all other aspects of language are intact. The functions of the angular gyrus in auditory-visual associations may be quite dramatically brought out by considering an even more restricted lesion, that of the so-called "pure word-blindness without agraphia" (Dejerine, 1892; Geschwind, 1962). Here the left primary visual cortex is destroyed. The patient can thus see only with his right visual cortex. In addition, however, there is usually a destruction of the posterior end of the corpus callosum. This acts to cut off the right visual region from the left angular gyrus region, and thus the patient cannot understand written language. All other aspects of language are intact.

The disturbances in these patients can be summarized as follows: they lose the ability to comprehend written language, to read music, and to name colors (but they can still match colors

---

[7] See for example the discussion in Critchley (1953).

correctly and show other evidences of correct color perception by *non-verbal* means—see discussion in Geschwind, 1964). They tend to preserve the ability to name objects and to read numbers. How does one make sense of this constellation of impaired and preserved visual tasks? Reading is learned nearly always after speaking. While one learns in speaking to name objects with which one has had both tactile and visual experience, learning to read is almost exclusively dependent on pure visual-auditory connections (particularly after the earliest stages). When these pure connections are cut off the patient can no longer read. He can still copy the words he cannot read (which effectively rules out almost any perceptual theory of this disturbance) because visuo-motor connections in the right hemisphere are still intact. He can name objects because these arouse tactile associations further forward in the right hemisphere and a connection can be made to the speech regions across an intact part of the corpus callosum lying forward of the damaged part.

Color-naming and music-reading are lost with word-reading because they are very pure visuo-auditory tasks—we can identify an apple by its form or texture, but we cannot identify a color by these. Finally, number-reading is preserved because numbers are usually associated with a powerful somesthetic reinforcement (counting on the fingers) through a considerable part of childhood, a form of reinforcement not available for words.

The thesis presented here is that the development of object-naming depends on the presence of anatomical structures in man which are absent or poorly developed in the monkey. The assertion that object-naming depends on visual-auditory transfers is of course an old one in linguistics. Wittgenstein (1953) opens his *Philosophical Investigations* with a quotation from St. Augustine's *Confessions:* "When they (my elders) named some object and accordingly moved towards something, I saw this and grasped that the thing was called by the sound they uttered when they meant to point it out. . . ."

Can we expand the theory presented here to more than object-naming and can we somehow use the same approach to help us with grammar? We may appropriately quote Wittgenstein's comment on the above passage, "Augustine does not speak of there being any difference between kinds of word. If you describe the learning of language in this way you are, I believe, thinking primarily of nouns like "table", "chair", "bread", and of people's names, and only secondarily of the names of certain actions and properties; and (*sc.* you are thinking) of the remaining kinds of word as something that will take care of itself.". But, of course, Wittgenstein implies, and we must agree, that the other words will not take care of themselves.

How would you teach a child the use of the word "if" by the method described by Augustine?

I do not have a solution to offer at this moment. It would be difficult to conceive of grammar as depending on intermodal transfers in the straightforward manner that object-naming does. Grammar appears at first glance to be something that grows up within the auditory association system itself, to depend on intramodal, auditory-auditory associations (which can then be transferred *en bloc* to written language by use of the cross-modal association system we have discussed).

This answer is, needless to say, hardly satisfactory, but our earlier discussion may give a clue as to some useful future approaches. We began this paper by stressing the exact method by which a monkey learns to choose a circle over a cross. Similarly, we have discussed the exact mechanism of object-naming in man. We can answer questions as to how we would teach certain things to a monkey and how we could teach a child the name of an object. Let us consider the possible applications of the method to grammar. We have some important facts, gleaned in important studies in recent years, on the child's acquisition of grammar. These facts, however, are still concerned mostly with the age of acquisition of certain grammatical features, their order of acquisition, and the learning of distinctions between features that might at first be accepted as equivalent. To some extent we can specify what rule the child follows at each age. I would suggest, as a supplement and by no means a substitute to these very important studies, that some attention be paid to the actual act of learning by the child and that some experiments be devised to study the elementary situations in which children learn to use certain words. At its origin grammar may well be acquired by mechanisms as naive as those of object-naming. Once these elementary associative steps are passed the acquisition of the more complex structures presents less difficulty. It is the very first steps which are the vital ones. Once speech is developed, it can develop an autonomy from the outside world that is all too familiar. If our studies on learning by monkeys and object-naming in man are to be of use, they should teach us to study not what grammatical rule is acquired by the child at a given age but *how* he has acquired this rule and how we could teach it to him.

SUMMARY

Certain aspects of the anatomy of the nervous system in man and other primates were reviewed. The distinction was pointed out between the **limbic system** (those structures lying in general in the "core" of the brain and involved in the motor and sensory aspects of feeding, drinking, elimination, aggression, flight and reproduction) and the **non-limbic** regions of the brain. It was pointed out that anatomically the major connections in sub-human primates from the non-limbic sensory zones (vision, touch, audition) are to the limbic regions and that therefore learning in these animals should consist mostly of associations of non-limbic to limbic stimuli. By contrast the non-human primates lack adequate anatomical structures for the development of associations between non-limbic modalities, and in fact such associations are not formed readily in them.

It was then pointed out that object-naming is in fact acquired by learning an association between two non-limbic stimuli (visual-auditory) and that the development of language in man has in fact been dependent on his acquisition of the ability to form non-limbic cross-modal associations. Reasons were given for the view that this ability depends on the great development of the **posterior parietal region** in man (the **angular gyrus region**).

There was some brief discussion of evidence in favor of this theory and a very brief mention of the possibilities of extension of this kind of theory to other aspects of linguistic behavior. In particular stress was placed on the importance of studying the process by which a child learns a grammatical rule and experimentally devising techniques for teaching these aspects of language in order to learn the mechanisms of acquisition.

BIBLIOGRAPHY

Bailey, P. and von Bonin, G., *The Isocortex of Man* (University of Illinois Press, 1951).

Bonin, G. v. and Bailey, P. in *Primatologia,* edd. Hofer, H., Schultz, A. H. and Starck, D., Vol. II/2, (1961) Lieferung 10.

Butler, R. A., *J. Comp. Physiol. Psychol.,* 46, (1953), 95.

Dejerine, J. *Mém. Soc. Biol.,* 3, (1891), 191.

Dejerine, J. *Mém. Soc. Biol.,* 4 (1892), 61.

Ettlinger, G. *Behaviour,* 16, (1960), 56.

Flechsig, P. *Lancet,* II, (1901), 1027.

Geschwind, N. in *Reading Disability,* ed. J. Money (Baltimore, Johns Hopkins Press, 1964).

Geschwind, N. (1964) "Disconnection Syndromes in Animals and Man". In Press.

Goldstein, K. (1927) in *Handbuch der Normalen und Pathologischen Physiologie,* volume 10, Berlin (Springer).

Sugar, O., French, J. D. and Chusid, J. G. *J. Neurophysiol.,* 11, (1948), 175.

Wittgenstein, L., *Philosophical Investigations,* translated by G. E. M. Anscombe (New York, 1953).

A FILE FOR A TECHNICAL DICTIONARY

H. A. GLEASON, JR.

Hartford Seminary Foundation

In recent years the terminology of linguistics has grown rapidly and chaotically. It has become a major problem to everyone in the field from the beginning student to the seasoned professional. A popular way to meet this problem, common to all disciplines, has been the preparation of special dictionaries of technical terminology. About four years ago, I started on a dictionary of linguistics. There are certain features of my procedure which may be of interest. I hope that my experiences may contribute in some small way to the discussion of the technique of lexicography.

Such a lexicon is an ideal small scale experiment in dictionary making. It is "unabridged" in its depth of coverage in that I plan to include all the generally used terminology in its field. Yet it is small. Some parts of the labor of dictionary preparation are proportional to the square of the size. Anything much larger than this proposal would be beyond the capacity of one man. Sometimes I wonder if this limited project isn't too much!

Specialized dictionaries must justify their existence. That is not always as easy as it may seem. The great unabridged dictionaries commonly give as full or fuller coverage. By the time mine is out, a third edition of Webster's New International will have appeared. The present one, published in 1934, and of course compiled a bit earlier, dates from before Bloomfield's *Language*. It is not very useful for the technical terminology of linguistics, but we should not forget that in 1934 it was excellent. The new one will, for a few years, be as up-to-date as a dictionary can be. The defining will have been done with care on the basis of a really phenomenal collection of evidence. It will have been edited by highly competent career lexicographers. I cannot hope to produce anything that will be better done, hardly anything more complete, but only to produce something different. The venture will be worthwhile only to the extent that I can profitably exploit the special opportunities of a specialized dictionary.

I have a more specific public in mind. This gives a certain flexibility in design that is not permitted to a general dictionary. I am not bound to any appearance of consistency of form between linguistic entries, chemical entries, art entries, and ordinary every-day basic words. Not, of course, that the unabridged dictionary imposes any dead uniformity, but the range of variation in form of definition is limited. I will be defining only one type of term, and will have liberty to determine what is the best form for that type without reference to any other. There can be finer meaning discriminations. My tentative definition of *accent* has nine meanings distinguished. Webster's 1934 also has nine, but only five of them are pertinent to language. There is opportunity for tighter tying together of entries and subentries. One particular meaning of *prosodic* can be tied in with a specific meaning of *phonematic*. At best this would be cumbersome in a general dictionary. There can be more entries for phrases, items like *secondary articulation, to mix levels, item, and arrangement.*

Perhaps the greatest difference is that the scope is totally different, not merely smaller. Webster's New International is a dictionary of the English language. It includes linguistics terms only as they are part of the English vocabulary. Mine will be a dictionary of linguistic terminology. This is not really English at all, but an international vocabulary manifested sometimes in English, sometimes in French, or in various other languages. *Phoneme* and *phonème* are not two words, but two spellings of one word contextually determined. One occurs after *the;* the other after *le.* As far as linguistic terminology is concerned we are compound bilinguals. I am accordingly not restricting my gathering to material in English. I do not yet have as strong representation of French usages as of English, but that is largely because I have had the assistance of typists who know only English. The imbalance must be remedied, not simply to have adequate representation of French but of certain authors or schools who write mostly in French. The language difference is incidental.

The definitions will be written, not for the intelligent general public, but for linguists. I shall attempt to give them the information that they will want. I leave it to Webster's to serve the general public.

Basically, the compilation of a dictionary involves little more than the selection of the proper entries and the writing of their definitions. But neither can be done without copious information about the possible entries. Defining then comes relatively late in the process. The first major operation is the building of a file of citations of usages. In the case of a literary language—and I am dealing with the language of linguistic publications—this consists of material excerpted from the literature. To gather such a file is an extremely long and expensive process. Hence it is one that needs a great deal of advance planning, effective control, and periodic assessment.

Once a lexicographer has a file well started, his die is cast. Knowing this, he starts by laying careful and detailed plans. He does a great deal of estimation and no little experimentation. (I wrote out several hundred slips in each of several formats before I settled on one and scrapped the rest.) The dictionary planner tries to foresee every possible contingency. Every eventuality he fails to provide for will rise up and plague him later.

His planning must be based on some fairly clear idea of the kind of dictionary wanted, its probable size, and the general characteristics of the material to be covered. Otherwise it will be impossible to estimate how much material will be needed, of what kind, and in what form it can best be handled. Before I began, I compiled a list of ten distinct types of terms that I thought should be included. I have had to make only small additions since, and those mostly very early in the work. In excerpting one must follow the rule: when in doubt, take it. It is expensive to take very many citations that might be foreseen to be useless, but it is disastrous to skip over items that will prove to be needed. A reasonably precise definition of scope from the beginning will produce a very much more effective collection of materials.

Planning centers around two problems, efficient excerpting, filing, and later handling of the material, and adequate but not wasteful sampliing of the universe. The first one is a matter of physical forms, efficient procedures, and close calculation of costs in time and money. The physicial form of a file is the least flexible thing about the work. But it also has a tremendous effect on every operation. Have you ever noticed the difference in sorting a pile of 4 x 6s and a pile of 3 x 5s? The first takes a larger table and longer reach. It is slower and more tiring. The larger paper size means higher costs, more space. On the other hand, slips must be large enough to contain the citations to be taken. They must have space for recording their subsequent handling. Perhaps the larger size will be worth the extra cost in time and materials. I so judged and I now think

I was right. But for a different sort of dictionary, I might use a smaller size.

It is the matter of time that needs the closest attention. One second per slip in the size file I contemplate amounts to nearly two full working days—no small matter. A few seconds in marking, in typing, in checking, in sorting, in filing, in reading, or any of the many processes each slip must go through means a great deal in the long run. These savings can be realized only by careful planning based on experimentation.

The second basic problem in building a file is one of sampling. What is wanted is a collection of material which represents with some reliability the universe to be described. It must tell when a term is in general use, and what the meaning or meanings are. To do this the sample must be drawn from every part of the literature to be covered—different subject matters, different terminological traditions, different theoretic positions, different dates, different types of writing. It must give some extra prominence to work that has been highly influential, but it must not neglect the writings of the relatively unknown authors. These will be most effective in indicating how the innovations of the leaders have been accepted.

The sample must be large enough that any term in sufficiently wide use to qualify will show up from three or four authors. Common terms must be represented fully enough that the range of meanings and usages will be clear. The whole file should be planned to get this result with the minimum total material.

Items are excerpted with a context. This should preferably be just adequate to provide the desired information. If insufficient context is given, it will be extremely expensive to refer back to sources. If excessive context is taken, this increases both the costs of excerpting and the time required in reading the slips when defining. Careful planning and good judgement are required here.

The second requisite for good filing is effective control. Information must be available to show how the planned sampling is progressing at any time. This means careful records of what material has been read and how many slips have been written.

I have done this by preparing record slips for each book or paper. These are made in quadruplicate. One is filed under the author. This is the easiest place to check against duplication. The second is filed by the periodical and volume. The third is under the language group. The fourth is under the branch of linguistics. I can, for example, find out rather quickly how many slips have been taken from the writings of any given linguist. Or, I can find that 1587 slips have been taken from BSOAS, and 959 from TPS. Together with some other items these indicate a fairly adequate representation of recent British work. Or, 811 slips from papers devoted to Romance languages indicates fairly good coverage (there is, of course, a great deal more Romance material covered in general books), whereas 115 slips for Greek and Latin points out a weak spot that needs strengthening.

Some lacunae are large and serious. But I have the information by which I can find them and plan to fill them. Without this control, the sampling could only be erratic and often very inadequate.

At rather long intervals during the course of the work it is desirable to go through the records and to examine a fairly large sample of the file to assess the progress of the collection. May I give you some idea of what can now be found?

The file now contains about 29,000 slips. These represent about 7,000 terms. That works out to an average of four citation slips per word, but, of course, such an average is very nearly meaningless. Seven tenths of the words are represented by less than the average number of slips, indeed nearly half, by only one. Many of these latter will ultimately be omitted. Some will not be found to be in general use; a possible example is *back mediodorsal*. Some terms are questionably technical, as *imbalance* found in a context where it was not clear whether the author intended it as a specifically linguistic term or not. Some are proposed for specific features in some particular language, and will not qualify unless they are found to be commonly chosen for similar features in other languages; a possible example is *leap-frog concord*. Some, though well known in neighboring disciplines are probably not firmly established within linguistics, as *negentropy*. Some, of course, are simple errors. All such things must be excerpted and filed so that they can be fairly judged. Support from several sources will indicate inclusion; the present unique exemplification suggests exclusion.

Examination of such a tabulation and of the items involved makes it possible to arrive at a more accurate prediction of the ultimate size of the vocabulary. The indications now are for something like 3,500 to 4,000 main entries. That is higher than my original estimate of 3,000 terms. It suggests a revision upward of all the original calculations. They projected a final file of about 50,000 slips.

Two other developments, however, revise the estimate downward. One of these new developments has been the appearance of
the CIPL glossaries. Those of Vachek and de Felice will very appreciably cut the amount of excerpting required in the literature of
the Prague and Neolinguist schools. Hamp's *A Glossary of American
Technical Linguistic Usage* came too late to save as much. Many of
the works he examined had already been excerpted. But his excerpting gave a very significant check on my own.

The second is that I seem to have attained to a higher efficiency
in excerpting than I had figured on. Obviously, in any process like
this, many of the citations taken are going to prove useless. Some
represent items that will finally be excluded. Others are redundant.
The real measure of a file is not the total number of citations, but the
number that actually contribute some useful information. Recent
examination of a fairly large sample suggested that about 15 percent
of the slips are redundant and about another 15 percent represent
words that will be excluded. That means an over-all efficiency of
70 percent. If that can be maintained, a total of 40,000 slips will be
better than the 50,000 with 50% useful on which the original plan
was based.

Of course, as the file grows, so do the opportunities for citations
to be redundant. More excerpting on the same basis will inevitably
depress the efficiency of the sampling. It must be more carefully
planned and controlled. But if this care can save writing a few
thousand slips, it may well be worth it. I now have hope that 40,-
000 to 45,000 slips will adequately support the lexicon that I have in
mind. Further excerpting will be done on a new and tighter plan
that will be designed to fill the present deficiencies with 10,000 more
slips. If I can do that, it will represent a tremendous over-all saving
in labor, expense, and elapsed time. A later assessment will tell if I
have been successful.

Or we can look at the problem from another direction. On the
basis of a probable vocabulary of 3,500 entries, how adequate is the
present file? Certainly some entries are sufficiently well documented
to give no difficulty at all. For these further excerpting should be
rather strictly limited. There is always the possibility of finding additional meanings, or more support for poorly represented meanings,
even in the most heavily documented entries. It is therefore not
possible simply to set up a list of words that will be hereafter off

limits.   But for these items, it will be desirable to exercise extra care in excerpting.

On the other hand, about 1000 of the expected 3500 entries are as yet inadequately covered.   To a certain extent, I can supply the deficiency from my own knowledge of the terminology, but I would hesitate to rely heavily on this for anything approaching 30 percent of the total vocabulary.   Further filing must be concentrated on obtaining fuller documentation for these items.   Familiarity with the present file can be of great value in accomplishing this.   The actual writing of definitions, still in an experimental stage, can sharpen up a feeling for what is needed.   Accordingly, from time to time I write a few definitions.   Several hundred have been written so far.   These serve two important functions.   First they help me appraise the present collection of material.   Secondly, they constitute the necessary experimentation on which planning of the later work will be based.

This preliminary drafting affords another significant set of statistics.   I expect about two-thirds of the entries to have only a simple definition apiece.   Another sixth will have two.   The most complicated that I have written so far has nine, one of them subdivided into three.   This range of complexity must be taken account of in any planning.   Present experience shows an average of 1.7 definitions per entry.   That means a total of 6,000 to 7,000 definitions.   It is really this, rather than 3,500 entries that is significant in calculating needed support.   A bit of arithmetic will show that 40,000 slips will be adequate only if I can succeed in maintaining a fairly high efficiency and good distribution.

All of these considerations enable me to guide my reading and filing.   Lacunae of various sorts come to attention, and a basis is provided for planning to fill them.   Excerpting is a haphazard process at best; without careful control it can become extremely unproductive.

I do not want to hold my own procedures up as a model.   I am sure that they can be improved in many ways.   But I do want to emphasize my conviction that a good dictionary file requires careful planning, effective control, and periodic searching assessment.   I started my present project with a minimum of past experience. Planning had to deal with a great number of imponderables.   If I were starting another dictionary, many of the things that then required a great deal of guess work would be known in advance.   I could certainly by-pass a number of the more complex problems. But my experience would lead me not to less planning but to more. I would establish even more careful controls. I think I could thus produce a better file for less work. Perhaps the improvements, percentage wise, would look small. But a dictionary is a huge undertaking. Small savings are multiplied by very large factors. A dictionary file is no place to leave the outcome to chance.

THE ORGANIZATION OF LANGUAGE: A STRATIFICATIONAL VIEW

H. A. GLEASON, JR.

Hartford Seminary Foundation

A language can be viewed as an apparatus for the transduction of information from one form to another. It enables a human user to produce a sequence of vocal sounds in response to his perception of an event, for example, in such a way that a second human user may reconstruct from the sounds a useful approximation [1] to the original perception of the event. The apparatus is symmetrical, in that the transduction can proceed in either direction, from experience to sound and from sound to experience. Indeed, a language apparatus is significant simply because it does provide for both operations. It is asymmetrical, however, in that the two directions of transduction are clearly distinguishable—they are, in fact, converses one of the other.

Language is sharply delimited from other phenomena. As a result, it can profitably be studied autonomously, as linguists are accustomed to doing—that is, with minimal dependence on phenomena outside language. This study may issue in statements that successfully exclude all other factors, yet are able to give a consistent, coherent, and insightful description. Such a result would hardly be possible if the autonomy of language were wholly

---

[1] There are of course, indeterminacies in any linguistic recoding operation. In one direction we customarily call these "free variation" or "style", and feel that they are of no great consequence. That is, we do not feel that a grammar is necessarily called upon to specify all free or stylistic variants, and certainly not to distinguish between them. We are similarly cavalier about cheap variations (the ones that are almost free). In the other direction indeterminacies are most often called "ambiguities", and we react very differently. Both phenomena, however, are significant in the communication system, and certainly such disparity of treatment is myopic. Moreover, we tend to get an entirely unbalanced idea of both. Neither occurs with such frequency or in such ways as to produce unavoidable serious interference with the process of communication. It can still go on effectively, making use of both transductions. All that is required in most instances is an approximation. Language users, in fact, have some control over the closeness of approximation.

fictional. Rather, it is a reflection of two crucial facts. First, language is highly organized, all of the central components being related directly or indirectly to each other. Second, in sharp contrast with most other phenomena with which it has contact, language is entirely quantized; it is a "digital" apparatus, excluding the gradience prevailing in both sound and event.

While cleanly delimited, it is not isolated. Rather, a language has essential contacts across at least two [2] regions of its boundary, one with sound and one with a vast range of phenomena which can be labeled broadly as "experience". We may call these regions **interfaces** because, intimate as the contacts may be, the boundary is not broken. A language maintains its characteristic internal organization entirely intact right up to the interface. Beyond it another type of structure, or a real or apparent lack of structure, takes over. There is no intergradation or mingling.[3] The boundary is not broken, but is, in these two regions, permeable. The membrane in the classical model of the living cell is an excellent metaphor.

From another, wider, point of view, the autonomy of a language within its own boundaries is only formal. While it can be described without external reference, the whole complex organization seems to be determined (in broad outlines) by the external phenomena contacted through these interfaces. It is, as it were, adjusted to its environment. At each end, a

---

[2] Some languages have only two, others have three, the third being with some complex of graphic marks, i.e. writing. In recent years (!), linguists have overlooked or even denied the existence of the latter. Nevertheless, a large and significant sector of language organization (at least one entire stratum, the **graphemic**) is missed. A full discussion of the organization of language would have to examine also the case of a language which has three interfaces (i.e., is both spoken and written). It would have to state the relations between such pairs of strata as the phonemic and the graphemic. It would be appreciably more complex than that which is described in this paper, but only a few additional basic principles would be involved.

A stratificational model provides a framework for a much more satisfactory treatment of writing systems than do other models, as I tried to show in a paper delivered to the Yale Linguistic Club on April 15, 1963, entitled "Structure in Writing Systems".

[3] In particular, it is not useful to conceive the phonetics of a language as an area of structure in which linguistic methods of study gradually give way to physical, physiological, or other methods, or in which these are mixed indiscriminately. Phonetics deals, among other things, with the way in which a language structure is projected onto a speech signal. To study this requires a basis both in language description and in physics or physiology. But the two remain separate. Phonetics, in spite of having a one-stem name, is actually a hyphenated science, comparable in every respect to psycho-linguistics, bio-chemistry, etc. As such, it must employ the results and methods of the two sciences in such a way that each supplements the other. It cannot be considered as a branch of linguistics.

language must possess an apparatus able to produce a useful digital model for the largely gradient material outside itself. Between, the language organization must be such as to facilitate a transduction from one quantization to the other. There may be more than one plan that might serve these ends, but clearly there cannot be many of them. The function of language, transduction of information between sound and experience, imposes severe restrictions upon its organization. The latter can only be understood in the light of these requirements.

SOUND AND PHONEMICS

Just outside one end of language is speech sound. This is dominated by an inexorable linearity in time. Yet it is more than simply linear. There are a number of parameters, each varying in time, so that speech sound is better compared to a bundle of strands. These are not fully discrete, but merge into each other in complex ways. In most parameters, any non-linguistic examination will find gradience.[4]

Across the interface, within a language, is a digital device modeling speech sound. This can best be labeled a **phonemics** or a **phonology**.[5] It also is dominated by a temporal-like linearity, and it also consists of a bundle of more or less independent parameters. There are a fixed number [6] of these in any one language, perhaps of the order of a dozen. Each is a small subset of contrasting units, the **phonons**,[7] sometimes called "distinc-

---

[4] For example, most of the problems of phonetics and phonemics are different in kind, not merely in degree. The problem of phonemic segmentation is in principle soluble, and we do in actual practice approach a solution. The problem of phonetic segmentation is in principle insoluble, and all that can be done is to set up a convenient ad-hoc organization of the data without theoretical justification of any kind.

[5] Neither of these terms is wholly satisfactory. "Phonemics" and the related adjective "phonemic" seem to give too great centrality to the phoneme. "Phonology" might seem more appropriate as a label for the study or description of the subcode than as a label for the subcode itself. There are similar difficulties with comparable pairs, e.g. "morphemics" and "morphology". Here, as at several other places, the terminology in this paper must be understood to be tentative, adopted by necessity rather than conviction, and subject to revision.

[6] The picture presented in this paper is a static one. Languages change, and in the process may pass through a stage where the number and identity of the phonons is temporarily not fixed. This indeterminacy, while certainly frequent in language, is never large, is generally transient, and is never basic to language organization. A fuller statement than is possible here would, however, have to make provision for this matter, but here it must be passed over almost as if it did not exist.

[7] The term "phonon", all other uses of the suffix "-on" 'a minimal unit of', much of the other terminology, and many of the ideas in this presentation I owe to Sydney

tive features".[8] The phonemics is more than a set of phonons organized into contrasting subsets. It includes also a set of patterns of combinations of phonons in two dimensions. There are restrictions as to what combinations can occur simultaneously [9] and what successively. These restrictions constitute the **phonotactics** of the language. The phonotactics specifies a hierarchy of units of various sizes. The **phoneme** [10] is a unit of this sort, as is the **syllable**, the **phonologic word**, the **microsegment**, etc.

Looked at phonologically, an utterance consists of a sequence of bundles of phonons, or alternatively, of a bundle of sequences of phonons. Geometrically this is best represented as a **matrix**, a two-dimensional array, one dimension being time, the other the list of phonon subsets.

Two basic operations occur at the interface between phonemics and speech. In one, the language apparatus has somehow generated a sequence of phonon bundles accordant with the phonotactics of the language. By some neuro-physiological process the user produces a span of vocal sound which corresponds in some significant way to this phonemic structure. Con-

---

M. Lamb. However, at certain points my interpretation of the material and hence my use of terms varies slightly from his.

[8] The term "distinctive feature" is rejected for several reasons. Prominent among them is the strongly phonetic implication. Another is the desire to indicate the close parallelism between phonon, morphon, and other units, by the common suffix.

The term "distinctive feature" has come to be associated with the claim that these occur in pairs, or that single distinctive features are either present or absent. The arguments for this binary interpretation, being in part neuro-physiological, are not really relevant here, but apply, if they apply at all, to the relations extending through the interface. That is, they are phonetic or psycho-linguistic, but not purely linguistic.

[9] Phonemes are sometimes defined in a form equivalent to "bundles of simultaneous phonons". This is not a definition of a phoneme. Rather, it is, indirectly, a definition of "simultaneous". Two phonons are simultaneous if, and only if, they are co-constituents of a phoneme. They are successive if they are constituents of successive phonemes. No appeal to physical (substantial) simultaneity is relevant here. Phonemes are not to be defined in terms of substance, and neither are phonons. Indeed, empirically, the projections of the phonons (acoustic features) do not have any such temporal relations as "simultaneity", taken literally, would suggest. If we do not recognize this fact, we are left with the intriguing result that in English there are three phonemically distinct kinds of total silence /p t k/, and that these are audibly distinguishable. Shades of Mr. Psmith!

[10] It must be emphasized that the phoneme is *not* the basic unit in the phonology. Rather it is a unit composed of phonons and playing a prominent role in the relations between morphemics and phonemics. In general, the phoneme is the realization of a morphon. It is this that justifies appeal to morphology in determining phonemes. Similarly, a morpheme is, in general, the realization of a lexon, and a lexeme the most usual realization of some sememic unit, the smallest unit for which realizations are generally stateable.

sidering this operation, the phonons can be thought of as "commands" to the articulatory apparatus. One might be glossed as "turn on glottal voice", its partner as "turn off glottal voice". This, however, is not a **linguistic** formulation.[11] The phonons are, linguistically, elements in a code, not neural impulses.

In the other operation, speech perception, a complementary neurophysiological process enables the human user to determine a sequence of phonon bundles which bears—hopefully—the same relationship to the heard sound as did the speaker's original matrix. From this point of view, phonons might be thought of as abstractive labels for features of sound. The same pair mentioned above might now be glossed something like "energy present at the fundamental" and "energy absent at the fundamental". Again, this is not a **linguistic** formulation. The phonons are coding units in the language, selected in response to such acoustic stimuli in a way that is accordant with the restrictions of the phonotactics. This operation is not a simple one. That it works at all is only because there are severe and largely systematic phonotactic restrictions.[12] As the hearer sets up a phonemic matrix it must be checked, repaired, and filled out. The phonemics, specifically the phonotactics, provides the first such check.

While the general organization of the phonemics is determined by the necessity of providing a feasible transduction to and from sound, many details are not. Every language has phonons, but no two necessarily have the same set. Every language has a phonotactic system, but very probably no two have the same.[13] The restrictions can be severe, both in inventory

---

[11] It is, perhaps, a useful psycho-linguistic or phonetic formulation, however; though probably over-simplified. Linguistics does not contain any physical or physiological component. Hjelmslev is quite right in maintaining a sharp distinction between "form" and "substance".

[12] The role of this redundancy in encoding and recoding must be emphasized. Any model of language that does not set up sets of tactic rules at a series of points along the path of language transduction finds itself hard put to account for the bidirectionality of language operation. A unidirectional model not only needs no phonotactics, it also needs no phonemes, nor phonons (or, at least, it does not need to label them as it passes by!). However, this fact does not mean that phonemics (in the sense of a subcode containing an inventory of phonons and phonemes and a phonotactics) has no place in language, or even in a complete language description.

[13] I have used the word "has" deliberately. I mean to assert that the organization of language here proposed has an appreciable measure of reality. Strata, I am asserting, exist, and the associated subcodes are necessary to account for the strata: "Network," "string," and various other terms may be metaphoric, but there is something about language such that "network" is a better metaphor than "string" in one case, and conversely in another. Terms like "phonon" and "phonotactics" are not meta-

and in tactics, because no language needs to provide a phonemic mapping for any sounds except those which have been produced on the model of a phonemic structure in the same language. That is to say, a language can and does select the sound features which its users employ in speaking.[14]

EXPERIENCE AND SEMEMICS

The phenomena contacted by the other end of language are much more various. They cannot be characterized in any useful simple way, only exemplified: a fly walking across a table, a solar eclipse, a destructive earthquake, the decay of a pion, a pattern in the clouds, a sudden pain, a wide-ranging generalization. Some of these are clearly structured; many are not. In any case, there is no single characteristic kind of structuring that they all share.[15] They range from trivial to cosmic, from familiar to catastrophic, from simple to hypercomplex. They grade along any parameters we might impose and the parameters fade into one another. Time may be a factor, but if so the dimensions vary from nanoseconds to megayears. Language does not exert any gross selective control.[16] Anything which

---

phors, but labels for some of the things that make these metaphors possible and useful.

[14] This means that the non-linguistic sound features used in projecting a phonologic structure are so closely determined by the latter that they are easily mistaken for part of it. Hence the familiar definition: "A language is a system of arbitrary vocal signals . . ." This must be abandoned. An improvement might read "A language is a system of arbitrary signals which may be given vocal realization . . ." But, perhaps, it would be better to give up the effort to find a definition.

[15] It is, of course, a basic assumption of science that most phenomena are structured. However, always several structurings apply to any arbitrarily selected bit of experience. From this point of view, there still is no over-all structure; "events" are a jumble of structurings. The first operation of a science is to extricate one putative system of structure from the phenomena, "ceteris paribus". In this sense, language (I do not mean linguistics) is a science, or sciences are special languages. The problem of the ways and extent to which science and natural languages differ is an intriguing one, but obviously not within our present scope. That a science can be called a "metalanguage" is suggestive, however.

[16] That is, language does not control what sorts of phenomena can enter human experience. It certainly does, with the provision of certain limited sets of alternatives, determine **how** the observed features are related in a narrative or a description. The latter controls, however, are also included in the language code of the hearer, and in his reverse transduction these may be decoded like any other part of the language code. In addition, a language may determine what features of experience are most readily and regularly observed. This, then, is the one really significant control, and it results in an effective though not unavoidable, linguistic determination of certain aspects of experience, and particularly of reconstructed experience. This would seem to be much less than Whorf claimed, though enough to be crucial in human com-

catches the idle curiosity of a human observer, anything which intrudes forceably into his life, anything he himself creates, in fact, anything at all may stand across the interface in contact with language, and so impose its requirements upon language organization.

Just within the boundary of language, adjacent to this interface, must be a digital apparatus capable of erecting a suitable model of any segment of this tremendous variety of intergrading and tangled phenomena. This part of a language is best labeled as a **sememics** or a **semology**.[17] It cannot be dominated, as is the phonemics, by a general and necessary linearity. Its organization must be quite different in many ways from that at the other end of language. Yet there are basic similarities. First, there is a set of contrasting units, the **semons**. Some of these fall into small contrastive sub-sets—binary as English 'singular' and 'plural', or many-membered as that distinguishing 'red, orange, yellow, green, blue, purple; pink, brown, black, gray, white'. Some semons merely contrast with their own absence, as does 'past' in English. Some subsets are restricted; others have open membership.

There are also patterns of combinations of semons. These constitute the **semotactics** of the language. For example, in Latin 'subjunctive' and 'future' do not co-occur.[18] There is no time dimension along which semotactic patterns are laid out. Time is an option. It is expressed, if at all, by the inclusion of a semon or semons specifying time. Nor is there linearity. The topologic model most appropriate is that of a multidimensional **network**. Points occupied by semons are connected to one another by **valences**. Two points may be connected, directly and indirectly, in several ways. The network is presumably the most flexible organization available to a language.

---

munication, and hence well worth investigating. The problems localize around the sememic-experience interface. A stratificational approach with a structural semology would seem to be prerequisite to their investigation.

[17] Sememics or semology has in many respects the same relationship to "semantics" (or to one application of this chameleon label) as does phonemics to phonetics. They should not be confused, as they often have been. Semantics I would take to be the hyphenated discipline that relates semology to percepta.

In my *Introduction to Descriptive Linguistics,* 1955, I used the term "content" for what is here labeled "sememics". The term, but little more, was from Hjelmslev. At that time I had no ideas of semotactics whatever, nor did many other linguists. But I was convinced that phonology and morphology did not exhaust the structured material in language. The chief mistake was the grouping of phonology and morphology as "expression" on the assumption that these two are somehow more immediately open to observation.

[18] 'Future' is very probably a semon; 'subjunctive' is very probably more complex.

And flexibility is a prime requisite, since the phenomena to be quantized by the sememic apparatus are so various.[19]

Recurring combinations of semons must compose sememic units of various kinds. As yet we know very little about these. In a few instances we can identify semons and some of their constitutes. In others we know putative units whose constituency is not yet established.[20] We can expect, in due course, to identify a variety of units and understand the hierarchy that exists among them. Presumably one of the significant construction types will profitably be labeled **sememe**. We suspect that sememes are often the semologic units which can be thought of as standing behind "words".

CODE AND STRATUM

There are three distinct processes in the total transduction by means of a language. A diagram is given in figure 1. Consider the top line. At the right is a fragment of experience. A sememic network is built to correspond with what are abstracted as the significant features of this experience. Since language is a code, the process is conveniently called **encoding**. At the other end, left on the diagram, there is an opposite operation. We might call this "decoding", but this would put the emphasis in the wrong place. It is not so much a transduction out of language as one into sound. We will designate it, therefore, as **projection**. We have pointed out two different subcodes, sememics and phonemics. Between the two there must be a process of **recoding**. Encoding and projection refer to the external operations of a language. Recoding is completely internal—of the three, it alone is purely linguistic.

---

[19] It must be emphasized that the structure must be flexible, not simply chaotic. There are restrictions—many of them—but there is also a high measure of flexibility.

[20] Native speakers are no more aware of semons than they are of phonons, so we need not be distressed if we have found it difficult to identify them, even in our own language. It is, after all, no easy task to find the phonons either, in spite of our much greater experience with this sort of analysis and the certainty that the job is inherently simpler anyway. (The phonons are a small, closed set; the semons are many times more numerous.)

Moreover, we should be very much surprised if the first work should turn up the basic units. The first recorded phonologic work (i.e. the development of certain early writing systems) only slowly came to recognize a consistent set of units, and these were not minimal. An instructive recent example is the creation of the Cherokee "alphabet", a highly successful bit of amateur phonologic analysis. The units found, however, were neither phonons nor phonemes, but "syllables". After some stumbling around, linguists should be expected to come up with some real sememic units. Then gradually these will be sorted out, brought to some consistence of level, further analyzed, etc. A full picture of the semons should emerge rather late.

THE ORGANIZATION OF LANGUAGE

THE TWO TRANSDUCTION PROCESSES

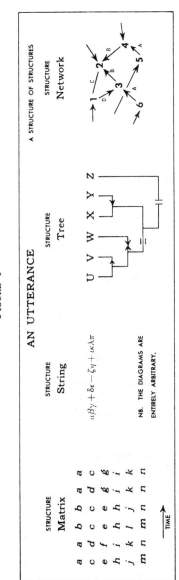

FIGURE 1

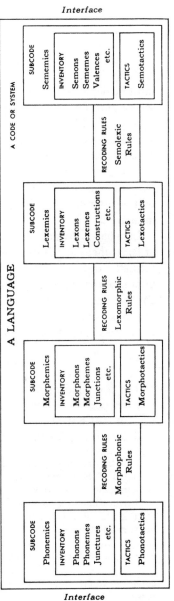

FIGURE 2

Encoding produces a structure—a network or a matrix as the case may be. Projection produces a non-linguistic correlate of a structure. Recoding adds one structure to another. In an utterance, a sample of language use, several structures co-occur superimposed one on the other.

Language is a code which stands behind the processes of recoding, and partially behind encoding and projection, guiding them. A language code must be described in terms of three kinds of major components: **inventories,** sets of units out of which structures can be built; **tactic rules,**[21] specifications of ways in which units can be used to build structures; and **recoding rules,** specifications of the relations which obtain between co-occurrent superimposed structures. Each inventory is associated with its own tactics. Such a combination is a subcode, the structure which it defines is a **stratum.** We have described two strata, the phonemic and the sememic. The organization of utterances and of a language in terms of these major units is shown in figure 2.

Languages do not recode in a single step. Instead, in some languages at least, there are three steps.[22] These join four distinct strata. The intermediate strata seem to be necessary largely because the topology of an utterance structure in the phonemics and that in the sememics are so different that there is no feasible device for direct mapping of one onto the other. One is a bidimensional matrix with one dimension linear in time; the other a complex multidimensional network with no necessary linearity.

LEXEMICS AND MORPHEMICS

The two middle subcodes will be designated **morphemics** or **morphology,** and **lexemics** or **lexology.** The first pair of terms is quite familiar. However, it will not necessarily be used in exactly the familiar way. Recent tradition [23] has, for the most part, recognized just two "levels", "articula-

---

[21] To say that a language has rules is a fiction. Languages have patterns that can be stated in the form of rules. But the looser wording is convenient—and harmless, if the meaning is not forgotten.

[22] With some languages it is possible to produce a fairly good grammar with only three strata. Possibly, even in these cases, an additional stratum (i.e. discrimination between morphemic and lexemic) will permit either simplification or further precision in statement. It is not known whether there exist languages requiring more than four strata for effective statement. No a priori reason for such an organization is currently visible, and our empiric experience is still too limited to generalize with complete confidence. Basically, the question is whether there is more than one feasible scheme for recoding between network and matrix, and if so, do languages use more than one. If the answer is yes, this would be a typologic feature of great interest and significance.

[23] The older tradition, represented for example by L. H. Gray in *Foundations of Language* (1939), recognizes three sectors, phonology, morphology, and syntax. A

tions", or "planes". Commonly these have been designated "phonology" and "morphology". There is no serious difficulty with the first of these, but "morphology" and related terms have been far from uniformly applied. They may refer to one of three remaining strata, two of them, or all three.[24] We are restricting terms with the stem "morph-" to that stratum most directly related to the phonemics.

The units of the lexemics are **lexons**, **lexemes**, and various larger sequences. The **lexotactics** characteristically produces **trees**. A tree differs from a network in that no two points are multiple-connected. There may be repeated branchings. At the ends of the final branches stand the lexons.[25] Each node represents a constitute of lexons, perhaps a lexeme. Nodes are "labeled" with designations for construction types. This is, of course, the now familiar picture of a "constituent structure grammar", though perhaps differing in some details from the way this is usually formalized by its critics.

The process of recoding from a semologic network to a lexologic tree can be crudely pictured as the breaking open of the network—that is, the elimination of multiple connections. Certain valences remain as connections in the tree, but others are represented by lexemes. In any language there seem to be a number of lexemes with just this latter function. The familiar distinction between "function words" and "full words" is in part

---

superficially similar tripartite organization was long standard in "Bloomfieldian" linguistics, but with a difference. Bloomfield redefined syntax in a way that made it only the upward extension of morphology, thus reducing the sectors of language to two, de facto. Gray, however, describes syntax in a way that sets it off, at least partially, from morphology. His description is not entirely clear, but it does suggest an awareness of some of the features here assigned to sememics and a crude effort to say something about them. They are not sharply separated, but are mixed with some bits of lexemics and some non-linguistic material. Gray's treatment might have provided a starting point for a development quite different from what did take place. That is to say, scraps of morphemic and lexemic material might have been excised, the limitation to strictly linguistic phenomena sharpened, and the whole gradually developed toward a third stratum with its own inventory and tactics. Instead, the semologic fragments were excised (and largely just discarded!), making a separate syntax non-functional and leading to its ultimate abandonment as a separate compartment in language organization. Gray's chapter on Syntax is worth a careful, sympathetic restudy.

[24] For example, Henry Hoenigswald in his *Language Change and Linguistic Reconstruction* (1960), speaks of a morph as "filling a morpheme" in such a way as to raise the suspicion that his morpheme is close to, or includes as a special case, what is here called a sememe. See also the discussion of Nida's treatment in this paper. Other authors are less precise, using "morpheme" for any "basic unit" which is not phonologic.

[25] Alternatively, the lexemic structure might be described as a dependency tree. The two types are nearly (!) interconvertible.

a crude statement of this fact.[26] Most of the relationships in the sememic network are recoverable from the lexemic tree with its more open structure just because lexemes or lexons may recode valences.

This picturing of the recoding operation is misleading. The sememic network is not altered or distorted to transform it into a lexemic tree. Rather, a tree occurs as an additional structure within the same utterance. It is patterned after the sememic network as the inter-stratal relations allow. These relations can be formulated in a set of rules; we will call them **semolexic realization rules**. We will say that a certain lexeme or tree feature realizes [27] a certain portion of a network.

In one mode of operation of a language, a tree is built following the lexotactic rules. From place to place these offer options. At each such place the semolexic rules specify a way to make the choice that will conform the tree appropriately to the network. The result will have been subject to two sets of language constraints, sememic and lexemic. In the other mode of operation, a network is built conforming to the semotactic rules of the language, choices being guided by the same semolexic rules.

There remains one very important feature of lexotactic rules to mention. At each branching, they impose a specification of left or right.[28] I say "impose" because there is no ordering of any comparable sort, that is, no orientation, in a semologic network. Valences may be directional (e.g. glossable as "A is dependent on B", which is different from "B is dependent on A"), but there is no before or after. Not only do lexotactic rules impose this elementary kind of order (a first step toward the dominant linear order-

---

[26] Stratificational grammar, therefore, gives promise of providing an adequate formalization of the notion of "function word", or at least a significant critique of it. That the term itself will prove useful in stratificational description is not so certain.

[27] One of the most serious difficulties with recently prevailing linguistic practice in America has been the notion that morphemes are "composed of" phonemes, or that phonemes are "composed of" sounds. The proper relationship is quite otherwise. A number of terms have been used to indicate this: "represents", manifests", "realizes", "is an exponent of", etc. I have used two sets of terms for much the same relation: **recode** and **realize** and their derivatives. I mean to make a subtle but significant distinction. "Recode" emphasizes the symmetry of the process; "realize", the asymmetry. Thus a tree may recode a network and a network recode a tree. A tree realizes a network, while a network is realized by a tree. "Recode" is more appropriate to discussion of transduction; "realize" to the structural relationships in an utterance, or to the rules describing these in a grammar.

[28] A very interesting paper might be written, I suspect, tracing the appearance and acceptance by linguists of this terminology. It is so evidently derived from some graphic substance, a source that might easily have been considered out-of-bounds on either or both of two counts. It is used here in a purely conventional and non-substantial way.

ing in a phonemic structure), but the semolexic rules have a part in the assignments. That is to say, order is a device which can be used to realize valences. (E.g. a valence indicating that A is dependent on B in some specified way may be realized (in part) as A' precedes B'.)

The second operation of recoding makes use of a set of **lexomorphic realization rules** to guide the choices that come up in a set of **morphotactic rules**. (In the other mode, lexomorphic rules guide the application of lexotactic rules.) The topology of the morphemic stratum is largely linear. Lexons are, in general, realized by **morphemes**. These are in succession, one after another. But the transition from morpheme to morpheme can occur in more than one way. We shall say that between pairs of morphemes there are **junctions**. There is a ranked set of these, one taking precedence over another and indicating a less close connection. The junctions serve to mark structure in the sequence of morphemes. This is conveniently described as a **string**. Morphemes are composed of **morphons**, and these are generally in linear arrangement within the morpheme.

Finally, we come to the **morphophonic rules** which state the recoding relations between morphemic strings and phonemic matrices. These seem familiar, but there is a significant difference from the usual view of "morphophonemic rules". The latter are based on the assumption that morphemes are composed of phonemes. Morphophonemic rules are, therefore, required only for those morphemes which have allomorphs, and indeed only for those parts of morphemes that vary from allomorph to allomorph. The rules can conveniently be stated in terms of "morphophonemes", a strange sort of variable phoneme. However, morphemes are composed of morphons, and these are units in the morphemic stratum not the phonemic, nor are they any sort of bridge between the two strata. Morphons are realized, in general, by phonemes. This is true whether a given morphon has one consistent realization or some very complex pattern of realizations varying from context to context. A morphophonic rule is needed in either case. These rules do more than merely relate units; like the other two sets of rules, they map one topology onto another.

This picture of the organization of language in terms of four strata can conveniently be called **stratificational**.[29] As a very minimum, a stratifica-

---

[29] Such a label no more implies that this is the only model using strata than does "structuralism" that other linguistic movements reject the notion of structure. As an arbitrary label, however, it will serve to distinguish an approach (a "theory" if you choose, though such a label has too often been used pretentiously in liguistics). One possible justification for the term is that this approach does clearly distinguish between stratum and level (i.e., within each stratum there is a hierarchy of levels), whereas many others have indiscriminately called both dimensions "levels".

tional model is one that recognizes at least three strata and corresponding subcodes, all of them totally within language, linearly ordered, and related by recoding operations. Each stratum contains an inventory proper to itself [30] and a tactics. Each stratum has a characteristic topology.

THE "BLOOMFIELDIAN" MODEL

Presented abstractly, a stratificational model of language is certainly more complex than the familiar "Bloomfieldian" model. One might reasonably ask some justification for preferring the greater complexity. There are several, but only major ones can be mentioned here.

Greater complexity in the abstract does not necessarily mean greater complexity in the description of any specific language. Consider a model still simpler than the two-stratum one of most recent practice. This can be obtained by abandoning the distinction between phonology and morphology. In this model, a linguist would seek simplemindedly to show how sequences of phonemes signal complex meanings. This, however, makes description hopelessly complex. More apparatus is required for even a workable fragment of a sketch. Three strata might produce a less complex statement than two. Whether this maneuver is successful or not depends on whether we can find a "natural" division; that is, one which gives similar treatment to similar phenomena, and different treatment to different. We think that there is reason to believe that four strata reflect some significant facts about language, and should, therefore, give the optimum description.

A familiar fact about linguistics is perhaps also indicative. Phonology has long been easier to handle than morphology, and morphology than syntax. The traditional explanation has been basically historical: linguists have worked longer on phonology. They are working their way up the ladder progressively from the natural entry point in sound. The methods developed at one level must be carried up to the next. It is only a matter of time before syntax will be handled as well as phonology.

I would like to suggest an alternative hypothesis: Phonology has been relatively easy to describe because we have been dealing here with a single stratum (though often bits of phonetics and scraps of morphology have contaminated the experiment). We have had some success with word-morphology because we have been able to focus on small problems where in some cases only lexemic and in other cases only morphemic strata figure prominently. Of course, it has been difficult to fit the pieces together into

---

[30] That is to say, no unit is a member of two inventories. A lexon may be consistently realized by a morpheme in a simple one-to-one relation. They are not, however, to be identified.

one consistent picture. We have had immense difficulty with syntax because here we must look at broader vistas, and every problem has components in three strata. The difficulties with syntax in a two-stratum model are exactly the same as those with all problems in a completely unstratified model. Syntactic analysis may not simply be difficult on this basis, but insoluble until the strata are sorted out.

Nida's *Morphology* [31] has gone through two editions. Unfortunately, few read the first any more; it is a valuable counterpoise to the second. The two are far apart in theory (within a two-stratum model), and their comparison throws certain cruxes into relief. In the first, Nida restricts "morpheme" to classes of allomorphs in phonologic complementation. Morphologic complementation defines groups of "supplemental morphemes". In the second, both kinds of complementation group allomorphs into morphemes, but an effort is made to keep the two separate by different symbols. Neither solution is wholly satisfactory, and the problem has continued to plague linguists. Allomorphy is, in stratificational terms, a matter of recoding. There are two separate and very different recoding phenomena involved. A two-stratum theory can provide no comfortable place for the two. Separation of morphemic and lexemic strata is required.

Of the chapters in Hockett's *Course*,[32] twenty-nine, "Surface and Deep Grammar" is perhaps the most difficult, at least for a person coming to it with a background in linguistics. Many linguists have been at a loss to know what to make of it. The argument seems plausible, but it suggests notions that have no place in our standard view of language organization. Hockett gives some examples with what amounts to lexologic tree analyses, and then shows that there are further relationships with grammatical significance but cutting across the sentence structure as diagrammed. These relationships are labeled as "deep grammar". They are semologic valences, not directly realized in the lexemics, but still recoverable from it. They can be given a place easily enough if a network structure is seen underlying the tree.

I have given two examples of fundamental matters of language organization which are left unaccounted for in the conventional two-stratum

---

[31] Nida, Eugene Albert, 1946, *Morphology; the descriptive analysis of words,* and 1949, *Morphology; the descriptive analysis of words, second and completely new edition, based on actual-language materials.* The complete change in the character of the problems seems to have diverted attention from the equally complete change in the theoretical base.

[32] Hockett, Charles F., 1958, *A course in modern linguistics,* pp. 246-260. (There are revealing additional examples in chapter 30.)

"Bloomfieldian" model. Stratificational grammar can handle these easily and naturally.

THE TRANSFORMATIONAL-GENERATIVE MODEL

Something like the last argument is the now familiar chorus of the more zealous transformational-generative linguists. They claim that their model will account for certain aspects of language structure or behavior that "constituent structure grammar" will not. In this they are right. But when they assert that all other than transformational-generative grammars are "constituent structure grammars" they are clearly wrong.[33] Stratificational grammar, for one, definitely is not. Moreover, a stratificational grammar can be shown to have all the "power" that a transformational-generative grammar has. The rules of a transformational-generative grammar can be rearranged, with appropriate modifications in form but not ultimately in effect, to fit into a stratificational framework. The result is a stratificational grammar of a crude sort. Indeed, certain developments in transformational-generative theory and practice since 1957 have been movements in precisely that direction.[34]

But transformational-generative and stratificational grammars are not simply equivalent in power, differing only in the arrangement of the rules. There are some basic differences and these justify certain claims that I will make on behalf of stratificational grammar, even though space does not permit the full discussion that they merit. Each of them can now be partially demonstrated; all will, I am confident, in due course be fully established. Any one of them alone would constitute evidence for the superiority of one model over the other.

1. A stratificational grammar can provide a workable basis for understanding and formalizing the processes of **both** transductions through lan-

[33] See for example, Postal, Paul, 1964, *Constituent structure: a study of contemporary models of syntactic description*. Postal's understanding of stratificational grammar completely misses the point. Lamb's "representational rules" (here called "realization rules") **do** "affect generative power" (p. 32) precisely because they do "map one type of representation into another".

[34] For example, Noam Chomsky, if I understood a brief oral presentation at the CCCC meeting in New York, March 27, 1964, now holds that a language has a "surface structure" relatable to the phonetics, and a "deep structure" relatable to the semantics. (I do not know whether these terms come from Hockett, but they seem to parallel his usage very closely.) The two are related through a set of transformational rules. This much of the model looks very much like a lexemic and a sememic stratum and a set of semolexic realization rules. Most transformational rules find their counterparts in a stratificational grammar in realization rules.

guage. A transformational-generative grammar has insuperable difficulty with one of the two.

2. A stratificational grammar can provide a simple and natural treatment for such phenomena as anaphora, and so for many of the grammatical features extending beyond the sentence. Transformational treatment is labored and counter-intuitive at best.

3. Postal lists eight points where "constituent structure grammars" are said to fail. His last is: "8. PSG cannot handle overlapping selectional restrictions without extraordinary and inelegant complexities and repetitions. The complexities are due to the cross-classifications of categories found in language".[35] In the discussion on the following page he says, "Flaws of the 8th type cannot be overcome by transformational rules since they are found in the part of the grammar which must be correctly characterized before transformations apply. At the moment there is, I think, no completely adequate way of dealing with them". Stratificational grammar should have no trouble with this type of restriction. Indeed, it is precisely this which most clearly indicates the necessity for a sememic stratum distinct from the lexemic, each governed by its own inventory and tactic rules.

4. For a reasonable and useful degree of comprehensiveness, a stratificational grammar will prove simpler and clearer than a transformational-generative grammar.

A transformational-generative grammar is theoretically designed to do just one thing—to generate sentences. Actually, few advocates have been able to maintain consistence in distinguishing "generate" in the sense of 'enumerate' or 'define' from "generate" in the sense of 'produce'. In fact, their grammars are readily adaptable to a second function, the random production of sentences. All that is necessary is to read the arrow as "rewrite as" instead of "consists of" or the like.

To achieve efficiency in this function or functions, various shortcuts are taken. For example, the phoneme is by-passed by a set of rules which go directly from morphophonemes, alias "phonemes" (and roughly our morphons), to phonetic specifications. Such shortcuts inevitably complicate other possible functions of a grammar, or render them impossible. The formalization of the transduction from phonology to semology seems to be one casualty, and to my tastes, a most lamentable one. If a grammar user wishes to program a grammar for a restricted use, he is free to by-pass any part of the apparatus which he does not need. But such curtailments should not be built into the **theory** of grammar, and the full apparatus must be provided for in any scheme for the design of specific grammars.

---

[35] Postal, Paul, 1964, *Constituent structure*, pp. 74, 75.

I may seem to have denied my claim of greater simplicity. Avoiding these shortcuts will bring some additional complexity into the grammar. However, transformational-generative grammars have so much excess ad hoc complexity that it is meaningless to speak simply of adding apparatus. A change of form can be expected also to render some apparatus unneeded. The substance of my claim is that any additions of **appropriate** machinery can easily be off-set by greater savings.

Transformational-generative grammars are like "Bloomfieldian" two-stratum grammars in confusing strata and intermingling rules of very different natures,[36] though there are great differences in the ways this is done. If a language is tightly and systematically organized, this should most certainly introduce artificial complexity. A look at a sample of the rules in any of the more copious transformational-generative grammars of English seems to confirm this. And we must remember that all of them are very far from complete in coverage. Their complexity is such that small extensions in scope have become very major undertakings, not so much in finding the facts as in integrating them into the statement.[37]

---

[36] For example, Lees' rule 1 ($S \rightarrow Nom + VP$) and his rule 5 ($V_{cop} \rightarrow \{V_p, V_{ac}\}$) are quite different. Rule 1 is properly read something like "S is composed of $Nom + VP$"; rule 5 is properly read something like "V_{cop} contains two subclasses, V_p and V_{ac}." Other rules combine the two relationships in various ways. The rules in transformational-generative grammars are said to be segregated largely on the basis of the type of rule. But at least two very distinct relations are mixed in the "phrase structure component". Moreover, the units are of more than one kind. In rule 8 ($V_{tr} \rightarrow \{V_t, V_x + P, V_T + C\}$), most of the symbols represent, in tagmemic terms, filler classes, but C is clearly a slot designation as it merely marks a spot that will later be filled by a transformational rule. (All examples from Lees, Robert B., 1960, *The grammar of English nominalizations*. Other grammars available to me have similar problems.)

That transformational-generative grammars confuse strata is more difficult to demonstrate briefly. However, the elaborate devices used to attain proper selection of collocated subclasses of nouns and adjectives, for example, seem far better interpreted as misplaced semotactic rules. With a strict tree structure, the "phrase structure component" seems basically to represent lexotactic rules. It is clear that much of the complexity in transformational-generative grammars arises from the efforts to restrict collocations, such as those of nouns and adjectives, to ones that are felt to be acceptable. It would be much more natural, and very likely much more simple, to separate this function from that of "generating" a phrase structure, that is, to distinguish sememic and lexemic strata, each with its own appropriate set of tactic rules.

[37] A model transformational-generative grammar of the dimensions of that presented in Chomsky, Noam, 1957, *Syntactic Structures,* can be quite misleading. As such grammars grow in size, they quite rapidly increase in complexity. Rules become longer and the symbolization more complex. The ones that I have been able to examine all contain dead-ends, disconnected segments, duplicate rules, or

There is, of course, a remedy. That is to sort out the rules into more natural blocks and to eliminate some of the artificiality in statement of some of them. But this means, in effect, to approximate the stratificational model. Transformational-generative grammatical theory can be moved toward what we are here describing. Therein lies its hope.

REALIZATION RULES AND MULTIPLE CONNECTEDNESS

As that approximation goes forward, sooner or later some rather radical changes will have to be made. One of these must be to replace ordered transformational rules (or certain of them [38]) by unordered realization rules. In another paper in this symposium, Sydney M. Lamb discusses this point in some detail. It is, therefore, unnecessary to do more than mention it here and to point out that the conception of realization rules correlating co-existent structures is fundamental to stratificational grammar and basic to some of the claims made in its behalf.

Another necessary change will be to introduce multiple connectedness

---

other errors of statement. These are not due simply to carelessness. I have tried to write such grammars and I have tried to repair these. I find it a task very nearly at the limit of intricacy with which I can cope. In particular, it seems especially difficult to expand an existing grammar without leaving scars of old connections now severed.

That writing a grammar is difficult is no argument against any form of grammar. Language is complex, and we must reconcile ourselves to finding that grammars are complex too. However, much of the difficulty with transformational-generative grammars seems to be in their form, rather than in the facts that they describe. The burden will become intolerable as they approach the coverage of the standard one-volume handbooks unless some major breakthrough in grammar-writing technique is achieved.

Part of the trouble is in being too rigorous too early. Granted rigor is a desirable end, it does not follow that a rigorous statement of a small fragment of the whole is necessarily a step toward a rigorous statement of the whole. If rigor is attained by the use of ad hoc rules, it may very well erect nearly impenetrable barriers to further progress. This seems to me to be the case with transformational-generative grammars of English.

[38] The heterogeneity among the rules in the transformational component of some grammars is extraordinary. For example, Lees' rule T24 (Pl → S) hardly seems to meet the standard definitions for a transformation! The difficulties with the constituent structure rules mentioned in footnote 36 can be multiplied in the transformational component(s). We are told by one transformationalist that "A rule of grammar may perform any of the following operations: deletion . . . , replacement . . . , expansion . . . , reduction . . . , addition . . . , permutation . . . T rules may perform any of them in any combination". (Bach, Emmon, 1964, *An introduction to transformational grammars,* p. 70.) Actually, this statement does not recognize the basic types of grammatical rules at all: constituency, realization, class membership, mutation, instantiation. Transformational rules confuse all of the first four.

into the first set of tactic rules. That is, to make the operation of sentence generation start in the sememic stratum with rules of appropriate form, rather than in the lexemic with random fragments of semology tied on. Here is one of the significant differences between a transformational-generative grammar rearranged into a crude stratificational form and what we are suggesting as a superior model. The network structure is significant, among other reasons, because it provides a direct approach to anaphora and various related phenomena. It makes it possible to be explicit at some points where transformational-generative grammars are inexplicit.[39] In providing a better treatment of anaphora, it opens a real possibility of handling all the grammatical features of discourses.

I recently put together a rough sketch of a stratificational grammar of a non-European language.[40] My objective, at first, was the quite traditional one of generating sentences, and I was able to do this at least as satisfactorily as in any of a number of previous attempts on a variety of models. Then, quite by accident, I discovered that the grammar would cover whole narratives as well as single sentences. Less had to be added to expand the coverage than could be deleted as no longer required. In this language, the stratificational grammar of whole narratives seems to be actually simpler than that of sentences abstracted from narrative and examined separately.

This may be a special case, but I am not ready to concede that it is. After all, a narrative is a much more natural unit of language than is a sentence. Native speakers produce narratives with ease. We cannot claim to have accounted for the sememics-to-phonemics transduction, much less

---

[39] For example, transformational-generative grammars derive a sentence such as 'The man cut himself' from an underlying string of the general form: 'the + man + -ed + cut + the + man' (with appropriate phrase marker). To do so it is necessary to require not merely that 'the + man' be identical in form in the two occurrences, but that it be identical in **reference**. Otherwise the resulting sentence must be 'The man cut him', or the like. A stratificational grammar would generate these sentences from two distinct sememic networks: (Some details have been omitted for convenience.)

'The man cut himself.' 'The man cut him.'

More complex examples indicate more clearly the advantages, but would require more space to present.

[40] The language is Kâte of New Guinea. This grammar is not in publishable form, being only a very preliminary sketch based on a quite limited corpus and on a previous traditional grammar. In addition, the best form of statement for the semotactic rules has not yet been established.

the event-to-sound transduction until we can handle the linguistic features of whole narratives satisfactorily.

This leads me to my final claim—one that is not susceptible of proof or disproof, a matter, perhaps, only of taste. But aesthetics has as essential a place in science as demonstration, for without it proof may readily become vacuous. My fifth claim is this:

Stratificational grammar gives an intuitively more satisfying picture of language organization than any other proposal yet made. I am not claiming final answers or ultimate and indisputable truth. I am claiming a step forward in our understanding, or, at least, the first tentative feeling for the solid ground on which that step will be planted. Over the years to come, many of the details I have here proposed will be corrected or completely replaced. But I am confident that there will be no return to the place whence we started. There will come a new view. As we have built on "Bloomfieldian" principles, so I expect it to be built on stratificational.

LINGUISTIC REPERTOIRES, GRAMMARS AND SECOND LANGUAGE INSTRUCTION

JOHN J. GUMPERZ

University of California, Berkeley

In his Postulates for a Science of Language, Leonard Bloomfield defines a language as the totality of utterances that can be made in a speech community (1926). His statement emphasizes the view that the sounds and grammatical patterns we study are always abstracted from social activity. They form part of a complex of communicative symbols, produced by members of particular societies interacting in specific social settings in accordance with culturally defined norms of behavior. Few linguists would disagree with this formulation. In asserting that speaking is a form of social interaction, Bloomfield is merely following long established tradition. But so far, such assertions constitute little more than professions of faith. The important contribution of modern linguistic scholars lies in their analysis of verbal signs in terms of their purely linguistic environment. Bloomfield and his followers were able to achieve the explicitness and reliability of statement for which they are justly famous largely because of their insistence that segmentation and classification of verbal forms be based on observable sound. Source data for linguistic analysis were, to be sure, collected from native informants, but once recorded, items were grouped purely on the basis of their formal similarities and differences. Meaning and context were left aside for later consideration.

The last decade has seen a radical break with the basic position of post-Bloomfieldian linguistics. The modern view of grammars as theories of a language rather than as classifications of pre-existing elements has also brought about important changes in the nature of linguistic descriptions. No matter what our opinion regarding these new developments, it is evident that these grammars cover a considerably broader range of phenomena than the earlier formal statements. Along with phonology and morphophonemics, syntax and semantics have once more become an integral part of linguistic descriptions. But the expansion in scope of

179

linguistic description is also accompanied by new efforts to reassert the independence of formal linguistic analysis. A recent article on semantic theory by Katz and Fodor (1963) makes a major contribution toward the incorporation of semantics into grammar, but in this article the authors also go to great lengths to argue that information about what they call sociophysical settings should be excluded from linguistic descriptions. The semantic theory they envisage is, among other things, capable of dealing with cases of homonymy in sentences such as "The bill is large," where the noun subject may refer either to a bird's beak, a document demanding payment, or to a currency note. On the other hand, the difference in meaning between the objects of the sentences "This store sells horseshoes" and "This store sells alligator shoes" is declared to be outside the scope of linguistics, since knowledge of the difference is a matter of personal experience, and thus not subject to formalization. Despite the increase in the scope of linguistic descriptions, therefore, the new theory continues to make sharp distinctions between grammars and the social context in which utterances are used. Linguists and social scientists operate with similar source data, but the products of the linguists' analysis remain independent entities whose relationship to social facts we are unable to specify in any clear terms.

In work on grammatical theory or internal reconstruction of proto-languages there is, of course, little need to go beyond the ordinary grammatical statement. But claims for the applicability of formal linguistics are usually much broader.

Since the 1940's, for example, the importance of descriptive analysis in the construction of foreign language texts has been emphasized. This emphasis has been justified to a large extent. Contrastive analysis of grammatical systems serves as the basis for drill materials which have been strikingly effective in teaching the ability to produce grammatical sentences in a new language. But it is also fair to say that we have not been completely successful in providing students with the linguistic ability they need to communicate effectively in speech communities where these languages are spoken. Problems of this type are especially severe in Asia, where the learners encounter a radically different cultural environment.

Consider the case of an American who, after completing the conventional language course and having attained reasonable fluency in spoken Hindi, arrives in New Delhi, the capital of India. In his background reading he has most probably learned that Hindi is not the only language spoken there, that many of the educated classes speak English, and that in addition Urdu, Punjabi, and a variety of other local dialects are used.

Since he has grown up in a monolingual community, however, he has little idea of what this multilingual situation implies for day-to-day communication. He therefore tends to be unprepared for the problems he finds.

A typical difficulty, which is the subject of frequent complaints by returning students, concerns the lack of opportunity to use and practice the Hindi that had so laboriously been learned. Wherever the Westerner goes, in hotels, in shops, at parties, in public offices, Indians address him in English. Their English may be barely intelligible but, nevertheless, he is given little opportunity to switch to Hindi. On occasion, when with a group of Indians, he may find his companions talking among themselves in highly abbreviated, idiomatic Hindi, or even in what seems like a mixture of English and Hindi. Nevertheless, they address him only in English, almost as if they were capitalizing on the language barrier in order to exclude him from the intimacy of their in-group relations.

When, in spite of all this, the Westerner does insist on speaking Hindi, he is frequently misunderstood. Some interlocutors will object to the conversational forms he has learned on the grounds that they are Hindustani, sometimes called *khaanaa khaaoo,* "eat your food," forms. These were used by the English in their relations with Indian servants, but are not regarded as suitable for free India. On the other hand, the Westerner's attempts to employ expressions such as *maaf kiijiyee,* "excuse me," as mere politeness formulas are inappropriate, as Indians use such expressions only to beg forgiveness for a real wrong. Similarly, polite forms of address when used with porters, waiters and similar service personnel, produce awkwardness rather than appreciation.

When questioned about the appropriateness of particular forms, native speakers commonly give conflicting responses. Interminable arguments may arise over the proper form of the subject pronoun and the direct object in sentences such as "he knows it," in which Hindi has several alternates:

$$
\left\{ \begin{array}{l} \text{wah} \\ \text{woo} \end{array} \right. \quad \left\{ \begin{array}{l} \text{us-koo} \\ \text{us-ee} \end{array} \right. \quad \text{jaantaa hai}
$$

he   it-to   knows.

Since native speakers contradict each other, the Westerner hardly knows where to turn.

In sum, learning appropriate Hindi usage in a modern Indian city is a difficult and frustrating task—almost as difficult as learning the grammar in the first place. Since our textbooks provide no guidance for this task, the result is that an unusually large proportion of Westerners in India tend after a while to drop their efforts at mastering the vernacular and revert to using English on all occasions. It seems necessary, therefore, at least for the purposes of applied linguistics, to reopen the question of the relationship between linguistic and social facts. More specifically, the question arises: given a grammatical analysis of the languages involved, what additional information can the sociolinguist provide in order to enable the language teacher to give his students the skills they need to communicate effectively in a new society?

This discussion suggests a somewhat different approach to the problem than that taken by Katz and Fodor. They, along with most linguists, tend to be concerned primarily with the cognitive functions of language. They look at language almost exclusively in terms of the way in which objects and concepts are encoded through verbal signs. In language instruction, however, our concern is also with behavior, as it affects language usage. The question, then, is not how to specify the relation between words and sociophysical settings in more detail, but rather, given several alternate ways of formulating a message, which of these is most appropriate according to the social norms of the particular occasion. Contrastive analysis furnishes the relevant grammatical patterns; what we need is information on the social factors which govern the employment of grammatically acceptable alternates.

Modern social anthropologists have formulated a set of concepts for the study of social interaction which seem general enough to apply to linguistic as well as to non-linguistic behavior, and which may be useful for the present discussion. In this framework the actions of individuals within particular settings may be analyzed in terms of their status, i.e., the positions they occupy within the social system, as defined by the rights and duties which the culture assigns to such positions. A person may act as a father, as a friend, as a judge, a customer, etc. In each case his behavior is determined by different norms. The term 'social relationship' may be used to describe interaction between two or more statuses. Every society has a finite number of such relationships, and each carries certain social norms. Some common examples are the father-son, customer-salesman, husband-wife relationships, etc. The daily round of activities in a society can be regarded as segmented into a series of distinct social occasions (Goffman, 1963)—more or less closely defined behavioral routines which are kept separate by members of a society. For example, we eat breakfast, travel to the office, participate in meetings, go out on dates, etc. In each such social occasion only a limited number of social relationships may occur. Thus, behavioral norms applying to any particular speech event should be predictable from knowledge of the social occasion and of the social relationships involved. What follows is an attempt to apply some of these concepts to problems of language usage.

Basic to the present approach is the assumption, also suggested in the work of scholars such as Brown and Gilman (1960) and Fischer (1958), that language usage reflects the quality of social relationships in particular social occasions. In dealing with linguistic phenomena in this way, we are thus operating in a new "ethnographic" dimension (Hymes, 1964) where linguistic alternates are grouped not in terms of their purely linguistic similarity, but in terms of the norms which govern their usage. We therefore introduce the concept of linguistic or verbal repertoire (Gumperz, 1964 and 1965), defined as the totality of linguistic forms regularly employed within the community in the course of socially significant interaction. Repertoires in turn can be regarded as consisting of speech varieties, each associated with particular kinds of social relationships. In monolingual speech communities, such as we find in the highly industrialized societies of the West, repertoires tend to be co-extensive with the linguists' grammars. The difference is that many of the speech varieties which must be recognized on social grounds are so similar linguistically that they have not been noted in ordinary grammars. In linguistically diverse speech communities like the one we find in Delhi, on the other hand, constituent varieties may require separate though related grammars. Switching among languages in communities of the latter type has the social function similar to stylistic switching in monolingual communities (Rubin, 1961). The linguistic repertoire, therefore, is a general concept which allows us to compare any two communities in terms of the way in which internal speech distribution reflects social structure, regardless of any pre-established criteria of linguistic homogeneity or heterogeneity.

To make formal statements of the relationship between social norms and language choice would, in view of our present limited knowledge, be a formidable task. It would require ethnographies much more detailed than we now have available. For the purpose of language instruction, however, the anthropologists' experience, based on several years of participant observation of interaction in typically Indian small town and village contexts, can at least provide a useful approximation. The Hindi teaching materials prepared at the University of California (Gumperz and Rumery, 1962) attempt to utilize this experience to make at least a beginning in the direction of introducing realism of social context into a language course.

A brief survey of common encounter types found in Indian and American societies reveals some important differences. Dating, parties governed by complete informality of relations, casual gatherings in doctors' offices or other public locations such as have been described by Hall in his popular *The Silent Language* (1959) are, for example, unknown in India. On the other hand, some common Indian practices have no Western counterpart. Consider, for example, the *puja,* or meditation period, which many Indians observe daily and which involves a half hour or more of silence. A Western visitor arriving during such a period will be completely ignored. If he is familiar with the local custom, he will leave without speaking and return later, or he will sit unobtrusively until the meditation period is over. Lack of acquaintance with such behavior, on the other hand, may cause awkwardness or misunderstanding. In other instances, what on the surface seem like similar encounters carry radically different behavioral norms in the two societies. It is, for example, usually inappropriate in India to discuss an interlocutor's wife and family in a casual encounter.

A crucial characteristic of Indian society in this respect is the importance placed on the interlocutors' formal status in most types of interaction. In the bulk of encounters outside the family and close friendship circles individuals are treated as occupying statuses, rather than as individuals. This fact is, as a rule, symbolized by verbal clues. Different greetings and different modes of address are used for Hindus, Muslims, officials, friends, respected elders, etc. A switch from Hindi to Urdu to English may have similar status-marking functions.

The need for such status markers is dropped only in personal interaction among friends. In view of the severe social barriers to interpersonal friendships, however, such friendship relations are considerably more difficult to achieve in Indian society than in Western societies. In a sense, therefore, we can say that the Indian's persistent attempts to use English in interaction with Westerners serves as a boundary maintenance device marking the social differences involved. This can be overcome only after long periods of close contact.

It might be objected that since selection of linguistic form is ultimately a matter of individual choice, individuals might easily be induced to change their attitudes. Ethnographic experience suggests that this is easier said than done. Behavioral norms such as those referred to here are, as a rule, deeply ingrained since childhood. They form part of unconscious linguistic behavior (Levi-Strauss, 1964) in much the same way that purely linguistic habits do. They are violated only at the risk of considerable social disapproval, and such violation usually results in extreme conflict on the part of individuals involved. The recent 'foul speech' controversy at the University of California in Berkeley, involving the public use of four-letter words, is a case in point. On the surface, all the individuals involved did was to exercise their freedom of choice. But in doing so they violated one of our most firmly held social norms governing conduct at public meetings, exposing themselves thereby to the ire of all concerned. Reactions to the foreigner's stylistically inappropriate speech in India is, of course, never so extreme, but nevertheless it may cause considerable discomfort.

An important task in constructing a socially realistic conversational sequence is, then, to isolate those encounter types in which a newly arrived Westerner might have occasion to use his Hindi. Since much of the Westerner's life is spent in Western-type, specially constructed, insulated residential colonies and modern shopping districts which confine him to contact with the Western-trained elite and keep him from intimate contact with typically Indian society, this proves to be not as simple as it may seem. Here the Westerner is restricted to meeting Indians who are bilingual in English and who, for the reasons explained above, tend to have little understanding of his efforts to practice Hindi. When contact with the few monolinguals who penetrate these enclaves becomes necessary, a host of bilingual intermediaries are ever ready to interpret and thus preserve him from direct contact with them.

Special efforts will therefore have to be made to find monolingual Indian settings where these difficulties may be overcome. The Westerner will have to seek out native bazaars or small provincial towns and learn to insist on dealing with monolinguals, avoiding English-speaking intermediaries. Only after considerable length of stay in the country and after acquiring a knowledge of the situational proprieties of language usage, when he has established close friendship ties with Indians, can the Westerner expect to converse freely in Hindi with his interlocutors.

After setting up a list of likely conversational situations and identifying each with respect to their cultural labels, these situations and the statuses of participants can then be graded in terms of their social complexity and in terms of the amount of knowledge of the culture that they require. The Indian bazaar behavior provides a convenient starting point for such an arrangement. In a country as diverse as India, the bazaar provides a neutral meeting place, where distinctions of caste and ethnic background remain suspended in social interaction. All actors become vendors or customers, regardless of their social background. Bazaar language thus shows relatively simple lexicon and sentence structures and avoids complex patterns of greetings and social introductions and politeness formulas.

Beginning with bazaar situations, it is possible to establish a range of complexity ranging from interaction with uneducated service personnel such as shoemakers and washermen, dealings with drivers of horse- or bicycle-drawn public conveyances, tourist guides in out-of-the-way places, conversations with fellow passengers on trains, to informal friendship relations with social equals and discussions on literary and political topics, towards the end of the scale.

As a next step in the preparation of the text, each encounter was enacted on the scene with a Westerner and actual Indian shopkeepers, service personnel, etc., as actors, and recorded by means of sequence photography. A set of color slides was then selected to represent conversation content somewhat in the way in which comic strip artists represent action. Texts to fit each slide set were then written by linguist-native speakers associated with the project. The conversations served as the basis for pronunciation and grammar drills such as those found in ordinary spoken language texts.

The Berkeley Hindi materials have now been in use for about two years at a number of institutions throughout the country. On the whole, native speakers tend to agree that the texts are appropriate to the social occasions illustrated. Students returning from India have commented on the 'realism' of the course. But the contextual approach also has a number of advantages for the purely linguistic content of the course.

Linguists, for example, have long objected to the educator's preference for word frequency counts, claiming that they are time-consuming and do not necessarily produce significant results. The procedure followed here makes word frequency counts unnecessary. If the encounter type is accurately defined, then the vocabulary which is appropriate to it by definition also has the proper frequency distribution.

More importantly, the association of stylistic variants with visual and social clues provides the student with a natural introduction to the social factors which underlie the style switching which is so important in India. English loans and even entire Indian English slang phrases will appear natural in student conversations. Urdu pronunciations and lexicon will correlate with Muslim dress and gestures, etc. It is even possible to switch styles within the same encounter and change from what Indians call 'chaste' Hindi to Westernized Hindi to Urdu within the same conversation, provided such changes are justified by the status relationship of participants within the encounter. Thus a speaker may use the Urdu *tashriif rakhiyee* in asking a Muslim to sit down, and then turn to someone with the Hindi equivalent, *padhaariyee,* for the same message.

The initial assumption regarding the dependence of linguistic form on social setting receives partial confirmation from the fact that in our text grammatical grading of conversational material emerges as a natural consequence of contextual grading. For example, among the important grammatical distinctions between Hindi and English are case-gender-number agreement of nouns and verbs and the verbal tense-mood system. Agreement is more basic to the system since it affects both nouns and verbs. It would be ideal therefore if problems of verb morphology could be left aside while agreement is practiced. The bazaar situations allow us to do just that with natural Hindi conversations, since the only verb forms that appear are the morphologically simple request forms.

In other cases our approach provides criteria for choosing among what would otherwise seem freely alternating modes of expression. Thus sentences like the *woo us-koo jaantaa hai* 'he knows it,' cited above, alternate with *pataa hai* (literally, 'knowledge exists'). The former occurs frequently in texts elicited by the usual linguist-informant interview method. With its subject-object-verb structure it is a relatively close translation equivalent of English and hence it might seem natural on grounds of ease of learning to emphasize it in drill materials. The latter expression shows a noun plus auxiliary type predication, somewhat more difficult for Americans to learn. It is, however, very common in informal Hindi, and furthermore has close parallels in local dialects and other South Asian languages. In general, wherever alternate Hindi expressions are possible, contextual eliciting tends to select those alternates with more direct translation equivalents in other Indian languages, whereas linguist-informant eliciting technique yields a higher proportion of English-like constructions.

Our examination of social interaction has revealed some important differences between behavioral norms in the American and North Indian speech communities. Further work in South Indian, Dravidian-speaking speech communities seems to indicate that behavioral norms there are quite similar to those in North India. Thus Tamil-speaking informants, when shown slide sequences taken in North India, seem to have no difficulty in producing natural conversations to fit these sequences. Indications are, therefore, that while the contextual approach requires considerable additional work, once an analysis is made it may at least in part be transferable to other speech communities within that culture area, resulting in a considerable gain in generality.

REFERENCES CITED

Bloomfield, Leonard (1926) "A set of postulates for the science of language," *Language* 2:153-156.

Brown, Roger W. and H. Gilman (1960) "The pronouns of power and solidarity," *Style in Language,* Thomas A. Sebeok, ed. New York, Wiley, p. 253-276.

Fischer, John L. (1958) "Social influences on the choice of a linguistic variant," *Word* 14:47-56.

Goffman, Irving (1963) *Behavior in public places.* Glencoe: Free Press.

Gumperz, John J. (1964) "Linguistic and social interaction in two communities," *American Anthropologist* 66: no. 6, 137-153. (1965) "Some desiderata in South Asian areal linguistics," *Indian Linguistics,* in press.

Gumperz, John J. and June Rumery (1962) *Conversational Hindu-Urdu.* Berkeley, Institute of International Studies, University of California.

Hall, Edward T. (1959) *The Silent Language.* Garden City, New York, Doubleday and Co.

Hymes, Dell (1964) "Toward ethnographies of communication," *American Anthropologist,* 66, no. 6, 1-34.

Katz, Jerrold J. and Jerry A. Fodor (1963) "The structure of a semantic theory," *Language* 39:170-210.

Levi-Strauss, Claude (1964) "Structural analysis in linguistics and anthropology," in *Language in Culture and Society, A Reader in Linguistics and Anthropology,* Dell Hymes, ed. New York, Harper and Row.

Rubin, Joan (1961) "Bilingualism in Paraguay," *Anthropological Linguistics* 4:52-58.

SYNTAX AND THE CONSUMER

MICHAEL A. K. HALLIDAY

University College London

At the Seventh Annual Round Table Meeting, held at the Institute of Languages and Linguistics in 1956, Professor Archibald Hill read a paper entitled 'Who needs linguistics?'. In it he referred to "the kinds of people who can now be shown to be in need of linguistic knowledge for practical reasons", including among them teachers of foreign languages and of the native language, literary scholars and those concerned with the study of mental disorders. His concluding paragraph contained the words "It is the linguists who need linguistics. . . . It is we who have the task of making linguistics sufficiently adult, and its results sufficiently available so that all people of good will, who work within the field of language, language art, and language usage, can realize that there are techniques and results which are of value to them".

Professor Hill could, if he had wished, have added others to the list; what he was emphasizing, as I understand it, was that any benefits which those other than the linguists themselves may derive from linguistic work depends on the linguists' own pursuit and presentation of their subject. Within those areas of activity, often referred to as 'applied linguistics', in which languages are described for other than purely explanatory purposes, the linguist's task is that of describing language; and he will not, for example, attempt to tell the language teacher what to teach or how to teach it, nor claim to be a pediatrician because his work may contribute to studies of language development in children.

While recognizing the limitations on their own role, however, linguists are not unaware of the needs of the consumer. Language may be described for a wide range of purposes; or, if that is begging the question I want to ask, there is a wide range of purposes for which a description of language may be used. The question is: do these various aims presuppose different ways of using the same description, or are they best served by descriptions of different kinds? Is there one single 'best description' of a language, or are there various possible 'best descriptions' according to the purpose in view?

One of the many important contributions made by Chomsky has been his insistence that linguists should define the goals of a linguistic theory. According to his own well-known formulation, the grammar should provide a complete specification of an infinite set of grammatical sentences of the language, enumerating all sentences and no non-sentences, and automatically assign to them structural descriptions. The theory should include a function for the evaluation of grammars, so that a choice can be made among different grammars all of which fulfill these requirements. The grammar can then be validated for compatibility with the given data and evaluated for relative simplicity.[1]

Associated with this is the underlying aim that "the formalized grammar is intended to be a characterization of certain of the abilities of a mature speaker"; "we would like the structural description to be the basis for explaining a great deal of what the speaker knows to be true of speech events, beyond their degree of well-formedness".[2] Compare also Katz and Fodor's formulation: "Grammars answer the question: What does the speaker know about the phonological and syntactic structure of his language that enables him to use and understand any of its sentences, including those he has not previously heard?",[3] and Chomsky's summing-up: "As I emphasized earlier, the central problem in developing such a theory is to specify precisely the form of grammars—the schema for grammatical description that constitutes, in effect, a theory of linguistic universals and a hypothesis concerning the specific nature of the innate intellectual equipment of the child".[4]

The evaluation of a linguistic description means, naturally, its evaluation in the light of the goals recognized for the theory. A formalized grammar is evaluated for its success in achieving the aims of a formalized grammar, or of that particular formalized grammar; the relevance of this evaluation to any other aims will depend in part on the extent to which a formalized model yields the kind of description that is most appropriate to them. That

---

[1] See for example Noam Chomsky 'Explanatory models in linguistics', *Logic, methodology and philosophy of science* (Stanford: U.P., 1962); 'On the notion "rule of grammar" ', *Structure of language and its mathematical aspects* (Providence: American Mathematical Society, 1961); 'The Logical basis of linguistic theory', *Proceedings of the Ninth International Congress of Linguists, (to appear)*.

[2] 'Explanatory models in linguistics' pp. 531-2.

[3] Jerrold J. Katz and Jerry A. Fodor 'The Structure of a semantic theory,' *Language*, 39, 2, (1963), 172.

[4] 'Explanatory models in linguistics' p. 550.

there are other possible aims is not, I think, in question; to quote Chomsky again, "I do not, by any means, intend to imply that these are the only aspects of linguistic competence that deserve serious study",[5] to which I would like to add that linguistic competence is not the only aspect of language that deserves serious study: the explanation of linguistic performance can also perhaps be regarded as a reasonable goal and one that is still, as it were, internal to linguistics. But I would also wish to include, among the possible goals of linguistic theory, the description of language for the purpose of various specific applications; goals which may be thought of as external to linguistics but for which linguistics is part of the essential equipment.

This is not of course to question the validity and importance of the goals defined by Chomsky; nor is it to suggest that, given these specific goals, the model that provides the 'best description' will not be of the type he specifies. But we should not perhaps take it for granted that a description in terms of a formalized model, which has certain properties lacking in those derived from models of other kinds, will necessarily be the best description for all of the very diverse purposes for which descriptions of languages are needed.[6] In assessing the value of a description, it is reasonable to ask whether it has proved useful for the purposes for which it is intended; and such purposes may be external as well as internal to linguistics.

There tends no doubt to be some correlation between the model a particular linguist adopts for his own work and the place where he grew up, linguistically speaking. Nevertheless I would defend the view that different coexisting models in linguistics may best be regarded as appropriate to different aims, rather than as competing contenders for the same goal. One may have one's own private opinions about the relative worth and interest of these various aims, but rather in the same way as most of us probably like the sound of some of the languages we study better than we like that of others. Estimates of the relative attainability of different goals may be more objective, although even here the criteria for the assessment of one goal as more difficult of attainment than another can probably be made explicit only where the two are basically different stages in the pursuit of a single more general aim. It is difficult to measure the relative demands made on a theory by requirements such as, on the one hand, that "the structural description of a sentence must provide an account of all gram-

---

[5] *Ibid.* p. 530 n.

[6] This is of course a different question from that of the relative evaluation of different formalized grammars.

matical information in principle available to the native speaker" [7] and on the other hand that the grammar should be of help to the student learning a foreign language or to the pediatrician in his diagnosis and treatment of retarded speech development; nor is it any easier to measure the degree of success of a description in meeting these demands.

Yet in spite of the difficulty of measuring attainment linguists 'intuitively' —that is, by their experience as linguists—recognize a good description, and most of them seem to agree in their judgments. This is not in any way surprising, but it illustrates an important point: that linguistic theory is no substitute for descriptive insight. Naturally different descriptions of a language will follow when different models are used to describe it; but the differences imposed by the model tend to obscure the similarities, and also the differences, in the linguists' interpretation of the facts. It is true, in the first place, that two descriptions will differ precisely and directly because different models are being used and these impose different kinds of statement. In the second place, however, the descriptions may differ because the linguists disagree at certain points in their interpretations. And in the third place the models themselves may impose different interpretations, either because one solution is simpler in one model and another in the other or because they have different terms of reference and different aims.

For example, transformational grammars of English recognize a passive transformation relating such pairs of sentences as *the man eats cake* and *cake is eaten by the man*. The analogue in a 'scale-and-category' grammar (to use a name by which the version of a system-structure grammar that my colleagues and I have been working with has come to be known) would be a system at clause rank whose terms are active and passive: as for example the question transformation is paralleled by a clause system whose terms are affirmative (transformational grammar's 'declarative') and inter-rogative. In fact no system of voice at clause rank is introduced into our present description of English. We could say that this is because it does not represent our interpretation of the facts. But the question is: what 'facts' are being interpreted? The 'system' implies proportionality: given a system whose terms are a, b, c, then the set of their exponents a_1 a_2 a_3, . . ., b_1 b_2 b_3 . . ., c_1 c_2 c_3 . . . are proportionally related: $a_1 : b_1 : c_1 :: a_2 : b_2 : c_2$ and so on. This holds good, it seems to us, to a reasonable extent (such that the simplicity of the general statement is not outweighed by the complexity of further statements that are required to qualify it) of affirmative and interrogative in the clause, and of active and passive in the

---

[7] Paul Postal, *Constituent Structure, IJAL,* 30, (1964); Publication 30 of the Indiana University Research Center in Anthropology, Folklore and Linguistics, p. 3.

verbal group where the description does recognize a system of voice; but not of active and passive in the clause. In other words, *John was invited by Mary, this house was built by my grandfather, the driver was injured by flying glass, John's been dismissed from his job* and *it was announced that the committee had resigned* are not explained as all standing in the same relation to a set of their active counterparts. Such a relationship is shown, but indirectly (as the product of a number of systemic relations) and not always by the same route.

But this does not necessarily imply different notions about English; it may simply mean a difference in what is being required of the description. While there may be some similarity between the system in a scale-and-category grammar and the transformation in a transformational grammar, in the sense that instances of the two often correspond, they are not and cannot be saying the same thing, because these are different kinds of model.[8] The nature of a grammatical description, in fact, is determined as a whole by the properties of the model in which it has status, as well as being conditioned by the goals that lie behind the model.[9]

If I were asked to characterize the work in which I have been engaged together with some of my colleagues, I would say that our aim is to show the patterns inherent in the linguistic performance of the native speaker: this is what we mean by 'how the language works'. This presupposes a general description of those patterns which the linguist considers to be primary in the language, a description which is then variably extendable, on the 'scale of delicacy', in depth of detail. It involves a characterization of the special features, including statistical properties, of varieties of the language used for different purposes ('registers'), and the comparison of

---

[8] The issue is **not** whether, as Katz and Fodor say ('The Structure of a semantic theory' p. 206) "sentences that are related to each other by the passive transformation . . . have the same meaning, except perhaps in instances where quantities are involved". The system does have implications for the grammatical semantics, but not this one; it implies that exponents differing only in respect of the selection in question (i) differ in meaning but (ii) differ in a regular way. Thus exponents of different terms in a system by definition have not the same meaning; but this merely illustrates the fact that the line between 'have' and 'have not the same meaning', like that between grammar(/lexis) and semantics, is drawn by the theory (or rather, by the description and in the light of the theory).

[9] Compare Chomsky, on the procedures by which different structural descriptions are assigned ('Explanatory models in linguistics' p. 534), "These specifications must involve no appeal to the intelligence or linguistic intuition of the reader because it is just this that we are attempting to characterize". I use here the term 'grammatical description' in preference to Chomsky's 'structural description' since in this model the description of an item is (by definition) structural-systemic.

individual texts, spoken and written, including literary texts. This in turn is seen as a linguistic contribution towards certain further aims, such as literary scholarship, native and foreign language teaching, educational research, sociological and anthropological studies and medical applications. The interest is focussed not on what the native speaker knows of his language but rather on what he does with it; one might perhaps say that the orientation is primarily textual and, in the widest sense, sociological.

The study of written and spoken texts for such purposes requires an analysis of at least sentence, clause and group structures and systems, with extension where possible above the rank of sentence. The analysis needs to be simple in use and in notation, variable in delicacy and easily processed for statistical studies; it needs to provide a basis for semantic statements, and to handle with the minimum complexity grammatical contrasts such as those in English expounded by intonation and rhythm; and it should idealize as little as possible, in the sense of excluding the minimum as 'deviant'. Idealization of course there is; as Putnam has said, "I shall assume here that some degree of idealization is inevitable in linguistic work, and I shall also assume that the question of how much idealization is legitimate is one that has no general answer. . . . Anyone who writes a grammar of any natural language is . . . automatically classifying certain sentences as non-deviant, and by implication, certain others as deviant".[10] For our purposes it is important that as much as possible of ordinary speech should be shown to be—that is, described as—non-deviant; in this analysis spoken English is much less formless, repetitive and elliptical than it might appear in another kind of description. But there are deviant utterances, and it is important to specify in what ways they are deviant.

For a brief, and necessarily oversimplified, illustration of one feature of the sort of description that we are attempting I shall refer to the **scale of delicacy** which, besides being of theoretical interest in providing a measure of the status of a given contrast in the language, and of the degree and kind of deviation of deviant utterances,[11] has proved of value in textual analysis because it provides a variable cut-off point for description: the analyst can go as far as he wishes for his own purpose in depth of detail and then stop. Delicacy can be illustrated with reference either to structure or to system; the present example relates it to the category of system.

Delicacy is in effect a means of having things both ways: that is, of saying that two utterances are both like and unlike each other at the same

---

[10] Hilary Putnam, 'Some issues in the theory of grammar', *Structure of language and its mathematical aspects,* p. 26.

[11] This is analogous to the procedure suggested by Chomsky in 'Some methodological remarks on generative grammar', *Word,* 17, (1961), 236-7.

time. Any two utterance tokens, of any extent, may be alike in one of two ways: they may be occurrences of the same formal item (tokens of the same type), or they may be different formal item exponents of the same grammatical categories (tokens of different types with the same grammatical description).

Both types of likeness are properties of the description: that is, it is the linguist who decides what are occurrences of the same item and what are different items with the same grammatical description. One possible decision of course is always to aim at maximal differentiation of tokens into types: this seems to be the point of view taken by Katz and Fodor when they write "almost every sentence uttered is uttered for the first time", since this can presumably only mean that the criteria adopted for token-to-type assignment should be such that almost every sentence uttered will be **described** as being uttered for the first time.[12] This would no doubt reflect a desire that the description should be capable of making all distinctions that the native speaker recognizes; this does not provide criteria, though it may be used to test their adequacy.[13] But token-to-type assignment is one point where the native speaker's intuitions tend to be most uncertain,[14] and this uncertainty reflects the multiple nature of the type-token relation in language: two utterances may be tokens of the same orthographic type

---

[12] 'The Structure of a semantic theory' p. 171. Such an assertion cannot be 'substantiated': it is true or false by definition, as is shown by the suggested procedure for its substantiation, "checking texts for the number of times a sentence is repeated". On any reasonable interpretation of the grammatical type-token relation the repetition rate for sentences would obviously be low, although it might be predictably rather than indefinitely low. (Extrapolation from the repetition rate for morphemes, words and groups in English in a manageable sample of texts would permit the prediction of at least the order of magnitude of the average repetition rate of clauses and sentences; there is no reason to assume that the sentence is unique in this respect—the group already admits recursive structures, for example.) Cf. Dwight L. Bolinger, 'Syntactic blends and other matters', *Language,* 37, (1961), 381: "At present we have no way of telling the extent to which a sentence like *I went home* is the result of innovation, and the extent to which it is a result of repetition, countless speakers before us having already said it and transmitted it to us in toto". To say this is of course in no way to deny or minimize the ability of the fluent speaker "to produce and understand sentences never before encountered"—and, one might add, clauses, groups and words.

[13] The point is made by Chomsky with regard to grammaticalness: see 'Explanatory models in linguistics' p. 533.

[14] That is, his intuition as to what are tokens of the same type and what are grammatically similar types; cf. Putnam, 'Some issues in the theory of grammar' pp. 36-37. Putnam concludes his discussion of this point by remarking "here we are reminded that linguistics is after all a social science and that its fundamental concepts have the same kind of dispositional and human character as do the fundamental concepts of any other social science".

but not of the same phonological type (the same 'expression'), or vice versa, and neither determines whether or not they are tokens of the same formal type (grammatical or grammatico-lexical, according to the model).[15]

Whatever the criteria adopted for token-to-type assignment, the question whether these items (types) are or are not assigned the same grammatical description is one to which it may be useful to be able to answer 'both yes and no'. What this means, however, depends on the ordering in delicacy of the systems by which they are related and differentiated. Suppose for example that, of a set of clauses (items of clause rank) in English, it is required to describe each of those in set (1) as distinct from all the others, but without taking into account any further related distinctions such as that represented in set (2).

(1) 1 *the Smiths are having a party this evening*
     2 *it's the Smiths that are having a party this evening*
     3 *a party the Smiths are having this evening*
     4 *it's a party that the Smiths are having this evening*

(2) 1 *the Smiths are having a party this evening*
     5 *they're having a party this evening the Smiths.*

Out of the total set of systems operating in the system-complex of 'theme', in which selection is made by the clause in English, it would be possible to isolate the systems shown in (3).

(3)

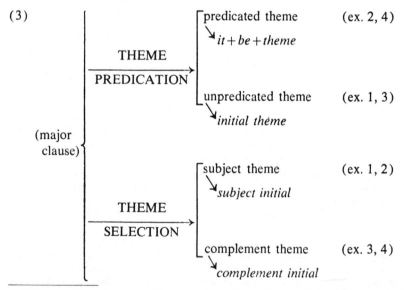

――――――
[15] One could perhaps specify that where two utterance tokens have potentially (with maximal delicacy) different formal descriptions they are shown ipso facto to

With the cut-off at this point, the clauses in set (2) have the same grammatical description. In order to discriminate between them, the further distinction shown in (4) may be introduced; the members of set (2) will then have different grammatical descriptions.

(4)

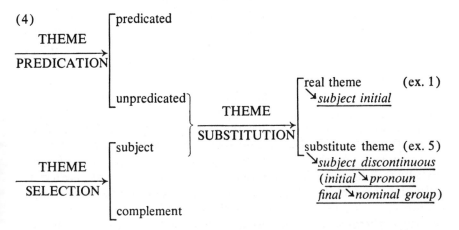

(Notes to (3) and (4)) The right-facing brace indicates simultaneous selection; the left-facing brace multiple (conjunct) derivation; the right-facing square bracket indicates the terms in a system. Names of systems are shown in upper case, names of terms in systems in lower case. The horizontal arrow means 'is related by delicacy to'; the diagonal arrow 'is related by exponence to (is expounded by)'. For simplicity, generalized statement of exponents (shown in italic), relating only to affirmative clauses, has been substituted for the structural notation.[16]

---

be tokens of different types; but if we go no further than this it is at least questionable whether almost every sentence uttered will be described as being uttered for the first time. The native speaker may not always go as far. He might well consider *he helped me do it* and *he helped me to do it* as 'different sentences', though their distinction can be ignored at least until a very late stage in delicacy, but //1 ∧ he / helped me to / *do* it// and //4 ∧ he / helped me to / *do* it //, or the former and //1 he / *helped* me to / do it //, or all three (notation as in my 'The Tones of English', *Archivum Linguisticum*, 15, (1963), as 'the same sentence', although these contrasts are of a high order of generality and should, in my opinion, be reflected in the assignment of tokens distinguished in this way to different types. Here the observer is likely to be in the familiar position where his intervention modifies the observation, since an inquiry will call attention to the distinction.

[16] Only nominal themes have been considered here; in fact the theme selection system covers also the selection of non-nominal elements as thematic. Other related systems have been omitted, for example that of **information focus** expounded by tonicity, which distinguishes // ∧ the / Smiths are / having a / party this / *evening* // from // ∧ the / Smiths are / having a / *party* this / evening // and so on.

Substitution as such is not of course restricted to the **thematic element:** compare *a party they're having this evening the Smiths, we've invited them the Smiths, I call it a good idea to do that;* but the thematic element can be 'substitute' only if it is both subject and unpredicated, and this would justify the treatment of **theme substitution** as a separate system.[17] Theme substitution is required, incidentally, to explain a number of ambiguities, as for example *they're leaving the others* (as ex. 1, or as ex. 5) and *it's the truth that we don't know* (as ex. 4 'what we don't know is the truth', or as ex. 5 'that we don't know is the truth').

Each system represents a dimension of potential discrimination in the grammatical description of items. Thus where one system is shown as derived by delicacy from a term in another—that is, as hierarchically ordered in respect of another—this represents a point at which the analysis may either proceed further or stop short. At this point a pair of items distinguished only in the higher-order system have not yet been differentiated: they have the same description. When the lower-order system is taken into account, however, they have different descriptions, and are thus shown to be distinct. Here therefore the answer 'both yes and no', to the question whether such items have or have not the same grammatical description, means as it were 'first yes, then no'.

The ordering of two systems in this way, by derivation in delicacy, means that freedom to select in the lower-order system is conditional on the selection made in the higher-order system. The illustration above shows multiple derivation, in which two higher-order systems are involved: only the conjunction of **subject theme** with **unpredicated theme** permits selection between **real theme** and **substitute theme.** Simple derivation could be illustrated by **theme polarity,** where freedom to select positive or negative depends on the selection of predicated theme in the **theme predication system:** *it's a party the Smiths are having this evening* contrasts with *it isn't a party the Smiths are having this evening.*

Where two systems are simultaneously ordered in delicacy as are theme selection and theme predication above, this means that they are shown as being related (derived from a common point of origin) but with no restriction on the combination of their terms. Each item that selects in the one system thus selects also unconditionally in the other. If two items

---

[17] In other words *it's they that are having a party this evening the Smiths* and *(it's) them that we've invited the Smiths* are regarded as representing different selections, since they seem to demand double tonality (two tone groups). If in fact they are no different from other 'substitute' clause-types, they are fully accounted for by 'substitution' as a simultaneous system.

are differentiated in the one system but not in the other, the question whether such items have or have not the same grammatical description might still be answered 'both yes and no', but here this would mean 'partly yes, partly no', or 'in this respect yes, in that respect no'.

These two kinds of ordering in delicacy, the hierarchical and the simultaneous, may be used to represent the simple relations of dependence and independence between systems: fully dependent systems are ordered hierarchically, fully independent systems simultaneously. More often than not, however, the linguist is faced with systems displaying one or another of various kinds of partial dependence, where selection in one system is partly conditional on selection in another: the relation of theme substitution to the other two systems above is in fact one of partial dependence.[18] Such systems may be shown either as hierarchical or as simultaneous in delicacy; nor are they necessarily all to be treated in the same way, since they fall into different types.[19]

Perhaps I might conclude with an illustration from familiar material in English of a grammatical feature which is connected with one kind of partial dependence between systems: this is the apparent 'neutralization' (in one of the many senses of this word) of systemic distinctions. Such 'neutralizations' are related to, though not exactly coterminous with, Bolinger's category of 'syntactic blends'.[20]

Clauses in English containing, as predicator, a verbal group in the passive and, as adjunct, a prepositional group initiated by *by* yield examples such as *he was deceived by a trick* where it does not seem to matter whether the prepositional group is considered as agentive or as instrumental: whether, in other words, the voice/theme contrast is with *a trick deceived*

---

[18] Partial dependence of this kind is indicated as hierarchical derivation with the derived system having as 'unmarked term', here 'real theme'. The difference between the selection of an unmarked term in a system and non-selection in the system in question is that the former implies choice: thus while *the Smiths have invited us* contrasts with *they've invited us the Smiths,* there is no parallel clause-item corresponding to *the Smiths we've invited.* A similar example would be the restriction of thematic selection in 'WH- clauses': *who did he ask, where did he go* contrast with *he asked who, he went where,* but there is no corresponding item in contrast with *who did it.*

[19] Systems in partial dependence are well described by the use of matrices as developed by Pike: see Kenneth L. Pike, 'Dimensions of grammatical constructions', *Language,* 38, (1962); from the point of view of ordering in the scale of delicacy this represents a form of simultaneity. Partial dependence may also be manifested statistically, where the selection in one system affects the relative probabilities of selection of the terms in another system.

[20] 'Syntactic blends and other matters'. Cf. *Generality, gradience and the all-or-none,* Janua Linguarum, 14, (Mouton, 'S-Gravenhage, 1961), 21.

him or with *they deceived him by a trick*. Other examples are *he was comforted by their reception of him, this is proved by Gödel's theorem* and *he was killed by a blow on the head*.

These are of course quite distinct from the ambiguities, involving agentive or instrumental on the one hand and locative on the other, such as *he was knocked down by the wall* or *she was comforted by the warm fire*. Each of these represents two discrete items and two grammatical descriptions are required, any occurrence being assigned to one only. This ambiguity arises also with active verbal group: *I'll toast it by the fire* may mean 'I'll use the fire to toast it' or 'I'll go near the fire while I toast it'; compare *hold it there by the handle* and *he came out by the back gate*.

The point at which neutralization occurs may be regarded as the intersection of two unrelated systems in partial dependence: voice in the verbal group and what we may call **agency** (agentive and instrumental) in the prepositional group, agency combining only with passive. Exponents of active and passive are of course monovalent (unambiguously identifiable), but both terms in the agency system may be expounded by prepositional group with *by*.[21]

There are restrictions, in one direction, on the classes of verb and noun: some verbs and some nouns cannot occur with the instrumental, so that *suggest* and *colleague* in *this is suggested by Gödel's theorem* and *this is proved by my colleague* seem to make these uniquely agentive. Of the two, the noun class seems the more obvious one; but animate and even human nouns can occur with active verbal group and therefore, on this criterion, instrumentally: *they make their money by their travelling salesmen, he does his correspondence by a secretary.* Moreover in many instances it is difficult to specify what marks a particular item as clearly agentive: this often seems to result from the collocation of noun and verb together.

Since the word-class restriction is both indeterminate and one-way, it seems useful to consider agentive and instrumental as systemically contrasting classes of the prepositional group operating at the same place in clause structure. Since further the contrast between agentive and instrumental is one which can be neutralized, unlike that between these two on the one hand and locative on the other, the former is best treated as more delicate than the latter: that is, agentive is shown as distinct from instrumental only after the two together have been separated from the locative

---

[21] It might be considered that the agentive always has *by,* and that items such as *he was overcome with sleep* and *he was misled through his own stupidity* are 'blends' in Bolinger's sense (the latter, for example, being perhaps a crossing of *he was misled by his own stupidity* with *they were able to mislead him through his own stupidity*).

and other classes of the prepositional group. In other words, combining these two requirements, the description may show a system of agency in the prepositional group, with terms agentive and instrumental, which is in partial dependence with the system of voice in the verbal group, instrumental combining with active and passive but agency only with passive; [22] agency is in turn fully dependent on a higher-order system contrasting agentive/instrumental with locative (and others), which is fully independent of voice and where multivalent exponents are in fact ambiguous. In an analysis which stopped short of the system of agency, the ambiguities would have different grammatical descriptions but the 'neutralizations' would not.

Instances of this kind, where a systemic contrast appears to be 'neutralized', may perhaps be thought of as those where the answer 'both yes and no' to the question whether or not two items have the same grammatical description means 'both yes and no at the same time'. In other words, *by his colleagues* and *by his efforts* are both alike and different in respect of the same variable. Here possibly one single token might be said to be at the same time a token of two grammatical types: the clause occurrence *this is proved by Gödel's theorem* would represent two items with different grammatical descriptions. Be that as it may, it seems appropriate perhaps that systems which yield 'neutralizations' of this sort should appear at a lower order of delicacy than those which yield ambiguities.

This brief discussion of the scale of delicacy has been meant to serve a twofold purpose. I have hoped both to illustrate one aspect of the current work of a small group of linguists with whom I am associated, bearing in mind here the title of the present panel; and to exemplify my earlier point that the features of a description, and therefore of the model that lies behind it, are relatable to the aims of the model and through these to particular applications of linguistics. In this instance the concept of delicacy proves useful in providing a means whereby the linguist analysing a text can select a point beyond which he takes account of no further distinctions and can specify the type of relation between the different systems in which he is interested.

In speaking about one possible approach to a particular type of pattern in language, I am not implying that we handle it more effectively than other linguists working with different models, but intending to show how its treatment links up with other features of a model conceived with the specific aims we have in view. Other models will handle such patterns differently in the light of their own goals. But while accepting, and indeed

---

[22] Where, as in this instance, the systems concerned are shown as unrelated, their partial dependence appears in the description as a feature of exponence.

applauding, the fact that linguists today are working with models of different kinds, I would at the same time underline one point of which no teacher of linguistics needs to be reminded: that there exists a vast store of knowledge which is just linguistics, and common ground to all linguists whatever model they happen to be using. And I can think of no better place for saying this than at a Roundtable Meeting of this Institute, where so many of the varied interests of our subject have been and continue to be represented.

SCHIZOGLOSSIA AND THE LINGUISTIC NORM

Einar Haugen

University of Wisconsin

When I received the invitation to participate in this panel on bilingualism, I decided to take as my topic the kind of bilingualism which exists in every complex civilized community, and which I decided to call schizoglossia. While we are all familiar with it under various other names, it has not usually been considered in this connection. This led me on to ponder the conflict which arises within the individual speaker when he becomes uncertain as to what he ought to say and write because the same linguistic item is presented to him in more than one way. This raised the question of a linguistic norm and its place in society, a question which has occupied me recently in connection with a book I am writing on language planning in Norway. Not until I got the printed program of the conference did I discover that a whole section was being devoted to such problems. By this time I was stuck with my title, and if this paper would seem to belong rather in tomorrow's than today's panel, you will now understand the reason why.

Schizoglossia may be described as a linguistic malady which may arise in speakers and writers who are exposed to more than one variety of their own language. Under favorable or more precisely, unfavorable conditions, the symptoms may include acute discomfort in the region of the diaphragm and the vocal chords. If the patient refuses to "leave his language alone," we are assured by Robert A. Hall that he may also be afflicted by general insecurity, which expresses itself as "false humility" and "needless self-depreciation." The damage to his character, we are told, may be "incalculable." [1] Pursuing this thought, I may add that the victims of schizoglossia are often marked by a disproportionate, even an unbalanced interest in the form rather than the substance of language. In extreme cases they may even turn into professional linguists, just as schizophrenics sometimes become psychoanalysts in order to study in others the symptoms of their own ailment.

---

[1] Robert A. Hall. *Leave Your Language Alone.* (Ithaca, New York, 1950) p. 236.

Schizoglossia is endemic in American society, which was founded by speakers from various parts of the British Isles. It flares up at times, especially when new editions of standard dictionaries are published. Sufferers are especially common in a society where most people are socially mobile and very few know exactly where they stand. Since its germ or virus has not yet been isolated, its cure, like that of the common cold, has mostly been undertaken by quacks and other well-meaning but financially interested persons. A flourishing industry exists for the purpose of supplying the country with remedies, ranging from pocket handbooks to improve your English through evening courses in diction to huge and costly tomes of scholarship. Dr. Noah Webster diagnosed the malady to his own interest in the early years of the Republic, and set himself to rescue the populace from its Babylonic babble. With patriotic devotion this Noah of our linguistic deluge followed in the footsteps of Dr. Johnson, who in 1755 had expressed the hope that by his dictionary he might "retard what we cannot repel, palliate what we cannot cure."

The malady which Dr. Johnson wished to cure was not precisely schizoglossia, but linguistic change in general. He was realistic enough to see that codification would not inhibit it completely. The medical metaphor which I have been developing was anticipated in his Preface, where he wrote: "When we see men grow old and die at a certain time one after another, from century to century, we laugh at the elixir that promises to prolong life to a thousand years; and with equal justice may the lexicographer be derided, who being able to produce no example of a nation that has preserved their words and phrases from mutability, shall imagine that his dictionary can embalm his language and secure it from corruption and decay, that it is in his power to change sublunary nature, and clear the world at once from folly, vanity and affectation." Nevertheless, he stoutly declared his desire to make an effort: "Life may be lengthened by care, though death cannot be ultimately defeated: tongues, like governments, have a natural tendency to degeneration: we have long preserved our constitution, let us make some struggles for our language."

This point of view, so typical of the eighteenth century, is one which few American linguists would endorse today. In fact, the prevailing attitude is rather the opposite, that not only is schizoglossia not a problem, but that it is positively harmful even to try to eliminate it. Bloomfield's remarks in the last chapter of *Language* pointed the way, which has been well-trodden by his followers, including such eminent scholars as Charles C. Fries and Robert A. Hall, Jr. Hall exhorted his readers in the previously cited book to "abandon entirely the old dogmatic, normative, theological approach of traditional grammar and of social snobbery; and to substitute the relativistic, objective approach of scientific study and analysis." [2] In another passage he makes an even more sweeping condemnation of the concern of the rhetorician with what is "right" and "wrong:" "The merit of what a person says or does is not in any way affected by the way in which they say or do it, provided it is the most efficient way of saying or doing it; and to accept or reject someone just because of 'correct' or 'incorrect' speech is to show oneself superficial, lazy, and snobbish." [3]

It will be my contention in this paper that the case of linguistic relativism has here been vastly overstated, and that there is no warrant in linguistic science for the wholesale condemnation here made of normative grammar. In his eagerness to neutralize the ill effects of Miss Fidditch's rigidity, Hall has thrown out the baby with the bath. It takes only a modest amount of discourse analysis to show that in these two passages the word "normative" has been associated rhetorically with pejorative terms such as "dogmatic," "traditional," and "snobbery," while "relativistic" has been associated with favorable terms like "objective" and "scientific." It also seems unrealistic to declare that merit is unrelated to the way in which something is done. Many would hold that the manner of doing may be more important than the doing. "Correctness" may not be synonymous with grace or charm, but together with these it is a significant element in what we think of as civilized behavior. For linguists as a group to put themselves in a position of opposing normative standards is to invite a charge of cultural barbarism. In recent discussion of Webster's Third New International Dictionary it has even been contended that "structural linguistics" is behind its supposed betrayal of standards. [4]

It needs to be clearly understood that "scientific" is not necessarily identical with "tolerant." A plea for tolerance may be laudable from a moral or ethical point of view, but does not of itself follow from the premises of science. A botanist may have private opinions about the plants he studies, such as that some taste better or are more sightly than others, but in expressing these he is not speaking

2 Op. cit., 248.
3 Op. cit., 236.
4 Dwight MacDonald. New Yorker, 10 March 1962.

as a scientist and his opinions have no more validity than anyone else's. The problem of linguistic correctness involves dimensions of human behavior that are not provided for in the models which linguists usually build. I venture to go so far as to maintain that when Robert Hall tells the non-standard speakers that "there is nothing inherently wrong with your language," he is no more scientific than Miss Fidditch. He is doing his bit to eliminate snobbishness, which does honor to his good heart, but he is not being either objective or scientific.

The conflict between the dual role that linguistic scientists are sometimes called to play has been painfully evident in recent years in Norway, where schizoglossia is not endemic, but epidemic. Although there are two official written languages, it is rather a case of schizoglossia than of diglossia, since these are little more than divergent dialects of one language. The official government policy during the past 25 years has been to promote the fusion of these two languages into one compromise norm. In 1952 a Language Commission was established by act of parliament which should advise the government. The directives given to this Commission declared that its function should be to give this advice "on the basis of scientific research" and thereby "promote the mutual approach of the two written languages on the basis of Norwegian folk speech." The humanistic faculty of the University of Oslo at first refused to nominate representatives to the Commission on the plea that this formulation committed them to a particular linguistic policy which would be inconsistent with their freedom as scientists. In its comment on this stand the Ministry of Education emphasized that "a distinction must be made between linguistic research and linguistic normalization and guidance. The latter has to build on scientific research and take its results into account, but is not in itself a purely scientific problem. It is in equal, or greater, degree a national, social, or practical-pedagogic problem." [5]

The distinction made by the Ministry of Education's adviser is one that it would be hard for any linguist to reject once he thinks more closely about it. In countries where he is asked to assume partial responsibility for language normalization, he has to face the same conflict of conscience as the atomic scientist in our country. No matter how well versed he may be in linguistics, he cannot then plead that everyone's language is equally good or that it it does not matter how a thing is said or written. Every dialect or every lan-

---

[5] *Stortingstidende 1950*, St. prp. nr. 1, Tillegg nr. 3.

guage may be equally entitled to exist in a historical sense and equally capable of expressing what its users wish to say. But within the nation Hall's goal of "the most efficient way of saying or doing" something is precisely promoted by uniformity of code rather than by diversity.

It is along this dimension that our understanding of linguistic normalization must proceed. If we do not keep our gaze one-sidedly turned on the linguistic structure itself, but lift up our eyes to see the society in which we really live, I think we have a model on which we can build. Linguists seldom consider the nature of the pressure that creates the high degree of uniformity among the speakers of what Bloomfield called a "speech community." Anyone who has observed the process of child learning of language will not fail to note the numerous instances of mutual ridicule and intolerance on the part of the still untutored savages. Schizoglossia is rooted out among them by constant correction, which goes far beyond the minimum needs of communication and virtually insists on identity of code. If it were not for this kind of insistence, there would be no language structure and no language history.

The introduction of writing made possible the infinite extension of the language community beyond the immediate reach of the voice. It made possible the building of nations and empires, which in their turn became extended speech communities. Within these the pressure against schizoglossia was directed above all at the normalization and standardization of writing, but with the growth of other means of communication through travel, it came to embrace also speech at least of those who travelled. Only by reducing what Hockett has called the noise of the code could the institutions of modern societies be built. From the prime community of children and savages over the secondary communities of classes and professions to the great states of modern times the basic model of communication remains the same, and the need for uniformity of code wherever communication is to be rapid and unimpeded is constant. The role of the written word in this connection has barely begun to be understood. Perhaps even the much reviled "spelling pronunciations," which Bloomfield (p. 501) called "ugly," may be found to have their virtues.

It seems to me that all the activities of rhetoricians and normative grammarians, from Samuel Johnson to the lowliest schoolmarm in American rural schools, need to be reevaluated in terms of this model. Dialects, whether regional or social, have their charms, but they hamper communication by calling attention to features which which either are or ought to be irrelevant to the message. They label their man by his social history, and their maintenance is often advocated precisely by those who wish to maintain a snobbish distinction of class. If dialects are to be tolerated, the teaching of tolerance must begin with other and more basic feaures of inequality in society than the purely linguistic one. In spite of the evidence piled up in Fries's American Grammar concerning the failure of the schoolmarm to impose her norm in certain areas, I am convinced that the comparative uniformity of American linguistic usage has been greatly facilitated by her activities. There is no nation in the world where the dictionary has entered daily life to the extent of ours, or where the teaching of "correct" grammar has touched as many lives. It is not difficult to see in this activity a reflection of the basic faith of Americans, however unrealistic it may have turned out to be, in equality of opportunity for all. In other countries one could learn the best usage only by associating with an aristocracy, which generally meant being born into one; here culture could be learned from a book.

There is an interesting difference of attitude among the Scandinavian countries in this respect. In Sweden the firmness of the written standard language has led to its dominance over speech. While the colloquial standard in many ways escapes from this dominance, the formal standard is strongly marked by it. While there are regional varieties, a recent investigation of the school practices showed that they were being reduced. Those pronunciations which come closest to the spelling are favored. In Norway the opposite condition prevails. The fluidity of the written standard has led to widespread toleration of dialectal speech on the stage and in private life. But the effects of widespread communication are nevertheless apparent in the mutual adjustment of speakers from various parts of the country to one another. And one may surmise on the basis of various tendencies that if once the written norm is unified, a concerted effort will follow through the schools to impose a common standard of pronunciation.

In conclusion, then, I note that there are two courses one can follow to meet the problem of schizoglossia in modern society. Linguists who do not regard it as a problem may of course take a laissez-faire attitude to it. But they cannot claim that they do so because this is the scientific position. The scientific position is to recognize that a problem exists, that it needs research and study in terms of social goals, and that mere toleration is not really a remedy. Normalization, which aims to provide a common code for those who need one, is a remedy, and linguists can make a contribution by seeing to it that it is a good one. It would be nice if we could persuade polite society to accept Eliza Doolittle as she is, but in our heart of hearts most of us would prefer to associate with her after Dr. Higgins has straightened out her aiches.

THE ROLE OF PARAPHRASE IN GRAMMAR

H. Hiż

University of Pennsylvania

The goal of grammar is a formally correct and empirically adequate account of various grammatical structures of the language under study. The sentential structures have an especially important role in grammatical theories. A grammar, to be empirically adequate, must describe the set of admissible sentences. It must also deal with regularities commonly felt and obeyed by those who speak the language. Some similarities and differences of sentence structures and certain relations between the structures are recognizable more or less uniformly by speakers of the language. This does not mean at all that the speakers have an explicit theory of the grammar of their language. On the contrary, people seldom know their own grammatical habits. They only have the habits. It is up to the grammarian to discover and describe them. To make his task practical the grammarian may start by exploring two fundamental facts about the language, facts that are more accessible to empirical study than are the latent grammatical structures. One of the facts is the presence in the language of ambiguous sentences, i.e., sentences with more than one meaning. The other is the presence of paraphrases, i.e., pairs of sentences with identical meanings.

Here someone may object and say that the proposed starting point is not properly chosen because meaning is less concrete and harder to handle scientifically than are syntactic structures. Such an objection would miss the point. To be sure, it is difficult to say what meaning is and to determine the meaning of any given phrase scientifically. However, we are asking not for the meaning of a phrase but only whether the meanings of two phrases are identical. It is true that we do not get reliable answers to the question what the meaning of a given phrase is, but to the question concerning the identity or difference in meanings of two phrases we can obtain reliable reactions. It may even be true that there are phrases with no meaning. But if any phrases have meanings, the sentences do. Besides, whether there are meanings of sentences or of any phrases is of no consequence for gram-

211

matical considerations. What matters is only that the speakers recognize a sentence as saying the same as another sentence. This "saying the same" is just a relation between two sentences and it does not presuppose something else, the "thing" said in each sentence. The ability of asserting a relation between two objects does not require the ability of recognizing in each object separately a property which makes them so related. If somebody still objects that we base the grammar on semantic rather than purely syntactic components we may reply that this is unavoidable if our grammar is to be empirically adequate. It is better to localize, control, and restrict the use of semantics in grammar than to pretend that there is none. Furthermore, it is a rather small part of semantics that is used for grammar. The more powerful concepts of semantics, such as truth and denotation, are not used here at all. To determine the meanings of phrases one must employ those powerful concepts; meaning depends on truth. But equality of meanings does not. The weak semantics considers the comparison of sentences as to their semantic equality or difference, and declares whether some sentences are ambiguous or not. Empirically, if a speaker considers a sentence ambiguous, he should be able to give two different readings of it, two paraphrases which are not paraphrases of each other. The judgment of ambiguity reduces therefore to two pronouncements about identity of meaning and one about difference of meaning. If on the other hand a sentence were judged unambiguous by a speaker, this would be equivalent to his saying that no two sentences which are not paraphrases of each other are paraphrases of it. But to assert this would require an examination of a very large number of sentences, which is not feasible. That is why people often fail to realize it when a sentence is ambiguous. When they do realize the ambiguity of a sentence we can trust them only if they are able to give two different readings of it. It is better not to rely on their mere feeling. The negative answer to the question whether a sentence is ambiguous will be not used in grammar. The positive answers, if backed by performance, give information enough to construct the totality of grammar of the language.

It must be understood that only one sort of ambiguity is of interest here, the sort which is called grammatical ambiguity. There are other kinds of ambiguity, or other senses of the word 'ambiguity'. Thus we say that a sentence is occasionally ambiguous when it has the property that it may be true when said by one person, in a given place, or at a given time, and false when used by another person, in a different place, or at a different time. E.g., *It's cold* is sometimes true, sometimes false, depending on the occasion of its use. Secondly, there is the phenomenon of the so-called dictionary ambiguity. It occurs when a word has two different meanings. Thus the sentence *Springs are useful* has more than one meaning because the word *spring* has many meanings. Our grammarian may not be much concerned with this sort of ambiguity, though it is an open and fascinating problem whether the dictionary ambiguities are reducible to the grammatical ambiguities. The distinction between a dictionary and a grammatical ambiguity is made mainly by the fact that in the case of a dictionary ambiguity we give paraphrases that contain different words (dictionary definitions) from those present in the ambiguous sentence, whereas in the case of a grammatical ambiguity we come up with a paraphrase which contains only words already appearing in the ambiguous sentence. The only exceptions are those words which are among the so-called grammatical constants. Their list is limited and their use is unlimited; they occur independently of the topic of the discourse.

When we say that the sentence

(1) *John cuts easily*
is ambiguous because it either says that

(2) *It is easy for John to cut*
or is paraphrasable by

(3) *It is easy to cut John,*

we are using the same words: *John, easy, cut.* The changes introduced in paraphrasing are only those of word order and insertion or omission of: *it, is, to, -ly, -s,* the constants of the grammar. (The list of constants in a grammatical theory, although assembled arbitrarily in principle, is in fact determined by their systematic occurrence in paraphrases. They must be those segments which help in formulating the rules of paraphrasing: the segments which are usually omitted or inserted among the component words.) It may happen that an ambiguous sentence is paraphrased into two sentences which in turn are paraphrases of each other. Such data fail to expose the ambiguity and further paraphrasing is needed. Possibly somebody may consider (2) and (3) paraphrases. But (2) and not (3) is a paraphrase of

(4) *It is easy for John to cut somebody or something.*

(1), (2), and (4) are paraphrases of

(5) *John cuts; It comes to him easily,*

(5) is not a paraphrase of (3) or of

(6) *It is easy for somebody or something to cut John.*

The presence of the word *easily* is essential for this analysis. When it is absent, as in

(7) *John cuts,*

or when it is relegated to another sentence, as in (5), there are no paraphrases like (6). However, the word *easily* does not have this effect in the sentence

(8) *Glass breaks easily.*

If we imitate the operations performed on (1) we obtain among others

(9) *Glass breaks; It comes to it easily,*
and

(10) *It is easy to break glass,*

and they may all be considered paraphrases of each other. To put it in more traditional terminology the verb *break* takes the middle whereas the verb *cut* takes the middle only in presence of adverbs, like *easily*.

To take another example of an ambiguous sentence.

(11) *There are numbers which are roots of a polynomial.*
It may be paraphrased either as

(12) *There are numbers such that all of them are roots of the same polynomial.*
Or it may read as

(13) *There are numbers such that for each of them there is a polynomial of which the number is a root.*

As was the case in (5) we sometimes paraphrase a sentence by a text of two, or more, sentences. In further discussion, for simplicity, we shall often treat this text as if it were a single sentence.

Among many sentences into which a given sentence is paraphrasable there are sets of sentences which are all paraphrases of each other. Let us call such a set a **paraphrastic set.** E.g. (1), (2), (4), and (5) form a paraphrastic set, but (1), (2), (3), (4), (5), (6) do not. A paraphrastic set is called a **maximal paraphrastic set** if it is not included in another paraphrastic set. It may be that in practices we rarely, if ever, reach maximal paraphrastic sets and have to be satisfied with approximations to them. We may be uncertain whether we have exhausted all possible mutual paraphrases. The maximal paraphrastic sets, as well as their practical approximations, differ considerably in size. There are maximal paraphrastic sets that contain more than twenty sentences, others consist of a single sentence, a sentence which does not admit a paraphrase except itself. The size of a maximal paraphrastic set to which a sentence belongs is an indirect indication of the complexity of the sentence, independently of its possible ambiguity.

The family of all maximal paraphrastic sets is not a partition of the set of all sentences. For there are ambiguous sentences and they belong to more than one paraphrastic set. The maximal paraphrastic sets are therefore not disjoint, and the relation of being a paraphrase is not transitive.

A grammarian compares paraphrastic sets with each other and finds similarities between them. He observes that in many of them the same constants appear or that the constants occur in the same combinations. He records that the repetitions or permutations of non-constant phrases coincide with the appearance of particular constants. The descriptions of those similarities constitute the **rules of paraphrasing.** For such comparisons it is helpful to arrange the sentences of a paraphrastic set into an order. We can then say that the change between, e.g., the first and the second sentence of one paraphrastic set is the same as the change between the first and the second sentence of another paraphrastic set. The order in which we arrange the paraphrastic sets is arbitrary and a given paraphrastic set may be ordered differently for comparisons with different paraphrastic sets.

We find many paraphrastic sets each containing, say, four sentences of the form

(14) $a_1\ a_2\ C_1\ a_3\ C_2$; $C_3\ C_4\ a_3\ C_5\ a_1\ C_6\ a_2$; $C_3\ C_4\ a_3\ C_6\ a_2\ a_1$; $C_6\ a_2\ a_1\ C_4\ a_3$.

For instance the paraphrastic set consisting of sentences (1), (2), (3), and (15), is of this form. And so is the paraphrastic set consisting of sentences (8), (16), (10), and (17).

(15) *To cut John is easy.*

(16) *It is easy for glass to break.*

(17) *To break glass is easy.*

We call -*s:* C_1, -*ly:* C_2, *it:* C_3, *is:* C_4, *for:* C_5, *to:* C_6. (14) is the common form of the two paraphrastic sets, each taken as an ordered quadruple of sentences. Much fewer combinations of variables and constants actually occur as forms of paraphrastic sets than are possible, even after we limit them in length and consider only such combinations which are forms of some sentences. A form of a paraphrastic set P is, therefore, a set of ordered n-tuples of sentences, each n-tuple being a paraphrastic set, one of which is P, where the n-tuples differ only in non-constant phrases. The form can be represented symbolically as in (14). A form of a paraphrastic set is sometimes called a **battery of paraphrastic transformations** (a terminology from my paper "Congrammaticality, batteries of transformations, and grammatical categories", in *Proceedings of Symposia in Applied Mathematics,* vol. XII, American Mathematical Society, 1961).

Innumerable paraphrastic sets containing two sentences each may be of the same form. In other words, some single, paraphrastic change applies to very many sentences. On the other hand, few maximal paraphrastic sets are of the same form. The number and variety of forms which we may obtain from noticing some similarities between paraphrastic sets makes the set of all forms a description of language which is not transparent. To make it more operative and more significant we have to impose a condition on choosing the forms for our grammar. A reasonable condition for a successful grammar may be to choose the forms in such a way as to have the smallest number of forms representing all the sentences of the language and all empirically given approximations to maximal paraphrastic sets. But here scientific good taste must play the crucial role, though it is not excluded that a procedure for finding an optimal set of forms will be established. Let us suppose that such a set F of forms of paraphrastic sets is chosen.

In F every sentence is represented and ambiguous sentences more than once. A sentence is represented in F by a place in a form which is the place the sentence occupies in the paraphrastic set of this form. Now it is easy to formulate precisely what is ordinarily meant by a sentence as read in a particular way. It is an ordered triple consisting of the sentence, the form of a paraphrastic set, and a place in this form: the place occupied by the sentence in the paraphrastic set of that form. Thus if $R(S)$ is a **reading** of a sentence, then

(18) $R(S) = \langle S, f, n \rangle$ where S is the nth element of a paraphrastic set of the form **f**.

$R(S)$ is in a (weak) sense a **meaning** of S and thus (18) can be taken as a definition of one of many possible concepts of meaning. It applies to sentences only.

A set of readings of sentences which are members of a paraphrastic set is called an **abstract paraphrastic set.** And, similarly, an abstract paraphrastic set is maximal if it is not a proper subset of another abstract paraphrastic set.

Theorem 1. A is a maximal abstract paraphrastic set if and only if there is a maximal paraphrastic set P of form f such that for every S in P if n is the position of S in P, the ordered triple $\langle S, f, n \rangle$ is a member of A.

Theorem 2. Maximal abstract paraphrastic sets form a partition of the set of all readings of all sentences of the language.

For further considerations we restrict our attention to those forms f which are elements of an (optimally) chosen set F of forms. Then we say that two readings R_1 and R_2 of sentences S_1 and S_2 are of the same type if and only if

$R_1(S_1) = \langle S_1, f, n \rangle$
$R_2(S_2) = \langle S_2, f, n \rangle$
and f is a member of F.

Theorem 3. The types of readings of sentences form a partition of the set of all readings of all sentences.

Now we come to an important grammatical concept. If a sentence is transformed into another within a paraphrastic set to which they both belong, or if it is transformed into a sentence with reading of the same type, or if those transformations are performed successively in any order, we will reach only sentences which have some global similarity to the starting sentence. From an indicative sentence we will not obtain a command or an interrogative. Nor, usually, from a singular, a plural sentence (though some plural and singular forms of words—but not entire sentences—may be exchanged, as witnessed by (11) and (13)). The concept we are dealing with now is more extensive than the concept of mood of the traditional grammars. Still the word **mood** can be properly used in this new role. We will say that two sentences S_1 and S_2 in their **readings** R_1 and R_2 respectively are immediately of the same **mood** if there is a sentence S_3 and its reading R_3 and there is a form f belonging to F such that either $R_1(S_1)$ and $R_3(S_3)$ are both represented in f and $R_3(S_3)$ is of the same type as $R_2(S_2)$ or else $R_2(S_2)$ and $R_3(S_3)$ are both represented in f and $R_3(S_3)$ is of the same type as $R_2(S_2)$.

Theorem 4. The relation of being immediately of the same mood is reflexive (take $R_1(S_1) = R_2(S_2) = R_3(S_3)$) and symmetrical.

But this relation may not be transitive. A transitive relation of being of the same mood is given by relation of **immediate mood** repeated a finite number of times. Thus, two sentences $R_1(S_1)$ and $R_2(S_2)$ are of the same mood if there is a sequence of sentences $R_n(S_n)$, $R_{n+1}(S_{n+1})$, . . ., $R_{n+m}(S_{n+m})$ such that $R_n(S_n) = R_1(S_1)$, $R_{n+m}(S_{n+m}) = R_2(S_2)$ and for each $R_i(n \leq i \leq n+m)$ $R_i(S_i)$ is immediately of the same mood as $R_{i+1}(S_{i+1})$.

Theorem 5. The moods form a partition of the set of all readings of all sentences.

Every sentence with a reading is of one and only one mood. The totality of sentence readings is divided into disjoint areas. The partition into moods depends in an essential way on the choice of the set F of forms. If all the forms of F are descriptions of nearly maximal paraphrastic sets, there will be more different moods than in a case where F contains forms corresponding to relatively small subsets of the maximal paraphrastic sets. One is tempted to choose several sets of forms, F_1, F_2, etc. and starting from each of them separately to perform the division of sentences into types, readings, and moods. It may be that a comparison of different grammars obtained from different sets of forms will lead to a deeper grammatical theory of a higher order.

Language contains many paraphrases. The same thing is said in many ways. One may feel that this is redundant. This alleged redundancy is intrinsically connected with the presence of ambiguities. We explain ambiguities by paraphrases. And we understand the presence of paraphrases better by studying the role they play in resolving ambiguities. It may be strongly suspected that every pair of paraphrases is used in explaining some ambiguity, so that each of them is actually needed for clarification of our utterances. This can be stated in a slightly weaker way.

Hypothesis. For every form f in F there is a set G of pairs of elements of f, i.e. pairs of types of sentences, which satisfies the following conditions:

1) Every element of f belongs to a pair of G, thus all types appearing in the form f are present in one or another pair of G;

2) For every pair $\langle h, k \rangle$ in G there are paraphrastic sentences α and β of types h and k respectively such that the ambiguity of α is partially explained by paraphrasing α into β, i.e. there is a sentence γ which is a paraphrase of α and not of β.

GREEK DIGLOSSIA

FRED W. HOUSEHOLDER, JR.

Indiana University

A. The purpose of the present study is not to recount the history of the "language question" in Greece, a fascinating story which could not be adequately told in any reasonable compass, full of the most remarkable human passions and incredibly illogical behavior; it is to specify as accurately as possible the linguistic marks of katharevousa and dhimotiki, the various degrees and shades of each and the typical situations in which each is used.

B. In this section we shall present the main distinguishing features of the two written standards, classified in two ways: (a) as spelling, inflection, vocabulary (subdivided into derivation and stems), or syntax; and (b) as obligatory, criterial, regular, occasional, and forbidden. An indication 1 (K1, D1) will indicate that the form in question is regarded as extreme, i.e., archaic in the case of K, dialect (O.K. for poetry and dialog) or conversational in the case of D; 2 (K2, D2) indicates a criteral form—i.e., any text with a K2 form in it is surely K, with a D2 form D; 3 (K3, D3) marks forms which are normally K or D but sometimes occur in the other language (D or K); 4 forms belong freely to both languages.

1. Spelling

a) The two most striking and frequent elements distinguishing D and K are points which involve both spelling and inflection. The first is final -*n*. Several forms which in K (and Ancient Greek) obligatorily end in -*n*, plus one or two which optionally do so with high frequency, never do so in D. The chief forms are: A. sing. in -*on*, -*an*. -*in*. N.-A. sing. neuter in -*ion, -on,* first person plural active in -*men*, third person singular past in -*en* (or -*e*). An average page of 300 words or so of Greek will have 50 or 60 examples of this presence or absence of final -*n*, or about two in every line.

The other, slightly less pervasive difference, lies in the preposition meaning "to, at, in," which in ordinary katharevousa is obligatorily a separate word *is* but in dhimotiki appears in three forms: *se* before consonants in general, *s'* before vowels, and combined with the definite article as *sto, sto(n), sti(n), stou, stis, stous,* and *sta.* This occurs about 10 or 15 times on an average 300-word page of text. In recent years this has begun to turn up occasionally in the mildest form of K, but otherwise is a mark of dhimotiki.

b) Of all the other orthographic cues, certain differences in accentuation are probably the most pervasive, occuring (on the average) about seven times on a page. These fall into several classes. (1) There are occasional instances where K regularly uses a circumflex accent, whereas official D (as laid down in Triandaphyllidhis' grammar) uses an acute. (2) The D accent is on a different syllable from the K accent: (a) because the D accent persists through all or most of a paradigm, as in the feminine forms (and genitives, and masculine accusative plurals) of most adjectives including comparative degree forms and in many nouns; (b) because the K accent is on an iota which becomes non-syllabic in D, inducing a shift to the following vowel (D pedhyá, etc., K pedhía, etc., D kardhyá and many other feminines in-yá —K kardhiá, etc.); (c) because of differences like D amerikánikos, K (and D) amerikanikós where D has developed a suffix which differs only in accent from another shared by K and D. But in addition to actual minimal pairs, there are many more cases per page where D has a purely D word whose accentuation is contrary to K rules (e.g. andílalus, gháydharos, etc.) but which would be replaced in K by a different word, or conversely cases in K of accentuation contrary to D rules where D would use a different word or form.

c) About five or six times per page there will occur a consonant cluster which will have one form in D and a different one in K. There are two main classes: the cluster of two voiceless obstruents (stops or fricatives) and the cluster of nasal plus obstruent. In the first case (two obstruents) K allows three types: stop plus stop or s e.g., pt, ps), fricative plus fricative (e.g., fth) and fricative plus stop or s (e.g., ft, fs). The ideal "pure" spoken language would allow only two, fricative plus stop (e.g. ft) and stop plus s (e.g. ps); D has, in fact, borrowed numerous words from K and from foreign languages which have reintroduced the other types, but there still remain many words in which K has (e.g.) pt or fth, where D has ft, kt or xth, where D has xt, fx where D has fk, fs, where D has ps, etc.

In the second case (nasal plus obstruent), K allows the obstruent to be a voiced stop, or a voiced or voiceless fricative, whereas "pure" vernacular Greek allowed only the voiced stop (for both stop and fricative of K), and dropped the nasal before a voiceless fricative. When nasal plus voiced fricative was reintroduced at a later date, spoken Greek dropped the nasal here too. D has reintroduced the K clusters in some words, and both K and D also have occasional sequences of nasal plus voiceless stop in loans from other European languages. However, many contrasting pairs remain.

d) Many items in D (and even more in S) differ from their K equivalents by the absence of an initial unaccented vowel or, in other cases, its replacement by another. This can occasionally cause trouble in looking up words in a dictionary, because not all the shortenings are recognized in every dictionary—though the most common and important ones are, of course. The unstressed syllabic augment, e-, is seldom used in D but regularly in K.

e) The preposition *ya* and the forms *yatí* "why," *yatí* "because," and *yana* "in order to" occur at least three times per page of D. The K equivalents for *ya* are varied: sometimes *dhiá* with acc.; sometimes a dative, sometimes *metá* with gen., sometimes *pros* with acc.; and there are others. *Yatí* "why" is rendered as *dhia tí*, but *yatí* "because" is *dhi' óti* and *yana* is simply *ína* most of the time, though *dhià na* occurs in "simple" K.

Virtually all the spelling differences (basically phonological differences in most cases) listed above belong to categories D1 and D2, i.e., they are used *only* in D, so their presence proves D while their absence does not prove K. A few of them, however, (e.g., the accent of comparatives) are almost criterial in both directions, like final *n* and *yá*.

Inflection

A. If we allow (for the moment) identity of forms with and without final -*n*, then a large proportion of noun-adjective endings and a fair number of verb forms are identical in the two dialects. (1) In the old first declension (stems in -a and -i) feminines are mostly the same in the singular and G. pl., but differ in the plural N.-A. (K N. -e, A. -as, D N.-A. -es). Feminines which are third declension (consonant stems) in K will have the same forms in D in the A. Sing., and N. G. Pl.: A. Sing. -a, N. Pl. -es, G. Pl. -on, while the other forms differ (K N. S. -s, G. -os, A. Pl. -as, D N. S. -a, G. -as, A. Pl. -es). The old i-stems present a different picture; here the whole plural is the same (N.-A. -is, G. -eon) and the acc. sing., as usual, differs only by an -n, while the genitive singular is commonly the same, espe-

cially in longer and more elegant words (-eos); but otherwise the
singular is different: in D N.-A. -i, G. -is, in K N. -is, G. -eos, A. -in.
(2) Masculines of this declension are like feminines, except that D
and K have now the same nominative (in -is or -as), but different
genitives (D -i, -a, K -u), although many proper names in K use the
D genitive. Two variations occur in D: some agent nouns in -is or
ís have added-syllable plurals in -idhes, -ídhes, or ádhes, and some in
-tís, recently borrowed from K, use the whole K plural. Those masculines which are third declension in K are declined like the K feminines of that type, with the same three cases like D, while the D N.
Sing. is in -as, G. Sing. in -a. There is an important type of agent-
noun which in K runs S -éfs, -éos, -éa Pl. -ís, éon, -ís. Normally D
here shares the A. sing. and the whole plural, reshaping the N. Sing.
to -éas and the G. to -éa, but a few of these words appear also in a
fully demoticized form -yás (etc.) with the extra-syllable plural in
-yádhes, etc. (like the feminines). (3) Old second-declension masculines are nearly identical in K and D (allowing for the final -n of
the A. Sing.). A few words (chiefly given names) take the (D)
vocative singular in -o instead of -e, but most of these names have a
different shape in K. Feminines of this declension are exactly like
masculines in K, and this declension may be preserved also in D.
But some old S. words (chiefly names with no plural) shifted to the
regular type in N.-A. -o, G. -os. Neuters, too, are generally the same
in D as in K except for the -n. But there is a D type in Sing. -í, yú,
Pl. -yá, -yón which corresponds to K S. -íon, -íu, Pl. -ía, -íon. However, K frequently avoids these nouns (even when they are good classical Greek), because they are so common in D and spoken Greek.
But moderate or "simple" K is sometimes willing to use them (even
with the D declension occasionally). (4) The old neuter s-stems are
also the same in D as in K: Sing. -os, -us, Pl. -i, -ón, except that K
uses an optional G plural in -éon for a few of these nouns. A large
group of neuter t-stems is identical in K and D, those which end in
Sing. -ma, -matos, P. -mata, -máton. D also has a productive de-
verbal noun suffix -simo which is declined in the same way, Sing.
-simo, -símatos, Pl. -símata, -simáton. This formation is not admitted
in K where it is replaced by -sis, -ma, -mós or the ancient infinitive
used as a noun. (5) Among adjectives, D has one new masculine
type (S. -ís, -yú, Pl. yí. -yón, -yús; where the irregularity lies in the
nominative singular (a noun would have -yós); the feminine is like
any noun in -yá, the neuter like neuters in -í. The corresponding K
type runs M. Sing. -ís, -éos, -ín, Pl. -ís, -éon, -ís like the common
feminine noun type except for the accent and the spelling; D has a

type with ordinary o-stem masculine and neuter and normal feminine plural, but with a feminine singular in -yá, -yás (instead of -í, -ís). Many of these can also be declined either like ordinary adjectives in the feminine with -í, -ís or like the -ís, -yú adjectives in masculine and neuter. In K they are all regular of one or the other type. Finally, D has a type with M. Sing. -is, -i, Pl. -idhes, -idhon, F. Sing. -a, -as, Pl. -es, -ikon, N. Sing. -iko, -iku, Pl. -ika, -ikon, with a few possible variants in F. and N. These words are always replaced by synonyms in K (and many of them are classed as D1, extreme Dhimotiki).

B. The inflection of verbs is a different matter; here a large proportion of the endings used in K and D are different and criterial. (1) In the active primary endings (except for certain "contracted" present types) everything is the same except for the final -n and sometimes the thematic vowel of the first plural. But in the third plural, D has a longer variant -une which is quite common in conversation, and K has also an extreme type in -usi or -usin, (-osi/n for subjunctives). (2) In the middle primary endings of the same class, four endings agree: -o-me, -e-se, -e-te and 3 Pl. -o-nde; D has 1Pl. o-maste, 2Pl. -e-ste and K 1Pl.-o-metha, -e-sthe. The difference in the second plural is one of the systematic phonological differences (reducing fricative plus fricative to fricative plus stop in D) between K and D. (3) In the past tense D has only one active set of endings (-a, -e-s, -e, -a-me, -a-te, -a-n or a-ne) which differ from the primary ones only in the quality of the (first) vowel (a instead of e, o, u; e for i), and they occur in the imperfective past active and the perfective past (aorist) active and passive. In K these three tenses differ, so that only 2 Sing. and 3 Sing. come out identical in the imperfect (-e-s, -e), while in the aorist everything except the 2 Sing. is the same (D -e-s , K -a-s), with the usual allowances for final -n (K) in 1Pl. and the optional final -e in 3Pl. In the aorist passive D has a characteristic -k- between these endings and the -i-, -ti- or -thi- which marks the paradigm, while K drops the first vowel (a or e) of the endings and adds the remainder directly after -(th)i-, introducing new suffixes -n for 1 Sing. and -san for 3 Pl. So of 18 forms, 11 are different. (4) The secondary middle set of endings (used only for the imperfective past) differ absolutely: K -ó-min, -e-so, -e-to, -ó-metha, -e-sthe, -o-ndo, D -ó-mun,   -ó-sun, -ó-tan, -ó-maste, -ó-saste, -o-ndan. There are several spoken variants in the D set, but all are even less like K than these. (5) In the imperative the agreement is nearly perfect, K having adopted three (out of 8) forms from D in place of ancient types. The only remaining difference (aside from -sth- vs. -st-) is in the plural aorist active, where D adds -te directly to the final consonant of the stem (usually s), or (in more elegant forms) uses -e-te, while K has -a-te. (6) While K has a complete set of two active and three passive participles (extreme archaistic Kl may have even more) all fully declined, D matches the K imperfective active participle with an indeclinable gerund or converb in -ondas (which coincides in form with the masculine accusative plural of the K participle) and otherwise has only the equivalent of the K perfect passive participle in -ménos. Here there is variation in K: many of these p.p.p's are identical with D, but others are reduplicated in K (e.g. *dhedheménos*) though never in D (*dheménos*) except for sporadic borrowing of common expressions from K. Vamboulis and Zoukis give lists of participles which must be, may be, and cannot be reduplicated (Pars. 275-280), but the general impression is that the lines are shifting so that more and more unreduplicated participles are coming into K. (7) In the so-called contract conjunctions, of which D essentially has only one (and part of a second), where K2 has three (though the mildest sort of K omits one), there are various other differences. The normal present active agrees with the alpha-contract verbs of K throughout, except for first-person plural, D -úme or sometimes -áme, K-ómen. But D has also an alternative 3 Sing. -áy (K and D -á), and a 3 Pl. -án, -áne (K and D -ún, D-úne), while Kl has an alternative 3 Pl. -ósi(n). And many verbs conjugated in this way in D are conjugated as epsilon-contract verbs in K.

This latter pattern also exists in D, and (in the present active) agrees completely with the K pattern (barring the final -n of lPl.). Many verbs in D and S fluctuate between the two patterns, some speakers and writers preferring (e.g. patí and others patáy). (8) The present middle or passive forms of D and K can easily be separated into a thematic affix followed by personal endings. The personal endings of contract verbs are the same as those discussed above in (2); the thematic affixes, however, are different. Nearly all D verbs use -ye- before singular endings and 2Pl. -ste, -yú- before 1Pl. and 3 Pl. (optionally and in some dialects also before 1 Sing.); K alpha-contract verbs have -ó- before 1Sing., 1 Pl., and 3Pl., but -á- before the rest, while epsilon-contract verbs have -ú- in 1Sing., 1Pl., 3Pl., and -í- for the rest. A small class of verbs recently borrowed by D from K agrees with K in this (e.g. mimúme "I imitate"); an even smaller class (e.g. thimúme "I remember") combines the two K types, having -ú- for 1Sing., 1Pl., 3Pl. but -á- for the rest (also, optionally, -á- for the 1S). (9) The formation of the active past (imperfect) of contract verbs differs widely in the two languages. In K alpha- contract verbs in the active have in the singular '-on, '-as, '-a and in the plural -ó-men, -á-te, '-on, while epsilon verbs go '-un, '-is, '-i, -ú-men, -í-te, '-un. In D all these verbs, regardless of the present tense formation, form their imperfect with a stem-affix -ús- or, in some dialects and some literary styles -agh- (with the accent always on the antepenult), followed by the regular endings mentioned under (3) above. The formation with -ús- appears occasionally in simple K now. (10) In the imperfective past middle (or passive) of such verbs, K and D differ both in thematic affix and in the endings (which are as in (4) above). For alpha verbs K uses the affix -ó- in 1Sing., 1Pl. and 3Pl., -á- elsewhere (just as in the present); for epsilon verbs, again as in the present, -ú- in 1Sing., 1Pl., 3 Pl., -i- elsewhere. In D, verbs which form their present with -ye- / -yú- add -yó- throughout for the past; those whose presents have -ú- and -í- use -ú- throughout the past, while those few with -ú- / -á- in the present have -ó- throughout the past.

In general we may say that inflection provides as strong criterial evidence as final -n; average pages show between 30 and 45 items per page (whether in K or D) which guarantee the dialect, and the amount of optional use of D forms in K, or K forms in D is usually slight, even in "simple" K or "journalistic" D.

Vocabulary

This is the realm where "simple" K and "moderate" D may, on occasion, approach each other very closely but, on the other hand, extreme forms of the two languages may differ almost one-hundred percent. In general, as we have already remarked, D feels free to borrow any K item that it needs, while K is self-conscious about borrowing a D word without first somehow cleaning it up a bit.

The most striking vocabulary differences between K and D are in the realm of basic or every-day vocabulary: prepositions, frequent verbs, body parts, kinship terms, common animals, etc. Here K adopts the D word only very rarely, when (a) the AG word would now be a monosyllable beginning with a vowel or (b) it is homonymous with some other word which might often occur in the same context, or (c) the D word did exist in AG where it had a slightly narrower or broader sense, or (d) the D word is of such very high frequency that it would be altering the essence of the language to change it (e.g., *dhén* "not," *nà* "that, to," *tòn* "him," *etc.*) not that earlier K writers didn't try. Out of over 200 basic vocabulary items, only some half-a-dozen or so have been taken from D or S by K, whereas about 25 have come into D from K.

	D.	No.	K.	No	Reg. Phno.	Irreg. Ana.	Deriv.	Stem
1. I	ἐγώ	4	ἐγώ	4				
2. thou	ἐσύ	2	σύ	2		X		
3. we	ἐμεῖς	3	ἡμεῖς	2		X		
4. this	αὐτός	4	αὐτός	4				
	τοῦτος	2	οὗτος	3		X		
	ἐτοῦτος	2				X		
5. that	ἐκεῖνος	4	ἐκεῖνος	4				
6. who	ποιός	3	τίς	1				X
			ποῖος	2	X			
7. what	τί	4	τί	4				
8. not	δὲ(ν)	3	δέν	4				
	μὴ(ν)	3	μὴ	4		X		
9. all	ὅλοι	4	πάντες	2				X
			ὅλοι	4				
10. many	πολλοί	4	πολλοί	4				
11. one	ἕνας	3	εἷς	2		X		
	μιά	2	μία	4	X			
	ἕνα	3	ἕν	2		X		
12. two	δυό	2	δύο	4	X			
13. big	μεγάλος	2	μέγας	2		X		
14. long	μακρύς	2	μακρός	2		X		
15. small	μικρός	4	μικρός	4				
16. woman	γυναίκα	3	γυνή	2		X		
17. man	ἄντρας	2	ἀνήρ	2		X		
18. person	ἄ(ν)θρωπος	4	ἄνθρωπος	4				
	πρόσωπο	3	πρόσωπον	3				
19. fish	φάρι	2	ἰχθύς	2				X
20. bird	πουλί	2	πτηνόν	2				X
21. dog	σκύλος	3	κύων	1				X
	σκυλί	2						
22. louse	φείρα	2	φθείρ	2			X	
23. tree	δέντρο	2	δένδρον	2	X			
24. seed	σπόρος	4	σπόρος	4				
	σπέρμα	4	σπέρμα	4				
25. leaf	φύλλο	2	φύλλον	2				
26. root	ρίξα	4	ρίζα	4				

27. bark	φλοιός	4	φλοιός	4				
	φλούδα	2			X			
28. skin	πετσί	2	δέρμα	4				X
29. flesh	κρέας	4	κρέας	4				
	σάρκα	2	σάρξ	2	X			
30. blood	αἷμα		αἷμα					
31. bone	κόκκαλο	2	ὀστοῦν	2				X
32. grease	λίπος	4	λίπος	4				
	γράσο	1						X
oil	λάδι	2	ἔλαιον	2		X		
33. egg	αὐγό	4	αὐγόν	4				
			ᾠόν					X
34. horn	κέρατο	2	κέρας	2	X			
35. tail	οὐρά	4	οὐρά	4				
36. feather	φτερό	2	τερόν	2	X			
	πούπουλο	1						X
37. hair	τά μαλλιά	2	ἡ κόμη	2				X
	τρίχα	2	θρίξ	2		X		
38. head	τό κεφάλι	2	ἡ κεφαλή	3			X	
39. ear	αὐτί	2	ὠτίον	2		X		
			οὖς	1				X
40. eye	μάτι	2	ὀφθαλμός	2				X
41. nose	μύτη	2	ῥίς	2				
42. mouth	στόμα	4	στόμα	4				
43. tooth	δόντι	2	ὀδούς	2		X		
44. tongue	γλῶσσα	4	γλῶσσα	4				
45. claw	νύχι	2	ὄνυξ	2				X
46. foot	πόδι	2	πούς	2				X
47. knee	γόνατο	2	γόνυ	2	X			
48. hand	χέρι	2	χείρ	2				X
49. belly	κοιλιά	2	ἡ γαστήρ	2				X
			κοιλία	2	X			
50. neck	λαιμός	4	λοιμός	4				
			τράχηλος	2			X	
			αὐλήν	2				X
51. breasts	τά βυζιά	2	οἱ μαστοί	3				
			οἱ μαζοί	1				X
52. heart	καρδιά	2	καρδία	4	X			
53. liver	συκώτι	2	ἧπαρ	2				
54. drink	πίνω	4	πίνω	4				
55. eat	τρώω	2	τρώγω	3				
56. bite	δαγκάνω	2	δάκνω	2	X			

57. see	βλέπω	4	ὁρῶ	1			X
			βλέπω	4			
58. hear	ἀκού(γ)ω	4	ἀκούω	4			
59. know	γνωρίζω	4	γνωρίζω	4			
	ξέρω	3	γιγνώσκω	1			X
			ἐξεύρω	3	X	X	
60. sleep	κοιμοῦμαι	3	κοιμῶμαι	2	X		
61. die	πεθαίνω	2	ἀποθνήσκω	2	X		
62. kill	σκοτώνω	4	σκοτώνω	4			
	ξεκάνω	1	φονεύω	2			X
	θανατώνω	3	θανατῶ	3			
63. swim	κολυμπῶ	2	κολυμβῶ	2	X		
64. fly	πετῶ	4	ἵπταμαι	1			
			πετῶ	4			
65. walk	περπατῶ	2	βαδίζω	2			X
			περιπατῶ	2	X		
66. come	ἔρχομαι		ἔρχομαι				X
67. lie	ξαπλώνομαι	2	κατακλίνομαι	2			X
68. sit	κάθομαι	2	κάθημαι	2	X		
69. stand	στέκομαι	2	ἵσταμαι	2		X	
70. give	δίνω	2	δίδω	3	X		
71. say	λέω	2	λέγω	2			
72. sun	ἥλιος	4	ἥλιος	4			
73. moon	φεγγάρι	2	σελήνη	4			X
74. star	ἀστέρι	2	ἀστήρ	2		X	
	ἄστρο	3	ἄστρον	3			
75. water	νερό	2	ὕδωρ	2			X
76. rain	βροχή	4	βροχή	4			
			ὑετός	1			X
77. stone	πέτρα	4	λίθος	2			X
			πέτρα	4			
78. sand	ἄμμος	4	ἄμμος	4			
79. earth	γῆ	4	γῆ	4			
	χῶμα	2	χοῦς	2			X
80. cloud	σύννεφο	3	σύννεφον	2			
			νεφέλη	2			X
			νέφος	2			X
81. smoke	καπνός	4	καπνός	4			
82. fire	φωτιά	2	πύρ	2			X
83. ash	στάχτη	2	τέφρα	2			X
			σποδός	1			X
84. burn	καίω	4	καίω	4			

85. path	μονοπάτι	2	ἀτραπός	2			X
			τρίβος	1			X
86. mountain	βουνό	3	ὄρος	2			X
87. red	κόκκινος	2	ἐρυθρός	2			X
88. green	πράσινος	4	πράσινος	4			
			χλωρός	2			X
89. yellow	κίτρινος	4	κίτρινος	4			
90. white	ἄσπρος	2	λευκός	3			X
91. black	μαῦρος	2	μέλας	2			X
92. night	νύχτα	2	νύξ	2	X		
93. hot	ζεστός	3	θερμός	3			X
94. cold	κρύος	2	φυχρός	3			X
			κρυερός	2		X	
95. full	γεμάτος	2	πλήρης	2			X
96. new	καινούργιος	3	νέος	3			X
97. good	καλός	4	καλός	4			
98. round	στρογγυλός	2	στρογγύλος	2	X		
99. dry	στεγνός	2					X
	ξερός	2	ξηρός	2	X		
100. name	ὄνομα	4	ὄνομα	4			

Because of the possibility of muliple choice in many cases, it is perhaps wiser to state a range rather than a single figure. For the 100 words above there is between 63 and 77 percent agreement. If these were two related languages which had been isolated from each other, the lexicostatistician would say that they had diverged somewhere between 430 and 1090 A.D. Their non-isolation would lead him to push the date even further back, say 100 B.C. to 650 A.D. It is, of course, the fact that K is not a living language which is responsible for this peculiar result; a lexicostatistical comparison of K with Ancient Greek would lead to a divergence date around 1850 (A.D.), or (at the earliest) 1700.

Substantial differences also exist in many other more specific areas of every-day vocabulary: of food, meals, cooking (here K often simply gives up and avoids the subject); (2) every-day crafts and trades (sailing, building, smith-work, garage-work, etc.); (3) names of ordinary plants, animals, birds, fish, etc.; (4) words for common aspects of human emotion and behavior; (5) the home and everything about it; (6) Christian names and nicknames; (7) common adverbs, prepositions, and similar grammatical words (several are on the list, but there are many more); (8) words having to do with time of day, seasons, weather, etc.; (9) most recent foreign loanwords in any field. On the other hand, realms in which there is very little difference between the two are very much the same as those where French resembles English; (1) terms belonging to a science or learned profession (including religion, to a large extent); (2) words of government or politics; (3) words in journalistic writing on general subjects; (4) most geographical names; (5) certain rather vague but dignified words of common occurrence in journalese. Unlike the French-English parallel, however, are the major classes of words not originally borrowed by D from K: (1) the essential grammatical words (many, but not all of them), like dèn "not," óchi "no, not," thà "will" eímai "me," many prepositions, some pronouns, some common adverbs, etc.; (2) certain items which have remained sufficiently unchanged in the spoken language tradition so that they can still be spelled exactly as in Ancient Greek; this includes some items which also fall in the first category, such as many forms of the article, some conjunctions, pronouns, etc., but also a number of verbs, nouns, and adjectives.

Syntax

In large measure the syntax of the two languages is identical so that (especially in simple journalistic material) a text in K and the corresponding text in D *might* differ only in phonology, spelling, and morphology. But there are a few striking differences in most styles which are confined almost exclusively to one language or the other.

K tends to use longer, more complex sentences, and D to use more parataxis. On an average page of K, the conjunctional particle *ke* (*ky*) occurs about 7 times; on a page of D, about 16 times, or more than twice as often. This is in part because it has in D a number of special functions (sometimes subordinating) not found in K.

A second frequent difference noticeable in K is the free use of participles in virtually every way in which they were employed in AG, including even the genitive absolute and the future participle of purpose. A count of several pages of K text selected at random shows an average of eight participles to the page, used in many different ways, of which four will be present participles, two aorist, and two perfect (including in all cases both active and passive forms). Less than three of the eight will be used as adjectives or nouns. In a page of D, on the average, there will be four participles, all perfect passive, and nearly all used as adjectives; gerunds in -ondas are less than one per page.

A third rather striking syntactic feature of K is the frequency of nominal genitives in many functions not possible in D. A sample count yields the following figures: K has an average of about 15 genitive nouns per page, D about 6. Several factors are involved here. D has, in general, long avoided the use of plural genitives and neuter genitives as much as possible. K, on the other hand, has no self-consciousness about genitives, and has, in addition, borrowed a number of genitive constructions from AG. One of these, the genitive absolute, was briefly mentioned above; its (rare) D equivalent is a nominative absolute (of the noun; the gerund in -ondas is, of course, uninflected). Of the fifteen normal D prepositions, none is regularly construed with nouns in the genitive; of 30 regular K prepositions, 18 take the genitive, including a group of "improper" prepositions whose D equivalents take sè, apò (or less often nè) when followed by nouns. D has only a handful of verbs which govern a genitive (mostly cases where Kl would have a dative), but in K there are dozens of such verbs. D rarely uses verbal nouns with subjective and objective genitives (though it is less rare in journalese D, of course), but K is extremely fond of these constructions. The construction of phrases like "glass of water" involves agreement in D, but a partitive genitive in K; and various other less common phrases differ in this same way.

Intermediate Languages

It is often alleged or implied that, if one chose a thousand modern Greek documents at random and sorted them according to language and style, these documents would form a single perfectly continuous series ranging without a break from extreme K to extreme D, and that there would be in the middle at least a few dozen items which could not easily or fairly be classified as one or the other. This is, of course, quite false. Any Modern Greek document can be unambiguously assigned to K or D on the basis of a half-dozen lines or less (in fact, a half-dozen words is normally enough), with very few exceptions.

The two readers prepared by Professor Pappageotes of Columbia University under contract with the Office of Education provide a very good sample of the total range of variation of each language.

There are (chiefly in the K reader) a number of selections whose language is in some measure mixed. Of this "mixed" language there are two main types: (1) a form of D which has been mildly purified by writing *dhià* for *yà* and *ís* for *s(è)*, adding a respectable number of final *n's* and augments, and occasionally one or two K verb forms (the favorites seem to be -*metha* for -*maste*, imperfective middle participles in -*ómenos, íto* and *ísan* for *itan*), and spelling all or most clusters in the K manner; (2) a form of K which has been "popularized" by using a few D words (neuter nouns in -i are most favored), including one or two D prepositions and particles (ya for dhià and particularly *mésa*), a few D inflections (especially N.-A. Pl. of feminines in -es, third plural forms in -ne often where literary D would not use them—, imperfective pasts of contract verbs in -úsa), and omitting an occasional -n or augment.

In some cases it is very difficult to say which sort of mixture is being used, but such cases are rare. If we separate the possible differences into four classes, we can, by counting, arrive at ratios or indices of Demoticity or Katharevusianism. The four are: (1) particles (mainly prepositions and conjunctions) and syntactic constructions; (2) inflectional affixes (including augments and reduplications); (3) vocabulary items (chiefly nouns, verbs, and adjectives, and only those where K and D each have an established word in regular use; (4) spellings. Of the four, inflection is without doubt the most important. In what follows we will give a sample of typical counts (per page, in general) of these items (in the form K/D), first in indubitable K documents, then in pure D, then slightly modified K and D, and finally problematical mixed-dialect cases, all selected from the preliminary drafts of Pappageotes' two readers.

Item and p. (*K Reader*)	*Synt.*	*Aff.*	*Voc.*	*Sp.*
editorial, 49	27/9	50/2	11/0	9/0
Xenopulos, 54	24/1	61/3	1/3	15/0
Nirvanas, 59	26/3	57/2	12/2	4/0
Melas, 61	25/1	48/0	3/0	12/1
Anninos, 65	9/2	58/0	9/1	14/0
Vamvas, 69	27/1	69/0	19/0	11/0
Karamanlis, 73	21/0	59/0	14/0	11/0
(article), 74	22/0	45/0	10/0	1/1
(article), 78	27/0	69/0	16/0	2/0
Papaconstandinu 91	14/3	30/2	4/1	3/1
Average for pure K	22.2/2	54.6/.9	9.9/0.7	8.2/0.3

D Reader:

G. Kazantzaki, 4	3/23	1/85	0/8	1/13
Papantoniu, 6	0/24	0/56	3/9	0/21 .
Megas, 11	3/32	6/69	1/28	0/30
Poriotis, 17	1/18	13/49	4/13	3/15
Palaiologhos, 20	4/20	5/62	12/12	6/12
Papadopulu, 26	0/15	5/54	1/33	7/30
Matsas, 32	3/17	1/68	1/11	3/10
Basias, 38	2/31	3/87	6/9	2/31
Michalopulos, 44	3/24	7/60	10/9	3/5
Kontoghlu, 57	0/48	1/131	1/44	1/33
Average for pure D	1.9/25.2	4.2/72.1	4.8/17.6	2.6/20

From a glance at these figures, it is obvious that pure D is more strongly characterized (in all four ways) than pure K; i.e., K uses more neutral forms and items than D does. It is also clear that D accepts a few more inflections and words from K than vice versa.

Now a sample of mixed forms: first predominately K, then mildly K, then predominately D, and finally one or two where the figures are almost equal.

K Reader:

(newspaper filler), 5	11/7	41/5	9/4	1/1
Moraitidhis, 20	34/6	65/5	6/15	17/1
Dhamveryis, 23	21/5	34/3	5/4	12/2
Khadzopulos, 27	22/4	78/9	15/10	25/2
Mitsakis, 201	45/5	75/9	18/17	4/2

In this group the uses of D items are principally of two kinds: in most of the selections a number of D vocabulary items are used for various special effects, and the other D forms result mainly from the principle of agreement or harmony; in the other selection there is a small amount of dialog, and dialog is generally (in K texts) composed either in good S or in a mildly purified D.

With more D mixture, but still K. (K Reader)

Cheropulos, 19	30/8	88/19	13/13	26/8
Petmezas-Lavras, 25	10/7	48/10	11/3	8/4
(Letter from Nea), 35	19/4	43/10	10/0	1/4
Papaconstandinu, 47-8	32/2	66/12	8/10	6/0

| Kokkinos, 63 | 28/9 | 59/13 | 6/12 | 17/1 |
| Theotokis, 67 | 21/7 | 54/9 | 6/2 | 21/0 |

Here the types of D material are the same; the proportion is just a little higher. The first two selections use D principally in dialog, but all show some instances of phrasal harmony.

The next group already includes a few which might be considered modified D, or at least "mixed."

K Reader:

Kosmas, 12-13	18/17	65/29	6/26	48/16
Skokos, 14	20/10	45/23	5/19	17/5
Xenopulos, 17	6/12	36/22	3/13	12/13
Nirvanas, 30-32	12/13	27/22	9/26	8/2
Trikupis, 71	16/5	51/26	12/4	11/2
Kolokotronis, 180	4/10	11/11	0/8	17/2

Note that almost all of these have a high D vocabulary ratio. Three of these (the first and the last two) are quite old, and all are earlier than Triandaphyllidhis. Hence it becomes important to consider not only how many, but what forms are used and how consistently. Kosmas the Aetolian is represented by four selections. The first (*On Charity*) is just about as pure D as one could expect in the 18th century: there are seven final n's, two *is*, and a *dhiá*, but otherwise (except for a K phrase "in word and in deed") everything is D. The other three have a little more the appearance of K.

The funeral oration on Byron by Trikoupis is K only to the extent of final n's, is, dhid, and certain spellings; the contract imperfect is always in -úsa, a-stem plurals are always in -es, aorist passives in -ika, active participles in -ondas. The brief speech attributed to Kolokotronis likewise has only dhia, is, final -n (not consistent), and a few spellings to justify the K label. Much the same applies to Laskaratos, who omits many final -n's, uses always the -ika aorist passive, the -ondas gerund, and the -es plural (except for one tas). Skokos, on the other hand, uses two -thi aorists, several -os adverbs, and two participles in -on (as well as many final n's), and even one dative phrase, but the basic pattern is clearly D. Xenopulos uses perhaps fewer peculiarly K forms than Skokos, but inserts the D items only singly, here and there, except in dialog, so that the impression is of a basic K style with a little spicing of D. This is a pretty fair sample of what is meant by "simple" K.

It is interesting that there are very few specimens with ratios (for endings) between 1/1 and 1/2. The best are these two:

Laskaratos, 15	19/18	17/28	1/5	16/2
Ghavrielidhis, 150	10/15	22/28	2/30	3/3

Both are unquestionably D, though not yet strictly according to Triandaphyllidhis. The K element consists chiefly of final n's and augments (though each selection has one feminine accusative article tas, induced by harmony with a following K noun ending in -is,) while the D elements include -ika forms, -ondas, many forms without final n, stin, stus, etc.

Laskaratos, 11	6/7	4/29	1/2	8/1
Laskaratos, 16	5/20	10/48	4/21	4/24
Oekonomakis, 33	7/31	19/49	2/9	10/8
Psathas, 36-7	2/31	8/41	2/10	18/2
Kondihylakis, 181	12/35	31/72	2/18	5/7

Most of these are pre-1900 and represent pretty good D for those days. The slight K coloring of the Oekonomakis selection is attributable to the journalistic nature of the subject and treatment. If we turn for a moment to the D reader, we can find selections with ratios very much like those in the last set.

Sykokis, 2-3	2/22	13/47	0/27	11/24
Angelomatis, 51	3/20	15/38	1/13	5/7
Vrachas, 59	3/27	7/53	13/7	2/14
Emmanuel, 60	5/25	11/68	6/5	5/3
Melas, 63	12/15	15/64	5/2	3/1
Churmuzios, 67	4/16	8/57	2/4	6/6
Pallis, 98	5/17	8/29	6/3	7/2
Symeonidhis, 128-9	3/20	8/38	2/3	2/3

All but one or two of these represent recent journalistic style, where the commonest K elements are augments, middle participles in -ómenos, an occasional third-declension nominative (esp. -sis, ótis), or genitive (-os, -eos). Pallis has some accusative plurals in -as; Churmuzios and Angelomatis several final n's.

Typical ratios from the recent reader by Sapoundzis, Sapoundzis and Hodge:

Page	P	E	V	S
5-6	2/25	0/55	2/21	2/8
26-7	1/28	3/52	0/17	2/9

42-3	4/27	4/91	5/27	7/7
53-4	2/22	2/114	1/18	5/6
75-6	1/37	0/82	0/32	3/9
91	5/20	4/53	5/17	6/0
119-20	1/32	3/86	0/32	11/5
149-151	4/26	10/103	7/20	19/9
178-9	8/52	16/159	10/26	11/14
219-20	6/30	30/85	12/19	14/2
248-9	33/3	75/0	6/0	3/0
280-282	23/49	53/169	4/26	13/6

Until the last three, these are all fairly pure D (in spite of the implication that this Reader is for a third language, neither D nor K), and the next-to-last one in pure K. The other two are substantially D, with phrases and sentences of K embedded (in one case fairly naturally, by references to a book).

There remain two selections in the K reader where the mixture is very difficult to classify because of wild inconsistencies.

Moraitinis, 21-2	12/11	28/29	11/18	17/3
Vlachu, 40-41	16/23	27/23	5/3	3/3

The Moraitinis selection is over 20 years old, uses forms with and without final -n, nominatives in both -sis and si, plurals in -es and -e (but no A's in -as) numberous iota subscripts, both sè and ís, both yà and dhià. A sentence will start D and end K. Or one sentence will be good K, and the next good D. This must be called truly "mixed," considered as a whole, but individual sentences or phrases are either clearly D or clearly K.

The Vlachu selection, on the other hand, is recent journalese with an obvious K base. The third declension types (especially the abstracts in -sis and -ótis) are consistently declined as in K (-sis, -seos, -sin, -ótis, -ótitos, -ótita, etc.) and augments are consistently added. But there are other inconsistencies. First and second declension accusative singulars occur both with and without final n; first declension plurals are given in both styles (D -es, -es, K -e, -as); the adverb is formed either in -os or in -a. There are gerunds in -ondas, contract imperfects in -úsa and third plurals in -ne. Both ya and dhia are used, both is and se, both boró and imboró, both aerodhrómio and aerodhrómion, for example. However, since most of the D items appear singly or in short (harmonizing) phrases embedded in longer stretches of K or neutral forms, the general impression is not as schizophrenic as the Moraitinis selection.

The vast majority of Greek writers, then, adopt a language which is either clearly D or clearly K; a few K writers (principally journalists) mix in occasional D words and inflections, and a few D writers adopt some K forms. Virtually no modern writers leave any doubt as to which language they are using, and there is no such thing as a *consistent* intermediate language. The net result of these mixtures is clearly that, as time goes on, K will replace more and more of its peculiar features with corresponding D ones, until, barring external influences, K as a distinct language will disappear. D, on the other hand, shows no strong disposition to borrow anything but vocabulary (nouns, verbs, adjectives).

The Uses of K and D

Pappageotes' K reader has a section called "Literary Texts" about 40 pages in length. It is instructive to note the nature of the 14 selections given here. The first (Kondhylakis) is actually in a mildly purified D, as we noted above, and another one (Mitsakis) is in a K with strong D admixture. Both were written before 1900; most of these selections were written before 1930, (indeed that is the case with over half the selections in the whole book). Two or three of the short pieces used as fillers are not properly literary at all, but encyclopedia articles or the like. Several selections have the character of memoirs; none are in verse.

In the D reader, on the other hand, half the selections are classified as literary; 123 pages of prose (chiefly fiction) and 22 of verse. In both readers the section called "Elementary Texts" (69 pp. in the K reader, 58 pp. in the D) consists mostly of literary pieces; again there is no verse in the K section, but there are seven poems in the D. Furthermore, as we have seen, four or five of the selections in this section of the K reader are either in D or have a heavy D mixture. So we may say:

(1) All verse, prose fiction (including plays) and (personal) essays are in D.

In the sections called "Articles" in the two readers there are several bits of literary criticism or art criticism or essays about writers: four (pp. 154-161) in the K volume, of which three are pre-1930, and the fourth by a member of the Academy, and nine (60, 67-84) in the D volume. This represents the facts pretty well.

(2) All or nearly all criticism—on art, literature, the theatre, etc.
—is nowadays written in D. Articles on art in the newspapers are
sometimes in K.

A number of the first few selections (pp. 2-9) in the D reader
are from Greek Readers used in the elementary school; there are no
such items in the K reader. On pp. 236-246 of the K reader there
are selections from a number of science textbooks. This does not
quite mirror the facts, but does so partially.

(3) In school, the prose in readers for the first three grades
(and most of the poetry in all readers) is in D; nearly all other textbooks, from fourth grade through graduate school, are written in K,
though there are now a few in D. This is also the case with most
reference books, particularly encyclopedias, and learned works on
most (but not all) subjects.

In the D reader there are letters on pp. 12-15, in the K reader
on pp. 6, 35. But the K letters on p. 6 are formal social notes, and the
one on 35 is a formal protest in a letter to the editor (and has a considerable D admixture, at that), whereas the letters in the D reader
include some personal letters and two "letters to the editor," both
couched in an informal style.

(4) Informal letters to friends or to periodicals are commonly
written in D; social or business letters and some "letters to the editor" are written in K.

The D reader contains one selection which might be called religious (p. 40), and that one is a newspaper article; in the K reader
(aside from Kosmas the Aetolian) there are three religious selections
(67, 102, 106), of which two are from newspapers.

(5) The official language of the Church is K, and most sermons,
theological treatises, serious articles on religion, etc., are in K. Occasionally a non-conformist preacher may use D, and the popular
press will include some religious pieces in D (particularly for children).

In the K reader a whole section (pp. 70-87) is labeled *Official
Texts*. In addition, pieces by (or about) leading politicians or by
King Paul appear on pp. 99, 107, 113, 119, 130, 142 and 210. Pp. 2-
10 include a variety of announcements, classified ads, programs, and
the like. In the D reader there are only two somewhat political pieces
(pp. 63 and 144), and both are quite unofficial and journalistic.

(6) The official language of government, politics, and law is K, and all official documents (licenses, diplomas, certificates, receipts, etc.), official and semi-official announcements, and classified ads, etc., public statements by political figures, laws, legal proceedings, court decisions, decrees, legal announcements, debates in parliament, proclamations, etc., and many political speeches are in K.

Among the "Articles" in the D reader, mostly taken from newspapers and magazines, are five on recent or current history, three on earlier (Byzantine to modern) history, six on the language question and four on science for the layman. In the K reader, besides the political and religious articles already mentioned, there are seven on historical topics, six on the language question, and three (not recent) on literature.

(7) In a few fields articles are written (and books as well, for that matter) with almost equal likelihood in both K and D: history, art history, biography, contemporary problems, science. In some cases the choice of language depends upon the stand taken: obviously a proponent of Katharevousa is not going to argue his case in Dhimotiki; and in politics a conservative Monarchist is not likely to write in D. In history, the period of the Revolution is more likely to be treated in D than are the wars of ancient Athens or Sparta.

Very few selections from the news columns of the daily press are included in these readers (in fact, other collections have been published exclusively of such material). But the D reader does have (291) one account of a basketball game.

(8) In most newspapers all principal news stories and editorials are in K; sports news, social columns (and many special columns) are in D.

To all this it must be added that spoken (or read) K exists in certain formal situations, particularly politics, law, church, and the classroom. And the proponents of K are particularly vigorous in pointing out that the Communists use and advocate D, so much so that, some years ago, one's stand on the language question was of basic political importance. Though the situation today is not quite as bad as it was, it is still the case that few right-wing believers are public users of D, and few socialists or liberals are violent advocates of K. Of course the most loyal supporters of K are the poor people who don't know it and can't use it.

A CHAPTER OF SEMOLOGY IN THE ENGLISH VERB

University of Wisconsin

Quite a few of us are old enough to remember some of the linguistic quarrels of the 1930's. One that particularly sticks in my mind had to do with the beginnings of phonemic theory. It seems that there were two words spelled *candied* and *candid,* and the problem was to prove that they were different words. Bloomfield transcribed the first of them with /ij/ and the second with plain /i/. Now that was a sufficient solution; but was it also a necessary one? Bloomfield himself said that it was not a necessary solution: "Any transcription that works" is a good one, he said; provided that it works through the whole lexicon and is not wasteful of symbols. Daniel Jones pointed out that the two words could be transcribed with the same vowel symbols, and *candied* with a hyphen before the final consonant, and that then both the British standard identity of the two words and the American difference between them would emerge from the single rule that before a hyphen one pronounces the same as at the end of the word *candy.* The Bloomfield theory of the day had no defense against that proposal; in fact, Bloomfield himself was not above using hyphens on occasion.

How did we get out of that jam? By instituting the principle of the Separation of Levels. That hyphen was a grammatical symbol, and it had no business intruding into a phonological description; and by the same token, nothing specifically semantic should be allowed to intrude into a grammatical description. It was an easy principle to defend, for we could simply remark that every mixing of levels amounted to begging the question. First, we said, the complete phonemic description without grammatical contaminations was a prerequisite to beginning to describe the grammar of a language; and then the complete grammatical description would be a prerequisite to beginning the study of meaning.

By the early part of the second world war we were erecting defenses on both flanks of this principle of the separation of levels. On one flank were ranged the literary critics—remember Leo Spitzer twenty years ago in Language?—who kept sniping at us for denying that meaning exists;

that forced us to say that we meant to use meaning only differentially: we promised to confine ourselves to asking whether two things had the same or a different meaning. One bold defender, Zellig Harris, undertook to show that even that employment of meaning was unnecessary for phonology and grammar; but most of us conceded that life would be too complicated on those terms. On the other flank were those who pointed out that even the differential use of meaning was not enough for a practical discovery-procedure: there, the leader was Kenneth Pike with his Grammatical Prerequisites to phonological analysis; and we covered that flank by distinguishing between practical analysis with no holds barred, on the one hand, and on the other hand a publishable description for which we would maintain the separation of levels. Many of us still maintain that that can be done with the help of a long spoon, but we can't deny that it is difficult.

As far as phonemics goes, Bloomfield had issued a sight-draft: he said that his distinctive features, by which he meant phonemes, would be delivered by the phonetic laboratories in about ten years. I am not one of those who say that Roman Jakobson's distinctive features have paid up on that sight draft; besides, the only people who are conspicuously using them are the ones who want to abolish phonemics entirely as a separate picture of a language, and the same people say that the language needs no separate picture on the meaning side either, but that the grammar can be trusted to generate everything with the help of a still longer spoon. It is a fascinating sight to watch their spoon grow longer and longer, and from time to time a little something can be learned from them by people like me. But what we mostly do is something much more old-fashioned.

I stand here today as a representative of Signals Grammar, and that means several things of different sorts. For one thing, it means that I am an individualist; and that is a notion that can be applied in more than one way. First, I hold that no linguist has a duty to believe everything that another linguist has conclusively proved; instead, I simply remark that various linguists start out from different sets of axioms and that *de gustibus non est disputandum*. Or in a single word, I am pluralist, as any individualist with a conscience ought to be: I think that variety is a Good Thing. Second, I believe that subdividing and the search for Symmetry are good things within the description of a language too; indeed, that it is the symmetries **within** each sub-system of a language that ultimately justify the dividing of the structure of the language into sub-systems. Or in other words, when I find enough symmetries I don't feel uneasy about the shortcomings of phonetics-laboratory or sociological-sematic data as supports for the sub-systems I work out. Instead, I regard the Separation of Levels as a presumably unattainable ideal but an ideal nevertheless.

But the cardinal principle of Signals Grammar is an axiom—not a discovery, not something that can be proved, but an axiom, a 'postulate' as these things are called in modern mathematics or logic—that says simply this: 'Text signals its own structure'. That is my wording; as a pluralist I have no objections to other wordings, of course. Like most axioms in all sciences, this one underlies the work of a great many people who never put the axiom into this or any other wording; they simply do what feels right to them and leave to others the task of saying why they do things that way. Again, like certain other axioms, for instance Euclid's Axiom of Parallels or the Parity Principle in sub-atomic physics, startling and useful developments have resulted from denying this axiom; in our case, Generative-Transformational Grammar. That need not, as I have explained, keep me from seeing what develops from an axiom that others have usefully denied.

An individualist, then, doesn't need to be a secessionist, any more than medical researchers with conflicting theories about Immunity are barred from cooperating in defending the community from a plague. It is from this standpoint, then, that I now proceed to attack a problem that has been plaguing us all for several decades. When Leo Spitzer and his fellow-travelers accused us all of neglecting or denying meaning, our separation of levels and our limitation to differential meaning were not our only defenses. Like Leonard Bloomfield promising that the phoneme would emerge from the laboratory in due course, many of us made an equivalent and I think safer promise about meaning: we said that all we needed was time enough to complete the theory of grammar as well as the theory of phonology, and then we would get around to tackling the theory of meaning; first, however, we needed a solid grammar to back it all up.

When that promise was a quarter-century old, say in the 1950's, the state of affairs with respect to meaning in American linguistics was roughly this. The anthropological linguists, more or less, had done a great deal with semantic hierarchies, notably in kinship terminologies and in folk taxonomies such as color-names and the hierarchic naming of flora and fauna. The general theory of semantic systems, notably on the basis of the Field Theory of Jost Trier, was a lively topic in European linguistics and a good many Americans lent a hand in this too. The Discourse Analysis of Zellig Harris had gone up like a rocket, but no general solution was visible to the problem of extending it beyond the confines of a single document. Trager and Smith had started out from the Bloomfield notion of the class-meaning of a grammatical category and were, and have since remained, busy elaborating that into a semology intimately tied to formal grammar; from time to time we have been treated to a shower of sparks from their smithy, but we are still awaiting the finished product. And the generative-grammar workers are still reducing meaning to a lot of fine print in the grammar.

When it comes to name-dropping, as my acquaintances know, I am not one to let modesty delay the proceedings. In the summer of 1957, feeling that it was about time I found out something about semantics, I offered a Semantics Seminar in the Linguistic Institute. The last three weeks of it were devoted to working out the theory of subdividing a definition for an unabridged dictionary. One of our discoveries was that the definition of the one morpheme that we studied thoroughly—CODE as a noun, as a verb, and in derivatives like *codify*—could be subdivided elaborately and perfectly symmetrically, and that is presumably the most conspicuous result in the publication in Studies in Linguistics, 'Semology: A Linguistic Theory of Meaning', in the last 1958 number. More important by far, in my view, was the demonstration that it all came out of linguistic context without reliance on the outside-world or 'semantic' value of either the context or the morpheme itself. I have since returned to this single experience in other publications that have added nothing substantial. My friends, if not all my acquaintances, will I hope be pleased to hear that I am only amused that there have been no publications of other problems worked out similarly. For myself, I have been content with what I learned that time, and have gone on to still other things.

One of these is the working out of the semology of the English verb. The cardinal difference is that this time we are faced with the semology of a substantial part of the grammar of a language, rather than that of a tiny part of the lexicon. But first let me list what we can still use from the earlier experience.

First, of course, there is the promise that **if** the semology of a **lexical** item can be kept entirely within the linguistic description, without recourse to sociology, physics, or any other of the various subdivisions of the lore that lies outside the language itself, **then** the same ought to be true *a fortiori* of a chapter of semology that belongs to the grammar instead of to the lexicon. In other words, Signals Grammar is where semology ought to be particularly easy, if it can be done at all anywhere.

Second, it is surely unnecessary to abandon the most significant lesson learned in working out that lexical problem. This lesson is the analysis of the meaning-contribution that a lexical unit makes to the sentence in which it is used, the analysis into two components which I call respectively the **additive** and the **privative** contribution that it makes. It makes these two contributions at different places in the sentence. It makes its **additive** contribution where it is itself syntactically situated in the sentence; and it makes its **privative** contribution everywhere else: mostly within the sentence, perhaps, but there is no definite limit to how far away it can make its privative contributions, perhaps even outside the confines of the single discourse and as late as say half a century in other discourses. For the privative contribution is nothing less than a contribution to the life-history of anybody who has encountered that sentence, and that personal history is what deprives particular sentences of certain referents for each of us.

The **additive** contribution starts out from our experience that the lexical unit—for instance CODE—has in our experience been used to refer to a truly vast number of real-world items; from that experience, we must allow that in each further sentence where it occurs it **imports** into the sentence, at least latently, **any and therefore all** of that vast list of references. Or we can afford to be more modest and say that it 'tries to import' them all into the one sentence; and in those terms the statement is unchallengeable because it is tautological. Equally we must admit that each and every other lexical unit in the sentence does the same with its own list of more or less familiar references, and that is the additive contribution of each. The total additive contribution of **all** the lexical items in a sentence (however short it may be) is vastly too much; its ultimate reference consists of **nothing but residues,** as explained next.

But when these two or more lexical units occur together in discourse, the list that each imports is almost wholly **in fatal conflict** with the other lists: nearly all of each list is **incongruous** with nearly all of each other list of possible references. This point becomes clear from the examination of the extreme case where absolutely all the references are absolutely in conflict with absolutely all the references of another lexical unit. Such an extreme case would be the deliberate nonsensicality of the formula *rope of sand* used to signify a political tie that does not bind. From the use of that formula to mean exactly that, it has acquired as a whole the status of a lexical unit, an 'idiom' as Hockett properly calls that sort of thing; so that this time, and eventually, we have procured **some** meaning instead of the **no meaning** that could safely have been predicted from the complete contradiction between the two lists of possible referents, the *rope* list and the *sand* list. That is to say, the a-priori prediction was that the **privative** contribution of *rope* to the sentence would completely wipe out the **additive** contribution of *sand,* while at the same time the **privative** contribution of *sand* would much more conspicuously wipe out the **additive** contribution of *rope*—that asymmetry is in fact the meaning of the English preposition *of*—leaving no referential meaning for the combination at all;

and only the adequate and repeated employment of the whole *rope of sand* in political contexts could confer meaning upon the whole though no longer upon either part of it.

With the recognition of this outcome I may seem to have taken back with one hand what I gave with the other; but note that we can still do the same thing by repeating the maneuver: we can construct the new collocation *rigid rope of sand,* and once more the conflicts or 'incongruities' have become entirely fatal. This new collocation, then, has no referential meaning at all. Yet it can eventually—perhaps as one result of reading this paper—acquire an idiomatic meaning; it could, for example, become another way of saying 'non-existent item' like that favorite of logicians the King of France who can safely be said to be bald. This is the ultimate difference between semology on the one hand and grammar or phonology on the other hand: it is easy to annex new items to the semology of a language, very hard to annex new items to its grammar, and all but impossible to add anything to its phonology. This is only another way of saying that every language is in principle equipped to say anything at all; and that again is the reason why there can be poets, philosophers, and scientists, all of whom leave their communities different from the way they found them.

Most of that is only by the way, but this much is needed for my promised topic: we now have adequately defined the two terms **additive** and **privative,** and we have seen that the **double** contribution to the meaning of a discourse is characteristic of **lexical** items. In turning to the semology of the English verb, we now are naturally curious about the additive or privative or other semological values of the venerable Bloomfieldian class-meanings, the meanings of grammatical **morphemes** or whatever we ultimately recognize as having 'grammatical meaning'. Well, I don't mean to keep you in suspense unnecessarily; let me immediately say that in the English verbs those meanings are **privative** and **nothing but** privative. Whether the same will prove to be true of, say, the plurality morpheme of English nouns is in principle an open question: I have not completed the research on the nouns and so I can't say. I must admit the possibility that 'singular' and 'plural' are **equipollent** in English as the Prague School long ago taught us to say. But in the grammar of the English verbs, the semological opposition is always between something and nothing, between 'marked' and 'unmarked' terms of an opposition; and the **marker** is always **privative** in its referential meaning or indeed whatever sort of meaning we want to call their effective meanings.

This is a startlingly **clean** result. Of course I wanted clean results when

I attacked the English verb about twenty-five years ago. I got no stable results at all for close to twenty years, despite all the pondering and all the reading of learnèd books and papers, good as many of them are. It turns out that the difficulty essentially consists in determining **just how much** grammatical form **is one marker.** Most of the time I was befooled by grammatical tradition. For instance, like many other people I tried to find out what was the meaning of the word *shown* in the two sentences *I have shown it to her* and *It has been shown to her.* It would have to be, according to tradition, the lexical meaning of *show* as modified by the morpheme -*n.* Well, that has turned out to be a mythical beast, like the present King of France.

The morpheme -*n* of *shown* has no consistent meaning; and that means that for our purposes it has no meaning at all, like the vowel /i/ that occurs in *bit* and *sit* and *pit* and *bid* and all those other words. Tradition says that it means 'completion' or something of the sort; but if we were to admit that, we would still have to dismiss it as irrelevant to the semology of the English verb's grammar, or anyhow incompetent.

Quite unsurprisingly, it was the transformation-grammar people that put me on the right track. I say 'me', but of course a lot of the work, and especially the indispensable wrangling, was done by others; among them I ought to name especially W. Freeman Twaddell, David DeCamp, W. Nelson Francis, and Ian Catford: we spent a number of weeks on this in Austin, Texas, in the summer of 1960, together with Mary Lu Joynes. In the two sentences, the verb-markers that have grammatical meaning (privative, it turns out) are (1) that -*s* that means 'concord with a subject that has gender' in the second sentence and can safely be dismissed after that has been noticed; (2) the marker *have* -*n* signifying **perfect phase** in both sentences; (3) the marker *be* -*n* signifying **passive voice** in the second sentence.

Then the verb-phrase in the second sentence has the constitution -*s have* -*n be* -*n show,* and each hyphened bit is morphophonemically a **suffix** to the following item, thus: -*s have* = *has,* -*n be* = *been,* and -*n show* = *shown,* so that the sentence reads *It has been shown· to her.* The corresponding analysis of *I have shown it to her* is now obvious, and it is equally obvious that *shown* is semologically not an immediate constituent of either sentence no matter what its morphological status is.

The problem is familiar. Essentially the problem is to determine the compass, the limits, of grammatical items in such a way that they will have **consistent** meanings, and that is what has been done here. Once it has been done, it is not surprising that their meanings are also **simple** meanings. As a bonus, we learn that in the English verb they are purely **privative** meanings, as I will now point out somewhat in detail. To begin with, and only to dismiss it as of no further interest, the gender-concord marker -*s* is a privative marker. No English plural has gender (which incidentally is true in the Germanic languages generally in modern times); thus the gender of *we* and *they* and of *you* with plural reference or of any plural noun is nonexistent. And the gender of *I* and singular *you* is epicene. But the gender of the Quaker subject *thee,* of *he, she,* and *it,* or of any singular noun is **determinate** in principle, even though perhaps hard to determine in a particular instance. That is why we say in modern English *If anybody leaves their book at home they borrow one.* The simple verb *borrow,* not only here but in *I borrow* and *we borrow* and *you borrow* and *people borrow,* lacks the gender-concord marker -*s* because none of those subjects has determinate gender; but in *he borrows* and *she borrows* and *it borrows* the marker says that the subject has one of the English genders, and it does the same in the Quaker *thee borrows,* for in principle the speaker always knows the gender of the addressee.

Then -*s* is obviously a privative marker in the sense that the verb *borrow* without that marker can have subjects of any gender or of unknown or inconsequential or indeterminate gender; but *borrows* with -*s* can only have a subject of specific gender each time it is used. This specificity is a restriction, a narrowing; that is, a privative thing. What is left is only **a part of the range** that was there without the marker, and that is what is meant by **privative.**

Without the **passive** marker *be -n* an English verb can be indifferently 'active' or 'passive' in meaning, for we say both *They are selling like experts* and *They are selling like hotcakes.* With the marker, the verb-phrase *are selling* is **deprived** of its otherwise possible active meaning, leaving its **always-possible** passive meaning **as a residue.** In this instance, we first note that *be* after zero is *are* (unless the subject is *I*); then *be -ing sell* is *are selling.* Next, the rule is that the **passive** marker comes **last before** the verb-base, and the passive constitution of the verb is then *be- ing be -n sell.* Finally, because -*n sell*=*sold* (never mind the fact that -*d sell*=*sold* also), this gives us the explicitly passive sentence *They are being sold like X* and if *X*=*experts* the results is that we are presumably talking about a slave-market. The natural-actor quality of *experts,* we see, cannot prevail over the meaning of the passive marker; but in *They are selling like hotcakes* the natural-victim quality of *hotcakes* deprives *are selling* of active meaning while in *They are selling like experts* the natural-actor quality of *experts* equally truly deprives it of passive meaning! The phrase *are selling* has **no voice of its own.** Contextual words can deprive it of either active or passive meaning, in each case leaving the other as a residue; but the marker *be -n* deprives it always and only of active meaning so as to leave passive meaning as the residue. In short, the meaning of the English **passive voice** is **not** 'passive' in a positive or additive way, but only 'not-active'—that is what we mean by calling the 'passive' (more realistically 'not-active') marker *be -n* a privative marker.

The effects of contextual *hotcakes* and *experts* do not necessarily depend on their being in the same sentence or even the same discourse. For example *They are selling all right* is always taken by the addressee as having active meaning or else as having passive meaning; never, that is to say, as having indeterminate voice—or 'hardly ever' as the saying goes. This is a fact of experience, and if I had the space I would repeat here the story of how one learns by experience that no native speaker of English consciously hesitates about the tense of *The councillors all put their glasses on their noses* when he hears or sees it: he instantly and sub-consciously dismisses one of the two tenses, and then he is astonished when he discovers that another hearer has taken it as in the other tense. What made him dismiss one of them we usually can't guess; perhaps something visible in the room, perhaps what he had for breakfast. This is a cardinal principle of semology. For one thing, it tells us how words acquire mean-ings in normal native-language learing—acquire the meanings they get for the individual learner, that is—namely that they acquire them from the equivalence of two equally privative factors: (1) linguistic context, (2) practical context.

In the game of Twenty Questions we notice two equally valuable things: (1) Each answer to a yes-or-no question has a privative effect in narrowing the range within which the ultimate answer is situated, and the best ques-tion-and-answer pair is the one which is most strongly privative, with the familiar consequence that the best are the rarest; the most efficient questions are those which split the residue into fairly equal halves; (2) The skillful questioner is apt to win especially by profiting from the responder's glances at various objects in the room, from his hesitations, and so on: all such are non-linguistic privative factors that are equivalent to linguistic answers.

It is because of that equivalence—that 'diplonomy' as I call it when my interlocutor is ready for the term—that a linguistic analyst can determine the precise meaning of any sufficiently recurrent item at all, never quite sure whether he is getting it from the immediate context or from his knowledge of the topic gained partly from the same document and partly throughout his earlier life. It is handy to be able to point to other words in the immediate context, but for an unprejudiced native it is not necessary. Unfortunately, it is all but impossible to find a native speaker of English without grammatical prejudices, so that my book *The English Verb: Form and Meanings* (University of Wisconsin Press: 1964) has to rely on a large and widely accessible corpus of nearly ten thousand verb-occurrences and also on a good deal of rather polemic argument.

Here is a short list of results.

1. The meaning of English **passive voice** is only that the grammatical subject of the verb **does not designate the actor.**

2. The meaning of the **temporary aspect** (marker: *be -ing*) is that there is **limited duration;** with here-and-now reference, this means that the **validity of the predication** has limited duration; with other reference, and in subordinate clauses and in non-finites, this means that the **specified event** does not advance the plot but has a limited duration that makes it serve as **background** for plot-advancing predications.

3. The **perfect phase** (marker: *have -n*) gets its name from the fact that the specified event and its interesting effects are 'out of phase' with each other, which can only be true if those effects are delayed so as to be later than their cause: that event. The specified event, that is, is not mentioned for its own sake but solely for the sake of its effects. The effects are least delayed opportunities for other events: *I have shown it to her* so that now she is familiar with it, and her familiarity is what matters while the show-ing does not. Conversely, English perfect phase does not mean 'earlier event' as the perfects of most European languages do.

4. The **remote tense** (marker: only *-d*) means that the specified event is **absent from the scene** as the clause is spoken. This has two interpretations: (1) the event is situated in authentic past history; (2) the event is unreal: it is an event, not real but hypothetical, posited for the sake of being vanquished in fatal conflict with accepted reality: *If you showed it to her right now, what then?*

5. Without *will, shall, may,* etc. (list of eight modals) the assertion is **factual** even though perhaps unreal; with any of those markers, the asser-tion is **relative.** Factual assertions are all made at the risk of the speaker being called a liar instantly; the unreal example above was only a question, and the corresponding statement *If you showed it her right now she would be angry* is a factual assertion made at the same risk. In short, factual asser-tion has **a determinate truth-value** with respect to the occurrence of the specified event. Relative assertion has no such truth-value: none of the sentences 'I M not show it to her' (where M is any of the eight modals *will, shall, can, may, must, ought to, dare, need*) is spoken at the risk of being shown up for a liar on the spot. Relative assertion gets its name

from the feature that the predication does not assert that the specified event is a proper part of the referential world, but rather asserts a relation between that event and the referential world: some relation which specifies what may be called 'the terms of admission' upon which it eventually becomes a proper part of the referential world if it ever does. In general, 'time will tell' whether it eventually does; to this extent, **every** modal has a **connotation** of futurity, but **no** modal (not even *will* or *shall*) has any **denotation** of futurity: English has only two tenses, and 'future' is not one of them.

In depriving the assertion of factuality (truth-value with respect to the occurrence of the specified event), all eight modals have the same privative significance. But in comparison with each other, the eight modals are all equipollent: none of their differences in meaning are privative differences.

6. The differences in meaning among the eight modals are three-dimensional differences. One dimension opposes the **maximal** social matrix of events (*must, ought to, dare, need:* the **stable** modals which reject the tense-marker *-d*) to the **minimal** social matrix of events (*will, shall, can, may:* the **casual** modals, signifying that the cogent factors are all the product of chance and whim). The **maximal** matrix is co-extensive with **the community;** the cogent factors are equally valid everywhere and at all times: they are **the mores** or identically **absolute logic,** and they impinge upon **the actor** (not necessarily designated by the grammatical subject: in *He must have shown it to her* the actor is **the order of nature**) and the stable modal is uniformly employed to say that this actor **is in jeopardy,** that he risks being adjudged 'not a proper member of the community'. The **minimal** matrix is populated with **circumstances,** and there is always a **personal center** of this matrix who determines what items of the referential world are to be valid as **cogent** circumstances for him; in general, the weightiest circumstances are situated **inside him,** the others are all more or less **near him,** and anything **outside** his purview is irrelevant, incompetent, and immaterial: it cannot be a cogent factor in any decision of his. Unless otherwise noted, the center of the minimal matrix is **the speaker;** *They can't do that to you* shows him right at home in the center; a question projects the center to the situation of the addressee instead, and other projections are possible but not indulged in by many speakers very often: *It says here that students may not smoke in classrooms.* In contrast, the **maximal** matrix **has no center:** all men are equal under the Common Law, and in this frame of reference every citizen loses his general privilege of making himself the center of any other frame of reference. David Riesman has explained, conceivably correctly, why the English stable modals are obsolescent.

Another dimension opposes **assurance** (*will, shall, must, ought to*) to **potentiality** (*can, may, dare, need*) in modern English since the second half of the seventeenth century; the Shakespearean value of this dimension, as near as I can read it at this distance, was Probability (i.e. probity in the actor as the warrant of eventual performance) to Permission (i.e. social capacity: in the feudal world, every capability was 'a freedom' graciously granted and none was inherent). See next.

The third dimension opposes **adequate** (*will, can, must, dare*) to **contingent** (*shall, may, ought to, need*); the last two of these modals became markers of relative assertion only within the seventeenth century (before that, one was a real past tense of *owe* and the other an equally factual impersonal verb), and with that reservation I can say that it seems to me that Shakespeare instead opposed Authoritative to Subservient. The retention of the older oppositions, here or as above or both, gives us such archaisms as *the President shall appoint* and the traditional answer to *Mother, can I go out to swim?* which is *No, you may not.*

All these, and factual assertion too, emerge quite automatically from a homogeneous set of symbolic definitions. The symbolic vocabulary is very small: four nouns, a sign of negation, and a relational verb or 'operator' as mathematicians call it:

A means 'actor as a proper member of the community.'

E means 'specified event: what is designated by the whole clause minus this modal.'

o means 'what is mentioned before is consistent with what is mentioned next and vice versa,' so that B o *beta* means that B is consistent with *beta* and *beta* is consistent with B: they can both be 'members of the same set' as mathematicians say.

A bar printed over a symbol negates it. Then ō means 'is inconsistent with.' And Ā means 'actor who is not a proper member of the community.' Finally, Ē means 'non-occurrent event: event such that a factual assertion that it occurred would be a falsehood.'

C means 'all the circumstances: every cogent factor with none absent on the roll-call' with the understanding that what is a cogent factor for one person may be none for another person, as explained before.

c means 'some of the circumstances **but not all'.**

Now we need a set of rules of combination for these symbols which will give us all the English possibilities and no others. This set of rules is our equivalent of Euclid's geometrical definitions and axioms.

Def. 1. A negation-sign combines with any symbol but C or c.

Def. 2. Only one negation-sign combines with the same symbol.

Def. 3. The number of negations is even, perhaps zero.

Axiom 1. There are just **three** symbols in each definition.
Axiom 2. A consistency symbol is in the middle as a **relator.**
Axiom 3. The Actor is relatable only to the Event.
Axiom 4. Circumstances are relatable only to the Event.
Axiom 5. The tautology that Events are consistent with Events does not define any marker's meaning.

The first three are called definitions for good reasons. Thus circumstances can never be negated: this is the definition of English pragmatism. The second definition says that negation yields an absolute contrary, so that when two negations are combined both vanish: 'two minuses make a plus'. The third one says that all the definitions are affirmative: each is favorable to occurrence of the event. The reasons why the other five are called axioms seem obvious to me; I don't think I could explain them to anybody to whom that is not obvious, and that is only what we must expect of axioms. Anyhow, the complete list of eight restrictions gives us this set of sentences and no others; each sentence consists of three symbols of which the middle one is a verb, and everything printed after each sentence is empirical fact verified by the whole corpus of 1340 relative assertions and 6700 factual assertions:

Ē ō C = will 'adequate casual assurance'
E ō c = shall 'contingent casual assurance'
E o C = can 'adequate casual potentiality'
E o c = may 'contingent casual potentiality'
Ē ō A = must 'adequate stable assurance'
Ē o Ā = ought to 'contingent stable assurance'
E o A = dare 'adequate stable potentiality'
E ō Ā = need 'contingent stable potentiality'
E o E 'the speaker has not contradicted himself'.

If the definition of *need* seems devious, remember that it is never used in a flat positive statement: *I need show it to her* is not English, but *Need I show it to her?* asks whether that deed is inconsistent with my being an outcast—whether showing it to her protects me from possibly being in disfavor. The other definitions are surely obvious, with the understanding that they do not refer to any archaic usage or textbook rule, but instead to present-day usage among such people as use these modals freely. For instance, mature Englishmen who do not suffer from insecurity say *I will show it to her* when adequately assured of factually doing it in these circumstances, but *I shall show it to her* to allow that the assurance is only contingent: the disregarded residue (C minus c) of the circumstances may intervene to frustrate the deed. Hence *I will give it you: here it is* against *I shall give it to you tomorrow;* and *I will certainly show it to her* against *I think I shall show it to her.*

Finally, let us see what we can do with that ninth tautological sentence, which seems to say that truth-telling is a mere tautology. If E o E, then by virtue of that same induction which assures us of the sun's rising tomorrow, we can say every factual event is consistent with every other factual event and therefore with the totality of them: but this totality is simply our personal history of the world up to the present moment, or in other words 'accepted reality'. This can be written R, and we get, applying the negation-signs by rule, these four:

$\bar{\text{E}}$ ō R 'the speaker's assertion must be true'
$\bar{\text{E}}$ o $\bar{\text{R}}$ 'this ought to be true even if it doesn't seem so'
E o R 'I dare say he's telling the truth'
E o $\bar{\text{R}}$ 'that assertion needn't be a lie'.

These seem to be, as a matter of empirical fact, the only ways of accepting a factual statement. The second can also be interpreted as one way of accepting an unreal conditional statement, and the fourth as another way of accepting one, for instance *If I knew where to find her I'd show it to her.*

It will not have escaped an attentive reader that the four formulas are strictly parallel to the definitions of the four stable modals. This seems to be a significant fact about English-speaking cultures. They also summarize, by the same token, the way I expect my factual assertions to be accepted subject to verification under the usual pair of stipulations: (1) No scientific statement can be proved true; at best, it can survive verification, and verification consists in failing to refute while trying hard. (2) Only one hypothesis is to be verified at a time: scientific verification does not include pitting one hypothesis against another, though two hypotheses can be separately verified before judging whether one stands the test better than the other. In this instance, one example of an unscientific attempt at refutation would consist in refuting my definition of *shall* by confronting it with texts **either** edited **or** interpreted by the hoary textbook rule.

My corpus used for verifying all this: Sybille Bedford, *The Trial of Dr. Adams* (Black Cat Book BA-21 = Simon & Shuster; with other paginations same title in Time Reading Program and two British editions of *The Best We Can Do* [Collins and Penguin]) relying especially on unretouched official court-reporter's transcript and on Mrs. Bedford's magnificently illuminating notes on paralinguistic events and dramatic tensions.

THE SEMANTIC PATTERNING OF WORDS

Hans Kurath
University of Michigan

The lexicographer conveys typical meanings by translation, paraphrase or description; he illustrates typical constructions in which the expression occurs; he illustrates typical lexical contexts. He hopes that such treatment of words and phrases will be meaningful to the reader. Judging from the fact that dictionaries are much in demand and relied upon by scholars, the lexicographer feels that he is doing a useful job and that he achieves his purpose to a considerable extent.

Looking beyond his immediate objective, the lexicographer is apt to ask himself all sorts of questions. He may ask to what extent the 'typical meanings' that he points out are *inherent* in the words of the language he deals with, and to what extent he *introduces* semantic distinctions for the sake of speakers of another language, i.e., of the language of the reader.

To illustrate. The ME adverb *faste* occurs in context with such verbs as *stand, hold, join; run, attack, defend; start, stop; rain, blow; look, learn; sleep; love, fear.* When I gloss such ME verb phrases in MnE by 'stand fast', 'join firmly', 'attack vigorously', 'stop suddenly', 'rain hard', 'look sharply', 'sleep soundly', 'love dearly', etc., do I identify inherently different meanings of ME *faste,* or do I attribute MnE semantic distinctions to it? Should I say that ME *faste* has only ONE meaning, a vague SEMEME, that could be suggested by the MnE expression *intensely?* Should I say that it has different meanings when joined with verbs of rest, verbs of motion, verbs of mental activity, and verbs of emotion, assuming that rest, motion, mental processes, and emotional experiences are 'categories of thought' reflecting different 'spheres of reality'?

Let us look at another example. ME *daunten* (whence MnE *daunt*) occurs in a wide range of lexical contexts in which MnE requires a variety of verbs. We *intimidate* or *daunt* a person, *tame* a horse, *train* a dog, *defeat* an enemy, *conquer* a country, *pacify* a child, *flatter* a woman, *control* an impulse, *restrain* our tongue, *refine* our behavior. In all such contexts ME has, or can have, the verb *daunten.*

Does that mean that ME *daunter* has as many *referential* meanings as the number of suitable MnE translations would suggest? Shall we go to the other extreme and say that ME *daunten* has only ONE meaning (a SEMEME), which could be paraphrased by such a MnT expression as *exert influence in such a way as to control (something)*? Shall we say that the *referential* meaning attaches to the verb phrase as a whole, and that we cannot assign discrete meanings to the verb and to its object? If the latter, should the lexicographer bother with words? Should he not rather deal with phrases or with whole sentences? The answer would seem to be that ME *daunten* actually has a variety of *referential* meanings which the lexicographer manages to convey to the reader by giving suitable lexical equivalents and by pointing out typical contexts. 'Intimidating' a person, 'flattering' a woman, 'restraining' one's impulses, 'defeating' an enemy, etc., are different observable *segments of reality* in any society, though these actions may be variously regarded in different societies. But where shall we draw the line between referential meanings inherent in the source language and meanings pointed out by the lexicographer for the sake of speakers of another language?

Can we shed some light on such vexing problems by investigating the parrellel semantic patterning of antonyms, synonyms, and paronyms, or the parallel semantic behavior of word classes? Since such parallelisms *do* exist, it is not unreasonable to expect that they may reflect either culture-bound habits of analyzing reality for purposes of communication or effects of the grammatical structure of the language.

Parallel semantic patterning is perhaps most striking in antonyms.

Thus in ME both *bright* and *derk* are applied
    to a source of light, to color, and to the weather:
      'bright' vs. 'dark';
    to vision: 'keen' vs. 'poor';
    to utterances: 'clear' vs. 'obscure';
    to behavior: 'virtuous' vs. 'wicked'.

Their application diverges in that *bright,* but not *derk,* refers also to the appearance of persons: 'fair' lady, 'handsome' fellow; and to sound: 'clear, resonant'. On the other hand, *derk,* but not *bright,* is applied to mentality or mood: 'ignorant', 'despondent'; and to moral characteristics: 'malignant'.

It should be noted that the divergences in the range of applications of ME *bright* and *derk* may be apparent rather than real because the ME corpus of writings, though large, is limited.

Parallel patterning is also common in synonyms. Thus both ME *care* (from OE) and *distresse* (from OF) are applied to an emotional experience and to a situation that induces the emotion. Only *care* means also 'pain' and 'responsibility'; and only *distresse* means also 'coercion' and (in *law*) 'right of seizure'.

Paronyms (i.e. coordinated terms, terms belonging to the same sphere of reality) are apt to exhibit parallel patterning, as *eye* and *ear,* both of which designate (a) a sense organ as an anatomical entity; (b) the function of the organ (perception); (c) a mental operation: *eye* 'insight, opinion' (*have an eye for sth.*); *ear* 'attention' (*lend an ear*); (d) an object similar in shape or position to the organ: *eye* 'bud' (of a plant), 'hole' (in an object); *ear* 'protruding handle' (of a pot). The two terms have also a variety of similar figurative uses. Only *eye* is used in the sense of 'expressing or arousing an emotion or attitude', as in the expressions *lecherous eyes, kind eyes, evil eye.*

Such examples could be multiplied almost indefinitely for any language. The few that time permits me to present are indicative of what one finds in ME:

(1) A word can denote a complex reality, or any one of its several aspects, as *eye* in the senses 'organ of sight, an anatomical structure, vision', or *distresse* in the senses 'a threatening situation, an emotional experience induced by the situation, a situation with the emotional response to it'. The intended meaning is conveyed by the lexical context or the grammatical construction, but may remain ambiguous.

(2) A word denoting something perceived with the senses can be applied to mental or moral qualities, experiences, or activities, as when *bright* and *derk* refer both to light, color, and vision and to certain types of thought or behavior.

(3) A word can be transferred to something having a superficial or imagined similarity to its original referent, as when *eye* is applied to a bud or a hole, or *ear* to a projection on a vessel.

Such observations are by no means novel. They are the stock in trade of semanticists from Bréal, Paul, Wundt, and Nyrop to Kronasser and Ullmann. What I would suggest is that this whole matter be systematically investigated in a number of different languages by analyzing the semantic range of synonyms, antonyms, and paronyms with a view to establishing the extent of parallel semantic patterning. I suspect that marked differences between languages may turn up and give us new insight into the thought world' or 'world view' of different peoples.

I conclude by merely hinting at the fact that word classes, such as nouns or subclasses of nouns, often exhibit similar semantic patterning. Thus action nouns frequently denote both an activity or process and the result or product of the activity or process. For instance, ME *generacioun* means 'propagation of the species, divine creation, development (of an embroyo, a plant), generation (of heat) as well as 'progeny, ancestral line or pedigree, a breed (of dogs)'. In parallel fashion, ME *feigninge* denotes the 'act of inventing (sth.), composing a story)' and 'a thing invented or composed: an invention, a story, a legal fiction, a supposition, a false statement'.

One can perhaps argue that a process or activity and its result or product are complementary aspects of a complex reality and that action nouns come to be applied to the result or product of the process or action for that reason. But it seems equally possible that this type of patterning is somehow connected with the structural fact that in English verbs have, or may have, objects.

Thus I end, as I started, by posing a question. I hope that someone will have the skill and he persistence to follow up my implied suggestions.

ON THE MECHANISM OF LINGUISTIC CHANGE

WILLIAM LABOV

Columbia University

INTRODUCTION

This paper outlines the approaches to the explanation of linguistic change which are being followed in our current research within the context of the speech community. It is now clear that many theoretical problems of linguistic structure cannot be resolved without data from the speech community;[1] here I will focus on the converse proposition—that linguistic change cannot be explained by arguments drawn from purely internal relations within the system, even if external, sociolinguistic relations are recognized as additional conditioning factors. In the mechanism of linguistic changes which we have observed, the two sets of relations are interlocked in a systematic way.

The investigations which form the basis for the present discussion are studies of linguistic change on the island of Martha's Vineyard, and in New York City; the principal focus will be on the process of sound change. The chief techniques used in this research have been described in several previous papers and publications, along with a certain amount of the data and the findings.[2] The data to be presented here may be considered repre-

---

[1] This point of view is developed in detail in W. Labov, "The aims of sociolinguistic research," to appear in the report of the Sociolinguistics Seminar held at Bloomington, Indiana, in the summer of 1964, under the auspices of the Social Science Research Council.

[2] "The social motivation of a sound change," *Word* 19:273-309 [1963]; *The Social Stratification of English in New York City*, Columbia University Dissertation, 1964; "Phonological correlations of social stratification," in Gumperz and Hymes [eds.], *The Ethnography of Communication, American Anthropologist*, Vol. 66, No. 6, Part 2, December 1964, pp. 164-176; "The reflections of social processes in linguistic structures," in Fishman, J. [ed.], *A Reader in the Sociology of Language* [to appear, Mouton]; "Hypercorrection by the lower middle class as a factor in linguistic change," in Bright, W. [ed.] *Proceedings of the U.C.L.A. Conference on Sociolinguistics* [to appear]; "Stages in the acquisition of standard English", in Davis, A. [ed.], *Proceedings of the Conference on Urban School Dialects and Language Learning* [to appear].

sentative of a much larger set of facts and correlations derived from these studies.

The problems of linguistic evolution. Despite the achievements of 19th century historical linguistics, many avenues to the study of linguistic change remain unexplored. In 1905, Meillet noted that all of the laws of linguistic history that had been discovered were merely possibilities:[3]

> . . . it remains for us to discover the variables which permit or incite the possibilities thus recognized.

The problem as we face it today is precisely that which Meillet outlined sixty years ago, for little progress has been made in ascertaining the empirical factors which condition historical change.[4] The chief problems of linguistic evolution might be summarized as five questions:

1. Is there an over-all direction of linguistic evolution?
2. What are the universal constraints upon linguistic change?
3. What are the causes of the continual origination of new linguistic changes?
4. By what mechanism do changes proceed?
5. Is there an adaptive function to linguistic evolution? [5]

One approach to linguistic evolution is to study changes completed in the past. This has of course been the major strategy of historical linguistics, and it is the only possible approach to the first two questions—the direction of linguistic evolution, and the universal constraints upon change. On the other hand, the questions of the mechanism of change, the inciting causes of change, and the adaptive functions of change, are best analyzed by studying in detail linguistic changes in progress. The mechanism of linguistic change will be the chief topic of the discussion to follow; however, many of the conclusions will plainly be relevant to the questions of inciting causes and adaptive functions of change, and it will be apparent that more

---

[3] *Linguistique historique et linguistique générale,* [Paris, 1921], p. 16.

[4] There has actually been a retrograde movement in this respect, in the sense that treatments of linguistic change which are essentially ahistorical have become popular. Chronological detail is deliberately set aside in such articles as H. Pilch, "The rise of the American English vowel pattern," *Word* 11:57-93 [1955], and M. Halle, "Phonology in a generative grammar," *Word* 18:54-72 [1962].

[5] This question is all the more puzzling when we contrast linguistic with biological evolution. It is difficult to discuss the evolution of the plant and animal kingdoms without some reference to adaptation to various environments. But what conceivable adaptive function is served by the efflorescence of the Indo-European family? On this topic, see "The aims of sociolinguistic research," cited above, and D. Hymes, "Functions of speech: An evolutionary approach," in Gruber, F. C. [ed.], *Anthropology and Education* [Philadelphia, 1961].

complete answers to these questions will require methods similar to those used here.

An essential presupposition of this line of research is a uniformitarian doctrine: that is, the claim that the same mechanisms which operated to produce the large scale changes of the past may be observed operating in the current changes taking place around us.

A STRATEGY FOR THE STUDY OF LINGUISTIC CHANGES IN PROGRESS

Although answers to the three questions given above are the ultimate goals of our current research, they do not represent the actual strategy used. For the empirical study of changes in progress, the task can be sub-divided into three separate problems which jointly serve to answer the questions raised above.

[1] The *transition* problem is to find the route by which one stage of a linguistic change has evolved from an earlier stage. We wish to trace enough of the intervening stages so that we can eliminate all but one of the major alternatives. Thus questions of the regularity of sound change, of grammatical influence on sound change, of "push chains" versus "pull chains," of steady movement versus sudden and discontinuous shifts, are all aspects of the transition problem.

[2] The *embedding* problem is to find the continuous matrix of social and linguistic behavior in which the linguistic change is carried. The principal route to the solution is through the discovery of correlations between elements of the linguistic system, and between those elements and the non-linguistic system of social behavior. The correlations are established by strong proof of concomitant variation: that is, by showing that a small change in the independent variable is regularly accompanied by a change of the linguistic variable in a predictable direction.[6]

[3] The *evaluation* problem is to find the subjective [or latent] correlates of the objective [or manifest] changes which have been observed. The

---

[6] The concept of the linguistic variable is that developed in "The linguistic variable as a structural unit," paper given before the Washington, D.C. Linguistics Club in October, 1964. The definition of such a variable amounts to an empirical assertion of co-variation, within or without the linguistic system. It appears that the fundamental difference between an explanation of a linguistic change, and a description, is that a description makes no such assertion. In terms of a description of change, such as that provided by Halle, *op. cit.*, there is no greater probability of the change taking place in the observed direction, as in the reverse direction. Note that the embedding problem is presented here as a single problem, despite the fact that there are two distinct aspects: correlations within the linguistic system, and with elements outside the system. The main body of this paper provides justification for this decision.

indirect approach to this problem correlates the general attitudes and aspirations of the informants with their linguistic behavior. The more direct approach is to measure the unconscious subjective reactions of the informants to values of the linguistic variable itself.

With tentative solutions to these problems in hand, it would be possible to provide an explanation of a linguistic change which answers the three questions of inciting cause, mechanism, and adaptive function. As in any other investigation, the value of an explanation rises in relation to its generality, but only to the extent that it rests upon a foundation of reliable and reproducible evidence.

THE OBSERVATION OF SOUND CHANGE

The simplest data that will establish the existence of a linguistic change is a set of observations of two successive generations of speakers— generations of comparable social characteristics which represent stages in the evolution of the same speech community. Hermann obtained such data at Charmey in 1929, by developing Gauchat's original observations of 1899.[7] We have such data for Martha's Vineyard, adding the 1961 observations to the 1933 data of the Linguistic Atlas.[8] For New York City, we add the current data of 1963 to the Linguistic Atlas data of 1940; in addition, we have many other reports, including the excellent observations of Babbitt in 1896 to add further time depth to our analysis.[9]

Solutions to the transition problem proposed here will depend upon close analysis of the distribution of linguistic forms in *apparent time*— that is, along the dimension formed by the age groups of the present population. Such an analysis is possible only because the original simple description of change in *real time* enables us to distinguish age-grading in the present population from the effects of linguistic change.[10]

The evidence obtained in the research reported here indicates that the regular process of sound change can be isolated and recorded by observations across two generations. This process is characterized by a rapid

---

[7] "Lautveränderungen in der Individualsprache einer Mundart," Nachrichten der Gesellschaft der Wissenschaften zu Göttingen, *Phil.-his. Kl.* XI: 195-214 [1929]; L. Gauchat, *L'unité phonétique dans le patois d'une commune,* [Halle, 1905].

[8] H. Kurath et al., *Lingustic Atlas of New England* [Providence, 1941].

[9] Y. A. Frank, *The Speech of New York City,* University of Michigan dissertation, 1948; H. Kurath and R. A. McDavid, Jr., *The Pronunciation of English in the Atlantic States* [Ann Arbor, 1961]; A. F. Hubbell, *The Pronunciation of English in New York City* [New York, 1949]; E. H. Babbitt, "The English of the lower classes in New York City and vicinity," *Dialect Notes* 1:457-464 [1896].

[10] C. Hockett, "Age-grading and linguistic continuity," *Language* 26:449-457 [1950].

development of some units of a phonetic sub-system, while other units remain relatively constant. It affects word classes as a whole, rather than individual words: yet these classes may be defined by a variety of conditions, morphophonemic and grammatical as well as phonetic. It is regular, but more in the outcome than in its inception or its development. Furthermore, it appears that the process of sound change is not an autonomous movement within the confines of a linguistic system, but rather a complex response to many aspects of human behavior.

Some comment is required on the possibility of observing regular sound change, since arguments inherited from the neogrammarian controversy have impeded the progress of empirical research in this area. The inheritors of the neogrammarian tradition, who should be most interested in the empirical study of regular change in progress, have abandoned the arena of meaningful research in favor of abstract and speculative arguments. Indeed, Bloomfield and Hockett have maintained that phonetic change cannot in principle be observed by any of the techniques currently available.[11] Hockett has proceeded to identify sound change with a level of random fluctuations in the action of the articulatory apparatus, without any inherent direction, a drift of the articulatory target which has no cognitive, expressive or social significance.[12] All of the empirical observations of change in progress which have been reported are explained as the results of a complex process of borrowing, and are relegated to a type of linguistic behavior known as the fluctuation or conflict of forms. No claims are made for the regularity of this process, and so the basic tenet of the regularity of sound change has been deprived of all empirical significance. Furthermore, the changes which actually are observed are regarded as unsystematic phenomena, to be discussed with anecdotal evidence,

---

[11] *Language* [New York, 1933], p. 347, 365; *A Course in Modern Linguistics* [New York, 1958], p. 439, 444. Hockett writes: "No one has yet observed sound change: we have only been able to detect it via its consequences. We shall see later that a more nearly direct observation would be theoretically possible, if impractical, but any ostensible report of such an observation so far must be discredited." His theoretical proposal is that "over a period of fifty years we made, each month, a thousand accurate acoustic records . . . all from the members of a tight-knit community." The suggestion to multiply the data in this way is not necessarily helpful, as the experience of sociological survey analysts has shown: for relatively small numbers are needed to measure change in a population if the bias of selection is eliminated or minimized. Otherwise, we merely multiply the errors of measurement.

[12] According to Hockett, the variables responsible for sound change include "the amount of moisture in the throat, nose and mouth of the speaker, random currents in his central nervous system, muscular tics . . . the condition of the hearer's outer ear [presence of wax or dirt] . . ." *Op. cit.*, pp. 443-444.

subject to forces "quite outside the linguist's reach," factors which "elude our grasp," fluctuations "beyond our powers" to record.[13]

The evidence of current research suggests that this retreat was premature, that the regular process of sound change can be observed by empirical methods. The refinements in methodology called for are not the mechanical elaborations suggested by the writers cited above; for the mere multiplication of data only confounds analysis and perpetuates the bias of selection. It is rigor in the analysis of a population and in the selection of informants which is required. Furthermore, we need ingenuity in the resolution of stylistic variation, to go beyond the sterile method of endless dissection into idiolects. With such techniques, we find that regularity emerges where only confusion was seen before. Random fluctuations in articulation can certainly be found: indeed, this is the level of "noise" which prevents us from predicting the form of every utterance which our informants will make. But it would be an error to ascribe a major role to such fluctuations in the economy of linguistic change. The forces which direct the observed changes appear to be of an entirely different order of magnitude, and the changes take place much more rapidly than any process of random drift could account for.[14]

A single example of a sound change recently observed will be used to illustrate the general approach to solving the transition, embedding and evaluation problems. This example is one of the simplest cases—that of the centralization of (aw) on Martha's Vineyard. In the development of this case, some new evidence will be presented on the mechanism of sound changes which has not been published before.

THE CENTRALIZATION OF (AW) ON MARTHA'S VINEYARD

We begin with a clear-cut case for the existence of a linguistic change from observations in real time. In 1933, Guy Lowman found no more than the barest trace of centralization of /aw/; the significant variation observed was the fronting of /aw/ from [aʊ] to [æʊ]. In 1961, a comparable set of older eighth generation descendants of Yankee settlers

---

[13] Bloomfield, op. cit., pp. 343-368.

[14] Thus the following table contrasts the two points of view:

Neogrammarian:	sound change	fluctuation of forms	ultimate regularity
Present discussion:	sub-linguistic fluctuations	sound change	ultimate regularity

from the same villages showed a very pronounced centralization of /aw/—now clearly the variable (aw).[15]

The *transition* problem is studied through a detailed examination of the distribution of forms through apparent time—that is, through the various age levels in the present population.[16] The first step in the analysis is to construct a quantitative index for discrete values of the variable: [17]

$$
\begin{array}{ll}
\text{aw-0} & [a\text{U}] \\
\text{aw-1} & [a^{\perp}\text{U}] \\
\text{aw-2} & [\text{вU}] \\
\text{aw-3} & [\text{əU}]
\end{array}
$$

The index of centralization was constructed from this scale by averaging the numerical values assigned to each variant. Thus (aw)-00 would mean no centralization at all, while (aw)-3.00 would mean consistent centralization at the level of [əU]. This index was applied to interviews with 69 informants by rating each of the words in which (aw) occurred. The first approach to the transition problem can then be made by correlating average (aw) index scores for these interviews with the age level of the speakers. The first three columns of Table 1 show a regular correlation, in which the centralization index rises regularly for four successive age levels.

The over-all tendency of Table 1 represents an amalgamation of many different types of speakers and many different trends in the use of (aw). Figure 1 presents a more detailed analysis of the transition problem for a

---

[15] In the notation used here, parentheses indicate the linguistic variable, while slashes indicate bi-unique phonemes and brackets phonetic notation as usual. Thus (aw) represents the variable in general; (aw-2) is a particular value of the variable; (aw)-22 is an average index score for the variable.

[16] In this case, as in many others, the original sample was too small to allow us to study differences in age levels; only four informants were chosen on Martha's Vineyard in 1933.

[17] The original impressionistic scale had six levels. Instrumental measurements of a sample of these ratings indicated that four levels could be distinguished with a high degree of conformity to formant positions. See "The social motivation of a sound change," pp. 286-287.

TABLE 1

Centralization indexes by age level

Generation	Age Level	(aw)-	(ai)-
Ia	over 75	0.22	0.25
Ib	61-75	0.37	0.35
IIa	46-60	0.44	0.62
IIb	31-45	0.88	0.81

	(aw-) 0 1 2 3		(aw) index
Fig. 1-a Four LANE informants, av. 65 yrs.	15 1 1 22 1	___ C° else.	.06
Fig. 1-b Mr. H. H., Sr. 92 yrs.	15 2 14 1	___ C° else.	.10
Fig. 1-c Mrs. S. H., 87 yrs.	8 2 12 3	___ C° else.	.20
Fig. 1-d Mr. E. M., 83 yrs.	19 2 4 20 3 3	___ C° else.	.52
Fig. 1-e Mr. H. H., Jr. 60 yrs.	1 6 4 1 4 8 2	___ C° else.	1.18
Fig. 1-f Mr. D. P., 57 yrs.	1 3 10 9 15 3	___ C° else.	1.11
Fig. 1-g Mr. P. N., 52 yrs.	17 2 10 6	___ C° else.	1.31
Fig. 1-h Mr. E. P., 31 yrs.	9 9 7 2	___ C° else.	2.11

FIGURE 1

Stages in the centralization of (aw) on Martha's Vineyard, Massachusetts

critical sub-group. Here are displayed the percentage distribution of lexical items for eight individuals from 92 to 31 years of age. The horizontal axes show the four coded levels of the variable (aw). The vertical axes are the percentages of lexical items used with each variant. The vocabulary is broken into two sections that are tabulated separately: the solid line represents words in which (aw) is followed by a voiceless obstruent, as in *out, house, about, mouth;* the broken line represents all other words [and principally those ending in a nasal, as in *town, found,* or with no consonant final, as in *now, how*, etc.] [18]

The first diagram in Figure 1 is not that of an individual, but shows the composite results for the four Linguistic Atlas informants interviewed in 1933. They show only the barest trace of centralization. The second diagram, 1-b, is that of the oldest informant of 1961, a man 92 years old. The average age of the Atlas informants was 65 years; Mr. H. H. Sr. would have been 64 years old in 1933, and so he is of the same age group. His centralization profile is quite similar to that of the Atlas informants in 1-a. In Figure 1-c, we have an 87-year-old woman who shows only a slight increase in centralization. Figure 1-d, Mr. E. M., 83 years old, indicates a small but distinct increase in the occurrence of variant (aw-2). Mr. H. H. Jr., in 1-e, is considerably younger; he is 61 years old, the first representative of the next generation, since he is the son of Mr. H. H. Sr. Here we have a marked increase in centralization, with both classes of words centered about a norm of (aw-1). In Figure 1-f, Mr. D. P., 57 years old, shows a distinct difference between words ending in voiceless obstruents and all others; the first are now centered about a norm of (aw-2), while the second group is concentrated at (aw-1). This process is carried further in the speech of Mr. P. N., 52 years old, who shows perfect complementary distribution. Before voiceless obstruents, /aw/ has an allophone which is almost always (aw-2), while before other terminals it is usually uncentralized. And at this point, there is no overlap in the distribution. Finally, in 1-h, the most extreme case of centralization, we see an even sharper separation: this is Mr. E. P., 31 years old, the son of Mr. D. P. in 1-f.

On the right hand side of Figure 1 are the figures for the actual numbers of lexical items observed, and the composite index scores for each of the eight cases. It may be noted that (aw) is only one-third as frequent as (ay), and the regularity which appears here does not require a vast corpus

---

[18] The phonetic conditioning was actually much more complex than this, and both following and preceding consonants are involved. *Ibid.,* p. 290.

of observations. The regularity emerges through the controlled selection of informants, methods of elicitation, and of recording the data.

The eight diagrams of Figure 1 represent the most homogeneous type of population. All of the speakers are Yankee descendants of the original settlers of the island, all are interrelated, many from the same families, with similar attitudes towards the island. All had rural upbringing, and worked as carpenters or fishermen, with one exception. Thus the continuous development of centralization represents the very model of a neogrammarian sound change, accomplished within two generations.

The *embedding* problem was first approached by correlating the centralization of the obviously related variables (ay) and (aw)—that is, the change of (aw) was embedded in the system of upgliding diphthongs. The Atlas records indicate a moderate degree of centralization in the 1930's, so that we know that the centralized forms of (ay) preceded the rise of (aw). The fourth column of Table 1 shows a close correlation of the two variables, with (ay) slightly in the lead at first, but (aw) becoming more dominant at the end. This pattern was repeated when the variables were correlated with a number of independent extra-linguistic factors: the occupation, education and geographic location of the speaker, and most importantly, the ethnic group to which he belonged. The significant differences in the transition rates of these various sub-groups allowed the following statement of a solution to the embedding problem:

> The centralization of (aw) was part of a more general change which began with the centralization of (ay). This initial change proceeded from a moderate level of (ay) centralization which was probably a regional and recessive trait inherited from the original settlers of the island. The increase of centralization of (ay) began in a rural community of Yankee fishermen descended directly from these original settlers. From there, it spread outward to speakers of the same ethnic group in other occupations and in other communities. The structurally symmetrical variable (aw) began to show similar tendencies early in this process. The change was also adopted by the neighboring Indian group at Gay Head, and a generation later, spread to the large Portuguese group in the more settled sections of the island. In these two ethnic groups, centralization of (aw) overtook and surpassed centralization of (ay).

Figure 1 would lead us to believe that the phonetic environment of (aw) was a powerful factor in the initiation of the sound change. Moreover, we can observe that the centralization of (ay) also showed a strong tendency towards phonetic conditioning in Generation Ib, similar to that displayed for (aw) in Generation IIb.[19] However, phonetic restriction on (ay) was overridden in the following generation, so that Generation II shows a uniform norm for (ay) in all phonetic environments. This development would support the view that phonetic conditioning does not play a significant role as an inciting cause of the centralization of (aw), but acts rather as a conditioning factor which may be eliminated by further change.

On Martha's Vineyard, the *evaluation problem* was approached by analyzing a number of clues to the subjective attitudes towards island life which appeared in the course of the interviews. Attitudes towards summer tourists, towards unemployment insurance, towards work on the mainland, towards other occupational and ethnic groups, were correlated with data obtained from community leaders and historical records, and then with the linguistic variables. It appeared that the rise of (aw) was correlated with the successive entry into the main stream of island life of groups that had previously been partially excluded. It was concluded that a social value had been [more or less arbitrarily] associated with the centralization of (ay) and (aw), and that social value could best be expressed as "native status as a Vineyarder." Thus to the extent that an individual felt able to claim and maintain status as a native Vineyarder, he adopted increasing centralization of (ay) and (aw). Sons who had tried to earn a living on the mainland, and afterwards returned to the island, developed an even higher degree of centralization than their fathers had used. But to the extent that a Vineyarder abandoned his claim to stay on the island and earn his living there, he also abandoned centralization and returned to the standard uncentralized forms.

The solution to the evaluation problem is a statement of the social significance of the changed form—that is, the function which is the direct equivalent on the non-cognitive level of the meaning of the form on the cognitive level. In the developments described here, the cognitive function of /ay/ and /aw/ has remained constant. It is plain that the non-cognitive functions which are carried by these phonological elements are the essential factors in the mechanism of the change. This conclusion can be generalized to many other instances of more complex changes, in which the net result is a radical change of cognitive function. The sound change observed on Martha's Vineyard did not produce phonemic change, in which units defined by cognitive function were merged or split. But many of the

---

[19] This phonetic conditioning is more in the nature of a continuum than that for (aw). On page 289 of "The social motivation of a sound change" is given the complete data for a speaker of the same age and background as Mr. H. H. Jr. of Figure 1.

changes in progress that have been observed in New York City did
produce such mergers and splits on the level of the bi-unique phoneme.[20]
One such change is the raising of (oh), the vowel of *law, talk, off, more,*
etc., which will serve to illustrate many aspects of the mechanism of
linguistic change not relevant to the simpler example on Martha's Vineyard.

THE RAISING OF (OH) IN NEW YORK CITY

It was not possible to make a direct attack upon the transition problem
in New York City. Although the records of the Linguistic Atlas showed
sporadic raising of (oh) at a fairly low level, the Atlas informants in
New York City were not selected systematically enough so that we could
construct a comparable sample in 1963.[21] Furthermore, an over-all comparison of the usage of this variable by older and younger speakers did
not show the clear-cut and regular progression which we saw for (aw)
on Martha's Vineyard. It was suspected that the reason for this difficulty
was the greater tendency towards stylistic variation among New Yorkers,
and the heterogeneity of the population in terms of socio-economic class
and ethnic membership. Therefore it was necessary to attack the embedding problem first, before the transition problem.

The variable (oh) is a part of the system of long and ingliding vowels
in the vernacular pattern of New York City speech which is essentially
r-less: that is, where final and pre-consonantal /r/ does not occur as a
consonantal glide. Thus (oh) occurs in the word class of *law, talk,
broad, caught, off,* and *more, four, board,* etc. To establish a quantifiable
index, five variants were coded as follows: [22]

(oh-1)	[ʊːə]
(oh-2)	[oːˑɔˑ⁺ə]
(oh-3)	[ɔːˑ⁺ə]
(oh-4)	[ɔː]
(oh-5)	[ɒː]

---

[20] The far-reaching shifts and mergers observed in the long and ingliding vowel
system of New York City, to be discussed below, do not affect the morphophonemic
system. The detailed distribution of the variables in the process of change appear to
provide evidence for the systematic status of the bi-unique phoneme. See "The aims
of sociolinguistic research" cited above for discussion.

[21] Convenience was apparently a greater factor in the selection of Atlas informants
in New York than on Martha's Vineyard. The great bulk of the New York population was poorly represented in the sample, including the working class and lower
middle class. The old-family stock used for Atlas interviews represents only a very
small fraction of the ethnic composition of the city, at most one or two per cent.

[22] The codification of these variants can be assisted by the use of some modal
reference points. (oh-1) is at the level of the vowel of [r-less] *sure;* (oh-3) is the

The (oh) index score was established by taking the numerical average of the variants recorded in any given portion of speech, and multiplying by ten. Thus the consistent use of (oh-2) would give a score of (oh)-20, and a consistent use of (oh-4), a score of (oh)-40.

A method was developed in the New York City study for isolating a range of well-defined contextual styles in the speech of individual inform-ants, and average index scores were determined for each style. A system-atic approach to the sampling of a large urban population was utilized, embodying the techniques of survey methodology, and average index scores for various sub-groups of the sample population were determined for each style. The embedding problem was then attacked by correlating the five chief linguistic variables each with each other, and with other elements of the linguistic system, with the level of stylistic variation in which they were recorded, and with the independent variables of socio-economic class [occupation, education and income], sex, ethnic group and age level.[23]

Correlations of (oh) with socio-economic class revealed that the irregular distribution of (oh) in the population as a whole was partly due to the fact that the change had not yet affected all social classes. Figure 2 is a style stratification diagram for (oh) in which the transition state of this variable can be seen in synchronic section. The horizontal axis represents the ten socio-economic levels used for this analysis, grouped informally into lower class, working class, lower middle class, and upper middle class. The vertical axis represents the average (oh) index scores: the lower values of (oh) are at the top, representing the higher, closer vowels, and the higher values of (oh) are at the bottom, indicating more open vowels. The index scores for each socio-economic group are entered on the diagram for each stylistic context, and values for the same style are connected along straight lines.

Figure 2 indicates that (oh) is not a significant variable for lower class speakers, who do not use particularly high values of this vowel and show no stylistic stratification at all. Working class speakers show a recent stage in the raising of (oh): very high vowels in casual speech, but otherwise very little stratification in the more formal styles, and little tendency towards the extreme, hypercorrect (oh-4) and (oh-5). But lower middle class speakers show the most developed state of the sound

---

level of the most common Northern vowel in [r-pronouncing] *or, nor;* (oh-4) at cardinal I.P.A. [ɔ]; (oh-5) at the level of Eastern New England *cot.*

[23] The embedding problem is treated here as one problem, not two, in accordance with the general logic of this paper.

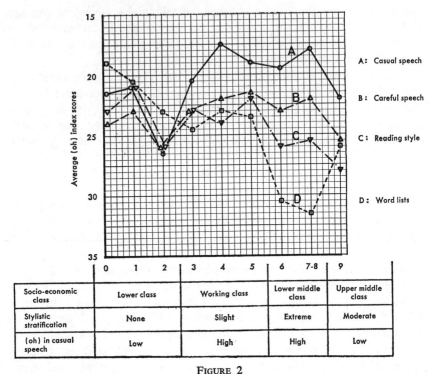

FIGURE 2

Style stratification of (oh) for nine socio-economic sub-classes

change, with high values in casual speech, and extreme stylistic stratification. Finally, the upper middle class group is more moderate in all respects than the lower middle class, still retaining the pattern of stylistic stratification.

The ethnic group membership of New York City speakers is even more relevant to their use of (oh) than socio-economic class. Figure 3 shows the differences between speakers of Jewish and Italian background in the treatment of (oh) in casual speech. For all but the upper middle class, the Jewish group uses higher levels of (oh).[24] Table 2 shows that both Jewish and Italian speakers have participated in the raising of (oh), but the increase seems to have reached its maximum early for the Jewish

---

[24] The Negro group does not show any significant response to the variable (oh), and shows a constant index of performance at a low level. As noted above, the lower class in general is similarly indifferent to (oh). Table 2 shows Jewish and Italian ethnic groups only, with the lower class excluded.

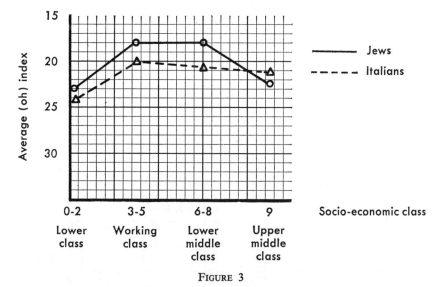

FIGURE 3

Class stratification diagram for (oh) by ethnic group in casual speech

group, and later for the Italian group. A separate solution for the transition problem is therefore required for each ethnic group.

The *transition problem* for the Italian group can be seen analyzed in Figure 4. The procession of values is not absolutely regular, since socio-economic membership, sex, and other factors affect the values; nevertheless, there is a steady upward movement from the oldest speakers on the right to the youngest speakers on the left. Within the present sample of New York City speakers, this is the finest resolution of the transition problem which can be obtained.[25]

---

[25] Figure 4 includes Italian informants who refused the original interview, and whose speech patterns were sampled by the television interview, as described in Appendix D of *The Social Stratification of English in New York City* cited above.

TABLE 2

Average (oh) Indexes by Age Level and Ethnic Group in Casual Speech

Age	Jews	Italians
8-19	17	18
20-35	18	18
36-49	17	20
50-59	15	20
60-	25	30

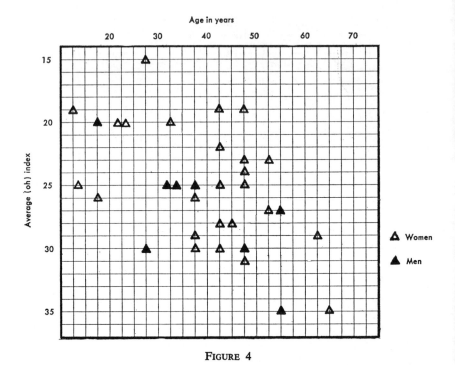

FIGURE 4

Distribution of (oh) index scores for Italian subjects by age

The *embedding problem* for (oh) requires an intricate set of correlations with other elements in the linguistic system, in addition to the extra-linguistic correlations exemplified above. We find that (oh) is firmly embedded within the sub-system of long and ingliding vowels, and also related structurally to other vowel sub-systems. Quantitative studies of these relations fall into five sets:

[1] There is a strong correlation between the height of (oh) and the height of the corresponding front ingliding vowel (eh) in the word class of *bad, ask, dance,* etc. This variable originated as a raising of /æh/, but early in the evolution of New York City speech it merged with /eh/, the word class of *bare, bared, where,* etc. The relation between (eh) and (oh) is strikingly parallel to that of (ay) and (aw) on Martha's Vineyard. The front vowel was raised first, as early as the 1890's in New York, and the back vowel followed. Like (aw) on Martha's Vineyard, the variable (oh) became specialized in the usage of a particular ethnic group: to the extent that the Italian group shows higher use of (eh) in casual speech,

the Jewish group shows higher values of (oh), until the difference is largely resolved in the youngest age level by merger of (eh) and /ih/, (oh) and /uh/.

[2] The variable (oh) also has close relations with the higher in-gliding vowel /uh/. As we observe higher and higher variants of (oh) in the casual speech of the younger informants, it becomes apparent that a merger of (oh) and /uh/ is imminent. This merger has undoubtedly occurred in the youngest speakers in our sample from the working class and lower middle class. In fact, we have many informants who show the merger even in the most formal styles, in the reading of isolated word lists, and we can conclude *a fortiori* that the merger exists in casual speech. Close study of the variants of their casual speech shows the merger as an accomplished fact: though most listeners who are not conscious of the overlap will hear *beer* as higher than *bear,* it is in fact indistinguishable out of context.

[3] There is also a close correlation between (oh) and /ah/, the long tense vowel heard in *guard, father, car,* etc. The variable (ah) represents the choice of back or center options for the subclasses of *hot, heart, hod* and *hard.* High values of (oh) are correlated with low back positions of *heart, hod* and *hard* [with the last two generally homonymous]; lower values of (oh) are correlated with low center positions of the vowels in these word classes. This correlation is independent of socio-economic class or ethnic group. Whereas (oh) is firmly embedded in the socio-linguistic structure of the speech community, /ah/ is not. As a linguistic variable, (ah) seems to be a function only of the height of (oh): a purely internal variable.[26]

[4] (oh) is also related to the variable height of the vowel in *boy, coil,* etc., (oy) in the front up-gliding system. The height of the vowels in *coil* and *call* seem to vary directly together in casual speech, but only (oh) is corrected to lower values in more formal styles. (oh) carries the major burden of social significance, and is the focus of non-systematic pressure from above.

[5] Finally, we find that (oh) and (oy) are jointly correlated with the variable (ay), which represents the backing or fronting of the first element of the diphthong in *my, why, side,* etc. High values of (oh) and (oy) are correlated with back values of (ay), and low values of (oh) and (oy) with low center values of (ay).

---

[26] The quantitative correlations are given in Chapter 12 of *The Social Stratification of English in New York City.* The relationship of (oh) and (ah) held even within a single ethnic group.

Beyond these immediate correlations, there are more indirect, diffuse relations with such variables as (aw) and /ih/, through which (oh) is connected with all of the other vowels in the vernacular system of New York City speech. This is not the place to pursue the full details of this intricate set of structural correlations within the linguistic system: however, it should be apparent that a full solution to the embedding problem will reveal the ways in which the internal relations of linguistic elements determine the direction of sound change.[27] We can summarize the most important relations that center about (oh) in the following notation, which defines the structural units on the left hand side of the equations as linguistic variables:

$$(oh) = f_1(St, C, E, A, Sx, (eh))$$
$$(ah) = f_2((oh))$$
$$(oy) = f_3((oh))$$
$$(ay) = f_4((ah)) = f_4(f_2((oh)))$$
$$(ay) = f_5((oy)) = f_5(f_3((oh)))$$

St = style
C = socio-economic class
E = ethnic group
A = age level
Sx = sex

In New York City, the *evaluation problem* was approached more directly than on Martha's Vineyard. The unconscious subjective reactions of the informants to each of the variables were determined. The details of this method have been presented elsewhere;[28] in general, we can say that the reliability of the tests can be measured by the high degree of uniformity showed by New Yorkers in contrast to the scattered results from those raised outside of New York City.

The subjective reaction responses to (oh) give us a clear view of the social significance of the variable, as shown in Table 3. The majority of informants responded to the test in a way consistent with the stigmatized status of high (oh).[29] Just as the solution to the embedding problem showed no significant stylistic response to (oh) for lower class speakers, here we find that lower class speakers showed no significant (oh)-negative response. The other groups showed (oh)-negative response in proportion to the average height of (oh) used in their own casual speech, and to

---

[27] In a manner which provides empirical confirmation for the view of linguistic structure expressed by A. Martinet, *Économie des changements phonétiques* [Berne, 1955].

[28] In addition to Chapter XI of the dissertation cited above, the most detailed presentation of this method is in "Subjective dimensions of a linguistic change in progress," a paper given before the Linguistic Society of America in Chicago, December, 1963.

[29] The (oh)-negative response shown here consisted of rating three speakers lower on a scale of job suitability when they pronounced sentences with high, close (oh) vowels, as compared to sentences with no significant variables. Those making the ratings were unaware that they were rating the same speakers.

TABLE 3

Percentage of (oh)-Negative Response by Socio-Economic Class and Age Level

Age Level	Lower Class [SEC 0-2]	Working Class [SEC 3-4]	Lower Middle Class [SEC 5-8]	Upper Middle Class [SEC 9]
20-39	25	80	100	60
40-59	18	60	62	57
60-	33	[00]	—	—

		N:		
4	10	11	5	
11	15	13	7	
6	1	—	—	

the degree of stylistic stratification in their speech patterns. This result illustrates a principle which holds quite generally in New York City: that those who used the highest percentage of a stigmatized form in casual speech were the most sensitive in stigmatizing it in the speech of others. Thus the lower middle class speakers between the ages of 20 and 39, who use the highest values of (oh) in their own casual speech, show 100% (oh)-negative response. Similarly, we find that the percentages of (oh)-negative response among Jewish and Italian speakers is proportionate to the height of (oh) in casual speech.

This solution to the evaluation problem can hardly be called satisfactory. It is not clear why a group of speakers should adopt more and more extreme forms of a speech sound which they themselves stigmatize as bad speech.[30] Some further explanation must be given.

First of all, it has become clear that very few speakers realize that they use the stigmatized forms themselves. They hear themselves as using the prestige forms which occur sporadically in their careful speech and in their reading of isolated word lists. Secondly, the subjective responses tapped by our test are only the overt values—those which conform to the value systems of the dominant middle class group. There are surely other values, at a deeper level of consciousness, which reinforce the vernacular speech forms of New York City. We have not yet measured these more obscure forms systematically, but through anecdotal evidence we can be sure of their existence—values which cluster about the themes of group identification, masculinity, friendship ties, and so on.

In the case of the alternate preference of Jewish and Italian ethnic

---

[30] Many subjects reacted to the test with violent and unrealistic ratings; as, for example, marking a person who used high vowels for *coffee* and *chocolate* as not even speaking well enough to hold a factory job.

groups for (oh) and (eh), we can put forward a reasonable suggestion based upon the mechanism of hypercorrection.[31] The influence of the Yiddish sub-stratum leads to a loss of the distinction between low back rounded and unrounded vowels in first-generation Jewish speakers of English, so that *cup* and *coffee* have the same vowel. In second-generation speakers of Jewish descent, the reaction against this tendency leads to a hypercorrect exaggeration of the distinction, so that (oh) becomes raised, tense and over-rounded. A parallel argument applies to Italian speakers. This suggestion is all the more plausible since hypercorrection has been demonstrated to be an important mechanism of linguistic change in a variety of circumstances.[32]

THE MECHANISM OF SOUND CHANGE

Solutions to the transition, embedding and evaluation problems have been illustrated by two examples, drawn from Martha's Vineyard and New York City. It is possible to apply the results of our work with these and other variables to a provisional answer to the question: what is the mechanism by which sound change proceeds? The following outline is based upon analysis of twelve sound changes: three on rural Martha's Vineyard, and nine in urban New York City.[33]

1. The sound changes usually originated with a restricted sub-group of the speech community, at a time when the separate identity of this group had been weakened by internal or external pressures. The linguistic form which began to shift was often a marker of regional status with an irregular distribution within the community. At this stage, the form is an undefined linguistic variable.

2. The changes began as generalizations of the linguistic form to all members of the sub-group; we may refer to this stage as *change from below,* that is, below the level of social awareness. The variable shows no pattern of stylistic variation in the speech of those who use it, affecting all items in a given word class. The linguistic variable is an *indicator,* defined as a function of group membership.

3. Succeeding generations of speakers within the same subgroup, re-

---

[31] I am indebted to Marvin Herzog for this suggestion.

[32] *Hypercorrection* is used here not to indicate the sporadic and irregular treatment of a word class, but the movement of an entire word class beyond the target point set by the prestige model. This mechanism is evident on Martha's Vineyard, as well as New York.

[33] The stages suggested here are necessarily ordered in approximately the manner listed, but there are some re-arrangements and permutations in the data observed.

sponding to the same social pressures, carried the linguistic variable further along the process of change, beyond the model set by their parents. We may refer to this stage as *hypercorrection from below.* The variable is now defined as a function of group membership and age level.

4. To the extent that the values of the original sub-group were adopted by other groups in the speech community, the sound change with its associated value of group membership spread to these adopting groups. The function of group membership is now re-defined in successive stages.

5. The limits of the spread of the sound change were the limits of the speech community, defined as a group with a common set of normative values in regard to language.

6. As the sound change with its associated values reached the limits of its expansion, the linguistic variable became one of the norms which defined the speech community, and all members of the speech community reacted in a uniform manner to its use (without necessarily being aware of it). The variable is now a *marker,* and begins to show stylistic variation.

7. The movement of the linguistic variable within the linguistic system always led to readjustments in the distribution of other elements within phonological space.

8. The structural readjustments led to further sound changes which were associated with the original change. However, other subgroups which entered the speech community in the interim adopted the older sound change as a part of the community norms, and treated the newer sound change as stage 1. This *re-cycling* stage appears to be the primary source for the continual origination of new changes. In the following development, the second sound change may be carried by the new group beyond the level of the first change.

[Stages 1-8 dealt with *change from below;* stages 9-13 concern *change from above.*]

9. If the group in which the change originated was not the highest status group in the speech community, members of the highest status group eventually stigmatized the changed form through their control of various institutions of the communication network.

10. This stigmatization initiated *change from above,* a sporadic and irregular correction of the changed forms towards the model of the highest status group—that is, the *prestige model.* This prestige model is now the pattern which speakers hear themselves using: it governs the audio-monitoring of the speech signal. The linguistic variable now shows regular stylistic stratification as well as social stratification, as the motor-controlled model of casual speech competes with the audio-monitored model of more careful styles.

11. If the prestige model of the highest status group does not correspond to a form used by the other groups in some word class, the other groups will show a second type of *hypercorrection:* shifting their careful speech to a form further from the changed form than the target set by the prestige group. We may call this stage *hypercorrection from above.*

12. Under extreme stigmatization, a form may become the overt topic of social comment, and may eventually disappear. It is thus a *stereotype,* which may become increasingly divorced from the forms which are actually used in speech.

13. If the change originated in the highest status group of the community, it became a prestige model for all members of the speech community. The changed form was then adopted in more careful forms of speech by all other groups in proportion to their contact with users of the prestige model, and to a lesser extent, in casual speech.[34]

Many of the stages in the mechanism of sound change outlined here are exemplified in the two detailed examples given above. The centralization of (aw) on Martha's Vineyard appears to be a stage 4 change from below. It may indeed have reached stages 5 and 6, but the techniques used on Martha's Vineyard did not provide the evidence to decide this question. There is no doubt, however, that the centralization of (aw) is a secondary change, produced by the re-cycling process when the centralization of (ay) reached stage 8.

To place the raising of (oh) in this outline, it is necessary to consider briefly the evolution of the New York City vowel system as a whole. The first step in the historical record is the raising of (eh). We have reason to believe that the merger of /æh/ with /eh/ began in the last quarter of the 19th century.[35] The upward movement of the linguistic variable (eh) continued beyond this merger, leading to the current cumulative merger of /eh/ with /ih/ among most younger New Yorkers. For the entire community, (eh) is subject to the full force of correction from above: the change has reached stage 11, so that the linguistic variable is defined by co-variation with social class, ethnic membership, age level, and contextual style. The raising of (oh) was the first re-cycling process which began when (eh) reached stage 8. The major burden of the raising of (oh) has been carried by the Jewish ethnic group; the extreme upward social mobility of this group has led to a special sensitivity to (oh) in

---

[34] We find some support in these observations for the idea that people do not borrow much from broadcast media or from other remote sources, but rather from those who are at the most one or two removes from them in age or social distance.

[35] See Babbitt, *op. cit.*

the lower middle class. Thus the merger of /oh/ and /uh/ has gone quite quickly, and (oh) has reached stage 11 for the lower middle class; yet it has hardly touched stage 1 for the lower class.

The third stage in the re-cycling process occurred when (oh) reached stage 8. The structural re-adjustments which took place were complex: (oy) and (ah) were closely associated with (oh), and were defined as linguistic variables only by their co-variation with (oh). Thus the raising of (oy) and the backing of (ah) were determined by internal, structural factors. Change from above is exerted upon (oh), but not upon (oy). In careful speech, a New Yorker might say [ɪts ɒːl tɪn fuːɪl], *It's all tin foil.* But the shift of (ah) and (oy) have in turn led to a shift of (ay), and this process has apparently begun a third re-cycling. Indeed, the backing of (ay) has reached stage 8 itself, and produced an associated fourth re-cycling, the fronting of (aw). There are indications that (ay) has evolved to stage 9, with the beginning of overt correction from above, although (aw) has reached only stage 4 or 5.[36]

It is evident that the type of structural re-adjustments that have been considered here require a linguistic theory which preserves the geometry of phonological space. The structural relations found here are strikingly parallel to those established by Moulton in his study of co-variation of mid and low vowels in Swiss German dialects.[37] The techniques, the area, the societies studied are quite different, and the coincidence of results provides strong empirical evidence for the view of phonological structure advanced by Martinet.[38] Nevertheless, the purely internal equilibria projected by Martinet do not provide a coherent theory of the mechanism of sound change. In the scheme that has been outlined here, they are only part of a more comprehensive process, embedded in the sociolinguistic structure of the community.

CONCLUSION

This discussion has focused on the theme that internal, structural pressures and sociolinguistic pressures act in systematic alternation in the

---

[36] Details are provided in Chapter XII of the dissertation cited above.

[37] "Dialect geography and the concept of phonological space," *Word* 18:23-33 [1962].

[38] Both studies show strong evidence for co-variation of low vowels along the front-to-back dimension with back vowels along the dimension of height. Distinctive feature theory, in the form utilized by Halle, *op. cit.*, dissolves the geometry of phonological space into a set of independent dimensions. Even if a phonetic form of distinctive features is provided with scalar values, distinctive feature theory has no rationale for co-variation of grave and acute with compact and diffuse.

mechanism of linguistic change. It can no longer be seriously argued that the linguist must limit his explanations of change to the mutual influences of linguistic elements defined by cognitive function. Nor can it be argued that a changing linguistic system is autonomous in any serious sense. Here I have attempted to carry the argument beyond the mere cataloguing of possibilities by introducing a large body of evidence on sound changes observed in progress. On the basis of this evidence, we can make the stronger claim that it is not possible to complete an analysis of structural relations within a linguistic system, and then turn to external relations. The re-cycling process outlined here suggests the kind of answer we can make to the basic questions of the inciting causes of linguistic change, and the adaptive functions of change, as well as the mechanism by which change proceeds. We can expect that further investigations will modify the outline given here, but that data from the speech community will continue to form an essential part in the analysis of linguistic change.

THE NATURE OF GENERAL PHONETIC THEORIES

PETER LADEFOGED

University of California, Los Angeles

There has been some discussion recently about the general theory of grammar, the categories which are involved, and their relations with one another. The phoneticians have taken little part in these discussions; and, in one sense, there are no theories of phonetics. The International Phonetic Association no longer presses the notion 'one sound, one symbol' (it had never formally defined what was meant by 'one sound'); and one of the principal adherents to the Distinctive Feature theory (Jakobson, Fant and Halle, 1951) has recently (Halle 1964a) been emphasizing the classificatory role of the features, rather than their descriptive power. But this lack of a general theory of phonetics does not negate the fact that the main business of a phonetician is to provide ways of relating linguistic descriptions with the observable phenomena of speech. We would undoubtedly like to be able to interpret our linguistic descriptions in a systematic way, ideally one that could be formalized in a set of rules. Thus we might want to have a rule:

$$[t^h] \rightarrow \text{voiceless aspirated alveolar plosive}$$

which would mean rewrite, or interpret, the complex symbol $[t^h]$ as consisting of the terms on the right of the arrow, where terms refer to specific, identifiable properties of sounds. The restrictions limiting the formal relations which may occur within the rules, together with all the permitted terms and their identities, constitute the general theory of phonetics. The particular set of rules which is applicable to a given language can be called part of the linguistic theory for the description of that language.

Linguists appear to disagree over the place in the description of a language at which it is appropriate to relate linguistic units to observable phenomena. Some linguists follow Firth (1951) in considering that the phonological description of a language should reflect a hierarchical structure in which each unit, except the smallest, is composed of an integral num-

283

ber of the units of lower rank. Thus, in describing English, Halliday (1963) has said that there are tone groups, which are composed of feet (stress groups), which are composed of syllables, which are composed of phonemes. Linguists of this school emphasize the fact that the larger units have directly observable correlates in the actual sounds. In their view each phonological unit is a theoretical construct which has at least two kinds of relations: the one with some observable properties of sound; and the other (which may be complex, and could be further analyzed) with the other units in the phonological hierarchy. These relations may be represented in a diagram as in Figure 1. Note that the items in the right hand column have no relation one with another. What matters for this theory is that there is some specific correlate in substance for each formal unit; but it is quite possible for the correlates of different units to involve different arrangements of the same physical events. The items on the left hand side, however, form a hierarchical structure so that a particular utterance may be partially represented by a tree, as shown in Figure 2. This tree designates an utterance in Igbira, a language of Northern Nigeria; some of the relevant phonology is given in Ladefoged (1964a). English was not used as the exemplifying language partly because this kind of representation would have involved the discussion of too many points of English phonology which are irrelevant to the theme of this paper, and partly because the use of a language such as Igbira demonstrates that in this phonological theory the formal units need not be the same as those required for English, which are as listed in Figure 1.

It follows from what we have said that the tree itself depicts only the

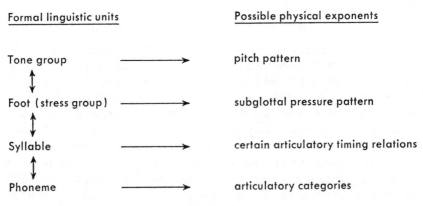

Formal linguistic units   Possible physical exponents

Tone group   ⟶   pitch pattern

Foot (stress group) ⟶ subglottal pressure pattern

Syllable   ⟶   certain articulatory timing relations

Phoneme   ⟶   articulatory categories

FIGURE 1

The relations between the phonological units of English and their exponents.

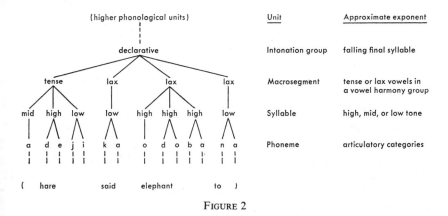

FIGURE 2

Part of a phonological tree for an Igbira (Northern Nigeria) utterance.

formal relations between units, and cannot show how the units are related to their physical exponents. The tree can be extended as indicated by the dashed lines at the bottom, so that, after the formal relations between the higher units have been shown, the smallest units may be linked with observable events. But an extension of this kind not only leaves out of account the links which this school continually emphasizes between the higher phonological units and their exponents, but also confuses the situation by not making clear whether these added items are formal units of a lower rank (as would seem to be the case for Halle's distinctive features viewed as a classificatory matrix) or exponents of the phonemes (which would seem to be the case for the Jakobson-Fant-Halle distinctive features, viewed as a descriptive matrix).

It could be largely irrelevant whether we hold to a Firthian view of phonology, or to one of the more common American views. But most linguists in the United States appear to disregard the possibility of a hierarchical arrangement of phonological units. They may, in describing a language such as English, abstract the intonation component, but all the other phonological features are represented by a single sequence of symbols, so that the representation of an utterance is not, from the phonological point of view, a tree structure, but (in Firth's terminology) a number of monosystemic marks arranged like beads on a string. But it should be noted that the symbols in this form of linguistic description need not be all of the same order; some may be segmental phonemes, and others junctures of some kind. So the possibility of a hierarchical structure may be implied. Or we may put this difference in viewpoints another way, and note that any hierarchical structure such as that shown in Figure 2 can be presented in terms of a linear sequence of symbols by writing appropriate brackets as shown in Figure 3a; these brackets may then be considered to be an alternative way of writing the junctures shown in Figure 3b. In many linguistic descriptions the juncture marks may not give as much information about the utterance as those in Figure 3b; but a terminal string with sufficient juncture marks could always be generated by a transformational-generative grammar. This would then be in accord with the formalization of the link between linguistic units and actual sounds required by the Firthian notion developed by Halliday in which a whole phonological tree rather than a terminal string is directly related to the sounds of an utterance.

The descriptive statements with which we are concerned will show even more information than the representations in Figures 2 and 3. They will contain not only the patterning of the higher phonological units and the phonemes, but also the subphonemic patterning, which we may consider for the moment in terms of the arrangement of allophones. We will want our phonetic rewrite rules to account for the difference between, for example, the [1] sounds in the English words *leaf* and *feel* which is certainly part of the sound pattern of English. But at this point we should be careful to distinguish between two kinds of allophones. Speech is a dynamic process and cannot be regarded simply as a succession of discrete events. Nevertheless all linguistic descriptions must consist of a sequence of items. In a very detailed transcription we might try to account for the continuous nature of speech by showing allophones which reflect the influence of the adjacent segments. For example, we could transcribe the English words *key* and *car* as $[k+i]$ and $[k-a]$ where the $[+]$ specified the advanced [k] allophone which occurs before the front vowel, and the $[-]$ the retracted [k] associated with the back vowel. But not all allophones are simply due to the process of accommodation or coarticulation between neighboring sounds. The different [1] sounds such as those at the beginning of *leaf* and the end of *feel* cannot be ascribed to the influence of the adjacent items in a simple way. These syllable-initial and syllable-final allophones each accommodate slightly to the neighboring sounds when in different phonetic contexts as in

(a)　　&[(a)(de)(ji)][(ka)][(o)(do)(ba)][(na)]&

(b)　　a−de−ji+ka+o−do−ba+na#

FIGURE 3

(a) A bracketed string of symbols showing the tree structure in Figure 2.
(b) The same information as in (a), using juncture marks instead of brackets, and tacit rules in a meta-theory concerning the rewriting of junctures.

leaf, lark, Luke and *feel, fall, fool;* but, as we shall see later, the differences between the two groups of allophones are such that we must regard them differently within a general phonetic theory. The distinction will be formalized at a subsequent point in this paper; but for the moment we may note that allophones which are due to the influence of the adjacent sounds may be called intrinsic; other allophones, which cannot be simply accounted for in this way, may be called extrinsic.

We must now discuss the exponents of extrinsic allophones and phonemes. The best way of doing this is in terms of a set of phonetic features. We may assume that if two sounds contrast either phonemically or as extrinsic rather than intrinsic allophones in any one language, then we will want them to have different feature specifications. It is more difficult to state the conditions under which we may identify two events in *different* languages as variants of the same feature. Jakobson and Halle (1956) have said that whenever two different phenomena (such as rounding and pharyngealization) never occur in contrast in a single language, then we may identify them as variants of the same feature. This dictum requires further elaboration.

We may begin by considering a particular body of data. Table I displays many of the consonants and semivowels which occur among some of the 94 languages that I have been able to examine at first hand in the last few years. Most of these data are from West African languages and have been described in detail elsewhere (Ladefoged, 1964b). We now have at the UCLA Phonetics Laboratory high-quality recordings; acoustic analyses; and physiological data such as X-rays, palatograms, linguagrams and air pressure and flow measurements, all of which enable us to characterize the sounds of a wide variety of languages fairly precisely.

The sounds which are represented by symbols in Table I may all be regarded as units in the sense that none of them involves a sequence of any two of the others. Affricates and prenasalized stops are thus not shown, although both of them operate as unit phonemes in many languages. Sounds with secondary articulations, such as the form of labialization which occurs mainly during the latter part of a segment and during its offglide but not its onglide, are regarded as sequences and are omitted. I have also left out many sounds which I have heard, such as the Danish stød, the Arabic emphatics, Korean fortis stops, Javanese and Indonesian 'lax' consonants, Zulu clicks, and others, either because I have not yet investigated these sounds myself sufficiently, or because I do not know how best to categorize them. Furthermore, I have followed a strict rule of leaving out of consideration altogether all sounds which I have not heard myself from an

TABLE 1

All the phonetic items shown contrast phonemically in at least one language with each adjacent item (irrespective of blank spaces), except for those items separated by heavy lines

(A) Upper articulator					lip & ridge	lip	teeth	teeth ridge		back of teeth ridge	hard palate	soft palate	and lip	palate & lip	uvula	vocal cords
(B) Lower articulator					lip & tip	lip	tip	tip or blade		tip / blade	front	back	and lip	front & lip	back	
(C) Name summarizing (A) and (B) →																
(a) Position of the soft palate	(b) Relation between the articulators	(c) Name summarizing (a) and (b)	(d) Position of unobstructed oral passage	(e) Action of glottis	labial alveolar	bilabial	labio-dental	dental	alveolar	post-alveolar	pre-palatal	palatal	velar	labial velar	labial palatal	uvular	glottal
raised	complete closure	stop	(none)	voiceless ejective		p'			t'			c'	k'				
				voiceless aspirated		ph			th			ch	kh				
				voiceless	p͡t	p		ʇ	t	ʈ		c	k	k͡p		q	ʔ
				voiced implosive		ɓ			ɗ				ɠ				
				breathy voiced		bɦ	dɦ	dɦ	ɖɦ			gɦ					
				voiced	b͡d	b		ȡ	d	ɖ		ɟ	g	g͡b			
				voiced laryngealised	ʔb͡d	ʔb			ʔd			ʔɟ					
lowered	nasal		(none)	voiceless		m̥			n̥			ɲ̊					
				voiced	m̃n	m		n̪	n			ɲ	ŋ	ŋ͡m			
raised	close approximation	fricative	central	voiceless		ɸ	f	θ	s	ʃ	ʂ	ç	x	ʍ		χ	
				voiceless ejective					s'								
				voiced		β	v	ð	z	ʒ	ʐ	ʝ	ɣ	w		ʁ	
			lateral	voiceless					ɬ			ɬ̡					
				voiced					l	ɭ		ʎ					
	open approximation	approximant	central	voiceless					ɻ̊					ʍ	ɥ̊		h
				voiced		ʋ			ɹ			j	ɰ	w	ɥ	ʁ̞	
				voiced laryngealised								ʔj		ʔw			
		trill		voiced		ʙ			r							ʀ	
		tap	(none)	voiced					ɾ								
		flap		voiced		ѵ̟			ɽ								

informant, and which are known to me only through the literature or by means of tape recordings or personal communication from colleagues. Because of my great ignorance of many of the well-known languages of the world (particularly in the Amerindian, Indian and Far Eastern areas) this means that the table is very incomplete. Its only virtue is that it represents data which I can vouch for myself with a fair degree of accuracy; and it is sufficiently complex to be interesting from the point of view of formalizing a theory of phonetics.

The data have been arranged so that, apart from pairs of symbols separated by heavy lines, each pair of adjacent symbols in either a row or a column represents a pair of phonetic items which contrast phonemically in at least one of the languages investigated, irrespective of blank spaces. Thus the voiced alveolar stop /d/ contrasts with a similar sound but with a breathy voice release (symbolized /dɦ/) in the Igbo of Owerri Province, with a dental stop /d̪/ in Isoko, with a laryngealized stop /ˀd/ in Fula, and with a postalveolar stop /ɖ/ in Ewe. Examples of these and other contrasts between pairs of similar sounds are given in Table 2.

The data in Table I can be specified by setting up categories in a number of different ways. One such scheme is implied by the labels shown. This is not the scheme which I would like to propose as an ultimate system of categories forming the features of a universal phonetic alphabet. But it does enable us to start noting some facts about possible categories. Phonetic features have certain relations determined by the physiological possibilities of the vocal organs. Thus the set of all stops excludes the set of all fricatives, since it is impossible for a sound to be simultaneously a stop and a fricative. A particular phoneme may be in one circumstance a fricative and in another a stop. But on the level of phonetic specification at a given moment a sound must be either a stop or a fricative. On the other hand the set of all stops includes some members of the set of all bilabials and the set of all voiceless sounds. Some feature sets can be grouped together so that they partition the field of possible speech sounds. This is true of the set of feature sets formed of the nasal, stop, fricative, approximant, trill, tap, flap, and vowel sets. There are no speech sounds which do not belong to one of these sets. A set of feature sets which has the property of partitioning the field of possible speech sounds will be called a type set. The set listed above is the one dependent on manner of articulation or stricture type.

Clearly, if two features are to be coalesced and regarded as variants of the same feature, they must both be members of the same type set. Only members of the same type set commute and can be guaranteed not to co-occur. I would also like to suggest a second criterion: two or more phenomena can be subsumed under a single feature if and only if they can be regarded as points on the continuum of that feature and can be described by numbers specifying the amount of the feature which they possess. Thus the difference between a fully voiced initial /b/ as in French and the English initial /b/ with slightly less voicing requires a specification of only the amount of the voicing feature which each of these sounds has. But the difference between the disparate states of the glottis required in the formation of ejectives and implosives cannot be specified in this way. To be in accord with the criterion suggested, these two phenomena would have to be

TABLE 2

Examples of contrasts between some of the items in Table 1

k'–k	Hausa:	wá:k'à	song	kà:ká	grandparent		
ts–tʃ	Nupe:	tsa	choose	tʃa	begin		
dz–dʒ		dzamı	bridle	dʒama	assembly		
tɕ–dʑ–ɕ	Gã:	étɕèò	it is ablaze	èdʑà	it is right	éɕá	sin
tɕʷ–dʑʷ–ɕʷ		etɕʷa	he struck	èdʑʷa	it's broken	éɕʷá	it is scattered
tʃ–tɥ–c –ch	Cama:	tʃa	stamp	tɥɛ	learn	cà chà	destroy pound
ph–th–kh	Igbo: (Owerri)	àphé	sharpening	àthá	blaming	ákhá	long
p–t–k		ápè	pressing	àtá	chewing	áká	hand
b–d–g		mbà	another town	ádà	crab	àgá	going
bɦ–dɦ–gɦ		mbɦá	boast	ádɦà	falling	àgɦá	being useful
ɓ–ɓɦ		àɓà	power	àɓɦà	jaw		
p̃–p–t b–d	Bura:	p̃á	*animal	pàkà bàrà	search want	tá dàwà	cook enemy
ʔbd–ʔb–ʔd		ʔbdà	chew	ʔbáłà	dance	ʔdà	eat meat
ʈ–d̪	Isoko:	òʈú	louse	úd̪ù	farm		
t–d–n		òtú	gang	údù	chest	òna	skill
f–θ–t	Sherbro:	faká	village	θàm	grandmother	tàmbàsé	sign
d–d̪–ɟ	Logba:	ɔ́dɛɛ	he scolds	ɔ̀d̪è	*clan	ɔ̀ɟándɛ́	gap in teeth
c–k	Urhobo:	écá	coming	ɔ́kà	maize		
k͡p–kʷ		òk͡pè	ugly	ɔ́kʷa	he packs		
ɟ–g		oja	soap	ɔ̀gà	illness		
gb–gʷ		og͡ba	fence	ɔ́gʷà	*yam		
ɓ–b–g͡b	Kala	aɓa	*girl	àbà	*fish	àg͡bà	offering
p–d–d	-bari:	àpà	fool	áda	dad	àda	eldest daughter
k–q–χ	Serer:	kor	man	qos	leg	χol	clean
m–n–ŋ	Idoma:	áma	bell	ànà	*fruit	ɔŋáɟ	rainbow
ɲ–ŋʷ–ŋ͡m		áɲà	quick temper	àŋʷà	divining pods	aŋ͡màa	body marks
ɸ–f	Ewe:			éɸá	he polished	éfá	it was cold
w–β–v		éwɔ̀	he made	èβè	Ewe language	èvè	two
s–ʔs–ʃ	Hausa:	wà:sá	play	s'à:s'à	rust	ʃáʃà:ʃá	fool
s–ʃ	Urhobo	ɔ̀sè	feather	èʃà	grey hair		
z–ʒ		òze	baisin	oʒa	suffering		
ʃ–ç–h	Bura:	ʃá	lost	çál	guts	hala	get old
x–h	Ora:	ɔ̀xà	story	ɔ̀hà	wife		
ɬ–ɫ–ɮ	Bura:	ɬábʷá	beat	ɫá	cow	ɮálá	cucumber
l ʎ		là	build			wúʎá	neck
l–ɹ–ɹ	Bini:	álázi	*monkey	aɹˤá	caterpillar	áɹába	rubber
ɺ				àɟà	burial ceremony		
l–ɹ–ɾ	Isoko:	òlá	jump	òɹá	flight	òɾá	yours
ʍ–ɥ–h	Birom:	ʍà	wife	ɥégèlèk	yesterday	hòm	cheek
jˤ–ɟˤ–ʔj	Margi:	jˤàjˤàʔdò	picked up	jà	give birth	ʔjà	thigh
wˤ–w–ʔw		wˤá	reach inside	káwà	sorry	ʔwáʔwí	adornment
ʝ–ɥ–w	Idoma:	ɔjá	width	ɔɥá	moon	ɔ́wá	redness
ɾ–ɽ	Hausa:	báɾà	begging	báɽà	servant		

regarded as separate features, each capable of generating different speech sounds.

This second criterion is entirely in accord with the theory of Jakobson, Fant and Halle (1951). One of the many excellent points in this theory is the observation that the distinctive features specify relative properties. What matters in the description of the sounds of a particular language is that if a sound is, for instance, + compact, then it possesses more of the feature compactness (whatever that may be) than a contrasting sound which is considered to be − compact. In another language the opposition compact—non-compact may be manifested by a pair of sounds with quite different degrees of compactness, such that the one which is considered to be + compact is most like the one which is considered to be − compact in the first language. In this way it is possible to limit quite considerably the number of features needed to specify all the languages of the world. But the technique will work only if the features specify clearly defined physical scales which can be observed and measured. One of my main difficulties with the theory proposed by Jakobson, Fant and Halle is that their descriptions of the features are not specific enough to be able to assign numerical values to all sounds in every case.

It may not be necessary to be so specific when discussing the linguistic organization of features. In these circumstances it may be legitimate to regard voiceless ejectives and voiced implosives or laryngealized stops as manifestations of the feature glottalized, as suggested by Jakobson (1962) on the grounds that no language has both voiced and voiceless ejectives or voiced and voiceless implosives; and Carnochan (1952) has shown that the linguistic description of a particular language, Hausa, is considerably simplified by classing all the glottalized consonants together. But as long as the difference between two phenomena is qualitative rather than a matter of degree, their coalescence is in some ways arbitrary. There does not seem to be any physical scale on the auditory, acoustic or physiological level of description which can be applied to ejectives and implosives such that their differences can be accounted for by a numerical specification of the amount of the quality which they possess. Nor can I find any physical continuum in which [i] and [u] differ from [a] which is the same as the physical continuum in which [p] and [k] differ from [t], and [m] and [ŋ] differ from [n]. The second criterion suggested here (and the view expressed in Jakobson, Fant and Halle, strictly speaking) does not permit the possibility of phonologically context sensitive rules which will allow us to rewrite the exponents of vowels in one way and consonants in another. Descriptions of this kind may be very elegant from a linguistic point of view; but they make it impossible to use non-arbitrary measurable distinctive features for phonetic specifications. Arbitrariness at the phonetic level can be avoided only by retaining the restriction that sounds should be considered to exhibit variants of the same feature only if the feature is a completely specified continuum and the sounds differ in the degree in which they have the feature.

We may now return to the consideration of when two allophones must be regarded as belonging to two different sound types in the universal phonetic alphabet. We previously noted that we would like to recognize the necessity of a different feature specification when the difference between allophones was such that it could not be ascribed to coarticulation with the neighboring sounds. This criterion can be put more formally by saying that whenever two allophones differ in the degree in which they exhibit a feature and the difference can be specified in terms of a simple numerical model which takes into account only the adjacent sounds, then we can say that the differences are those of intrinsic allophones. But all other differences are those of extrinsic allophones.

I prefer this criterion for distinguishing between the two types of allophones to that of Wang and Fillmore (1961), from whom I took the terms. For them intrinsic allophones reflect the structure of the speech mechanism in general, and extrinsic allophones reflect the speech habits of a particular community. Their terms are apt, but it seems better for the distinction to be based on the two types of allophones which must be recognized in a general phonetic theory, rather than on knowledge of whether a given difference between two sounds is a learnt speech habit or an inevitable consequence of coarticulation. In studying the phonetic structure of a wide variety of languages I am sometimes surprised by finding that speakers take care not to make an articulatory adjustment which I had considered to be an inevitable coarticulation and a language universal.

The distinction that is suggested here is motivated by the desire for economy in the phonological component of a grammar of a language. The experimental work of Lindblom (1963, forthcoming) and Ohman (1964, forthcoming) has shown that it is possible to specify 'target' positions for the formants and the vocal tract shapes of sounds which might be extrinsic allophones, and then, by the application of certain formulae, predict (or generate) the actual formant positions and vocal tract shapes which will occur when these sounds occur in context. They are thus able to account for the variations between intrinsic allophones which are due to coarticulation and which, in the particular language they are investigating, are not voluntarily controlled by the speaker. But they would need to specify extrinsic allophones as having different target positions, since such differences are made deliberately and are not simply ascribable to coarticulation.

In assessing the number of phonetic features required in a general theory of phonetics we must consider the extent to which variations in place of articulation can be taken to be variations in the degree of one or more features. In so far as the articulations shown as the column headings in Table I represent points in a continuum, we must have almost as many different place of articulation features as there are columns. The only possibilities for reduction are by identifying postalveolar and prepalatal (which are neighboring items which do not contrast in any language) and perhaps considering separately the double articulations labial alveolar (which may not have been placed at the appropriate place in the continuum), labial palatal and labial velar. We are then left with 8 columns in which the sounds could be regarded as differing in the degree in which they possessed the single feature nearness-of-the-place-of-articulation-to-the-glottis. In a general phonetic theory we will have to state that this feature has 8 possible states for generating sounds.

In passing I might note that I have been unable to find any additional parameters which could be used to account for variations in place of articulation. At least three binary distinctions would be needed to generate the subtle variations shown in Table I. But I cannot find a workable definition of even a single feature such as the one labeled grave-acute by Jakobson, Fant and Halle (1951). It is interesting that Halle (1959) in his excellent book *The Sound Pattern of Russian* notes that there are many difficulties in identifying consonants with respect to this feature; and Fant in his recent publications on phonetic specifications (1962, 1964) does not mention any features such as grave-acute and compact-diffuse, although he still uses features such as nasal-oral and voiced-voiceless to specify aspects of sounds roughly corresponding to manner of articulation and state of the glottis.

I am not yet prepared to give a definitive arrangement of phonetic categories, which will account for the data in Table I in the most economical way. There are, of course, more co-occurrence restrictions than the fact that a feature can never be combined with another feature in its own type set. Many of these are formalized in the present arrangement of Table I. Thus only stops have the full range of possible phonation types; trills and flaps cannot be voiceless; and the option voiced-voiceless is open only to lateral fricatives as opposed to lateral approximants. But, if we are to avoid generating many sounds which have not been observed, at least in the sample of languages represented in Table I, then we must find a way of stating additional restrictions. For example, we should have the option of choosing the voiceless aspirated feature only when we have already chosen both the stop feature and one of the features bilabial, alveolar, palatal or velar. Dependencies of this kind can be shown most easily by means of a finite state machine or by means of rules as in a phrase structure grammar; but no theory of phonetics has yet been formalized to this extent.

Some formal status should also be given to two different kinds of restrictions on possible combinations of phonetic categories; some, such as a lingual-velar trill, are physiologically impossible; others, such as an ejective dental fricative, can be produced comparatively easily, but have never been recorded in any language. (Since the proportion of languages with dental fricatives is small, and the proportion with ejective fricatives is also small, I would guess that there is almost certainly no language in which this particular combination occurs.) This is another aspect of phonetic theory which has not been fully investigated.

We must now reconsider the possibility of using Jakobson and Halle's distinctive features as part of a general phonetic theory. Note that we are not here concerned with the use of distinctive features as a classificatory matrix at the phonemic level, but only with the implications of trying to achieve phonetic specificability through the use of the same set of features in a phonetic matrix. Current distinctive feature theory (Halle 1964a) seems to be that there are about fifteen features. On the phonetic level these features are not necessarily binary; the rules of the phonological component of a grammar are said to be capable of assigning integers representing the different degrees of intensity which a feature may manifest. But the features are still viewed as representing 'the capacities of man to produce speech sounds and constitute, in this sense, the universal phonetic framework of language.' (Halle 1964a). If we consider the possibility of only presence or absence of a feature, which would be the minimum for requiring the feature in a phonetic framework, and disregard the added possibility of more subtle differences in degree, then this phonetic framework will generate 2^{15} or 32,768 sound types. Of these 8,192 are clearly irrelevant to our discussion of the data in Table I, since they are vowels (i.e. + consonantal and + vocalic). But 24,576 would be available to account for the 93 sounds shown in Table I.

All the accounts of distinctive feature theory have pointed out that there are some restrictions on the combinations of features which may occur. But if we subtract from the total number of consonantal sound types all those generated by impossible combinations of features as given in Jakobson, Fant and Halle (1951), Jakobson and Halle (1956) and Halle (1964), we are still left with a minimum of 12,288 consonantal sound types. This seems an unnecessarily large number.

We may also note that it seems most unlikely that the twelve features in Jakobson and Halle (1956) or the fifteen mentioned in Halle (1964) would be sufficient to account for the phonetic data represented in Table I. As Fant has said, 'The limitations of the preliminary study of Jakobson, Fant and Halle are that the formulations are made for the benefit of linguistic theory rather than for engineering or phonetic applications. Statements of the acoustic correlates to distinctive features have been condensed to an extent where they retain merely a generalized abstraction insufficient as a basis for the quantitative operations needed for practical applications.' (Fant 1962). Many of the sounds represented in Table I have never been discussed at all by addicts of distinctive feature phonetics.

But the main objection to the usual distinctive feature approach is that it is based largely on auditory criteria. It is sometimes claimed that acoustic (or auditory) descriptions are preferable to articulatory descriptions because 'the same acoustic phenomenon may be obtained by very different means' (Jakobson, Fant and Halle 1951). In fact such cases are not very well authenticated and need not occur at all if proper articulatory categories are set up. There are no two combinations of any of the categories illustrated in Table I which will give the same acoustic result. This being so, there seems to be no reason for preferring auditory criteria; and it is evident that if physiological criteria are used it is easier to state the inherent restrictions among phonetic features. It is not, for example, useful to consider the phonetic feature discontinuous as being opposed simply to the feature continuant. The feature discontinuous (or stop) is much more usefully opposed to all the other features of its own type set, such as nasal, trill, and vowel, but not to features of other type sets such as voiced and voiceless. This kind of relationship is implicit in the traditional classification of sounds in terms of place and manner of articulaton. Forgetting, for the moment, the possibility of a more elaborate general theory of phonetics which would include a formal set of dependency rules, we may note that even the traditional phonetic chart as in Table I provides a far more economical specification of possible speech sounds than Jakobson-Fant-Halle distinctive features phonetics. This is because all traditional phonetic charts are arranged so as to preclude a number of possible combinations of states of the glottis and manner of articulation. The restrictions implicit in Table I can be formulated in terms of a set of rules or a finite state automaton as shown in Figure 4. Table I uses 29 states in all (the 16 shown in Figure 4 and the 13 places of articulation) intersecting to form 273 categories, of which 93 represent sounds which actually occur in the languages represented in the corpus. As we have seen, distinctive feature theory has 15 features,

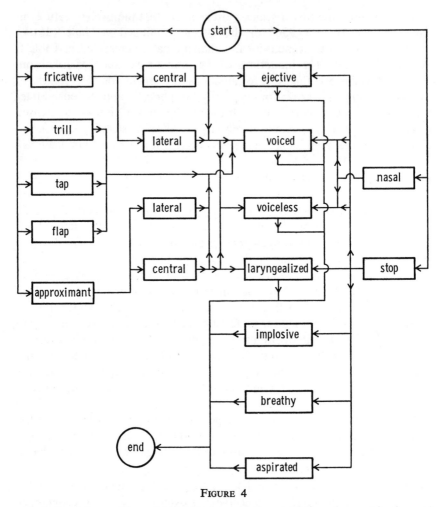

FIGURE 4

A finite state machine which will generate the restrictions in combinations of manner of articulation and state of the glottis for the data in Table I. (Note that these terms require specific definitions, which may not be the usual ones. Thus "breathy" denotes a specific state of the glottis, which is sometimes called "breathy voice"; and "implosive" denotes another state of the glottis including both a downward movement and a particular mode of vibration of the vocal cords.)

each of which must have, on the phonetic level, a minimum of two states, so that there are at least 30 states in this phonetic framework. Allowing for the stated combinatory restrictions, this apparatus generates 12,288 categories and even then probably does not account for all the 93 sounds.

I am entirely convinced by the arguments advanced by Halle (1964b) in favor of some set of distinctive features which can form the classificatory matrix required in the phonological component of a grammar; and I would also agree with him and Jakobson in the desirability of trying to establish a set of phonetic features which reflect some universals of language. But it seems to me that the Jakobson-Halle distinctive features can be shown to be most unsatisfactory as part of a general theory of phonetics.

BIBLIOGRAPHY

Carnochan, J. (1952) "Glottalization in Hausa" *Trans. Phil. Soc.* 79.

Fant, C. G. M. (1962) "Descriptive analysis of the acoustic aspects of speech" *Logos* 5, 3-17.

Fant, C. G. M. (1964) "Phonetics and speech research" in *Research Potentials in Voice Physiology* (ed. D. Brewer) New York: State University of New York.

Firth, J. R. (1957) *Papers in Linguistics, 1934-1951* Oxford: Oxford Univ. Press.

Halle, M. (1959) *The Sound Pattern of Russian* 's-Gravenhage: Mouton.

Halle, M. (1964a) "On the bases of phonology" in *The Structure of Language* (ed. J. Fodor and J. Katz) Englewood Cliffs, N. J.: Prentice-Hall.

Halle, M. (1964b) "Phonology in generative grammar" in *The Structure of Language* (ed. J. Fodor and J. Katz) Englewood Cliffs, N. J.: Prentice-Hall.

Halliday, M. (1963) "The tones of English" *Archivum Linguisticum* 15.1, 2-28.

Jakobson, R. (1962) "The phonemic concept of distinctive features" *Proc. IVth Internat. Congr. Phon. Sciences* 's-Gravenhage: Mouton.

Jakobson, R., Fant, C. G. M., and Halle, M. (1951, reprinted 1963) *Preliminaries to Speech Analysis* Cambridge, Mass.: M. I. T. Press.

Jakobson, R., and Halle, M. (1956) *Fundamentals of Language* 's-Gravenhage: Mouton.

Ladefoged, P. (1964a) "Igbirra notes" *Jour. W. Afr. Langs.* 1.1, 27-37.

Ladefoged, P. (1964b) *A Phonetic Study of West African Languages* Cambridge, England: Cambridge University Press.

Lindblom, B. (1963) "Spectrographic study of vowel reduction" *J. Acoust. Soc. Amer.* 35, 1773-1781.

Lindblom, B. (forthcoming) "Some temporal correlates of stress contours" *J. Acoust. Soc. Amer.* forthcoming.

Ohman, S. (1964) "Numerical model for coarticulation, using a computer-simulated vocal tract" *J. Acoust. Soc. Amer.* 36.5, 1038.

Ohman, S. (forthcoming) "Coarticulation in VCV utterances: spectrographic measurements" *J. Acoust. Soc. Amer.* forthcoming.

Wang, W. S-Y., and Fillmore, C. J. (1961) "Intrinsic cues and consonant perception" *J. Speech and Hearing Research* 4.2, 130-136.

ON ALTERNATION, TRANSFORMATION, REALIZATION, AND STRATIFICATION [1]

SYDNEY M. LAMB

University of California, Berkeley

FORMULATIONS FOR DIVERSIFICATION

Diversification is the term I use for one of the fundamental properties of linguistic stratification.[2] This condition is present wherever a linguistic unit has two or more alternate realizations on the next lower stratum. For example, phonemes have alternate phonetic realizations; morphons (i.e. morphophonemes) often have alternate phonemic realizations; the lexon ᴸ/good/ has alternate morphemic realizations in the forms *good, better, best;* the sememic combination

$$\Big/ \overset{\text{s}}{}\text{FARMER} \leftarrow \text{agt} \rightarrow \underset{\underset{\text{past}}{\uparrow}}{\text{KILL}} \leftarrow \text{gl} \rightarrow \text{DUCKLING}\Big/$$

is realized lexemically in a variety of ways in the expressions *the farmer killed the duckling, the duckling was killed by the farmer, did the farmer kill the duckling?, the killing of the duckling by the farmer, the farmer didn't kill the duckling, having killed the duckling, the farmer . . .,* etc. Instead of accounting for such phenomena in terms of stratification and realization, linguists have often attempted to deal with them by means of other formulations, which can be called **alternation, transformation,** and **classification.** To characterize them briefly, let us consider an abstract example in which there are two upper-stratum units A and B such that A has the single realization a while B has alternate realizations b and c. The alternative

---

[1] This work is supported in part by the National Science Foundation.

[2] For an account of these properties and examples see my "The Sememic Approach to Structural Semantics" *American Anthropologist, (in press).* In that paper I use the term 'representation' for what is here called 'realization'.

formulations are diagrammed in Figure 1, and a brief characterization of
each is given below.

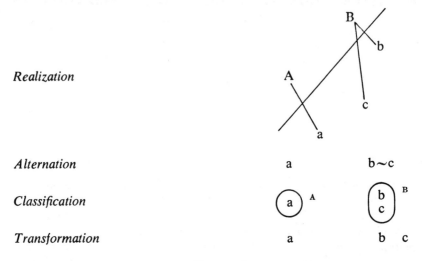

Realization

Alternation

Classification

Transformation

FIGURE 1

Alternation. This is actually only a partial formulation and one which
is clearly inadequate. Here the analyst simply says that b alternates with c.
This is approximately what Bloomfield did in part in *Language* (New York,
1933) when he characterized the morpheme as a combination of phonemes
and then observed that some morphemes have alternants (pp. 163-164).
(In part, however, Bloomfield used the transformation formulation.) He
did not really come to grips with the question of the nature of the morpheme, and he left its relation to the alternants and to the phonemes
unclear. Another example would be a statement that the above-cited
variations on the theme of *the farmer killed the duckling* are in some kind
of alternation with each other, without carrying the analysis to the conclusion that there must be some underlying unity at a deeper level of the
structure, of which the alternants are realizations. In other words this
formulation falls into the category of what I'm told Kroeber used to criticize
on the grounds that the analyst has cleared away the brush but hasn't cut
down the tree.

Classification. Here the analyst would say that b and c are members of
a class B. There are two versions of this formulation only one of which is
illustrated in the figure. In the one diagrammed, the analyst also says that
there is a class A, of which a is the only member, while the other version

would not have an A but would put a on a par with B. Thus the former version is more nearly stratified. It recognizes that at some structural level B can be treated as a single unit and that at this level the number of members of the classes A and B is irrelevant. The other version puts a at both levels so that it must serve in one relation to B and in another to b and c. The classification formulation is the one in which we would say that a phoneme is a class of phones and a morpheme a class of morphs. It can be shown to be inadequate since the relation of realization is more complicated than the class-member relation. The membership of a class may be specified by a list of the members, but the realization of a realizate requires for its specification the identification not only of the realizations but also of the conditioning environment for each of them.

Transformation. I am using the term 'transformation' here in a general sense to refer to the 'process' type of formulation at any level of linguistic structure. Rules of the type which are familiarly called transformations therefore exemplify just one type of transformation formulation. In this approach one of the alternants, say b, is picked as the basic one and it is sometimes (but not always) subjected to a transformation or process, which changes it to c, whereas when it is not so subjected it remains as b. On the other hand, a does not get subjected to any transformation and so remains. The items a and b thus serve in two functions, at two different periods in a fictional time span.[3] At the later period b alternates with c (and both are coexistent with a) whereas b also serves as the source of c and as such is in a different relation to a, which also exists at the earlier period. The process approach is more nearly adequate than the two preceding ones and is not as easily disposed of. The appropriate type of rule for this kind of formulation, like the realization rule (and unlike the class-member rule), includes specification of conditioning environments, and indeed it is undoubtedly because of this similarity as well as because modern synchronic linguistics grew out of diachronic studies that process formulations came to be used for stratificational phenomena.

In the case of the process relationship, the prior item, e.g. b, is differentiated from the resulting items, e.g. b and c, by its existence prior to the operation of the process. It must therefore be viewed as existing on the same stratum as the mutants which correspond to it; i.e. there is no need

---

[3] The more sophisticated practitioners of this approach are apparently aware that the time span which it uses is fictional and has nothing to do with either of the two aspects of real time passage which are relevant to linguistics, namely that of diachronic linguistics and that involved in the production and decoding of discourse (that which we reflect in linguistic notation by writing from left to right).

for stratificational distinctions as well. Thus, in process morphophonemics the morphophonemic processes are applied not to morphophonemes but to phonemes or, for some practitioners, to phonetic features. It is true that this practice is not universally followed, but one can easily rule out the use of both stratification and process to differentiate the "before" from the "after" as using two different entities where only one is necessary. And that, of course, is multiplying entities beyond necessity.

In other words, the essential difference between stratification and process is that the b which exists prior to the transformation is b and not a different entity B. Thus the thoroughly consistent process approach would be one in which phonetic features were used instead of phonemic, and in which they would be present also at what would correspond to the next higher stratum, and so on up to the highest stratum. In other words, a consequence of a consistent process approach is that at the highest stratum (at which we might appropriately want our units to have some direct relation to meaning) the units will consist of phonetic features. And we find that precisely this property is present in what I understand is the current version of Chomsky's theory. The distinctive features are now introduced at his deepest structural level, even before the transformations.[4] By contrast, in the stratificational approach the phonetic distinctive features are not introduced in a generative description until the conversion from the phonemic stratum to the phonetic.

The transformation or process type of formulation and its relation to realization are examined in detail in the remainder of this paper.

APPLICATIONS OF TRANSFORMATION FORMULATION

First we should distinguish the various ways in which transformation or process formulations have been applied in linguistics. They have apparently been used in four different functions:

1. **For Conflation of Concatenation and Realization.** The first involves a confusion or blending of two relations, namely realization and the one involved in tactic combination. There are two well-known ways in which this type of process formulation has been used, namely Sapir's morphological processes and Chomsky's optional transformations. Suppose that (in terms of a stratificational account) we are dealing with a lexon ᴸ/good/ which can occur with another lexon ᴸ/er/ and that there are realization rules (which define the realizations of the lexons in terms of their environ-

---

[4] In an earlier version presented in his paper in the preprints of the Ninth International Congress of Linguists, they were introduced right after the transformations.

ments) such that the realization of ᴸ/good er/ is *better*. We would account for *better,* using a stratified approach, in terms of two separate phenomena: (1) the fact that a particular lexon is combined with another, a tactic phenomenon, and (2) the fact of how this combination is realized on the next lower stratum. These two separate facts are combined into one in the morphological process approach, in which (if one is consistent and refrains from multiplying entities) there are no morphemes; instead there are two kinds of things, roots (which are phonetic or phonemic entities depending on whether a phonemic stratum is recognized) and morphological processes; and words are accounted for in terms of the application of morphological processes to roots, i.e. a process of suffixation plus suppletion in the case of *better,* in the case of *worse* just suppletion, in the case of *taller* just suffixation, and for *longer* just suffixation but of a different suffix than for *taller* (namely one which begins with *g*), unless the processist is willing to partially stratify and set up the root *long* in a basic form (having final *g*) which doesn't actually occur.

Most linguists (I hope) don't do this kind of thing any more at this level, but more recently it has been going on at a higher level, namely that of Chomsky's transformations (although Chomsky has now revised his theory so that this conflation is no longer present).[5] In a stratified account there are sememic units occurring in various combinations as specified by semotactic rules; and there are realization rules which specify how the sememic combinations are realized on the lexemic stratum. Instead of this the "lexological process" approach would have (similarly to the morphological process approach) two kinds of entities at the highest level, namely items and lexological processes (called transformations) to which these items can be subjected. For example, there would be a negative transformation which would be applied to a "sentence" to transform it from positive to negative (whereas the stratified account would have a negative semon occurring with other semons as specified by semotactic rules and, as a separate phenomenon, the realization of the combination as, say, *the farmer didn't kill the duckling*). Notice that just as morphological processes were applied to phonetic or phonemic entities, i.e. to things of the same kind as what emerges from the operation of the processes, so the lexological processes are applied not to semological networks, but to constituent-structure trees, i.e. entities which are like those found on the lexemic stratum.

As mentioned above, the new version of Chomsky's theory accounts for

---

[5] Chomsky presented this revision in a lecture given at the University of California, Berkeley, on 25 February, 1964.

these phenomena in a more nearly correct way. All the significant elements which will be present in the sentence are now introduced during the original constituent-structure rules, so that now the transformations have the sole function of converting from what he calls the "deep structure" to the "surface structure". They do not add any new material. There are no longer, in other words, any optional transformations. (Chomsky's system is still only partially stratified, however, since his interstratal conversion is done with rules of a process type instead of realization rules.)

So it may be safe to say that this first type of process formulation is not widely used any more, except perhaps by followers of Chomsky who haven't yet heard about his new system.

2. **For Concatenation and Classification.** In a stratified system there is a set of tactic rules for each of the structural strata, which characterize the set of well-formed combinations of units of that stratum. Each such rule is a statement about a set. On one side of the rule is given a symbol for the set, on the other side a specification of the membership of the set, either by listing (if it is a set whose members are ultimate constituents) or in terms of other distribution classes (whose membership is in turn specified by other rules). A specification of the latter type might be

$$A \; N \; ,$$

which means the set of all strings an such that a is a member of A and n is a member of N. Without going into such rules in detail I want just to state here that the only relations involved in tactics are the class-member relation and that of concatenation (or some other type of combination, in the case of a stratum on which units occur in non-linear combinations) and that each tactic rule is merely a statement about the membership of a set. This is a simpler type of rule than those required for realization and for mutation (i.e. the type of relation involved in linguistic change) and the tactic relations should of course be kept distinct from these more complex ones. But we find that Chomsky and his followers use replacement rules both for this function and as a substitute for realization (see ¶3 below), and one hears Chomsky making statements to the effect that a noun phrase, say, is "realized as" or "represented by" an article plus a noun.[6]

---

[6] It is true that Chomsky and the more sophisticated of his followers are aware of differences in the form of the different kinds of rules involved, and one might think they would thus be able to avoid confusion in their own minds despite the use of the same symbol (i.e. the arrow) and same set of locutions (is rewritten as, is replaced by, is represented by, is realized as) in all of the types of rule. But there is evidence that they are not entirely successful in this attempt, and it is quite certain that students and those followers who are not experts readily get confused.

3. **For Realization.** The process type of formulation is perhaps best known and most widely used in this function, and it is this application that I will be concentrating on below. Examples are the use of ordered rewrite rules for morphophonemics, and the transformational rules of Chomsky's new semi-stratified system, which convert from his "deep structure" to his "surface structure".

4. **For Mutation.** If we use the term 'mutation' for the relation involved in linguistic change, then it is for the mutation relation that ordered replacement rules, i.e. process statements, are properly used. Here the property that the items existing prior to the process are of the same kind as those resulting from it (e.g. both phonemic) is entirely appropriate. Of these four types of application of process, this is the one (and the only one) where it belongs. Process formulations and the study of process rules are valuable for that reason. But in synchronic linguistics they are out of place. (In the sequel I shall use the term 'mutation rule' interchangeably with 'process rule', 'rewrite rule', and 'replacement rule', and I shall focus on the differences between this type of rule and the realization rule.)

MUTATION AND REALIZATION

The function of a set of realization rules is to specify how the elements of a stratum are realized on the next lower stratum. Each such set of rules may be thought of as a code relating two neighboring strata. The names **semolexemic, lexomorphemic,** and **morphophonemic** may be used for the three sets of realization rules relating the four structural strata of a system with sememic, lexemic, morphemic and phonemic strata, and there are in addition the rules defining the phonetic realization of the phonons, i.e. the elementary units of the phonemic stratum. (To keep the terminology consistent these would be called phonophonetic rules, but I am not insisting on that term.)

The realization rule, in its simple form (some modifications are described below), consists of (1) a realizate, or the name of the rule, which is an element of the upper stratum, and (2) a list of one or more subrules. Each subrule specifies (1) an environment, expressed in terms of upper-stratum elements, and (2) the realization which the realizate has when it is in that environment. In some cases (where there is free variation) a set of freely-varying alternate realizations is given in the same subrule. In the notation which I use, each subrule is introduced by " || ", which may be verbalized as "when in the environment", and the realization (or set of freely-varying realizations) is introduced by " / ", which may be verbalized as "is realized as". An abstract example is the rule

$$w \parallel x\text{--}y \,/\, z$$
$$\parallel t\text{--}u \,/\, v$$
$$.$$
$$.$$
$$.$$
$$\parallel \text{---} \,/\, s \,.$$

Here w is the realizate; each of x, y, t, u, . . . is either (1) zero (i.e. nothing), meaning any combination of upper-stratum elements, or (2) a string of one or more symbols each of which is either an element of the upper stratum or a cover symbol;[7] "--" identifies the position of the realizate in the environment; "---" means "in any environment"; and each of z, v, . . ., s is a combination of zero or more elements of the lower stratum or, in the case of free variation, a set of such combinations. The ordering of the subrules is significant in that a given subrule applies only if none of the preceding ones does.[8] Thus the environment symbol "---" means "everywhere" if it appears in the first (hence only) subrule and "elsewhere" (i.e. in any environment other than those specified above) if it appears in the last. For some purposes it is convenient to adopt a notational convention whereby, if it is economical to write the realizate with the same symbol as that used for the realization given in the last subrule, that subrule may be omitted. (But note that since the realizate and the realization are on different strata, use of the same symbol does not mean that they are the same unit.)

Now one might ask if this is really different from the mutation rule. Isn't it the case, one might say, that we could restate the rule in the following way, in which the arrow means "is replaced by":

$$w \parallel x\text{--}y \rightarrow z$$
$$\parallel t\text{--}u \rightarrow v$$
$$.$$
$$.$$
$$.$$
$$\parallel \text{---} \rightarrow s \,,$$

---

[7] The restrictions on use of cover symbols are such that any preceding or following environment is a regular set, in terms of automata theory.

[8] Thus the list of subrules defines a partition of the set of all possible contexts in which w may occur, even though the sets of contexts as defined overtly by the individual subrules may overlap.

or even in the form

$$xwy \rightarrow xzy$$
$$twu \rightarrow tvu$$
$$w \ \rightarrow \ s\,.$$

Aren't these statements formally equivalent, and aren't these alternative symbolizations and their accompanying verbalizations just different ways of stating what is really the same thing? The answer is **no.** And one lesson to be learned from this answer is that one cannot know what the structure of a system is just by looking at the form of the individual rule. One has to look at the structure of the whole system and at the way in which the parts of the rule are defined. Or, one good way to see the difference is to look at the way the rules operate. This we shall do below in order to make the difference quite clear, but first it may be helpful to look at a couple of simple examples.

It is easy to see that the last formulation above leads to an entirely different result from that of the true realization rule. The realization rule above tells us only about the realizations of w, but tells us nothing about how x, y, . . . are realized. For all we know there are rules to the effect that

$$x \,||\, \text{--}w/p$$
$$y \,||\, w\text{--}/q,$$

in which case the realization of xwy is not xzy (as in the rewrite rule above) but pzq. This difference (between the correct result and the incorrect one) is a consequence of the fact that for realization the two strata are entirely distinct from each other, and the environments of the realization rules are stated in terms of the upper stratum, while the realizations are on the lower stratum. In other words, everything to the left of the "/" is on the upper stratum, while what is at the right of it is on the lower one. The set of elements of the upper stratum is disjoint from that of the elements of the lower one (except that both have the empty string as a member), and so a formulation of the type

$$xwy \rightarrow xzy$$

cannot be used since in it the x and y at the left of the arrow are the same units as those at the right. In other words this type of rule is possible only in an unstratified system.

Let us now consider a hypothetical morphophonemic example, in which the following rules apply:

$$i \,||\, \text{--} \ \#/\emptyset$$
$$t \,||\, \text{--} \ i/c,$$

where # is word juncture and Ø is zero (i.e. the empty string). Then the phonemic realization of the string ^{M}/kati/ when it is followed by ^{M}/#/ (assuming that ^{M}/ka/ is realized as ^{P}/ka/) is ^{P}/kac/, since both ^{M}/t/ and ^{M}/i/ are in the specified environments. But if we restate the rules as mutation rules we have

1. i || -- # → Ø

2. t || -- i → c;

in which I have written the rule numbers to call attention to the fact that rewrite rules are ordered. Applying these rules to the same string we get kati → kat. And there the process stops, because after rule 1 has operated, t is no longer in the proper environment for rule 2. But with realization rules the environment is on the upper stratum and it does not get replaced. The "output" of a realization rule does not replace anything; it belongs instead on the lower stratum.

Of course, to get the right answer one can state the rewrite rules in the opposite order:

1. t || -- i → c

2. i || -- # → Ø.

Then we get kati (when followed by #) → kaci → kac, which is correct.

Now, what if in some other dialect the phonemic realization is ^{P}/kat/? Then the ordering tried first above for the rewrite rules would be correct, and the proponent of ordered rewrite rules might wonder how we would handle this with unordered realization rules. Well, in terms of stratification, the situation is simply that the rule for ^{M}/t/ applies before non-final ^{M}/i/ but not before ^{M}/i#/. Thus the rules for this dialect would be written

i || -- #/Ø

t || -- i $\overline{\#}$/c

(and they could of course have been written in either order), in which $\overline{\#}$ is a cover symbol meaning "any morphon except #". At this point we can expect that the champion of replacement rules will say, "Aha! You have had to use an extra symbol in the statement of the conditioning environment, namely $\overline{\#}$." To which my reply would be, "Aha! **You** have had to use **two** extra symbols in your rules, namely the digits 1 and 2!". Those digits cannot be ignored. They are technically an integral part of the ordered rule, since the ordered rule is ordered. In other words, the ordering is not free, when we are computing degrees of complexity by counting symbols. An ordered set is a more complex object than an unordered one and, in particular, each rule of a set of ordered rewrite rules is, formally speaking, paired with a positive integer. So every rewrite rule has an extra symbol, namely the rule number.

So here we have another difference between the two types of rule. The realization rule does not have a rule number, except in the sense that the rule number is the realizate itself. And it is instructive to think of the realization rule in these terms. I stated above that the realizate could be considered the name of the rule. It can also be considered the rule number, which is equivalent, or the location of the rule in a production system. That is, the morphon $^M/t/$ is, structurally speaking, the name or number or location of the rule which provides certain realizations that speakers of the language treat as in some way equivalent. And the occurrence of a morphon is simply a specification that a particular morphophonemic rule is to be executed. If we wanted to we could number the realization rules but if we did so these numbers would replace the alphabetic symbols now used. Such a concept is not applicable in the case of mutation rules, for which the units corresponding to morphons are "objects" which get operated upon.

These considerations will become clearer if we consider the procedures for using the two types of rule. In the stratified system the encoding from one stratum to the next lower one can be accomplished in a single left-to-right pass through each string to be encoded. For each element e_i of the string $e_1 \ldots e_n$ to be encoded we go (directly) to rule e_i and execute it. Since the subrules are ordered, the execution consists of testing the environments specified in the successive subrules one by one until the one which applies is encountered, at which time we (do not rewrite e_i but instead) put out the realization (which is in turn a specification that one or more rules of the next lower code are to be executed).

In the case of mutation rules, on the other hand, **a separate pass must be made through the string for each rule.** Here the rule numbers specify the order in which the successive passes are to be made through each string. The execution of the individual rule is also more complicated, since it involves two parts. First, each element of the string must be looked at to see whether it is one to which the rule may apply. Whenever an element e_i is encountered to which it may, then the operations of testing the successive environments are performed as in the case of the realization rule. When an applicable environment is found, then e_i **is replaced by** the symbol or symbols specified by the subrule having that environment. Note that such rewriting destroys what was previously there, namely e_i, so that the formulator of the rules must have made sure that this e_i is not a part of a conditioning environment for any following rule. In other words, each rule must be placed into the ordered sequence in such a way that (1) no preceding rule has already altered the conditioning environment of e_i and (2) e_i will not be part of the conditioning environment in any following sub-rule. It is this property of rewrite rules which makes it essential that they be ordered and which evidently also accounts for various other complications in process descriptions. Thus much of the complexity seen in a transformational grammar is the result not of complexity in the language, but of an artificial restriction imposed by the type of rule being used.

There is another difference, one which at first glance might appear to favor the mutation rule. In the mutation rule it is not necessary that the subrules collectively cover all possible contexts in which the element can occur. If none of the subrules applies, then the element is not rewritten at all.[9] The corresponding situation is not possible for realization rules because the set of upper stratum elements and that of lower stratum elements are disjoint sets. Therefore there must always be a realization, even for elements which have the same realization in all environments. This consideration relates to Figure 1 above, in which we had separate units A and a even though a was the only realization of A. As I said, this difference might seem to favor the mutation rule, but only at first glance. For if the user of process rules wants to take advantage of this property of the process formulation he can do so only by having present at the earlier period in the fictional time span those elements that he has to end up with at the completion of the process. Thus in the Chomsky system the phonetic distinctive feature matrices are introduced very early in the generative heirarchy even though they are not needed (and in fact are very cumbersome) until near the end; whereas in a stratified generative system the phonons (i.e. the components of the phonemes) are not introduced until the time of the morphophonemic rules, and the components present at the top structural stratum are not phonetic but sememic.

Let us summarize the differences between mutation and realization by means of the following table.

Properties of Mutation Rules	Properties of Realization Rules
1. Ordered (i.e. each rule is paired with an integer). Consequence: multiple passes through string.	1. Unordered; realizates are names of rules; single pass through string.
2. "Output" of rule replaces input (which is no longer available as environment).	2. "Output" of rule is name(s) of other rule(s); input is unaffected.
3. Items can remain unchanged (but if they do their final composition must be present at beginning).	3. Every item has a realization (i.e. lower-stratum elements not present at beginning).

---

[9] This property is quite appropriate to the proper use of these rules, which is for mutation in diachronic linguistics.

REALIZATION FORMULATION VARIATIONS

The description of the realization rule given above characterizes what may be called the simple form of the rule. A slightly different form is needed for semolexemics, since the realizates here do not occur in strings but rather in networks. The specification of environments in subrules must therefore take a somewhat different form. In addition there are various modifications available which allow descriptions of certain phenomena sometimes encountered at lower levels to be somewhat simpler and more realistic than is possible for the simpler form of rule. These modifications buy simplicity of the rules when dealing with these phenomena, at the cost of additional meta-rules in the system which specifies the form of rules in a well-formed linguistic description. I will mention them briefly for the record although I cannot give full explanations in this brief paper.

First we may briefly consider the phenomena of portmanteau realization, empty realization, and anataxis,[10] all of which can be handled by the addition of one device which is apparently needed anyway for semolexemic rules. This device is the numerical superscript, to be attached to certain symbols appearing in the specification of environment in subrules. The function of a superscript is to specify a deviation from the usual order of execution of the rules. (Recall that the usual order is that in which the realizates occur.) For example, to take care of a case of metathesis for which a process treatment would use the rule

$$y(p,t,k) \rightarrow (p,t,k)y \,^{11}$$

which actually changes the order of the units, we would use superscripts to specify that the rule for the stop of the upper stratum is to be executed before that of y, as follows:

$$y \,||\, \text{--}^2(p,t,k)^1/y.$$

Here there is no reordering of elements, since realization rules do not ever change the realizates. The rule has merely specified that instead of the usual left-to-right order of putting out the realizations, that of the stop is to be put out before that of y.

Portmanteau realization can be handled without any special devices (and for that matter so can metathesis at the cost of a little simplicity and realism), by rules like these (which are lexomorphemic):

$$er \,||\, bad \,\text{--}/\emptyset.$$

---

[10] For descriptions and examples of these phenomena, see "The Sememic Approach to Structural Semantics" (cf. footnote 2 above).

[11] The expression in parentheses is an "ad hoc cover symbol" having the values p, t, and k. This example of metathesis is presumed to be present in Zoque on the basis of problem 52 in Nida's *Morphology*, (Ann Arbor, 1949).

But such a formulation tends to strike the intuition of native speakers as being less than completely realistic, since *worse* would seem to be the realization of the combination ^{L}/bad er/, not just of ^{L}/bad/, which indeed is why we call it a case of portmanteau representation. A convenient notational convention for this phenomenon (which can also be used for metathesis) would allow the rule

$$\text{bad er} \,\|\, \text{--}/\text{wərs}.$$

But it must be understood that this is merely a notational convention for what, strictly speaking, should be written

$$\text{bad} \,\|\, \text{-- er}^0/\text{wərs},$$

where the zero superscript indicates that the rule for this ^{L}/er/ is not to be executed at all (since the realization given in this rule is that of the combination ^{L}/bad er/). The notationally convenient form of this rule violates the requirement that the realizate for any rule must be a single element, a requirement which is necessary to the manner of operation of the rules described above.

In empty realization the realizate is zero. To handle this phenomenon without superscripts it is necessary either (1) to in effect deny it any special status and treat the empty realization as a part of the realization of the element preceding the zero realizate; or else (2) to have a rule with a zero realizate and to go to it (when encoding) after the execution of the rule for every non-zero realizate. In the formulation which allows superscripts, however, an environment expression can contain

$$\ldots \text{--} \, \emptyset^1 \ldots$$

to specify that rule $\emptyset$ (i.e. the rule for the zero realizate) is to be executed next. The superscripted zero would appear only in rules for elements which can precede the empty realizate. Thus the rule for the zero realizate is executed only when, as it were, specific instructions to do so are given.

The "output" part of a realization rule is a specification that certain other rules are to be executed, except where the realization is zero. In the rule as described so far these other rules are realization rules at the next lower level of coding. The following example illustrates a type of simplification that can be achieved by modifying this feature of the rule. These rules describe a morphophonemic situation in Monachi (or Mono), a Utoaztecan language of California. (Square brackets in the specification of an environment mean that the enclosed element(s) may be present or absent in that position.)

$$w \parallel (e,a,o)h\text{--}(a,e)/q^w$$
$$\parallel h\text{--}/k^w$$
$$k^w \parallel (e,a,o)[h]\text{--}(e,a)/q^w.$$

That is, $^M/w/$ is realized as a labialized stop when preceded by $^M/h/$ and the stop is velar or postvelar depending on the surrounding vowels; but $^M/k^w/$ is realized as $^P/q^w/$ in the same vocalic environment for which $^M/w/$ has that realization. (In some vocalic environments $^P/k^w/$ and $^P/q^w/$ contrast, so they are phonemically different.) The rules as stated in this simple form contain a redundancy in the specification of this vocalic environment, which can be eliminated by the adoption of a meta-rule which will allow us to state the rule for $^M/w/$ in a slightly different form.

First, however, let us pause to make a comparison with how this phenomenon could be treated by the mutation rule. One way to write mutation rules for it is:

1. $w \parallel h\text{--} \rightarrow k^w$
2. $k^w \parallel (e,a,o)[h]\text{--}(e,a) \rightarrow q^w.$

Here the vocalic environment has to be stated only once, since the second rule will apply both to "original" k^w and to the k^w which is "derived" from original w. But this economy is achieved at the cost of making these rules ordered.

We should also note here an important factor which has not been made explicit in the notation so far. In the process rules above, the symbols of the notation can be taken either as (1) denoting structural elements or as (2) convenient notational abbreviations for what are really bundles of phonons or of distinctive features. If the former alternative is chosen, then all the rules of this type must be followed by another list of rules which will convert the elements of the final output string into their components. For example, there would have to be rules such as the following (if phonons are used rather than binary distinctive features, which are more complicated):

$$k^w \rightarrow \begin{matrix} Cl \\ Vl \\ Lb \end{matrix}$$

$$q^w \rightarrow \begin{matrix} Cl \\ Pv \\ Lb \end{matrix}$$

where Cl stands for "closed", Vl for "velar", Lb for "labial", Pv for "postvelar"). If the other alternative is adopted then the components are the elements which are really present at the beginning of the sequence of morphophonemic rules, and all the symbols in the two ordered mutation rules above are really abbreviations. In other words, according to this formulation the rules are actually the following:

$$1. \quad Lb \parallel Gm \dashrightarrow \begin{matrix} Cl \\ Vl \\ Lb \end{matrix}$$

$$2. \quad Vl \parallel \begin{matrix} Vo \\ Lo \end{matrix} [Gm] \begin{matrix} Cl \ Vo \\ -- Lo \\ Lb \ \overline{Lb} \end{matrix} \rightarrow Pv.$$

In measuring the complexity of a list of rules it is of course the actual structural meaning of the rules which must be measured, not the notation.

What, then, is the relation between the notation and the actual situation for the realization rules above? The answer is implicit in the description of the realization rule already given. It is that each alphabetic symbol to the left of "/" stands for a morphon, which is an indivisible structural element of the morphemic stratum, while each phonemic symbol, i.e. each symbol at the right of "/", is an abbreviation for a bundle of phonons. Thus these rules may be stated without the use of any abbreviations or notational conventions as follows:

$$w \parallel (e,a,o)h \dashrightarrow (a,e) / \begin{matrix} Cl \\ Pv \\ Lb \end{matrix}$$

$$\parallel h \dashrightarrow / \begin{matrix} Cl \\ Vl \\ Lb \end{matrix}$$

$$\parallel \text{---} / Lb$$

$$k^w \parallel (e,a,o)[h] \dashrightarrow (e,a) / \begin{matrix} Cl \\ Pv \\ Lb \end{matrix}$$

$$\parallel \text{---} / \begin{matrix} Cl \\ Vl \\ Lb \end{matrix}$$

$$q^w \parallel \text{---} / \begin{matrix} Cl \\ Pv \\ Lb. \end{matrix}$$

Now we are ready to introduce the variation hinted at above, which allows us to let the "output" of a realization rule refer to another rule at the same level of coding in order to eliminate redundancy. For this type of reference we can use "$|$" instead of "$/$". Then the above rules can be restated as follows:

$$w \parallel h-- \mid k^w$$
$$\parallel ---/Lb$$
$$k^w \parallel (e,a,o)[h]--(e,a) \mid q^w$$
$$\parallel ---/\begin{matrix} Cl \\ Vl \\ Lb \end{matrix}$$
$$q^w \parallel ---/\begin{matrix} Cl \\ Pv \\ Lb. \end{matrix}$$

Whereas "$/$" is to be verbalized as "is realized as", "$|$" is to be verbalized as **"is realized in the same way as"**. In terms of the operation of the rules, the difference between the two types of output is simply a difference of whether the specified rule(s) to be executed are at the same level of coding or the next lower one. Notice that this elimination of redundancy is achieved without resorting to ordered rules, and that the properties of the realization rule described previously are still retained in this version.

To illustrate, let us take the form $^M/\text{?ahwehci}/$ 'her grey hair'. Alternative treatments by the stratificational formulation and by the last process formulation above (in which the phonons are already present at the beginning of the morphophonemic rules) are shown below.

Realization	Morphemic stratum:	?	a	h	w	e	h	c	i
	Phonemic stratum:	Gl	Vo Lo	Gm	Cl Pv Lb	Vo Lo Fr	Gm	Cl Gr	Vo Hi Fr
Mutation	Stage 0	Gl	Vo Lo	Gm	Lb	Vo Lo Fr	Gm	Cl Gr	Vo Hi Fr
	Stage 1	Gl	Vo Lo	Gm	Cl Vl Lb	Vo Lo Fr	Gm	Cl Gr	Vo Hi Fr
	Stage 2	Gl	Vo Lo	Gm	Cl Pv Lb	Vo Lo Fr	Gm	Cl Gr	Vo Hi Fr

Another version of the realization rule would be that which allows for indirect specification of conditioning environment. This device involves an extension of the cover symbol (which is available for the "simple" type of realization rule, but which isn't treated above for lack of space). The usual cover symbol (such as "V" or "C" in morphophonemic rules) can be construed structurally as a reference to another rule (unless it is an ad hoc or self-defined cover symbol, such as (e,a) in the rules above), namely a tactic rule which specifies the membership of the set V or C or whatever it may be. The indirect environment is like a cover symbol but it calls for reference to another realization rule rather than to a tactic rule. To illustrate, the first subrule for $^\text{M}$/k$^\text{w}$/ in the last formulation above, using this device, could be stated in the following way, where pointed brackets "$< \,.\,. \,>$" are used to enclose the indirect environment:

$$k^\text{w} \parallel \left\langle \begin{matrix} \text{Vo} \\ \text{Lo} \end{matrix} \right\rangle \text{[h]--(e,a)} \mid q^\text{w}$$

The symbol $\left\langle \begin{matrix} \text{Vo} \\ \text{Lo} \end{matrix} \right\rangle$ is a cover symbol for morphons whose realization has the components Vo (vocalic) and Lo (low). Whether this symbol is simpler than the alternative (e,a,o) for the same set of morphons is open to question, but there are circumstances in which the use of this device seems to provide clearly simpler rules.

BEHAVIORAL EVIDENCE FOR CONTRASTING FORMS OF BILINGUALISM [1]

W. E. LAMBERT

McGill University

It is a special pleasure for me, a psychologist, to be asked to talk to you about some of our work on language behavior. This is so because I have a personal conviction that neither linguists nor psychologists have become fully aware of the fact that both are studying often the very same phenomena of language with distincitvely different methods, schemes of analysis, and ultimate purposes in mind. In light of these differences, when linguistic and psychological facts or laws do make contact or coincide, their significance for each discipline becomes appreciably richer and more meaningful. Opportunities extended to me by the Social Science Research Council's Committee on Linguistics and Psychology to meet with linguists for long periods have demonstrated clearly the value of contact for both groups. I don't believe that the fruitful consequences of contact require that we know one another's business or jargon to any great extent as long as both groups are willing to share major ideas, stating them in simplified terminology.

I hope that what I have to say here about bilingualism will illustrate the psychological approach to this fascinating topic. I have been helped in my work by my contact with Uriel Weinreich and Einar Haugen. I responded to their linguistic perspective of bilingualism as a psychologist. Whether they or other linguists will respond in turn to my psychological interpretation of bilingualism, thereby completing the cycle of contact, I can't really judge, but I do hope so.

The phenomenon of bilingualism had been examined by the more speculative, former generation of linguists long before psychologists considered it of special interest. In an exhaustive review of the literature on this topic, Weinreich (1953) reports several publications in which two forms of bilingualism have been identified.

---

[1] The work discussed here has been supported by the Canadian Defense Research Board and more recently by the Carnegie Corporation by grants to the Language Research Group at McGill.

Linguists have used various names to distinguish the two, e.g. "pure versus mixed," "organic versus inorganic," "subordinative versus co-ordinative." The distinction between the two forms has been made on the basis of differences in linguistic behavior of bilinguals such as the general or specialized usage of one or both languages, proneness to translate from one language to the other, or differences in connotations of words which are supposedly equivalent in the two languages.

The psychologist's interest in bilingualism centers on the effect upon verbal behavior and thinking of the acquisition and usage of two systems of signs. Following Osgood's development of a theory of meaning (1953) which uses a mediation principle as its pivotal concept, Ervin & Osgood (1954) formulated a theory of bilingualism which incorporates the linguist's notion of a bilingual dichotomy and relates the two types to the manner in which bilinguals acquire and use their languages.

Ervin & Osgood argue that the "meaning" of a sign (or word) is identical to the representational mediation process which that sign elicits in the organism. The mediation process is some form of neutral-system replica of the original reactions made to the referent or object signified by the sign. A "compound bilingual" is defined as one who possesses two sets of equivalent signs (one in each language) for the same class of referents. For example, the meaning of the English word "house" is identical with the meaning of its French equivalent "maison" since both these signs elicit the same mediators. A "coordinate bilingual" is defined as one who possesses two sets of signs which have comparatively less equivalence because the situations in which the two languages were learned were contextually separated and in some cases the actual referents of signs in the two languages are not identical or equivalent. Thus, the word "house" elicits its appropriate mediation process, while the word "maison" elicits a mediation process which is different to some degree from that elicited by "house." The coordinate may learn to translate "house" by "maison" as well as note the similarities between the objects referred to by the two signs, but the meaning of these two words will remain different, usually being subjectively experienced as a difference in connotation or appropriateness of reference.

From these definitions, specific kinds of language experiences are conducive to the formation of compound and coordinate bilingual systems. Thus, the so-called "indirect" method of language learning (e.g., "maison means house," taught in the classroom) favors the development of compound billingualism since the new sign ("maison") is directly conditioned to the mediators already existing for the sign "house." It is evident that all meanings which are assigned are of the compound type. In contrast the "direct" method of language learning promotes coordinate bilingualism. Also, bicultural experience such as the use of French exclusively in France by an Englishman, favors the development of a coordinate system since the French signs tend to be conditioned or re-conditioned to new referents and experiences. "Specialization" in language usage (e.g. using French exclusively at home but English at work in bilingual communities) also promotes a coordinate system since the two languages are likely to become functionally independent.

We were first interested in testing the mediation theory of bilingualism by examining certain behavioral manifestations of the functional dependence or independence of bilingual language systems and relating these to the manner in which bilinguals learned their two languages (see Lambert, Havelka & Crosby, 1958). We contacted a large number of English-French bilinguals and interviewed them extensively in order to be confident in categorizing them either as *coordinate* if their languages were learned in situationally, culturally, or temporally distinctive settings, or as *compound* if the two languages were learned in essentially the same situation or through translation methods, or if they were used interchangeably. We also tested their comparative skill in the two languages and kept in our samples only those who were "balanced" in their bilingual skill (see Lambert, 1955).

Our first idea was to see how well compound and coordinate bilinguals would be able to keep their languages independent in a learning task. Each bilingual was given a list of 20 English words to memorize and then was given a second list to learn, the second list consisting of translation-equivalent French words for each of the original 20 English words. Here's the problem: from the theory, we predict that coordinates would keep their two languages separated in this task while compounds would show an interaction of the two languages. The results support this prediction clearly since compounds were able to profit from the interpolated French-equivalent list of words and *improved* their retention of the original English list while coordinates were disrupted by the translation equivalents and even forgot much of the original English list. That is, learning a series of words like "father, garden, church," etc., is more vividly remembered by compound bilinguals after they have rehearsed a series of equivalents such as "père, jardin, église," etc., while coordinates are bothered by the learning of the equivalents.

Our next prediction was that compound bilinguals would have more similar meanings for translated equivalents than would coordinates. Here we examined the two groups' patterns of meanings of translated equivalents using Osgood's semantic rating procedure (see Osgood, et al, 1957) which was designed to measure connotative meanings of words. The results are clear: if coordinate bilinguals learn their languages in culturally distinctive settings then they have comparatively different patterns of meanings for common words such as house and maison, poor and pauvre, me and moi than have compound bilinguals. That is, the meanings of equivalents such as "house-maison" or "poor-pauvre" are more distinct for coordinates who have learned their two languages in culturally segregated settings than for compound bilinguals. This finding does not hold for coordinates who have learned their languages in situationally segregated contexts within one cultural setting as in Montreal. Semantic distinctiveness apparently demands quite contrasting acquisition contexts whereas functional independence of the two language systems as noted in the memorization problem is developed more readily in a greater range of distinctive settings, not necessarily culturally segregated ones.

Our third test of the theory involves a new idea. Suppose we could by some method eliminate or reduce the meaning of a word in one language, what would be the effect of this meaning reduction for equivalents in the other language? We would predict that compounds would manifest the reduced meaning cross-linguistically whereas the coordinates should not show as much of any cross-linguistic effect from meaning reduction in one of their languages.

We have developed a method for reducing the meaning of a word by repeating it until its meaning is "satiated" (see Lambert & Jacobovits, 1960), for example repeatedly saying "house, house, house, etc." for a 15 second period. When measured on semantic rating scales, it is observed that the intensity of connotative meaning is systematically reduced by word repetition.

Groups of French-English coordinate and compound bilinguals were tested for cross-linguistic satiation. Concepts such as "cuisine" or "father" were continuously repeated by a subject for a 15 sec.

period and then the translated-equivalents ("kitchen" and "père") were presented one time and the extent of meaning change was measured for these translated-equivalents. The compound bilinguals behave as expected here: repetition of "cuisine" reliably reduces its connotative meaning and that of its equivalent, "kitchen." The co-ordinant bilinguals, however, show no reliable satiation of the meaning of repeated words nor do the translation-equivalents reflect a cross-linguistic satiation effect. In fact, continuous repetition of a word in language A actually *increases* the intensity of meanings of translation-equivalents in language B (see Jakobovits & Lambert, 1932). We have more work to do on this problem but at present we feel that these results are highly suggestive of quite different (and intriguing) processes underlying compound and coordinate biling-ualisms.

We have made other deductions from the psychological theory of bilingualism which were not supported and as a consequence of attempting to explain these cases, we have been led to new predic-tions and to likely modifications of the theory. I have only time enough to give you the general outline of these studies and the new ideas stemming from their findings. Compound and coordinate bi-linguals were asked to learn a mixed series of English and French words and to remember which words were associated with electric shock—a slight one administered to one finger. It wasn't long before the word "verte" or "boy," for example, would lead to a rapid press-ing of a key which eliminated the occurrence of shock. After this habit was well learned, we introduced (along with other new con-trol words) the translations of shocked words such as "green" and "garçon." Here we expected compound bilinguals to be more prompt than coordinates in pressing the key for the other-language equiva-lents of shocked words, arguing that the association of shock with "verte" for compound bilinguals would more likely also associate with "green" than would be the case for coordinates whose languages we assume function more independently. But we found no differ-ences between the groups here (see R. Olton, 1960).

In a further procedure (R. Olton, 1960) bilinguals learned a mixed list of English and French words and later were presented a longer list and asked to pick out the words memorized from among new words and translation-equivalents of those originally learned. For example, "glove" and "printemps" might have been on the list to be learned originally while only their translations ("gant" and "springtime") would be on the final list. Thus the subjects were forced to switch languages rapidly in memorizing the list but also remember which words appeared in which language. We would predict that compounds would make more errors in confusing "glove" with "gant" than would coordinates, but no reliable differences appeared. In both procedures all bilinguals showed cross-language generalizations, a finding of importance for the theory of mediated generalization. For the compound—coordinate problem, however, the results either indicate that these tests were too subtle or poorly executed, or that the procedures used prompted both groups to behave in a translation—alert manner, making coordinates appear as compounds.[2] This latter line of reasoning has led us to a new hypothesis concerning various procedures which involve rapid language switching and their effects on the thinking of bilinguals. The central notion under current examination is that experimental procedures which encourage a readiness to switch languages may modify the behavior of coordinate bilinguals and make them indistinguishable from compounds. We hope to be able to delineate such conditions, if they exist.

Psychology can of course make profitable contacts with other disciplines than linguistics. I have found it particularly interesting in the study of language to be sandwiched between linguistics on one side and physiological-psychology on the other. McGill University offers a splendid opportunity to learn about the important work of Hebb and Milner as well as Penfield and his associates. Donald Hebb in particular has encouraged me to think about the possible neurological implications of our work. In his recent book (D. O. Hebb, 1958, p. 104f) Hebb outlined one manner in which groups of neurological cells could function as either "fused" or "separated" systems—hypothetical neurological analogues of compound and coordinate systems.

Hebb's thinking suggested the possibility of indirectly testing the neurological features of compound and coordinate bilingualism. A long history of medical reports are available on bilinguals who have become aphasic, sometimes "losing" one of their two languages, other times "losing" both. We went through the published cases (mainly compiled in Europe) to determine if compound and coordinate classifications could possibly be made on the basis of how aphasic bilinguals originally acquired their two (or more) languages.

---

[2] This possibility might also account for our failure to find compound-coordinate differences in speed of translation mentioned in the Lambert, Havelka, Crosby study.

The findings of this study (Lambert & Fillenbaum, 1959) are of special interest because they suggest the possibility of someday linking linguistic, psychological and neurological principles. The argument here is that the functional relations of the bilingual's two languages have some systematic neurological representation in those areas of the brain necessary for language. In view of the behavioral evidence of functional dependence or independence of bilinguals' languages, we speculated that coordinate bilinguals should have more functionally separate neural structures underlying their languages than should compound bilinguals. Thus, concepts like "church" and "église" should be stored in neural elements which have some sort of greater functional discreteness for the coordinate bilinguals. It follows that brain damage which results in aphasia would be more likely to affect both languages of the compound bilingual but should lead to more selective disturbances for coordinates. The results of our analysis of aphasic patients are in line with these predictions: those cases which suggest a compound bilingual background typically show a generalized disorder affecting both languages whereas those cases with a coordinate bilingual background typically show more specific-language disorder following aphasia.

Throughout these studies, a psychological theory, based on the thinking of Charles Osgood and Donald Hebb, has functioned as an analytic guide. It generated a host of predictions, the testing of which has extended our understanding of bilingual behavior. The general picture is getting progressively clearer: converging evidence dealing with the learning and thinking processes of bilinguals supports the notion of functionally dependent language systems for those who acquire their two languages in a compound fashion and of functionally independent systems for those who acquire their languages in a coordinate fashion. Still there are certainly many intriguing features to be uncovered which have not even been conceptualized as yet.

REFERENCES

Ervin, Susan M. and Osgood, C. E. Second language learning and bilingualism. *J. abnorm. soc. Psychol.*, Supplement, 1954, *49*, 139-146.

Hebb, D. O. *A textbook of psychology.* Philadelphia: Saunders, 1958.

Jakobovits, L and Lambert, W. E. Semantic satiation among bilinguals. *J. exp. Psychol.*, in press, 1962.

Lambert, W. E. Measurement of the linguistic dominance of bilinguals. *J. abnorm. soc. Psychol.*, 1955, *50*, 197-200.

Lambert, W. E. and Fillenbaum, S. A pilot study of aphasia among bilinguals. *canad. J. Psychol.*, 1959, *13*, 28-34.

Lambert, W. E., Havelka, J. and Crosby, Cynthia. The influence of language-acquisition contexts on bilingualism. *J. abnorm. soc. Psychol.*, 1958, 56, 239-244.

Lambert, W. E. and Jakobovits, L. Verbal satiation and changes in the intensity of meaning. *J. exp. Psychol.*, 1960, 60, 376-383.

Olton, R. M. Semantic generalization between languages. M. A. thesis, McGill University library, 1960.

Osgood, C. E. *Method and theory in experimental psychology.* New York: Oxford University Press, 1953.

Osgood, C. E., Suci, G. J. and Tannenbaum, P. H. *The measurement of meaning.* Urbana: University of Illinois Press, 1957.

Weinreich, U. *Languages in contact.* New York: Linguistic Circle of New York, 1953.

TRANSFORMATIONAL PARAMETERS IN TAGMEMIC FIELD STRUCTURES

ROBERT E. LONGACRE

Summer Institute of Linguistics

0. In keeping with the theory of grammar here represented, this paper is interested in contrastive construction types and in relations between such types. In spite of many recent statements to the contrary, taxonomy, i.e. classification, is an abiding interest of science in general and of linguistic science in particular. The biological sciences botany and zoology continue to be flourishing taxonomic disciplines—even though they have also been concerned now for over a century with developmental hypotheses. The chemist is interested not only in chemical reactions and processes but in the identification, classification, and description of elements and compounds. The astronomer is concerned not only with schemes of stellar evolution but uses these very schemes as a means of classifying stars.[1] Linguistics—mainly classificatory in the previous two decades—has recently been enriched by bringing into focus transformational relations between constructions. But interest in transformations is not mutually exclusive with interest in classifying constructions and their parts. On the contrary, transformation relations between constructions are of considerable classificatory value. The fact that in astronomy a white dwarf star is a 'transform' of a red giant does not mean that we are no longer interested in distinguishing the two types of stars. Rather, the posited development is useful in classifying these two and other types in a coherent taxonomic scheme.

On the other hand, having granted the taxonomic significance of grammatical transformations, we find that admitting them as a classifying device has some important implications: (1) Transformational relations are not the only parameters which relate constructions. Rather transformations belong to a system of relations which includes non-transformational param-

---

[1] Morton S. Roberts, "Hydrogen in galaxies," *Scientific American* 208.6.94-106 (June 1963); Bart J. Bok, "The large cloud of Magellan," *Scientific American* 210.1.32-41 (January 1964).

eters as well. (2) A given coordinate, e.g. transitivity, in a system of contrasting types may involve both transformational and non-transformational parameters. (3) Transformations therefore do not comprise a separate level and need not be segregated in a separate section of the grammar.

This paper also attempts to show that certain concepts and notational conventions of tagmemics are useful in formulating linguistic transformations.

Relations between grammatical constructions within a language may be conceptualized as a field structure, i.e. as space in *n* parameters (or parameter classes).[2] This can be conveniently represented in a graph with a system of coordinates provided that the coordinates which characterize an entire system do not exceed three. A fourth coordinate characterizing an entire system may be represented by two or more related three-dimensional graphs. Parameters which do not characterize an entire system can be represented more conveniently as sub-divisions within another coordinate.

In conceptualizing grammatical systems in this fashion care should be taken to insure that the various constructions thus charted are, in Pike's words, "well-delineated constructions." [3] Well-delineated constructions are obtained not only by attention to systemic considerations of the sort discussed here but by attention to contrasting internal structures of constructions and to their distribution within other constructions. The constructions grouped into such a system may be from any level, i.e. the system may be a system of word types (morphological constructions), of phrase types, of clause types, or sentence types, or even conceivably of paragraph and discourse types.

The field structures here described are systems of clause structures in Ostuacan Zoque, Sierra Popoluca, and Tlahuitoltepec Mixe. In that these three languages are genetically related we find certain resemblances among the three field structures alongside considerable variety. Zoque is the simplest system; Sierra Popoluca, the most involved; and Mixe, the most symmetric. Of necessity these systems will be described with a minimum of actual linguistic data. The data for Zoque and Sierra Popoluca are published and easily available. A description of Tlahuitoltepec Mixe is now in the hands of the editor of IJAL.[4] Zoque and Sierra Popoluca display very similar systems of clause types. Mixe is strikingly divergent.

---

[2] Cf. Kenneth L. Pike, "Dimensions of grammatical constructions," *Language* 38.221-44.

[3] Pike, *Language* 38.231-42; Longacre, "Trique clause and sentence: A study in contrast, variation and distribution" (submitted to IJAL).

[4] Ralph Engel and Robert E. Longacre, "Syntactic matrices in Ostuacan Zoque," IJAL 29.331-43; John Lind, "Clause and sentence level syntagmemes in Sierra

	Non-transitive	Intransitive	Transitive	Ditransitive Referential	Ditransitive Causative	
Declarative	X	X	X	X	X	
Subordinate	X	X	X	X	X	
Interrogative	X	X	X	X	X	
Imperative		X	X	X	X	

DIAGRAM I: ZOQUE CLAUSE TYPES
(adopted from Engel and Longacre IJAL 29.332)

1. Zoque has an open-ended system comprising at least nineteen clause types. This system may be graphically represented in reference to two coordinates (as in diagram I): (1) mood; and (2) transitivity.

Mood is a variable with four values: declarative; subordinate; interrogative; and imperative. The latter three moods are transforms of the declarative. Specifically, a declarative clause is transformed to a subordinate clause by preposing a conjunction and/or suffixing the verb; the six sub-types of subordinate require separate transformation rules. Interrogative and imperative are obtained by inversion transformations (permuting the predicate to the fore of the clause) plus employing one of fourteen question words in the interrogative; and plus use of a specifically imperative form of the verb in the imperative.

Transitivity is a variable with an ordered succession of values: zero grade, i.e. non-transitive; grade one, intransitive; grade two, transitive; grade three, ditransitive; and scattered instances of higher grades of transitivity in rare clauses which are possibly of marginal grammaticality. For this reason the system of Zoque clause types is considered to be open-ended. A third parameter, that of referential versus causative, divides clauses of transitivity grade three on up the scale.

In non-transitive clauses transitivity is irrelevant. The clauses are

---

Popoluca," IJAL 30.341-54; Shirley Lyon, "Tlahuitoltepec Mixe clause structure" (submitted to IJAL).

Also of relevance are: Don D. Lyon, "Tlahuitoltepec Mixe verb syntagmemes" (submitted to IJAL); William L. Wonderley, "Zoque I: Introduction and bibliography," IJAL 17.1-9; "Zoque II: Phonemes and morphemes," IJAL 17.105-23; "Zoque III: Morphological classes, affix list and verbs," IJAL 17.137-61; "Zoque IV: Auxiliaries and nouns," IJAL 17.235-51; "Zoque V: Other stem and word classes," IJAL 18.35-48; "Zoque VI: Text," IJAL 18.189-202; Benjamin Elson, Gramática del Popoluca de la Sierra, Universidad Veracruzana, Jalapa, 1960; Larry Clark, "Sayula Popoluca morpho-syntax," IJAL 28.183-98. Terrence Kaufman, "Mixe-Zoque diachronic studies" (unpublished) has a section that is a good beginning in comparative Mixe-Zoque syntax.

descriptive or equative and have non-verbal (nominal, attributive, or participial, predicates), e.g.

(1) mihci mbyanemcete *you* (are) *a priest*

Intransitive clauses have one dramatis persona: the subject. Transitive clauses have two dramatis personae (both of which need not be animate): subject and object. Ditransitive referential clauses have three dramatis personae: subject, object, indirect object (only third person). Ditransitive causative clauses also have three dramatis personae: subject, causative object, object. In higher grades of transitivity a benefactive object ('for someone') as well as an indirect object ('to someone') may occur—and both may co-occur with causative object. Thus, such a Zoque clause as the following with transitivity grade five (quadruple transitive) is probably the extreme of complexity generated by the system (and of marginal grammaticality):

(2) te pʌ'nis mi ndʌ 'akñci'ay 'ʌ ⁿune te paŋ *the man made you give my child bread for me* (S: te pʌ'nis *the man;* CO: mi *you;* BO: ndʌ *me;* P$_{t4}$: 'akñci'ay *caused-to-give-to-in-behalf-of;* IO: 'ʌ ⁿune *my child;* O: te paŋ *bread*).

Grades of transitivity from one on up (intransitive, transitive, and ditransitive) are in partial transformational relationship. Nevertheless, the transitivity scale is more basic than the transformations that partially characterize it. Thus, there are verb stems that are inherently intransitive (e.g. min *come*), others that are inherently transitive ('a'm *see*), and still others that are inherently ditransitive (verbs of delivery, such as ci' *give*). There are a few verbs that function as both transitive and intransitive. These various verb classes determine kernel clauses on all three grades of transitivity. But there are intransitive clauses whose verbs are derived from transitive.[5] Regular transformations derive transitive clauses from intransitive, and ditransitive clauses from transitive. Thus both kernel and derived clauses are found on all three lower grades of transitivity (although grades of transitivity higher than three are non-kernel). The ordered increase in number of dramatis personae is more basic to the transitivity scale than the transformations.[6]

---

[5] In the joint paper with Engel we do not mention that intransitive verbs may be derived from transitive. Wonderly, however, mentions a suffix 212 —'oy which intransitivizes transitive verbs in Copainnalá Zoque (IJAL 17.150).

[6] In Trique, e.g. there are three grades of intransitivity: meteorological clause (zero grade); intransitive (grade 1), and transitive (grade 2). Nevertheless, there are not many patterns of verb derivation from intransitive to transitive verb. One suffix dV-

The transformations presented here and in subsequent sections of the paper are given in modified tagmemic notation. Each clause-level tagmeme (functional segment of the clause) is represented by two symbols separated by a colon. The colon is normally read "given function manifested by following set." In a tagmemic formula the manifesting set is often given in terms of the construction types (syntagmemes) of a structurally lower level. Thus, clause-level functions are commonly manifested by various phrase types. The colon may, however, be used to indicate particular lexical manifestations. Thus, in example (2) the symbol-colon-symbol sequence is used as an analytic device for a particular clause (e.g. S: te pʌʔnis *the man* means "subject function manifested by the particular Zoque noun phrase which follows"). In transformation rules employing tagmemic notations the colon may be followed by a symbol (e.g. NP=noun phrase) which has a subscript (NP_1). If the same symbol with the same subscript occurs beyond the arrow, this indicates that the same lexical item found preceding the arrow occurs also in the indicated function following the arrow. If somewhere following the arrow, a symbol occurs with a new subscript this indicates something added in the course of the transformation. Thus, the symbols labelled with subscripts may be used to keep track of particular lexical exponents of various tagmemes. Use of this tagmemic notation obviates the necessity of giving the transformational rule in two stages.[7] Furthermore, use of the tagmemic notation keeps better account of the functions involved, especially in languages like the three here presented where permutations of clause-level tagmemes are relatively free.

Addition of -hay *benefactive* suffix to a verb boosts that verb and its clause one grade in the scale of transitivity by adding one further dramatis persona, the benefactive object. Thus, an intransitive clause may be transformed to a transitive:

(3) $+P_i:V_i \quad \pm S:NP_1 \Rightarrow +P_t:V\text{-hay}(_t) \quad \pm S:NP_1 \quad \pm O:NP_2$ (where P_i=intransitive predicate, S=subject, P_t=transitive predicate; O=object, V_i=intransitive verb; V-hay=transitive verb formed by

---

causative serves to transitivize some intransitives. But causative verbs often have patterns of lexical selection quite distinct from those of the corresponding intransitives. Consequently, while there is word-level derivation there is little clause-level transformation. The transitivity variable in Trique is an ordered sequence of values but with little transformational relation along the sequence.

[7] Cf. Bach's formulation of the 'passive optional' transformation in English (Bach, *An Introduction to Transformational Grammars*, 62):

Structural analysis: NP — Aux — V — NP
Structural change: $X_1 - X_2 - X_3 - X_4$
$\Rightarrow X_4 - X_2 - $ be $-$ en $- X_3 - $ by $- X_1$

adding -hay *benefactive,* and NP=noun phrase, with subscripts keeping track of identity of phrases in the transformation).

By a similar rule the transitive clause is transformed to ditransitive referential; only verbs inherently transitive participate in the transformation:

(4) $+P_t{:}V_t +S{:}NP_1 \pm O{:}NP_2 \Rightarrow +P_{t2}{:}V\text{-hay}_{(t2)} \pm S{:}NP_1 \pm O{:}NP_2$ $\pm IO{:}NP_3$ (where subscript $_t$ marks transitive predicate manifested by transitive verbs; where $_{t2}$ marks ditransitive predicate manifested by ditransitive verbs; and where IO=indirect object).[8]

Addition of another prefix ʔak- *causative* also boosts a verb and its clause one grade in the scale of transitivity. The transformations are more complex in that addition of this prefix shifts the noun phrase manifesting subject to object or causative object (agent) and adds a new dramatis persona as subject. An intransitive clause may be transformed to transitive in this manner:

(5) $+P_i{:}V_i \pm S{:}NP_1 \Rightarrow +P_t{:}\text{ʔak-}V_t \pm S{:}NP_2 \pm O{:}NP_1.$

(6)   toks te nʌ *the water boiled* ⇒pegruʔs ʔak-tʸoks te nʌ *Peter caused-to-boil the water* (pegruʔs *Peter;* ʔak-tʸoks *caused to boil;* te nʌ *water*).

Similarly, a transitive may be transformed to ditransitive causative:

(7) $+P_t{:}V_t \pm S{:}NP_1 \pm O{:}NP_2 \Rightarrow +P_{t2}{:}\text{ʔak-}V_{t2} \pm S{:}NP_3 \pm CO{:}NP_1$ $\pm O{:}NP_2.$

Thus the Zoque

(8)   ʔʌc mi ncaŋu *I hit you* ⇒heʔtis ʔʌ mi ʔak-ncaŋu *he caused-to-hit-me you* (heʔtis *he,* ʔʌc~ʔʌ *I, me;* mi *you*).

2. Sierra Popoluca is characterized by an open-ended system comprising at least thirty-two types of clauses (diagram II). In spite, however, of the

---

  [8] The transformational rule given in (4) is set up so that only inherently transitive verbs (V_t) may be derived to transitive by adding -hay benefactive. Present data available to me are insufficient to clarify the co-occurrence privileges of ʔak-*causative* and -hay *benefactive.* Both occur on the same form in verb ciʔ *give* of example (2) above; but this may be as exceptional and marginal as the fifth grade of transitivity there exemplified. Zoque data at present available to me also indicate that ʔak- can be prefixed to an intransitive (such as kaʔ *die*) to make a transitive (such as ʔahkaʔ *kill*) and this may in turn be given another ʔak- to make a ditransitive (such as ʔakʔahkaʔ *cause to kill*). These co-occurrence possibilities, when thoroughly understood, need to be built into the tagmemic-transformational rules. The function-set notation makes it comparatively easy to build such constraints into the rules. Thus the rule given in (8) could be modified to read $+P_t{:}V_t/\text{ak-}V_t.$

			Intransitive	Transitive	Ditransitive Referential	Ditransitive Causative	Tritransitive Referential	Tritransitive Causative	
Independent	Verbal	Declarative	X	X	X	X	X	X	--
		Indefinite	X	X	X	X	X	X	--
		Imperative	X	X	X	X	X	X	--
		Obligatory	X	X	X	X	X	X	--
		Reciprocal	X	X	X				
	Non-vb.	Stative		Possessive			Factive		
			X		X			X	
Dependent		General				Time			
			X				X		

DIAGRAM II: SIERRA POPOLUCA CLAUSES
(adopted from J. Lind IJAL 30.342)

greater complexity of the system it is in many ways similar to that of Zoque. As analyzed by Lind, the system first splits into dependent versus independent clauses, with but two types comprising the former: general dependent clauses, and time dependent clauses. General dependent clauses consist of two parts: a relator (such as hu·t^y *where,* iga *that,* hu$^?$uc *like,* and hučïs *when;* and an axis consisting of any clause type except imperative. Time dependent clauses similarly consist of two parts: a relator (mu *when* or suffix -pa·m/-wï·m on verb, *time subordinator;* an axis consisting of any clause type except imperative, plus the special constraint that intransitive clauses which manifest axis tagmeme to time dependent clauses do not prefix to their verbs the pronoun series otherwise characteristic of intransitive clauses, but rather take a series found in transitive verbs.[9]

Lind next divides independent clauses into non-verbal and verbal. While Zoque has but one non-verbal type which is easily handled as zero value of the transitivity variable, and which has three values of the mood variable, SP has three types of non-verbal clauses: stative, possessive and factive,

---

[9] Lind's analysis of dependent clauses may be compared with the Engel-Longacre analysis of Zoque subordinate clauses. In Zoque, since the system of clause types is of modest proportions and since most subordinate clauses involve affixal modification of their verbs, it seems feasible to set up a whole vector consisting of subordinate clause types in one-to-one correspondence with the declarative types. In SP, where the system is of considerable complexity, and where not only declarative but indefinite, obligatory, and reciprocal clauses can be made subordinate it seems simpler to adopt the alternative analysis here summarized. As co-author of Engel's paper and linguistic consultant for Lind and Shirley Lyon, I bear the opprobrium for whatever inconsistency may be present among the three analyses.

and is better handled as a separate coordinate. Thus such a noun as kï·pi *wood* may be predicate of a stative clause:

(9) kï·pi (it is) *wood.*

With suffixation of -ï?y *possessive predicate marker* and pronouns, this same noun can be the predicate of a possessive clause:

(10) kï?ïbï?y *he-has-wood.*

Possessive clauses can be transformed to possessive noun phrases by deleting the -ï?y suffix and changing the person marker series. Still a third clause type, the factive, can be built on such a noun as *wood* by suffixing -a·/-a·p *factive predicate marker:*

(11) sï?ïp mikï-ïba·p *now you-are-wood-chopping.*

Factive clauses are not transformable to any phrase type.

The remaining twenty-seven SP clauses are verbal. They constitute a sub-system in the same three coordinates as seen in Zoque: (1) mood; (2) transitivity; (3) referential versus causative. Mood is a variable representing the set: declarative, indefinite, imperative, obligatory and reciprocal. While subordinate is considered to be a mood in Zoque it is handled as a broader and more basic dimension in SP. Interrogative patterns as a mood on the clause level in Zoque, but seems to pattern better on the sentence level in SP. Both Zoque and SP have declarative and imperative moods. SP has also the indefinite, obligatory and reciprocal. The five SP moods are exemplified here by minimal clauses consisting only of predicates manifested by verbs; all examples are intransitive:

(12) anïkpa *I-am-going* (declarative);
nïknï·mpa *someone-is-going* (indefinite);
nï·gï *go!* (imperative);
nïgiñ *he-should-go* (obligatory);
nanïkta· *he took himself away.*

In the transitive, indefinite mood is often passive in thrust:

(13) kocta· *he-is-hit;*

and reciprocal involves two subjects:

(14) nakocyahta· *they-hit-each-other.*

The transitivity variable has an ordered succession of four values: grade one, intransitive; grade two, transitive; grade three, ditransitive; and grade four, tritransitive. In contrast to Zoque where grades of transitivity higher than three are difficult to document and of marginal grammaticality, SP clauses of transitivity grade four are not uncommon. In both Zoque and SP, however, transitivity grade five is probably the extreme of productivity of the system. Furthermore, the higher grades of transitivity seem to be confined to the verb *give* (ciʔ in Zoque; či in SP). The SP example, given by Lind, of grade five transitivity is:

(15) heʔm čo·mo ikčiʔaʔypa pe·to iyo·mtï-wï heʔm wïdʸa·ya iša·mñi
      the old woman caused Peter to give the old man's bananas to his
      sister. S: heʔm čo·mo *the old-woman;* P₍ₜ₄₎ ikčiʔaʔypa *she-caused-*
      him-to-give-his (*another's*)-*it-to-her* (*another*); CO: pe·to *Peter;*
      IO: iyo·mtïwï *his sister;* BO: heʔm wïdʸa·ya *the old-man;* O:
      iša·mñi *his-bananas.*

Dramatis personae in the various grades of transitivity are much as in Zoque: subject in intransitive clauses; subject and object in transitive; subject, object, and benefactive object in ditransitive referential; subject, object, and causative object in ditransitive causative; subject, object, indirect object and benefactive object in tritransitive referental; subject, object, causative object and benefactive object in tritransitive causative. Verb roots occur as inherently intransitive or inherently transitive; a few verbs belong to the intersection of both classes. Verb inflection and clause structure of intransitive and transitive clauses are sufficiently distinct that a clean partition of the two is possible. Some intransitive verbs are derived from transitive by addition of -oʔy *intransitivizer*. Presumably, certain transitive clauses can be transformed into intransitive by addition of the affix to the verb and deletion of the object. Apparently only one verb, či *give* is basically ditransitive (referential) in contrast to a set of *delivery* verbs in Zoque.

Much as in Zoque any of the affixes ak- and na- *causative* prefixes, and -aʔy *benefactive* suffix, on being added to a verb, boost that verb one grade in the scale of transitivity. Only ak- and na- are added to intransitives to derive transitives. The third suffix -aʔy *benefactive* is added to a transitive (which may have been derived from intransitive by addition of ak-/na-) to form ditransitive referential. Inherent transitives plus ak-/na- become ditransitive causative. From the ditransitive referential the tritransitive types are derived: addition of a further -aʔy *benefactive* (resulting in a repeat sequence -aʔyaʔy for all verbs except či which is inherently ditransitive referential and adds but one -aʔy) gives the tritransitive referential. Addition of ak-/na- *causative* to a ditransitive referential gives tritransitive causative. Two specific transformation rules follow with analyzed examples.

The first rule derives ditransitive causative from transitive; the second derives a tritransitive causative from a ditransitive referential.

(16) $+P_t:V_t \pm S:NP_1 \pm O:NP_2 \Rightarrow +P_{t2c}:ak\text{-}/na\text{-}V \pm S:NP_3 \pm CO: NP_1 \pm O:NP_2$.

(17) he?m makti ihokspa ika·ma *the spirit being hoes his field* $\Rightarrow$ he?m makti inihokspa ika·ma *he caused the spirit being to hoe his field*.

In the former clause he?m makti *the spirit being* is subject and ika·ma *his field* is object; in the transform he?m makti is causative object and a new subject (specified only vaguely in the verb affixes) is brought in.

(18) $+P_{t2r}:V\text{-}a?y \pm S:NP_1 \pm O:NP_2 \pm BO:NP_3 \quad +P_{t3c}:ak\text{-}/na\text{-}V\text{-}a?y \pm S:NP_4 \pm CO:NP_1 \pm O:NP_2 \pm BO:NP_3$.

(19) ikoca?y ima·nïk he?m ika·wah *his son hit his (somebody else's) horse* he?m šiwan ikkoca?y ima·nïk he?m ika·wah *John caused his son to hit his (somebody else's) horse*.

In the first clause ima·nïk *his son* is subject; he?m ika·wah *his horse* is object, and there is an implied (but unstated) third dramatis persona, the benefactive object, which is possessor of the object and as such distinct from the subject.[10] In the transform, he?m šiwan *the John* is the subject, and ima·nïk *his son* is causative object, while the other relations are undisturbed.

3. Tlahuitoltepec Mixe has a closed system of twenty-two clause types in four coordinates (and an extra systemic non-verbal type not illustrated here): (1) voice; (2) transitivity; (3) mood; and (4) orientation. Voice is a variable with three values: active (with fourteen clause types); imperative (with four clause types); passive (with four clause types). Imperative and passive clauses are transforms of the indicative. Transitivity is a coordinate with a succession of values much like in Zoque and SP. The last two coordinates are specific to Mixe. Thus Mixe 'mood' has nothing in common with mood in the other two languages of the family. I first describe these latter two parameters which are peculiar to Mixe, then transitivity, and finally voice.

Mixe has a kernel system of six clause types distinguished by the presence in the verbs of six differing sets of pronominal prefixes indicating first,

---

[10] In SP the one 'for whom' something is done and 'on whose possession' something is done are expressed by the same grammatical device. Both are here termed benefactive object (BO) —a name which obviously fits only the former usage well. But approximate labels are sufficient in any taxonomic science provided that they receive proper meaning in the context of description. The expression of "benefactive object" and "object possessed by a person other than subject" by the same grammatical category is not uncommon in Mesoamerican languages.

second, and third person: (1) n-, m-, y/t-; (2) n-, š-, t-; (3) š-, m-, #;
(4) š-, m-, y-; (5) #, m-, #, and (6) n-, m-, y-. The six pronoun series
are in one-to-one correspondence with the six clause types which are
assigned the same numbers. The verbs of clause types (1), (3), and (5)
contrast with the verbs of clause types (2), (4) and (6) as to choice of
allomorphs of the tense-aspect-mood morphemes and the intricate morphophonemic changes which accompany these various allomorphs. Furthermore, clauses (1), (3) and (5) occur either without an introductory
tagmeme or with an introducer (I') comprised of a limited list of interrogatives, relatives, conjunctions, and adverbs (midiʔ *which,* ti *what,* pʌn *who,*
whom, pʌnʌ *if,* paty *for this reason,* kumʌ *since,* neʔekʌ *better,* sumʌ
always. By contrast clause types (2), (4), and (6) occur with an introducer tagmeme (I") which is obligatory except under very special and
specific conditions. The set of items comprising I" shows very little intersection with that comprising I': suco *how;* tiko *why,* pʌn *who, whom,* mɔ
where, sɔ *how,* wʌntem *when* (future interrogative), wʌnti *when* (past) paty
for this reason, haʔakʌsp *because,* neʔekʌ *better,* ku *when,* hʌc *and,* shac
and then; as well as any phrase or particle expressing negation, location,
time, or manner.[11] Only the particles pʌn *who, whom,* paty *for this reason,*
and neʔekʌ *better* characterize both lists. The wealth and variety of introducer items in clauses (2), (4), and (6) plus the all but obligatory status
of the introducers indicates that these clauses are in some way dependent
on the introducers. They are termed therefore *conjunct* clauses. Clauses
(1), (3), and (5)—not so dependent—are called *non-conjunct.* The distinction is similar to that of dependent and independent clauses in some
languages but more subtle and arbitrary in that particles of the sort usually
found in dependent clauses are found in both lists of introducers. Furthermore, interrogatives are found in both lists. Therefore, neither dependent
versus independent nor declarative versus interrogative are considered to
be relevant parameters to the system of Mixe clauses. The contrast non-
conjunct versus conjunct gives the two values of the variable here called
mood.

The occurrence of the six contrasting pronoun series is, however, only
partly explained by reference to mood. A second variable with two values
is *orientation.* I quote here Shirley Lyons: "A clause may be oriented
towards its actor, its goal or its subject. The first two orientations occur

---

[11] Searle Hoogshagen, in an unpublished study of Coatlán Mixe, analyzed negation,
location, time, and manner in introducer function in conjunct clauses as permutations
of the same clause-level tagmemes. Lyon's analysis sets up an intersection of manifesting classes between I" and certain other clause-level tagmemes.

with transitive. With a transitive verb and a given set of dramatis personae the selection of actor orientation versus goal orientation is predictable, according to a hierarchy of importance. In this hierarchy six persons and categories rank as follows (from greater to lesser importance): first person, second person, third person definite, third person indefinite, animal, thing. The dramatis persona of highest rank in a situation may be represented by a noun phrase and cross-referenced to the prefixes of the verb manifesting predicate, or the latter device may be used without the former. When the actor or the initiator of the action outranks the goal or recipient of the action, the clause will be actor oriented. If the goal outranks the actor the clause will be goal oriented." [12] This difference is illustrated by the following examples: in each pair of examples the first clause is clause (2)—actor oriented conjunct; and the second is clause (4)—goal oriented conjunct. All examples are conjunct in that tʌ *past time* occurs clause initial:

(20) tʌ ʔʌhc ha hɔɔʔy nwopy *I hit the person* (ʔʌhc *I,* ha hɔɔʔy *the person,* nwopy *I-him-hit*) versus tʌ ʔʌhc ha hɔɔʔy šwopy *the person hit me* (šwopy *he-me-hit*).

(21) tʌ mehc ha hɔɔʔy šwopy *you hit the person* (mehc *you,* šwopy *you-him-hit*) versus tʌ mehc ha hɔɔʔy mwopyʌ *the person hit you* (mwopyʌ *he-you-hit*).

(22) tʌ paat ha hɔɔʔy twopy *Peter hit the person* (paat *Peter,* twopy *definite-indefinite-hit*) versus tʌ paat ha hɔɔʔy wyopyʌ *the person hit Peter* (wyopyʌ with metathesis of y- and stem-initial w, *indefinite-definite-hit*).

(23) tʌ paat ha hʌyuhk twopy *Peter hit the animal* versus tʌ paat ha hʌyuhk wyopyʌ *the animal hit Peter.*

The two coordinates mood and orientation (plus transitivity which distinguishes clauses 5 and 6 versus clauses 1-4) now enable us to distinguish and label the six kernel clauses which are in one-to-one correspondence with the six pronoun series: (1) non-conjunct actor oriented; (2) conjunct actor oriented; (3) non-conjunct goal oriented; (4) conjunct goal oriented; (5) non-conjunct subject oriented; and (6) conjunct subject oriented. In clause (5) and clause (6) which are intransitive, a subject tagmeme is considered to occur in contrast to the actor tagmeme of the transitive clauses (1)-(4).

In the kernel clause system, transformation is of varying relevance to the three coordinates, *mood, orientation* and *transitivity.* While actor oriented

---

[12] From the unpublished paper referred to in fn. 3.

and goal oriented clauses are very similar they are not transformations of each other. There is here nothing analogous to the choice possible in English between 'I was hit by Bill' and 'Bill was hit by me.' 'I' outranks 'Bill,' and such a Mixe clause can be only actor oriented. (Mixe passives are a separate consideration and are summarized briefly below.) The kernel system prohibits rather than facilitates transformations between these obviously related structures. Transformation is of some relevance to mood. Thus by permuting a time expression to the fore of a clause the clause may be transformed from non-conjunct to conjunct. Choice of certain introducers determines, however, the choice of mood. Transitive versus intransitive within the kernel clause system of Mixe involves inherent verb classes as well as transformation from one grade of transitivity to the other (chiefly intransitive to transitive).

The remaining features of Mixe clause structure can be outlined only in the most summary fashion: (1) Clause types (1-4) are regularly transformed to clause types (7-10) *instrumental* clauses (with the same distinction of mood and orientation) by adding an instrumental prefix ta- to the verb and by adding an optional instrumental tagmeme in the clause. The verb moˀ *give* is inherently instrumental without the addition of a prefix (cf. ciˀ in Zoque či in SP *give*—which is inherently ditransitive referential). In the Mixe equivalents of the clauses, 'I cut the person with a machete,' and 'I give the person a gift,' 'I' is actor in both clauses; the 'person' is object, while both 'with a machete' and 'a gift' are instrumental. Objects tend to be animate, and instrumentals inanimate in these instrumental clause types.[13] These Mixe clauses (7-10) are somewhat parallel to Zoque and SP ditransitive referentials.

(2) Clause types (7-10) now may be transformed to clauses (11-14) *agentive instrumental* (with the same distinctions of mood and orientation) by further prefixing tuk *agentive* before the ta- *instrumental* found in clauses (7-10) and by adding an optional agentive tagmeme in the clause.

Thus a clause 7, instrumental actor oriented non-conjunct, may be transformed to a clause 11, agentive instrumental actor oriented non-conjunct as here exemplified:

(24) ha paat macyet y-ta-pootpy ha hɔɔˀy *Peter cuts the person with a machete* (ha paat *the Peter,* macyet *machete,* y-ta-pootpy *definite-indefinite-instrumental-cuts,* ha hɔɔˀy *the person* ⇒ ˀʌhc ha paat

---

[13] Hoogshagen has cited for me an example of instrumental clause where 'the husband hit the wife with the baby' (i.e. picked up the baby and used it to strike the wife). Both situationally and linguistically such use of an animate as an instrument is unusual.

macyet n-tuk-ta-pootpy ha hɔɔʔy *I cause Peter to cut the person with a machete.*

Here, as in Zoque and SP causative transformations, the original subject becomes the 'causative object' or 'agent' and a new dramatis persona is introduced as subject. Mixe clauses 11-14 are somewhat parallel to the SP tritransitive causative clause type.

The above exemplify an ordered succession along the transitivity co-ordinate in Mixe from intransitive (clauses 5-6) to transitive (clauses 1-4) to instrumental (clauses 7-10) to agentive instrumental (clauses 11-14). The number of (mentioned or implied) non-predicate nuclear tagmemes (dramatis personae plus instrumental) increases from one to four as in SP.

(3) The sub-system so far sketched comprises the indicative. The voice variable has three values: indicative, imperative and passive. Each of the grades of transitivity—a sub-system of two clauses (5-6) in the intransitive; and sub-systems of four clauses in the transitive (1-4), instrumental (7-10) and agentive instrumental (11-14)—is transformed to one corresponding imperative clause type. This is expressed by Shirley Lyons as follows:[14]

"Multiplication of kernel clauses 1-4 by still another constant, Imp (deletion of most clause level tagmemes and stripping the predicate of most of its affixes), gives but one further clause type, the transitive imperative clause (cl. 15). This results from the fact that multiplication by Imp deletes the identifying features of clauses 1-4 (contrasting orientation and contrasting moods). Similarly multiplication of clauses 5-6 . . . by Imp gives an intransitive imperative clause type (cl. 16). Derived clause types cl. 7-10, when multiplied by Imp give the instrumental-imperative clause (cl. 17) while derived clause types (cl. 11-14) times Imp gives the agentive instrumental imperative clause (cl. 18)."

In brief, in each case a sub-system of kernel or derived kernel clauses gives, by deletion transformation, but one resulting type, i.e. the indicative and imperative clauses are in many-to-one relation. By deletion of the subject or actor an imperative clause has at least one less dramatis personae than the corresponding sub-system of the same grade of transitivity.

Four passive clauses (cl. 19-22) constitute the passive system. The non-conjunct transitive clauses, actor oriented (cl. 1) and goal oriented (cl. 3) both become transitive non-conjunct passive (cl. 19) by: (a) prefixing yik-*passivizer* to the transitive predicate; (b) deleting the subject of the transitive clauses and replacing pronoun set 1 with set 5; and (c) making

---

[14] From the unpublished paper referred to in fn. 3.

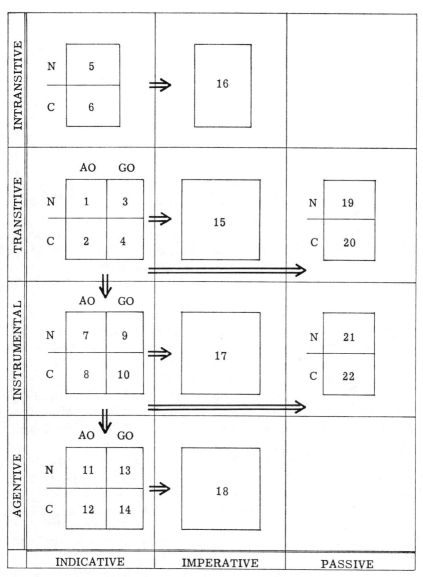

DIAGRAM III: MIXE CLAUSE TYPES
(N = nonconjunct; C = conjunct; AO = actor oriented; GO = goal oriented)

the object of the kernel clause the subject of the transform. Similarly, the two conjunct transitive clauses (cl. 2 and cl. 4) transform to transitive conjunct passive (cl. 20) with pronoun set 2 replaced with set 6. Again the kernels and transforms are in many-to-one relation in that the passive transformation obliterates the orientation distinction found in the indicative. In the following (non-conjunct) example cl. 1 ⇒ cl. 19:

(25) ʌhc ha paat nwohp *I hit Peter* ⇒ paat yik-wohp *Peter was hit.*

Similarly, cl. 7 and cl. 9 (instrumental non-conjunct clauses) transform to instrumental non-conjunct passive (cl. 21) with pronoun set 5; while cl. 8 and cl. 10 (instrumental conjunct) transform to instrumental conjunct passive (cl. 22) with set 6.

In diagram III the total system of Mixe verbal clause types is presented as a field structure in four coordinates. The voice coordinate with three values is represented as a succession of three columns, the indicative, imperative, and passive systems. The transitivity coordinate is represented as a sequence of four rows with the lowest grade of transitivity at the bottom. Mood and orientation coordinates are both relevant within the lower three rectangles of the first column. Mood is relevant to the top rectangle of the first column, and to the third column. Transformational relationships are indicated by arrows. Numbers indicate clause types. Lack of internal partition in the rectangles 16-18 indicates the deletion transformations whereby whole sub-systems of clauses are transformed to single types in the imperative. Lack of vertical partition in the rectangles filled by 19-20 and 21-22 indicates deletion of the contrastive orientation parameter of the indicative in the transformation to the passive.

4. Tagmemics can gain many valuable insights from transformational grammar. Transformational grammar could learn some things from tagmemics as well: more explicit functional orientation; use of function-set notation to clarify transformational rules; and sufficient attention to field structures to fit transformations into adequate context. From the prejudiced viewpoint of the writer of this paper, tagmemics is the most adequate expression of taxonomic linguistics. Transformation grammar is, on the other hand, the most sophisticated attempt made to date to represent linguistic structure exhaustively in formal rules. It would be mutually profitable to both schools to engage in thoughtful dialogue rather than in ideological warfare.

METHOD ANALYSIS
A Survey of its Development, Principles and Techniques

WILLIAM FRANCIS MACKEY

Laval University

0. INTRODUCTION

The purpose of this survey is simply to give a general idea of what has been done in the field of method analysis—the elaboration of principles, development of techniques, adaptation to mechanolinguistic analysis, and the making of method profiles.

What is the place of method analysis in the field of language didactics? Of what practical use is it? When and where was it developed? What are its basic principles?

0.1 *Method Analysis in Language Didactics*

One of the most important and at once most neglected branches of language didactics is the analysis of language teaching. One of the reasons why language didactics has for centuries remained a matter of opinion rather than of fact is that it has not yet developed its own principles and techniques of analysis. For without analysis, no scientific study of language teaching is possible.

The analysis of language teaching rests on two fundamental distinctions —(i) between language teaching and language learning, on the one hand and (ii) between these and the methods used in language teaching and learning, on the other. For the language learning process is obviously quite distinct from the language teaching process; in each case, what has to be analyzed is not at all the same thing. Language learning is in no way dependent on language teaching, and language teaching does not necessarily result in language learning.

Secondly, both the teaching and learning of a language are quite distinct from the methods used. Two teachers, using the same method, may produce quite different results. There are therefore three separate fields of analysis—learning, teaching and method. It is only after having analyzed these processes separately that any cause-effect relationship may be established between their constituent elements.

Of these three fields of analysis, it is the latter, method analysis, with which we are here concerned.

0.2 *The Uses of Method Analysis*

Method analysis has not only an obvious theoretical relevance to the study of language didactics, it has also a great deal of practical usefulness in the choice and application of language teaching materials.

Ever since the invention of printing, the materials put into the hands of language learners have been assuming more and more importance. In recent years, with the increase in the extent and ease with which recordings and pictures are disseminated, the language learning material is rapidly becoming the chief vehicle of language instruction.

Every year, departments of education, curriculum directors, and the teachers themselves are faced with the problem of choosing the language materials best suited to their needs. They are continually being asked to abandon old methods and to adopt new materials, without always being sure of what is old and what is new, and of what the changes would involve. In some parts of the world, the possible choices of elementary language texts approaches the hundred mark—ranging from locally produced regional efforts, which are not necessarily bad, to the lavishly published national courses, which are not necessarily better.

The choice of the language materials is sometimes made by a committee of experienced teachers who have tried out a number of methods in class. Since there are no standard criteria, the various results are not comparable; since not all possibilities are studied, the choice is limited; and since so much weight is given to teacher opinion, the conclusions are subjective. Even if such efforts were valid as experiments, interpretation of the results would have to be based on an analysis of the methods themselves. It is for these reasons that techniques of method analysis had to be developed.

0.3 *The Development of Method Analysis*

This development of method analysis goes back to the 1940's, when a series of proposals were made in London for a descriptive rather than prescriptive approach to language teaching. These later came out as a group of articles in the 1950s. During the 1950s, the content of these articles, which was simply programmatic, was largely expanded, made more rigorous, and presented in the form of a book which was completed in 1960, sent to press in 1961, and due to appear in 1965. In recent years there have been further expansions and refinements, especially in the framework of differential description, language restrictability, typology of repetition, and in the field of mechanolinguistic method analysis, the general procedures of which had already been established (*Language Teaching Analysis*, pp. 453-463).

At the very outset it was evident that much of the confusion in the battle of methods was due to the way the term itself was being used. Administrators thought they could set up experiments to find out whether one method was better than another—whether, for example, the Direct Method was better than the Informant Method, the Basic English Method, the Mimicry-Memorization Method, or the Army Method. They did not seem to realize that, in each case, the term "method" meant something different, sometimes referring to what was taught and sometimes to how it was taught. Since the *what* and the *how* were not mutually exclusive, and features of one method easily combined with features of another, such proposals to discover the best methods by means of experimentation were virtually meaningless.

It was therefore necessary to limit the meaning of the term "method" to the particular set of materials to which the language learner is exposed—texts (including workbooks and readers), recordings (including tapes and disks), and pictures (including films and film-strips). The analysis of such sets of materials in language courses was termed "method analysis." It is not to be confused with "method specification," which tells how effective teaching materials are prepared.

0.4 *The Principles of Method Analysis*

Method analysis is the objective study of the basic constituents common to all methods and the measurement of all their factors. What are these basic constituents? What are the elements which all methods, by their nature, must contain—elements by which one method may be distinguished from another?

Methods differ in what they teach, the order in which they teach it, the way they convey their material and the way they convert it into a skill. In other words, all methods, whether good, bad or indifferent, must have a certain selection, gradation, presentation and repetition. Selection, because it is impossible to teach the whole of a language; we are forced to a limited choice. Gradation, because what has been chosen cannot all be conveyed at once; something must come before or after something else. Presentation, because what has been selected must be transmitted by some means to somebody. Repetition, because in order to be acquired, a skill must be used. (*The Meaning of Method,* p. 3)

It is therefore through these four basic constituents—selection, grada-tion, presentation and repetition—that language teaching methods may be analyzed and measured.

1. SELECTION

The analysis of selection is the answer to the question, What and how much is taught?

Methods teaching the same language do not all teach the same things. This is even true of the beginning courses supposedly limited to the basic elements of the language. What is taught may depend on the purpose, level and duration of the course and, in each case, on the dialect, register, style and medium of the language.

To determine what and how much is taught requires a linguistic analysis of the material—a description of the phonological, grammatical and lexical units and structures included. Method analysis is thus dependent on linguistic analysis.

The first and most obvious question to ask in analyzing a method is, How much does it cover? How much of the phonology, grammar and vocabulary of the language does the method teach? In calculating the amount of phonology included, inventory is made of all the units and structures of articulation, catenation, rhythm and intonation taught through tapes, disks and sound-film.

The results of the phonological, grammatical and lexical computation may be expressed as percentages of the total number in the language as far as this is known. When we know how much of everything has been included, we next have to find out how useful it is.

The usefulness of an item has nothing to do with its facility. No matter how many easy items a method may teach a learner, he is wasting his time as far as learning the language is concerned if these are of no use to him. There are four measures of usefulness, viz. range, frequency, availability and coverage. The applicability of each depends on the degree of restrict-ability of each level of language and on the completeness and reliability of the statistics. The restrictability of an item may be anywhere from zero, as in the case of many phonemes, to more than 99% in the case of certain vocabulary items.

Fortunately, most of the language statistics and other indices are in the area in which the language is most restrictable, that is, in vocabulary. We already have indices of range and frequency for the vocabulary of

French, English, Spanish, German, Russian, Dutch, and other languages. Some are based on speech samples, some on written texts, some on both.

As for availability, there are figures at present only for French. As for coverage, there is as yet no index for any language, but some are being elaborated.

To calculate the usefulness of a selection we add and average the index figures for each class of items—vocabulary, inflections, structure words, etc.—to obtain the mean range, frequency, availability and coverage of the items included. The measures of usefulness of what is taught can be adjusted to the purpose and level of the course.

2. GRADATION

In all methods, regardless of their quality, the items of the language appear in a certain order; each item also occurs in company with other items. This sequence and grouping of items in a method constitutes its gradation. An item may be a unit of one of the systems of the language, or it may be one of its structures. We may present the inter-relationship thus:

	Sequence	Grouping
Systems	Which units come before which?	What goes with what?
Structures	Which structures come before which?	What goes into what?

2.1 *Sequence*

Which units and structures come before which, and how many? Do the easier, more frequent and more useful items come before the difficult, less frequent and less useful?

2.1.1 Sequence in the System

The sequences in which units of a language appear help determine the facility and speed with which the language is learned. Certain things come naturally before others because the latter are dependent on them. For example, surface nouns like *table, shelf* and *floor* might usefully be presented before the preposition *on,* since they help teach its meaning. Under this heading we analyze such things as the order in which the determinatives, regular and irregular inflections, and different types of words are first introduced.

2.1.2 Sequence of Structures

Sequences of structures differ in direction, expansion, variation and length.

The direction of a sequence of structures depends on where it leads. To lead up to a given structure by using a number of given elements it is possible to pass by a number of different routes. To go, for example, from a structure like *It's here* to the structure of the sentence *The keys are on the table* a sequence may pass through the structures represented in such sentences as *This is a key, The key is here,* etc. Or the sequence may proceed in the opposite direction.

A sequence progresses through expansion and variation. Methods differ in the extent to which they expand the number of units in a sequence of structures. Here is one example of an expansion: *He's leaving. He's leaving home. He's leaving home at noon. He's leaving home at noon today.*

The gradualness of the expansion depends on the extent to which the elements in each structure are varied before the next structure is introduced. For example, between the second and the third structure of the above sequence one might have: *He* (She, It, John) *is* (was, will be) *leaving* (coming, going, driving) *home* (here, there).

The length of a sequence depends on the number of expansions and variations in a given direction. If the direction of two sequences is the same, the longer one is probably the better graded.

A measure of the gradualness of a sequence is its rate of intake, which is an indication of how much comes in at a time. The general formula for intake is

$$I = \frac{\text{Tokens (to)}}{\text{Types \ (ty)}}$$

It applies to units and structures at all levels of language. At the lexical level, for example, it represents the number of running words divided by the number of different words. It also applies within each level. Verb intake, for example, is the total number of verbs in the text divided by the number of different verbs in the vocabulary:

$$VI = \frac{V \text{ to}}{V \text{ ty}}$$

It can be calculated for any point in the sequence. By calculating it for a number of points we get a curve of the rate of intake of any element or combination of elements.

2.2 *Grouping*

Methods group their items in different ways; not all groupings are equally effective. Grouping in the system is analyzed by techniques different from those used to analyze grouping in the structure.

2.2.1 Grouping in the System

An item in a language is learned by the company it keeps. It is learned better when grouped with some items rather than with others. At all levels of language we ask the question, What goes with what, and why? The question applies to all units in the system and to all relationships between them.

It applies to such semantic relationships as exist between prepositions and certain surface nouns, for example, between *on* and *table, shelf, floor, wall, ceiling*.

2.2.2 Groupings of Structures

To what extent are the units in a method grouped so as to fit into the relevant structures? For example, when the phrased structure *preposition+determinative+noun* (e.g., *on the table*) is first introduced, how much of the preceding vocabulary can it absorb?

The measure of a grouping is its productivity. Productivity answers the question, How much can you say with what you have? The productivity (P) of a gradation (G) is the sum of the productivities of all its sentence structures (s):

$$PG = \Sigma Ps_1 \ldots Ps_n$$

The productivity of a sentence structure (Ps) is the product of the productivity of each clause structure (c) that fits into one of its position:

$$Ps = Pc_1 \times Pc_2 \times \ldots Pc_n$$

The productivity of a clause structure (Pc) is the product of the productivity of each phrase structure (p) that fits into one of its positions:

$$Pc = Pp_1 \times Pp_2 \times \ldots Pp_n$$

The productivity of a phrase structure (Pp) is the product of the number of words (Nw) that fit into each of its positions:

$$Pp = Nw_1 \times Nw_2 \times \ldots Nw_n$$

In comparing methods, however, total productivity is not alone significant since the difference may be due to the number of structures used. We get a better idea of the relative efficiency of the gradation by calculating the average productivity per structure, the median, and the degree of deviation, computed according to the usual statistical formula.

If we wish to know how well a method exploits its possibilities, we calculate its productivity differential (PD) by subtracting the actual, or textual productivity (TP) from the general, or combinatorial productivity (CP):

$$PD = CP - TP$$

But the productivity of each point in the gradation is different. It is useful to know at what rate the possibilities of a method increase. By calculating the productivity at regular intervals of, say, 500 tokens, we get a productivity curve representing the rate of increase in productivity.

If we wish to know the extent to which this increase is exploited, we superimpose at each point the actual number of sentences used, and obtain a second curve. The gap between both curves is a measure of how well the method exploits its possibilities as the course progresses.

3. PRESENTATION

Presentation answers the question, How does the method get the language across? A method may present all or part of the language, leaving the teacher the job of doing very little of the presentation, or most of it.

It is important here not to forget that it is not the presentation done by the teacher that is being analyzed, but rather that done by the method through its texts, films, and recordings. What is there to present? Either the method or the teacher must present both the form of the language and its corresponding semantic content.

3.1 Form

A method may present either the spoken or written forms of the language—or both of them—for purposes of expression or of comprehension only. In other words, a method may present any or all of the four basic skills—listening, speaking, reading, and writing.

Methods differ in the way they transmit the forms of the language and in the way they stage its basic skills.

3.1.1 Transmission

A method may transmit the spoken forms of the language through recordings on disk, tape or film. Some of these recordings present material which is not available in written form; others are simply recordings of all or part of the written text which appears in either orthography or in phonetic notation. Some methods have elaborate sections—entire volumes—devoted to pronunciation; others ignore it completely.

The transmission of the written form has to do with the script or alphabet of the language and the spelling of its words. Methods intended for learners unable to read the script used may present it in a separate section, ranging from a single page to a whole book. Some methods make no systematic effort to present the orthography of the language they teach; others devote special sections to it either in their main text or at intervals in their workbooks.

3.1.2 Staging

Methods also differ in the number, order and spacing of the stages in which the basic skills are presented.

Some methods limit themselves to one or two of the basic skills; others may present all of them—listening, speaking, reading and writing.

They may divide the task into any number of stages, according to the components of each skill; for example, listening may be presented in such stages as: rhythm identification, phoneme identification, identification of phonetic sequences, auditory comprehension, tempo.

These stages may follow one another in a block or they may be interspersed throughout the phases of other skills, so that the learner may, for example, start on the first stage of one skill before having completed all the stages of the other skills, starting to read, for instance, before having covered all the stages of listening comprehension. The first thing to analyze, however, is the order in which the basic skills are first introduced. Is it listening (L), speaking (S), reading (R) and writing (W), or is it LRSW, or LRWS, or RLSW, or which of the other possible orders of staging?

The order in which skills are staged, however, is not the only variable; there is also their spacing. The question here is, How much of one stage before the next begins?

Staging may be measured by listing the number of stages in the order of their appearance and computing the number of tokens in each stage.

3.2 Content

As for the presentation of the content, there are four possible ways of getting meaning across. Only one of these, ostensive procedure, is not available to the method since it involves the use of actual objects, actions and situations. Any or all of the others—pictorial, differential and contextual procedures may be used by a method to convey the meaning of the forms taught. In analyzing a method it is important to find out which of these semantic procedures are used, and in what proportion.

3.2.1 Pictorial Procedures

Some methods use pictures to get most of their meaning across; others make no use of pictures whatsoever. It is difficult and most time-consuming to determine exactly how much of the meaning in a method is taught through pictures. But a good idea of the relative importance of pictures in the teaching of meaning may be had by counting the number of semantic pictures and expressing the total as a percentage of the total number of word tokens.

3.2.2 Differential Procedures

Some methods convey the meaning of the forms presented by exploiting the differences between the language being learned and the native language of the learner. This may be done through translation and through explanation.

We may determine how much of these is used and the proportion of each by figuring the total tokens in the first or native language and expressing the results as a percentage of the total tokens in the text— exclusive of drills and exercises. Of the total tokens in the native language we determine what proportion is devoted to translation and what proportion to explanation.

3.2.3 Contextual Procedures

Teaching meaning through verbal contexts involves the use of known words to teach the unknown. Instead of checking every new semantic item to find out whether or not it is made clear by the surrounding words, we can establish a reliable notion of the relative importance of verbal context in a method by the use of two statistical measures: (i) How many units and structures first appear in environments in which all other items have already been used. In other words, how many unknowns are presented exclusively through the knowns. (ii) How many different items precede and follow each item taught. In other words, in how many environments does each semantic item appear. Both measures are necessary; applying only the first would, of course, be invalid.

4. REPETITION

The final distinguishing characteristic of methods is the way they convert into linguistic habits the material which they present. This is done through repetition.

Methods differ in the amount, ratio, type and variety of repetition which they use.

4.1 *Amount*

In measuring the amount of repetition in a method the actual number of repetitions must be distinguished from their distribution.

The number of repetitions may be calculated from the intake figures, dividing tokens by types to give the average number of repetitions per class—nouns, verbs, prepositions, etc.

The distribution is calculated by dividing the text into blocks of running tokens, the size of the blocks to depend on the degree of refinement required. For our purposes, blocks of 500 seemed to be the optimum. After determining in which block an item occurs for the first time, we find out the percentage of all subsequent blocks in which the item recurs, and its distribution.

4.2 *Ratio*

This has to be calculated by skill and by medium. What proportion of the total repetition is devoted to listening, to speaking, to reading and to writing? This is simply a matter of adding the number of tokens occurring in sections of the method devoted to each skill and of figuring the proportion.

What proportion of each medium of transmission does the method use? How much of the material appears in the form of recordings, pictures and printed texts? This is also a matter of adding up tokens and of figuring out proportions.

4.3 *Type*

There are four types of repetition—rote, incremental, variational and operational. What percentage of the repetition in the texts belongs to each type? This is a matter of adding tokens for each type and expressing the results as percentages of the whole.

4.4 *Variety*

How many sorts of drills and exercises does the method use? What percentage of the repetition is devoted to each? After counting the number of different sorts of drills and exercises used, we total the tokens for each and express them as percentages of the whole.

Figures for all factors are reduced to percentages, and plotted on a circular graph, producing a profile of the method based on all its measurable variables.

5. MECHANOLINGUISTIC METHOD ANALYSIS

After trying out the above analytic techniques on scores of methods, it became evident that a complete analysis could be done much better through the use of computers.

We therefore set about elaborating a procedure for converting these techniques into a system of computer programmes. This made it necessary to divide the operation into three stages—pre-editing, machine analysis, and post-editing. We were then able to program another machine to do part of the pre-editing, and found out that most of the post-editing could be done by a special graph-drawing attachment to the computer system. This makes it possible for us to feed an entire method into one end of our computer system and extract its profile from the other end. The profiles would look something like those in the following diagrams.

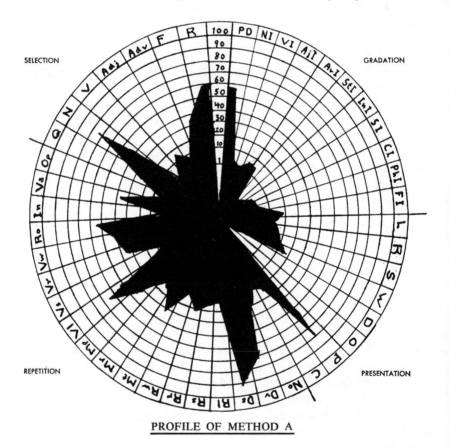

PROFILE OF METHOD A

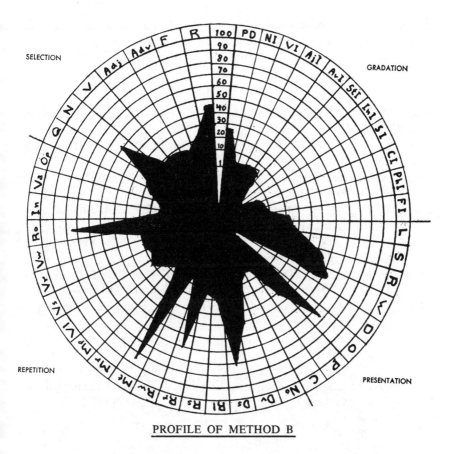

PROFILE OF METHOD B

The profile may be read in the light of the specific requirements of a given group of teachers and learners.

6. WHAT REMAINS TO BE DONE

We still need to extend and refine some of our measures and to find out the extent to which the teaching and learning of a language is modified by changes in each of the factors. It will be necessary to correlate each of these variables with those determined by similar analyses of language learning and language teaching, whenever these become available.

Once this is done we should be able to measure and to predict what sort of results a certain method may have on a given group of learners working for a given period of time under a certain type of teacher. When we can do this it will be possible to put language didactics on a scientific basis. It is hoped that our efforts to establish principles and techniques of method analysis may in some measure contribute to this end.

REFERENCES

1949   W. F. Mackey, "Rola gradacji w nauczaniu językow obcych," *Wiadomości Nauczycielskie* 5:4-10.
1950   W. F. Mackey, "The meaning of method," *English Language Teaching* 5:3-7.
1953   W. F. Mackey, "What to look for in a method: Selection," *English Language Teaching* 7:77-85.
1954   W. F. Mackey, "What to look for in a method: Grading," *English Language Teaching* 8:45-58.
1955   W. F. Mackey, "What to look for in a method: Presentation," *English Language Teaching* 9:41-56.
1957   W. F. Mackey, "The theory of structural gradations," *Proceedings of the Eighth International Congress of Linguists,* Oslo. 847-849.
1958   W. F. Mackey, "Un calcul de la productivité," *Les annales de l'Acfas* 24:111.
1961   W. F. Mackey, *Language Teaching Analysis.* London: Longmans (in press).
1962   W. F. Mackey, "Parameters of restrictability," Paper read at the annual meeting of the Canadian Linguistic Association (unpublished).
1965   W. F. Mackey, Indices of coverage (in preparation).

THE FOUNDATIONS OF A FUNCTIONAL SYNTAX

ANDRÉ MARTINET

University of Paris

If every one concerned agreed as to the meanings and implications of the terms "function" and "syntax", there would be no need to explain what is meant by a functional syntax and to discuss what the foundations of such might be. Linguists have, by now, become aware of the necessity of re-defining the technical terms they use every time they face a new audience. We all remember widely divergent uses of the word "function" within the domain of our science, and no general agreement has so far been reached regarding the respective domains of syntax and morphology.

My own conception of function in language is closely akin to the one that underlies everyday usage, that of "role played by some person or object", and if, from the function of linguistic items, we pass on to the func-tion of language itself, I should describe that function, in naive terms, as what we do with language, what we use it for. It would seem that the main, if not the sole, aim of language is communication of one's experience to others. Thereby I do not necessarily and exclusively mean an attempt to make one's interlocutor participate in that experience. If one experiences a craving, the most economical way of making others aware of it will probably be in the form of a request or a demand. But when what is at stake is securing the satisfaction of one's needs, a bare nudging and pointing may suffice. Farthest from this inarticulate form of communication is the typi-cally linguistic achievement that consists in communicating a large share of experience as felt.

It is not the task of the linguist to determine and describe the processes through which man experiences the world around him and within him. But whose duty but the linguist's is it to observe and describe the behavior of bilingual persons when they try to communicate the same experience in different languages to two successive audiences? This type of observation indicates that, depending on what language is used, the same experience is broken down differently into items corresponding to the successive units of each utterance. This implies that, prior to an effort to communicate it linguistically, the experience is a largely amorphous whole which the subject might want to communicate in its entirety and amorphousness. But this is probably impossible: grunts, moans, or gestures will convey its amorphousness, but hardly its entirety and specificity. A recourse to language will never enable man to communicate the whole of his experience, but he will get closer to it then with the help of grunts, moans, and gestures. In the process of transmission, the somewhat nebulous experience will be transmuted into a succession of neatly identifiable speech segments, each one corresponding to one particular aspect of the total experience. The number of such favored aspects will vary according to whether the speaker is being casual, or is intent upon communicating his experience in its specificity. When passing from one language to another, the number may vary for the same degree of specificity.

Hearers belonging to the same speech community as the speaker will record that succession of speech segments as an experience. Their behavior, linguistic or non-linguistic, may show that this experience is close enough to the original one for the participants to be satisfied that the transmission has been successful.

Any linguistic communication implies the use of such a succession of speech segments each corresponding to one aspect of the total experience, and the basic linguistic problem is to determine how the hearer is in a position to piece them together. Here we have a linear succession out of which he will have to reconstruct an experience in terms of a three-dimensional world. Those linguists who concentrate on utterances as such and are loath to consider what they stand for, have devised the theory of immediate constituents which is a binary approach to the problem and, like all binary approaches, establishes as a descriptive model what is nothing but the necessity, for the investigator, to compare two and only two things at a time. What immediate constituent analysis and the so-called trees derived from it seem to overlook is the fact that, within the linear succession of speech are to be found all the hints that will enable the recipient to reorganize the communication into a coherent non-linear whole, and that this whole is neither conceivable nor presentable as a plain succession. When we hear a statement like *Peter gave Jane a kiss under the mistletoe,* we grasp it as a whole, and the hierarchy we, as linguists, might be tempted to establish among the various segments or phrases involved (*Peter* apart as subject, *Jane* and *kiss* as central, *under the mistletoe* as circumstantial and peripheral) would be based upon the nature of the very tricks employed to transcend the linearity of speech.

These devices are of three types, each of which will now be considered separately.

Every one of the segments corresponding to one aspect of the experience to be communicated may suggest not only that aspect, but also the relation of that aspect to the rest. In many African languages, the word referring to a forest may be used by itself not only to indicate that a forest is part of the experience, but also to point out that a forest is where the event experienced by the speaker is (or was or will be) located. In simpler terms, "forest", in such languages, may mean (and usually does) all by itself "in the forest". Linguistically, this segment bears upon the clause as a whole or upon whatever element happens to be its head (the so-called predicate). Its relative position in the succession may be largely regulated by tradition. But position does not always suffice. Besides, should any speaker deviate in that respect, the contribution of the segment to the whole would be the same, very much as the function of *last night* is the same whether it stands initially or finally in the clause.

One could imagine a language where all relations would be marked in that way. But it would be so uneconomical that there is no likelihood that such a language exists, has existed or will ever exist. If a given unit always meant "in the forest" we would have a different unit for "forest as the object of some action", another one for "through the forest", another one still for "over the forest," and so forth. In actual languages, only relatively few units are thus used for expressing both what they stand for, and their relation to the rest of the utterance. Besides, these are also found in contexts where their relation to the rest is expressed by some other means, so that the unit itself implies nothing but what it stands for, and no longer any preferential relationship: *forest,* in a language where it means **all by itself** "in (the) forest", may thus be used with the bare meaning "forest", its relationship to the rest of the utterance, as for instance its use as subject, being then indicated by some other device.

Such uses are generally called adverbial. In most European languages there are a handful of primary adverbs, usually indicative of time or manner, which carry their functions in themselves: French *hier, demain, vite.* English adverbs of motion such as *up, down, out,* also belong here. Such phrases as *last night, next summer, the day before,* behave in just the same way: each one of their components refers to some aspect of experience, but none of them implies by itself its relation to the context; yet, the whole of each phrase is sufficiently reminiscent of time to dispense with any recourse to explicit marking, such as *in* in, e.g., *in winter.*

What is traditionally called an adjective is quite often shown to be used as an attribute or a predicate through its location in the context. But in many languages, French for instance, its identification, when it functions as an attribute, is based upon its "adjectival" meaning, so that it can be said to carry in itself some indication of its relation to the rest of the utterance: French *une élégante personne* and *une personne élégante* may have different stylistic implications, but are grammatically identical; *élégante* has to be in the neighborhood of *personne* if it is to be interpreted as its determinant, but the fact that *élégante* is the determinant and *personne* the head is only made clear by the "adjectival" meaning of *élégante* (and the "substantival" meaning of *personne*).

The meaning of a unit may also happen to be indicative of its function when, e.g., a language with declensions lacks, for some words, a distinction between the so-called nominative and accusative cases and relies, for the distinction between subject and object functions, on the contrast between the active connotations of the word used as the subject and the passive connotations of the one meant as the object, added to the semantic implications of the predicate. This would be the case in Latin with the neuter nouns *animal* and *gramen* in combination with the verb *pascitur,* where the beast would, beyond any doubt, be munching the grass and not the reverse.

Another way of making explicit the relation between one aspect of an experience, as represented by a linguistic unit in the chain, and the rest, as manifested by the other units of the utterance, consists in placing these units in such an order as to suggest the nature of their mutual relationships. Since segmental units can only appear before or after one another, the number of distinct relationships that can be expressed in this way may seem very limited. Starting from the experience to be communicated, it would seem that the most obvious procedure would be to choose one of its central features. This would be matched linguistically by an element becoming the head of the utterance. Another aspect of the experience would furnish another linguistic element which would be tagged to the head, either before or after it, depending on whether, in that language, subordinate elements should come before or after the head. We shall call the type of linguistic relationship existing between the head and the second element one of **determination,** the element added to the head being the **determinant.** Whether a third element, standing according to the rules of the language before or after the former group, would determine that group as a whole, or only the head, or only its immediate neighbor, the first determinant, would not be explicated through the respective positions of the three units involved. If we designate the head as H, the two determinants as D_1 and D_2, and determination as $\rightarrow$, the speaker might want to imply either

$$(1) \ D_2 \rightarrow \boxed{D_1 \rightarrow H}$$

$$or \ (2) \ D_2 \rightarrow \boxed{\begin{matrix} \ \\ H \\ D_1 \rightarrow \end{matrix}}$$

$$or, \ still, \ (3) \ \boxed{D_2 \rightarrow D_1} \rightarrow H.$$

If H meant 'building', D_1 'house', and D_2 'village', (1) would mean 'village house-building', (2) 'village [and] house building', and (3) 'village-house building'.

Suprasegmental solutions of the problem thus raised are fairly obvious: in (1) D_2 and D_1 might receive greater prominence than H, in (2) the three elements might have equal prominence, in (3) D_2 and H might have greater prominence than D_1. Or, if pauses were used, (1) would have a pause after D_2, (2) two pauses: one after D_2 and one after D_1, (3) a pause after D_1. But, of course, such suprasegmental features should count as linguistic units in their own right, and they actually belong to the third type of relationship indication, the one we shall consider below, where some specific segment is used for that purpose.

It is clear that both the positions before and after the head cannot be used with different implications in the same language, unless the head is marked as such irrespective of its location among the determinants, a possibility we have not considered so far. In what precedes, the head was identified as such only through its position in relation to the determinants: H, in the patterns, is recognized as such because it is final. Should the head be identifiable as such through its meaning in much the same way as *last night* was, above, identified as a temporal complement or *down* as an adverb of motion, it becomes possible to attribute different functions to the position before and the position after it. In French, *tue* being known as a verb, i.e. an element whose only function is that of a predicate, or head of a clause, the element preceding it will be identified as the subject, the one following it as the object, e.g., in *l'homme tue la bête*.

Pure and simple determination, expressed either by pre-position or post-position as the case may be, goes a long way towards indicating the most diverse actual relationships when it combines with whatever is hinted, in that respect, by the meanings of the elements in presence. Nothing is more different than the relationship between *gold* and *smith* in *goldsmith* and that between *gold* and *fish* in *goldfish,* the former amounting to '[smith] who deals in [gold]', the latter to '[fish] that looks like [gold]'.

This indicates what services the simple device of respective position can render toward the reconstruction by the hearer of the experience which is being communicated. Yet it is hard to imagine how a full-fledged language could work without recourse to some more sophisticated way of indicating syntactic relationships.

This way consists in using certain units for specifying the nature of the relationship between a given element and the rest of the utterance. Whenever their history can be traced back, these units are, more often than not, found to be adverbial in origin and bearing in themselves the indication of their connection with the environment. When tagged to the segments whose relationship with the rest has to be shown, they assure an unambiguous expression of that relationship, which becomes totally independent of the position of the phrase in the context. These functional indicators correspond to the cases as well as to the prepositions and conjunctions of traditional grammar. The phrases resulting from the combination of a functional indicator and the element whose functions are at stake, with or without determinants, can be dubbed **autonomous.** Syntactic autonomy is established beyond any doubt when an autonomous phrase can be shifted from one environment to another within the clause without change in its relation to the context: *he went down the hill, down the hill he went.* But syntactic autonomy exists prior to this permutation test. In some languages the order of the successive segments of the clause may be strictly regulated, so that permutations are not to be encountered. But autonomy exists all the same as long as the nature of the relationship of a segment to the rest is unambiguously marked by a specific indicator.

As soon as we have at our disposal this most supple and varied means of marking syntactic relations, we might conceive of a break-down of experience into different aspects, each corresponding, in speech, to an autonomous phrase, so that the utterance would consist in a free succession of such phrases, all on an equal footing. Let us start from an expanded version of Sapir's famous sentence: *Last Monday, the farmer killed the duckling with a hatchet.* If we eke out our prepositional system by means of functional labels, a fully analytic version of this would read as follows: *date last Monday, agent the farmer, action killing* (N. B.: not a predicate), *patient the duckling, with* (or, more specifically, *tool*) *a hatchet.*

Of course, no such syntactic pattern is on record. It is so much more economical to dispense with one, two, three or more of the proposed labels. One of the items becomes the head in reference to which all the others have to be organized. The head is what is called the predicate. The predicate may be identified as such because it is known by all the members of the community as never having any function but the predicative function (cf. French *tue* above), in which case we call it a verb. In the case of a verb-noun homonymy or polysemy (a *table, to table*) the verb may be identified on the basis of its relative position and the presence around it of specific (grammatical) determinants such as (*-ed; tabled*). In other cases the predicate is shown to be the head because of the behavior of the other items as its satellites.

In some languages, there exist ways of modifying the verbal predicate so as to compel the other items to change the nature of their relationships to it: thus in English the normal active voice may be replaced by the passive voice, whereby the item normally characterized by its position after the predicate (object) assumes the function and position of the pre-posed item (subject).

It must be pointed out that the assumption of the universal existence of predicates is the first inductive one we are making here. Whatever was said, in what precedes, regarding the three types of function marking was, of course, illustrated by reference to existing languages, but deductively arrived at when starting from a definition of a language as a doubly articulated set of vocal habits employed for the communication of experience.

It may not be needless to stress that assuming that a predicative head is everywhere to be found in language does not imply in the least that predicates are always verbs or that the noun-verb dichotomy is universal. Neither does 'predicate' necessarily imply 'subject'. Traditionally and semantically, the subject is considered the theme about which something is predicated, and consequently the preservation of the term 'predicate' as the designation of a universal feature of language might seem to imply that the subject is universal too. As a matter of fact, when we consider what is called 'subject' in the languages for which the term was invented, we notice that its only permanent characteristic, in contradistinction to the so-called complements, is the fact that in normal, non-elliptic and non-injunctive speech, an item with all the marks of a certain function (be it a given type of ending or a definite position) must necessarily accompany the predicate; all other items are complementary, hence their designation as 'complements'. They may, in some contexts, be unavoidable, but many complete utterances exist without complements of any sort. In these languages, the subject may assume very different and, at times, elusive forms: it may be a noun, a phrase, a pronoun, a verbal ending, or, as for instance in Italian or Spanish singular 3rd persons, a 'zero ending' revealed as subject by some ulterior reference (*su,* in Spanish *quiere a su madre,* implying a subject in *quiere*) or some transformation. But it is always there. In *the child is drinking a glass of water, a glass of water* can be left out without destroying the sentence as such, but . . . *is drinking a glass of water* is nothing but a maimed utterance. Many languages are on record where verbal predicates need a subject, but where non-verbal predicates can dispense with it. When investigating whether a language has a subject or not, care should be taken not to let the absence of a functional indicator be interpreted as a proof that we have to do with a 'subject' case.

A consciously functional approach to phonology normally entails that the labeling and grouping of facts will be determined by the role they play in the process of communication more than by the physical nature of those facts: pitch is, from a physiological standpoint, a neatly circumscribed phenomenon; stress is less easy to pin down, but, on the plane of phonetic observation, stress and pitch do not overlap. Yet, from a properly linguistic standpoint, pitch may function word-distinctively as tones (or tonemes) as an ingredient of accent, i.e. as a contribution to syntagmatic structuration, or as intonation, i.e. on a level where sound features contribute directly to meaning. In its accentual function, pitch normally combines with some stress.

In the same way, a consciously functional approach to syntax will entail that formal resemblances be subordinated to functional identity. What is really essential is not whether the indication of the function of a noun is secured by means of a declensional ending or through a preposition; in both cases we obtain an autonomous phrase, e.g. Latin *homini,* or English *to the man.* The only fundamental difference between these two phrases lies in the existence in English of the specification corresponding to the definite article. The fact that some linguistic significant units are not represented in the spoken chain by any unambiguously delimited segment, as in the case with the dative in *homini,* should by no means be more disquieting than the well accepted fact that one and the same meaningful unit ('morpheme') may be represented, in different locations, by totally different segments ('morphs'). If we accept to operate with the fiction of a zero 'morph' of the preterite 'morpheme' in *he cut,* it is hard to see why we should balk at assuming an amalgamated 'morph' of the dative 'morpheme' in Latin *homini* and *hominibus.* We are of course all agreed that no linguistic unit can be posited unless its presence corresponds to some phonological difference in the utterance, but we know that *he cut* is a preterite and *he cuts* a present without being able to point out a segment corresponding to the expression of the preterite.

Operating with the concept of amalgamation amounts to freeing ourselves of the self-imposed task of finding a well-delimited segment for any one of our linguistic units. One of the main reasons why I decided to use the term **moneme** as a designation of the minimal significant unit in language instead of the now well-established **morpheme,** was that in the minds of a majority of structuralists, that word automatically suggests some speech segment, whereas it may happen that a moneme cannot be precisely located in the utterance. The functional standpoint makes us thus independent of the vagaries of linguistic forms. We become far less reluctant to operate with discontinuous units of all sorts. Such patterns of agreement as we find, for instance, in French *les grands animaux dorment* /legrãzanimo dorm/ where the choice of the plural instead of the singular shows in four different places (/...e...z...o...m/) are just one aspect of the formal predictability of monemes. There are just as many monemes in an utterance as there are meaningful choices, whatever the number of distinct formal accidents each choice may entail.

Another implication of the functional approach is that when a distinction which obtains in certain contexts is found not to function in others, it is felt that no amount of formal identity should compel us to posit the distinction as generally valid in the language. In other words, the concept of neutralization is based upon a functional view of language. In the same way as the formal difference between [t] and [d] is relevant in Russian *tom, dom,* but neutralized in [pat ˈkoməm] *pod komom,* [pad ˈgorədəm] *pod gorodom,* the significant difference between indicative and subjunctive which is relevant in French in certain contexts is neutralized in those where only the subjunctive form or only the indicative form is to be found and where, as a consequence, no choice is left to the speaker.

In our present approach, functional indicators have early been set aside as a very special type of moneme. They figure of course in the traditional categories of prepositions, case endings, and conjunctions. All of these belong to grammar rather than to lexicon, which does not mean that some of them do not appear as specific entries in dictionaries, e.g. English *for, with, as.* Inclusion in grammar is often reserved to what appear, from a formal standpoint, as the problem children among the monemes: those that cannot be neatly delimited from the context and consequently alphabetically listed. Even if prepositions and conjunctions are sometimes listed in grammars, few people ever bother to look for them there, unless the choice of one of them determines some further modification of the context. It is useful to have, in a Latin grammar, a list of prepositions, which, like *sine,* require in the following amalgam the accident characteristic of the ablative. Where no such complications exist, in English for instance, listing *without* and congeners in the grammar serves no useful purpose. Yet, contemporary linguists have retained the traditional distinction between grammatical and lexical elements, trying of course to give a formal non-semantic basis to the distinction. Calling limited inventories 'grammatical' is generally found to be satisfactory, and it undoubtedly tallies with ideas of grammar as a part of language description where all relevant items are presented without any *etc.* and which is reserved to the really structured aspects of language. Even if making a complete inventory of all the functional monemes and phrases of a language (cf. English *onto, up to, in view of,* etc.) may be no easy task, if we want to avoid arbitrary decisions as to what should belong there, we cannot avoid including functionals in grammar. How would a Latin grammar look if we did not include cases in it? But, of course, all grammatical items, the ones that belong to limited inventories, are not functionals: singular, dual, and plural, definite and indefinite articles, tenses and moods, 'persons' of verbs, the so-called possessive adjectives are not meant to indicate in what way the non-grammatical item to which they are attached is connected with the rest of the utterance. They may imply a reference to what has been said before, as when a definite article reminds the audience that the following item is one that was referred to before, or when *his* recalls an aforementioned masculine being. But neither *the book* nor *his book* indicates what relation exists between the item *book* and the rest of the clause; or if we transfer all this on a non-linguistic plane, how the aspect of the experience corresponding to the book ties up with the experience as a whole. In other words *the book, his book,* as well as *a book* or *her book* may be the subject or the object or any complement, but before we can tell which, we will need some information derived from the position of the phrase or the addition to it of a functional. Such units as *the* or *his,* or the plural moneme, or the preterite are nothing but additional specifications to what is conveyed by their neighbors. They are cheaper, more routine, often less informative specifications than what would be contributed by such an adjective as *red* or a phrase like *John's,* but they belong to the same general functional type of determinants, whether they belong to the same class, as is the case with *the, his,* and *John's,* or a different class like *red; the, his,* and *John's* are indeed mutually exclusive, whereas *red* can combine with any of these.

The reason why the basic difference between the functionals and the grammatical determinants which I propose to call **modifiers** has not generally been pointed out so far is that linguists, traditionalists and structuralists alike, have mainly been engrossed by the formal vagaries of their units. Both functionals and modifiers belong to grammar; both are on the average considerably more frequent and consequently shorter than lexical items;

both are closely attached to some lexical item, or group of such, and therefore likely to be amalgamated with it; both are likely to feature jointly in cases of agreement. They have thus too much in common from a formal standpoint, for people who concentrate on form to become aware of their fundamental functional difference.

One important consequence of the subordination of form to function and of the use of the blanket operational concept of amalgam to cover cases when segmentation raises problems, is that there is little need left for the word as a unit intermediate between the moneme and the sentence (i.e. the main clause and its appendages): if we decide that *homini* and *to the man* are, above all, autonomous phrases and that the formal differences between them are covered by reference to amalgamation, there is no need to add that *homini* is one word and *to the man* three. When describing a language like Latin where amalgamated autonomous phrases are normal features, it would be pedantic to insist on designating them as such instead of using the short and handy term "word". Therefore I am not tempted to exclude the term "word" from the technical vocabulary of functional linguistics. But it is important to stress that we are under no obligation to segment all utterances of any language whatever into an exhaustive succession of words. An implication of this is that the status of morphology should be reconsidered. Morphology used to be the study of formal variations of words: since *homini* was said to be "the same word" as *homo* and *hominibus,* it was necessary to explain under what conditions and for what purposes the word had to suffer such drastic changes; hence morphology. If we now look at *homini,* not as one avatar of a unit, but as the amalgam of three units, the necessity remains of investigating under what form the moneme of dative will appear in combination with that of singular or plural, and that of 'man' or any other noun of the Latin language. There is no reason why we should not call this 'morphology'. We will then have to define morphology as the study of the formal variations of monemes. Applied to a language like Latin, this morphology would hardly differ from what we find in traditional grammars: the declensional and conjugational patterns are probably the most economical way of presenting the formal variations of Latin monemes. What we will exclude from morphology is any reference to the uses of the various grammatical categories, the function of a moneme having no direct connection with its formal variations. Derivation and composition, which are sometimes included in morphology, had better be dealt with in a different chapter, with a morphological section where whatever formal deviation incurred by the moneme, in the process of composition or derivation, should be accounted for; e.g., *deep* becoming *dep-* in *depth*.

Out of this, syntax emerges as the study of the combinatory latitudes of monemes, beginning with the combinations of modifiers with their lexical supports and ending with the building up of sentences. By **combinations,** we mean the faculty of coexisting on different levels, in some cases irrespective of the actual position of the elements in the chain, and with absolute disregard of any formal variation. Here again, and in spite of different formulations, we come pretty close to traditional practice: as soon as syntax begins, no one is supposed to worry about *tulit* being the perfect of *fero* and *went* the preterit of *go*.

This particular approach to linguistic analysis, syntax, and morphology has not, so far, been elaborated in all details. The theoretical presentations available to date are to be found in Chapter 4 of *Elements of General Linguistics* (London, Faber and Faber, 1964), and Chapter 3 of *A Functional View of Language* (Oxford, Clarendon, 1962). Among the few articles devoted to the subject, only one deserves to be mentioned here, namely my contribution to the De Groot Festschrift, *Studia Gratulatoria* (Amsterdam, North-Holland Publishing Co., 1962), entitled "De la variété des unités significatives," pp. 280-288. The underlying method has been applied to the description of a number of African languages. Two of them are available: Jacqueline Thomas' *Le parler ngbaka de Bokanga,* Ecole pratique des Hautes Etudes (Paris, 1963), and Charles Vandame's *Le ngambay-moundou,* Mémoires de l'Institut français d'Afrique Noire, No. 69 (Dakar, 1963). A third one, Maurice Houis' *Etude descriptive de la langue susu,* will be published this spring. According to the same method, Geneviève Corréard N'Diaye is preparing a description of the Basque dialect of Maya, Guipuzcoa, and Denise François that of spoken Parisian French.

INDIAN AND LADINO BILINGUALISM: SOCIOCULTURAL CONTRASTS IN CHIAPAS, MEXICO

Norman A. McQuown
University of Chicago

The data on which the present paper is based were gathered by the field-workers, both linguists and social anthropologists, of the University of Chicago's projects among the Tzeltal and Tzotzil-speaking *Indians* of Chiapas, Mexico and among the Spanish-speaking non-Indians (*Ladinos*) of the same area (see Figure 1). There are considerable numbers of bilinguals in both groups, although the incidence of bilingualism varies greatly from place to place within the area. In the southern and southwestern portions of the territory, where there are large numbers of Ladinos, there are many Indian bilinguals and practically no Ladinos who know anything of the indigenous language. In the northern and, in particular, in the northeastern parts of the area, these proportions are reversed. There are very few Ladinos, and these are, for the most part, bilingual. The agents of acculturation in the north, are, in great part, the Ladinos who speak the Indian language. In the south, on the other hand, such agents are to be found among the Indians themselves.

What such general statements fail to specify, however, is why some Ladinos in the north and some Indians in the south are very poor, some very good, agents of culture change, and what are the specific indices, both linguistic and sociocultural, of such differences in individual personality, differences which account for the selection process whereby some are chosen to lead and some are not. It is the purpose of this paper, in the concrete linguisitic, sociocultural, and personality data available on five individuals, distributed over this continuum, to attempt to discover such specific indices, and, having discovered them, to try to rationalize the particular roles which individuals so distinguished play in the life of their changing communities. I am especially grateful to the social anthropologists Charles E. Mann of Stanford University, María Esther Alvarez de Hermitte of the University of Chicago, and Marcelo Díaz de Salas of the Mexican National School of Anthropology, and to the linguists Gerald E. Williams of Stanford University, and R. Radhakrishnan, and Harvey B. Sarles of the University of Chicago for having made

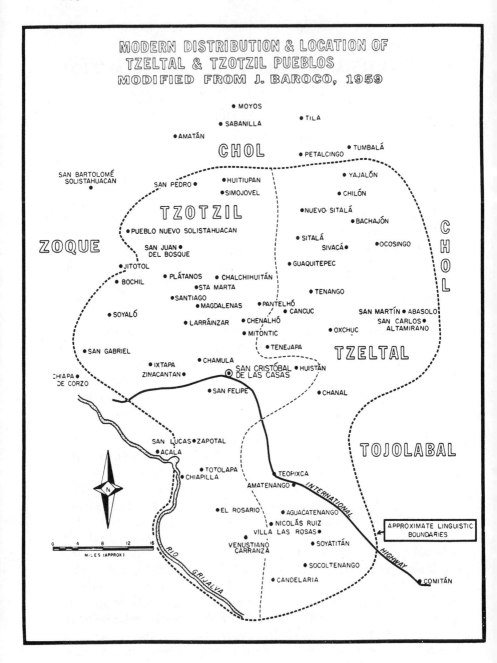

MODERN DISTRIBUTION & LOCATION OF
TZELTAL & TZOTZIL PUEBLOS
MODIFIED FROM J. BAROCO, 1959

CHOL

• MOYOS
• SABANILLA   • TILA
• AMATÁN
                                  • PETALCINGO   • TUMBALÁ

SAN BARTOLOMÉ   • YAJALÓN
SOLISTAHUACAN   • HUITIUPAN
           SAN PEDRO • • SIMOJOVEL   • CHILÓN

TZOTZIL   • NUEVO- SITALÁ
                                                • BACHAJÓN
• PUEBLO NUEVO SOLISTAHUACAN
                                   • SITALÁ
ZOQUE   SAN JUAN •   SIVACÁ •   • OCOSINGO
                DEL BOSQUE
        • JITOTOL   • GUAQUITEPEC
          • BOCHIL   • PLÁTANOS   • CHALCHIHUITÁN
                        • STA MARTA   • TENANGO
                    • SANTIAGO
                      MAGDALENAS   • PANTELHÓ   SAN MARTÍN • ABASOLO
    • SOYALÓ   • CANCUC   SAN CARLOS •
                     • LARRÁINZAR   • CHENALHÓ   ALTAMIRANO
                            • MITONTIC   • OXCHUC
      • SAN GABRIEL   • TENEJAPA
                                                        TZELTAL
                        • IXTAPA   • CHAMULA
CHIAPA •   ZINACANTAN •   SAN CRISTÓBAL • HUISTÁN
DE CORZO   DE LAS CASAS
                               • SAN FELIPE   • CHANAL

                                                        TOJOLABAL
              SAN LUCAS • ZAPOTAL
                 • ACALA

                    • TOTOLAPA
                 • CHIAPILLA   • TEOPIXCA
                            AMATENANGO •   INTERNATIONAL
                                                        APPROXIMATE LINGUISTIC
                    • EL ROSARIO   • AGUACATENANGO   BOUNDARIES
                             • NICOLÁS RUIZ
                             VILLA LAS ROSAS •
                    VENUSTIANO   • SOYATITÁN
                    CARRANZA
    0   4   8   12 16   • SOCOLTENANGO HIGHWAY
    MILES (APPROX)   RIO
                        GRIJALVA   • CANDELARIA   • COMITÁN

CHOL (right side)

available to me the sociocultural, linguistic, and projective test materials on which this study depends. I have made use of taped 200-word vocabularies, both for Spanish and for Tzeltal-Tzotzil, and of the responses (in Spanish) to two types of cultural projection tests (the conventional T. A. T.'s, and a photo-test for cultural perception devised especially for the Chicago Chiapas projects by Murial Eva Verbitsky de Hunt of the University of Chicago). In addition, I have had available to me a variety of socio-cultural census data on the five individuals in question (one Ladino, and four Indians), all of whom are bilingual in varying degrees which will be here carefully specified.

Since the features which I have here isolated as indices of bilingual adaptation are in considerable number phonological, I present first, in brief outline, the phonological systems (Figures 2-11) of the dialects involved, followed by the lists of features, so that the factual selection among the features found in these systems in the usage of each of the individuals under study as well as the rationale of such selection may be made clear.

Figure 2

OCOSINGO TZELTALZ

p	t	¢	č	k	ʔ			i		u
p̓	t̓	¢̓	č̓	k̓					e	o
b	d		g						a	
	s	š	x							
m	n								a	á

w	y		CV	CVC
l			CVh	CVhC
			CVʔ	CVʔC
r			CVVC	CVʔVC
			CVhVC	CVS*VC
*S = Semivowel			CVʔCVC	

The Ocosingo Tzeltal (Figure 2) of Informant No. 1 (Ladino) contains, among others, the following phonological peculiarities which stamp it as *non-Indian*:

(1) absence of glottalization (in all positions);
(2) absence of glottal stop (in CVˀCVC);
(3) absence of stop articulation (in /b̵/);
(4) assimilation of e.g. [š] to [ž] before voiced item;
(5) replacement of [Vˀb̵] by [Vb]; of [ˀβɸ] by [vf].

The following represent instances of *hyper-Indianism*:

(1) [. 'xak̂ . k̂a .] instead of normal [. xaˀ . ˀa̧ .] 'agua';
(2) [. t ɛn . 'tsum .] instead of normal [. tɛn . 'tsun .] 'chivo';
(3) [. tu . 'miŋ .] instead of normal [. tu . 'min .] 'algodón';
(4) [. ta . 'k̂in .] instead of normal [. ta . 'kin .] 'seco';

On occasion, however, other, *genuinely Indian*, features *do* appear:

(1) utterance-final glottal stops (regularly);
(2) glottalization (properly placed) (sporadically);
(3) [ˀø] where it *should* occur;
(4) CVxC (regularly) (but with a strongly fricative [x̤] in this position.

One or more of these genuinely Indian features occurred not as re-actions to the linguist's elicitation formulae, but rather as echo re-actions to Indian responses to the formulae. In such cases the chain Spanish-speaking elicitation—Tzeltal response in Spanish context was broken, and a genuinely Tzeltal reaction was in order.

Figure 3

OCOSINGO SPANISH

p	t	č	k			i		u
b	d		g				e	o
f	s	š	x					a

m n ñ   a   á

w   y   CV

l   CVV   pr   tr   kr

r   r̃   CVVV   br   dr   gr

The Ocosingo (?) Spanish (Figure 3) of Informant No. 1 (Ladino), as evidenced by the text of the informant's reactions to the individual photographs in the P[hototest for] C[ultural] P[erception], departs very little from the Central Mexican phonological norm, although there are numbers of grammatical and lexical provincialisms and an occasional vulgarism. Among *provincialisms,* we note:

(1) ad-verbial *muy* (*no muy se distingue*);
(2) *ir a* without *a* (*se va casar*);
(3) feminine en *-anta* (*ó alguna acompañanta ó alguna visitanta*).

As a *vulgarism* we observe the pronunciation [. tsɛk. ' tal.] in place of the usual [. tsel. ' tal] in *de raza tzectal.*

Inspection of the content of Informant No. 1's Spanish-language PCP reactions produces clear evidence of his Ladino identifications:

(1) his use of the term *indito* for the human figures in the photos;
(2) his use of the term *choza* for their houses;
(3) his use of the term *indumentaria* for their clothing.

On the other hand, his constant use of the diminutive in *-ito* or *-ita* evidences his kindly tolerance and good will (*dos inditos, su chocita, este chamaquito, está contentito, se conoce muy apuradito, chamulitas, son inditas*) toward Indians, as does his use of *señora* of an Indian woman. Other words and phrases for identifying Indians are typically Ladino in their avoidance of more direct labels (*indigenas, de raza tzectal, de raza indigena, un chamaquito . . . asi de la región, es del carácter de ellos*). His almost exclusive reliance on clothes as providing the distinguishing line between Indian and Ladino is again typical, although it gets him into trouble when he tries to reconcile Ladino trousers and shirt with bare feet and a kerchief tied around the head. Shift of clothing from the Indian to the Ladino norm is characterized as progressive (*más adelantados, una familia bastante* *decente y arreglada, pero ya indigenas más civilizados*). The use of pewter bowls is a mark of progress (*por lo tanto, ya están bastante adelantados*). The refusal to recognize, among the photos, either of the curing ceremonies as such, on the other hand, indicates Indian-Ladino common sentiment on witchcraft and curing. Full identification with the non-Indian (*ahorita si se ve que está muy contento*), however, is manifest in Informant No. 1's reaction to the last of the twenty PCP photos.

Figure 4

PINOLA TZELTAL

p	t	¢	č	k	ʔ		i	u
ṗ	ṫ	¢̇	č̣	k̇				
							e	o
b	d		g					
							a	
	s	š	x					
m	n						a	á
w		y					CVx	
	l						CVʔ	
	r						CVĊ	

The Pinola Tzeltal (Figure 4) of Informant No. 2 (Indian) contains the following special characteristics which mark it as *innovating* and *hispanicizing*:

(1) complete lack of noun-classifying numeral prefixes (with only one exception, the personal *tul*, in only one instance);

(2) almost exclusive use of [b] allophone of /b̓/ (only one instance of /ʔb/ in utterance final);

(3) use of -/Vl/ final (adjectival) instead of nominal root initial members of the Tzeltal equivalents of Spanish adjective-noun phrases (*¢ahal lum, tohol beh, sikil ʔakabal, yačil nah*).

Other features may be interpreted as indicating a tendency toward slavish literal translation (*yakat yučil haʔ* : estás bebiendo agua, *ha ȼiʔe štiʔawan*: los perros muerden); the grasp of the second language is, however, not always adequate (tokal lom ʔip: *not* cayó una lluvia fuerte *but* hay una neblina fuerte).

Figure 5

PINOLA SPANISH (INDIAN)

p	t	č	k		i	u	pr	tr kr
b	d	g					br □	gr
				e	o			
f	s	š	x					
				a				
m	ᴘ	ñ						
w	y			a á			Cía	CVx
l							Cío	CVVx
r	ř							

The Pinola Indian Spanish (Figure 5) of Informant No. 2, notwithstanding his tendency toward innovation in Tzeltal, departs quite widely from the Central Mexican norms for Spanish:

Phonetic Features:

(1) the voiceless stops are usually aspirated ([kʻ] *amino largo, a*[kʻ]*i*) (but occasionally not; [k]*acho*;

(3) post-nasal voiced (*está Usted cor*[d]*ando zacate*) or lenis (*tem*[**p**]*lo*);

(5) the /ř/ is fricative (*cerro, barriga*);

(6) the final vowels are followed by voiceless echo vowels (*grande* [e̥], *zope* [e̥]);

(8) utterance final /a/ is occasionally centralized (mi mano derech[aʌ]).

Morphophonemic Features:

(15) nasals usually fail to be homorganic with following stops or fricatives (*u*[n] *perro, u*[n] *piojo*) but occasionally do assimilate (*nara*[ŋ]*jas, u*[ŋ] *caballo*);

(19) cluster /gr/ replacing /dr/ (*una piegra, un cegro*);

(20) cluster /xu/ replacing /fu/ ([x]*uego* instead of *fuego*);

(21) cluster /ie/ replacing /ue/ (*carne del pierco*);

(22) *ia* or *io* vowel clusters instead of *illa* or *illo;* (*mi rodía, amarío, martío, un amarío, gargantía*) (for *rodilla, amarillo, martillo, armadillo,* and *gargantilla* respectively);

(24) loss of [d] (¿*onde 'estabas? se 'espiertan*);

(25) loss of initial vowel (*'stá seco, 'l ombligo*);

(26) loss of final vowel (*lech' de vaca*);

(27) loss of final syllable (*mi mano zur'* instead of *mi mano zurda*).

Grammatical Features:

(35) plural endings are omitted (*somo' chiquito', dos pájaro', 'stán bueno', dos mes', cuatrociento'*), as are other final *s*'es (*'stá lejo'*);

(36) plural number in possessive adjectives refers to plurality of possessor rather of thing possessed (*sus ojo' Ustedes, sus hombro'*);

(38) possessive phrases lack both the article preceding the thing possessed and the preposition *de* which connects it with its possessor (*polvo los camino', tronco los palo'*);

(39) feminine gender concordance fails (*no andan los criaturas, un hoja verde, manta blanco, está enfermo su mujer*);

(40) special forms of the second person singular of verbs (those compatible with the pronoun *vos,*) frequently occur (*vos sos, no sabés, dormite*) but not to the exclusion of the usual Central Mexican forms compatible with the pronoun *tú* (¿*qué quieres?*).

Lexical Features:

(60) special lexical items (**calca** *del palo, mi* **pescuezo,** *un* **lucero,** *cayó una helada* **doble,** *mi* **carne,** *un* **zope, tzilica, murciégalo**) (for *corteza, cuello, estrella, fuerte* or *espesa, cuerpo, zopilote,* and *chilacayote,* respectively).

   Nine items (5, 19, 20, 22, 24, 25, 26, 40, and 60) are characteristic of local Indian Spanish, five items represent special solutions to difficult problems of shift from Indian speech habits to Spanish speech habits, and *six* items (1, 3, 6, 8, 15, and 35) are clearly transfers of Indian linguistic habits into Spanish speech.

   Inspection of the *content* of Informant No. 2's Spanish language T.A.T. reactions produces clear evidence of his distance from the Ladino world:

(1) he fails totally to recognize the *violin* and the sheet music in Picture No. 1 and concentrates instead on the alleged sadness and sleepiness of the figure;

(2) he fails to recognize the *books* carried by one of the two women in Picture No. 2;

(3) the *female figure* in Picture No. 3BM is identified as a man (perhaps because of the short hair-cut), and its emotional state is identified as drunkenness;

(4) *grief* in Picture No. 3GF is not recognized as such, but is identified as illness of physical origin;

(5) he fails to identify the *resistance* of the male in Picture No. 4 to female advances;

(6) and the woman in Picture No. 5 is merely identified as such and her *expectant* attitude is not clearly specified.

In short, in language which continues to represent consistently Informant No. 2's special brand of Indian Spanish, this informant regularly misses standardized cues to Ladinos mores and morals.

Figure 6

PINOLA TZELTAL

p	t	¢	č	k	ʔ		i	u
p̓	t̓	¢̓	č̓	k̓			e	o
b̓	d		g					a
		s	š	x				
m	n						a	á
w		y					CVx	CV¢́
	l						CVʔ	CVʔC
	r							

The Pinola Tzeltal (Figure 6) of Informant No. 3 (Indian) contains a number of features which clearly mark this informant as fairly *conservative*:

(1) the use of nominal classifiers in place of (tulát ˙sos cris-
tiano') or prefixed to numerals (túlʔán¢ 'una mujer', kóht
¢íʔ 'un perro', péh téʔ 'un palo', hṗís tón 'una piedra');

(2) the use of classifiers /h/- and /š/- (hkóht š-č úč 'una rana');

(3) clear glottal (/ʔb/ and glottalization (/b̓/) in the reflexes of
/b̓/ (hoʔé[ʔb] čáy 'cinco pescados', čéʔb mf̓ 'dos pájaros', hkaʔbtik 'nuestras manos', hún ha ʔbíl 'un año',
čín [b̓]éh 'caminito', ya š-b̓áh ta milél 'lo van a matar,
htáʔ[b.øą] 'veinte');

(4) Tzeltal stress in Spanish loans (krisyanóh 'gente', man¢anáh
'manzana', hkóht čiwóh 'un chivo', merkadóh 'mercado',
pwersáh 'fuerza') (except for: ʔalagúnaéh 'la laguna',
šléče waká 'la leche de la vaca', túnah ~ tunáh 'nopal',
segúro, 'seguro').

There is, on the other hand, a small number of features which
mark No. 3 as *innovating* or *hispanicizing*:

(1) occasional straight numerals (without the nominal classi-
fier prefixes) in situations which normally require such
classifiers (hoʔéʔb čáy 'cinco pescados', čéʔb mút 'dos
pájaros', ʔoséb tomút 'tres huevos');

(2) homorganic nasal (in position where the local Tzeltal does
not normally have it) (čí[m]b̓éh 'caminito').

Figure 7

PINOLA SPANISH (INDIAN)

p	t	č	k		i		u		pr	tr	kr
b	d		g			e	o		br	□	gr
f	s	š	x			a			Cía		
m	n	ñ				a	á		Cío		
w		y				CVx					
	l					CVVx					
	r	ř̓									

The Pinola Indian Spanish (Figure 7), of Informant No. 3, is, on the whole, even more *conservative* than that of Informant No. 2, and is characterized by the following special features:

Phonetic Features:

(1) the voiceless stops are occasionally aspirated (*un* [kʻ]*aminito, se 'stá hinchando mi* [pʻ]*ie, el*[pʻ]*olvo del* [kʻ]*amino*);

(2) use of [v] allophone of /b/ (*es muy* [v]*i*[v]*o*);

(4) failure of /s/ to assimilate to voiced allophone before voiced consonant (*e*[s] *muy vivo*);

(5) fricative /r̃/ (*una rana*);

(6) the final vowels are occasionally followed by voiceless echo vowels (*la sangr*[εε̥], *el hues*[oo̥], *lo* '*ist*[εε̥] *la ceniz* [aḁ], *es redond*[oo̥];

(7) very open allophone of final /e/ (*la sangr* [εε̥], *sus pi*[εε̥], *lo* '*ist*[εε̥], '*stá cortando zacat*[εε̥], *manta dobl*[εε̥], *veint-*[εε̥], *caf*[έε̥], *camot* [εε̥]) or /e/ elsewhere (*despu*[έ]s, *las nub*[ε]s, *una pi*[ε]*gra, ar*[ε·]*na, ci*[ε·]*go*);

(8) final /a/ is occasionally centralized (*una piegr*[aȧ̂], *aren*[aȧ̂], *la ceniz*[aȧ̂], *l*[aˆ] *muchach*[aˆ],*manzan* [aˆ] *pogrid*[aȧ̂]);

(9) introduction of a voiceless vocoid initial in a Spanish word (or perhaps final in a preceding item) (*la* [i̥]*iel*).

Morphophonemic Features:

(15) failure to assimilate a nasal to homorganic position (*so*[n] *buenos*);

(16) misspeaking of a labial (*los pájaros muelan* instead of *vuelan*);

(17) introduction of a nasal into a consonant cluster (*y un ingle-sia* for *y una iglesia*);

(18) cluster /ky/ replacing /kr/ (*las* [ki̯]*aturas no andan* instead of *las criaturas . . .*);

(19) replacing of cluster /dr/ by /gr/ (*una piegra,* manzana *pogrida, un cegro*);

(20) replacing of cluster /fu/ by /xu/ (*el* [x]*uego*);

(22) *ia* or *io* vowel clusters replacing *illa* or *illo* (*la semía, la rodía, amarío, martío*), but: *se 'stá riyendo de mí* instead of *se está riendo de mí*);

(23) omission of preconsonantic /s/ (*y 'eamos comiendo*);

(24) loss of [d] (y *si 'spiertan temprano* = *y se despiertan temprano*);

(26) loss of final vowel (*carne de coch', por la noch'*).

Grammatical Features:

(35) plural endings are omitted (*somos chico', cinco pescado', dos pájaro', nuestra' oreja', sus nariz', sus pie', sus corazon'*) as are other final *s'es* (*lejo*[ǫ]*'*);

(36) plural number in possessive adjectives refers to plurality of possessor rather than of thing possessed (*sus nariz', sus pie', sus barriga', sus corazon', sus hígado'*);

(37) use of the article before the possessive adjective (*está mala la su mujer*);

(39) feminine gender concordance fails (*el orina, un inglesia, la ropa es blanco, 'stá muy frío la noch'*);

(40) special forms of the second person singular of verbs (*vos sos ¿quién sos? ¿cómo te llamás?*), although the Central Mexican forms also occur (*¿qué quieres? ¿porqué no vienes? no lo sabes*);

(41) misplacing of grammatical agreement in imperatives (*duérmate* in place of Central Mexican *duérmete* or Chiapanec *dormite*).

Lexical Features:

(60) special lexical items (*una* **mata** *de palo, la* **cáscara** *del palo, carne de* **coch'**, *una* **tijera**, **tzilicayote**) (*for árbol, corteza, puerco, tijeras*, and *chilacayote*, respectively).

Accuracy of Translation:

(70) occasional poor translation equivalents (sbak̓ te hsitik ≠ sus ojos de Ustedes, kakantik ≠ la rodilla, hsitik ≠ tu cara).

Nine items (5, 19, 20, 22, 23, 24, 26, 40, and 60) are characteristic of local Indian Spanish, *three* items (18, 36, and 39) represent special solutions to shift difficulties between the two languages, and *twelve* items (1, 2, 4, 6, 7, 8, 9, 15, 16, 17, 35, and 37) are clearly transfers of Indian linguistic habits into Spanish speech. Item 41 constitutes an unresolved problem (what to do wtih a special imperative form which reflects a status difference?). Item 70 tells us that Informant No. 3 occasionally strays from the translation stance (the three Tzeltal examples all contain the first plural possessive affixes, although none of the elicitation forms do).

Analysis of the content of Informant No. 3's Spanish-language responses to the T.A.T. pictures reveals clearly his own even greater remove from a Ladino frame-of-reference:

(1) he totally fails to see the *violin*, in Picture No. 1, does not note the half-closed eyes which indicate either sadness or weariness, and subsequently identifies the young male figure as happily relaxing, and proud of his cornfield; he suggests that the figure may be that of his *compadre*, disregarding age, situation, and objects in the picture, treating only those things the viewer has imaginatively attributed to the figure;

(2) his only suggested reason for hypothetical sadness of one of the two female figures, in Picture No. 2, is illness;

(3) the short-haired female figure in Picture No. 3BM is identified as male, and the attitude as due to a crippling infirmity;

(4) the female figure in Picture 3GS is said to be weeping from sadness at having lost some possession;

(5) he totally misses male resistance to female advances in Picture No. 4 and characterizes them both as happy;

(6) reaction to the female figure in Picture No. 5 is solely to her physical attitude—her environment, characteristically Ladino, is totally ignored;

(7) the female figure in Picture 6BM is identified as male, the house interior is identified as a park, and the thoughtful attitude of the young man is characterized as conceit;

(8) in Picture 6GF, the short-haired lip-sticked female figure is identified as a boy, and the pipe-smoking middle-aged figure behind her is described as a little old man smoking a cigar, and the living-room in which they are talking is said to be a summer-house in a garden;

(9) the doll in the hands of the pre-adolescent girl in Picture No. 7GF is said to be a baby, and the girl's mother (the baby's grandmother) is advising her to feed it, since it is crying;

(10) the scene with the men (one of whom is holding a knife) hovering over a prone figure, in Picture No. 8BM, with a thoughtful young man in the foreground, is interpreted as a post-violence scene in which the prone figure is the body of a man who has been murdered, and the formal clothes of the young man are said to be mourning-dress.

All of these reactions are typically non-Ladino, and the Ladino attributes of attitudes and environments are nowhere perceived.

Figure 8

PINOLA TZELTAL

p	t	¢	č	k	?			i		u
,	,	,	,							
p̓	t̓	¢̓	č̓	k				e		o
b̓	d		g						a	
		s	š	x						
m	n								a	á
w		y						CVx		CVC̓
	l							CV?		CV?C
	r									

The Pinola Tzeltal (Figure 8) of Informant No. 4 (Indian) contains certain features which mark this informant as *extremely conservative*:

(1) the very frequent use of nominal classifiers prefixed to numerals (*h-htúl ?ánç* 'una mujer', *ho?kóht čay* 'cinco-pescados', *hpéh té?* 'un árbol', *?ošpis tomút* 'tres huevos', *hpíh tón* 'una piedra', *hč̓iš ?asarón* 'un azadón');

(2) clear glottal /?b/ and glottalization /b̓/ in the reflexes of

/b̓/ (*k̓ešam k̓a?bal* 'mano izquierda', *yak ta s-b̓ohel ?ak* 'está cortando zacate');

(3) the Spanish loans which appear are almost all completely assimilated (*mantáh* 'tela', *manç̓anáh* 'manzana', *?asarón* 'azadón', *tešelešetík* 'tijeras', *kapéh* 'cafe', *tunáh* 'nopal', *nalašetík* 'naranjas', *tulesnáh* 'durazno').

On the other hand, there are also several features of his Tzeltal which mark him as *innovating* (under Spanish influence):

(1) use of some unassimilated loans (*kristyánoh* 'gente', *spulmoník* 'sus pulmones');

(2) use of plurals of items in circumstances in which plurals would not, in Tzeltal, normally be used (*ya s-ti?awan*

či°etik 'muerden los perros', *tokaletik* 'las nubes', *tane-tik ka°al* 'ceniza', *tešelešetik* 'tijeras', *nalašetik* 'naran-jas').

Figure 9

PINOLA SPANISH (LADINO)

p	t	č	k			i		u	
b	d	g				e		o	
f	s	x				a		a	á
m	n	ñ							
w	y								
l					CV	Cíya	pr	tr	kr
	r	ř			CVV	Cíyo	br	dr	gr

The Spanish (Figure 9) of Informant No. 4, however, shows hardly any influence whatsoever, either of Pinola Tzeltal or Pinola Indian Spanish:

(4) failure to assimilate /s/ to a following voiced consonant (*tre*[s] *huevos*);

(19) replacement of /dr/ by /gr/ (*una piegra*);

(28) insertion of /y/ in intervocalic hiatus (*se está riyendo de mí*: normal *riendo*);

(5) omission of final /s/ (*cuatrociento'*).

On the contrary, many of the features characteristic of local (Indian) Spanish are not found in this informant's speech:

(5) his /ř/ is a clear trill;

(20) his *fuego* is pronounced with an /f/;

(22) his *illa* and *illo* pronounce their *ll*;

(24) his [d] is *not* lost.

This informant presents very precise translation equivalents in what is otherwise very good Central Mexican Spanish. (*kehtikik* 'nuestros dientes', *tukel layalbon* 'él me dijo', *ha° °ačišeh* 'la muchacha', *yakon ta °a°tel ta hkal* 'estoy trabajando en mi milpa'. Informant No. 4 contrasts with Informants No. 2 and No. 3 not only

negatively, in the precision of his translation, where they are imprecise, but also positively in having as prevalent allophones of /w/
[yṷ] and [gṷ], characteristic of neither of his two languages alone, but
found in *both*.

Analysis of the *content* of Informant No. 4's responses to the
T.A.T. pictures shows a considerable sophistication in things Ladino
and an accentuation of Ladino ideals of conduct:

(1) the thoughtful boy, in Picture No. 1, is described as an orphan, having his music, as studious and hard-working, in preparation
for becoming a great man;

(2) the man with a horse, in Picture No. 2, is said to be very
industrious; the young female figure is described as being a teacher
with a book;

(3) the short-haired female figure, in Picture No. 3BM, is described as a sad young man (or a drunken young man), who is an
orphan;

(4) the woman covering her face in picture No. 3GF is said to
be weeping because she cannot earn enough money to make a living;

(5) the scene of the reluctant male, in Picture No. 4, is described
as a scene of marital bliss in which a loving husband and wife, faith-
ful to each other, are in constant fear, lest one or the other die;

(6) in Picture No. 5, all the emphasis is on the material possessions in the house of the woman of affluence, who is good, and intelligent, too;

(7) in Picture No. 6BM, both female and male figures are correctly identified as to sex; the former is given the role of mother, the
latter that of a studious, intelligent son who cares for her needs;

(8) the female figure in Picture No. 6GF is identified as male,
and in him our informant sees a studious son and a loving father,
and expatiates on the advantages of having a father to care for one;

(9) in Picture No. 7GF, the mother and daughter are identified
as such, but the doll is described as the daughter's baby, and much
is made of the possibility that the baby might die;

(10) the knife scene, in Picture No. 8BM, is described as involving doctor hired by a dutiful and loving son to operate on a loving
father suffering from a serious illness;

(11) the smiling young lady of Picture No. 8GF is said to be
sad because she is an orphan;

(12) the resting workers, in Picture 9BM, are made the motive of a discourse on the salutary effects of rest for the tired body;

(13) the two women of Picture No. 9GS are said to love each other like sisters;

(14) in Picture No. 10, marital bliss is again extolled;,

(15) in Picture No. 11, the informant sees an elephant, of whom people are wrongly afraid, and some vultures which are held in check by a man;

(16) in Picture No. 12M, God has sent a priest to bless a dying person, whom He will take, if that is His will;

(17) in Picture No. 12F, an old woman is seen side by side with her son (here a female figure is misidentified as a male), and the virtues of filial piety are extolled;

(18) in Picture No. 12BG, a pool for bathing in a summer scene is identified;

(19) in Picture No. 13MF, a man is said to be mourning his deceased wife;

(20) in Picture No. 13B, the child is said to be eating fruit without a care in the world, and the advantages of having parents who care for one is indicated;

(21) in Picture No. 13G, a child is climbing stairs;

(22) in Picture No. 14, a carpenter is working in darkness;

(23) in Picture No. 15, a man is described as standing among crosses and squares;

(24) the blank Picture No. 16 motivates a long discourse on the baptism of a child;

(25) the rope-climbing naked figure, in Picture No. 17BF, is motive for a discourse on the use of ropes to climb trees with low branches;

(26) the Picture No. 17GF (of the sun shining on the bridge and the boat-docks) gives rise to a discussion of the shape of the world and of night and day;

(27) the man held by hands, in Picture No. 18BM, is said to represent an ill person supported by friends;

(29) the cabin-in-the-snow scene, in Picture No. 19, is said to represent a tractor;

(30) the hatted figure beneath a street-lamp, in Picture No. 20, is said to represent a man who went out to buy medicine at a late hour.

This informant sees Ladino goals in almost all subjects. His preoccupation with orphanhood, and with death through illness, how-

ever, as well as his failure to recognize dolls and short-haired fe-
males mark him quite clearly as an Indian in his perception of the
Ladino world.

Figure 10

SAN BARTOLO TZOTZIL

p	t	¢	č	k	ʔ		i	u
ʼp	ʼt	ʼ¢	ʼč	ʼk			e	o
b̕	d		g					a
		s	š	x				
m	n							
							a	á
w		y					CV	CVʔ
	l						CVx	CVĊ
	r							

The Tzotzil (Figure 10) of Informant No. 5 likewise presents
features which mark him as carefully *conservative*:

(1) use of nominal classifiers prefixed to numerals (*hwo ʔán¢*
'una mujer', *hkot ¢íʔ* 'un perro');
(2) use of * čul* 'holy, sacred' with the names of numerous objects belonging to the category of revered natural phenomena (trees, seed, sun, moon, star, rain, stone, clouds,
fire, night, sky, day, fog, year, cornfield, drum, God);
(3) use of *čin* 'small' as a similarly reverential diminutive for
other objects (feather, bird, frog, butterfly).

His translation equivalents for the Spanish elicitation formulae are

exact (*ʔasátik hoʔošúk* 'sus ojos de Ustedes', *sb̕ákel ketík* 'nuestros
dientes', *hkót ʔikál ¢íʔ* 'un perro negro', *čul čáwokil tók* 'la neblina
(santa nube del rayo)'.

Figure 11

SAN BARTOLO SPANISH (INDIAN)

p   t   č   k   i   u

b   d   g
                                    e   o
f   s   š   x
                                       a
m   n   ñ

w   y   a   á

        l   CV

        r   ř   CVV

The Spanish of Informant No. 5 is, in general, near the Central Mexican norm, but departs from it in some respects:

(5) his /ř/ is fricative (reboso, corral);

(19) replacement of cluster /dr/ by /gr/ (*en una piegra*);,

(42) omission of *a* in the expression *ir a* (*hacer algo*) (*lo va calentar*);

(43) use of general object form *lo* not in agreement as to number or gender with those of the objects to which it refers (*él lo está cuidando las cositas que tiene, lo va calentar una taza de agua*);

(60) lexical pecularities (*está* **poco** *triste*, **pos**, **ansí**, *apuntando* **en** *el dedo*, **saber** *de dónde* for *algo, pues, así, con, quién sabe*);

(61) gender shift (el *costumbre*, but also la *costumbre*).

Noteworthy is the careful use of *tampoco* which not even all native speakers of Spanish use in its required context.

Indian Informant No. 5's perceptions of the Indian world, found in the photographs of the P.C.P., differ considerably from those of Ladino Informant No. 1:

(1) in P.C.P. No. 1, Informant No. 5 sees the girl as being from cold country (by contrast with San Bartolo);

(2) in P.C.P. No. 2, he sees the couple as Chamulas from Amatenango (which is Tzeltal, *not* Tzotzil);

(3) in P.C.P. No. 3, he sees the old man as sad and everyone as solemn as if in church (it is a wedding);

(4) in P.C.P. No. 4, he sees the old man as from Aguacatenango (he is in fact from Pinola), and as guarding his possessions;

(5) in P.C.P. No. 5, he sees the ladies as supping, as in a house, as Ladinos from Pinola (they are Pinola Indians in a grave-yard on All Souls' Day);

(6) in P.C.P. No. 6, he sees a Ladino lady as about to heat a cup of water (she is an Indian from Pinola);

(7) in P.C.P. No. 7, he sees an Indian boy with a sling-shot as Ladino (because he has good trousers);

(8) in P.C.P. No. 8, he sees a Ladino house in San Cristóbal (it is in fact to be found in Pinola);

(9) in P.C.P. No. 9, he sees a man blowing the fire with his head tied up like a chef's (it is, in fact, a curing ceremony);

(10) in P.C.P. No. 10, he sees old men (Chamulitas) playing the fife and drum (they are in fact Pinola Tzeltal, not Chamula which is Tzotzil);

(11) in P.C.P. No. 11, he sees a lady from Ladino Soyatitán as a Chamula redressed as a Ladino.

Our San Bartolo Informant No. 5 sees a clear line between San Bartoleños and others, some from cold country. The line between redressed Indians and Ladinos, however, is not so clear to him, nor is the line between one cold-country Indian and another. For the rest, his description of the content of the P.C.P. photographs is relatively colorless. He, like the Ladino from Ocosingo, fails to identify curing ceremonies as such. He himself, as revealed by his reactions to the P.C.P., is a relatively dispassionate person, who reacts without great involvement to external stimuli.

In the Spanish, as we have seen in these test responses, of Informants 2, 3, 4, and 5, all Indians, only one feature (19) is shared by all four, and only two features (5 and 35) are shared by three (by 2, 3, and 5, and by 2, 3, and 4, respectively), but eleven are shared by Informants 2 and 3, and two by Informants 3 and 4 (1, 6, 8, 15, 20, 22, 24, 26, 36, 39, 40, and 4 and 28, respectively). Of the 11 shared by Informants 2 and 3, features 1, 6, 8, 15, 22, 26, 36, and 39 are Indianizing features, features 20, 24, and 40 are local or substandard Spanish, and the combination characterizes a special *Indian Spanish* dialect. Features 3, 21, 25, 27, 38, and 60 are limited to Informant 2, features 2, 7, 9, 16, 17, 18, 23, 37, 41, and 60 are limited to Informant 3, whereby it is apparent that no two individuals, even those speaking what is essentially the same dialect, make exactly the same selection of Indianizing (or, for that matter, Hispanicizing) features.

Informant No. 1, who speaks good Central Mexican Spanish with only a slight local rural tinge, speaks fluent but inaccurate local Tzeltal, and identifies himself, by his reactions to the P.C.P., as a benevolent but undoubted Ladino. His job is that of local Commissioner of Indian Affairs.

Informant No. 2, who speaks Pinola Indian Spanish with wide departures from the Central Mexican norm, nonetheless speaks a Pinola Tzeltal which is innovating and, in some respects, hispanicizing. His transfer from one to the other is, however, difficult, and his translations lack precision. His reactions to the T.A.T. show clear evidence of his considerable distance from the Ladino world, and his attempts at fluent Spanish never progress beyond the Indian Spanish level. He is caught between his desire for Ladinization and his inability to attain it. He is a local curer.

Informant No. 3, who speaks a conservative Pinola Indian Tzeltal, on rare occasions innovates or hispanicizes. He speaks an Indian Spanish which departs even farther from the Central Mexican norm than that of Informant No. 2, and contains further special features not found in the speech of No. 2. His reactions to the T.A.T. are far removed from the Ladino frame-of-reference, and he repeatedly misses in the pictures Ladino attitudes and environments. He is a local farmer.

Informant No. 4, who speaks an extremely conservative Pinola Indian Tzeltal, has, nonetheless, certain minor features which mark him as innovating (under Spanish influence). His Spanish, on the other hand, is closer to the Central Mexican norm than that of either of his two fellow Pinoltecos. Indeed, it betrays only very occasional traces of departures from this norm, not even in the direction of local Ladino Spanish. He transfers quickly from one language to the other, and his translation equivalents are extremely precise. He has, both in his Tzeltal and in his Spanish speech, a single feature, the fricative /w/, which sets him apart from his fellows. His responses to the T.A.T. show great sophistication in things Ladino and in Ladino ideals of conduct, although his private themes of orphanhood and the fear of death through illness frequently recur, and his failure to recognize items such as dolls and short-haired women betray his Indian origin. He is an orphanned tubercular who is employed as a town-clerk and interpreter and functions as a kind of communications officer between Indians and Ladinos.

Informant No. 5, finally, is in his Tzotzil speech conservative, in his local San Bartolo Spanish fluent, and in his translation equivalents exact. His perceptions of his fellow Indians in the P.C.P. differ considerably, as one might expect, from those of Ladino Informant No. 1. He is, nonetheless, imprecise in his identification of Indians elsewhere, and, in some cases confuses them, since dress seems to be his primary index, with Ladinos. His responses to the P.C.P. do not strongly identify him with the Indians from elsewhere when he sees them, and he reacts somewhat dispassionately to other stimuli in their environment. He is employed as informant to the anthropologist who is working in San Bartolo.

Informant No. 1 is the only Ladino among our bilinguals and plays his role well.

Informants No. 2 and No. 3 both innovate and hispanicize, the former frequently, the latter rarely, in their Tzeltal. Both speak fluent Indian Spanish, but the speech of both of them departs widely from the Central Mexican norms. Although No. 2 still strives to approach that norm, No. 3 is blissfully unaware of its existence. Bilingualism with No. 2 is a means for change, but he finds himself completely at home in neither sociocultural community. For No. 3, bilingualism seems to have no important function at all—it would be hard to be more monocultural and yet bilingual.

Informants No. 4 and 5, on the other hand, both speak an Indian language which is even more conservative than that of Informant No. 3. At the same time, their Spanish departs only slightly from the Central Mexican norm. No. 4, in his reactions to the T.A.T., shows himself to be a good interpreter of Ladino culture, although not fully identified with it. No. 5, however, although like No. 4 in most other respects, is dispassionate toward it, and is quite happy to keep his distance.

Only Informants 1 and 4, therefore, succeed as mediators between the two cultures, the first by virtue of his attitude more than through his performance, the latter by skillful manipulation of the communication media of two worlds.

WHAT STANDARD FOR DIGLOSSIA?
THE CASE OF GERMAN SWITZERLAND

WILLIAM G. MOULTON

Princeton University

If such a thing is possible within the brief space of three years, I think it is fair to say that Charles A. Ferguson's 1959 article on "Diglossia" [1] has already become a classic. It has achieved this status not because it presented us with any new data, but rather because it identified and described a particular type of linguistic situation which can arise quite independently in widely separated geographical areas, and which—if we may be allowed to speculate—has probably arisen many times in the past. Stated briefly, and in Ferguson's words, "Diglossia is a relatively stable language situation in which, in addition to the primary dialects of the language (which may include a standard or regional standards), there is a very divergent, highly codified (often grammatically more complex) superposed variety, the vehicle of a large and respected body of written literature, either of an earlier period or in another speech community, which is learned largely by formal education and is used for most written and formal spoken purposes but is not used by any sector of the community for ordinary conversation" (p. 336).

Among the various examples of diglossia which Ferguson describes—Arabic, Swiss German, Haitian Creole, Greek—Swiss German stands out as being, apparently, much the most sophisticated and self-conscious. [2] Ferguson reports that, through a kind of self-deception, many speakers of Arabic and of Haitian Creole go so far as to deny the very existence of the dialect speech which they use almost exclusively in everyday life. Such an attitude would be unthinkable in Switzerland. Every adult speaker is fully conscious of the distinction between standard and dialect, even though some do not control the standard very well. Further, the more educated and

---

[1] *Word*, XV (1959), 325-340.

[2] My knowledge of Swiss diglossia comes in part from the literature on the subject, in part from a year's residence in Zurich (1958-1959) during which time I worked with the materials of the *Sprachatlas der deutschen Schweiz*. I would like to express my gratitude to the editor of the *Atlas*, Professor Rudolf Hotzenköcherle, for his kindness in letting me use these materials; and to the American Council of Learned Societies for a grant which made my year of Swiss dialect research possible.

sophisticated a speaker is, the more he tries to make the distinction between standard and dialect as sharp and clear as possible. Like so much else in Swiss life, the use of language is well regulated, and each mode of speech is neatly assigned to its proper place within the general scheme of things.

This complete awarness of the distinction between dialect and standard is reflected in a number of phenomena which seem to be unique to Swiss diglossia. Scholarly interest by the Swiss in the analysis and description of their many local dialects extends back over a century and a half, beginning with the work of Franz Joseph Stalder.[3] In 1862, motivated partly by a mistaken fear that dialect speech was on its way toward extinction, work was begun on a far more ambitious national dialect dictionary, the *Schweizerisches Idiotikon*. Publication began in 1881, and is still continuing; it is carried on by a full-time staff of scholars in Zurich. A landmark in the history of dialectology—whether in Switzerland or elsewhere— was the publication in 1876 of J. Winteler's *Die Kerenzer Mundart des Kantons Glarus* (Leipzig & Heidelberg, 1876), a work which to a considerable extent anticipated modern phonemics and even the theory of the over-all pattern. The 20th century has seen the publication of large numbers of dialect descriptions, notably the 20 volumes of the *Beiträge zur schweizerdeutschen Grammatik* (Frauenfeld, 1910-1941), edited by the late Albert Bachmann; and the 11 volumes—to date—of the *Beiträge zur schweizerdeutschen Mundartforschung* (Frauenfeld, 1941 ff.), edited by Rudolf Hotzenköcherle, Bachmann's successor at the University of Zurich. As I was writing the first version of this paper, I received a prospectus announcing that the first volume of a linguistic atlas of German Switzerland, edited by Hotzenköcherle, would soon be off the press.

Works of this type, written for a scholarly audience, prove only that the distinction between standard and dialect in Swiss diglossia is clearly recognized by Swiss scholars. But there are other signs that this awareness extends throughout the whole population. As early as 1921 there appeared a textbook written specifically to teach the local dialect: Karl Stucki, *Schweizerdeutsch: Abriss einer Grammatik mit Laut-und Formenlehre* (Zürich, 1921). (There is, of course, no such dialect as "Schweizerdeutsch;" what Stucki's book teaches is Zurich German.) This was followed in 1948 by Albert Weber,

---

[3] *Probe eines schweizerdeutschen Idiotikon,* Aarau, 1806. Revised and enlarged as *Versuch eines schweizerischen Idiotikon,* 2 vols., Aarau, 1812. Cf. also *Die Landessprachen der Schweiz, oder schweizerische Dialektologie,* Aarau, 1819.

Zürichdeutsche Grammatik (Zurich, 1948), a work which bears the significant subtitle: *Ein Wegweiser zur guten Mundart* ("A Guide to Good Dialect"). I do not know whether this book found the wide popular audience which its author hoped it would. But I *do* find it highly significant that the publisher (Schweizer Spiegel Verlag) was sufficiently encouraged by its sales to follow it with several more books of the same sort. A guide to good Lucerne dialect was published in 1960 (Ludwig Fischer, *Luzerndeutsche Grammatik*); this was followed in 1961 by a "Zurich German Dictionary for School and Home" (Albert Weber and Jacques M. Bächtold, *Zürichdeutsches Wörterbuch für Schule und Haus*); and a combined grammar and dictionary of the dialect of the canton of Zug has been announced for the near future.

I mention these various works because I gather they would be inconceivable in the other diglossias which Ferguson describes. But there is more to come. During the 1940's there was a successful "Swiss German School" in Zurich, where *Auslandsschweizer* (native Swiss who have spent most of their lives abroad) and foreigners could learn how to speak the local dialect. [4] This was desirable from a social point of view, since only dialect is spoken at normal social gatherings, whether of humble folk or of the cocktail set. But —a very significant point—it was also necessary for more practical reasons. Any candidate for citizenship in the canton of Zurich— and, thereby, for federal citizenship—is required, as an earnest of his intentions, to demonstrate at least some knowledge of local dialect. Again, I gather that such a thing would be inconceivable in other diglossias.

All of the things I have described are clear evidence that the diglossia of German speaking Switzerland is extremely stable. Ferguson is surely right when, in his prognosis for the next two centuries, he gives to Swiss German the label "relative stability" (p. 340). Such prognoses are, of course, hazardous. Just 58 years before Ferguson, in 1901, another linguist made precisely the opposition prediction for Swiss diglossia. Taking due account of the high percentage of foreigners in the large cities at that time—28% in Schaffhausen, 29% in Zurich, no less than 35% in Basel—and recognizing the greater prestige which standard German enjoyed among

---

[4] Cf. Paul Zinsli, "Hochsprache und Mundarten in der deutschen Schweiz," *Der Deutschunterricht*, VIII (1956), ii, 61-72, esp. p. 65. This article is full of valuable information on Swiss diglossia.

all segments of the population, Ernst Tappolet[5] predicted, more in sorrow than in anger, that the diglossia of German Switzerland would not outlast another half century. "For," he wrote, "where a dialect is in conflict with a written language—and I believe I have shown this to be the case in German Switzerland—the standard language will win out if political conditions remain unchanged" (p. 39).

What happened in the half century following 1901 to prove Tappolet's prediction so wrong and to make Ferguson's seem so right? The answer can be given in three short phrases: World War I; Adolf Hitler; World War II. During each of these three major catastrophes of 20th century Europe, the Swiss firmly held themselves aloof—first refusing to be embroiled in the senseless conflict of World War I, next repulsed and horrified by the inhumanities of Nazism, and then stubbornly maintaining their neutrality in World War II even though all the world knew where their sympathies lay. As an indication that this fierce neutrality still continues today, let us note the fact that Switzerland joined the economic group called the "Outer Seven" only with the greatest reluctance, and that it still refuses to join the United Nations. A people with this passion for independence will not soon give up its local dialects.

Diglossia depends, of course, both on the maintenance of local dialects *and* on the continued acceptance of a separate but related standard language. Is Swiss independence so strong that it will abandon diglossia by rejecting the standard language of Germany in favor of a new standard of its own? Again, predictions are hazardous; but at the moment such a development seems unthinkable. The only possible candidates for a standard Swiss German are the dialects of Basel, Bern, and Zurich; but the whole Swiss Federation would have to collapse before a Baseler would be willing to learn Bärndütsch, a Berner learn Züritüütsch, or a Zuricher learn Baaselditsch. This would be the most inconceivable development of all. Secondly, the Swiss are too practical and reasonable: they accept standard German as a kind of necessary evil because it would be unreasonable for so small a country to add yet another standard language to a world that is already overburdened with them. Finally, the Swiss are proud of their own share in the great cultural heritage which is recorded in standard German. In this connection it is worth noting that the only two really first-rate dramatists writing

---

[5]*Über den Stand der Mundarten in der deutschen und französischen Schweiz*, Zurich, 1901; = *Mitteilungen der Gesellschaft für deutsche Sprache in Zürich*, Heft 6.

in the German language today are both Swiss: Friedrich Dürrenmatt and Max Frisch.

Though the Swiss are too practical and too proud to abandon standard German as their second language, they are also too independent to feel that they must accept it in exactly the form that it has in Germany. For over 60 years now, the phonology of standard German has been carefully codified in a work generally known as the *Siebs*, after its first editor, Theodor Siebs. [6] To oversimplify, the type of spoken language prescribed by the *Siebs* might be said to consist of south German phonemes pronounced with north German allophones. And it is precisely this north German element in standard German which the Swiss cannot stomach. It strikes them as too sharp and too racy, it carries overtones of Prussian militarism, and it even bears a suggestion of concentration camps looming in the background. [7] This type of German must be avoided at all costs. They are willing to accept—indeed, they demand—a neutral sort of standard German on the stage; but in all other situations they wish to use a German which is standard, to be sure, but which nonetheless clearly sounds Swiss rather than German. [8]

In order to codify such a Swiss version of standard German, a special "Swiss Siebs Committee" was established in 1954. Three years later the results of its deliberations were published in a little booklet which I shall refer to as the *Boesch*, after its editor, Bruno Boesch. [9] If I were to give this booklet a frivolous title, I would call it: "How to Speak German Without Sounding Like a German"—or, more accurately, " . . . and Still Sound Like a Swiss." In the re-

---

[6] First edition 1898. Latest edition: *Siebs, Deutsche Hochsprache, Bühnenaussprache*, edited by Helmut de Boor and Paul Diels, 16th ed., Berlin: Walter de Gruyter, 1957.

[7] Cf. the following in the *Boesch* (see below): "Die Hochsprache ist unserem Gemüt, besonders in ihrer norddeutsch-umgangssprachlichen Färbung, wie wir sie im Kino und sogar gelegentlich im Theater vorgesetzt bekommen, zu 'preussich', zu schneidig, zu schnittig. Gewiss, das sind Gefühlsmomente, die schwer zu umschreiben sind; aber sie sind vorhanden, nicht nur bei Schweizern, auch bei Bayern, Schwaben, Österreichern. Dazu lassen politische Gründe aus der Vergangenheit in vielen Kreisen noch heute keine rechte Freude an der gepflegten Hochsprache aufkommen" (13). Cf. also the reference on p. 7 to the "überspitzte norddeutsche Aussprache."

[8] Cf. the following in the *Boesch*: "Beim Schauspieler ist es uns peinlich, den Schweizer herauszuhören; in allen andern Sprechsituationen ist es ebenso peinlich, ihn *nicht* zu vernehmen, ganz besonders peinlich ist es aber, wenn er sich nach gewundenen Anstrengungen schliesslich doch verrät" (14).

[9] *Die Aussprache des Hochdeutschen in der Schweiz: Eine Wegleitung*. Im Auftrag der Schweizerischen Siebs-Kommission herausgegeben von Bruno Boesch. Zurich: Schweizer Spiegel Verlag, 1957. Pp. 46.

mainder of my remarks I should like to compare the phonemic systems of *Siebs*-German and *Boesch*-German, to show the interesting ways in which they differ.

Siebs-German has the following vowel system, presented here in terms of distinctive features:

Lax	Tense	Diphthongal	Unstressed	Long	Nasalized
ɪ ʏ ʊ	i y u				
ɛ œ ɔ	e ø o	ɔø	ə	ɛː	ɛ̃ œ̃ ɔ̃
ʌ	a	ae ao			ã

Redundant features and other details:

(1) The *Siebs* describes lax vowels as short, non-lengthenable, open (except /ʌ/), and as joined closely to a following consonant (*fester Anschluss*); they are also centralized, i.e., /ɪ/ is lower and more central than /i/, /ʊ/ is lower and more central than /u/, /ʌ/ is higher and hence more central than /a/, etc. Distributionally they are checked: they occur only before consonants.

(2) The *Siebs* describes tense vowels as short when unstressed, long when stressed, lengthenable, close (except /a/), and as joined loosely to a following consonant (*loser Anschluss*); they are also de-centralized, i.e., /i/ is higher and farther front than /ɪ/, /u/ is higher and farther back than /ʊ/, etc. Distributionally they are free: they occur before consonants, before vowels, and in word-final position. The *Siebs* describes /a/ as being only very slightly lower than /ʌ/, and treats length as if it were the relevant opposition between the two, writing /a/ vs. /aː/. The opposition between these two phonemes is suspended in unstressed position.

(3) The *Siebs* states clearly that the only two vowels in which length is the sole distinguishing feature are /ɛ/ and /ɛː/; it does not indicate whether this opposition is to be maintained in unstressed position. It should be added that /ɛː/ is a very unstable phoneme for many speakers of standard German: it is prescribed wherever the spelling shows the letter *ä* representing a long vowel, but many speakers—especially in the north—frequently substitute /e/ for it.

(4) The nasalized vowels occur only in words borrowed from French. *Boesch*-German has the following vowel system:

Short	Long	Diphthongal	Unstressed	Nasalized
$\begin{bmatrix} i \\ ɪ \end{bmatrix}\begin{bmatrix} y \\ ʏ \end{bmatrix}\begin{bmatrix} u \\ ʊ \end{bmatrix}$	i: y· u:	(iə yə uə)		
e	e: ø: o·		ə	
ɛ œ ɔ	ɛ·	ɔe		ɛ̃ œ̃ ɔ̃
a	a:	ae	ao	ã

Discussion:

(1) Two deviations from *Siebs*-German are minor and unimportant. First, where the *Siebs* prescribes /ɔø/, with lip rounding maintained throughout, the *Boesch* prescribes ɔe/, with rounded syllabic vowel but unrounded glide. (This is also the commonest prounuciation in Germany, despite the *Siebs*.) Secondly, *Boesch*-German uses the ingliding dipthongs /iə yə uə/ only in Swiss names spelled with *ie, üe, ue* (*uo*): *Brienz, Flüelen, Hueb* (*Ruoff*). These are therefore "foreign phonemes," used only in dialect loans, much like the nasalized vowels which are used only in French loans.

(2) Far more interesting are the following two differences between *Siebs* and *Boesch*: (a) where the *Siebs* prescribes lax (and, redundantly, open and centered) [ɪ ʏ ʊ], the *Boesch* permits either open [ɪ ʏ ʊ] (presumably not centered, following Swiss articulatory habits; the *Boesch* does not mention this feature) or close [i y u], depending on what the speaker uses in dialect speech; (b) the *Boesch* prescribes a contrast, similar to that in the dialects, between close /e/ and open /ɛ/:*Esche* vs. *Wäsche, Held* vs. *hält, wetten* vs. *hätten, Netz* vs. *Schätze*. These two deviations from the *Siebs* produce three structural changes in the system of the monophthongs. First, the vowel inventory is increased by one, through the addition of /e/. Secondly, the system of distinctive features is changed in that the opposition "short ≠ long," which is redundant in *Siebs*-German (except for /ɛ/ vs. /ɛ:/), now becomes relevant, replacing the opposition "lax ≠ tense." Thirdly, the long /ɛ:/ of *Siebs*-German is no longer structurally isolated (and hence unstable), but is now well integrated (and hence stable). (The *Boesch* mentions the common north German use of /e/ for /ɛ:/—[špe:t] *spät* rather than [špɛ:t]—as one of those north German prounuciations which are particularly offensive to Swiss ears.)

(3) Distribution. In *Siebs*-German, the lax vowels are checked, and hence occur only before consonants. In *Boesch*-German, the corresponding short vowel are checked in native words, but short open /ɛ/ occurs in word-final position in such French loans as *Bud-*

get, Couplet, Filet. (*Siebs*-German uses tense /e/ in words of this type.)

(4) Incidence. Though the short and long vowels of *Boesch*-German generally correspond, respectively, to the lax and tense vowels of *Siebs*-German, there is some difference in incidence. For example, the stressed vowels of the following words are tense in *Siebs*-German but short in *Boesch*-German: *Jagd, Krebs, Obst, Nische, düster, pusten, Art, Pferd, Geburt, Fabrik, Notiz, Wuchs.* Contrariwise, the stressed vowels of the following words are lax in *Siebs*-German but long in *Boesch*-German: *brachte, Rache, rächen, Amboss* (2nd syllable).

(5) Glottal stop. Previous to 1933, the *Siebs* prescribed the north German practice of using for all vowels in syllable initial position an allophone consisting of glottal stop plus vowel: [ˈʔʌlt] *alt,* [ˈʔoːnə]*ohne,* [fɛrˈʔaen]*Verein* [ˈʔübərˈʔʌl] *überall,* etc. In 1933 it made the glottal stop optional, but still prescribed a clear onset of the vowel (i.e., open juncture): /fɛr+ˈaen/, /ˈyːbər+ˈʌl/. The *Boesch* prescribes ONLY the latter treatment, without glottal stop. (Though the *Boesch* does not specifically say so, the glottal stop is another north German feature which the Swiss find objectionable.)

Siebs-German has the following consonant system, presented here in terms of distinctive features:

Stops,	voiceless	p	t		k	
	voiced	b	d		g	
Fricatives,	voiceless	f	s	š	[ç~x]	
Nasals						h
Liquids		v	z	ž	j	
		m	n			ŋ
	voiced	1	[r~ʀ]			

Redundant features and other details:

(1) Voiceless stops and fricatives are fortis; voiceless stops are also aspirated except when they are in close juncture with a following fricative.

(2) Voiced stops and fricatives are lenis. Distributionally they do not occur in word-final position.

(3) [ç] and [x] are in complementary distribution: [ç] occurs initially, after front vowels, after liquids and nasals, and in the diminutive suffix *-chen;* [x] occurs after non-front vowels. However,

[ç] has quasi-phonemic status: first because it occurs in -*chen*, regardless of what precedes it (i.e., even after non-front vowels); secondly because it is the voiceless counterpart of voiced /j/.

(4) The *Siebs* specifically describes /j/ as a voiced palatal fricative, corresponding to voiceless [ç], and states that it should not be pronounced as a semivowel. (This is contrary to widespread usage, especially in the south.)

(5) Though the *Siebs* sanctions the use of both apical [r] and uvular [ʀ], it expresses a preference for the former. Previous to 1933 it prescribed only [r]. It should be added that, though the ͏ *Siebs* condemns such a practice, popular pronunciation uses the allophone [ɐ̯] (non-syllabic, lower and farther back than [ə]) for postvocalic /r/. This is consistently used after tense vowels: ['tʰi:ɐ̯] *Tier* (vs. prevocalic [r~ʀ] in ['tʰi:rə~'tʰi:ʀə] *Tiere*). After short vowels it is used in free variation with [r~ʀ]: ['vɪɐ̯] or ['vɪr~ vɪʀ] *wirr* (vs. *prevocalic* [r~ʀ] in 'vɪrə~vɪʀə] *wirre*). Postvocalic /ər/ regularly gives the phone [ɐ] (syllabic), in which the syllabicity may be ascribed to the /ə/, the quality to the /r/: ['bɛsɐ] = /'bɛsər/ *besser* (vs. prevocalic [ər~ əʀ] in ['bɛsərə~ 'bɛsəʀə]=/'bɛsərə/*bessere*).

(6) The phoneme /ž/ occurs only in loanwords.

Boesch-German has the following consonant system:

Stops,	fortis	p	t		k
	lenis	b	d		g
Fricatives,	fortis	f	s	š	[ç~x]
					h
	lenis	v	z	ž	
Nasals		m	n		ŋ
Liquids		l	[r	ʀ]	
Semivowels		w		j	

Discussion:

(1) Stops. In *Siebs*-German, the relevant opposition which distinguishes /p t k/ from /b d g/ is "voiceless ≠ voiced;" redundant oppositions are "fortis ≠ lenis" and, in part, "aspirated ≠ unaspirated." In *Boesch*-German, on the other hand, all stops are voiceless. The relevant opposition which distinguishes /p t k/ from /b d g/ is therefore "fortis ≠ lenis." (On the redundant opposition "long ≠ short," see below.) Following the *Siebs*, the *Boesch* states that /p t k/ should be aspirated (presumably everywhere except in close juncture with a following fricative; details are not mentioned). This is in sharp

structural contrast with the dialects, where [pʰ tʰ kʰ] are clusters of two phonemes, and not allophones of single phonemes. For example, the phoenetic sequence [tʰuːt] gives three phonemes in *Siebs*-German /tut/, *Boesch*-German /tuːt/ (*er*) *tut*; but it gives four phonemes in dialect /thuːt/ *d'Huut* 'the skin' (standard *die Haut*).

(2) Fricatives. The only fricatives which the *Boesch* describes clearly are /s/ and /z/, and here *Boesch*-German differs from *Siebs*-German in just the same way as in the case of the stops. In *Siebs*-German, the relevant opposition which distinguishes /s/ from /z/ is "voiceless ≠ voiced;" the opposition "fortis ≠ lenis" is redundant. In *Boesch*-German, on the other hand, both /s/ and /z/ are voiceless; the relevant opposition which distinguishes them is therefore "fortis ≠ lenis." (On the redundant opposition "long ≠ short," see below.) The same opposition also distinguishes fortis /š/ (as in /ˈtaošen/ *tauschen*) and (voiceless) lenis /ž/ (as in /baˈgaːžə/ *Bagage*). Though the *Boesch* might not approve (it does not discuss the matter clearly), the same opposition is commonly used also to distinguish fortis /f/ (as in /ˈžlaːfen/ *schlafen*) and (voiceless) lenis /v/ (as in /ˈhaːvən/ *Hafen* or /ˈsklaːvən/ *Sklaven*). Some dialects likewise have an opposition between fortis /x/ and (voiceless) lenis /ɣ/; possibly their speakers also carry this habit over into standard German.

(3) [r∼ʀ]. The *Boesch* expresses no preference for either apical /r/ or uvular /ʀ/, but suggests simply that each speaker continue to use whichever allophone he already uses in his dialect speech. It is worth noting that the Swiss dialects do not show the allophone [ɣ] which is so common for postvocalic /r/ in Germany and Austria. Hence Swiss speakers have no trouble in following the *Siebs* prescription of [r] or [ʀ] even in postvocalic position.

(4) Long consonants. In the Swiss dialects, length is a redundant feature of fortis obstruents. Roughly speaking, fortis obstruents are long after short vowels: [ˈofːə] = /ˈofə/ *offen,* and half-long after long vowels: [ˈšlaːfˑə] = /ˈšlaːfe/ *schlafen,* and after consonants: [ˈhælfˑə] = /ˈhælfə/ *helfen.* Length is also a redundant feature of fortis nasals and liquids in those dialects which extend the opposition "fortis ≠ lenis" to this part of the consonant system: [ˈšwümːə] = /ˈšwümmə/ *schwimmen,* etc. The *Siebs* (p. 59) strongly condemns all such long allophones; the Boesch (p. 27) just as strongly supports them wherever the standard spelling writes double letters. Hence *Siebs* [ˈɔfən] = /ˈɔfən/ *offen* vs. *Boesch* [ˈɔfːən] =

/'ɔfən/; *Siebs*['gʌsə]=/'gʌsə/ *Gasse* vs. *Boesch*['gas:ə]=/'gasə/; *Siebs* ['štra:sə] = /'štrasə/ *Strasse* vs. *Boesch* ['štra:s·ə] = /'štra:sə/; etc.

(5) Semivowels. The *Siebs* states that /j/ should be articulated as a voiced palatal fricative, and thus classes it as an obstruent; the *Boesch*, on the other hand, states that it should be articulated as non-syllabic *i* and thus classes it as a semivowel. Concerning the phoneme represented by the letter *w*, the *Boesch* is less clear. The *Siebs* describes it as a voiced labiodental fricative, and hence makes of it an obstruent, transcribed /v/; the *Boesch*, on the other hand, states merely that *w* "ist stimmhaft und kräftig zu artikulieren" (p. 29). This description of *w* as "voiced" indicates that it is not an obstruent, since all *Boesch* obstruents are voiceless. Accordingly, I have classed *w* as a second semivowel, transcribed /w/. Presumably the *Boesch* accepts its dialect articulation as a non-syllabic vowel with slight bilabial and/or labiodental friction.

(6) *Siebs* /f/—/v/, *Boesch* /f/—/v/—/w/. In both word-initial and intervocalic position, *Siebs*-German shows only the two-way opposition /f/—/v/: voiceless /f/ in /'faen/*fein*,/ 'høfə/*Höfe;* voiced /v/ in /'vaen/ *Wein*, /'løvə/ *Löwe*. In word-initial position,*Boesch*-German also shows only a two-way opposition; but since fortis /f/ does not occur word-initially, it is not /f/—/v/ but rather /v/—/w/: (voiceless) lenis /v/ in /'vaen/ *fein*, (voiced) semivowel /w/ in /'wain/ *Wein*. In intervocalic position, however, *Boesch*-German shows the three-way opposition /f/—/v/—/w/: fortis (long) /f/ in /'ɔfən/ *offen*, (voiceless) lenis (short) /v/ in /'o:vən/ *Ofen* and /'høvə/ *Höfe*, (voiced) semivowel /w/ in /'løwə/ *Löwe*. *Siebs* /v/ regularly corresponds to *Boesch* /w/ (for some differences in incidence, however, see below); but *Siebs* /f/ corresponds both to /f/ and to /v/ in *Boesch*. As a result, *Boesch*-German has one more consonant phoneme than *Siebs*-German.

(7) Distribution. In *Siebs*-German, the opposition "voiceless ≠ voiced" is suspended in word-final position, where only voiceless obstruents occur. Thus, to illustrate with the examples cited in the *Boesch*, the words *grob, Sod, genug* end not in voiced /-b -d -g/ but in the same voiceless (and aspirated) /-p -t -k/ as *Stopp, Lot, Spuk*. In *Boesch*-German, on the other hand, the corresponding "fortis ≠ lenis" opposition is maintained in world-final position: the first three of these words end in (voiceless) lenis /-b -d -g/, the second three in fortis (and aspirated) /-p -t -k/. Though the *Boesch* does not mention it,

we may assume that fricatives also maintain the opposition "fortis ≠ lenis" in word-final positions: fortis /f/ in /ˈžaːf/ *Schaf* vs. lenis /v/ in /ˈbraːv/*brav;* fortis /s/ in /ˈhaes/ *heiss* vs. lenis /z/ in /ˈaiz/ *Eis.*

(8) Incidence. We have seen above that *Boesch*-German generally renders the *Siebs* voiced fricative /v/ with its voiced semi-vowel /w/: *Wein, Löwe,* etc. In a good many words of foreign origin, however, *Boesch*-German renders the *Siebs* voiced /v/ with its voiceless lenis /v/: *Klavier, November, Provinz,* etc. (Cf. *Boesch,* p. 29.) A far more striking difference in incidence concerns the suffix spelled *-ig.* Though *Siebs* /g/ is otherwise unvoiced to /k/, in this one suffix it is usually to be unvoiced to/ç/: voiced medial /g/ in /evɪgə/ *ewige,* but unvoiced final /ç/in /ˈevɪç/ *ewig.* This is yet another north German practice which is offensive and unacceptable to the Swiss. The *Boesch* therefore prescribes voiceless lenis /g/ both medially and finally: /eːwig/ *ewig* just like /ˈeːwigə/ *ewige.*

LINGUISTIC GUIDELINES FOR INTERMEDIATE FOREIGN LANGUAGE MATERIALS

PATRICIA O'CONNOR

Brown University

Nowadays, when we are asked to point to some contributions of linguistics to foreign language learning, we have a fairly impressive body of evidence. Since the days of the Army Specialized Training Programs, linguists have taken leading roles in the planning and preparation of materials for both teachers and students of foreign languages. Perhaps these contributions have been most impressive in the two fields of teaching English as a foreign language and teaching the "unfamiliar" or "exotic" languages to Americans, but linguistically-oriented materials have also been produced for the teaching of the "familiar foreign languages" in the schools and colleges of this country.

Gratifying as it is to observe these productions, covering a wide range of languages and teaching situations, it is still somewhat embarrassing to recognize that so far, linguistic insights have been very largely exploited only on the introductory phase of the language learning process. The Bloomfieldian doctrine of overlearning in beginning language study has been, as far as I know, unanimously accepted by linguists, and increasingly accepted by the general teaching profession, abetted by the development of electro-mechanical devices. It is probably fair to say that nowadays there is a fairly general competence in the profession to construct linguistically sound elementary language materials. There is now available an arsenal of drill devices and procedures, either "live" or on tape, to insure this habit formation through overlearning, mixed and varied with different degrees of pedagogical skill.

But beyond this introductory or lower-intermediate stage of habit formation, the linguist has not conspicuously contributed to an intelligent and functional transition from drill *on* the language to the ability to *use* the language. There are, of course, numerous reasons and justifications for the linguists' apparent lack of interest in the intermediate and advanced phases of the language learning process, but it is not our business today

401

to go into them. We can simply observe that as far as the teaching and learning public is concerned, we have had a lot to say about how to get started, but very little to say about what to do next. Tacitly, we have been like the mother in the "sick joke" of several years ago: in answer to the question "Mommy, when do we get to Europe?" She replies "Shut up and keep swimming!" And we know that far too many of our students quit swimming somewhere short of halfway across and never reach Europe, or anywhere else, linguistically.

Is it true that linguists can apply insights from their science only in the introductory, habit-forming phase of language study? Are there no insights in linguistics which can serve as guidelines for intermediate language learning? Let's be honest about it—to a certain extent, the answer has been "yes." The linguists' professional interest is in the formal system of the language—the expression system, the code. And the habits that the elementary learner must form are, beyond the phonology, very largely those of redundancies within the code: phenomena of agreement, order and phrase morphology.

The complex process of language habit formation has been institutionalized into five distinguishable stages. The first stage, recognition, involves the identification of the parts of a new word, construction, or idiom (the sounds or letters, the stems and/or endings, the parts of constructions and idioms) and the association with its meaning. The second stage, imitation, involves the learner's immediate echoing of a model performance. Stage three, repetition, is the learner's performance on the basis of his memory of his own earlier performance. The fourth stage, variation, involves the learner's performance, under close guidance, of phrases or sentences differing minimally from the ones he has previously imitated and repeated. Selection, the final stage, is the learner's choice of the particular phrase or sentence that is meaningfully appropriate to a particular situation from the repertory of statements, questions and requests he has mastered through the previous practice.

It will be observed that the three middle stages of imitation, repetition and variation, which, incidentally, account for approximately eighty per cent of classroom time on the introductory level, are sheer drill, aimed overwhelmingly at practicing the code, with relatively little attention to the "content" or "message" aspects of the language. For example, the various forms of the so-called pattern or substitution practice have as their object the manipulation of the code and are obviously unnatural as a succession of messages. Indeed, the typical pattern practice is a violation of the normal semantic redundancies of natural language: one deliberately chooses a "stem" which is compatible, though rarely inevitable, with each of a half-dozen variables. This overt focusing of attention on practice of the code is even more pronounced in the preceding stages of imitation and repetition, where the genuine message content is practically zero.

In the first and last of the five stages, recognition and selection, the learner is at least approximating real language behavior. The expert user of a language performs recognition with a very high degree of unconscious skill when he listens or reads and, as a speaker or writer, he performs processes of selection often of such complexity as to invite the descriptive label "generation." But during the introductory phases of language study, these linguistic behaviors are stringently controlled and guided. The students' success in recognition is made almost inevitable by the use of every pedagogical trick in the bag—gestures, pictures, native language glossings, or paraphrasings. And in many materials, the systematic recurrence of both lexical and grammatical items artificially averts the natural problem of partial or total forgetting. Practice of selection, too, is so carefully guided as to be almost a mockery in the elementary phases, for the students are led to "select" only those sentences which we know they have previously practiced through all the preceding stages.

The foregoing comments are certainly not intended as strictures. The introductory level is very properly one of concentration on structural habit formation through drill, and at this stage, attention on message-sending and receiving must yield at attention upon phonology and grammar. We all know that the danger of infractions of the code are greatest when the beginner is allowed freedom in the construction of messages and we must be primarily concerned with reinforcing control of the structures, rather than with the production of messages for their own sake. Naturally, the more this concentration on structure can take the form of imaginable and, if possible, interesting messages, the better—particularly for our younger, less carefully selected, less motivated learners. But in the grand strategy of language learning, drill on the code is the focus of the introductory phase. The degree of sugar-coating of the materials will vary according to the age and motivation of the beginning learner, but the pill is the same —drill to build up structural habits.

But despite the fact that the linguist's professional competence is primarily in the structure of the code, linguists do have knowledge about and interest in language as communication, and linguists can offer guidelines for the intermediate and advanced stages of language learning. In fact, the guidelines have existed for a long time; it is simply that only recently has it been possible to exploit them in the preparation of language teaching materials. If we remember that the intermediate stage of the language learning process is that of transition from a predominance of drill to a predominance of use of the language as communication, it follows that of the five stages, the middle three—imitation, repetition and variation— should gradually be allowed to atrophy on the second level of language learning. Correspondingly, the development of the skills in normal language behavior of recognition and selection must increasingly become primary objectives.

In the intermediate stage, it is above all the skill of recognition which requires development. Largely as a consequence of the attempt to eliminate the burden of lexical memory during the introductory phase so as to facilitate the formation of sound phonological and grammatical habits, the intermediate student has not had practice in using the clues of semantic and grammatical redundancy as means of recognition. The primary goal of the intermediate course is to develop these skills, and there are linguistic insights which are relevant.

One of these is the linguist's appreciation of the high redundancy of messages, the very considerable predictability of a particular item in a message, given the rest of the message as context. The linguist is also aware of the high degree of correlation in practical speech between the linguistic message and the factual, practical environment. We know that the user of a language is skilled in using such clues for recognition of the content of a message and can very nearly always "understand" by supplying a meaning even when an apparently important element of the message is lacking, be it a word with which he is not familiar, or a word acoustically obliterated by a slamming door or a loud sneeze. The linguist also knows that in natural language continua, most of the vocabulary has a very low frequency of occurrence. For example, of all the different word forms in a given continuum, between forty to fifty per cent of them occur once and only once, and approximately thirty per cent occur twice and only twice. Thus one can say that three-quarters of the different word forms in any "real" text or natural language continuum will occur within the text fewer than three times. When our language learner has become a user of the language and is no longer protected by the artificialities of our constructed language materials, he must be prepared to cope with this fact of language. We cannot possibly supply him in advance with *all* the vocabulary of *any* real text that he may read or any conversation that he may overhear or participate in. What we can and should supply is the skill in using the inner redundancy of messages and the correlation between linguistic messages and the real world.

Clearly, then, in the intermediate stage the artificial guidance to recognition must give way to practice in actively using all relevant clues; what we did for the student in the introductory stage, he must begin to do for himself. Of course, the shift cannot be an abrupt one; the withdrawal symptoms are too horrible. One symptom is panic. Other, probably related, symptoms are the compulsive dependence on a bilingual dictionary in which every unfamiliar word is looked up, or the faith-healing ritual of memorizing bilingual word lists and the shuffling of vocabulary cards. All of these, as language teachers know and linguists could predict, are fatal to the development of any usable skill in recognition.

Thus, the linguist's insight into the internal redundancy of messages and the frequency structure of a vocabulary determine the procedures of the intermediate language course as far as the development of the skill of recognition is concerned. They also call for some classroom procedures and devices of a rather new kind. Students will do what they are rewarded for doing. If we want them to develop skills in exploiting the internal redundancy of messages, we must reward them for doing just that, or even for trying to do it. The phrases "sensible guessing" and "toleration of vagueness" may be anathema in many classrooms, but they could well be slogans in an intermediate language course. Needless to say, there is every reason to continue in the intermediate course some degree of vocabulary control in order to reinforce the budding habit of using grammatical and semantic clues as an aid to recognition. But the purpose of the control is to maximize success at first, and to place upon the learner increasing responsibility for making sense out of the messages. A judicious use of pictures can help to simulate the correlation between a linguistic message and the practical environment. In practical life, if I hear the sentence "Look at that Cadillac with the funny XYZ on its roof!" I will know what an XYZ is as soon as I look at the roof of the Cadillac. As a language learner, if I see that sentence in print together with a picture of an XYZ on a Cadillac, I am similarly enlightened.

Two further aspects of intermediate course strategy for which the linguist can provide helpful guidelines are those of culture and stylistics.

As to culture, linguists have maintained an awareness of cultural anthropology inherited from the time of Boas, Sapir and Bloomfield, and, of course, professionally exemplified in many of our colleagues today. Hence, linguistics prescribes a realistic component of cultural content in a complete language learning program. It is obvious that an awareness of cultural patterns is an important component of skill in exploiting the semantic redundancy of messages. For example, we would want our students to be able to draw the proper conclusions from these two sentences: "Mr.

Cadwalader entered the room, followed by his devoted XYZ." (in which XYZ might be either a beagle or a butler), and "Mr. Yamamoto entered the room followed by his devoted XYZ." (in which XYZ is very probably Mrs. Yamamoto).

Many applied linguists are of the opinion that it is unwise to introduce drastically different cultural content at the beginning of a language course, especially for younger learners. There is enough shock in the performance of nonnative phonology and grammar in itself, and only after the learner has developed some confidence in the use of the language is it desirable to add differentness of culture as well. But the intermediate stage seems to be indicated as the proper one for the development of cultural sensitivity. Here too, a judicious selection of visual materials can go a long way in suggesting the differences and the similarities between the learner's culture and that of the foreign language.

As for stylistics, linguistic analysis reveals some considerable variation in both vocabulary and structures, corresponding to what we may call stylistic levels. Linguists are aware that stylistic distinctions are not random, nor matters of individual whim. They are not content with a simple dichotomy between standard and nonstandard, and insist that a useful command of a language must include an awareness of stylistic differences in, and control of, at least the two styles of formal written prose and cultivated, practical conversation. The widespread adoption of an aural-oral approach is ultimately justified by both linguistics and pedagogy on the grounds of the primacy of speech and of the greater effectiveness of oral practice in establishing grammatical as well as phonological habits. As a corollary, the content of the introductory language course is usually in a conversational style, and for a considerable time at the beginning of a total language program, it is probably advisable to work wholly or largely on one style level. But the beginning of practice on the level of formal prose, narrative and expository, should not be postponed indefinitely.

In various languages the conversational and formal styles show a considerable range of differences. We already know something about some of the important differences and are finding out more through computer-based research. As an observation of the practicalities, it seems fairly clear that in French, the formal prose style presents relatively less difficulty for the American learner than does authentic conversational material, while in German, the situation is certainly the reverse. Obviously a linguistically-based appraisal of learning needs and difficulties in the stylistic dimension is a guideline for the construction of intermediate language teaching materials.

It would be unrealistic to assume that the language habits practiced on the elementary level will automatically be maintained or improved with subsequent study of the language. Linguists are aware of the still insecure control of foreign language habits, many of them conflict with native language habits even after several hundred hours of guided and supervised practice. And linguists understand *why* there is often a retrogression, especially on the phonological level, as the primary focus of attention changes from practice on the code to practice with messages. As the learner becomes increasingly skillful in recognition and as his vocabulary increases, some of the foreign language morphemes and structures do indeed become habitual. This involves the danger that the very familiarity on the morphemic level may invite a resurgence of the native language pronunciation habits.

The basic shift, on the intermediate level, from the use of speaking-practice as a basis for reading to that of the use of more extensive reading to provide a basis for speaking is partly responsible for this problem. As Nelson Francis has pointed out, there is a significant and almost mutational evolution from "reading" in the sense of making noises in response to printed symbols to "real reading" skill within a tiny domain of controlled lexicon and structures. It may be noted parenthetically that while in "real reading" there is probably a nonvocalized accompaniment of the syntactic intonations, in "skimming," this accompaniment is missing. In any event, desirable as this direct association of printed image with language may be, the linguist is aware that it involves the elimination of the detour via speech: a "real reader" does not move his lips while he reads. Thus it may contribute to the problem of phonological retrogression as a concomitant of morphological and lexical progress. Awareness of the possibility of retrogression suggests that intermediate foreign language materials should include provision for systematic review and confirmation of desirable pronunciation habits at the known troublesome conflict points.

It is ironical to reflect that despite the general acceptance of the aural-oral approach, we must still be on guard against the grammar-reading method which made grammar a bore and reading a puzzle. As we know, the grammar-reading method is becoming extinct on the introductory level, but it is all too often revived later as the only available framework.

These observations suggest that the linguists' contribution to language learning need not end with the elementary phase of structural habits focussed on the code, but that on the contrary, linguistic insights on the nature of messages can supply guidelines for the intermediate level as well.

'SEQUENCE' AND 'ORDER'

F. R. PALMER

University College of North Wales, Bangor

Both speech and the linguist's description of it are, or at least are often considered to be, unidimensional, the first in time, the second horizontally along the written page. The problem to be discussed here is, in its simplest terms, 'How far if at all, ought this shared feature of unidimensionality to determine linguistic analysis?' To distinguish between the single time dimension of speech and the single horizontal dimension of linguistic structure, J. R. Firth used the terms 'sequence' and 'order'. The terms are not clearly defined by Firth; the relevant quotations are "In these structures one recognises the place and order of the categories. This, however, is very different from the successivity of bits and pieces in a unidimensional time sequence.", and "Elements of structure, especially in grammatical relations, share a mutual expectancy in an order which is not a sequence.".[1] A more detailed statement, which I believe to be a fair interpretation of Firth, is to be found in M. A. K. Halliday. "Structure is made up of elements which are graphically represented as being in linear progression; but the theoretical relation among them is one of 'order'. Order may, but does not necessarily have as its realisation, sequence, the formal relation carried by linear progression; sequence is at a lower degree of abstraction than order, and is one possible formal exponent of it. A structure is thus an arrangement of elements ordered in 'places'. Places are distinguished by order alone; a structure XXX consists of three places." [2]

Sequence, then, is of the observable speech events, **order** of the linguist's constructs. The problem is to decide to what extent sequence is, or should be, an **exponent** of order (I use, with Firth, the term 'exponent' for what Trubetskoy called 'realisation' and Pike 'manifestation'—Halliday's use is a little different). I am not suggesting that all features of speech in their

---

[1] J. R. Firth, "A synopsis of linguistic theory", *Studies in Linguistic Analysis* (Special volume of the Philolical Society, Oxford, 1957), 5 and 17.

[2] M. A. K. Halliday, "Categories of the theory of grammar", *Word*, 17, 3 (1961), 254-5.

most directly observable form are in sequence. It is merely that we are here concerned with those features that **are** sequential. For there can be no denying that in the utterance 'cat' the velar plosive precedes alveolar plosive and in *John hit Bill, John* precedes *Bill*. Nor, of course, am I unaware of the fact that not all linguistic statements are made in terms of an 'ordered' (linear) structure.

Two extreme views are obviously possible on the question 'What is the relation between sequence and order?'. First, we may say that order is wholly determined by sequence, the order of the linguistic elements is identical with the sequence of those parts of the speech events they are intended to characterize. This is implicit in what C. F. Hockett [3] has called the 'size-level' view of language, in which elements at each level occupy the same relative position as clusters of lower level elements of which they are composed. Secondly, we may say that order is wholly independent of sequence; if sequential features are relevant to the linguistic statement they are characterised by some means other than order. The point of view here is taken to its logical extreme by Hjelmslev and Uldall who say "in glossematic, as in logical algebra, ab is the same as ba . . . and the order in which functives are written should not be taken as having any significance.".[4] Unfortunately this is never developed; they go on "since . . . order is utilised as a distinguishing feature in the linguistic expression . . . it is obviously necessary to devise some means of differentiating, e.g. *fist* and *fits;* but that is a problem which does not concern us here and which will be dealt with later". But it is never dealt with.

The first view, though once firmly held, cannot be justified if we wish to make a statement in terms of ordered structure about any of the following characteristics of a language.

(a) Features such as discontinuity and conflation. The first implies that what is a single item in the structure has as its exponents two or more elements that are separated in sequence. Conversely the second implies that two or more items in the structure have a joint set of exponents that cannot be sequentially divided.

(b) Non-contrastive variations of sequence. If we do not wish to indicate these variations by a variety of structures we may set up one structure only, but clearly the order of the elements of this one structure cannot correspond to the variety of sequences. Halliday,[5] for instance, considers *The man came*(,) *from the Gas Board* where *the man . . . from*

---

[3] C. F. Hockett, *A manual of phonology, IJAL* Memoir 11, (1955), 15.

[4] L. Hjelmslev & H. J. Uldall, *Outline of glossematics* (Copenhagen, 1957), 45.

[5] Halliday, "Categories of the theory of grammar", 255, n. 33.

the Gas Board is a nominal group, contrasting with (and differing intonationally from) *The man came from the Gas Board* where *from the Gas Board* is an adjunct. The structure of the first is SP, of the second SPA. Unless I completely misunderstand him he is asserting that the first sentence is structurally the same as *The man from the Gas Board came*. It then follows that in no structural statement can the order of the elements correspond to both sequences.

(c) Contrastive variations of sequence. It is possible to handle these together in a single ordered structure, but in that case it again follows that the order of the elements cannot correspond to the varying sequences. An example is to be found in Hockett [6] when he suggests that *The body was found by a troop of boy scouts* may be regarded as *A troop of boy scouts found the body* and the morpheme {passive}. Clearly the structure cannot correspond to both sequences (and the morpheme {passive} has no corresponding element in sequence).

We have good reasons then for not trying to handle everything in terms of linear structure. (b) and (c) are indeed a justification for transformational analysis, but I will return to this later.

The second view, which disassociates order from sequence has, as far as I know, never been put fully into practice. It is obviously uneconomical. If our linguistic symbols are written in order, it is convenient to make order significant, and the simplest use is to indicate sequence. A different use of order is found in the Arabic numeral system; the Arabs realised, though the Greeks did not, that order alone could distinguish units, tens and hundreds. If order is not made significant, moreover, some arbitrary rule will be needed, so that we shall not indiscriminately write the same symbols in various orders, for this would create confusion. An arbitrary rule of this kind is found in chemistry where H_2O and not O_2H is written though nothing different could be indicated by the latter. But there is no point in having an arbitrary rule of this kind, if a non-arbitrary (and useful) rule is available. Yet there may be parts of the linguistic description where the disassociation of sequence and order is forced upon us.

If more than one linguistic level is recognised, we may, of course, make different decisions concerning the relations of sequence and order at each level. In phonology, for instance, we may decide that order is wholly determined by sequence, while in morphology it may be wholly independent of it. In that case, it will follow that there is a difference between the order of the elements at each of the two levels. When considering grammar, then, we may handle the problem not in terms of relations between order and

---

[6] Hockett, "Linguistic elements and their relations", *Language,* 37, 1 (1961), 51-2.

sequence, but of relations between the order of the grammatical elements. But it must not be assumed that there are no sequence/order problems in phonology. On the contrary there are problems of discontinuity, conflation and non-contrastive variation.[7] Contrastive variation is, as far as I know, not attested, but it could happen in theory; it might be convenient in a language to treat forms such as /pæt/ as an inverted form of /tæp/, /bæk/ of /kæb/, and so on.

Because of these difficulties, those linguistic theories that are in terms of linear structure compromise between the two extreme views. Order is **to some degree** determined by sequence. But there are two dangers here, one of saying too little about the relation of sequence and order, the other of saying too much.

First, there is the danger of not stating clearly when order is indicative of sequence and when it is not. Hockett [8] has insisted that morphemes are not **composed** of phonemes but are **represented** by them. It would have been consistent for him to continue with the statement that the order of the morphemes is not identical with the order of the phonemes (and therefore not with the sequence of the linguistic events), but that even between order at one level and order at another the relation is a representational one. In fact his notion of representation makes such a view inevitable. The morphemes of *took* and *liked* clearly cannot both be in the same order as the phonemes represented by them. It is worth contrasting here a consistent size-level interpretation such as that of B. Bloch.[9] Bloch interprets *took* as /tuk/ + /Ø/. Such an interpretation allows for the morphemes of both *took* and *liked* to be in the same order as their constituent phonemes.

The second danger is a more serious one. It is, or should be, fairly obvious that if order is made indicative of sequence, we cannot, without confusion or redundancy, further establish a linguistic element whose exponent is sequence. Yet this is done. Z. S. Harris [10] for instance, talks about morphemic order, even of 'morphemes of order'. Between the sentences *You saw Fred* and *Fred saw you* there is for Harris a difference consisting of a morphemic element. But these two sentences are not at all closely related linguistically. All that needs to be said to characterize them is that there is a structure in English which we may characterize NVN, and that *Fred* and *you* are both members of class N. The sequential features

[7] For a contrary view see A. Martinet, "Elements of a functional syntax", *Word*, 16, 1 (1960), 2.

[8] Hockett, *A manual of phonology*, 15.

[9] B. Bloch, "English verb inflection", *Language*, 23 (1947), 399-418.

[10] Z. S. Harris, *Methods in Structural Linguistics* (Chicago, 1951) 185-6; and "Discourse analysis", *Language* 28, 1 (1952), 18.

are taken care of by writing the two N's in different places in the structure; in a similar way the difference between /kæt/ and /tæk/ is handled by writing CVC, and noting that both /t/ and /k/ are members of C. There is not something called 'morphemic order' or 'phonemic order' over and above the statement in terms of the elements N and C and their class membership. Similarly, of course, there is no important mathematical relation between 14 and 41, except that the same symbols are used in a different order. Moreover the fact that order is significant implies that the same symbols **are** being used in different places in the structure.

The confusion is perhaps seen more clearly still in Halliday,[11] who has elements of structure S, P and O —Subject, Predicator and Object; one possible structure is SPO. But a 'crucial criterion' of S (and presumably of O) is its place in sequence. The mere fact, therefore, of writing the symbols in an order is sufficient for their differentiation. Nothing is gained and clarity is lost by writing **different** symbols; instead of S and O we need one symbol placed in the first and the third position. Because he distinguishes between S and O, Halliday is compelled to add yet another kind of distinctive symbolisation. He writes arrows over the symbols S and the P (S P) in order to indicate that sequence is an exponent of S, but it is only because he has distinguished between S and O that he now needs the arrows—to show that, except in terms of sequence, they are not different at all. If different symbols had not been used the arrows would not be necessary. We have then a double redundancy here, the second made necessary by the confusion created by the first. Of course, it may be argued that the justification for writing the separate symbols S and O is that it is not merely sequence that distinguishes them, but that there are the additional exponents of concord with the verb and of the form of the pronoun, and, indeed, that these are more important than sequence. For if we ignore intonation and juncture we can identify the subject and object of *Lots of money has she*. But if we treat concord, pronominal form, and sequential position as exponents, we no longer require order. We may write SPO, SOP, PSO, etc., without distinction. Here, then, at this level perhaps we should disassociate sequence and order. Why, then, does Halliday need two different symbols? There is a strong suspicion that S and O are not structural features of English, but some kind of universal (and notional?) feature of language. For he compares the English pattern in terms of S, P, and O with that of Latin; in Latin, of course, sequence is not an exponent of the distinction between the two.

Similar considerations hold for K. L. Pike's tagmemes, as long as a

---

[11] Halliday, "Categories of the theory of grammar", 257-8.

tagmeme is defined in terms of a particular place (slot) in a particular structure.[12] Yet some kind of tagmemic statement is essential if we wish to identify places in different structures, if for example (to use wholly traditional terminology) we wish to identify the object of an active verb with the subject of a passive one, or the subject of the first with the 'agent' of the second. Such identification is legitimate and indeed forced upon us if we undertake a transformational statement. We can use a set of symbols with subscripts, for instance, N_1 and N_2 such that *John* is N_1 and *Bill* N_2 in both *John saw Bill* and *Bill was seen by John,* but since it is customary in linguistics to use notionally informative labels for formally defined categories, terms such as 'actor' and 'goal' seem more appropriate.

Transformational analysis might seem to offer a solution (perhaps **the** solution) to all our problems. Ought not all that part of linguistic description that can be dealt with in terms of an order dictated by sequence be handled in the constituent structure rules and the remainder in the transformation rules?

In fact, this simple solution is not adopted and perhaps it cannot be adopted. For categories that involve sequence are included in the constituent structure section and the sequential problems are handled in the morphophonemic section of the grammar. An obvious example in the English progressive will be the rule Prog. → BE + ING and a morphophonemic rule that transfers ING to the end of the verb.

The basic difficulty is that sequential and non-sequential features of language are often exponents of closely related formal categories.[13] In English, for example, negation, if formally defined in terms of the /nt/ verbal formation, is closely connected with interrogation, if this is defined in terms of the change in the order of the subject and the verb. For both categories involve the auxiliary verbs. But while the former can be handled with no more difficulty (perhaps even less) in terms of linear structure than the past tense forms of the verb, the latter must be in terms of contrastive variations of sequence. (I do not think that the problem is seriously complicated by the introduction of DO since this can be treated morphophonemically as zero except where associated with /nt/.) Ought not, then, negation to be dealt with in the constituent structure rules and interrogation in the T-rules? N. Chomsky[14] does not do this, but recognises the structural relations between negation and interrogation and handles them together. But this means that he is forced to treat them both in the T-rules

---

[12] K. L. Pike, "A syntactic paradigm", *Language,* 39, 2 (1963), 216-230.

[13] C. E. Bazell, *Linguistic Form* (Istanbul, 1953), 57.

[14] N. Chomsky, *Syntactic Structures* ('s/Gravenhage, 1957), 61-65.

in spite of the fact that negation would so much more naturally belong to the constituent structure section of the grammar. R. B. Lees [15] on the other hand treats negation in constituent structure but interrogation in the T-rules and so fails to indicate the close relationship between the two categories.

Similar considerations hold for voice in English, for active and passive, vis-à-vis the other verbal categories of tense, progressive, and perfect. All of these are formed in English by means of the auxiliaries BE and HAVE. A grammar that brings out the structural relationships between them ought to handle them all together, but voice involves sequential relations of a much more complicated kind than those associated with the other categories. All four categories could, of course, be handled together either in the constituent structure rules or in the T-rules, but the solution offered by transformational grammars simply fails to handle them together at all; voice goes into the T-rules and the other categories into the constituent structure rules. [16]

One can therefore have a great deal of sympathy with Hockett when he suggests that passive could be treated as a morpheme in English. It is easy enough, of course, to show that this would greatly complicate the morphophonemic statement and this is obviously the reason why transformational grammars do not handle it in the constituent structure section. But if one talks, as Chomsky does, of "deep underlying regularity", [17] or as P. M. Postal does of "accounting for formal structures", [18] it is surely necessary that passive should be handled together with past, perfect and progressives. One can argue with some conviction that these categories differ only in the nature of their exponents.

Leaving aside the entirely different problem of embedding transformations, we may well ask what in principle distinguishes constituent structure rules and T-rules if the order/sequence relation does not. It seems that the distinction relies upon the **word** in that morphophonemic rules involving sequence are permitted **only** where there is change of sequence within the **word** (as with negative, progressive and perfect), and not between words

---

[15] R. B. Lees, *The Grammar of English Nominalizations* (Publication of the Indiana University Research Center in Anthropology, Folklore and Linguistics) (second edition), 19 & 36.

[16] Lees op. cit., C. J. Fillimore, "The position of embedding transformations in a grammar", *Word,* 19, 2 (1963), 225 & 228.

[17] Chomsky, *Syntactic Structures,* 68.

[18] P. Postal, *Constituent Structure: a study of contemporary models of syntactic description* (Publication 30 of the Indiana University Research Center in Anthropology, Folklore and Linguistics, 1964), 74.

as with passive and interrogation. The distinction then rests upon a definition of the **word** or its acceptance as given in its traditional form. The usual explanation is that in constituent structure rules we are limited to the rewriting of one symbol at a time. But this does not help make the distinction. For we can easily handle passive interrogation, etc., in this way merely by leaving the more difficult order/sequence problem to the morphophonemics. A different point is made by Lees,[19] that the constituent structure section allows us to formalize the notion of grammatical category; but this too is not a satisfactory explanation since passive and negative are as much grammatical categories as past, perfect and progressive.

Transformational grammar, then, disguises the problem of the relation between sequence and order. It does not answer it. The problem is still there though it may have been banished to the unexplored field of what C. E. Bazell has called "pregrammatical statement", which is "neutral with regard to different grammatical statements and indeed basic to . . . them".[20] Perhaps we need a pre-grammatical statement in which order is utterly divorced from sequence. Here and here alone, moreover, may we make 'God's truth' judgements about what are 'correct' and 'incorrect' interpretations of structure (in the widest sense), leaving us free for the sake of 'simplicity', 'economy', etc., to make 'hocus-pocus' statements based upon this interpretation in the grammar proper. For there is no reason to suppose that the criteria of simplicity and correctness will converge. Perhaps we should say, then, that it is only in the grammatical statement in this very restricted sense (where we are concerned with the purely practical task of stating formulaically our findings), that the problem of 'To what extent is order determined by sequence?' should arise.

---

[19] Lees, *The Grammar of English Nominalizations*, 2.

[20] Bazell, *Linguistic Typology* (School of Oriental and African Studies, University of London, 1958).

SOME ASPECTS OF CHINANTEC GRAMMAR:
A TAGMEMIC VIEW

CALVIN R. RENSCH

Summer Institute of Linguistics

In the literature dealing with grammatical structure, a wide variety of theoretical frameworks is represented. One system, the tagmemic view, recognizes the tagmeme as the basic unit of grammar. Pike describes this unit as "the functional slot with its class filler." [1] Longacre elaborates: "Of considerable importance here is the correlativity of substitution point and class. A substitution point does not exist apart from the occurrence of some linguistic item or sequence belonging to some class. On the other hand, class itself has no reality apart from occurrence of items and sequences at certain substitution points." [2]

Another element of the tagmemic system is the hypertagmeme. [3] The hypertagmeme is a grammatical structure composed of one or more tagmemes which is itself a unit on some level of analysis and which functions as a distributional matrix for tagmemes on the same or other levels of analysis.

The analytical levels commonly include word, phrase and clause, but for any particular language may include levels above, below, or between these. The number of levels is determined by the language under attention, not by an a priori figure. The hypertagmemes of the language are the contrasting types of words, phrases, clauses, etc.

The concept of the tagmeme is applied at the various levels without initially recognizing a morphology-syntax division. Further analysis may demonstrate that the distinction between word and phrase levels must be recognized for a given language; but uniform procedures are, nevertheless, applied throughout the range of grammatical levels.

---

[1] K. L. Pike, "Grammemic Theory," *General Linguistics,* II (1957), 36.

[2] Robert E. Longacre, "String Constituent Analysis," *Language,* XXXVI, 1 (1960), 63.

[3] The hypertagmeme of Longacre differs somewhat from the obligatory complex structure of Pike. Cf. K. L. Pike, *Language in Relation to a Unified Theory of the Structure of Human Behavior* (Santa Ana, 1st ed. 1954), and Longacre, *op. cit.*

One of the tasks of grammatical description, then, consists of describing the contrasting hypertagmemes together with a presentation of their tagmemic constituency. It is a fragment of this task to which this paper addresses itself: a study of the contrastive clause-level hypertagmemes of Lalana Chinantec,[4] an Amerindian language of southern Mexico. Although only the independent affirmative clauses—taken from a considerable body of text—are under attention at this time, the present description is intended to be indicative of the manner in which the total grammar of a language may be analyzed.

One of the areas of greatest interest in tagmemic studies has been that of developing and consistently applying criteria for distinguishing hypertagmemes, i.e., for deciding when two structures are in contrast. The various writers are not unanimous as to their criteria, but Longacre states: "A criterion may be framed as follows: two strings on the same level are hypertagmemically distinct if (1) they exhibit at least two structural differences relative to each other, and (2) if these differences are relevant either to both obligatory and optional tagmemes in the two strings, or to more than one obligatory tagmeme." [5]

In accordance with Longacre's criterion, the equational type clause of Lalana Chinantec can be distinguished from other independent affirmative clause-level hypertagmemes. First, in the equational clause no verbal element is obligatory or, for that matter, normally present. In the other clause-level hypertagmemes, however, the only obligatory grammatical slot is that filled by a verbal element. Secondly, the equational clause type—by its very nature, the identification of one item with another equivalent item—requires two tagmemes. In the other types, only one tagmeme, the Predicate, is obligatory. Thus, by Longacre's criterion, the equational clause type of Lalana Chinantec contrasts with other independent affirmative clause types of the language because (1) two structural differences exist between this and other clause types and (2) these differences are relevant to more than one obligatory tagmeme.

Grammatical structures can be described by tagmemic formulae. The structure of the equational clause type of Lalana Chinantec may be described in a formula [6] as follows:

$$\text{Eq cl} = +\,\text{Iden}:\text{N} + \text{Item}:\text{Nom dep cl}/\text{N}/\text{pro}$$

---

[4] A Chinantec clause is a "non-co-ordinating, nonsubordinating" construction with a single predicate or predicate-like tagmeme. Cf. Longacre, *op. cit.*, and B. F. Elson and V. B. Pickett, *Beginning Morphology-Syntax* (Santa Ana, 1962).

[5] Longacre, *op. cit.*, p. 75.

[6] A simple system of abbreviations is normally adopted to shorten the formulae,

The Equational clause is tagmemically composed of an obligatory Identification slot filled by a Noun phrase and an obligatory Item slot filled by a
Nominal dependent clause, a Noun phrase, or a pronoun.

The Equational clause type may be illustrated by sentence 1.

1. ši³yu̧·³   kye·n²³ma̧²na̧¹   ʔnȩ·ʔ²³
    baby   my   you (pl.)
    'You are my babies.' [7]

The remaining independent affirmative clause types of Lalana Chinantec,
which may be termed Verbal clause types, are further subdivided into
Declarative and Imperative groups. There are a number of structural
differences which distinguish these two groups of clause types. First, the
Predicate slot of the Imperative clauses is filled exclusively by Imperative
verb phrases, whereas the Predicate slot of the Declarative clauses never is.
The following are ways in which the Imperative verb phrases are distinguished from other verb phrases: (a) different forms of the negative
occur: the ʔa²³ form is used in Imperative verb phrases as opposed to the
ʔa²³hyaʔ³ form used in Declarative verb phrases; (b) the verbal modifier
slot filled by adjective stems follows the verb in Imperative verb phrases,
whereas it precedes the verb in Declarative verb phrases; and (c) verb
forms can occur with only one prefix, ri³-, which appears only with the
negative in the Imperative verb phrases, whereas fuller lists of prefixes occur
in Declarative verb phrases. Secondly, the rarely occurring optional Subject
tagmeme of the Imperative clause types must follow the Predicate tagmeme,
whereas in the Declarative clause types the optional Subject tagmeme may
precede the Predicate or follow it.

Inasmuch as there are several types of Imperative and Declarative

---

although, of course, terms can be written in full. In the formula for the Equational
clause type, for example, Eq cl refers to 'Equational clause', Iden to 'Identification
slot', N to 'Noun phrase', pro to 'pronoun', Nom dep cl to 'Nominal dependent
clause'. Although systems of notation vary among writers, the following conventions are generally followed: To the left of an '=' is placed the designation of the
hypertagmeme under attention; to the right are listed the constituent tagmemes of
that structure. '+' preceding a tagmeme symbol indicates that that tagmeme is
obligatory to the hypertagmeme; '±' indicates that that tagmeme is optional to the
hypertagmeme. ':' is placed between the slot and the filler of a tagmeme. '/' is placed
between alternate fillers of a slot. Capital letters are used to symbolize clause- or
phrase-level slots and also filler classes whose analysis is relevant on the clause or
phrase level.

[7] Raised numerals following each syllable indicate the tone pattern of that syllable; ¹ indicates the highest of three tone levels. Other symbols are used with their
common values.

clauses, formulae and illustrations will await the description of the individual types.

Four Declarative clause types are distinguished: Transitive, Intransitive, Impersonal and Adjective clause types. The first evidence for differentiating these clause types is that of the differing kinds of verb phrases which fill the Predicate slots. These verb phrases are distinguished principally by differing groups of verb stems and, also, by the affixes with which they co-occur. Those verb stems occurring in Transitive verb phrases filling the Predicate slot in Transitive clauses are labeled stems *a* and *b'*. Those occurring in Intransitive verb phrases are labeled stems *b* and *c*. Thus, stems *a* occur only in Transitive phrases and stems *c* occur only in Intransitive phrases. Stems *b,* however, occur in Intransitive phrases and stems *b'* occur in Transitive phrases. Stems *b'* are so labeled because they consist of the roots of stems *b* plus a tone and/or vowel replacive morpheme. Those stems occurring in Impersonal verb phrases are labeled stems *d* and those occurring in Adjective verb phrases stems *e*. Correlated with these differences in stem sets is the difference in affix sets. In Transitive verb phrases set A affixes occur. In Impersonal and Adjective verb phrases, set C affixes occur. In Intransitive verb phrases, some verb stems occur with set C affixes and others occur with set B which is identical with set A, plus the additional affix si^3- 'habitual action' which does not occur with Transitive verb phrases.

These different verb phrases, established as contrastive by the above and other criteria, correlate with other differences in the clause to separate the four Declarative clause types. Thus, in the Transitive clause type the optional Subject tagmeme is rare and no more than one other tagmeme, besides the obligatory Predicate and the Object, regularly occurs, be it Subject or other optional tagmeme. In the Impersonal clause type, only the optional Subject occurs in addition to the Predicate. In the Adjective clause type, the optional Subject tagmeme regularly occurs and, at times, one other tagmeme has been observed. Finally, in the Intransitive clause type, the Subject occurs in a majority of the illustrations observed and in addition to the Predicate and Subject, up to three optional tagmemes occur.

The Transitive clause type is further distinguished by occurrence of an optional Object, which never occurs in the other three types. The Intransitive clause type is further distinguished by occurrence of an optional Accompaniment tagmeme which never occurs in the other three types.

The various criteria by which the four Declarative clause types are distinguished are now summarized:

Transitive clause type: Transitive verb phrase with stems *a* or *b'* and affix set A; optional Object; rarely occurring Subject or one other tagmeme other than Object; no Accompaniment tagmeme.

Intransitive clause type: Intransitive verb phrase with stems *b* or *c* and affix set B or C; no Object; usual Subject plus up to three other optional tagmemes; optional Accompaniment tagmeme.

Impersonal clause type: Impersonal verb phrase with stems *d,* affix set C and no person-marking suffixes; no Object; usual Subject but no other optional tagmeme.

Adjective clause type: Adjective verb phrase with stems *e* and affix set C; no Object; optional Subject with one other optional tagmeme permitted.

The structure of the Transitive clause type of Lalana Chinantec may be formularized as follows:

$$\text{Trans cl} = +\text{P:Trans } V \pm \text{O:Cl/N/pro} \pm \frac{\text{S:N/pro}}{\text{L:Loc cl/N}_{\text{loc}}\text{/Loc/nom}}$$

The Transitive clause is tagmemically composed of an obligatory Predicate slot filled by a Transitive verb phrase; an optional Object slot filled by a Clause, a Noun phrase, or a pronoun; and (1) an optional Subject slot filled by a Noun phrase or a pronoun, or (2) an optional Location slot filled by a Locational (dependent) clause, a Noun phrase with a locational noun as head, a Locational (prepositional-type) phrase, or a nonexpandable nominal, or (3) neither of those tagmemes.

To the formula for the Transitive clause should be appended the following statements:

(1) The Object may precede the Predicate with focus on the Object; when filled by a clause or a Noun phrase containing the Quantifier tagmeme, the Object slot regularly precedes the Predicate.

(2) More rarely, the Subject or Location may precede the Predicate.

The Transitive clause type may be illustrated by sentences 2, 3 and 4.

2. bi²³   ka²³hmẹʔn²³   mịh³   kyeʔ²   za³   he²   hen³¹nạ¹   nị̈³
                              his-   where
   very mistreated   woman house person   live-I   there
   'The man where I live really mistreated his wife.'

3. ka²³teʔn²teʔ²³   ʔwvh²³
   they-made-fall   ground
   'They made him fall to the ground.'

4. bi²³   mạ²³ʔnẹ³   ñụ·hn³   hmị·h²   rị̈²hmẹ·²ra²
                         many
   very   exceedingly   days   we will do
   ta²   kyeʔ²   nụ·³
   work   of   jungle
   'For very many days we'll clear land.'

The structure of the Intransitive clause type of Lalana Chinantec may be formularized as follows:

Intrans cl $= +$P:Intrans V $\pm$ S:Loc cl/N/pro $\pm$ Acc:Acc
$\pm$ L:Loc cl/N_{loc}/Loc/nom

The Intransitive clause is tagmemically composed of an obligatory Predicate slot filled by an Intransitive verb phrase; an optional Subject slot filled by a Locational (dependent) clause, a Noun phrase, or a pronoun; an optional Accompaniment slot filled by an Accompaniment phrase invariably introduced by the form kyą?[2] 'with'; and an optional Location slot filled by a Locational (dependent) clause, a Noun phrase with a location noun as head, a Locational (preposition-type) phrase or a nonexpandable nominal.

To the formula for the Intransitive clause should be appended the following statements:

(1) The Subject may precede the Predicate with focus on the Subject; when filled by a Noun phrase containing the Quantifier tagmeme, the Subject slot regularly precedes the Predicate.

(2) The Location may precede the Predicate but does not normally do so when the slot is filled by a Locational (dependent) clause.

(3) Not uncommonly, the Location tagmeme is repeated; both occurrences may follow the Predicate or one may precede it.

(4) The Locational (dependent) clause has not been observed to fill both the Subject and Location slots in the same clause.

The Intransitive clause may be illustrated by sentence 5.

5. tah³   la²³   ñę?n²³ną²³   kyą?n²³²ną¹   ši³yų·³
    early   I-go-home   with-I   baby
    kye·n²³ną²³   ?a³mį²?a·h²³
    my   tomorrow
    'Early tomorrow morning I'm going home with my baby.'

The structure of the Impersonal clause type may be formularized as follows:

Impers cl $= +$P:Impers V $\pm$ S:Ind cl/N

The Impersonal clause is tagmemically composed of an obligatory Predicate slot filled by an Impersonal verb phrase and an optional Subject slot filled by an Independent clause or a Noun phrase.

To the formula for the Impersonal clause should be appended the following statement:

Commonly, the Independent clause filling the Subject slot is discontinuous if some constituent tagmeme of the clause precedes the Predicate tagmeme, inasmuch as the Predicate:Impersonal verb phrase tagmeme immediately precedes the Predicate of the Independent clause filling the Subject slot.

The Impersonal clause type may be illustrated by sentence 6.

6. ?a²³hya?³   li·h²   ri̧²hi·²ra²   nu̧?²   kye?²te?²³
    not   is-   we-will   brush-   of-them
                 permitted   clear   land
    'We aren't permitted to work their land.'

The structure of the Adjective clause type of Lalana Chinantec may be formularized as follows:

Adj cl = + P:Adj V ± S:N ± Loc:Loc cl/N_{loc}/Loc/nom

The Adjective clause is tagmemically composed of an obligatory Predicate slot filled by an Adjective verb phrase; an optional Subject slot filled by a Noun phrase; and an optional Location slot filled by a Locational (dependent) clause, a Noun phrase with a location noun as head, a Locational (preposition-type) phrase, or a nonexpandable nominal.

No variation from this order has been observed; this is probably because the sequence of classes noun-adjective would be interpreted as a Noun phrase rather than as constituents of a clause construction.

The Adjective clause type of Lalana Chinantec may be illustrated by sentence 7.

7. li²?o̧·³   mi̧³¹gwi·³   šu̧n²³na̧²³   hmi̧·h²   mi̧²ho³
    dark   sky   all   day   back-then
    'Back then the sky was always dark.'

In addition to the four Declarative clause types described above, the Verbal clauses of Lalana Chinantec include two Imperative clause types: the Transitive and Intransitive imperative clause types.

The evidence by which these types are distinguished from each other is similar to that by which the corresponding Declarative types are distinguished. The presence or absence of an optional Object tagmeme is correlated with the use of the Transitive imperative verb phrase and the Intransitive imperative verb phrase respectively. Imperative clauses are sufficiently rare as to leave uncertain which additional tagmemes occur, but probably the composition approaches that of the corresponding Indicative types.

The Transitive imperative clause type of Lalana Chinantec may be formularized as follows:

Trans imp cl = + P:Trans imp V ± S:?ni̧³ ± O:N/pro

The Transitive imperative clause is tagmemically composed of an obligatory Predicate slot filled by a Transitive imperative verb phrase and an optional Subject slot filled by the pronoun ?nį³ 'you' and an optional Object slot filled by a Noun phrase or a pronoun.

The Transitive imperative clause type of Lalana Chinantec is illustrated by sentence 8.

8. ku³?en³   kye·²³   kye?²   za³
   go-pick   flesh   of   person
   'Go pick off some human flesh!'

The Intransitive imperative clause type of Lalana Chinantec may be formularized as follows:

Intrans imp cl = + P:Intrans imp V ± S:?nį³

The Intransitive imperative clause is tagmemically composed of an obligatory Predicate slot filled by an Intransitive imperative verb phrase followed by an optional Subject slot filled by the pronoun ?nį³ 'you'.

The Intransitive imperative clause type is illustrated by sentences 9 and 10.

9. gwʌ?n³
   go-home
   'Go home!'

10. gwɨn³   ?nį³
    sleep   you
    'Sleep!'

In the course of this discussion of contrastive clause-level hypertagmemes, only occasional reference has been made to internal composition of lower level hypertagmemes, such as phrases and words, and this only to distinguish between contrasting fillers of diagnostic tagmemes in the various clause types. Of course, a complete statement would include such treatment. Likewise, a complete statement would draw attention to the distribution of hypertagmemes in differing matrices as a means of establishing structural differences. It would also utilize differences of transformational relationship to distinguish structural types. These methods, as well as those demonstrated in this paper, are useful in presenting the grammatical structure, not only of clause-level structures, but also of structures at all levels of the grammatical hierarchy.

GRAMMATICAL MODELS AND LANGUAGE LEARNING

Sol Saporta, Arthur L. Blumenthal and Donald G. Reiff

Presented by Sol Saporta

University of Washington

The ultimate purposes of a series of studies currently being conducted at the University of Washington are two-fold: (1) to provide behavioral correlates for three theoretical models of grammatical description and (2) to demonstrate how in a specific language-learning situation, certain models facilitate second-language acquisition.[1]

Chomsky has demonstrated that essentially three models underlie most generative grammars: a finite state model, a phrase structure model and a transformational model. He has pointed out the limitations of the first two both from the point of view of generative potential and overall simplicity of description. That the three models are increasingly powerful seems clear. Indeed, it is apparent from a simple characterization of them that this must be the case, since a phrase structure grammar does not preclude a finite state type of rule, but rather adds a different type of rule as well, and similarly for a transformational grammar.

Consequently, we are not trying to provide additional evidence of a purely logical sort for what we feel has already been adequately demonstrated. Rather, we accept the proposition submitted by Chomsky and ask what kind of experimental situations can be set up which will show differences in learning behavior which correspond to the different grammatical models. Phrased in the most general terms, we are concerned with demonstrating that, all other things being equal, the learning of language can be affected by the grammatical model underlying the presentation, and, of course, that the difference will be in the predicted direction.

The following grammatical drills may serve as illustration of the different approaches:

a) *FS:* Students are given a stem, e.g., *The man saw*—, and are asked

---

[1] This study is supported under contract OE-2-14-010 with the Office of Education under title VI of the National Defense Education Act.

to provide appropriate items such as *John* (*The man saw John*), *him, trees, poorly* (*The man saw poorly*), etc. The process of formulating grammatical sentences is thus viewed as a series of selections of items from some inventory, each selection of subsequent events being conditioned by antecedent events.

b) *PS:* Students are presented with a particular pattern and expansions of one segment of the pattern for substitution in the appropriate position: thus, for example, with a model *The man saw John,* the student might be asked to substitute *his friend* for *John* (*The man saw his friend*), *his good friend, his very good friend,* etc. Underlying such a drill, is the view that what is essentially the same pattern may be represented by different combinations of word-classes, introducing a hierarchy of levels, according to which, for example, *John* and *his very good friend,* of different internal structures, may nevertheless substitute for each other in larger sequences. The two are essentially different representations of the same construction, in this case a noun phrase.

c) *T:* Students are presented with a pattern and are required to perform a number of changes necessary to convert it into a different but related pattern. Thus, presented with a stimulus, *The man saw John,* a student must make a response indicating awareness of the relationship of patterns: *Did the man see John?,* or *John was seen by the man,* etc. In addition to the hierarchical levels of PS, this drill is based on exploiting relationships between sentences.

Now the above are drills, not grammars, and the current studies are not concerned with questions of pedagogy or of certain teaching techniques. The variable which we are concerned with isolating is the underlying grammatical model.

It soon became clear that there were at least two notions about which we had made assumptions, but about which we had not been sufficiently explicit. Our first job then was to define what kind of behavior could appropriately be called 'learning a language' and furthermore, to determine in what sense and to what extent we could talk about 'all other things (except the underlying model) being equal'. The preliminary pilot studies described here are aimed at clarifying these questions.

We assumed that we could write two grammars for the same corpus: say, a finite state grammar and a phrase structure grammar and then use these grammars as a basis for presenting material to two groups of subjects.

Such a requirement seemed to provide the best kind of experimental controls, since it made it possible in theory at least to eliminate all variables but the underlying grammatical model. But in so doing, we diluted the advantage of the phrase structure model, since we were now restricted to use languages which could be described adequately by either generating device, and, as Chomsky has pointed out, the advantage of a phrase structure grammar is precisely that it can account for certain properties of language which can not be handled by a simpler theory. In effect, then, we were arguing that if we could demonstrate that a phrase structure presentation could facilitate learning for languages which both models could describe, then it would follow that such a presentation would *have* to facilitate learning for a language which only the phrase structure model could describe. Figure I shows two such grammars which are the basis for the studies described here. Each grammar is presumably the simplest one in keeping with the model and each generated the same corpus, a total of 40 sequences of varying lengths.

The difference between the grammars is that for a finite state grammar all symbols to the right of the arrow are terminal symbols, whereas in a phrase structure grammar, the symbols A and B which occur to the right of the arrow and subsequently to the left of the arrow are not terminal symbols, but reflect something of the abstract nature of immediate-constituent analysis. In both cases, braces represent obligatory elements; angles represent optional elements. The branching diagram represents the derivation of one sequence, namely GNXNS.

In the first experiment, nonsense symbols were substituted for the

FIGURE I

A. Finite State Grammar

$$S \rightarrow \langle G \rangle N \begin{Bmatrix} X(\langle G \rangle N) \\ S \end{Bmatrix} \left\langle \begin{matrix} X(\langle G \rangle N) \\ S \end{matrix} \right\rangle$$

B. Phrase Structure Grammar

1. $S \rightarrow A\ B\langle B \rangle$
2. $B \rightarrow \begin{Bmatrix} X\langle A \rangle \\ S \end{Bmatrix}$
3. $A \rightarrow \langle G \rangle N$

C. Sample Derivation

terminal symbols, G being represented by #, N by ||, X by § and S by /. These symbols were substituted to avoid any built-in associations that the letters might have which might prejudice the data. But this results in a rather odd use of the word 'language'. In fact, the sequences of nonsense symbols lack both a phonological component and a semantic component, since they are neither pronounceable nor particularly meaningful. But they do have a syntactic component, since there are clear restrictions on the combinatorial possibilities. Hence, what we are concerned with at this stage is not so much the learning of language, but the learning of syntax.

The first three experiments, which, incidentally, yielded negative results may serve to illustrate the nature of the problem.

In the first experiment, subjects were shown each one of the 40 sequences generated by the grammars at a rate of 5 seconds each. After this, subjects saw 80 sequences composed of the same nonsense symbols. Forty of these were the same sequences as shown before, and 40 were new arrangements of the symbols not dictated by the grammar, that is, non-grammatical sequences. The two groups of sequences had been randomly mixed to form a list of 80 which was then presented to each subject on a memory drum. The subject's task was to identify those sequences that he recognized as having been shown before, that is, to distinguish grammatical from ungrammatical sequences.

The independent variable which distinguished three groups of subjects consisted of three different systems of placing spaces between symbols within the various sequences originally shown to the subjects. In group one, a space appeared after each symbol so that only a finite state description was immediately apparent for a particular sequence. In group two, a space appeared between those symbols which were divided by the major immediate constituent boundaries which derive from the phrase structure grammar. In group three, spaces were inserted between symbols at random, using a table of random numbers. Here, the number of spaces that occurred per sequence was equated with those in group two. Thus, three types of groupings of symbols were arranged on the basis of three different schemes: (1) a finite state arrangement, (2) a phrase structure arrangement and (3) a random arrangement. An analysis of variance statistic computed for differences between the three groups yielded no significant differences under the three conditions.

The second experiment was a replication of the first with one change. Instead of using the four nonsense symbols as vocabulary items, four numbers, 3, 5, 2 and 8 were used. It was hoped that this would reduce the extreme differences among subjects in the use of mnemonic devices.

Indeed, we found that although we had tried to eliminate the phonological and semantic variables by the use of nonsense symbols, subjects almost invariably resorted to naming the symbols—presumably in order to facilitate recall. In any case, substituting numbers yielded no significant difference among the groups.

We then felt that perhaps the 80-item test list might have been inadequate. It was biased in favor of the finite state group, since no spacing was used on the test list. This is, on the test, the phrase structure group saw the same list as the finite-state group, and the immediate constituent boundaries were not indicated on the test sequences. Therefore, it was decided to replicate experiment 2 with test lists appropriate to each group. Essentially, for the phrase structure and random groups, spaces were maintained in the 40-test list sequences and spaces were inserted at random in the 40 ungrammatical items within the list. The difference in the test items in experiments 2 and 3 is illustrated in Figure II. The analysis of variance results approached, but did not reach statistical significance.

These three pilot studies demonstrate a number of things including the obvious fact that it is possible and almost easy to design poor experiments. It should be made explicit that the negative results reflect on the inadequacy of the experimental design and not on the proposition that a phrase structure grammar is superior to a finite state grammar, a proposition convincingly demonstrated on independent theoretical grounds. At best, such experiments can only demonstrate that, in searching for empirical evidence, there may be limitations to the kind of learning situations in which this superiority is relevant.

FIGURE II

A. Experiments 1, 2, 3
$$G = \# = 3$$
$$N = \| = 5$$
$$X = \S = 2$$
$$S = / = 8$$

B. Experiments 2, 3

Test lists in Experiment 2 all groups	Test lists in Experiment 3 Te FS	PS	Random
3 5 8	3 5 8	3 5 8	3 5 8
*2 8 5	*2 8 5	*2 8 5	*2 8 5
2 3 8 5	2 3 8 5	23 8 5	2 3 85
5 2 5 2 5	5 2 5 2 5	5 25 25	5 2 525
. . . .	. . . .	. . . . . .	. . . . . .

* = ungrammatical.

Implicit in the previous studies was the view that the learning of syntax was essentially the ability to distinguish grammatical from ungrammatical sequences after only one presentation. The next attempt had a different orientation.

Using the same grammars as previously, a random selection of ten of the 40 sequences was made with the constraint that strings of all lengths be included, this time using the letters rather than nonsense symbols or numbers. Each of three groups of subjects was presented with one set of ten strings which were either (1) spaced evenly, (2) spaced according to immediate constituents, or (3) spaced randomly, with the number of spaces per sequence equalling the immediate constituent spacing. The inclusion of the third group was aimed at demonstrating that it was not merely grouping that was a factor, but the systematic grouping which characterizes immediate constituent analysis. The three lists are shown in Figure III.

The subjects were all undergraduate students from introductory psychology courses. The three groups were of ten subjects each. The subjects were told nothing about the method of constructing the lists and were told it was important to remember the correct order of the letters without regard to the occurrence of spaces. The sequences were typed in capital letters on 3 x 5 inch cards. The subject was seated across the table from the experimenter who laid the cards face up in front of each subject at a rate of one card every five seconds. After all ten cards in the list had been presented, the experimenter, who laid the cards on the table, picked up the deck of cards and shuffled it while the subject wrote, in any order, all the sequences he could recall. When the subject finished, the experimenter removed the response sheet and proceeded to the next trial. Ten such trials were given, and the order of the cards was varied in the same way after each trial. Response sheets were scored for the number of correct sequences

Figure III

Finite State	Phrase Structure	Random
N X S	N X S	N X S
N S X N	N S XN	N S XN
N X N S	N XN S	N XN S
G N S X	GN S X	G N SX
N X N X N	N XN XN	N X NXN
G N X N G N	GN XN GN	GNX N GN
N X N X G N	N XN XGN	N XN XGN
N X G N X	N XGN X	NX GN X
G N X G N S	GN XGN S	G NX GNS
G N X G N X G N	GN XGN XGN	GNXGN XG N

recalled. The acquisition curves for the three groups are shown in Figure IV. Analyses of variance were performed for each trial. The significance of differences between group(s) means is shown for trials 8 through 10. The acquisition of the phrase structure group in contrast to the other groups

FIGURE IV

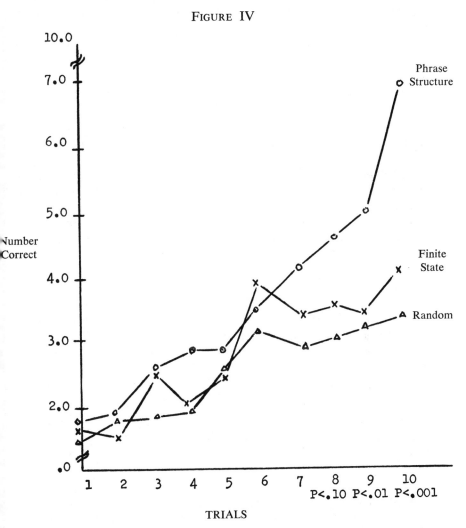

TRIALS

Averages for three groups of ten each.

One trial consisted of a one-at-a-time presentation of all 10 sequences of a sequence group. After each trial, the subject attempted to write as many sequences as he could recall. The order of presentation was varied haphazardly on each trial.

shows how organization into immediate constituents aided recall. The lack of difference in the performances of the finite state group and the random spacing group suggests that mere grouping is not of itself beneficial. A summary of the statistical analysis is included as Figure V.

By this time, we were so delighted to get any positive results that we overlooked one possible interpretation of the results. It was pointed out to us that one might consider that the groups were presented with a vocabulary of 5 items G, N, S, X and space. In such a case, the systematic introduction of spaces for a phrase structure group would increase the redundancy as opposed to the random introduction of spaces which carry more information in the sense of communication theory. However, we had explicitly told the subjects not to worry about recalling position of spaces. Undoubtedly, the spaces facilitate the grouping of symbols into higher-level units, but we did not feel we had to apologize for this fact, since it is precisely what immediate constituent analysis purports to do.

It is clear that these results cannot be safely generalized. However, once a convincing case can be made for a particular experimental design, it is hoped that similar results can be attained with the learning of material more closely approximating natural languages—with the only relevant variable being the model underlying the presentation and with no regard for the actual pedagogical devices or method of instruction.

FIGURE V

SUMMARY OF ANALYSIS OF VARIANCE

Source of Variation		Sum of Squares	Degrees of Freedom	Mean Square	F
A:	Spacing	67	2	33.50	6.11 (p<.01)
	Error (A)	148	27	5.48	
B:	Trials	325	9	36.11	38.01 (p<.001)
Ax B:	Spacing-Trials Interaction	61	18	3.39	3.57 (p<.01)
	Error (B)	231	243	.95	
	Total	832	299		

The three significant values indicate: (1) Spacing: that the number of correct recalls differed significantly among the three groups (P.S: 36.0, Finite: 28.0, Random: 24.8); (2) Trials: the group averages differed from trial to trial; (3) Spacing-Trials Interaction: there is a significant difference in the rate at which the three groups improved over the ten trials. For discussion of the statistical technique involved, see Edwards, A. L., *Experimental Design in Psychological Research*, New York: Rinehart, 1960, pp. 227-232.

SYNTAX AND SEMOLOGY

Henry Lee Smith, Jr.

State University of New York at Buffalo

[The following is an expanded version of the original paper. Perhaps it would more accurately be titled "Aspects of Phonology, Morphology and Semology," with the subtitle, "A look at the 'triadic' frame for the analysis of language." The author apologizes for the extremely condensed handling of certain points and for not being able, owing to space limitations, to develop sufficiently all pertinent aspects of the theory. The table in footnote 1 exemplifies the symbology used throughout the article.]

Microlinguistic analysis of a specific language or of language in general presupposes that all human beings use linguistic systems that fulfill the same functions. Though each language is uniquely different as a *structure,*

---

[1] Symbology employed in this article is demonstrated in the following examples:

√ = á·w =	kernel vocalic nucleus
√b./, √iy./	consonantal and vocalic morphophone units
√b.ó·.y.	free primary base
√ᵒ1.á·y.m.–	bound primary base
√k.á·.n. ⊢	prebase (as in *con*tract)
√ ·é·y.t.–	postbase (as in sublim*ate*)
√–iⁿ·./š.–	subbase (as in boy*ish*)
√–Z¹	morpheme (paradigmatic suffix)
ªV–ɨz	allomorph (of paradigmatic suffix)
√ð. ⊢	prefix (as in *th*is)
√ ⊣t–	postfix (as in tha*t*)
√ ᵒy.k–	non-derivational affix (as in part*ic*ular)
√–Z¹	macro-morpheme class
ˢʃ̰	stem component
ᴾʃ	phrase word
ᶜʃ	word phrase or "compound"
ᵀʃᐱ+'	tactical phrase superfix
ᴸʃ'+`	lexical phrase superfix

433

all languages may be described by similar techniques of analysis, since all languages, as cultural systems, are the same *kinds* of structures.

Charles F. Hockett, in Chapter 64 of his *Course in Modern Linguistics,* notes that human languages all share certain *design features* which are lacking in all other modalities of communication, animal *or* human. Principal among these is that feature he terms "duality of patterning." Put in other terms, languages have a phonological level and a morphological or grammatical level. The phonemes /p/ and /t/ have no "meaning" in and of themselves, but when "looked at" in the base morphemes in the words *pin* and *tin* they serve to make a contrast between two different words. So, too, though the phonemes /s/, /z/ and /ɨz/ have no "encapsulated meaning," the occurrences of /-s/ in *rats,* /-z/ in *dogs* and /-ɨz/ in *horses* serve the same grammatical purpose; they are non-contrasting *allomorphs* of the morpheme √-Z¹, all of whose members contrast with the phonemes /t/, /d/, /ɨd/ *when seen as* allomorphs of the *contrasting* morpheme √-D¹—"he *horsed* around," "he *dogged* my footsteps," "he *ratted* on his friends."

Traditionally, these morphemes have been termed *plural* (of the noun) and *past tense* (of the verb), and the morpheme as a construct of the linguistic analyst has been generally defined in some such terms as "the smallest recurring patterned partial of linguistic structure *that has meaning.*" The linguist is quick to assert that the term "meaning" here does not imply *referential* meaning but *grammatical* or *structural meaning.* But the non-initiate's reaction is that "past tense" *means* "past time" and "plural" *means* "more than one." Using a definition of the morpheme which substitutes the wording *"has grammatical significance"* for "has meaning," we can put off the problem of what "grammatical meaning" or "structural meaning" implies until we have gotten out the morphemes of the language seen only as recurring *contrasting classes* of grammatically significant components. The informant tells us that *dogged* /dóhgd/ is not the same *dogs* /dóhgz/ and also the *dogs* in "he *dogs*" is not the same as *dogs* in "two *dogs*" or "no *dogs.*" Thus /z/ belongs to two contrasting morphemes, √-Z¹ and √-Z³. At this point we are not concerned with anything but an identification and a labeling of the morphemes which are of several different kinds— paradigmatic suffixes, derivational morphemes of various types, bases, etc. Each class and each member of each class has grammatical significance and hence in various distributions demonstrates what we may term a "message-sending potential." It is the determination of how messages can be sent and are sent that is the domain of *semology;* it is the study of how language is able to *make sense. Morphology* is the study of the *shape* of the structure, the *substance* of language, while phonology has to do with the determination of the *units* or the "building blocks" of the substance, the selected classes of sounds that form the basis of all human languages.

Thus language conveniently or, perhaps, inevitably, yields to a *three*-level analysis rather than a two-level analysis, and all languages can be seen to possess three basic "properties"—*sound, shape* and *sense,* as Trager puts it. Further examination of these implications might well necessitate positing "triality" rather than duality of patterning as the essential design feature of human language. An analysis that proceeds from this assumption takes as data the actual linguistic occurrences and looks at them from three different points of view or *aspects,* and the resulting description is termed an *aspectual analysis.*

A glance at figure 1 shows a further subdividing of each of the three major areas into three more levels, and, finally, each of these is again broken down into three levels, making a total of twenty-seven. In each case, the second of the three levels is taken as the substance and is the *entry point* for looking at the data at that level. The first levels compose the units or *diacritics,* to use Joos' term, of the substance, and at the third levels, which have been termed, *system, pattern* and *distribution,* we examine the systematic patterning of the substance and arrive at the classification of the substance, noting particularly permitted and prohibited distributions.

FIGURE 1.

Classification of an Extended Qualificative Nominal Collocation

1	2	3	4	5	6	7	8	9	10	
	those my John's such etc.			additional remaining etc.	good wretched etc.		aged	brown etc.	French	
All |	the |	ten |	other |	similar |	fine |	old |	aging |	gray |	stone |	houses ||
Designative	Indicative	Quantitative	Contrastive	Comparative	Qualitative	Temporative	Aspective	Chromative	Technitive	#
A			B		C					
Indicating			Classifying		Qualifying					

* Junctures following each qualifying word above are single bar /|/, the terminal juncture is double cross /#/, or double bar /||/.

To exemplify this, the area of Phonology would be entered at II, where we concern ourselves with the *phones* as the basic substance. These are seen as real events in the physical world, and the study of the composition and structuring of the phones is studied in *phonetics*. But the phones themselves are not "atomic," but are seen as "bundlings" of *articulations* or "sound features" such as "stopness," "spirantness," voicing, "bilabialness," "lenisness," "fortisness," aspiration, etc., and the study of the kinds of articulations a language selects and of the features which are permitted to occur with each other or are prohibited from so doing is the province of what might be termed *phonics*. In the case of English, for instance, aspiration may occur with voicelessness and "stopness" but does not occur with "stopness" and voice. "Bilabialness" may occur with "stopness" and nasalization but does not occur with spirantization. As a consequence, English has no voiced aspirated stops and no bilabial spirants in its inventory of phones. In phonetics the *kinds* of phones—*vocoids, contoids,* etc.—are seen as the diacritics of the substance, the inventory of the occurring phones is the concern of phonetics 2, and in phonetics 3, the permitted and prohibited distributional patterning of the phones is examined. Thus, to single out only a very small number of examples, we find that voiceless stops are always aspirated in initial position and generally unreleased finally and lose their fortisness and aspiration when preceded by a voiceless spirant. Spirants and stops that follow any voiced phone must themselves be voiced, and when following voiceless phones all spirants must be voiceless. Statements similar to these result from the complete examination of the material.

Thus a complete treatment of the material in Phonology I and II prepares us for the classification of the phones into phonemes, which is the province of *phonemics,* the system level of Phonology. Here the tremendous number of phones are gathered together into the familiar kinds of phonemes —vowels, consonants, semi-vowels, stresses, pitches, or tones, and the transitional or junctural phonemes. The inventory of the phonemes occurring for the *language as a whole* (the overall-pattern) is listed in phonemics 2, and the statement of the prohibited and permitted distributions of phoneme with phoneme is the concern of phonemics 3. (It will be noted that the statements made in both phonetics 3 and phonemics 3 are part of what A. A. Hill has termed *phonotactics.*)

Returning to a look at the three basic aspectual areas, it becomes apparent that Morphology II, which concerns itself with the study of morphemes, is the *principal entry point,* into the analysis of any language. The study of the various kinds of morphemes, their composition and classification, is the concern of *morphemiçs*. Here, too, we examine how the morphemes enter into those kinds of *lexical items* which may be termed *true words*. For English, there are two kinds of true words built from base morphemes, *simple* and *complex*. *Simple true words* are composed of a single *free base* morpheme, which is described as having as part of its composition a *strong stress* (phonemically, a primary) and may be combined with one or two *paradigmatic suffix* morphemes. Thus the base morpheme √bóy-yields the true word ʷ√bóy and ʷ√bóy may be combined with the suffix morpheme √-Z¹ in the allomorph shape ᵃ√-z to yield the true word ʷ√bóyz. *Complex true words* are formed by the addition of *derivational subbase* morphemes to simple true words. Thus ʷ√bóy is combined with √-iš- to give ʷ√bóyiš ('boyish'), and ʷ√bóyiš can be combined with √-nis- to give ʷ√bóyišnis ('boyishness'). It is important to note here that subbases and suffixes are characterized by never, under any circumstances, occurring except with weak stress. Hence, other derivational morphemes that occur with tertiary stress or with primary stress form a different class of morphemes to which the term *postbase* is given. The '-ize' of *realize*, the '-ee' of *employee*, the '-ist' of *realistically* are examples of *postbases*, and morphemes like the 'con-' of *contract* (noun) and of *contract* (verb) are termed *prebases*.

All ten kinds of English morphemes cannot be exemplified because of limitations of space, but it is important to note the lexical items in the language can be classified by the kinds of derivational morphemes and/or suffix morphemes present. Thus all words that take the subbase √-nis- (-'ness') can be combined with √-Z¹ and √-Z² and are called *nouns*. If, however, as in *witnessed*, the morpheme √-D¹ and/or √-D² is identified as final, the word is classed as a *verb*. All words that can take the subbases √-ər- and √-ist- (the "endings of the comparative and superlative") are termed *adjectives* in morphemics regardless of the fact that many such compared words will be seen to have a *syntactic role* which will at that level be termed *adverbial* as in the *tactical phrase rân+fáster*. Space limitations also prohibit a detailed examination of the *four-slot derivational matrix*, but the following series—*long, length, lengthen, lengthener; long, length, lengthy, lengthiness; long, length, lengthy, lengthily*—show the *direction of derivation* to be adjective, noun, adjective, noun; adjective, noun, verb, noun; adjective, noun, adjective, adverb. In other words, adjectives yield both nouns and adverbs, adverbs are derived *only* from adjectives, and verbs yield nouns, but verbs that are true words are never derived directly from adjectives. The series *steal, stealth, stealthy, stealthiness* and *steal, stealth, stealthy, stealthily* show a verb in the first slot as the source of a noun and the resulting second-slot noun as the source of an adjective. *Grease, grease, greaser* and *grease, greasy, greasily* show a second-slot noun as the source of a third-slot verb as well as of a third-slot adjective. *Grease* (n.), *grease* (v.), *greaser*, along with *breath, breathe, breather* and *life, live, liver* show a *zero occurrence* of the third-slot verb-making derivational subbase (compare the presence of $\sqrt{}$-en- in this slot in the series *long, length, lengthen*). In each set examined except the one beginning with *grease* (n.), vowel alternation (*ablaut*) is present in the derived verb and there is voicing of the spirant. (Speakers like the writer voice the spirant in *grease* (v.) and in the adjective *greasy*, as well.) This comparison establishes the fact that the *zero occurrence* of the third-slot derivational subbase is sufficient to indicate the verb, and the occurrence of ablaut variation in the presence of a zero morpheme is analogous to that which accompanies the zero *suffix* morphemes (*not* allomorphs) present in the "irregular" nouns and verbs—*ride, rode; foot, feet*. It is necessary to point out here that I have become convinced that there have not been enough level distinctions in the description of morphemes. The '-en' of *oxen* is not an *allomorph* of $\sqrt{}$-Z^1 but constitutes a *separate morpheme,* $\sqrt{}$-N^1, with allomorphs ${}^a\sqrt{}$-in~${}^a\sqrt{}$-n. Since I am also convinced that allomorphs are properly analyzed as being composed of *phonemes* and since there are no zero phonemes because there are no zero *phones,* zero cannot be an *allomorph* of any morpheme but must be seen as a morpheme *in its own right* and as one of the members of a larger morpheme class, or *macromorpheme*. Therefore, the macromorpheme $\sqrt{}$-Z^1 has several *constituents* or *morpheme alternants,* including the productive morpheme $\sqrt{}$-Z^1: ${}^a\sqrt{}$-s~${}^a\sqrt{}$-z~$\sqrt{}$-ɨz, the non-productive $\sqrt{}$-N^1 mentioned above, and $\sqrt{}$-Ǭ (in *sheep,* and with ablaut in *feet,* etc.). Similarly $\sqrt{}$-D^1 has, among others, a productive $\sqrt{}$-D^1:${}^a\sqrt{}$-d~${}^a\sqrt{}$-t~$\sqrt{}$-ɨd, a non-productive $\sqrt{}$-T (compare *burn, burned* with $\sqrt{}$-D^1, vs. *burn, burnt* and *sleep, slept,* with $\sqrt{}$-T), and a $\sqrt{}$-Ǭ in *hit, hit.*

By using the criteria of suffix morphemes and derivational subbases, five principal morphemic word classes or morphemic "parts of speech" may be listed and ranked in a hierarchy. First in rank is the verb, whose paradigm displays the largest number of productive paradigmatic suffixes. Next comes the noun, and third in line the personal pronoun, which is ranked below the noun since all of the suffixes in the paradigm are non-productive. The words in the pronoun paradigm also show a different kind of structure from those constituting the verb and noun paradigms. Where the latter show a base and affix composition, the pronoun yields to a *prefix, kernel vocalic, suffix* analysis. For example, such forms as *him* and *them* show the *prefixes* $\sqrt{}$h⊢ and $\sqrt{}$ð⊢, respectively, a kernel vocalic

$\sqrt{}=\acute{\imath}=$ and $\sqrt{}=\acute{e}=$ and the object case suffix $\sqrt{}$-M². The pronoun form, *I,* would show a zero occurrence of a prefix ($\sqrt{}$ℚ⊢), *me* and *my* would show a prefix $\sqrt{}$m   and kernel vocalics $\sqrt{}=\acute{\imath}y=$ and $\sqrt{}=\acute{a}y=$, respectively, and zero occurrences of the object case and of the first possessive case, respectively. *Mine* shows an occurrence of $\sqrt{}$-N³ (ⁿ$\sqrt{}$-n), one of the second possessive morphemes, as does *thine* and the non-standard *hisen* and *hern*. *Its* shows a zero prefix, an $\sqrt{}=\acute{\imath}=$ kernel vocalic and a *postfix, not* a suffix, $\sqrt{}$⊣t- followed by a first possessive $\sqrt{}$-Z⁴ (ª$\sqrt{}$-s). If there were a second possessive form for the pronoun *it,* it would be a zero occurrence of the macromorpheme of the second possessive. Pronouns, in the nominative case, are analyzed like nouns and verbs in their *name forms* in that it is assumed they have *nothing* morphemically after them. Thus the paradigm is seen to have four *cases,* an unmarked nominative, an objective, and a first and second possessive marked by suffixes. There are also six *persons* marked by prefixes, and the third person has three forms, distinguished by contrasting prefixes ($\sqrt{}$h⊢, $\sqrt{}$š⊢, $\sqrt{}$ℚ⊢) which, later on in the analysis, are seen to be marked for *semological gender.* Also later there will be seen to be two *semological numbers* exhibited in the paradigm.

Below these first three word classes in the hierarchy are ranked the adjective and its derivative the adverb, classified, respectively, by the productive subbases of the comparative and the superlative and by the *final,* or fourth-slot subbase, ⁴$\sqrt{}$-liy-, which must be distinguished from the third-slot subbase ³$\sqrt{}$-liy-, which forms adjectives, as in *kindly* and *lowly.*

Following these first five word classes is a second group of five which are set off by virtue of their prefixes. All these words are like the personal pronouns in that they are analyzed as having prefixes, kernel vocalics and, like *it,* postfixes. However, their classification rests principally on their prefixes. For example, all words beginning with /ð/, which are not classified among the personal pronouns are taken as showing a prefix $\sqrt{}$ð⊢ and are designated *demonstratives.* Examples are *then* ($\sqrt{}$ð⊢, $\sqrt{}=\acute{e}=$, $\sqrt{}$⊢n-), *though, than, there,* etc., and the pair *this* and *that.* These latter show a non-productive constituent of the macromorpheme $\sqrt{}$-Z¹ in *these* and *those,* and therefore must also be classed as nouns, but their $\sqrt{}$ð⊢ prefixes and their kernel vocalics $\sqrt{}=\acute{\imath}=$ and $\sqrt{}=\acute{æ}=$, respectively, and their postfixes $\sqrt{}$⊣s- and $\sqrt{}$⊣t- necessitate a double classification—*demonstrative nouns.*

The prefix $\sqrt{}$(h)w   sets a class called *relatives—which* ($\sqrt{}$(h)w⊢, $\sqrt{}=\acute{\imath}=$, $\sqrt{}$⊢č-), *what, when, where, why,* etc., and the minimal pairs *where* and *there, when* and *then, whence* and *thence* (these latter showing *two* postfixes $\sqrt{}$⊣n-, $\sqrt{}$⊣s-) furnish the basis for a "pseudo-paradigm."

The prefix √hr established the *locatives—here, hither, hence,* and the prefix √n⊢ the negatives—*no, not, never, neither, nor,* etc. The *positives* are arrived at by the *absence* of a prefix in such minimal pairs as *or* vs. *nor, either* vs. *neither,* etc. The eleventh morphemic word class is termed *unclassified* and constitutes all the remaining true words in the lexicon which cannot be conveniently classified by the morphemes which compose them. Here, for example, are all the words that *later* in syntax through distributions in binary phrases will be classified as *conjunctionals* and/or *prepositionals—in, of, through, over, as, if, so,* etc.

At this point in our discussion it will be necessary to return to the unit or diacritic level of Morphology, which treats the *morphophones* under *morphophonics.* The material handled at this level has traditionally been called *morphophonemics,* but since the morphophones have no *"allo's,"* an "-eme" designation for this level is not an accurate one. From the point of view of our theory, the level is of paramount importance, since our frame of reference indicates that phonemes do not enter *directly* into morphemes, but morphemes must be seen as being composed of morpho-phones as their units, or, to put it another way, all morphemes must have a *basis* in morphophones. But looking at the phonemic level, it is also obvious that this system level of Phonology must comprise the units for the whole of the language, so the problem may be stated as one of seeing how entities on one level—the phonemes of Phonology—enter into the morphemes of Morphology. Further, there is abundant evidence that linguists, by their failure to recognize the morphophonic level for what it is, have confused phoneme with morphophone and thus have failed to see how Phonology "feeds in" to Morphology. For example, C. C. Fries and K. L. Pike have stated that English has eleven vowel phonemes and three *clusters* or diphthongs, and Eugene Nida, as quoted by Gleason in the revised edition of *An Introduction to Descriptive Liguistics* (pages 326-7) saw his idiolect as having fourteen vowel phonemes, seven simple or short— /i, e, æ, u, ə, o, a/, and seven complex or diphthongal—/iy, ey, ay, oy, uw, ow, aw/. The Pike-Fries and Nida statements agree in listing the same fourteen "counters" but differ in that Nida is seeing all the complex nuclei as structural diphthongs while Pike-Fries give diphthongal status only to /ay/, /aw/ and /oy/. But those who follow Trager's and my statements of the over-all pattern of the vowel phonemes in English syllabic nuclei as set forth in *An Outline of English Structure* last thirty-six: nine *simple* or *short* vowel nuclei—/i, e, æ, ɨ, ə, a, u, o, /, and the combination of each of these with each of the three semivowels—/y, w, h/, to make twenty-seven possible *complex* (diphthongal) nuclei. The idea of a "common core" put forth by Hockett as early as 1952 and restated in his

Course in Modern Linguistics (pages 332-337) can now be seen as not lying within the province of Phonology but rather as a matter to be seen and handled in Morphology under morphophonics. By the same token, Nida's phonemic analysis of the vowels of his idiolect and the Pike-Fries statements of English phonemes can be seen to be quite good statements of the *vocalics* of a *morphophonic* rather than a *phonemic* "common core."

To bring the problem into focus and understand the reason for making the last statement, we must see the relationship between idiolect-dialect and the language as a whole. The linguist's job is to write a description of the *language* which will include and, of course, be based on the examination of the several dialects. Fries asserts that his eleven vowel phonemes and three diphthongal clusters are for "English," that is, the language over-all, while Nida sets up his fourteen "counters" as the situation pertaining only to his idiolect. Fries' statement simply closes the door to handling such contrasts as the Central Atlantic Seaboard speaker's *can* (v.) /kǽn/ vs. *can* (n.) /kéhn/, *sorry* /sáriy/ vs. *sari* /sáhriy/ or *bomb* /bám/ vs. *balm* /báhm/, *hurry* /hə́riy/ vs. *furry* /fə́hriy/, and gives no way of seeing the phonemic structuring of the New Yorker's *first* /fə́yst/, the southern Middle Westerner's *ash* /ǽyš/, *push* /púyš/, the New Englander's *home* /hóm/ vs. *pot* /pɔ́t/ seen against the New Yorker's /hówm/ vs. /pát/, or of the Chicagoan's *caught* /kɔ́t/ vs. the Philadelphian's /kóht/. Nida's statement, on the other hand, simply says his *idiolect* needs no further "counters" simply because these contrasts or these structurings don't exist in his dialect. But to handle all the phonemic contrasts and structurings for the language as a whole, the total number of thirty-six possible syllabic nuclei need to be posited, even though no one dialect need make use of all the possibilities.

The situation becomes more interesting when we realize that certain dialects and idiolects may use more than one phonemic "actualization" for the same word. For example, in Buffalo *sorry* is said with five different selections, any speaker regularly using three of these is what seems to be free variation—/sáriy/, /sɔ́riy/, /sáhriy/, /sɔ́hriy/, /sóhriy/. Obviously there is no contrast possible here between /sáriy/ (*sorry*) and /sáhriy/ (*sari*) as is the case with the Easterner, and the Eastener must *calibrate* his /sáriy/ with *any* of the five Buffalo pronunciations. The Buffalonian hears no *essential* or "real" difference between any of the five and finds it surprising to learn the Easterner insists on making "needless" distinctions.

Thus an important fact emerges: speakers of various dialects with different phonemic selections in the same words must calibrate these differences into "sames" at the same time that they recognize phonological "sames" in another dialect are separated and kept distinct as "differents" in their own. It is perhaps this matter of "same" becomes "different" and "different" becomes "same," as we pass from level to level of the description, that is the very essence of the nature of a linguistic system, and is, perhaps, basic to the hypothesis of *triality* rather than simple *duality* of patterning.

It is suggested that the inventory of morphophones be posited in such a way that all phonemic distinctions that carry a *functional load* for *all* dialects be recognized as constituting a *common core*. Thus the short vocalics √i./, √e./, √æ./, √u./, √ə./, √a./ constitute an absolute minimum as heard in contrast in *pit, pet, pat, put, putt, pot,* respectively. When the northern Middle Westerner makes contrasts between /kæt/, /kát/, /kɔ́t/ (*cat, cot, caught*), another short morphophone √o./, must be added to the inventory, giving seven, arrangeable as follows:

√ i.   u.   (N.B.   Morphophones are symbolized by the root sign
   e.   ə.   o.   preceding the syllable and the slant line following, with
                    a period after the symbol itself.)
   æ.   a./

We have now come out with the Pike-Fries and the Nida short vocalic "counters," which they termed phonemes. /ɨ/ and /ɔ/ are eliminated from the inventory as carrying no *functional load* at the level of the morpheme. That is, /ɨ/ and /ɔ/ can be seen to be *diamorphophones* of √i./, √e./ and √o./, √a./, respectively. That is, the New Englander's /pɔ́t/ calibrates completely with the Philadelphian's /pát/ in *pot,* and the Baltimorean's variation between /jɨ̇st/, /jést/ and /jə·st/ for *just* (adv.) cancels out /ɨ/ as a necessary counter in the morphophonic common core.

By the same reasoning, the sever complex morphophone units √iy./, √ey./, √ay./, √oy./, √uw./, √ow./, √aw./ need to be posited for the *common core,* since, first, *all* dialects make true contrasts between such items as *Pete, pate, height, Hoyt, boot, boat, bout* and, second, since all dialects show *productive morphophonic alternation* between these *complex morphophonic units* and several of the *simple units,* when in the *morphophonic environment* of morphophone √y./ and √i./ with the morphophone of strong stress (√'./) on the syllable in question. Note the following examples: √iy./~√e./ in *extreme, extremity;* √ey./~√æ./ in *sane, sanity;* √ay./~√i./ in *sublime, sublimity;* √oy./~√ə./ in *join, junction;* √uw./~√ə./ in *assume, assumption;* √ow./~√a./ in *verbose, verbosity;* √aw./~√ə./ in *pronounce, pronunciation.*

It becomes quite simple to see, then, that such dialectically different occurrences as those appearing in say, the four phonemically contrasting pronunciations of *house*—/háws/, /hǽws/, hə́ws/, /héws/—are *dialectical equivalents,* and hence may be termed *diamorphophones* of the complex pronunciations of *house*—/háws/, /hǽws/, /hə́ws/, /héws/—are *dialectical* morphophone unit √aw./, since they calibrate completely, one with another, and no *morphemic* contrast is involved. These differences, seen inside the *base morpheme* √h.á·w.s.-, constitute *diamorphs* of the morpheme, *not* allomorphs, and the alternation in the base morphemes in *all* dialects, in the cases like *sublime, sublimity,* again do not constitute *allomorphs* but, rather, *altermorphs* of the bases. One step further leads us to the term *dialog* for the various non-contrasting dialect equivalents of true words in the lexicon. (All these "dia-" forms constitute *equivalences* when we get to Semology III.2. and will ultimately be classified according to levels of *style.* It must be remembered that *equivalence* is *not identity,* but different *selections* of equivalences carry a "message sending potential.")

Before leaving the level of morphophonics, it must be pointed out that the fourteen vocalic units in the common core are *not* a sufficient number of counters to handle all of the contrasts made within and between morphemes in all the dialects. Minimal contrasts like /kǽn/ and /kéhn/ and /baðer/ (bother) and /fáhdər/ (father) necessitate setting up an √eh./ and √ah./, and the fact that the Easterner has a contrast between /dóhg/ (*dog*) and /lág/ (*log*) and has only /óh/ when the Middle Westerner has only /ɔ́/ (in *caught, short,* etc.) would indicate the necessity of setting up an √óh./ for these speakers and also indicates that the Easterner lacks completely the short unit √o./. This suggestion is further substantiated by the situation in Western New York, where /ǽ/ *never* occurs, but /éh/ occurs in the place where other dialects have /ǽ/. These speakers, then, lack short √æ./ and have √eh./ in its place.

The morphophonic inventory for the *language* over-all would then require the addition of the three complex units with "h," making a total of seventeen vocalics. No "pure" dialect seems to utilize more than sixteen—e.g. East Coast U.S. and Southern British—and the northern Middle West shows only fourteen, the smallest number of units, in fact the exact number of counters posited for the common core, no more and no less.

Space limitation prohibits a detailed treatment of other morphophonic "changes," such as *shortening,* as seen in the /kríyk/, /krík/ (*creek*), /rúwm/, /rúm/ (*room*) situations, where √iy./~√i./ and √uw./~√u./, or *lengthening* where a simple unit may be lengthened by the addition of √h./, √r./, √y./, or √w./,—cf. /wáš/ vs. /wáhrš/=/w.a.š/ vs. /w.ā.h.r.š./ when both the short √a./ and the combination of √ā.h.r./ are taken as diamorphophonic equivalents of the short unit √a./. Note here, too, the New Englander's lengthening of √ə./ in an unstressed syllable as in "Cubar." Limitation of space also makes it impossible to treat in detail the alternations of *palatalization* and *affrication* between t. to š. and č., respectively, in the presence of √y./ and √y.uw./—cf. *fraction* and *fracture* and similar alternations of √d./, √t./, √g./, and the *voicing* of √f./, √θ./ and √s./ must be passed over as well. But we must note the interesting facts about the morphophonic *semivocalics* √y., w., h., r., l./, which form a group showing similar properties. All may alternate with each other (except that √h./ never alternates with √r./), and all may alternate with √Q./ as does /+./. The alternation between √y./ and √Q./ explains the Cockney's " 'ead" for *head* and the Marylander's " 'east" for *yeast* and the same alternation after an alveolar morphophone explains the difference in pronunciation in such words as /lyúwt/ vs. /lúwt/, /nyúwz/ vs. /núwz/ = √l.y.~Q.ú·w.t./, √n.y.~Q.ú·w.z./.

It becomes apparent after a little reflection, that the English writing system, though based on the *alphabetic principle* of "one phoneme, one grapheme" is, in actuality, essentially a morphophonically based script. We are writing, or trying to write, one *graph* for one morphophone. Thus in *fraction* the *i* represents the √y./ which is palatalizing the variable consonantal √t./ to √š./. In the graph sequence ⟨ute⟩, ⟨une⟩ etc., the ⟨u⟩ followed by the consonant graph, followed by the ⟨e⟩ stands for the √y./ which may alternate with √Q/ after a graph standing for an alveolar consonantal morphophone—⟨tune⟩, √t.y.~Q.ú·w.n./. But when a graph for a *bilabial* or *velar* precedes—cf. ⟨moot⟩, ⟨mute⟩; ⟨coot⟩, ⟨cute⟩, the spellings ⟨ute⟩ vs. ⟨oot⟩ regularly indicate the presence or absence of √y./. The spelling system is amazingly regular in its representation of morphemes in its *morphographic* aspects and of lexical items in its *lexographic* aspects. The author is becoming increasingly convinced that further close study of the writing system as one essentially *in practice* based on "one morphophone, one graph" will be richly rewarding.

Up to now, with the exception of the examples of the *sublime, sublimity* type, we have been concerned with examining our "triadic" frame of reference only in connection with the various types of true words with their subbases and suffixes, prefixes and postfixes. But English has two other types of *lexical items, phrase words* and *word phrases.* As the terms imply, they are kinds of *phrases,* which means they lie actually in the province of syntax, where the basic substance of syntax 2. is the *phrase.* A phrase has been previously defined by Trager and me in the *Outline of English Structure* as a stretch of material containing more than one *word,* and the word has been defined as having only one (primary) base morpheme. In our earlier treatment, we added that a word to be complete must be combined with a *word superfix,* or "stress pattern." I have become convinced that *true words* need not be thought of as being combined with word superfixes, since bases and kernel vocalics are *by definition* accompanied by a morphophone of strong stress ($\sqrt{'\cdot/}$), while subbases and suffixes, *never* have anything but a morphophone of weak stress ($\sqrt{\check{}\cdot/}$) as inherent in their composition. Therefore the "stressing" in true words is always completely predictable. However, when we are dealing with combinations of *more* than one entity of *base status* in a lexical item, that is, with more than one *primary base* or with *primary bases* and/or the types of morphemes designated below as *prebases, postbases* and *non-derivational affixes,* we must posit the operation of a *lexical phrase superfix.* This is necessitated by the fact that items of base status may appear in completed *phrase words* or *word phrases* with any of the four phonemes of stress—primary, secondary, tertiary, or weak. *Phrase words* differ from *word phrases* in that the former have only one *primary base* morpheme but may have a number of *secondary* bases—*postbases* or *prebases.* The *postbases* may attract to them derivational subbases and the whole *phrase word* may terminate with a paradigmatic suffix. In addition there are *non-derivational affixes,* such as the $\sqrt{-\acute{y}\cdot}$.k.- of *particular,* which can take the stress of a lexical phrase superfix but these can never terminate a *phrase word.*

For example, such a maximum occurrence as *decompartmentalizationalistically* shows two prebases, $\sqrt{d.\acute{i}\cdot y.}\vdash$ and $\sqrt{k.\acute{a}\cdot.n.}\vdash$ (the maximum number permitted) preceding the one primary base $\sqrt{p.\acute{a}\cdot.r.t.}$-, which, in turn, is followed by the postbases $\sqrt{\cdot m.\acute{e}\cdot.n.t.}$-, $\sqrt{\cdot \text{æ}\cdot.l.}$-, $\sqrt{\cdot \acute{a}\cdot.z.}$-, and $/\cdot\acute{e}\cdot y.t.$-. $/y.\check{\eth}\cdot.n.$- is a subbase, which like $\sqrt{-\breve{i}\cdot y.}$- of the fourth slot only combines with bound primary bases or with postbases. Next comes $\sqrt{\cdot\check{\text{æ}}\cdot.l.}$- again, followed by the postbases $\sqrt{\cdot\acute{i}\cdot.s.t.}$- and $\sqrt{\cdot\acute{y}\cdot}$.k.-; then $\sqrt{\cdot\check{\text{æ}}\cdot.l.}$ again and, finally the fourth-slot adverb derivational subbase $^4\sqrt{-l.\breve{i}\cdot y.}$-. It will be noted that this long *phrase word* can be "broken up" at certain points. That is—*compartment, compartmental, compartmentalize, compartmentalization, compartmentalizational, compartmentalizationalist, compartmentalizationalistic, compartmentalizationalistical* and finally, *compartmentalizationalistically.* Of course, the first *prebase,* $\sqrt{d.iy}\vdash$ can be combined at least as early as with the string *compartmental.* Consequently, a matrix for the *derivational postbases* can be set up, *analogous* to that for the subbases. The first slot forms nouns ($\sqrt{\cdot m.\acute{e}\cdot.n.t.}$-), the second, adjectives ($\sqrt{\cdot\check{\text{æ}}\cdot.l.}$-), the third in two parts, verbs ($\sqrt{\cdot\acute{a}\cdot y.z.}$- and $\sqrt{\cdot\acute{e}\cdot y.t.}$-), and the fourth nouns ($\sqrt{\cdot\acute{i}\cdot.s.t.}$-). This fourth slot item can be followed by the postbase $\sqrt{\cdot y\cdot}$.k.-, an adjective maker and again, by

√·ǽ·.l.-, another adjective maker, which can always be *first* combined with the fourth-slot subbase ⁴√-l.ï·y.-, the abverb maker.

The observations of the composition of *phrase words* indicates that though the one primary (bound) base is always the *node,* or most important constituent, the *strings* that have been put together into the final composition must be seen to be recurring *stem words* of the phrase word and must be handled first. Thus in the phrase word *atheistic* we have a prebase √é·y.⊢, a bound primary base √·θ.í·y.-, a postbase √·í·.s.t.- and a postbase √·y·.k.-. Now √·í·.s.t. must first be combined with √·y·.k. under ᴸ∫'˜ to give the stem word ˢ∫ístĭk which is *then* combined with ˢ∫θí·y⟨√·θ.í·y.- under ᴸ∫'⁺' or ᴸ∫'˜' to give the phrase words ᴾ∫θìy+ístik or ᴾ∫θïyístik. It is important to note that the √y./ always "pulls" the stress to the syllable immediately preceding it and hence controls the position of the one primary stress in the resulting phrase word. To put in another way, once √·í·.s.t.- and √·ý·.k.- have been combined, √íst-/ keeps the primary stress. After ᴾ∫θìy+ístik, ᴾ∫θïyístĭk is formed, √é·y.⊢ can be combined with either under ᴸ∫'⁺' to give ᴾ∫èy+θìy+ístĭk or ᴾ∫èy+θïyístik. In the above, the symbol is to designate that the superfixes and the resulting phrase words are on the level of *syntax,* not *morphemics.* It is essential to note here that the phrase superfix is *not* a morpheme but a "taxeme" or syntactic *operand* that has the power or valence of reducing a morphophone of strong stress on a base, postbase, prebase or non-derivational affix to a *phoneme* of stress *below* the rank of primary. Also all operations involving phrase superfixes are *binary* operations, that is only two items of base status can be combined at a time. Hence our ˢ∫ístik must be combined with √·ǽ·.l.- under ᴸ∫'˜ to give ˢ∫ístĭkəl and √·ǽ·.l.- must first be combined with ⁴√-l.iy.- to give ˢ∫ǽliy before combination with ˢ∫ístik to give ˢ∫ístĭkəlïy. By the same kind of analysis the string ˢ∫éyšĭnəl is arrived at and put together with (*de*) *compartmentalize before* ˢ∫ístĭkəlïy is combined with the material before it. In other words, the analysis of *phrase words* procedes from the *end* of the complete string, taking *stem words* (themselves phrase words) step by step and combining them *binarily* with a series of lexical phrase superfixes until the string containing the one primary base and its "satellites" is reached.

With *word phrases* (traditional "compounds") the procedure is reversed. Here there are always at least *two* primary bases, and the typical examples like *Whíte+Hòuse, Lóng+Islánd, líghthouse+kêeper* contain *free true words.* Here we start with the *first* of the items in the composition—∫wáyt & ∫háws·ᴸ∫'+'→ᶜ∫wáyt+hàws. This formula is to be read: the word /wáyt/ as a member of a lexical phrase, combined with the word

/háws/ as a member of a lexical phrase, operated on by the lexical superfix ᴸʃ'+' results in the *word phrase* ᶜʃwáyt+hàws. *Long+Islánd, ice+créam,* etc., have the lexical superfix ᴸʃ'+' rather than ᴸʃ'+ˇ. In the *extended word phrase* ᶜʃlíght+hòuse+kêeper, the whole *word phrase* ᶜʃlíght+hóuse is combined with /kíyper/ under ᴸʃ'+ˆ to give the result ᶜʃláyt+hàws+kîypər. *Word phrases* can be composed of a maximum of three primary bases, and such items as *psychological, biographical,* etc., etc. are *word phrases* composed of the *bound* primary bases, √·s.á·y.k.-, √·b.á·y.-, combined with the non-derivational affix √÷ow. put together under ᴸʃ'+', or ᴸʃ'+ˇ to give ˢʃsáy+kòw, ˢʃbáy+òw, or ˢʃsáy+kə, ˢʃbáy+ɔ̌, which then are combined under ᴸʃ'+' with ˢʃlájĭkɔ̌l, ˢʃgræ̆fĭkɔ̌l, respectively. These latter are composed of ˢʃláǰ & ˢʃíkəl under ᴸʃ'⁓ and ˢʃgræf & ˢʃíkɔ̌l under ᴸʃ'⁓. The /ɔ̆i/ is, of course, the form of the postbase √·æ.l.- which was *first* combined with the postbase √·y·.k.- under ᴸʃ'⁓. (Note that bound primary bases are symbolized by √°y, postbases by √·, and non-derivational affixes by √÷.)

But, of course, the main concern of syntax is the *tactical* rather than the *lexical* phrase. Here the phrase superfixes are putting together two or more words in binary or extended phrases that do not form lexical items but phrases that are termed *constructs* and *constructions*. A *construct tactical phrase superfix* never has a secondary stress as the partner of the one obligatory primary stress—ᵀʃ'+', ᵀʃ'+', ᵀʃ'+', ᵀʃ'+ˇ, ᵀʃ'⁓, ᵀʃ°⁓, etc., whereas these tactical superfixes with *secondary* stress as the primary's partner are termed *construction* phase superfixes. Note that *stresslessness* in such a tactical phrase as *'tis* counts as one of the two parts of the binary phrase superfix—ᵂʃít & ᵂʃíz·ᵀʃ°⁓→ᵀʃtíz.

It should also be noted that normal transition, ˇ, though *not* a phoneme counts along with /+/ as the binary division point of both lexical and tactical phrase superfixes.

The three steps of syntactic analysis cannot be covered in any detail here, but step one *converts* the eleven *morphemic* "parts of speech" into *syntactic* "parts of speech" and notes the phrase superfixes that have put the material together, dividing the lexical items from the tactical *construct* and *construction* phrases. Step two concerns itself with the syntactic *relationships* between the *immediate,* or *intra-phrasal, constituents* of the binary tactical phrases. For example, the phrase *whîte+hóuse* is a *tactical phrase* (in contrast to Whíte+Hòuse) since ʃˆ+' always forms a *tactical construction*. (Lack of space prevents a detailed listing of the tactical versus the lexical superfixes in relation to the nature of the morphemic material being phrased.) The relationship between *any* material phrased with a tactical superfix before a syntactic *nominal* (morphemic noun) is termed *prenominal*. Among the eleven such relationships within binary tactical phrases are *anteverbal* (nominal or pronominal material *preceding* verbal material, and *postverbal* (nominal or pronominal material *following* verbal material), and when relationships like the *anteverbal* and *postverbal* (^{2}Jôhn + ^{3}rán^1#, ^{2}hît + Bíll^2#) are put together so that the phonological indication is a *terminal juncture,* (^{2}Thĕ bîg ^{2}bóy ^{2}/ ^{3}rán^1#, ^{2}Jóhn ^{2}# ^{2}hít ^{2}/ ^{2}thĕ bîg ^{3}bóy ^{1}#), the terminal junctures mark *principal constituents* of the *syntactic sentence.* There are four such principal constituents—∫*subject,* ∫*predicator,* ∫*complement,* ∫*adjunct.* The sentence ^{2}Jôhn$_s$ ^{2}hít$_p$^{2}/ ^{2}Bíll$_c$^{2}| ^{3}hárd$_a$^{1}# shows all four *principal constituents.* It must not be concluded that only terminal junctures signal *principal constituents;* for example, the syntactic sentence ^{2}Jôhn + ^{3}rán^1#, shows the *anteverbal relationship* which always, in the third step of syntactic analysis, is the indication of the two principal constituents of *syntactic subject* and *syntactic predicator.* In syntactic analysis, the distinction between *major* (/#/, /‖/) and *minor* (/+/, /|/) junctures is of primary importance. For instance, such distinctions as those between *subordinate* material—phrases and clauses—and *subordinated* material are signalled by the contrast between major and minor terminal junctures. Thus in ^{2}Thèy ^{2}décorated ^{2}/ ^{2}thĕ ^{2}gírl ^{2}/ ^{2}wĭth thĕ ^{3}flówers ^{1}# versus ^{2}Thèy ^{2}décorated ^{2}/ ^{2}thĕ ^{2}gírl ^{2}# ^{2}wĭth thĕ ^{3}flówers ^{1}#, the single bar juncture, /|/, signals the difference between an *adnominal phrase, included* in the *syntactic complement* and the *attached* syntactic *adjunct,* signalled by the /#/. The difference between pitch phonemes, that is /2/ vs. /3/, is not a matter of concern at the level of syntax, though the fact of pitch *generation* can be an indication of immediate and/or of principal constituents.

After all the *syntactic relationships* have been handled and all the various types of syntactic sentences have been classified and their *principal constituents* indicated, we can go on to *Semology* where we take first, in Semology I, certain *occurrences* (from Semology II.2, "Phemics") having no more than a single bar included in a stretch terminated by a major juncture. Within these stretches, which are termed *collocations,* if they have no verbal material, and *colligations* if verbal material is present, the semes are determined. Some are direct conversions from morphemics; for example the macromorphemes $\sqrt{}$-Z^1 and $\sqrt{}$-D^1 are seen to carry the semes traditionally designated *plural* and *past tense.*

Figure 2. shows the matrix of a maximally extended *qualificative collocation,* and will give some indication of how the first level of semological analysis is done. It will be noted that the items in this series can be said with no more than single bar juncture separating them and that if the order

FIGURE 2.

PHONOLOGY (A)			MORPHOLOGY (B)			SEMOLOGY (Γ)		
I.	II.	III.				I.	II.	III.
Articulations	*Phones*	*Phonemes*	*Morphophones*	*Morphemes*	*"Taxemes"*	*"Semes"*	*"Phemes"*	*"Rhemes"*
"Phonics"	Phonetics	Phonemics	Morphophonics	Morphemics	Syntax	"Sememics"	"Phemics"	"Rhemics"
1 2 3 ←	1 2 3 ←	1 2 3 ←	1 2 3 ←	1	1 2 3 ←	1 2 3 ←	1 2 3 ←	1 2 3 ←
inventory of articulation features	Identification of phones	Phonemic Inventory ("Over-all Pattern")	Morphophonic Inventory	Kinds of morphemes	Phrases, Lexical and Tactical, and Syntactic relationships	Collocations and Colligations	Occurrences	Equivalences
				2 Morphemic Inventory				
				3 Classification of morphemes and of true words				

is changed to put a slot-seven item, say, before a slot-five item, a major juncture must intervene. Also, if more than one item from any of the slots is uttered, it, too, must be preceded and followed by a major juncture. This leads to the conclusion that *every* item that can go into any of the ten slots shares at least one *seme,* that of the column as a whole, with every other member found in that slot. It may seem at first blush that the labels given to the slots—*quantitative, chromative, technitive,* etc.—are selected because of referential meaning, but this is *not* the case. Even though all *chromatives* (slot nine) refer to what we call colors, the slots could just as well be designated by the numerals 1 through 10. To exemplify, an item like the semological mass noun *stone* in the *technitive* slot (in *prenominal syntactic relationship*) certainly refers to a material used in our technology to build houses, but the semological proper noun *French* does not. However, our argument indicates that *stone* and *French* each contain the *technitive,* or column ten, seme in common. It is interesting to speculate, though, whether because of this occurrence of the proper noun in prenominal relationship in this semological matrix whether speakers of English *react* to *French* in this position in some such way as they react to *stone,* that is, that the "French" in "French wines" like the "Japanese" in "Japanese cameras" is really referring to the *materials* entering into the product. Such questions are relevant to the further testing of the Sapir-Whorf hypothesis.

The other classifications of noun collocations—the *general* and the *partitive* cannot even be exemplified owing to the limitations of space—and the classification of the *colligations*—the *tenses, aspects, phases, modes, moods* and *voices* of the English *syntactic predicators* can only be referred to as having been quite thoroughly handled. But some mention must be made of the statements and concerns in Semology II as a whole. Here the occurrences are looked at again but not limited to stretches with only single bar junctures within them. And here, too, pitches *qua* pitches are of primary importance, because in Semology II.3. all the *semological functions* are gotten out. Semological *functions* furnish an excellent example of the principle of "sames" on one level becoming "differents" on another. For example, a syntactic subject now is seen to have more than one *semological function* depending upon its *distributional* environment. A syntactic subject of a semological *transitive active* verb is the semological *actor,* but the semological subject of a verb in the semological *passive voice* is designated the semological *patient.* Verbs themselves are classified as *stative, active, transitive, intransitive,* as well as *motive, affective* and more than a dozen other such categories by virtue of what kinds of distributions they are permitted. For example, *He taught the dog to bark* versus *He heard the dog bark,* not "to bark," indicates that the verbs belong in different semological classes, and verbs showing distributions similar to *teach* go into the "instructive" class, and verbs following the distribution patterns like *hear* can be classified as "sensitive;" they carry different *phemes* though both are *active* and *transitive.*

Further, such a contrast as that between ²Thĕ ³kíng ²# ³Jóhn ²# ²ĭs ³déad ¹# vs. ²Thĕ ³kíng ²# ²Jóhn ²|| ²ĭs ³déad ¹# signals, by virtue of the contrast in both pitch and terminal juncture, the difference between the *semological functions* of *appositive* vs. *vocative.* In Semology II.3. all sentences are "looked at" again and classified as to *statements, questions,* conditions of various kinds, etc., and what has traditionally been called grammar is completed. But the classification of *equivalences,* the substance of Semology III, remains to be done. As we have indicated, equivalences are *not* identities and what *constitutes* equivalences must be determined at this final level, or before it. *Dialogs* are one kind of equivalence, and of course the *selection* of, say, a semological *active voice* vs. a *passive voice* constitutes another kind of equivalence. *Selection* of equivalences is the province of Semology III and in Semology III.3. the *classification* of all such selections is done in order to arrive at statements of *style.* This can be done only when all the prohibited and permitted distributions are thoroughly understood and stated at the lower levels, but it *must* be done since every *selection* carries "message sending potential."

Language looked at and analyzed in this triadic frame allows us to see, step-by-step, how language can carry messages. No longer are "lexicon" or "morphophonemics" left out in "left field," and no longer is the linguist embarrassed by where "semantics" fits into his description. In the "final analysis" he has not overlooked *any* of the data, and the data—the actual occurrences—are always the beginning and the end of his concern. Followed through, such a triadic analysis and description shows how we *can* get to *meaning* through *structure,* and gives a really adequate basis for *pre*scription, nothing more or less than an adequate *de*scription.

REPAIRING THE GAPS IN THE VOCAL-AUDITORY SYMBOL SYSTEM

WILLIAM C. STOKOE, JR.

Gallaudet College

Although deafness presents special problems and teaching deaf persons offers wide scope for the application of linguistics, the deaf student in college and high school has exactly the same room for improvement in certain language skills as has his hearing counterpart. For, if the real numbers between zero and one represent degrees of language skill, zero of course represents no skill whatever and one is equivalent to (unattainable) perfection. One student's skill may be different from another's, say as 0.01 is different from 0.99; yet between each of these points and the number one there lie an infinite number of points. In having infinite room for improvement all possessors of any language skill are the same.

The language skills particularly pertinent here are, starting from the top, the ability 1) to compose discourse of quality and magnitude adequate to answer questions requiring both general knowledge and intelligently read specific materials; 2) to develop paragraphs that are more than mere collections of sentences; 3) to originate sentences appropriate to linguistic and situational contexts; 4) to construct grammatical sentences; 5) to produce grammatical, and reprocess ungrammatical, principal constituents of sentences; and 6) to select from a well-stocked memory words appropriate to the syntactic and semantic contexts of such principal constituents.

The native speaker with unimpaired hearing is expected to have begun moving up these stages even before reaching high school. But because there is infinite room for improvement in these skills and because the standard for judging proficiency in them is likewise variable, there is no need to abandon them as objectives for teaching the gifted student. And even if grammaticality were a strict matter of yes or no, human beings, like generative grammars, differ in efficiency of production.

The high school or college student who is not a native speaker but needs a native-like command of English is expected to master preliminary

453

audiolingual skills and a new writing system. Contrastive grammars and a wealth of machinery and printed material are available to help him.

However, between the deaf student's skills and the stages of skills named, there are gaps—gaps, that is, in the vocal-auditory symbol system. These gaps penetrate several layers of language structure. For the deaf student whose main detour around the auditory gap is lipreading, most of the phonemes of English are not phonemic at all. Here is the summary of a piece of linguistic research done at the John Tracy Clinic, where teaching the skills of lipreading and speech production to deaf children is a major emphasis. It deals not with repairing but with surveying this particular gap:

> A research program has been set up to apply the theory and method of structural linguistics to an analysis of lipreading processes. As the first step, perceptual differences among English initial consonants were tested. Stimulus materials consisted of pairs of phonemically identical and minimally different nonsense syllables, which provided a constant, nonredundant linguistic environment for the phonemes tested. Stimuli were presented to 185 experimental subjects, normal-hearing adult speakers of English, by means of a silent film. The test was administered also to smaller control groups by presenting the sound track alone, and by showing the complete film with both picture and sound. In place of the 24 initial consonants tested, results indicate that only four visually-contrastive units are available consistently to the lipreader.[1]

The partially hearing student, with or without electronic aid, may also fail to distinguish phonemes because there may be very slight phonetic or audible distance between two sounds that are phonologically different. But this person may encounter other gaps. He may fail at times to perceive anything to confuse with something else. Phonemes or sequences of phonemes under weak stress simply are not there for him.

The student for whom the language of signs is the main mode of interaction must come to English from a language in which verbs are not inflected for time nor nouns for number and in which an auxiliary verb, a negative morpheme, and a main verb—at least three morphemes in English—can be divided evenly into two, negative auxiliary and main verb.[2]

The deaf student whose teachers and fellows have always fingerspelled to him may habitually relax his eye-focus once the first few digital symbols

---

[1] Authors' summary, *dsh Abstracts*, 1(1961), 149, of M. F. Woodward and C. G. Barber, "Phoneme perception in lipreading," *JSHR*, 3 (1960), 212-222.

[2] Stokoe, "Sign language structure," *Studies in Linguistics*, Occasional Papers: 8 (1961); and "Appendix A" in *A Dictionary of American Sign Language* (Gallaudet College, fall 1965).

give him the lexical identity and before the inflectional or class deriving suffixes are signalled. For him a number of morphemes and syntactic systems may be confused or non-existent.

These gaps in the phonemic and morphemic systems are minor of course compared to the abyss that absence of the auditory function leaves. They are inherent in the substitutes used for the lost hearing, and they are troublesome enough, for they cannot be predicted and have not been explored by linguists or mapped except in the sketchy outlines presented here. It is reasonable to suppose that a combination of all or some of these substitutes: lipreading, residual hearing (and auditory training when appropriate), sign language, and fingerspelling should minimize the gaps. Such a combination is used at Gallaudet College, for only this simultaneous method of communication can reach students from every kind of methodological preparation. Working against an earlier use of multi-channel approaches, though, is the much to be deplored exclusiveness that advocates of each substitute system militantly maintain.

The gaps inherent in the substitute systems are widened and not repaired by language teaching based on misapprehension of the relation speech bears to writing and on ignorance of the arbitrary, symbolic, and systematic nature of language. Reminiscent of the "Secondary and tertiary responses to language" which Bloomfield quotes (*Language* 20.45-55 [1944]) is this statement in a text still used in some centers that train teachers of the deaf:

> *The language of signs* is another form of communication. This is a system of conventional gestures of the hands and arms that by and large are suggestive of the shape, form, or thought which they represent.[3]

As much to be deplored is perpetuating, in teacher training and in classroom work with deaf students, the worst faults of traditional prescriptive grammar. The young hearing pupil may be confused and frustrated by what Miss Fidditch tells him about his language, but he has some defense. He knows what he hears. Outside the classroom he has the check of good solid linguistic reality on her absurdities. The young deaf pupil, however, has not the same language experience outside; and years later the deaf student may still be found using the fidditchisms he learned in school.

On the positive side, the deaf student who reaches college is one of nineteen or twenty in the educational output of his year instead of one in

---

[3] Hallowell Davis and S. Richard Silverman, *Hearing and Deafness* (New York, 1947) 419.

eight or nine in the hearing population. Both hearing and deaf college students are the cream of their age group, but the socio-economic-educational separator happens to be set now so that the cream is twice as rich among the deaf population. The deaf student's dependence on sight, moreover, has given him unusually good skill in spelling, and an accuracy in mechanical details that depend on eye-motor coordination. His exposure to mathematical symbolism is huge relative to his experience of vocal-auditory symbol systems. He therefore shows generally greater mathematical than language aptitude on standard tests and may have superior skill in handling abstract concepts, when they are presented in the precise and elegant language of mathematics. Of course possession of that language skill can handicap him with a teacher who says in effect: "When I use an abstract noun like *myth*, or *democracy*, or *evolution*, you must be thinking of the very same collections of concepts as I am or else you cannot think in the abstract." The deaf student is skilled in the ultimate abstractions: his visual perception of sameness and difference is preternatural.

The task of teaching him the six language skills under discussion here involves all the matters so far considered and many more, but the gaps in the vocal-auditory symbol system loom large. Major repair has to be made in morphology. He may be able to spell all the inflected forms of a noun or a verb but remain unaware of which to use in a given environment. He may have whole chapters of a traditional grammer memorized and score high on objective tests, yet, when he composes, make mistakes in concord, voice, number, tense, and order. He may connect many strings of letters with lexical meanings but perform most erratically in constructing grammatical sentences and principal constituents of sentences.

To teach him these skills it is first necessary to teach that there are principal constituents and how they function. When one has to speak and fingerspell simultaneously in teaching, the term *principal constituent* proves most cumbersome. We use instead, at Gallaudet, the term *field*. This has more than the obvious advantage of brevity. There is in American Sign Language a sign for 'field' ($\overline{\text{B}}$ B$_\text{v}\perp\cdot$), but it is most often used in the immediate language community to translate the academic phrase 'field of specialization.' It translates the English word *major* in its academic uses: as verb, 'to *major* in a field'; as adjective, '*major* courses'; as abstract noun, 'what's your *major*?'; and as personal noun, 'a math *major*.'

The term *field* as a synonym for *principal constituent* has been given a new sign (L$_\text{A}$·L$_\text{A}$ ÷), and a graphic symbol, the horizontal bracket (⌟___⌞). Because fields as principal constituents are the largest parts into which a sentence may be divided, they are (with a few explainable exceptions) consecutive strings of words, zero or more words long, with well defined boundaries. It is very convenient in teaching to use horizontal brackets to mark fields on paper or on the blackboard.

There is a further advantage in the use of the term *field* for the syntactic entity better known as the principal constituent. That is the advantage of using a term for a concept or process isomorphic with the linguistic one. In applied mathematics it is necessary to distinguish between data, the contents of some part of a computer, and the container. The ultimate unit of the container is the cell, which may contain something or nothing— an electric or magnetic charge, usually, or its absence. Every number and every other kind of information that a computer can handle is representable in this binary code of something or nothing. Of course for some data, many cells may be required. One cell can count only to two. Two cells can represent 1, 2, 3, and 4 or else 0, 1, 2, and 3. Eight cells can count to 256 and so on. A machine's memory or storage must have a great number of cells, but there must be a way of knowing for any given cell if and how it is related to others.

Suppose it were possible to look at six adjacent cells in an actual storage, and that they appeared like this (solid for something, one, and open for nothing, zero): • ○ • ○ ○ •. There is no way of knowing what number, if any, this string is supposed to represent. Only by specifying the computer system's "word" structure, the rules for reading cells and "words," can it have meaning. Suppose these six cells are in, or are, one computer "word": • ○ • ○ ○ •. Their meaning is either 37 or 41, depending on whether the system reads words from the left or the right. If they constitute two "words" of three-cell length, read from right to left, the words contain 5 and 1: • ○ • ○ ○ •. But there is still ambiguity: do '5' and '1' mean fifty-one or fifteen or the two numbers 5 and 1? The answer to such questions is given by field specifications. If the system reads words in a field from right to left, and if the six cells and two words are now specified to be in a field also read from right to left, there can be only one meaning, fifty-one: [4]

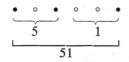

---

[4] Actually fifty-one read out of three-cell words should be treated as an octal number, since each word can contain no number larger than seven. Thus $54_8 = 41_{10}$ or 5 8's+1 one. Likewise $15_8 = 13_{10}$. The argument that fields so defined are system-isomorphic with principal constituents is strengthened by adding the translation from octal to decimal symbol systems.

To represent fifteen in the same system, the string of cells must change:

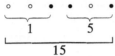

Fields thus defined are free to vary in length. With different field boundaries, the original string of cells and words may represent five and one:

but with word and field boundaries free to vary, many combinations are possible; this for instance:

In this generalization and simplification of numerical logistics, several points appear that are eminently useful in teaching language skills to deaf students. First, a field—either a numerical field or a syntactic field—may be as long as the system specifies. Second, a field may be as short as one word—a computer "word" or an English word. Third, a field may be no words long. This, in the last diagram, is the same as an empty one-cell word. An empty field in English has no word in it, but the field remains as a place that could be filled. Hence, the principle in teaching syntax and morphology to repair gaps caused by hearing loss is that English sentences have at least three fields, nominal, verbal, or neither (N, V, or X):

He saw the girl. She looked inviting.
N   V   N   N   V   X

He spoke. Ø   Ø "Come closer."   Ø "Scram!" Ø
N   V   X   N   V   X   N   V   X

A corollary principle is that a field may be extended or expanded to any appropriate length by the use of explicitly derived rules. (Appropriateness is an extra-linguistic or meta-linguistic consideration which may also be made explicit in a well-designed program of teaching language skills, as John Gumperz and others on yesterday's panel made clear.)

For explaining subordination the three kinds of fields provide a better apparatus than do the terms *phrase* and *clause* and the Protean concepts they stand for. And for showing structure graphically, the field concept symbolized by horizontal brackets is at least as effective as traditional diagramming besides leaving the sentence itself in normal order. Thus:

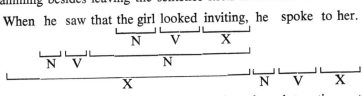

The major advantage is to give the student for whom intonation patterns are forever inaccessible a formal framework for the control of meaning that is in many respects isomorphic with mathematical systems he has learned. The native speaker of English knows the difference between *the thin edge* and *edge, the, thin* and the other four possible arrangements of these three words because he hears the stress, pitch, and juncture phenomena which make *the thin edge* a nominal field. By giving the deaf student a logical and mathematical explanation of field structure, it is possible to repair some of the gaps at the morphological level in the vocal-auditory symbol system. This may then help him to master language skills that allow him to assume a productive role in the educated class.

THE FUNCTIONAL DISTRIBUTION OF CREOLE AND FRENCH IN HAITI

WILLIAM A. STEWART
Center for Applied Linguistics

In an article published in 1959, Charles A. Ferguson directed the attention of linguists to a special kind of bilingualism in which a speech community may use two varieties of the same language under different conditions or for purposes.[1] To designate such a situation, Ferguson suggested use of the term *diglossia.* If this terminological refinement is accepted, then the term *bilingualism* itself can be reserved to indicate situations where the co-occurrent languages are sufficiently unalike in all ways as to be readily distinguishable from each other at any level, and where they may well serve as the linguistic aspects of two relatively autonomous and perhaps competitive cultures. Situations involving bilingualism, in this specialized sense, can be expected to be fairly unstable and to eventually result in the dominance of one of the languages over the other.

In contrast, a diglossia situation is one in which the juxtaposed linguistic systems are sufficiently alike in some ways to encourage their structural fusion at certain points. This, in turn, allows for enough mutual identification of the two systems on the part of their users that they may function as situational variants of each other. Such a functional complementation of two linguistic systems is characterized by more stability than is usual in other kinds of bilingualism, so that diglossia situations may endure for considerable stretches of time without any serious encroachment of one of the languages upon the domain of the other.

At about the same time that the Ferguson article on diglossia appeared, Martin Joos made a preliminary classification of English style variation in terms of five levels of usage, i.e. intimate, casual, consultative, formal, and frozen, ranging from maximum informality to maximum formality.[2] As isolated by Joos, style variation occurs largely wtihin that part of linguistic behavior which is usually de-

---

[1] Charles A. Ferguson, "Diglossia" *Word* 15.325-340 (1959).

[2] Martin Joos, 'The isolation of styles" in: Richard S. Harrell, ed., *Report of the Tenth Annual Round Table Meeting on Linguistics and Language Studies,* Georgetown University Monograph Series on Languages and Linguistics, No. 12, pp. 107-113.

scribed in structural analysis as "free" in that it not easily specified in terms of purely linguistic constraints (i.e. phonological, morphological, or syntactic rules). Yet, style variation is not really unspecifiable, once factors outside the language itself are taken into consideration. Thus style variation is like semantic differentiation in being functionally linked to extra-linguistic behavior.

It is somewhat surprising that in the aftermath of the Ferguson and Joos articles there has been almost no attempt made to investigate the relationship between diglossia and style variation, this especially in view of the fact that even a casual comparison of the two phenomena reveals striking functional similarities. [3] Perhaps these similarities have been obscured in part by the fact that the structural relationships between the linguistic subsystems in a diglossia situation bear an overall resemblance to the structural relationships between geographical or social dialects in other situations. It is understandable how this could lead to an assumption that the rationale of diglossia should be sought within the realm of dialectology, rather than elsewhere. Yet, there are some important differences between diglossia and dialect variation. In situations involving different geographical or socal dialects, each linguistic subsystem, or dialect, is in most cases used by its speakers to the exclusion of other dialects of the same type. That is to say, speakers of different geographical or social dialects do not normally have a command of each other's linguistic systems. Dialect differences, far from being part of the productive linguistic repetoire of the members of the wider speech community, are historically imposed upon individuals by their geographical provenence or group membership. [4]

In diglossia, on the other hand, the linguistic subsystems are like the style levels of a single language in that they are used together as interchangeable linguistic devices within the discourse of individuals throughout the wider speech community. Furthermore, as will be seen, the subsystems are linguistically differentiative in that the use of one or the other conveys speaker-intended meaning,

---

[3] A possible relationship between the two was suggested, though not elaborated along precisely these lines, for one kind of Arabic diglossia in the article by Haim Blanc, "Stylistic variations in spoken Arabic: a sample of interdialectal educated conversation" in: Charles A. Ferguson, ed., *Contributions to Arabic Linguistics,* Cambridge, Massachusetts, Harvard University Press, 1960.

[4] It is possible for originally different geographical or social dialects to come to be used coterminously in a diglossia relationship. But when this happens, the speech forms cease to be geographical or social dialects as such, and become instead the potentially common property of all members of the speech community.

rather than information about the speaker's background, as is the case with dialects.

It seems obvious, then, that the relationship of diglossia to style deserves further study. It will be the purpose of this paper to contribute to that study by examining such a relationship in the functional distribution of Creole and French in the diglossia situation of Haiti.

The Republic of Haiti is located on the western third of the island it shares with the Dominican Republic. Haiti's predominantly rural population is rather large, considering the size of the country (10,714 square miles), being placed by the last official census at some 3,097,000 persons and presently estimated to have reached three and one-half million. As the former French colony of Saint-Domingue, Haiti was the center of an Afro-French cultural complex which coincided with French domination in the Caribbean and extended from what is now the State of Louisiana down to French Guiana in north-eastern South America. Like most of the other areas which were once part of this complex, Haiti has inherited two languages. One is a French-based Creole which, though normally unwritten, has continued to be an everyday language for virtually one-hundred percent of the population. [5] The other, French, is the official and written language of the Republic. French, as spoken in Haiti, exhibits certain local characteristics when compared with, say, educated Parisian usage. As might be expected, many of these local characteristics are due to the influence of Creole. In its written form, however, there is little difference between the French of Haiti and that of the Continent. The number of French speakers in Haiti contrasts sharply with the number of Creole speakers, and although there are no figures available which show how many Haitians can speak French, the fact that it is the country's only written language allows one to take the approximate literacy rate of 12.5% for those over ten years of age as a rough indication of some formal exposure to French (although the number of persons who are really fluent in the language must be well below this). Of course, nearly all French speakers in Haiti are native speakers of Creole as well, and hence are bilingual.

---

[5] A brief survey of the historical development and geographical spread of French-based Creoles in the Caribbean, as well as their relation to non-French Creoles, is to be found in William A. Stewart, "Creole languages in the Caribbean" appearing in: Frank A. Rice, ed., *Study of the Role of Second Languages in Asia, Africa, and Latin America*, Washington, D. C., Center for Applied Linguistics, 1962.

All-important in the description of any diglossia situation is a statement of the structural relationships which the linguistic sub-systems have to each other. Perhaps the best place to begin such a statement of the structural relationships of Creole and French is with the phonological inventories which serve as their fundamental building blocks.

When one compares the phonologies of the two most mutually remote varieties of Creole and French in Haiti, namely the rural Creole (= RC) of a monolingual Haitian peasant with the Haitian French (= HF) of an educated urbanite, one finds surprisingly little difference in the basic phoneme inventories of the two languages. The greatest divergence is in the vowel systems, illustrated as follows:

Rural Creole				Haitian French		
i	u		**ORAL**	i	y	u
e	o			e	ə	o
ε	a	ɔ		ε	a	ɔ
ẽ	õ		**NASAL**	ẽ	ɔ̃	õ
	ã				ã	

Thus HF has the rounded front vowels /y ə ɔ̃/ contrasting with the unrounded front vowels /i e ẽ/, while RC has only the latter set, e.g. HF /dyr/ *dur* 'hard' vs. /dir/ *dire* 'to say', both of which are /di/ in RC.

In the consonants, HF has a rounded front glide /ɥ/ contrasting with the rounded back glide /w/, where RC has only the latter, e.g. HF /ɥit/ *huit* 'eight' vs. /wi/ *oui* 'yes', corresponding to RC /wit/ and /wi/ respectively. Otherwise, the main difference between RC and HF consonants lies, not in the inventories themselves, but rather in the combinatorial possibilities of their elements. Thus /r/ occurs post-vocalically in HF, while in RC it does not, e.g. HF /pɔrt/ *porte* 'door', RC /pɔt/. Also, HF can have final consonant clusters of the type /Cl/, /Cr/, and /st/, whereas RC has simply /C/ and /s/, e.g. HF /tabl/ *table* 'table', /livr/ *livre* 'book', /turist/ *touriste* 'tourist', beside RC /tab/, /liv/, and /turis/. Finally, it is worth noting that the allophonic conventions holding for like phonemes in

RC and HF are practically identical.[6]

In comparing the morphological characteristics of RC and HF, one must distinguish between grammatical morphenes, which are more properly dealt with as part of the grammatical systems, and other lexical items. Haitian Creole is referred to as a French-based Creole because its lexicon is obviously and overwhelmingly French-derived. There are, however, certain lexical differences to be found between RC and HF. Generally speaking, these are of three main types:

(1) Differences in the phonemic shape of lexical cognates, due to divergencies in the two phonological systems (exemplified above).

(2) Differences in the phonemic shape of lexical cognates, due to other (principally historical) causes, e.g. RC /šɛj/ 'chair', /zãmi/ 'friend', /blie/ 'to forget'; HF /šɛz/ *chaise*, /ami/ *ami(e)*, /ublie/ *oublier*.

(3) Differences where the direct semantic equivalents are non-cognate, e.g. RC /mẽ/ 'here (is)', /kaj/ 'house', /gumẽ/ 'to fight', /kuljea/~/kunjea/ 'now'; HF /vwasi/ *voici*, /mezõ/ *maison*, /kõbatr/ *combattre*, /mẽtənã/ *maintenant*.

Differences of type (1) are by far the most frequent, accounting for the vast majority of lexical divergencies in RC and HF. Type (2) differencees are much less common, and type (3) differences are fairly rare. Even rarer are cases where lexical items which are structurally cognate in RC and HF have different meanings, cf. RC /nɛg/ 'fellow', /bagaj/ 'thing' beside HF /nɛgr/ *négre* 'Negro', /bagaž/ *bagage* 'baggage'.

In grammar, the differences between RC and HF are more marked than in phonology or lexico-semantics. Without going into the extensive detail necessary for an accurate comparison of the two systems, it can be stated that among the more important grammatical differences are those of different arrangements of categories for

---

[6] This sub-phonemic behavior which is common to Haitian Creole and Haitian French is quite different from the sub-phonemic behavior of French anywhere on the Continent. In fact, it is largely through its allophones that Haitian French gets its characteristic sound. This sub-phonemic difference from Continental French is reinforced by a few actual phonemic differences as well. Thus HF normally has, like Creole, /$\tilde{\nabla}$m/. /$\tilde{\nabla}$n/, and /$\tilde{\nabla}$ŋ/ word-finally where Continental French has /$\tilde{\nabla}$b/, /$\tilde{\nabla}$d/, and /$\tilde{\nabla}$g/, e.g. HF /žãm/ *jambe* 'leg', /mõn/ *monde* 'world', /lãŋ/ *langue* 'tongue'; Continental French /žãb/, /mõd/, and /lãg/.

nouns, adjectives, pronouns, prepositions, and verbs in the two languages, as well as quite different syntactical structures. [7]

The foregoing comparisons have shown that Haitian Creole, in
its rural form, is structurally different from Haitian French at all
linguistic levels—phonology, lexicon, and grammar. However, there
also exists in Haiti another variety of Creole, which is spoken principally in the urban centers, largely (but not exclusively) by Haitians who know some French. Though generally ignored or discount-
ed by linguistic descriptions so far, this urban Creole (= UC) is of
practical importance because of the fact that it has much higher
social prestige than RC, even in the opinion of RC speakers themselves. In addition, UC is of linguistic importance because it, and
not RC, is the variety of Creole which is the normal co-participant
with French in Haitian diglossia.

UC differs from RC principally in being structurally closer to
HF in certain ways, so that many of the differences in form which
distinguish RC from HF do not hold for UC. For example, the
phonemes /y ə ə̃ ɥ/, absent in RC, occur in UC with much the same
lexical distributions as in HF. The same is fairly true for post vocalic
/r/ and, to some extent, for the final clusters /C/ /Cr/, and /st/
as well. Thus lexical differences from HF of type (1) above, so frequent in RC, are largely eliminated in UC. In addition, type (2) differences may also be eliminated in UC by the free use of HF forms
beside the RC ones, e.g. /šɛz/ beside /šej/, /ami/ beside /zãmi/,
etc. [8] Even the relatively rare lexical differences of type (3) are de-
emphasized by the general convention that, even where they are
non-cognates, French equivalents may be substituted for Creole forms
(but not vice-versa!).

Although phonological and lexical divergences from HF are thus
generally minimized in UC, the same is not true with respect to the
two grammars. Even in UC, accommodations to French grammatical
patterns are slight. For the most part, they involve the use of cer-
prepositional constructions, e.g. UC /m vwajaže də pɔrtoprɛs a
žakmɛl/ 'I travelled from Port-au-Prince to Jacmel', where RC would
be /m vojaže pɔtoprɛs žakmɛl/, the use of the subordinator /kə/,
e.g. UC /li di m kə l(i) ta fɛ sa pur mwẽ/ 'he told me that he would

---

[7] For more details about the basic grammatical structure of Haitian Creole,
the reader should consult Robert A. Hall, Jr., *Haitian Creole; Grammar, Texts,
Vocabulary*, Menasha, Wisconsin, 1953 (= Memoir 74, American Anthropological Association and Memoir 43, American Folklore Society).

[8] Sometimes the form in UC does not have the shape anticipated. Thus,
RC /vle/ 'to want' has a UC equivalent /vlə/, apparently as much on analogy
with HF /və/ *veux* as with the expected HF /vule/ *voulez*.

do that for me', for RC /li di m li ta fɛ sa pu mwẽ/, and gender accord for nouns and adjectives (signalled by morphological changes),
e.g. UC /nɛg sa-a se aisjẽ/ 'that fellow is a Haitian' vs. /fãm sa-a se
aisjɛn/ 'that woman is a Haitian', where RC would have /aisjẽ/ in
both cases.   In most other ways, however, Creole grammar remains
relatively little influenced by French.

The result of these similarities and differences is that UC and
HF stand, in the linguistic makeup of the bilingual Haitian, in an
interesting relationship to each other.   The two linguistic systems
are more or less fused at those points where they correlate with a
commonly shared part of the real world—once at the phonological
end, where language bhavior is correlated with the organs of speech
—again at the lexico-semantic end, where language behavior is correlated with its external referents.   This relationship can be illustrated schematically as follows: [9]

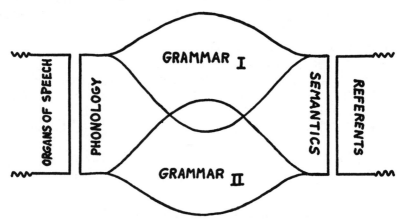

The two grammars remain distinct enough so that it is possible for
the speaker to select at will one or the other, and possible for the
hearer to tell at any given moment which grammar—and hence
which language—is being used. [10]

With the structural parameters of Creole and French outlined,
it is now possible to move on to the central concern of this paper—

---

[9] I am indebted to Martin Joos for this diagram, which he suggested in the
course of a private conversation about the diglossia situation in Haiti.

[10] In fact, one may occasionally hear such UC utterances as /mwa pa kɔnɛ
lɥi./ 'I don't know him, where all the constituent morphemes are perfectly French
(the phrase could be written *moi pas connais lui*) but which is immediately
recognized as Creole, simply because the construction is meaningful only in
terms of the syntax of that language, cf. RC and more usual UC /m(wẽ) pa
kõnẽ ni/ but French *je ne le connais pas*.

the functional distribution of the two languages within the Haitian bilingual community.

Certainly the most obvious kind of restriction on language use is that placed upon the speaker by immediate considerations of a purely linguistic or mechanical nature, such as the necessity to use Creole to a monolingual peasant, or French when addressing a foreigner or dictating correspondence.   However, such cases account for only a small fraction of the decisions which, in the course of his daily activities, the bilingual Haitian must make as to which language to use.   In most cases, his choice will depend largely upon non-linguistic factors, many of which relate to the immediate social context.   Observation has shown that two main kinds of behavioral variables play an important role as the determiners of language usage in any social situation.   These are:

Public (impersonal or representative) behavior
vs.
Private (personal and non-representative) behavior
and
Formalized (formally prescribed) behavior
vs.
Unformalized (not formally prescribed) behavior

The usual language distribution in terms of these variables is illustrated by the following chart, with the most frequently used language listed first in those cases where both can be used: [11]

	Formalized	Unformalized
Public	French	Creole~French
Private	French~Creole	Creole (~French)

It can be seen from the chart that French is the only appropriate language for public-formalized behavior, e.g. that involved in official ceremonies, legal and administrative procedures, formal education, and the like, while, at the other extreme, Creole is the usual language for private-unformalized behavior such as interaction between

---

[11] Another version of this diagram appears in William A. Stewart, *op. cit.*

friends or relatives, at informal gatherings or within the family. [12] In between, French is the more common language for private-formalized behavior, e.g., introductory conversations between strangers, and Creole is somewhat more common for such public-unformalized behavior as advertising, general bartering, etc.

Except for public-formalized situations, the social context itself is only a partial determiner of language usage in Haitian diglossia. In most situations, one of the languages is more commonly used, but the other can also be heard. Part of this variation is undoubtedly due to personality differences among individual speakers; conservative minded Haitians will lean toward the greater use of French, while more relaxed and progressive Haitians will prefer to use Creole whenever possible. Yet this is clearly not the full answer, since often the same individual can be observed to alternate between lanlanguages in cases where the social context appears to remain constant. It would seem that language usage in Haitian diglossia is to some extent determined by conditions which are relatively independent both of speaker personality and the social context. But then the inevitable question is—what conditions?

When I first went to Haiti, I quickly noticed that bilingual Haitians would often shift from French to Creole (or viceversa) and back again right in the middle of a conversation, and sometimes even in the middle of a sentence. Although I had already caught on to the differences in linguistic behavior which were clearly conditioned by the social context, I continued for some time to regard this other kind of fluctuation in language use simply as erratic behavior, produced by the two linguistic sysems in contact. Then one day, on a subsequent stay in the country, I was engaged in conversation with a Haitian friend with whom I had been on Creole speaking terms for some time. I happened to enquire about the health of his mother, who had only a short time previously been hospitalized because of an illness. I was surprised by the fact that my friend switched to French for his reply. Then it struck me that the changeover corresponded rather neatly to a shift which an English speaker would

---

[12] For the use of Creole in the family, exceptions to the rule may be found in those cases where parents use only French with their children, so that the latter will get accustomed to using the language. But the parents usually continue to speak Creole to each other, as well as to friends and servants. The children, on their part learn Creole from servants and playmates anyway, and usually speak it among themselves when not in earshot of their parents. In effect, what happens within such families is that French becomes the special medium for parent-child communication, while Creole continues to be used for all other family purposes.

be likely to make under similar circumstances from a colloquial to a more formal style of speech, say, from Joos' casual to consultative. It began to appear that my friend had used the change from one language to the other as a stylistic device to indicate a change in the mood of his discourse.

Subsequent observations have tended overwhelmingly to support this hypothesis. In particular, most of the language shifts which I have observed in conversations involving bilingual Haitians have corresponded to cases where a style shift would also be appropriate in English. Take, for example, part of a telephone conversation in which one Haitian businessman was overheard speaking (primarily in French) to another: "*Je comprends très bien pourquoi vous demandez l'argent d'avance,* /wap proteže tet u/". Compare a somewhat free English equivalent: "I certainly understand why you're asking for the money in advance—you've got to (= /gat+tə/ or /gatə/) look out for yourself, I guess." Note the consultative style of the sequence before the break, marked by the use of *certainly,* among other things, followed by a shift into casual, marked by the pronunciation of *got to* and the softener, *I guess.* Both the language shift in the Haitian conversation and the style shift in its English equivalent are devices used by the speaker to communicate information to the addressee—in this case, a message of voluntary identification and understanding.

If correct, this hypothesis about the nature of diglossia in Haiti has several implications. I will mention just two here—one for assumptions which are often made about Haitian French, and another for the theory of diglossia itself.

In the first case, foreigners who have visited or resided in Haiti have often remarked that Haitian French seems to them to be stuffy and bookish, and lacking the relaxed, fluid quality which it often has when used by Frenchmen. The foreigners tend to assume from this that French is not well spoken in Haiti. Haitians, on their part, have noticed this characteristic of their French, too. However, they explain it differently—saying that French usage in Haiti is simply more "pure" than in France. What is probably the case, however, is that Haitian French tends to lack equivalents for Joos' casual and intimate styles, since where a Frenchman would use his French counterparts for these styles, Haitians normally switch to Creole. This characteristic of HF is matched by a converse one in UC. I have noticed that the Creole of bilingual Haitians seems to lack the special kinds of styles which monolingual Creole speakers use in certain formalized activities, such as the recitation of folk tales, religious ceremonies, etc. This is probably because in his own formalized situations the bilingual Haitian will not normally use Creole at all—he will use french.[13]

As regards the theory of diglossia, a situation has been described in this paper in which the two related linguistic systems function, for bilinguals, as stylistic variants of each other. Eventually, if the term *diglossia* is not to degenerate into just a somewhat fancy synonym for bilingualism, it will be necessary for linguists to formalize a little more definitely the ways in which diglossia differs from other kinds of bilingualism. The diglossia situation in Haiti sugggests one possible difference. If subsequent examinations of diglossia situations elsewhere reveal style function as a similar factor, it may well serve as a central criterion for the general definition of diglossia as a unique sociolinguistic phenomenon.

[13] In RC, a style with many of the characteristics of Joos' frozen style has been developed for newspapers, educational broadsides, pedagogical materials, religious tracts, etc., written in Creole. This style of Creole is not really identical with any spoken form of the language.

LINGUISTICS AND MODERN PHILOSOPHY

C. I. J. M. STUART

Georgetown University

From the earliest times philosophers have undertaken analysis of key expressions as a preliminary to philosophic investigation proper. British empiricists from the seventeenth century until well on into the nineteenth provide a notable example of this tendency in the philosophy of empiricism. Modern analytical philosophy, on the other hand, takes the analysis of language as its primary task. Its historical roots are in inquiries concerning the foundations of mathematics and closely related investigations in the development of modern systems of logic, and in interpretations of physical science. With the exception of ordinary-language analysis, the main branches of analytical philosophy are predominantly concerned with the language of empirical science in an attempt to make explicit the meaning of scientific propositions and the structure of scientific thought. To this end, analytic philosophers make considerable use of mathematical logic in constructing artificial languages in order to correct the ambiguities and reduce the complexities of natural language.

It is precisely this last feature which causes many linguists to challenge the value of analytical philosophy for investigations in empirical linguistics. Among the more coherent forms which this objection takes, we may mention the following by way of illustration. No logistic language is known for which typical natural language corpora, such as provide data in empirical linguistics, can stand as a domain of interpretation. Moreover, it is not likely that any such logistic system or calculus will meet this requirement, if only because systems of formal logic are obtained from natural language. That is to say, the metalanguage in which formal logics are constructed is always a natural language, and not vice versa. In this respect, we may add that all known systems of formal logic have been developed within the Indo-European languages.[1] The question as to whether or not quite different

---

[1] This fact was pointed out to me by I. M. Bocheński when I suggested to him that natural languages may well turn out to be axiomatic systems. Bocheński then went on to point out a possible relation between the above mentioned fact and my

logics may be developed within languages of fundamentally different structure thus points out the further question as to whether or not the structural
devices of natural language, which are closely related to modes of conceptual
relations, may fix limits for parameters of relation in logistic systems
derived from natural language.

An objection is valid only in case it applies. In what follows, I want to
discuss a frame of reference with respect to empirical linguistics in which
the objection I have mentioned, whatever particular form it might take,
does not apply, and to go on to outline certain issues which come to attention
when one looks at linguistics from within this frame of reference.

The linguist's attempt, either in descriptive or in explanatory terms, to
account for phenomena of design in natural language is represented in
sets of activities which constitute the process of investigation, though
different activities would have to be specified as between different 'schools'
of linguistics. These activities are, in turn, represented in sets of statements
that the linguist makes about them. The order in which the different
activities may be undertaken is subject to a great deal of variation, but it is
always possible to direct attention to relations between the corresponding
statements so as to draw general conclusions independently of the activities
themselves. The general schema which I outline below is, perhaps, novel
in certain respects, but it does no violence, that I am aware of, to the
actual practices of individual linguists so long as we remember that it
involves no more than possible reorderings of statements of a kind actually
made by linguists.

The construction of a conceptual scheme is represented in definitions
which specify analytical terms and the kinds of relations in which they stand.
It is through the conceptual scheme that the data are observed and
interpreted, but individual devices are needed for the particular observational
acts. Such devices are obtained in the form of *protocols* which are statements of steps to be undertaken in the process of analysis. Since protocols
are the immediate observational devices of linguistics, their construction is
a task of great importance. Any distortion of the terms and relations of the
conceptual scheme which might occur in protocol construction will result
in a skewing of observation relative to the conceptual scheme through which
observed states of affairs are subsequently to be interpreted. This difficulty
can in large measure be controlled if we require that the protocol contain,
in addition to statements of steps to be undertaken, statements as to the

---

suggestion: the classification of language types on the basis of their inherent logics
may prove far more illuminating with regard to the origins of language than an
approach based upon strict phylogeny.

interpretation to be given to the results obtained at each step. That is to say, the protocol will consist of a series of ordered pairs of statements; the first statement of a pair tells the analyst what to do, and the second tells him what result he will obtain, having done it, in terms of the initial conceptual scheme. Analysis itself consists in applying to the data each step in the protocol. Each such step in the analysis constitutes an *observational act* and is represented in an *observation statement*. The result obtained from each observational act, thus corresponding to the second member of a *protocol pair,* constitutes a theory-directed interpretation of the data, and is represented in a *protocol statement*. Several layers of protocols may be needed in the course of certain observations.

In terms of this schema, there are at least two broad categories of statements in empirical linguistics: those which justify observational acts and the results obtained from those acts and those which specify what is observed as a result of particular acts of observation. Such statements, which form part of linguistic discourse, are themselves a subject for analysis if we are interested in the meaning of linguistic statements, how they acquire meaning and how the language of linguistic discourse is structured. This last problem concerns logical relations among the terms which occur in the individual statements of linguistics and systemic relations as between the individual statements. Analysis of this kind, which is part of theoretical linguistics, is concerned with the logic of linguistics as an empirical science, and its primary justification lies in the extent to which we attach importance to the problems it deals with.

It is in this kind of analysis that clear relations are established between empirical linguistics and modern analytical philosophy. The most immediate of these relations lies in the fact that the procedures of empirical linguistics are inadequate for the task of analysing the logical structure of linguistic discourse. The objection I mentioned earlier seems to lose its force when we recognize this limitation on our empirical procedures and when we recognize that the subject of investigation is the language of linguistic statements, not the language about which linguistic statements are made, the objection seems to me to be irrelevant.

To say, however, that analysis of the logic of linguistic statements is itself irrelevant to the goals of linguistics is tantamount to a claim that linguistic statements are justified in so far as they correspond to the facts vested in utterance corpora. Such a view of the objectivity of empirical fact is not very satisfactory; however, since it would imply our regarding science as consisting in a body of methods by which these 'facts' are discovered, and which establishes a body of 'factual knowledge'. In this respect, let me remind you that in my account of empirical linguistics I spoke of protocol statements as representing interpretations of the data as directed by the initial conceptual scheme. Close examination of the schema will reveal that there is no other way of accounting for protocol statements. This is because science is essentially an intellectual activity in which our experiences of empirical states of affairs are organized within the formal restraint of a logical system.

That this is an accurate account of science may be seen by reference to the case of an empirical theory for which a calculus is specified. Assuming standard modern accounts of the structure of theory, we should say that the language in which observations are recorded is formally determined by the logical structure of the theory. That is to say, statements of what is observed must be capable of occurring as empirical interpretations of formulae derived within the calculus. So that what is observed is an interpretation in the logical sense, and what we experience is that aspect of the empirical state of affairs to which attention is directed by the formal constraint of theory. From this we should conclude that scientific experience in such cases is always relative to the theoretical structure from which observation takes place. But this is to say that science is vested in experience of empirical states of affairs within a logical system. Another way of putting this is to say that the experience is not empirically founded, but just so much of the empirical state of affairs is the object of experience as may be correlated by rules of interpretation with the logical structure of the language of theory.

It is on this account that scientific knowledge, represented in statements about scientific experience, cannot properly be said to be correct. And this is true not only in the case of theories where the initial conceptual scheme is a linguistically ordered one, as in a calculus, and in such cases as the schema which I gave for empirical linguistics, but applies with equal force in the extreme case of pure description. Here the only terms which may occur in statements are those which are taxonomic labels for directly observed entities, and the only relations admitted between statements are those which represent observed states of affairs, and similarly with regard to relations between the taxonomic labels within statements. In such a case the structure of statements is relative not to the gross empirical state of affairs, but to those particular isolates in the crude data to which definitions are attached.

In spite of recent claims to the contrary, there is no way open for us mechanically to evaluate contending theories in linguistics or elsewhere in science. This obtains in the three cases we have discussed and in theories which lie at various points between, including logical constructions from taxonomic theories of the latter kind. Given two distinct theories, they can only be evaluated in relation to sets of conditions, whether linguistic inventions or taxonomic isolates, which provide the initial frame of reference. In such circumstances we say that this theory, rather than the other, accounts more adequately for the sets of conditions. But this leaves us hanging in the air, so to speak, as to the ultimate status of these conditions. Given, on the other hand, two distinct sets of conditions and a theory relative to each set, there is no mechanical way in which we may decide that one of the theories is better than the other unless we can show, in a mechanical way, that one set of conditions is better than the other. But this can only be done by appeal to some further set of conditions which subsumes the other two, in which case we should still be left to account for the criteria by which this new set of conditions is established.

Such considerations point to the inadequacy of the view that certain theories are 'correct' and that others are 'incorrect' in the absolute sense that we have come to hear from certain proponents of transformation theory. To know the full set of truth conditions for any field of inquiry, and to know that it is the full set of truth conditions, is to obviate the need for science. As I have tried to indicate, science is not vested in empirical states of affairs, but in the mind of the individual scientist whence it takes on public form in statements which correspond to this experience. The extent to which certain of these statements, those which specify what is observed, also correspond to empirical states of affairs is not only a measure of the adequacy of theory, but is also precisely the extent to which these empirical states of affairs constitute interpretations, in the logical sense, of these statements. Hence, scientific experience has to do with particular interpretations which form the empirical basis for the way in which we interpret, in the sense of providing explanation or description, the world about us. Thus, to claim for a particular theory that it specifies the 'truth' is to indulge in a particularly unrewarding form of mysticism.

In the case of empirical linguistics the problem is dimensionally different from that of most other fields of inquiry. Elsewhere, the parameters of investigation are fixed between the initial conceptual scheme and the empirical data. But in linguistics the data constitute a representational form for a semantic, or behavioral, state of affairs: the matrix of ordinary experience. The physical corpus which the linguist analyses may be viewed as incorporating, in some sense or other, the logic of this further dimension. Accordingly, the conditions of grammaticality in the physical data, E_1, may be viewed as specifying the relations under constraint of which experience coheres in the second dimension, E_2. In this sense, a natural language is regarded as a *system of natural logic* with regard to the matrix of ordinary, non-scientific, experience for a given community. Grammaticality is a matter not only of the formal properties of utterances as formula-types in the natural logic which underlies E_1, but is concerned also with these formulae as specifying the constraints under which experience coheres in the E_2 matrix. Thus, possible interpretations for E_1-formulae, within E_2 as the specified domain of interpretation, constitute sets of relational or structural meanings. That is to say, we specify a *relational or structural meaning* as a member of a set of possible interpretations in E_2 for a formula-type which underlies the data in E_1. A *non-relational or isolative meaning* is specified as a set of possible interpretations for lexical items which occupy positions in E_1-formulae.

In this way, I think we can overcome the problem of semantic contamination in empirical linguistics. The value of protocols here is that we may use them to determine when recourse to the second dimension, in order to get through an impasse in the first dimension, is viciously circular or not. There is, then, a two-way traffic between empirical linguistics and analytical philosophy; the latter provides a frame of reference in which we can undertake the logical analysis of linguistic statements, and the former may be instrumental in adding to our knowledge of non-deductive systems of inference by investigation of systems of natural logic.

FUNCTIONAL SYNTAX AND SYNTACTIC OPERATIONS

A. G. F. VAN HOLK

University of Groningen

1. If it is the aim of general linguistics to understand "how language works" by establishing the general principles of its mechanism, the linguist who seeks to achieve this without transcending the bounds of the observable will naturally concentrate his attention upon what Martinet circumscribes as "that stretch of the communication process that lies between the lips of the speaker and the ears of the listener".[1] We may take this to mean that only the utterance, or perhaps the sequence of utterances that makes up a continuous text, is to furnish the material for linguistic experiment, to the effect that no property or function, semantic or other, should be attributed to language unless it is, to quote Martinet once more, "expressed somehow in the utterance".[2] Accepting this restriction of our field of research has considerable theoretical implications, inasmuch as it constrains us to base our picture of the mechanism of communication, and of linguistic structure in general, on the **syntagmatic** patterns embedded in the flow of speech, and on the distribution of linguistic elements over those patterns.

> [This preoccupation with the linear arrangement of the message does not imply a neglect of the paradigmatic aspect of language: it merely enables us to replace the familiar concept of the unordered paradigm by a more promising view of paradigmatic extension as organised by the **literary** structure of a continuous text.]

In this paper I propose to take up the analysis of syntactic structure from a "functional" standpoint which, in its pivotal tenets, owes much to Martinet's recent publications on what he calls "functional syntax". A novel element with regard to Martinet's approach is the use of certain operations, such as the hypotactic and paratactic combination and the

---

[1] André Martinet, "Elements of a Functional Syntax", *Word,* 16 (1960), 4.
[2] Ibid.

neutralisation of functions, with the aim of deriving new functional dimensions from a given set of primary functions.

The term 'function' (beside 'functional level' and 'dimension') will be used throughout this paper in the familiar sense, conforming to which an entity is said to fulfill a function if it contributes, directly or indirectly, as a meaningful or distinctive feature, to the expression or transmission of semantic content by virtue of the status of that feature in a given pattern. Thus, for instance, an expression may perform a lexical function owing to its phonemic identity, and as a lexical entity it may in turn figure as a modifier relative to another entity of the same text.

2. De Saussure has called attention to the peculiar property of language, that we are so often at a loss to delimit its units (unités concrètes), despite their obvious role in the mechanism of language.[3] In syntax especially, one faces the problem which entities are to be taken as the ultimate constituents of syntactic patterning, and what size are its **maximal** units.

> [Several contemporary linguists in the Netherlands have adopted an approach to syntax pivoted on the polar contrast between the word as the minimal independently meaningful unit and the sentence (defined in Bloomfield's terms) as the maximal unit.[4] In a functional approach, the core of the problem is to assign each unit, such as the phoneme, the word, the clause, its proper place in the study of a particular kind of phenomenon. Thus the **word** as a unit is certainly fundamental in studying the combinatorics of phonemes,[5] whereas in syntax the basic units will rather be the clause and the sentence.]

For our present purpose we shall define the clause as a subject-predicate expression or an equivalent impersonal variety of this type, possibly containing one or more objects and an arbitrary number of omissible con-

---

[3] F. de Saussure, *Cours de linguistique générale* (Paris, 1949), 149.

[4] Cf. for instance E. M. Uhlenbeck, "Traditionele zinsontleding en syntaxis", *Levende Talen*, 193 (1958), 18-30, and A. W. de Groot, *Inleiding tot de algemene taalwetenschap tevens inleiding tot de grammatica van het Nederlands,* (Groningen, 1962), 51 (definition of the sentence) and *passim.*

[5] One may think, for instance, of the exclusive use, in Dutch, of the apicals /t,d,s,n,r/ together with the vocalic archiphoneme /ə/, to form flexional endings (*mooi, -er, -st; kom-t, kom-e(n), nieuw-s,* etc.) and of the necessity to distinguish between mono and polymorphemic frames in discussing the distribution of phonemes. Thus, in Dutch, the functional difference between stops and spirants involves the location of a morpheme boundary : /-pt, -kt/ differ from /-ft, -xt/ in that they normally—apart from loanwords—contain a morpheme boundary, so that the stops in Dutch could be defined as **closers** of a morpheme, while the spirants lack this property. Cf. A. Cohen, C. L. Ebeling, K. Fokkema, A. G. F. van Holk, *Fonologie van het Nederlands en het Fries* ('s-Gravenhage, 1961), ch. IV.

stituents; by a sentence we shall understand, following Bloomfield's use of the term, a clause in absolute position.[6]

3. The functions entering into combination within the frame of the sentence can be adequately defined in terms of **three** [7] primary functional levels.

In the first place may be mentioned the **lexical function** of the phonic material of a sentence. The sound level of language enters into syntax on account of its capacity to identify the lexical sphere of a meaningful expression. This fact was well understood by Bloomfield when he extended the term **lexical** "to cover all forms that can be stated in terms of phonemes, including even such forms as already contain some grammatical features (e.g. *poor John* or *duchess* or *ran*)" and defined the phoneme as a "lexical" unit of linguistic signaling.[8]

Now we notice that, although the syntactic components of a sentence practically all—with the possible exception only of certain "empty" words like *of* in *the conquest of the North*—perform a lexical function, only **one** type of expressions performs no other function besides: these expressions may be called **substantive phrases.** Thus, in *my brother gave her a fan,* the substantive phrases *my brother, her,* and *a fan* will be specified by their exclusively lexical function.[9] On the contrary, the finite verb of a clause like *they manned the boat,* although decidedly endowed with lexical function, as we gather in this case from the inclusion of the cognate noun stem *man-,* yet performs other functions besides, as appears from the presence of the past tense suffix in *manned,* as well as from the syntactic latitudes of this class of forms in general. Thus the lexical function of an expression in our present approach represents, still in keeping with the tenor of Bloomfield's formulation, the total contribution of the root morphemes to the identification of a sentence.

In expanded clauses, a substantive phrase will in general occupy a definite **position** relative to other substantive phrases. The difference in position reflects a **lexical** relation, as between the agent and the patient of an action, and this relation is not expressed segmentally, but, depending on the language, by a feature of order relative to the finite verb or by a meaningless position-marker in the shape of a case-suffix, a subject-particle,[10] or the like.

---

[6] Leonard Bloomfield, *Language* (New York, 1933), 11.1.

[7] **Four** if intonation is included; see end of this section.

[8] Bloomfield, op. cit., 16.1.

[9] Cf. Martinet, op. cit., p. 5, where these units are described as "non-autonomous" phrases.

[10] See for example A. A. Fokker, *Inleiding tot de studie van de Indonesische syntaxis* (Groningen-Djakarta, 1951).

At this point it is necessary to recall an important syntactic distinction made by Ebeling [11] (and applied with much success by A. H. Kuipers to the case-system of Circassian),[12] namely, the distinction between "parallel" and "non-parallel" linguistic elements of the spoken chain. According to Ebeling, two elements are parallel if they point to the same portion of reality; otherwise they are called non-parallel (or divergent). Ebeling's idea may be interpreted to mean that two lexical positions approach a state of complete non-parallelism, i.e. of orthogonality, to the degree that the elements in those positions can be selected **independently.** Applying this notion to the lexical structure of the clause, it appears that the three participants of the action expressed by the finite verb in a clause of the general form

$$X \text{ } gives \text{ } Y \text{ } to \text{ } Z \text{ or } X \text{ } gives \text{ } Y \text{ } Z,$$

are mutually perpendicular in the sense specified above (they are also treated that way by Ebeling himself in his analysis of the Russian construction *dat' knigu učeniku* 'to give the book to the pupil').[13] In such English constructions as *the dogs barked furiously* the adverb *furiously* may be decomposed into a suffix *-ly,* which is parallel with the verb *barked,* and a stem *furious-,* which is parallel with *dogs.*

The next primary function to be discussed now is the **time of utterance.** In syntax, the typical unit endowed with time function is the sentence. Unlike the lexical function, the time level of language does not occupy a syntactic position: its units, for instance the successive sentences of a novel, are completely determined by their place in the sequence, whereas an entity with lexical function is determined both by its place in the paradigm [14] and by its relation to other lexical entities of the same clause.

Finally, among the primary functions we should include a special **actualising function.** In a personal clause of the substantive plus finite verb type, e.g. *the boys are playing chess,* the actualising function is expressed by the so-called subject; in other clause types, such as *it is raining,* and German: *es wird getanzt,* Dutch: *er wordt gedanst,* Russian: *vse nebo*

---

[11] Carl L. Ebeling, "On the semantic structure of the Russian sentence," *Lingua,* IV (1954), 207-222, esp. p. 211.

[12] A. H. Kuipers, "The Circassian Nominal Paradigm: A Contribution to Case-Theory," *Lingua,* XI (1962), 231-248.

[13] Ebeling, op. cit., p. 218.

[14] The analogy between place in the paradigm and place in the time sequence becomes more obvious if we consider this paradigm as the set of parallel expressions relating, for instance, to a given personage of a novel and thus making up the "path" of that personage through the "narrated space" of the novel; cf. F. C. Maatje, *Der Doppelroman* (Groningen, 1964) (diss.), part I, ch. 2, and Summary, p. 149.

tučami zavoloklo, Polish: *gdy go pytano, czyja to miaya być ręka* (Sienkiewicz), and many others, the actualising function is performed by the clause as a whole. The difference between the personal clause type and the various impersonal varieties regards the internal structure of the clause and is closely linked up with the so-called **voice** of the verb. Going into this would lead us too far afield; all that can be said here is that the actualising function in general may not be expressed by any **one** constituent of the clause, but be contained in, or divided over, the entire **lexical** extension of the clause. This means to say, that all possible differences in lexical position are **neutralised** [15] with respect to the actualising function.

[If our functional analysis of the sentence should include the linguistic functions of sentence intonation, in particular its deictic and modal functions, the above list of primary functional levels is to be enlarged with one more function, the function of the so-called **shifters,**[16] which establish a relationship between the text and the speech situation. In this paper these functions are not dealt with.[17]]

4. The three primary functions we have been able to identify so far can enter into combination with one another to form new, **derived** functions.

Taking the clause as the basic unit of syntax, we are naturally led to regard the semantic function of this unit as the basic type of **meaning** to be dealt with in syntactic analysis. Since we have to do with a structured entity, i.e. a construction or combination of constructions, it seems altogether justified to define the meaning of such an entity in Worth's terms, as a "transformation potential".[18] This potential clearly corresponds to the **distribution** of an unstructured entity (such as a morpheme or a word). It is worth mentioning in this connection that Lees in his *Grammar of English Nominalizations* [19] considers the possibility that **all** English sentences should be of the subject-predicate form, either explicitly or after transformation. Some examples may be welcome to illustrate the above-mentioned identification of meaning and transformation potential.

[Consider an expression like *she covered the floor with a rug.* The grammatical status of the preposition phrase *with a rug* could be described here as a transform of the semantic potential of

---

[15] See for a discussion of this notion § 4.

[16] See especially the penetrating treatment by Roman Jakobson in *Shifters, Verbal Categories, and the Russian Verb* (Cambridge 1957).

[17] See the author's paper "Referential and Attitudinal Constructions," *Lingua,* XI (1962), 165-181.

[18] Dean Stoddard Worth, "Transform Analysis of Russian Instrumental Constructions," *Word,* 14 (1958), 247-290.

[19] Robert B. Lees, *Grammar of English Nominalizations, IJAL* 26 (1960), p. 24.

a rug covered the floor. The preposition phrase expresses here a particular type of 'instrumental' function, characterised by the fact that the noun [*a*] *rug* can occur as the subject of the same verb. Cf. Russian *kover pokryvaet pol* beside *pokryvaju pol kovrom,* and also constructions like *nebo zavolokli tuči* beside *nebo zavoloklo tučami.*]

We proceed now to show how the grammatical meaning or potential of the clause can be derived from, how it is related to, the primary functions we have delimited before: the lexical function, time of utterance, and the actualising function.

Let us first consider the **finite verb function.** As stated before, the finite verb in general performs a lexical function like the substantive; however, unlike the latter, it combines this function with another function, which we now wish to ascertain.

Consider two autonomous expressions like *he was busy* and *the window was shut.* Both expressions may be used as a sentence, and there is no grammatical restriction on their order in time, so that the lexical function of the two expressions uttered in succession will depend on their order, AB and BA being lexically different utterances. If we now devise a transformation which will unite the lexical functions of the consecutive verb phrases *was busy* and *was shut* into a single finite verb form, we obtain a new utterance like *he shut the window,* and in the finite verb *shut* of the new utterance the free order of the original lexical entities is **neutralised:** the action of 'shutting the window' and the resultant state of 'being shut' appear in the given verb, in an unalterable order. Conversely, if we are given a clause like *he went to town* or *he grew old,* we describe the underlying constructions, in the line of Worth's transformational approach, by decomposing the given expression into two other expressions, thus:

he went to town → (1) *he was going* + (2) *he was in town*

he grew old → (1) *he was growing* + (2) *he was old.*

The result of this transformation is a sequence of expressions in a definite order, which is now free, since the expressions have been raised to the level of autonomous sentences.

I am well aware of a possible objection here. Taking *he was busy* and *the window was shut* as our initial lexical strings, why do we unite these into the single finite verb form *shut,* rather than, say, into a composite clause like *he was busy shutting the window* or *he finished shutting the window?* The answer to this objection is that the finite verb is the **simplest** type of expression the given transformation can lead up to: such strings as *busy shutting* or *finish shutting* are all of a more complex type, involving one or more subsidiary constituents of the clause. These will be discussed presently.

The transformation T_1 which unites two consecutive expressions into a single form, and the transformation T_2 which decomposes that form into two consecutive expressions, obviously **undo** each other's results;[20] therefore, they may be regarded as each other's **inverse.** In particular, if T_2, which raises an entity in included position to absolute position, is interpreted as **multiplication** by the time function, then T_1, the neutralisation of order, will represent **division** by that function. Thus the complete functional dimension of the finite verb may be represented as **lexical function divided by time of utterance.** Writing V for the finite verb function, L for lexical function, and T for time of utterance, we obtain for V the formula:

(i) $V = LT^{-1}$.

To complete the functional analysis of the finite verb, we note that the forms of this class, although necessarily figuring as the center of a clause, yet alone do not produce a favorite sentence type, an autonomous expression, unless they contain, or are accompanied by, an element indicating the subject (if the clause is of the personal type) or whatever corresponds to the subject in a clause of the impersonal type. Taking the personal clause, in accordance with Lees' above-mentioned view, as the underlying form of all clauses, and noting that the finite verb in such a clause is actualised by a non-paratactic combination of the verb with the subject, we conclude that the function of the personal clause results from the non-paratactic combination of the finite verb function and the actualising function (discussed in § 3). If we further interpret the non-paratactic combination of two functions as a special case of **multiplication** (cf. the multiplication by the time function), and write P for the personal clause function and A for the actualising function, we obtain for P the formula:

(ii) $P = AV = ALT^{-1}$.

5. So far, I have confined myself to the consideration of only the simplest type of clause; a more general, expanded form of the clause will contain one or more subsidiary constituents, in the function of a **modifier.** Examples are the participle in *she kept smiling,* the adjective in *she bought a new hat,* and in *she married young,* the preposition phrase in *he lived in London,* the infinitive phrases in *you may leave us* and *they began to play Beethoven,* and the adverb in *tomorrow he will leave.*

---

[20] Cf. Zellig S. Harris, "Co-occurrence and Transformation," *Language,* 33 (1957), 332-334, on multiplication and addition of transformations, and Kenneth L. Pike, "Dimensions of Grammatical Constructions," *Language,* 38 (1962).

The common function of these subsidiary constituents can be analysed in the same way as the finite verb function. If V_1 and V_2 are two finite verbs in consecutive sentences, with relevant time order, then the transformation uniting these into a single modifier amounts again to the neutralisation of the original free time order of the verbal expressions. Compare, for instance, the two sentences *he is working* and *he is in his room,* with free order on the time axis. Uniting the finite verb phrases *is working* and *is in his room* into a modifier-modified construction *he was working in his room,* we notice that the free order of the original strings is abolished, and replaced by a structural order of subsidiary relative to nuclear constituent. Whatever freedom of time order may be left in the resultant string—note, for instance, the possibility of interchanging the modifier and the modified, giving *in his room he was working*—does not affect the syntactic relation between the modifier and the modified; it bears only on the intonational content of the sentence, the localisation of the 'theme' and the 'propos', relative to the word material. We conclude from all this that the function of the modifier will have the form of a **finite verb function divided by the time of utterance**; in symbols:

(iii) $VT^{-1} = LT^{-2}$.

The multiplication of this function by the actualising function A symbolises the use of a modifier in a particular type of clause, especially its **indirect** combination with the subject of the basic personal clause type. Thus in *the dogs barked furiously,* the finite verb *barked* is connected directly with the subject, whereas the modifier *furiously* is connected indirectly, via a transformation like *the furious dogs,* with the subject. The function of an actualised modifier may accordingly be symbolised by the formula:

(iv) $F = AV$.

Thus the difference between actualised and non-actualised modifiers answers exactly to the difference between finite verb and clause.

> [Noting that the class of finite verbs **outside** the clause occurs only as a morphologic category, whereas the clause itself is obviously a syntactic category, it seems likely that the actualising function also differentiates the modifier as a syntactic unit from the corresponding morphologic category of **adjectives,** defined by their syntactic "valence",[21] and not by their actual application. Such a view would suggest a possible solution for the analysis of constructions like Russian *sčitali ego uže umeršim* 'they considered him dead already', *ona malen'kaja umerla* 'she died young', where the predicate agrees in gender-number with the object or subject of the clause, but does not make up a syntactic constituent

---

[21] De Groot, *Inleiding,* p. 241.

with either of these. The feature of concord would indicate here an **unactualised** modifier-modified construction, i.e. a construction with **morphologic** (rather than syntactic) status.]

6. It was pointed out before (§ 5) that the grammatical content of a clause, conceived as a transformation potential, can be transformed in various ways into expressions which belong to other functional levels. Conversely, the grammatical content of the clause can be obtained by combining certain functions in a definite way. I shall confine myself here to mentioning the two fundamental constructions whose meaning contributes to the grammatical content of the clause as a whole.

(1) The hypotactic (non-coordinative) combination of a modifier and a substantive into a predicative or attributive construction, e.g. *she* and *young* in *she married young*, and *young* with *a . . . woman* in *a young woman*. As before (§ 3), we interpret a hypotactic combination as a **product**; thus, writing G_s for that portion of the grammatical meaning of the combination of modifier and substantive, we obtain the formula:

(v) $G_s = FL = ML^2 T^{-2}$ (from § 5).

The attributive construction differs from the corresponding predicative construction especially in the possibility of **amalgamation** (or idiomizing), as in *red herring* beside *fresh herring*, French *œil-de-bœuf, face-à-main*. The process of amalgamation is probably to be described as a partial **conversion** of the grammatical meaning of a construction into **word** meaning.

[If the modifier is not completely parallel with the noun it modifies, as in Turkish: *kapını yeşile boyadım* 'I painted the gate green', which can be derived from *kapı yeşildir* 'the gate is green', only that part of the predicate that is parallel with the noun, say *yeşil*—without the case suffix, can yield a meaningful combination with the noun (*yeşil kapı* 'the green gate'). Likewise in *the dogs barked furiously*, only the part of *furiously* that is parallel with *dogs*, i.e. the stem *furious*—, will contribute to the grammatical meaning of the clause, when it is combined with *dogs*, as in *the furious dogs*. On the contrary, in *we saw her* no part of the complement *her* is parallel with the subject *we*, so that the co-occurrence of these constituents within the same clause does not contribute to its grammatical content.]

(2) The hypotactic combination of a finite verb with another constituent, both parallel with the subject, and forming a close-knit phrase. Examples are the finite verb phrases in *the boy is tall, she kept smiling, you may leave, he can go*, Russian *ja budu rabotat'*. The two constituents of such a construction do not separately combine with the subject, so that a clause of this type contains the actualising function only **once**. Further, the non-

finite constituent is a modifier (*tall, smiling, leave, go,* Russian *rabotat'* in the above examples) raised to the level of the finite verb, whereas the copula or auxiliary approaches the state of an 'empty' expression, so that it contributes to the meaning of the construction only with a small fraction of the full verb function. Thus the grammatical meaning G_v of the verb phrase can be expressed as the product of two verb functions V and one actualising function, A giving the formula:

(vi) $G_v = AV^2 = AL^2 T^{-2}$.

In concluding this paragraph it may be remarked that the meaning of a combination does not enter into relations of parallelism or non-parallelism with the meaning of other combinations of the same clause. This is especially apparent from such idiomized combinations as *red herring, prime minister, Court of Justice,* and so on: while both members of such a combination considered in its non-amalgamated state, occupy a definite syntactic position relative to one another, the meaning of the combination, which is the result of the amalgamation, does not figure in a definite syntactic position.

7. Summarising the results of the foregoing discussion, we can say that the functional levels of syntactic entities display a certain hierarchy, as shown in the table below.

	oriented	non-oriented
I	L	A,T
II	V,P	
III	F	
IV		G

The primary functions (A,L,T) naturally occupy the lowest rank; next come the finite verb and personal clause functions (V,P); then follows the modifying function (F); the highest rank is held by the level of meaning (G). Finally, the table indicates the distinction made throughout this paper between "oriented" functions—those occupying a definite position relative to one another, and "non-oriented" functions, which are not so characterised.

The functional approach outlined in this paper may contribute, it is hoped, to gain insight in the general interdependences of linguistic functions. In particular, the choice of lexical function and time of utterance, the former associated directly with the phonemic level, the other indissolubly linked up with prosodic features, at least opens up the possibility of a unified approach to whatever is structured in both sound and meaning.

LANGUAGE AND THE EPISTEMOLOGICAL FOUNDATIONS OF THE SOCIAL SCIENCES

J. F. Glastra van Loon

University of Leyden

I

One of the ways in which the peculiar nature of the social sciences can be indicated is by pointing out the fact that social scientists can disagree, not only about facts and theories, but also about the question of whether particular social phenomena can only be adequately described in the language of the actors with whose behavior they are concerned, or also and equally well (or even better) in another one. Is it, for instance, possible to give an adequate description and analysis of classical Roman law in the terminology of the modern civil lawyer or is one, by so doing, already and inevitably imputing anachronistic concepts to the Romans? [1] Can one, to give another example, adequately analyse 18th century European political institutions in the terms of 20th century political science or is one thereby inadvertently distorting history? The problem is further complicated by the fact that the authors of particular documents may have used one of a number of different language systems without it being indisputably clear which is the most relevant one for their interpretation. Should one, for example, when interpreting a chronicle or a testament, take as the appropriate contextual system the language which the author was wont to use when addressing himself to a small group of intimates, or rather the official language which was used by a wider circle of persons who may also be considered to have been among his addressees?

These questions require analysis. Part of my paper will be concerned with the general methodological problems arising in connection with that analysis. First of all, however, I want to insist that the fact that these questions can arise at all is symptomatic of a fundamental methodological (not merely technical) problem which is peculiar to the social sciences. To

---

[1] Cf. H. R. Hoetink, "Les notions anachronistiques dans l'historiographic du droit", *Tijdschrift voor Rechtsgeschiedenis/Revue d'Histoire du Droit, t.* XXIII, 1955.

be sure, a number of social scientists believe that social phenomena can be dealt with in fundamentally the same way as any other kind of phenomena. These authors will hold that, by raising the question just mentioned to the status of a fundamental problem, I am in fact prejudging the issue. It seems to me that this objection can be returned with equal force and that, therefore, the matter cannot be dealt with quite so simply.

The point at issue is whether (and in how far, and in what way) the referential systems of the agents whose behavior one is studying has to be taken into account or can be ignored by the social scientist. By systems of reference I mean interrelated regularities of behavior (possibly also, sometimes exclusively, but not necessarily, verbal behavior) in terms of which individual agents define the relations between themselves and their environment and between elements of their environment. Language as a social fact, to put it in the words of Alf Sommerfelt, is "le moyen par lequel la société non seulement agit sur le monde qui l'entoure, mais en outre conçoit le monde".[2]

In order to avoid misunderstandings about what seems to me to be the real nature of the problem concerning such systems, I shall first mention another form in which it has frequently been presented in a discussion between Watsonian behaviorists and physicalists on the one hand, subjectivist relativists on the other hand.

The *objectivist realists* (as I shall call the former group of social scientists) have stressed the fact that science can only be concerned with what is open to inspection by others as it is to the individual agents themselves. These authors contend that there can, therefore, be no fundamental methodological differences between the social and other sciences, but only technical differences concerned with the observation and authentication of data, the control of variables, etc. Processes of interaction between an organism and its environment, they will say, are overt phenomena which can be studied in fundamentally the same way as any others. There is no methodological difference between finding out the predictable outcome of putting a flame to gunpowder and establishing regularities of human behavior.

The point is well taken. There is, indeed, as I shall argue further on, a long stretch which the social sciences can cover along lines running virtually parallel to the path taken by the physical sciences. This, however, does not preclude the possibility that the social sciences must also cover an area which has no parallel in the physical sciences. One of the ways in which the actual existence of such an area can be demonstrated is, I submit,

---

[2] Alf Sommerfelt, *La langue et la société* (Oslo, 1938), 3.

through an analysis of the part which is being played by the referential systems of different actors in processes of interaction. That part, I further submit, is that of a 'constitutive element'. Or, more precisely: it is a variable which we must take into account in our analysis of such processes in order to achieve cross-cultural and transhistorical comparability of social phenomena. This contention is, in fact, supported by what the methodology of the physical sciences reveals concerning the role of referential systems in these sciences when they are seen, not as stocks of knowledge piled up somewhere in a mental storehouse, but as social enterprises which have to be kept going through co-ordinated activities of individual scientists. I shall come back to this in a moment.

The very opposite view to that of the objectivist realists has been defended by other social scientists (especially historians and cultural anthropologists), to whom I shall refer as *subjectivist relativists*. A number of these have denied the possibility of acquiring nomothetic knowledge in their field of research on account of the incomparability of the phenomena which they are studying. The usual reply to this contention has been that, by using words for the description of these phenomena, the ideographically inclined social scientist is already specifying and classifying them, and that it would therefore be inconsistent with his actual practice to deny the possibility of comparing them. Now, to my mind, this objection misses the target. The subjectivist relativist can admit the generality of meaning of his descriptive terms and yet insist on the uniqueness of the configurations of the phenomena which he is thereby describing without contradicting himself.

The point which is missed by both parties in this controversy is, it seems to me, that, if the subjectivist relativists were right, if in other words they were really concerned with what constitutes the uniqueness of their objects, and nothing else, it is quite unclear in what sense they could be said to be concerned with *social* phenomena.

As is so frequently the case with extreme opponents, the underlying assumptions of subjectivist relativists and objectivist realists overlap each other on a central issue. Both, in fact, assume that the meaning or significance of social acts is, or derives from, something subjective, mental or psychic, private, internal and not open to public scrutiny. It is in the conclusions which they draw from this assumption that they part company, the ones putting their faith in procedures of aesthetic 'empathy', the others forging ahead with the gestures of the physical scientist—without further reflection on the conditions which must be fulfilled in order that their own work may proceed as an intersubjectively repeatable, objectively corrigible and at the same time innovating process. It is the basic assumption underlying these two views that is the main target of this paper.[3]

Briefly put, my position is that what characterizes social phenomena as the object of the social sciences is that they possess 'meaning' or 'significance' in an intersubjective sense, the determination of which involves the taking into account of referential systems of actors participating in social processes. Now, methodology, as a discipline which is concerned, not with the substantive contents of particular sciences, but with the way in which knowledge is being obtained, has something in common with the social sciences which is relevant to my position.

This *common element* is contained in the concern of the methodology of science with referential systems, their logical properties, and their potentialities for the descriptive and explanatory ordering of environmental events. The *characteristic difference* between methodology of science and the social sciences, on the other hand, consists in the fact that whereas the former is studying referential systems in their cognitive function only, the social sciences are studying them generally as variables in processes of interaction.

For a clarification of this point, I want to distinguish two dimensions of referential systems: (1) They define a number of elements of the environment in relation to each other as objects of cognition, manipulation, affection, etc.; I shall call this their *designatory dimension*. (2) They also regulate relationships between actors in interaction; I shall call this their *co-referential dimension*.[4]

The relations between these two referential dimensions can be determined in a number of different ways. The most important criterion for the differentiation of referential systems from the social scientist's point of view is the way in which they make possible the substitution of individual agents in social processes with regard to the designatory objects. Thus a scientific referential system is characterized by the fact that it makes possible complete substitution of individual scientists relative to the definition

---

[3] The mentalistic, as opposed to the operational, conception of knowledge is complementary to an ontologistic view of reality as a system of facts inherent in nature which can be known through a process of 'mirroring' in the mind, in which the individual organism is only passively involved. In this conception of reality on the one hand, knowing or knowledge on the other hand, there is no place where 'significance' or 'meaning' can be located, except in the minds of individuals. It is clear that once they have been relegated to those ethereal spheres, their scientific fate has been decided upon: they are not intersubjectively accessible, not open to inspection to the one as to the other, etc.

[4] The term 'co-referential' has been suggested to me by R. A. V. van Haersolte, who also helped to clear up some muddles in my thinking.

and determinateness of the objects of research in the context of that system. The co-referential dimension of the system is thereby, as it were, reduced to a single role or point of view. With regard to the objects of designation of a scientific theory, all actor-scientists in the field function in one and the same role, i.e. in terms of the same set of mutually consistent expectations which are held together by the same referential system. Insofar, moreover, as sets of phenomena can be said to be defined in terms of more than one referential system, they can only be said to be the same objects of scientific research as their definitions can be translated in terms of a single theory which encompasses or unifies the others.

Methodology of science, then, is concerned with referential systems which are characterized by the fact that they each determine a single role which can be interchangeably occupied by any number of individual scientists. Methodology is, indeed, confronted with these systems in the plural. It is not, however, concerned with processes of interaction between scientists as occupants of different roles. This is so precisely because scientific enterprise, as a purely cognitively oriented activity, is directed towards the suppression or neutralization of differences between such roles, where and whenever there appears one.

The object of research of the social scientist, on the contrary, is exactly such processes of interaction between the incumbents of different roles. He is concerned with behavior as it is oriented by systems of reference whose co-referential dimension interrelates a variety of roles and whose designatory dimension far exceeds a merely cognitive scope.

The preceding remarks can be summarized as follows. The difference between social and other phenomena is not that the former are, whereas the latter are not, uniquely but, rather, specifically determined; nor is it that the former are, whereas the others are not, open to inspection by one individual as they are to others, or that the ones are, whereas the others are not, mental or dependent on mental processes. This last distinction is one which runs across the borderline separating the social and other sciences; it will give rise to differences of technique in observational and verificational procedures, not, however (at least not necessarily), to differences of a methodological nature. The difference between social and other phenomena rests on the fact that social action is defined in terms of systems of reference which differentiate roles in interaction, whereas non-social phenomena are not thus defined.

My position should not be misunderstood as implying that it would be impossible to study certain phenomena according to the methods of the physical sciences. Nor am I suggesting an ontological distinction between two mutually exclusive classes of concrete entities. My contention is, rather, that the study of social phenomena is complicated by the fact that they are studied in terms of cognitive systems of reference which include referential systems amongst the variables which determine their objects of designation.

II

How is the social scientist to relate his system of reference to those of the individuals whose behavior he is studying in order that the phenomena which constitute his object of research will become amenable to intersubjective, cross-cultural, cross-societal, etc., comparison? The solution of this problem must, it seems to me, be looked for in the context of a division of the research procedure in phases which are related to each other in roughly the same way as an object-language is related to a meta-language.

Let us, for an illustration of this point, look at the case in which one would want to find out the rules of a game without being able to do so by simply asking for an explanation from someone who already knows them. Now, surely, insofar as the behavior of a number of individuals is indeed in conformance with a particular set of rules, it should be possible to get to know these rules by taking the appropriate steps of observation, description, classification, hypothesizing, interrelating hypotheses, deductive inference of new hypotheses, correction of hypothetico-deductive systems on the basis of actual findings, etc., until a sufficiently consistent set of statements shall have arisen on the basis of which the behavior of the players in the relevant situations can be predicted with sufficient accuracy.

The knowledge thus acquired would amount to an ability to take part in the game as a player, or to supervise it as a referee. One would, in other words, be able to 'generate' all possible moves of the game on the basis of a systematically arranged set of rule-of-the-game statements. This in itself would amount to a verification of the inductively acquired 'understanding' of the game. The fact that one might be using completely different terms for the designation of the moves in the game, that one might have classified them in an altogether different way, and might have arranged the rules in a different system or order than the players themselves—all such variations from the 'original' would not in the least detract from the adequacy of this knowledge of the rules of the game. No need, in other words, to take a peep into the minds of the players concerned; no need even, as far as knowing how to play the game is concerned, to be able to speak their language.

So far, then, the case presents us with no methodological peculiarities. From the social scientist's point of view, however, the case of the game itself is a rather special one. A closer look at what makes a game a game will show us why. The main characteristics of the game are that it is being played according to rules which have been fixed in advance and that all the activities which are relevant to the game are taken to have no other consequences than those foreseen by the rules. In other words, in the case of a game, the system of reference in terms of which the behavior of the players is defined has been detached from all other possible contexts in such a way that their multiple interpretability has been excluded completely or at least to a very high degree. All the 'meaning' there is to an act or move or sequence of acts in this context is determined by the logically possible relations between the elements of the system. Any move outside the range of these possibilities has been 'ruled out': it has been branded in advance as 'co-referentially meaningless'.

It is clear that this sort of unequivocalness is a great asset to the orderly procedure of social interaction. No better example of this than the role of mathematics as a provider of systems of exclusively implicitly defined terms in the development of science! A certain degree of it must be presumed in all orderly ongoing social processes. In some areas of behavior (say, road traffic) the adherence to the 'rules of the game' is generally as strict as in the case of field games. In others we find regularities of behavior which are less strictly (and therefore less exclusively) determined in accordance with a particular set of co-referential postulates. In those cases it will not be possible adequately to predict or to explain the behavior of individual agents in those terms, but it is yet possible to regard the total results arising from interaction processes as having, on the average, been determined by specific co-referential rules. Economics could not be the valuable social instrument it is, if this were not the case.

It is in these areas then, that the social sciences can proceed along methodological lines which run parallel to those of the physical sciences. One would, however, draw an altogether too idyllic picture of social *reality* and an oversimplified and too restricted one of the social *sciences,* if one were to leave it at that. Society is not merely an ongoing concern or a system in stable equilibrium. It is also shot through with ambiguities, conflicts, innovating activities, etc., which cannot be adequately described, let alone explained, as mere 'deviations from the general pattern'.

I want to stress that what I am saying is not that it would be *impossible* to define such aberrations in those terms. I even want to go one step further and say that, in an initial phase of research concerning a particular society, it is *necessary* to handle one's data in such a fashion. I only want to add to this, that this first phase must be followed by another one. It is this other phase which involves methodological considerations which play no part in the physical sciences.

I shall try to expound this in four points. Two of these are more fundamental than the others. They are: (1) the inherent ambiguity or *multiple interpretability* of social phenomena in general; (2) the fact that what is being determined by the inductive procedure just mentioned, taken as a system or structured whole, is itself an *unique social phenomenon*. Let me try to clarify this.

(1.a.) I shall first mention a point which is a relatively minor one, but which leads up to a major one. Instances of behavior which can be adequately defined as deviations from a general pattern at one moment may, in the course of time or even abruptly, develop into regularities of such a scope that it becomes doubtful whether they can still be accounted for as deviations from the pattern or should rather be considered as constituting a *change* of the pattern.

(1.b.) Another point, closely connected with the previous one, is that processes of change frequently can only be adequately described as arising from, or even constituting, conflicts between two or more competing or at any rate mutually incompatible referential systems operating in one and the same society. What these two points amount to is that social phenomena may be equivocal, i.e., amenable to interpretation in terms of different (non-isomorphic) referential systems, each or some of which define some phenomena as 'deviations' which are defined as 'conforming behavior' in terms of one or some of the other referential systems operating in a particular interaction process.

(1.c.) Now this difficulty is further complicated by the fact that the social scientist must, at any time, face the possibility that the inductively acquired systems of reference have been based on selections and classifications of phenomena which have themselves been determined by his own pre-conceived system of reference. The source of this ambiguity is not one which only erupts occasionally or accidentally. It is flowing continuously and it lies at the root of the social sciences. It is, indeed, implied by the very definition of social phenomena as such, namely, as *phenomena which are determined by,* amongst other things, *the regularities of verbal and other behavior in terms of which human beings orient themselves in interaction processes.*[5]

---

[5] The physicist, as compared with the social scientist, presents us with an exceptional case. His case is exceptional in two respects. First, from the *methodological* point of view, on account of the fact that his concepts are defined in terms of the system of reference which he himself constructs only. He does not, in other words, as the social scientist does, introduce one or more referential systems as variables in

In this context, it seem relevant to point out that the case of the game with which I started this analysis is a special one in a similar way as languages are special cases of action systems. I am using for this purpose a quotation from Sapir: "Of all forms of culture, it seems that language is that one which develops its fundamental patterns with relatively the most complete detachment from other types of cultural patterning. . . . In ordinary life the basic symbolisms of behavior are densely overlaid by cross-functional patterns of a bewildering variety. It is because every isolated act in human behavior is the meeting point of many distinct configurations that it is so difficult for most of us to arrive at the notions of contextual and non-contextual forms in behavior. Linguistics would seem to have a very peculiar value for configurative studies because the patterning of language is to a very appreciable extent self-contained and not significantly at the mercy of intercrossing patterns of a non-linguistic type.".[6] It is because the latter is, indeed, the case with regard to most other social phenomena that the special problems of methodology to which I am referring do arise in the social sciences.

(2) Now over from the first fundamental point, i.e. the one concerning the multiple interpretability of social phenomena, to the second one. This leads us, as it were, to the opposite extreme. The point is that what constitutes a pattern or system of generically defined phenomena on one level of analysis (such that each individual phenomenon is determined as an instance or value of a variable which has been contextually defined by the system of reference), on another level of analysis is an *uniquely defined social phenomenon*. The point has, I believe, never been put more simply and clearly than in the following words from Charles Peirce: "There will ordinarily be about 20 *the*'s on a page, and of course they count as 20 words. In another sense of the word 'word', however, there is but one 'the' in the English language. . . ."[7] A word or a language, a move in chess or the game as a whole, are each in a sense uniquely determined.

---

his own system, in terms of which the other variables are defined. In the second place, he is exceptional from the point of view of *social science*, i.e. as a social phenomenon, in that all physicists, at least on principle, are incumbents of one and the same role, i.e., that the distinction of *ego* and *alter* is being cancelled out relative to their objects of designation. The blind spot in the objectivist realist's methodological manner of seeing things consists in the fact that he cannot conceive the possibility of another method of research which involves the taking into account of systems of reference of the scientist's objects of designation.

[6] E. Sapir, "The Status of Linguistics as a Science", *Language*, 5, (1929). The quotation is taken from *Culture, A Critical Review of Concepts and Definitions*, A. L. Kroeber and Clyde Kluckhohn, eds., (Cambridge, Mass., 1952).

[7] Charles S. Peirce, *Collected Papers*, Charles Hartschorne and Paul Weiss, eds., (Cambridge, 1931-35), vol. 4, p. 537.

Just as, therefore, one must first have acquired sufficient *know how* of a language or of the rules of a game in order to be able to determine the number of times a particular word or a particular gambit is being used in connection with a specific other phenomenon, one must also first possess sufficient understanding of the referential system according to which the members of a particular society are interacting in order to be able to acquire *knowledge about* the quantitative correlations which obtain between particular social phenomena. Thus we must already know the referential determinateness of a *corporation,* or a *sale,* or a *manslaughter,* or a *suicide,* in order to be able to determine their relative frequency over time, etc. In the social sciences, quantitative induction must be preceded, or at any rate supported, by qualitative induction.[7a]

There is yet another conclusion which can be drawn from the previous analysis, viz., that phenomena which have been defined in terms of different systems of reference cannot be directly compared with or related to each other. It would, for instance, be highly misleading to take the fact that a legal institution in one society and another one in another society are respectively referred to in those societies by words which can be lexicographically translated into one another, as a sufficient basis for their comparison. The social scientist who would translate, say, "propriété" into "property" and then do comparative research about the phenomena thus designated in France and England would obviously get involved in gross misconceptions. What he will need is not only sufficient technical knowledge of the legal systems of both countries, but also an artificially constructed system of reference in terms of which both legal systems can be analysed. A good example of this can be found in the set of implicitly defined terms which has been suggested for this purpose by Hohfeld.[8] If

---

[7a] Cf. J. F. Glastra van Loon, *Norm en Handeling.* Erven T. Bohn N. V., Haarlem, 1956; E. V. W. Vercruijsse, *Het ontwerpen van een sociologisch onderzoek,* (van Gorcum, Assen, 1960), 9 ff.

[8] W. N. Hohfeld, *Fundamental Legal Conceptions as applied in Judicial Reasoning and other Essays,* W. W. Cook, ed., (New Haven, 1923). Hohfeld defines a set of eight "jural opposites and correlatives" as the "least common denominators" for the analysis of legal relations. Cf. Julius Stone, *The Province and Function of Law* (Sydney, 1946), 115 ff., and E. Adamson Hoebel, *The Law of Primitive Man* (Cambridge, Mass., 1954), 46 ff.

Another important contribution to the problem of meta-systematic analysis of legal systems has been made by E. M. Meijers, *De Algemene Begrippen van het Burgerlijk Recht* (Leyden 1948). Meijers develops and clarifies the method of definition by means of "normal types", first suggested by Sigwart. A "normal type" is conceptually constructed by an enumeration of analytic characteristics which may or may not be together applicable to actual legal institutions. The point is, that actual

his interest goes beyond a comparison of the legal systems as such, if he is also interested in finding out about their relations to other social phenomena, then he will need a similar terminological device for the comparative description and analysis of those other phenomena as well. Talcott Parsons' set of pattern variables immediately comes to mind in this connection.[9]

Inter-systematic comparison of social phenomena requires the taking of a meta-systematic point of view. This can only be realized by the construction of a meta-systematic frame of reference. I am stressing this point, because it has been more than just occasionally misunderstood by social scientists themselves. The nature of this misunderstanding can be gathered from the accusations which this kind of work has met of being too abstract and formal to be of any use, as well as from the insistence upon direct operational definition of the terms of the meta-system concerned.

These objections are based on the mistaken assumption that a meta-systematic system of reference constitutes a technical language in the same sense as, e.g., the language of the physicist. Or, in other words, that they are meant to designate phenomena by means of similar chains of operations as are represented by terms like 'weight', 'length', 'temperature', etc. They overlook the fact that these meta-systems do not *directly* designate social phenomena, but *indirectly;* i.e. as they are determined in the context of a particular system of reference which is operative in a particular society. A meta-system is an instrument of analysis; its terms become operational through non-physical operations of a kind which are similar to those involved in the analysis of a text in the technical terms of a grammar.

III

My remarks about the definition of meta-systematic terms should not be interpreted as denying the *possibility* of 'direct' operational definitions of social phenomena. What I am contending is that this will get us no further than descriptions of particular cases in statistical terms without providing a basis for cross-systematic comparison. Cross-systematic comparison requires meta-systematic terms which can be applied to social phenomena as they are defined in terms of the referential systems of the agents in the

---

legal institutions may now be characterized, and thus at the same time systematically ordered relative to each other, by defining them as instances of a normal type missing a particular one (or some) of its defining characteristics. This method of definition highly facilitates comparison of legal institutions both within the context of one legal system and cross-systematically.

[9] Talcott Parsons, *The Social System* (London, 1952).

field. Generally speaking, this means that they must be applicable to *qualitatively* defined phenomena.

A clear picture of the situation in which the social scientist finds himself after having determined and analysed his phenomena by means of *directly* operational terms has been given by Lazarsfeld. The social scientist, Lazarsfeld tells us, will first define his concept, say 'group cohesiveness', in terms of a number of indicators (expressions of friendliness by members about members of the group, relative frequency of instances of social inter-course between members with each other as compared with between members and outsiders, etc.). He will then collect statistical data by observing large numbers of groups and by describing each in terms of the indicators. "Each group will thus be characterized by a profile or response pattern. Using an appropriate statistical technique, the investigator will then compute the covariations between all the indicators taken over all the groups he is studying. His basic numerical material will be one or more matrices, the entries of which indicate how well pairs and perhaps triplets and quadruplets of indicators agree with each other in concrete situations."

Finally, these matrices will be submitted to mathematical analysis in order to establish the diagnostic value of each of the indicators. "There are quite a number of . . . models which can be used for this analysis. But they all have two features in common. They do not use an outside criterion. No one tells us in advance which groups should be considered more cohesive than others; we do not calibrate indicators against superior knowledge. . . . We pull ourselves up, so to say, by our own bootstraps. We end up by finding two things simultaneously: given that a group belongs at a certain point on the underlying continuum of cohesiveness, we can tell the probability with which it will manifest each indicator; and, given the profile or response pattern of the group, we can say with what probability the group belongs at various points along the intended classification." [10]

I have quoted Lazarsfeld at some length, because he so pungently puts across the fact that all one can get from statistical analysis of operationally defined data is a probabilistic descriptive ordering of phenomena in terms of one another, i.e. a classification of sorts. The trouble with these classifications is that, although they increase our knowledge about facts, they leave us in the cold with regard to the question of how these facts could be nomothetically related to other facts.

---

[10] Paul F. Lazarsfeld, "Philosophy of Science and Empirical Social Research," *Logic, Methodology and Philosophy of Science, Proceedings of the 1960 International Congress,* Ernest Nagel, Patrick Suppes, Alfred Tarski, eds., (Stanford, Cal., 1962), 467/8.

The decisive characteristic of scientific knowledge is that it is not merely practically useful but also theoretically fruitful. Regardless of how that knowledge may have been acquired, of how well it may have been confirmed, and of how accurately it has been determined, it will be fruitful only if we can derive or infer from it tentative views or hypotheses concerning other relations or covariations of phenomena than the ones which are determined by that knowledge. The empirical testing of the derived hypotheses should then give us grounds for changing the systematically related hypotheses and for looking for yet other possible correlations between phenomena, etc.[11]

The crux of the matter is that this procedure leads not merely to ever increasing accuracy in the determination of facts but also, and above all, widens the empirical basis on which we build our conceptual systems of reference. The situation now is no longer like that of a man trying to pull himself up by his bootstraps, but rather like that of a man holding on to bits of straw who finds that by plaiting them he can overcome the force of gravity. All the bits of straw separately floating around him will not support him, will rather be a hindrance to his movements. Their combined sustaining capacity, however, will be sufficient for lifting him out of the water.

---

[11] "Scientific knowledge has enormous self-propelling power because this sort of knowledge (in the sense of knowledge of laws) can be used as a means to create—in an objective sense—concepts which can be used to give descriptions of phenomena; acquired knowledge enables us not only to direct our activities in everyday life but also . . . to see deeper and further than was possible beforehand. . . .

"Once the concept 'resistance' has been instituted by an operational definition, one can, for instance, measure resistance as a function of temperature. In so doing one again finds a law. Now a sceptic can try to falsify this law by looking for pairs of values for resistance and temperature which do not fit into this law—but to do so, he has to presuppose that Ohm's law is valid. I mention this because it makes clear that the possibility of falsifying a law depends on the assumed validity of descriptions of a certain type which in their turn depend on a law: the 'objective value' of concepts is complementary to the validity of laws.

"Now this implies that one can state that somewhere . . . decisions have to be made. In doing so one can either assume that some concepts are sacrosanct or that some laws have an a priori status; this means one can assume that descriptions of a certain type are valid or that certain laws are valid. The first choice is made by empiricists of Humean origin—the latter by rationalists of the Aristotelian or Cartesian tradition who are looking for 'first principles'. But the scientist does not make this kind of decision: for him neither concepts nor laws are sacrosanct: he tries to form concepts, to learn how to make observations and to use words by means of laws—he tries to formulate laws by making observations and using words; moreover inquiry itself is a process of transformation and readjustment."—J. B. Ubbink, "Model, Description and Knowledge," *Synthese,* XII (1960).

I have intentionally been using loose language. My reason for this is that, although I am fully convinced that the hypothetico-deductive method is the only scientifically fruitful one, I also believe that by copying in the social sciences the forms in which it has been realized by the physical sciences, its propulsive capacity is being used the wrong way. It is like using a motorcar for travelling on water. What is being lost sight of in this way is that social phenomena are defined as such, and are specified as this or that particular social phenomenon, relative to the systems of reference of social agents in the field. The danger that this will be overlooked is enhanced if the development of highly sophisticated techniques of observation leads to definitions of findings which cannot be translated in terms in which those agents define their situations.

This does not mean that, in the social sciences, we should restrict ourselves to 'ordinary language', and the distinctions and classifications available in everyday speech. It does, however, mean that we must construct our models in terms which can be translated into those of the referential systems relative to which the agents in the field orient themselves, proceed in interaction, frame their expectations, suffer deceptions, are motivated to action or inaction, etc.

Every science must start its development from common experience. This is perhaps the broadest but definitely also the most vaguely determined system of reference which we possess. It is also, therefore, the one which, by itself, is least amenable to correction on the basis of empirical findings. Every science must, therefore, in order to accumulate the impetus which is necessary for its 'take-off' into self-corrective flight, artificially construct it own models and theories. The processes of direct induction from experience characteristic of the 'natural history' stage of development, however much refined by techniques of sampling and of statistical, multiple factor analysis, can never by themselves do this for us. The distinctive nature of every science depends on the nature of the theories which we construct, i.e. on the variables we select and choose to include in them. It definitely does not depend on the nature of "the facts themselves".

Thus, some of the most important ingredients of social theory are contained in our common social experience. What will make a social science into a distinct science will depend on what it admits from this welter of data into its constructed system of reference. The social sciences are concerned, not with a residue left over by the physical sciences on the one hand, psychology on the other hand, but with an object which is defined independently from either of these, namely, interaction processes between human beings in terms of roles which are themselves determined by a variety of referential systems. The social sciences, one might say, are anthropomorphic not by mistake or by default, but by definition.

The way we know about social interaction processes in terms of common experience, is that we can take the position of someone else *vis-à-vis* ourselves and thus understand the intersubjective meaning of his behavior from our point of view as we understand our own from his viewpoint. To the very extent that this is not possible there is a barrier to or a problem of interaction. Now, clearly, the very opposite of what the social scientist wants to achieve would be to exclude himself from the legion of potential participants in the processes which he is studying. Equally clearly, he wants to achieve more than that. The problem is, how to achieve the extra bit as an extension and perfection of what is already available, and not as an unconnected, separate chunk of knowledge (let alone as a pile of such chunks).

The link between *social experience* and *social science* can indeed be retained if we construct our models and theories as formalizations of interaction processes as we know them from social experience, instead of either trying to jump the fence and start off where the physical sciences have arrived (i.e. with ready made mathematical models which do not include qualitatively determined systems of reference of agents in the field amongst their variables), or by copying its research techniques without framing the conceptual instruments in terms of which the resulting data can be interpreted and interrelated.

Each formalization will take place at the price of one-sidedness. The nature of the one-sidedness determines the nature of the science. Every formalization also proceeds by introducing connections between phenomena which were not seen as thus interrelated in previous experience. It is precisely therein that lies its fruitfulness: it is these connections which will have to be put to empirical tests and which can thereby shed new light on what we already knew or thought we knew. The purpose of empirical investigation in this procedure is to put each of a number of systematically inter-connected hypotheses to the test, rather than to establish a measure, or order, or scale for the application of an isolated concept. The consequence of it is that the outcome of the investigation may now lead to corrections of the theory and thus contribute to scientific research as a progressing, and not merely accumulating, social enterprise.